SONG OF SOLOMON

by

Bernard of Clairvaux

Translated and edited by

Samuel J. Eales

WIPF & STOCK · Eugene, Oregon

Wipf and Stock Publishers
199 W 8th Ave, Suite 3
Eugene, OR 97401

Cantica Canticorum
Eighty-six Sermons on the Song of Solomon
By Bernard of Clairvaux, and Eales, Samuel J.
Copyright © 1895 by Bernard of Clairvaux, All rights reserved.
Softcover ISBN-13: 979-8-3852-3421-9
Hardcover ISBN-13: 979-8-3852-3422-6
eBook ISBN-13: 979-8-3852-3423-3
Publication date 9/24/2024
Previously published by Elliot Stock, 1895

This edition is a scanned facsimile of the original edition published in 1895.

CONTENTS.

	PAGE
TITLE - - - - - - - -	v
DEDICATION - - - - - - -	vii
INTRODUCTORY ESSAY - - - - - -	ix
TABLE OF SERMONS - - - - - -	xxv
PREFACE OF DOM JOHN MABILLON - - - -	1
SERMONS - - - - - - - -	7-528
INDEX - - - - - - - -	529

INTRODUCTORY ESSAY.

FOLLOWING his invariable custom, the learned and laborious editor of St. Bernard's collected works, F. John Mabillon, has prefixed to the 'Sermons on the Canticles' a critical Introduction, which is here translated. It is, however, both exceedingly brief, and does not include (what perhaps might have been expected from it) any information as to the general lines of interpretation adopted respectively by the very numerous commentators who have written upon the Song of Songs, and the relation to these in which the Sermons of St. Bernard will be found to stand; much less does he supply anything in the nature of a Bibliography of the subject. Yet without some help of this kind, it will not be easy for the reader to form a just idea of the place which these Sermons occupy in the history of interpretation; and it seems needful, therefore, to furnish here a sketch of the principal facts bearing upon these subjects.

Considerations of space would, in any case, make this necessarily a brief one, and that must prevent it from being complete, since the number of commentators upon the Song of Songs is very great, and their works, generally speaking, excessively lengthy. This is of the less consequence for our present purpose, as the critical editions of the Song of Songs are many and excellent, and we are not proposing to add another to them. Our purpose is a much simpler one, namely, to furnish sufficient information to enable the reader to come to the perusal of St. Bernard's Sermons with a general idea of the interpretations given to the book by other pious and learned authors, so that he may see at once the position among them taken up by the Saint.

II. There are to be distinguished four great schools of interpretation:

A. *The Jewish allegorical*, which is mystico-historical, and sees in the Song of Songs an allegorical description of various periods of the history of the Theocracy of Israel.

B. *The Christian allegorical*, which adopts a method of treatment similar to the former, and differs from it principally in referring the allegory to the Lord Christ, and His relations with either (*a*) the soul of the individual believer, (*b*) the Church, or (*c*) The Blessed Virgin Mary.

C. The *prophetic-mystical* or *chronological*. This regards the Song as being, so to speak, the Apocalypse of the Old Testament; that is to say, as affording a continuous view of human history, and being partly, therefore, historical, and partly prophetic; and which takes its scope as extending from the Creation to the Final Judgment and Consummation of all things.

D. The *literal* or *erotic*. This explains the Song as being an ordinary *epithalamium*, or love-song, which may have been founded upon actual fact or not; but in either case has no mystical character, is composed of a number of separate lyric poems, and is, in fact, a mere anthology of amatory songs, the Idyls or Bucolics of an earlier period.

III. As to A., there is no clear proof that the Song was interpreted in an allegorical manner by any Rabbi before the Christian era. The passage from the LXX. (Cant. iv. 8), adduced for this purpose, is apparently a mistranslation. Ecclus. (xlvii. 14-17) and the Book of Wisdom (viii. 2) have been referred to as showing that the Song was customarily understood in a mystical sense, but without any certain result, and it is even asserted that an allegorical mode of interpretation was the *conditio sine qua non* of its reception into the Canon; but of this there is no proof whatever.

R. AKIBA (lived in the first century A.D.) said that 'all the

Scriptures are holy, but this sublime Song is most holy,' showing that he regarded it as containing mysteries; but we do not know what he considered these to be. The Talmud of Jerusalem, and also that of Babylon, contain tracts in which passages of this Song (as i. 2; i. 3, 13, 14; and v. 13) are quoted and commented upon; and in the Targum or Chaldee paraphrase (pub. A D. 550) occurs the first complete commentary on the Song which has come down to us. It is in that on the five Megilloth, *i.e.*, Song, Ruth, Lamentations, Esther, Ecclesiastes. It 'explains the Song of Songs as an allegory describing prophetically the history of the Jewish nation, beginning with their exodus from Egypt, and detailing their doings and sufferings, down to the coming of the Messiah, and the building of the third Temple' (Ginsburg, *Introd.*, p. 28). It is not known who was the author.

(A.D. 892—942). After the Chaldee paraphrase there occurs a long interval of about 350 years, during which there was no Jewish literature of which we know anything. The Dark Ages exercised the same benumbing effect apparently upon the Jewish school of Biblical interpretation as upon every other kind of intellectual culture, and the next Rabbinical commentator is R. SAADIAS, who was born at Pithom, in Egypt, in A.D. 892. He was Gaon, or spiritual head of the Jews in Babylon, and executed a translation of the Old Testament into Arabic, of which the Pentateuch portion is inserted in Walton's Polyglot. He wrote, also in Arabic, a 'Commentary on the Song of Songs,' which was translated into Hebrew by some person unknown. He agrees with the Targum in the general view he takes of the scope of the Song, but differs widely from it in the details of his interpretation. He allows that there is a great diversity of opinions as to its meaning, and assigns as a reason for this that 'the Song of Songs is like a lock, the key of which hath been lost.'

(A.D. 1000—A.D. 1040). The allegorical interpretation was in course of time introduced into the Jewish Liturgical services, when they endeavoured to compose sacred hymns and poems upon it, to be said or sung at their feasts or fasts. 'The Song of Songs is used in a poetical paraphrase on the first and second morning services of the Passover feast.'

R. SOLOMON BEN ISAAC (RASHI), A.D. 1040—1105,
DAVID KIMCHI, A.D. 1190—1250,
IBN EZRA, d. A.D. 1167,
MOSES MAIMONIDES, d. A.D. 1204,

were the chief commentators of this school. With these may be mentioned, as agreeing in the main idea of their interpretations, a certain number of Christian commentators, *e.g.*, S. AUGUSTINE, *de Civitate Dei*, Lib. XVII., c. 8, 13, 20; LUTHER, *Brevis Enarratio in Cant. Canticor.*; J. BRENTIUS, LEON. HUG, KAISER, ROSENMÜLLER.

B. The *Christian allegorical*. This may be said, speaking generally, to comprehend all the Fathers and mediæval writers. Of these, both the earlier in point of time, and the larger in point of number, is that school (*a*) which 'sees in the Bride of the Canticles the soul pining for union with God, and in the Bridegroom the Divine Love which sanctifies, purifies, and elevates it to Itself' (Dr. Zöckler). We can only name the chief among these: ORIGEN (d. A.D. 253. His Homilies were translated by St. Jerome, and Commentary by Rufinus, but the latter is only extant in part); EUSEBIUS of CAESAREA, d. A.D. 340 (Comment. lost except a few questions); MACARIUS the EGYPTIAN (d. A.D. 390); GREGORY of NYSSA (d. A.D. 394); THEODORET, Bishop of Cyrus (d. A.D. 457); MAXIMUS CONFESSOR; WILLIAM, Abbot of EBERSBERG (d. A.D. 1085); HONORIUS of AUTUN, RICHARD of ST. VICTOR, ST. THOMAS AQUINAS, GERSON, ST. BONAVENTURA (Cardinal Bishop of Alba), ST. TERESA of JESUS, ST. JOHN of the Cross, and most of the Spanish mystics. Other names might be quoted, but the later writers seem to have borrowed a good deal from the earlier (as, for example, Madame Guyon, *Le Cantique des Cantiques, interpreté selon le sens mystique*—Grenoble, 1685), and to have few points of originality in their works.

It is to this class that the Sermons of St. Bernard on the Canticles are to be referred. From them, and from the works of St. Teresa, the Commentary of Madame Guyon, mentioned in the last paragraph, seems to have been in a great measure derived.

A *second* class (*b*) among Christian writers interprets the Song of Songs of 'the relation between Christ and His Church.' Of these the chief are:

ST. ATHANASIUS, *Expositio in Cant. Canticorum* (now lost).

EPIPHANIUS, *Commentarius super Cant. Salomonis* (of doubtful authenticity).

ST. CYRIL of JERUSALEM, *Catechesis* XIV.

CASSIODORUS, *Expositio in Cant. Cantic.* (of doubtful authorship).

JUSTUS ORGELITANUS, ISIDORUS HISPALENSIS, GENEBRAND, Bishop of Aix (d. A.D. 1597), HIERON. OSORIUS (*circa*

1600), JOHN PISCATOR (1647), JOHN GERHARD (1666, STARKE, Synopsis, Part IV.), M. F. ROOS (1773); and in modern times O. von GERLACH, KEIL, HÁVERNICK, HENGSTENBERG.

(c) A *third* class may be styled *Mystico-Mariological,* and takes Shulamith in the Song of Songs to be mystically the Blessed Virgin Mary. Among these are: ST. AMBROSE (*Sermo de Virginitate perpetuâ S. Mariæ*), who explains Cant. iv. 12, 'a garden inclosed . . . a spring shut up, a fountain sealed' of the perpetual virginity of St. Mary.

ST. GREGORY the GREAT, *Expositio super Cantica Canticorum.*

MICHAEL PSELLUS the younger wrote in the eleventh century a metrical paraphrase of the Song of Songs and a prose commentary on it—both in Greek.

RUPERT of DEUTZ extends the suggestion made by ST. AMBROSE in his Sermon (see above) to a continuous explanation of the whole book.

DIONYSIUS CARTHUSIANUS, GULIELMUS PARVUS, MICHAEL GHISLERIUS, SALMERON, carrying out the hermeneutical rule, then universally received, of the threefold sense of every part of Holy Scripture, interpret all that is said of the Spouse in the Song of Songs (1) To the Church; (2) To the soul of the individual believer; (3) To the Blessed Virgin. But the most striking example of this school of interpreters is CORNELIUS A LAPIDE (Van der Steen, d. 1637), who in his 'Commentary on the Song of Songs' deduces, indeed, a threefold sense; but while he makes the '*primus sensus,*' which he calls '*totalis et adæquatus,*' to refer to Christ and the Church, and the second '*litteralis et partialis*' to Christ and the holy soul, makes the third to be '*principalis,*' and to denote Christ and the Blessed Virgin. Like most of the mystical writers after the time of St. Bernard, he quotes freely from these Sermons.

A *fourth* kind of interpretation is ventured upon by a few writers, who imagine 'the figurative language of Canticles to have been the offspring of some esoteric doctrine or Egyptian hieroglyphical wisdom of Solomon' (Zöckler). It may be called the *Mystico-hieroglyphic* Interpretation. This idea is advocated by VON PUFFENDORF, '*Umschreibung des Hohenleides, oder die Gemeine mit Christo und den Engeln im Grabe*' (1776). ('Paraphrase of the Song of Solomon, or communion with Christ and the Angels in the Grave.') 'The object described is supposed to be the participation of the believers of the Old and New Testaments in the grave and death of

the Saviour, in which also their desire for His appearing is likewise represented, and the future of the Church until the general resurrection is prophetically prefigured' (Zöckler). KISTEMACHER, '*Cantic. Canticor. illustratum ex hierographiâ Orientali*' (1818).
    C. The chief writers of this school, beginning with ST. AUGUSTINE, have been named above.
    D. The *literal* or *erotic* school of interpreters may be said to comprise the majority of the moderns, beginning with 'the reformed humanist' SEBASTIAN CASTELLIO (1544), HUGH GROTIUS, J. D. MICHAELIS, LESSING, HERDER, Bishop LOWTH (*De Sacra poesi Hebræorum*), BOSSUET, Bishop of Meaux, EWALD, HITZIG; and still later ERNEST RENAN, J. F. THRUPP, Dr. Otto ZÖCKLER (in Lange's *Bibel-Werk*, and particularly the translation with additions by W. H. Green, D.D.: T. and T. Clark, 1870), Dr. CHRISTIAN D. GINSBURG ('The Song of Songs translated from the original Hebrew': 1857). The two latter works are especially rich in the bibliography of the subject. We have made much use of them here, and refer to GREEN's ed. of ZÖCKLER, and DARLING's 'Cyclopædia Bibliographica,' especially for lists of English commentators.

    We cannot omit to mention here that Bishop CHRISTOPHER WORDSWORTH ('Commentary on the Bible,' vol. iv., p. 3) regards our subject 'as a prophetic allegory, suggested by the occasion of Solomon's marriage with Pharaoh's daughter, and descriptive of the gathering of all people into mystical union with Christ, and the consecration of the world into a church espoused to Him as the Bride.'

    These Sermons of St. Bernard, then, may be reckoned among 'Christian-allegorical' works, in which the Song of Songs is so treated as to substitute a religious and mystical meaning for the apparent one, in which it is a drama, or series of lyrics, of human love. They do not constitute a Commentary upon it, as well for the obvious reason that throughout the eighty-six Sermons only chapters i., ii., and part of iii. are treated,[1] as also because no serious attempt is made to comment upon the Song as a whole. Each verse is considered, for the most part, independently. The preacher's usual method of proceeding is to *isolate* a verse, and to apply it in a way more or less arbitrary to some great spiritual truth; which he then proceeds to develop

---

[1] His disciple, Gilbert of Hoiland, in continuing the task in forty-eight sermons more, only carried it on to v. 10, little more than half the book.

independently, and most generally with great beauty and wealth of original thought. It is this strain of lofty and mystical teaching which gives to the Sermons their great attraction and principal value.

But there is one fundamental conception which runs through the Sermons, and gives them such unity as they have. St. Bernard never loses grasp of the idea that the Bridegroom in the Song is the Lord Jesus, and the Bride, either the soul of the individual believer, or the totality of such souls; that is, the Church. It is, however, the *individual* soul that he describes, that he analyzes, that he counsels and exhorts, habitually in these Sermons. His gaze turns from time to time upon the Church—it may be said to do so even frequently—but it always comes back again to the soul of the believer as to its proper subject. To him the Divine Life in the soul was a matter of the most awful sacredness. In his thought all spiritual forces, whether for good or for evil, converged upon the soul of each individual believer, and out of it, as the result of their working, came the issues of life or of death. That the soul needs to have a thirst for Divine wisdom, and that this opens to it or in it new perceptions, which enable it to transcend outward things, to have an intuitive discernment of spiritual realities, a dim, glorious vision of mighty secrets of the higher region of thought and life, he was never tired of repeating. This was, in his view, the essential operation by which the spirit of man was made one with the Spirit of God, and it was of a nature wholly inward and spiritual, entirely hidden from the external sight, independent of outward things, and known only to the soul and to God. Thus he says in Sermon I., *n*. 11: 'That canticle the anointing of grace alone teaches, and experience only makes the soul to be familiar with it. Those who have had experience of it know it well; let those who have not had that happiness earnestly desire, not to know it, but to experience it. It is not a cry from the mouth, but the gladness of the heart; not the sounding of the lips, but the impulse and emotion of joys within; not a concert of words, but of wills moving in harmony. It is not heard without, nor does it make a sound in the streets. Only she who sings, and He in whose honour it is sung; that is, the Bridegroom and the Bride, hear the accents of that song.'

This, then, he held to be the indispensable element in the process of the soul's transformation, and so emphatic was his conviction of this, that he seems to have regarded it well-nigh as the *only* element that was indispensable. Though no one ever believed more fully than St. Bernard in the vivifying grace of which the Sacraments are the channels, or valued them more devoutly than he, yet he is never more emphatically a Mystic than when treating of the Sacraments. No one was to neglect them or abstain from them; no one was to think lightly of them; but at the same time the near Presence of God was (he held) better than they, and the direct action of the Spirit in the soul more manifestly efficacious. Thus he could write of the Holy Eucharist in Sermon XXXIII., *n*. 3:

' I have the WORD also here below, but in the Flesh; the Truth also is set before me for nourishment, but in the Sacrament. An Angel is rendered fat with the finest of the wheat, and filled with the pure grain; but it behoves me [since I am on earth] to be content during this life with the Sacrament, as with a husk; with the Flesh, as with bran; with the letter, as with chaff; with faith, as with a veil [upon the truth]. And such things as these bring death in the tasting (Rom. viii. 6-13), unless they be seasoned in some degree with the firstfruits of the Spirit. Assuredly, I can find only death in the pottage, unless it be rendered sweet with the meal of the Prophet (2 Kings iv. 41). Indeed, without the Spirit even the Sacrament is received only to condemnation; the flesh profiteth nothing (John vi. 63); the letter killeth (2 Cor. iii. 6); and faith itself is dead. But it is the Spirit that quickeneth these [means of grace], that I may live in them. But with whatever abundance of the Spirit those things may be enriched, it is not possible to find the same sweetness in the husk of the Sacrament, and in the fatness of the wheat; in faith as in vision; in remembrance as in presence; in time as in eternity; in the reflection in a mirror as in the countenance itself that is reflected; in the form of a servant as in the Image of God.'

Yet he fully valued the sacramental principle, as priceless for edification and for training in righteousness. There may have been dimly present to his mind the consciousness that it was not given to all souls to dwell upon these lofty heights of serene contemplation and mystical rapture; and that for the vast majority of Christian souls, the Sacraments form both the necessary means of salvation, as well as the nearest approach they are capable of sustaining, in this life, to the Ineffable Presence. He would even have extended the principle farther, so as to invest a beautiful and symbolical usage of the Cistercian Order, the washing of the feet of the brethren—*pedum ablutio*—with somewhat of sacramental grace, and remarks: 'That we may have no lingering doubt regarding the forgiveness of our daily trespasses: we have a Sacrament which symbolizes it, the "washing of feet".... And that there is somewhat hidden in this which is necessary for salvation, is shown in that not even Peter himself had, without it, any part in the kingdom of Christ and of God' (John xiii. 8). (*Sermon in Cænâ Domini, n.* 4).

Doubtless it was this sentiment that the soul of man is the fittest tabernacle here below for the Divine Presence, that made him so uncompromising a Puritan with regard to Church architecture and art. For the beautiful in art he seems to have had no taste whatever; it was even repulsive to him; and ornamented Churches he blamed in the Cluniac and other orders, and positively forbade to the houses of his own Rule. ' O vanity of vanities,' he says of it in one place, ' and not more vain than foolish! The Church glistens on all its walls, but the poor are not there! It clothes its stones with gold, but leaves the poor, its children, to their nakedness. At the expense of the needy it feasts the eyes of the rich. The curious find what pleases them, but the wretched find nothing to give them succour.' (*Apolog. ad Guil. Abbat.* c. xii.)

This horror of outward ornament in things sacred he sedulously impressed upon his followers. While he lived, the Cistercian Abbeys were, in their Churches, vestments and ritual, the emphatic expression of a bare and unadorned simplicity. ' Scarcely any ornament was admitted; no sumptuous hangings, no splendid paintings or mosaic pavements, no crucifixes made of silver or gold and set with jewels. The chalice alone might be of silver, and the vestments of the clergy of plain linen only. Their Church windows were to be entirely of white glass without coloured enrichments. No bell-towers in their Abbeys, whether of stone or wood, were to be of immoderate height. Every detail of construction was to show a studied bareness and plainness.'[1] We know little of the appearance of the earliest Church of Clairvaux, which would enable us to judge how St. Bernard carried out this principle, so to speak, in his own house. But the Church of Fontenay, the second daughter-house of Clairvaux, which was founded in 1119, less than four years after he became an Abbot, is still extant, though secularized; and it exhibits, in the opinion of so

---

[1] 'St. Bernard, Abbot of Clairvaux,' p. 66, S.P.C.K.

competent a judge as M. Viollet-le-Duc, the true type of the primitive Cistercian basilica. 'Of extreme simplicity, of a robust and masculine beauty, it bears the deep impress of that rigorous asceticism which was the especial stamp of the new and growing institution. . . . Those austere cenobites, who waged with their senses a war without truce or mercy, who kept their eyelids lowered before the Pope and the splendours of his suite, who had fled from the world in order to be nearer heaven, and to obtain it the more quickly, took care to give to the architecture of their Churches the special character which it was intended, in their view, to discharge. It was apparently in their thought that the severe aspect of the building, and its wide bare surfaces, should conduce to grave meditation, should inspire a kind of religious awe, favourable to collectedness and pious contemplation.'[1]

The inward, not the outward, kind of beauty was to be the aim of all endeavour; and this aim the Saint, in these Sermons and elsewhere in his writings, was never wearied of urging.

If, then, the Holy Spirit, in his direct action upon the human soul, was to St. Bernard the *causa causans* of the new creation which issued in a perfect salvation and blessedness, and if some degree of spiritual aspiration and effort were the condition which rendered that action fruitful, he would never fail, in his exhortations, to insist also upon the necessity of *Charity or Love*. This he constantly teaches must be sincere, living, and continually increasing so as to have no limit; so as to surge over every obstacle, either in the nature or circumstances of the individual soul, or those of others, unless all progress in a spiritual direction was to be nugatory or even hurtful. Great gifts and lofty aspirations, if without charity, he holds to be, if not sins themselves, yet but too easily, or almost inevitably, the cause of sins. To these he traces the fall of the devil, and finds in him the perfect exemplification of knowledge and ability without love. (Sermon III., *Pro Dominica* i. *Novembris, nn.* 1, 2, 3, 4). 'In vain,' he says, 'does one who has no knowledge of love come to hear, or to read, the Song of Love, since it is in nowise possible for a cold and icy heart to comprehend a discourse fervid and glowing. As one who does not understand Greek comprehends nothing said by him who speaks in that tongue . . . so the language of love, to one who

---

[1] See Chomton, *St. Bernard et le Château de Fontaines-les-Dijon*, ii., p. 82. Dijon, 1894.

knows it not, will be (as it were) barbarous; it will be as sounding brass and a tinkling cymbal.' ('Serm. in Cant.' lxxix., *n.* 1).

Yet another striking characteristic of these Sermons is their *Scriptural character*. No reader of them can help noticing how small is the number of quotations in them from the writings of the Fathers, and how vast the number from every part of the Holy Scriptures. Of Bernard it may truly be said that, like the Psalmist, he might have declared, '*Lord, what love have I unto Thy law : all the day long is my study in it.*' There are not, throughout all these Sermons on the Song of Songs, a dozen quotations from any extraneous source whatever;[1] while those from the Holy Scriptures may be numbered by hundreds, so that in many passages his sentences form a continuous *cento* of Scripture language and phrases. He was so familiar with the text of the Vulgate, particularly in the Psalms and the writings of the Prophets, that their language became his own, and his thoughts naturally expressed themselves in it.[2]

[1] Generally speaking, and exceptions apart, the only Fathers that St. Bernard ever quotes are St. Augustine and St. Gregory.

[2] A magnificent MS. Latin Bible in two volumes folio, belonging to the first half of the twelfth century, was preserved at Clairvaux down to the time of the suppression of the Abbey in 1790-92, and thence transferred to the Municipal Library at Troyes, in which it bears the number 458. It is written in two columns to the page, and has the initial letters adorned in colours and gold, many of them also with pictures. At the beginning of the first volume is the inscription in Gothic characters, in a hand of the twelfth century :

Pars Prima Bible Beati Bernardi Abbatis Clareballis.

These details are extracted from a notice inserted in the *Mémoires de la Société Académique de l'Aube* (Troyes, 1842, p. 246), by M. Harmand, Librarian of the city of Troyes. It is known, therefore, as the 'Bible of St. Bernard,' and 'appears to have really belonged to that illustrious man' (D'Arbois de Jubainville, *Études des Abbayes Cisterciennes*, p. 97, Paris, 1858). It is said to have been that used by him when composing these 'Sermons on the Canticles.' In this Bible, the *Cantica Canticorum* occupies two leaves only. 'In examining them, it seems,' says a celebrated bibliophile, 'that the eyes still discern resting upon them the venerable hand which has almost worn them out with continually turning them over and over, while engaged in drawing from them those eighty-six sermons.' M. L'Abbé Serisier, Curé Doyen of Ervy (Aube), and formerly a *vicaire* of the Cathedral at Troyes, informs me that there are MS. notes on the margins of this Bible in the handwriting of the Saint.

In 1517 an ancient room in the Abbey of Clairvaux, panelled in wood above, was still shown and known as the *Chamber of St. Bernard*, in which he was said to have composed *Cantica Canticorum*, 'qui est de bois à la mode anticque, lambrissée dessus en manière d'église ... et joignant ladicte chambre y a ung petit oratoire, en manière d'une chapelle, appellée

But apart from that, his mind was too rapid and vigorous in its action to lend itself easily to the habit of discursive quotation which may delight a thinker of a more deliberate and leisurely character. He pioneered for the most part his own luminous track of thought, and there are very few provinces of the spiritual life, as conceived from the monastic point of view, which he does not find occasion to traverse. There is indeed this one obvious limitation. He was addressing an audience of monks; he looks at all things through the loopholes of the cloister; he treats of the occupations, the studies, the dangers, the besetting temptations, and the ideals of monks; and for each and all of these subjects he finds an occasion in the Song. Either he finds in it, or perhaps he not unfrequently reads into it, and extracts from it by a loving casuistry, the deepest lessons of Christian duty, the most touching and pathetic experiences of Christian life. The Sermons are tremulous with an incessant shimmer of allegories, allegories wholly arbitrary, in most instances wholly without foundation in the text treated of, and yet so rich in their spiritual suggestiveness, that they strike upon the mind like rays straight from heaven, and belonging to '*the light that never was on sea or shore.*' Thus he explains the kiss of the Mouth of God, desired by the Bride in the Song, of the Holy Spirit, by whom the mystery of the Holy Trinity is communicated to the Church (Sermon VIII.). Of the kiss itself of God (he distinguishes between the two), he says that it is the miracle of the Incarnation, in which the Divine Word is joined, in the Hypostatic Union, to human nature (Sermon II.). To kiss the Foot of God is the sign of *forgiveness;* to kiss His Hand, that of *sanctity* and *virtue;* but to kiss His Mouth is the sign of self-consuming spiritual fervour, perfect love, and mystical communion with the Divine Nature (Sermons III., IV.). The sense of religious hope, or fear in the soul, is the impress of mercy or of judgment; that is, of one or of the other Foot of God (Sermon VI.). The Breasts of the Bridegroom, that is, Christ, are, the one, the patience with which He waits for the sinner; the other, the willingness and kindness wherewith He receives him (Sermon IX.).

The three chief ointments of the spirit are contrition,

La Chapelle Sainct Bernard, sur le pas et marche de laquelle est escript ce mot : HIC : qui est le lieu où monseigneur sainct Bernard rendit l'esprit sur des cendres' (Record of a visit made by the Queen of Sicily, the Count and Countess of Guise, to Clairvaux in 1517, *L'Abbaye de Clairvaux en* 1517 *et en* 1709, Paris, 1866, p. 23 and note).—ED.

devotion, goodness. The first stinging, and giving pain; the second anodyne, and relieving pain; the third healing, which drives out the disease (Sermon X.). And so on, through a veritable forest of brightly-coloured allegorical fancies, hanging in a kind of Debatable Land, or *Limbo Puerorum*, between the earth of prosaic fact and the heaven of settled dogma. This is, in fact, a phrase of his own, as when he says: 'I thought that we should quickly traverse that forest, sombre and shady with allegories, and arrive, in a journey of perhaps one day, at the open plain of the moral meanings of our subject; but it has proved otherwise. . . . The eye of an observer at a distance traverses in a moment the tops of great masses of verdure, and marks the mountain peaks; but it cannot pierce into the vast depths of the low-lying valleys, or penetrate the obscure coverts of the thickets (Sermon XVI., *n.* 1).

Perhaps the most singular fact with regard to these wonderful Sermons, or, at least, that which strikes a modern reader of them with most surprise and astonishment, is that they have throughout, as a theme absolutely fundamental, just that very element in human life which was forbidden to every monk by the rigid conditions of his profession, which it was sin in him to desire, or even to make the subject of his contemplation: that is to say, the conjugal relation, the solace and the sweetness of the mutual affection of husband and wife. To the faithful monk this was forbidden ground. It was his strenuous endeavour eventually to root out altogether, and, in the meantime, to crush down with ruthless severity, every faculty and feeling, every regretful longing or momentary tenderness of thought which tended to render him like unto the general mass of human kind who 'marry and are given in marriage.' The ideal of his conventual profession, as well as the specific vows which he had taken upon him at entering it, equally forbade this. Yet in these Sermons we find the saintly Abbot, as if he had been addressing an audience of persons who were actually married, or who might hereafter be so, selecting for his subject the impassioned affections of a Bridegroom and a Bride, and making the ebb and flow of their feelings, the tender or romantic incidents of their attachment, the vehicle of his moral teachings. Surely this is the strangest paradox in the history of the pulpit, that St. Bernard should discourse upon marriage to those who could never be married, and paint before their eyes, in rich and glowing colours, idyllic pictures of an affection which they had all definitively renounced.

Upon this strange *tour de force* two observations may be made. First, that it is a glorified and idealized marriage which is his subject. It is but the terms of his narrative which he borrows from earth, for that which he uses them to describe belongs to heaven. All that is distinctive, all that is individual in sentiment, is merged in the deep and flowing stream of spiritual experiences. The saintly preacher is the opposite of Antæus in a well-known Greek myth, the antagonist of Heracles, for though he ever and anon touches the earth, his strength and his persuasiveness, the staple of his teaching, and that which gives to it its peculiar character, are altogether unearthly. 'He spoke to men,' says the historian Fleury, 'the language of Angels, and they were scarcely able to understand it.'[1] In the second place, if he addresses himself in a marked degree to that element which in the monastic character was, as it were, a force unappropriated and unused, it is that he may utilize it for good, and in employing it may transform it into something higher than itself. It has ever been the wont of the Church to make use of *all* the elemental forces of human nature, however far removed they may appear to be from her especial sphere. Thus there can hardly be any feeling farther alien to the character of the 'Gospel of peace' than the combative instinct which drives men on to war and bloodshed. Yet the Church (heedfully and warily, it is true) enlists it in her service, and teaches her people to sing:

> 'Onward, Christian soldiers,
> Marching as to war.'

The Christian is bidden to 'put on the whole armour of God.' He is to be 'Christ's faithful soldier and servant unto his life's end'; and thus the forces which give energy, and consistency, and patience to human effort are enrolled in the army of Salvation, and made to do yeoman's service against evil.

It is probably a similar utilization of the primitive forces of human nature that we are to see in these Sermons on the Canticles.

There is still another characteristic quality of these Sermons, that no attentive student of them will be able to overlook, that is to say, their prodigal wealth of imagination. 'One would hardly know,' says a recent lecturer on Bernard,[2] 'where to find a brighter example of the power which

---

[1] *Histoire Ecclesiastique*, vol. xiv., p. 193.
[2] Dr. R. S. Storrs.

is imparted to the preacher by this always noble, if sometimes misleading and dangerous, faculty. It is perpetually apparent in Bernard. Whatever else he is or is not, he is never commonplace. His mind is fruitful in large suggestions, and the text is often hardly more than the nest from which, like the eagle, he lifts himself on eager wing to touch, if he may, the stars of light. One of these Sermons on the Canticles, for example, treats of the angelical love toward God, according to the differing orders of angels; another, on the darkness and beauty of the Bride, discusses the question why it is that hearing is of more value than seeing in matters of faith; another, on the ointments of the beloved, exhibits the nature of four principal virtues; another presents the excellency of the Vision of God, and the measure in which the sense of the Divine Presence will vary in good men according to their varying aspirations; another still, impresses the truth that while knowledge of literature may be profitable for intellectual culture, the knowledge of one's own weakness is more profitable for salvation. There is hardly any theme of practical spiritual religion for which he does not find suggestion, toward which he does not take incentive, in the parts of the Song which come under his view' ('Bernard of Clairvaux,' p. 400).

Upon the whole, we cannot but think that every reader will find these, notwithstanding the old-world mould in which they are cast, emphatically helpful Sermons. The writer had the gift of spiritual sympathy in a marvellous and almost unexampled degree; his sentences palpitate, as it were, with an ardent love for souls. To teach, to reprove, to encourage, to warn his hearers; to lead them onward in ways of pleasantness, and along paths of peace,

> 'To warn the sinner, cheer the saint,
> To feed Thy lambs and tend Thy sheep,'

is the intention and object always present to the preacher. In him the pastor and the poet meet. 'Whatever his object, however familiar, or even apparently trivial, there is always a light thrown upon it by his imagination, which is like the light of golden brown or royal purple which rests upon Italian hills. Cottage and villa, the rocky cliff, the squalid town, are in that light as if transfigured. So the commonest theme stands to Bernard invested with an unworldly radiance, because connected with infinite truths and immeasurable destinies. Whatever his immediate point of view, he sees the glory of God before him, in Creation and Redemption, and the majestic meaning and pathos in all human life.'

Sermons of which this may be truly said cannot, however antique be their form, be altogether out of date; nor can they have wholly lost their power to attract and to influence readers of this generation. It is with the conviction that this is the case that they are here put before the English public.

SAMUEL J. EALES.

TABLE

OF

ST. BERNARD'S SERMONS ON THE SONG OF SONGS.

SERMON	PAGE
I. The Title (Cant. i. 1)	7
II. The Incarnation of Christ expected (Cant. i. 1)	12
III. What it is to kiss the Feet, the Hand, and the Lips of the Lord (Cant. i. 1)	17
IV. The threefold progress of the soul, arising from the kiss of the Foot, the Hand, and the Lips of the Lord (Cant. i. 1)	21
V. Of the Four Orders of Spirits; viz., the Spirit of God, of the Angels, of man, and of the beast (Cant. i. 1)	24
VI. Of the Supreme and Infinite Spirit, who is God; and of the sense in which mercy and judgment are called the Feet of God (Cant. i. 1)	29
VII. Of the ardent love of the soul for God; and of the care and attention that ought to be given to prayer and to psalmody (Cant. i. 1)	33
VIII. That the kiss of God is the Holy Spirit; and that the Church asks for this kiss, that she may have the knowledge of the Holy Trinity (Cant. i. 1)	38
IX. Of the breasts of the Bridegroom: of which the one is patience in waiting for the conversion of sinners; the other, benignity in receiving them (Cant. i. 2)	43
X. Of the three spiritual perfumes: namely, penitence, devotion, and piety (Cant. i. 2)	49
XI. Of two principal facts in human redemption: the manner in which it is accomplished, and the benefits which we derive from it (Cant. i. 2)	55
XII. Of the perfume of piety, which is the most excellent of all; and of the respect which those who are under authority ought to have for those set over them (Cant. i. 2)	60
XIII. That praise and glory is always to be rendered unto God, for all the good gifts which we receive of Him (Cant. i. 2)	67
XIV. Of the Church of faithful Christians; and of the Synagogue of perfidious Jews (Cant. i. 2)	74

SERMON		PAGE
XV.	In what manner the Name of Jesus is a salutary medicine to faithful Christians in all adversities (Cant. i. 2)	79
XVI.	Of contrition of heart: and of the three kinds of true confession (Cant. i. 2)	86
XVII.	That it is needful to observe with care the approach and the departure of the Holy Spirit ; and of the envy of the devil towards the human race (Cant. i. 2)	95
XVIII.	Of the two operations of the Holy Spirit, of which the one is called *effusion,* and the other *infusion* (Cant. i. 3)	100
XIX.	Of the nature, manner, and properties of the Angelical love towards God, according to the several Orders of Angels (Cant. i. 3)	104
XX.	Of the three ways in which we love God (Cant. i. 3)	109
XXI.	In what manner the Bride, that is, the Church, asks that she may be drawn to follow after her Spouse, who is Christ (Cant. i. 3)	116
XXII.	Of the four perfumes of the Bridegroom : and of the four cardinal virtues (Cant i. 3)	123
XXIII.	Of three ways of contemplating God, represented under the figure of three storerooms (Cant. i. 4)	130
XXIV.	Principally against the detestable vice of detraction : and in what rectitude in a man chiefly consists (Cant. i. 4)	143
XXV.	That the Bride, namely, the Church, is black, yet comely (Cant. i. 5)	149
XXVI.	St. Bernard laments the death of his brother Gerard (Cant. i. 5)	155
XXVII.	Of the adornment of the Bride : and in what sense the holy soul is called *heaven* (Cant. i. 5)	167
XXVIII.	Of the blackness, yet beauty, of the Bride : and in what manner hearing, rather than sight, avails in matters of faith, and to the knowledge of the truth (Cant. i. 5)	176
XXIX.	Of the complaint of the Church against her persecutors ; that is to say, against those who sow division amongst brethren (Cant. i. 6)	186
XXX.	That the faithful people, or the souls of the elect, are signified by the vineyards, of which the Church is called the guardian ; and that the prudence of the flesh is death (Cant. i. 6)	192
XXXI.	The excellency of the Vision of God. How at the present time the delight in the Divine Presence felt by holy men varies according to the varying desires of their soul (Cant. i. 7)	201
XXXII.	Christ communicates Himself to the holy soul as *Bridegroom,* and to the soul that is weak and imperfect	

SERMON		PAGE
	as *Physician*. Of the moods of the soul; how they differ from each other, and from what causes (Cant. i. 7)	207
XXXIII.	Of those things which a devout soul ought to seek without ceasing. What is to be understood by the word '*noon*,' and of four classes of temptations to be sedulously avoided (Cant. i. 7)	214
XXXIV.	Of humility and of patience (Cant. i. 8)	224
XXXV.	Of the sharp reproof which the Bridegroom gives to the Bride: and of two kinds of ignorance which are especially to be feared and avoided (Cant. i. 8)	227
XXXVI.	That the knowledge of literature is good for our instruction, but the knowledge of our own infirmity is more useful to salvation (Cant. i. 8)	233
XXXVII.	Of the two kinds of knowledge and the two kinds of ignorance: the evils or injuries caused by these (Cant. i. 8)	238
XXXVIII.	How from ignorance of God comes despair: and how the Bride is called the fairest among women (Cant. i. 8)	243
XXXIX.	Of the chariots of Pharaoh, that is, the devil; and of the chiefs of his army, who are malice, sensuality, and avarice (Cant. i. 9)	247
XL.	What is meant by the face of the soul; what constitutes its beauty or its deformity, its solitude and its modesty (Cant. i. 10)	252
XLI.	Of the great consolation which the Bride feels from the contemplation of the Divine Glory, before she attains to the clear vision of it (Cant. i. 10)	255
XLII.	Of two kinds of humility: the one born of truth, the other warmed by charity (Cant. i. 12)	259
XLIII.	How meditation on the Sufferings and the Passion of JESUS CHRIST enables the Bride, that is, the faithful soul, to pass uninjured alike through the prosperity and the adversity of this world (Cant. i. 13)	266
XLIV.	That correction ought to be adapted to the character of offenders, so that those of humble and complying disposition should be gently dealt with, but the stubborn and obstinate severely chastened to oblige them to reform (Cant. i. 14)	271
XLV.	Of the twofold beauty of the soul: how the soul speaks to God the WORD, and the WORD to the soul, and what language they employ (Cant. i. 15)	275
XLVI.	Of the state and composition of the whole Church. Also of the manner in which, by an active life spent	

SERMON		PAGE
	under obedience, the life of contemplation may be attained (Cant. i. 16)	281
XLVII.	Of the threefold flower [of holiness], namely, of virginity, of martyrdom, and of good works; and of the devotion with which we should participate in Divine Service (Cant. ii. 1)	287
XLVIII.	Of the praises which the Bride and the Bridegroom address reciprocally to each other; and how by the Shadow of Christ is to be understood His Flesh, and faith in Him (Cant. ii. 2)	292
XLIX.	How charity is regulated by discretion, so that all the members of the Church, that is, the elect, are held together by mutual bonds (Cant. ii. 4)	297
L.	Of two kinds of charity, namely, that of feeling and that of action: and how they are co-ordinated (Cant. ii. 4)	302
LI.	How the Bride makes petition that the fruits of good works and the perfumes of faith may be made to abound with her as flowers: and also concerning hope and fear (Cant. ii. 5)	308
LII.	Of that ecstasy, which is called contemplation: in which the Bridegroom causes the holy soul to attain peace and rest, being earnestly desirous of its blessedness (Cant. ii. 7)	314
LIII.	By 'mountains' and 'hills' are signified the heavenly spirits, over whom and through whom the Bridegroom passes in His Coming to earth; that is, in the Mystery of His Incarnation (Cant. ii. 8)	319
LIV.	Another interpretation; in which by *mountains* are signified Angels and men; and by *hills*, demons. Also of the threefold fear with which everyone ought to feel anxiety, lest he should lose the grace of acting rightly, which he has received from God (Cant. ii. 8)	324
LV.	How it is possible, through a true penitence, to escape the judgment of God (Cant. ii. 9)	332
LVI.	That sins and vices are as walls, interposing between God and the sinner (Cant. ii. 9)	335
LVII.	That the visitations of the Lord are to be carefully and reverently observed: and by what signs and tokens they may be known (Cant. ii. 10)	340
LVIII.	How the Bridegroom bids the Bride, that is to say, those men who are perfected, to undertake the rule and training of souls less perfect. Also of the cutting down of vices in them, that virtues may grow and increase (Cant. ii. 10)	347

knows it not, will be (as it were) barbarous; it will be as sounding brass and a tinkling cymbal.' ('Serm. in Cant.' lxxix., *n.* 1).

Yet another striking characteristic of these Sermons is their *Scriptural character*. No reader of them can help noticing how small is the number of quotations in them from the writings of the Fathers, and how vast the number from every part of the Holy Scriptures. Of Bernard it may truly be said that, like the Psalmist, he might have declared, '*Lord, what love have I unto Thy law: all the day long is my study in it.*' There are not, throughout all these Sermons on the Song of Songs, a dozen quotations from any extraneous source whatever;[1] while those from the Holy Scriptures may be numbered by hundreds, so that in many passages his sentences form a continuous *cento* of Scripture language and phrases. He was so familiar with the text of the Vulgate, particularly in the Psalms and the writings of the Prophets, that their language became his own, and his thoughts naturally expressed themselves in it[2]

[1] Generally speaking, and exceptions apart, the only Fathers that St. Bernard ever quotes are St. Augustine and St. Gregory.

[2] A magnificent MS. Latin Bible in two volumes folio, belonging to the first half of the twelfth century, was preserved at Clairvaux down to the time of the suppression of the Abbey in 1790-92, and thence transferred to the Municipal Library at Troyes, in which it bears the number 458. It is written in two columns to the page, and has the initial letters adorned in colours and gold, many of them also with pictures. At the beginning of the first volume is the inscription in Gothic characters, in a hand of the twelfth century:

Pars Prima Bible Beati Bernardi Abbatis Clareballis.

These details are extracted from a notice inserted in the *Mémoires de la Société Académique de l'Aube* (Troyes, 1842, p. 246), by M. Harmand, Librarian of the city of Troyes. It is known, therefore, as the 'Bible of St. Bernard,' and 'appears to have really belonged to that illustrious man' (D'Arbois de Jubainville, *Études des Abbayes Cisterciennes*, p. 97, Paris, 1858). It is said to have been that used by him when composing these 'Sermons on the Canticles.' In this Bible, the *Cantica Canticorum* occupies two leaves only. 'In examining them, it seems,' says a celebrated bibliophile, 'that the eyes still discern resting upon them the venerable hand which has almost worn them out with continually turning them over and over, while engaged in drawing from them those eighty-six sermons.' M. L'Abbé Serisier, Curé Doyen of Ervy (Aube), and formerly a *vicaire* of the Cathedral at Troyes, informs me that there are MS. notes on the margins of this Bible in the handwriting of the Saint.

In 1517 an ancient room in the Abbey of Clairvaux, panelled in wood above, was still shown and known as the *Chamber of St. Bernard*, in which he was said to have composed *Cantica Canticorum*, 'qui est de bois à la mode anticque, lambrissée dessus en manière d'église ... et joignant ladicte chambre y a ung petit oratoire, en manière d'une chapelle, appellée

SERMON		PAGE
	up their abode in it; and of the close relation that is thus entered into between God and the soul (Cant. ii. 16)	420
LXX.	Why the Bridegroom is called *Beloved;* and of the truth, the gentleness, the righteousness, and the other virtues, which are called *lilies,* and among which He is said to feed (Cant. ii. 16)	426
LXXI.	Of spiritual lilies, that is, good works: of which the fragrance is a right intention, and the colour a good reputation; and how the Bridegroom both nourishes these, and is nourished by them. Also of the unity of God the Father with the Son, and of the holy soul with God (Cant. ii. 16)	432
LXXII.	The meaning of the words 'The day breaks and the shadows flee away.' The various days in the lives of men expounded. That the righteous live in light, and that a brighter day awaits them; but that the wicked, who are devoted to works of darkness, can look forward only to eternal night (Cant. ii. 16, 17)	441
LXXIII.	How Christ shall come to judge in human form, that He may appear delightful to the elect: and how He is less than the Angels, yet loftier than they (Cant. ii. 17)	448
LXXIV.	Of the visitations of the Bridegroom, the WORD, to the holy soul, and the secrecy with which they are made. St. Bernard states his own experience of this, with great humility and modesty, for the edification of his hearers (Cant. ii. 17)	454
LXXV.	God is to be sought in due time, place, and manner. That now is the acceptable time, in which anyone may find God for himself by good works, and may work out his salvation (Cant. iii. 1)	461
LXXVI.	Of the glory of the Bridegroom, in which He sits at the Right Hand of His Father, and is coequal with Him. How careful, watchful, and discreet good Pastors ought to be in feeding the souls given into their charge (Cant. iii. 2)	468
LXXVII.	Concerning the bad pastors of the Church. Also how the Blessed in Heaven, and the Angels, come to the aid of the elect, who are still pilgrims upon the earth (Cant. iii. 2)	474
LXXVIII.	That the Bride, that is to say, the Church of the elect, was predestinated by God before all ages; and prevented by His grace that she should seek Him and be converted (Cant. iii. 2)	479

SERMON		PAGE
LXXIX.	Of the strong and indissoluble love wherewith the soul holds to its Lord ; also of the Return of the Bridegroom at the ending of the age, to save the Synagogue of the Jews (Cant. iii. 3)	483
LXXX.	An acute and profound argument respecting the Image or WORD of God, and the soul, which is created in that image : and concerning the error of Gilbert, Bishop of Poictiers (Cant. iii. 3)	487
LXXXI.	Of the similarity and likeness of the soul to the WORD, in respect of its identity of essence, its immortality of existence, and its freedom of will (Cant. iii. 3)	494
LXXXII.	How the soul, while still remaining like unto God, loses by sin a portion of its likeness to Him in its simplicity, immortality, and liberty (Cant. iii. 3)	501
LXXXIII.	Of the manner in which the soul, however corrupted it may be with evil habits, is still able, by a chaste and holy love, to recover its resemblance to the Bridegroom, that is, Christ (Cant. iii. 3)	507
LXXXIV.	That the soul, seeking God, is anticipated by Him : and in what consists that search for God in which it is thus anticipated (Cant. iii. 1)	511
LXXXV.	Of the seven needs of the soul, on account of which it seeks the WORD. When the soul is once reformed, it draws near to contemplate Christ, and to enjoy the sweetness of His Presence (Cant. iii. 1)	516
LXXXVI.	Of the caution and modesty becoming to the soul in seeking the WORD, and of the praise of modesty (Cant. iii. 1)	525

SERMONS ON THE SONG OF SONGS

PREFACE OF DOM JOHN MABILLON

(TO VOL. IV. OF HIS SECOND EDITION).

ALTHOUGH all the works of St. Bernard are filled with the sap of solid piety and sound doctrine, yet there are two of them which are especially valued by all, namely, the [five] 'Books on Consideration,' and the 'Sermons on the Song of Songs.' In the former work is, in fact, contained, in a form as elegant as it is concise, whatsoever is most sacred in the Holy Scriptures, and in the decrees of councils, as also whatsoever is most salutary in the writings of the ancient Fathers, and in the decrees of Pontiffs with regard to the government of the Church.

Similarly in these sermons will be found all that our holy Doctor has penned throughout all his other works for the purpose of forming a [religious] character and arousing piety; all that has relation to vices, to virtues, and to the whole of the spiritual life. All these subjects, I repeat, are treated anew in the sermons before us, and that with added solidity and loftiness. The preacher brings into view the mystical and allegorical senses of the text, and finds in them all the secrets of perfection, doing this in a manner as useful and delightful as it is sublime. So that these sermons may be considered, as it were, a treasury of chaste delights for pious souls. This manner of writing we call both delightful and useful. For this is, according to the testimony of St. Bernard himself, 'the condition, at once wonderful and pitiable, of human souls, that, although by the vivacity of their genius they are capable of perceiving so many things external to themselves, they nevertheless need corporeal figures and similitudes, in order that from these outward and visible things they may conjecture something of the invisible and inward realities.'[1] In attaining which object St. Bernard has admirably succeeded in the sermons before us.

2. St. Bernard made a commencement upon this remarkable work

---

[1] 'Sermons de Diversis,' vi. 1. But the passage is quoted in a condensed form, some sentences having been omitted.—ED.

in the year 1135, after his return from Aquitaine, as appears from his 'Life' ('Ernald,' Bk. II., c. 6): 'The man of God, having obtained an interval of quiet, occupied himself with other affairs; and, withdrawing into a bower formed of a trellis covered with sweet peas, he occupied himself in solitary meditations upon Divine things. And suddenly there came to him in that humble hermitage, as to one sitting in the Lord's dwelling, songs of love, and the feasts of spiritual nuptials. For a long time he poured forth his soul in meditation upon these things; he has expounded them in many forms; and it is manifest to all who read them how greatly he, who feasted daily upon those dainties, benefited thereby; and how great benefit we may also derive, for whom the remains of that blessing in [the study of] Scripture have been preserved.' Geoffrey also, in his continuation of the 'Life' (Bk. iii., c. 7), thus expresses himself: 'In the sermons upon the Song of Songs, he shows himself both a magnificent investigator of the mystical sense, and expounds the moral to edification.'

It is evident, from the exordium of the second of those sermons, that this book was begun during the Advent of the year named above, viz., 1135. For he speaks thus: 'Behold, how many there are who shall rejoice in this, His Nativity, which is shortly to be celebrated,' etc.

3. It is evident that Bernard des Portes, the Carthusian, was, if not the suggester, at least the encourager, of this undertaking; and this appears from the letter of Bernard (No. 153) to him, in which the Saint alleges his want of ability, in answer to his earnestly begging for an exposition, or some spiritual work upon the Canticles from his hand; yet at length yields to his fervent request, whether this is to be explained of the undertaking of the work, or the publication of one already commenced. The words of Ep. 153 favour this latter opinion: 'I yield to your importunity, so as to put an end to all your doubts. I am dealing with a friend. I no longer spare my modesty, and in doing what you wish, I will not think that I am committing a folly. I am having transcribed for you some sermons lately delivered on the beginning of the Canticles, and I send them to you as quickly as possible before they are made public. When I have time, according as Christ assigns me my tasks, I will endeavour to proceed with this work.' From which words it comes out clearly that Bernard des Portes had asked for some spiritual work from our Bernard, who had sent to him the first sermons on the Song of Songs. I do not know whether it is to this Bernard that the passage in Sermon I., *n*. 3, is to be taken as referring: 'I do not think that the friend who has come to us from his journey will have reason to murmur against us, when he shall have taken of that third loaf'; that I must leave to others to decide. Lastly, it was to Bernard des Portes that the earlier sermons were addressed, at the same time as Ep. 154, in which I read these words: 'I am sending on to you the sermons on the beginning of the Song of Songs, which you asked for, and I promised; and when you have read them, I beg you to give me your

advice as soon as possible, whether I ought to give them up, or proceed with them,' which may be understood indifferently of the planning out and of the completion of the work.

4. Although St. Bernard was in the habit of preaching almost every day to his monks at Clairvaux, yet he was not able, during the eighteen years which he lived after this, to complete the work which he had begun ; he found himself often distracted by various affairs both of Church and State, not to speak of the multitudes of eager visitors, of which he complains not once only, as at the end of Sermon III. : ' But the evil craft of the day calls me away. For those people, whose coming has just been announced to me, oblige me to break off, rather than to finish, a discourse which is agreeable to me. I must go out to our guests, that no offices of that charity, of which we speak, be left unperformed.' And in Sermon LII., *n.* 7 : 'Scarcely is an hour of intermission left to me by the visitors who come.' It is indeed wonderful that the holy Father, distracted as he was by the cares of a numerous community, and of a multitude of affairs which pressed upon him, was enabled to compose those sermons full of wisdom so deep, and to preach them daily. For he himself declares that he did this, in Sermon XXII., *n.* 2 : ' It is a task, not without some labour and fatigue, for me to come daily to draw from the streams, the open streams of Scripture, to give to each of you according to his need.' For he preached these sermons on festival days, even when these were almost continuous, as appears from Sermon LXXXIII., where he says that he has exhausted his strength in expounding one passage during three successive days. Furthermore, he delivered these sermons *vivâ voce*. Thus he says at the end of Sermon XLII. : ' My weakness, which you well know, does not permit me to go further.' And at the end of Sermon XLIV. : ' This suffices for the present. And, indeed, my weakness warns me to cease, as it frequently does.'

5. The Saint was wont to unite prayer to meditation to prepare the material of his sermons ; nevertheless, out of the abundance and fertility of his mind he sometimes preached them when not yet written, as is proved by various passages. For in various parts of his sermons there are many passages which were evidently spoken *ex tempore*. Such is that, for example, in Sermon XXXVI., in which he chides those who were sleepy, and says : ' I thought that I should be able to say to you in one sermon what I had promised, of the two kinds of ignorance; and this I should have done, if this discourse did not seem already too long to such as are fastidious; for I perceive some yawning, and others even asleep. I do not wonder at this ; the vigils of last night, which were indeed very long, are their excuse.' But there is no passage which affords proof so distinct that it was extemporaneous as one in Sermon IX., *n.* 6 : ' Another sense also occurs to me, which I had not thought of before, but which I cannot pass over.' Add to this that the Saint himself informs us in the following words that many of his sermons were written down by his disciples after he had delivered them : ' They have been written

down as they were delivered, in the same manner as other sermons also, so that, with the exception of the style, anything that may have been lost is easily recovered' (Sermon LIV., *n.* 1). To this also relates what we read in Sermon LXXVII., *n.* 2 : 'Even though what I say were perchance put in writing, they would disdain to read them.'

6. St. Bernard used to preach these sermons invariably in the auditorium of the Brethren, and even the Novices (Sermon LXIII., *n.* 6) were present, but not the 'Conversi,' who did not attend meetings of that kind at all. Wherefore he often asserts that his auditors were well skilled in the Scriptures ; and even more, he declares in his sermons that the 'rapid apprehension' of his hearers would 'anticipate' what he had to say (Sermons XV., *n.* 2 ; XVI., *n.* 1 ; XXXIX., *n.* 2). Again, as to the hour at which these sermons were delivered, it was sometimes in the morning, before the celebration of the Holy Eucharist (as was said with regard to other sermons in the preface to a former volume), and sometimes in the evening. It is apparent that it was sometimes in the morning, from two passages in which he brings the sermon to an end, because of their manual labour, and of the Divine office. Thus in Sermon I. towards the end : 'But the hour passes by,' he says, ' at which both our poverty and our settled rule summon us to the labour of our hands.' Still plainer in this respect is a passage in Sermon XLVII., which he, in fact, broke off because of the approach of the hour for the Divine office. As to the evening preaching, the testimony is clear in Sermon LXXI., *n.* 15 : 'But while I prolong this argument, the end of the day has come.' But enough has been said of these small matters, though here they are not altogether out of place.

7. St. Bernard had finished four-and-twenty sermons in the year 1137, in which year he set forth into Italy for the purpose of composing the schism. He returned thence in the following year, and at once betook himself to the work which had been interrupted, repeating Sermon XXIV. with another exordium and another peroration, by which has been occasioned a diversity of reading, which I shall treat of in its place. Sermons LXV. and LXVI, which begin from the exposition of that verse, 'Take us the little foxes ' (ii. 15), the Saint composed against the heretics of Cologne, having been induced to do this by a letter written to him by Everwin, provost of Steinfeld, which letter he seems on that account to have placed at the head of those two sermons. Finally, Sermon LXXX was delivered after the Council of Rheims in 1148, held in the presence of Pope Eugenius, in which was condemned the error of Gilbert de la Porrée, Bishop of Poitiers, which Bernard himself refers to in that sermon.

8. In most MSS. the sermons are in number eighty-six, in a few eighty-seven ; but this is either because they have repeated Sermon XXIV., as is the case with the Colbertine MS., or have divided another into two, as is done in our MS. of St. Germain. Of

five MSS., which our brother, John Durand, consulted at my request, one has only eighty-six sermons; but in another, bearing the number 665, is found a preface which no other MS. has, nor any edition. It begins thus : 'Preface of the blessed Bernard, Abbot of Clairvaux, to the Song of Songs. The highest incentive which God has proposed to virtue is that of the delight of future blessedness; just as pleasure is the most powerful spur to wrong-doing which the devil has discovered. Of the truth of each of these sentiments we have a proof in Adam, the chief of the human race, since he was placed by the Lord God in a Paradise of pleasure, that he might thus be attracted to virtue, and enjoy eternal felicity in future ages.' The writer goes on to say that the loss of innocence by sin was followed by the loss of happiness, but that this loss was repaired by the melody and sweetness of the Psalms and Song of Songs. There is not a word in this preface which approaches the style or genius of Bernard. This preface is followed by eighty-three sermons only, under this title : 'Exposition of the Song of Songs, by the blessed Bernard, Abbot of Clairvaux.' Another codex has, 'Bernard upon the Song of Songs,' and others, 'Treatise of the blessed Bernard, Abbot of Clairvaux, upon the Song of Songs.' One Colbertine MS. bears for title 'Treatise' instead of 'Sermons,' according to the ancient usage. But these are small details. That exposition breaks off in the third chapter of the Song of Songs at the verse, ' By night upon my bed I sought Him ' (verse 1), from which point Gilbert of Hoiland, who was himself a Cistercian of England,[1] continued it to this verse of the fifth chapter, ' My beloved is white and ruddy ' (verse 10), in forty-eight sermons. He was a man assuredly not much inferior to Bernard in the gravity and piety of his style. Death withdrew him from the world before he had carried his endeavour any further, as if he were indignant (if we are to believe Sixtus of Sienna) that the work of Bernard, which he had interrupted, should be continued a second time, and that Gilbert should dare even to wish to bring it to completion. Sixtus is mistaken when he says that this work was begun by Bernard ' in the last year of his life.'

9. Besides this exposition, Bernard dictated another and shorter one to William of St. Thierry, as William himself declares ('Life,' Bk. I., c. 12); but it will be a fitter place to speak of this when I shall refer to a brief comment on the two first chapters of the Canticles, drawn from St. Bernard's work.

10. In the first sermon of this longer exposition St. Bernard seems to hint that he had written commentaries on the Proverbs of Solomon, and on Ecclesiastes. He speaks thus (*n*. 2): ' For as to the words of Ecclesiastes, I believe that by the grace of God you are sufficiently instructed how to recognise and to contemn the vanity of this world. What as to the Proverbs ? Is not your life and conduct sufficiently formed and ruled on the teaching which they contain ?

---

[1] Mabillon says 'of Ireland,' but he has apparently confused the Abbey of St. Mary at Swineshed with that of St. Mary at Dublin.— ED.

Wherefore, having tasted of both of these, which you have accepted, nevertheless, as it were, two loaves offered from the chest of a friend, draw near and taste of the third also, and see if it be not still better.' But these words seem to signify only this, that the brethren of Clairvaux had been occupying themselves in reading the Proverbs and Ecclesiastes, and had adapted their conduct to the rules given in those books. Certainly Geoffrey, who has framed a list, sufficiently accurate, of the works of St. Bernard, has never attributed to him any commentaries on those books, nor has any contemporary author done so, as far as I am aware. Perhaps by that word 'of a friend' St. Bernard meant to refer to some author of that time, such, for example, as Hugo of St. Victor, who composed nineteen homilies upon Ecclesiastes.

11. I return to the sermons upon the Song of Songs. What Guerric, Abbot of Igny, and himself a most pious disciple of our holy Doctor, thought of these, he declares in his third sermon for the Festival of SS. Peter and Paul, in which he says : 'Our master, that interpreter of the Holy Spirit, resolved to explain to us the whole of that nuptial Song, and from those parts of his exposition which he put forth gave us good ground to hope that, if he had attained to treat of that passage, respecting which you inquire, "until the day break and the shadows flee away," he would bring those shadows into the light of knowledge. He shall tell us in the light that which was spoken, or shall be, in darkness.' These are the words of Guerric.

SERMON I.

ON THE TITLE OF THE BOOK: 'THE SONG OF SONGS, WHICH IS SOLOMON'S.'

O you, brethren, it is needful to speak of other truths than to those persons who are of the world; or, at least, to speak of them in a different manner. To them, if a preacher wishes to observe the order of teaching which the Apostle has prescribed (1 Cor. iii. 2), milk, not meat, is to be given. He himself teaches us, by his own example, to offer more solid nourishment to such as are spiritual, as when he says: 'We speak, not in the words which man's wisdom teacheth, but which the Holy Ghost teacheth, comparing spiritual things with spiritual.' And also: 'We speak wisdom among them that are perfect' (1 Cor. ii. 13, 6), such as I trust that you, my brethren, are; unless it is in vain that you have been long occupied in the study of heavenly things, in meditating upon the law of God day and night, and in training yourselves to arrive at a knowledge of the truth. Prepare, therefore, to be nourished, not with milk, but with bread. There is bread in [these words of] Solomon, and that white and delicate; I mean in this book which is called 'The Song of Songs.' Let us set it before us, and break it according to our need.

2. As for the Book of Ecclesiastes, you are, if I do not mistake,

sufficiently well instructed by the grace of God to recognise and despise the vanity of the world, which is treated of therein. And what as to the Proverbs? Is not your life and conduct sufficiently formed and ruled on the teaching which they contain? Wherefore, having tasted of both of these, which you have accepted nevertheless as [it were loaves] offered from the chest of a friend, draw near and taste of this third loaf also, and see if it be not still better.[1]

There are, then, two evils, which are the chief, if not the only ones which war against the soul, namely, the vain love of the world, and the excessive love of self. The two former books prescribe the remedy for each of these diseases, the former, by cutting away, with the sharp blade of discipline, whatever is corrupt in the character and superfluous in the desires of the flesh; the latter, by wisely penetrating with the light of reason the deceitful glamour of this world's vanity, and distinguishing it accurately from that which is real and solid. Finally, Solomon prefers the fear of God and the keeping of His commandments to the pursuit of human knowledge and of worldly desires. And rightly so. For the first of these is the beginning of true wisdom, and the second its consummation; if, that is to say, true and perfect wisdom consists only in departing from evil and doing good; and if, also, no one is able perfectly to depart from evil without the fear of God, as no one is able to do good without the keeping of His commandments.

3. These two evils having then been put to flight by the reading of those two books, it is possible to approach fitly in order to listen to that sacred and sublime discourse, which being, as it were, the fruit of both [the previous books], is not to be listened to except by ears and hearts which are chastened and wise. For otherwise, unless the flesh has been mastered by discipline, and subjected to the spirit; unless the burdensome pomp of the world has been despised and cast away as insupportable, the heart is impure and unworthy to peruse the sacred Song. Just as the pure light is poured, vainly and to no purpose, upon blind eyes, or upon eyes that are closed, so 'the natural man receiveth not the things of the Spirit of God' (1 Cor. ii. 14). For the holy spirit of discipline will flee from the deceitful (Wisd. i. 5), that is, from one who leads an unregulated life. Never will He, who is the Spirit of Truth (John xiv. 17), have part or lot with the vain things of this world. What alliance can there be between the wisdom which is from above, and the wisdom of this world, which is foolishness with God (1 Cor. iii. 19), or the wisdom of the flesh, which is positively hostile to Him (Rom. viii. 7)? But I think that the friend who comes to us from his journey[2] will have no reason to murmur against us, when he shall have taken of this third loaf.

[1] There is a reference here to Luke xi. 5: 'Friend, lend me three loaves.' Whether the words in the text imply that St. Bernard had made a comment upon those two books is discussed in the preface.

[2] There is a question whether this 'friend' may not have been Bernard des Portes. See the discussion in Mabillon's preface.—ED.

4. But who shall break it? The Master of the house is present; do ye recognise the Lord in the breaking of bread. What other is there who is capable of doing this? As for me, I am by no means so rash as to arrogate the task to myself. If you look to me, yet do so as looking for nothing from me. For I myself am one of those who await their meat from God; I entreat with you, for the food of my soul, the sustenance of my spirit. Truly poor and needy as I am, I knock at the door of Him who openeth and no man shutteth (Rev. iii. 7), to obtain a knowledge of the deep mystery which lies hidden in this book. The eyes of all wait upon Thee, O Lord. Thy little children seek bread, and there is no one to break it for them. From Thy goodness we hope for that blessing. O most merciful One, break Thy bread to the hungering souls that are before Thee: by my hands, if Thou shalt see fit, but by the strength of Thy grace.

5. Make known to us, we entreat, by whom, and of whom this verse is said, and to whom it applies (Cant. i. 1). Why is it so abruptly spoken that it seems to plunge the hearer suddenly into the mid-action of a drama? The speaker breaks forth suddenly, as if someone had spoken before, and as if a second character in the dialogue were then introduced, whosoever it may be, who makes this impassioned request. Then again, why is this unusual manner of speech made use of? But assuredly the very novelty and abruptness of this manner of beginning is not otherwise than very pleasing. Thus is it with the Holy Scripture; it has an attractive countenance, which wins upon us at once, and carries us on to the reading of it, in such wise that, however laborious it may be to investigate the hidden mystery which it enfolds, that labour becomes pleasure, and however great the difficulty of the inquiry, it does not weary, inasmuch as the sweetness of the discourse recompenses and charms the inquirer. Who is there whom that commencing without commencement, that novel mode of speaking in a book so old, would not render attentive? From this it appears that this work is not due to human powers, but was thus composed by the wisdom of the Holy Spirit; so that, however difficult it might be to understand, the searching out of its meaning might be a delightful task.

6. But are we to pass over the title in silence? By no means. We ought not to neglect the least iota, remembering that our Lord gave command that the fragments should be gathered together, that nothing might be lost (John vi. 12). The title is thus worded: 'Here begins the Song of Songs, which is Solomon's.' Observe first that the name of Solomon, that is, the Peaceful,[1] well becomes the beginning of this book, which commences by the sign of peace; and remark at the same time also that only *the peaceful* are invited to the consideration of this scripture, that is to say, those who have tranquil and peaceful souls, delivered from the agitation of evil passions, and the tumult of earthly cares.

---

[1] שְׁלֹמֹה = Shĕlômôh, the 'Peaceful One.'—ED.

7. Do not suppose either that it is without significance that the title of this scripture is not simply 'a song,' but 'the Song of Songs.' I have read many songs or canticles in Scripture, and I do not remember one on which such a title as this was set. Israel sang to the Lord a song of praise, because they had escaped both from the sword and the slavery of Pharaoh, because they had been at once wonderfully delivered, and avenged, as by a twofold miracle, at the Red Sea. But yet their song was not styled 'Song of Songs.' The Scripture says, if I remember rightly, 'Then sang Moses and the children of Israel this song unto the Lord' (Exod. xv. 1). Deborah, too; Judith, and the mother of Samuel, each gave utterance to a song. Not a few of the Prophets also raised their voices in song; but we do not read that any of all these called his canticle 'the Song of Songs.' You will find, I believe, that each and all of these sang to celebrate some advantage conferred upon themselves or their people; for example, because they had gained a battle, escaped from some peril, obtained some wished-for benefit, or object of that kind. They uttered their songs, then, each for some object more or less private, that they might not be found ungrateful for the Divine benefits, as it is written: 'When Thou hast blessed him he will praise Thee' (Ps. xlix. 18, Vulg.). But this King Solomon, who was endowed with admirable wisdom, exalted glory, overflowing wealth, and enjoyed profound peace, is known to have needed nothing, the attainment of which would have given him occasion to lift up his voice in this song of praise. There is no statement of Scripture anywhere which seems to suggest any such reason.

8. It was, then, by inspiration from above that he sang the praises of Christ and His Church, the grace of holy love, and the mysteries of everduring marriage; and at the same time gave expression to the yearning aspirations of the holy soul. Thus he has composed a nuptial song or epithalamium, rejoicing in spirit, and in an ornamental and figurative style. Doubtless he veiled his face, as it were, after the example of Moses (Exod. iii. 6), which was perhaps not less resplendent [in the glory of its meaning] as also because in that day there were few, or none, who were capable of sustaining that glory if fully revealed. Therefore I conclude that this nuptial anthem is named 'Song of Songs' for its surpassing excellence, just as He who is above all is for that reason called alone '*King of Kings and Lord of Lords*' (1 Tim. vi. 15).

9. If you consult your own experience,[1] after the victory which your faith has gained over the world, and at your coming forth from the abyss of misery and filthy bog, have not you also sung a new song unto the Lord, because He hath done wonderful things? Again, when He has set your feet upon a rock, and ordered your goings, I

---

[1] The MS. of Citeaux adds here: 'The songs which we ought to sing through at each advance;' which seems to be an error. (Or is there a reference to the 'Psalms of Degrees?')—ED.

think that then also in like manner, in thankfulness for the renewal of your life, a new song was put into your lips, even a thankfulness unto our God. And when, after your repentance for sin, He has not only put away your offences, but has even promised you rewards also, has not that joy with which you were inspired by the hope of future blessings made you to 'sing in the ways of the Lord, that great is the glory of the Lord'? Again, when some one of you who had found some passage of Scripture to be hitherto obscure and impenetrable has gained a certain degree of light upon it, then, without doubt, in thankfulness for the nourishment of heavenly bread which he has received, he should delight the Divine ear with the voice of gladness and the sound of one that feasts. Finally, in the struggles and combats of every day, which are at no time wanting to those who live piously in Christ, whether it be with the flesh, the world, or the devil, so that the life of man upon the earth is a continual warfare, as you experience incessantly in your own selves, it is needful day by day to raise new songs of thanksgiving for the victories which you gain. As often as temptation is overcome, vicious inclination restrained, imminent danger escaped, a snare of the tempter discovered, or some ancient and inveterate fault of the soul healed perfectly and once for all, or as often as some special favour long desired and frequently besought from God is at length obtained from Him, ought we not so often, according to the prophet's saying, to make the voice of joy and praise resound, thanksgiving, and the voice of melody (Is. li. 3), and at each of His benefits let God be praised in His gifts? Otherwise, he shall be counted as ungrateful in the day of judgment who is not able to say unto God: *Thy statutes have been my songs in the house of my pilgrimage* (Ps. cxix. 54).

10. I imagine that you have yourselves already noticed that in the psalter we have psalms called not 'Songs of Songs,' but songs or psalms 'of degrees' (Pss. cxx.-cxxxiv.) 'because in the measure that you make progress in the spiritual life, according to the steps upward that each makes in his heart, he ought to render songs to the praise and glory of Him who is the inspirer of them all. I do not see how in any other manner that verse could be accomplished: *The voice of rejoicing and salvation is in the dwellings of the righteous* (Ps. cxviii. 15), or that beautiful and salutary exhortation of the Apostle: *Speaking to yourselves in psalms and hymns and spiritual songs, singing and making melody in your hearts to the Lord* (Eph. v. 19).

11. But there is a canticle which, by its excellence and incomparable sweetness, rightly surpasses those which I have mentioned and all others, if there be any, and this I may call 'the Song of Songs,' seeing that it is itself the fruit of all others. That canticle the anointing of grace alone teaches, and experience only makes the soul to be familiar with it. Those who have had experience of it know it well; let those who have not had that happiness earnestly desire, not to know it, but to experience it. It is not a cry from the

mouth, but the gladness of the heart; not the sounding of the lips, but the impulse and emotion of joys within; not a concert of words, but of wills moving in harmony. It is not heard without, nor does it make a sound in public. Only she who sings, and He in whose honour it is sung, that is the Bridegroom and the Bride, hear the accents of that song. It is a nuptial song, which is expressive of the chaste and sweet emotions of souls, the entire conformity of character, the blending of affections in mutual charity.

12. But for the rest, this song is not to be sung or to be understood by a soul which is as yet a neophyte in the infancy of its virtue, and but newly turned from the world. It belongs to the advanced and instructed soul, which, by the progress in grace made by it through the power of God, has grown as far as to reach a perfect age, and, as it were, to have become marriageable (remember that I speak not of years, but of virtues), and fit for the nuptials with its heavenly spouse, such as will be more fully described in its place. But the hour is passing, at which both our poverty and the precept of our rule call us forth to the labour of our hands. To-morrow we will continue in the name of God what we had entered upon with respect to the opening verse, since the sermon of to-day has furnished the explication of the title.

SERMON II.

OF THE INCARNATION OF CHRIST, WHICH WAS ANNOUNCED BY THE PATRIARCHS AND PROPHETS, AND ARDENTLY EXPECTED BY THEM.

'*Let Him kiss me with the kisses of His mouth.*'—Cant. i. 1.

THINK very often of the deep earnestness and ardour with which the ancient Fathers desired the presence of Christ in the Flesh, and I am touched with a feeling of extreme grief and shame in myself, I am scarcely able even now to restrain my tears, so much am I ashamed of the coldness and insensibility of the unhappy times in which we live. Who is there among us that feels joy as great at the actual showing forth of this wonder of grace, as the desire and longing wherewith the ancient saints were fired at the promise only of so great a thing? How many there are who will rejoice at that Festival of His Birth, which we are soon about to celebrate! But would that their rejoicings were, not on account of vain things, but really on account of His Birth! This verse seems, then, to me to breathe the ardent desire and pious impatience of those great men.

The little band of those who then were animated by the Holy Spirit felt in advance how great would be the grace which would be diffused upon those Divine Lips. Therefore it was that speaking in the ardour of that desire, wherewith their heart was fired, they said these words, passionately wishing not to be deprived of happiness so great.

2. For each of these saintly souls would, as it were, say : To what end do these wordy[1] utterances from the mouths of the prophets come to me? Let Him rather who is fair beyond the sons of men, let Him come to me with the touch of His Lips. Not now do I listen to Moses : he has become slow of speech to me, and of a slow tongue (Exod. iv. 10). The lips of Isaiah are impure (Is. vi. 5). Jeremiah knows not how to speak, for he is a child (Jer. i. 6) ; yea, all the prophets are speechless. Let Him of whom they bear witness, let Him speak Himself to me. Let Him speak to me no longer in them or by their means, for their words are as a darkening cloud in the air of heaven ; but let Him whose presence is full of grace, whose teaching shall become in me a fountain of water springing up into eternal life (John iv. 14), let Him come to me with the touch of His Lips. Shall not He whom the Father hath anointed with the oil of gladness above His fellows (Ps. xlv. 8), pour upon me from His fulness a more abounding grace, if He shall indeed deign to do this? He it is whose speech, living and powerful, is to me as a kiss, and that not the mere meeting of the lips, which ofttimes is but a deceptive sign of peace in the heart, but rather the imparting of joys, the revealing of things hidden, and a certain wonderful, intimate, and wholly ineffable mingling of the heavenly light which enlightens the soul, and the soul which is illuminated by it. For *he that is joined unto the Lord is one spirit* (1 Cor. vi. 17). Rightly, then, do I receive neither visions nor dreams ; I turn away from parables and metaphors ; even angelic glories themselves I hold in disdain. For even these Jesus, who is mine, by His fairness and His attractiveness to my soul, far surpasses. Of no other, then, whether angel nor man, but of Him alone do I make his entreaty. Yet I have not the presumption to require to be kissed with His mouth. That is the unique privilege and incommunicable felicity of the Man whom the Word has assumed to Himself in the incarnation. My petition is more humble : and this is a privilege common to all who are able to say, *Of His fulness have we all received* (John i. 16).

3. Observe : It is the Word becoming Incarnate, who is the Mouth who gives the kiss. It is the Human Nature which is assumed which receives it. The kiss, which is perfected equally by Him who gives and Him who receives it, is that Person constituted of each nature, the Mediator between God and men, the Man Christ

---

[1] *Seminiverbia, i.e.,* σπερμολόγος, as in Acts xvii. 18. This is a rare word, and the corresponding Greek is used only this once in the New Testament.—ED.

Jesus. On this account none of the saints presume to say, 'Let Him kiss me with His mouth,' but only 'With the kiss of His mouth.' They reverently respected the sole prerogative of that [Nature] on which the adorable Mouth of the Word was impressed once for all, when the Fulness of the Godhead was united corporeally with it. Happy the sign, wonderful and stupendous the condescension, in which, not lip is pressed to lip, but God is united to Man. There, indeed, the pressure of the lip does signify the union of souls, but here a union of Natures joins that which is Divine and that which is Human, and reconciles those things which are on earth and those in heaven. *For He is our Peace, who hath made both one* (Eph. ii. 14). It was, then, for this that every saint of the old time longed, because they felt the assurance beforehand that upon Him joy and gladness were abundantly poured, and in Him were hid all the treasures of wisdom and knowledge (Col. ii. 3); and they earnestly desired to have part with Him and in His fulness.

4. I feel that what has been said meets with your assent; but listen to still another sense of the words. It was not hidden from holy souls, even before the coming of the Saviour, that God was meditating designs of peace towards the race of mortals (Jer. xxix. 11). Nor did He speak as regarding the earth without revealing His purpose to His servants the prophets (Amos iii. 7). Yet this saying was hid from many (Luke xviii. 34), for in that time faith was rare upon the earth, and hope faint among most of those who waited for the redemption of Israel. But those who had foreknowledge, predicted that Christ should come in the Flesh, and that with Him should come peace. Thus one of them says: *Peace shall be in our land when He shall have come* (Micah v. 5). Nay, more, they confidently predicted what they had learned from above, that men through Him should recover the favour [*gratiam*] of God. And this John, the Forerunner of the Lord, recognized to have been fulfilled in his time, and declared: *Grace and truth came by Jesus Christ* (John i. 17), an assertion of the truth of which the whole Christian people has experience at this day.

5. But though they foretold peace, yet, as the Author of peace delayed to come, the faith of the people was weak and tottering, there being none to redeem or to save. That brought men to complain of the delay, because the Prince of Peace, so oft announced, had not yet come, as He had for so many ages promised by the mouth of His holy prophets; and holding these promises, as it were, in suspicion, they eagerly demanded the sign of the reconciliation, that is to say, the Incarnation. As if one of the people should reply to the messengers of peace, 'How long do you hold our minds in suspense? You have long been foretelling peace, and it does not come; you promise every kind of good, yet behold trouble and misery. Behold, how many times and in what divers manners have angels announced this very thing to our fathers, and our fathers have handed it down to us, crying *Peace, peace*, yet there is no peace (Jer. vi. 14). If God desires

that I should be convinced of the determination of His good pleasure, which He so frequently promised by His messengers, but does not as yet make manifest, let Him come to me with the touch of His Lips, and the sign of peace shall be for me an assured pledge of peace. How can I put my trust any longer in words? It is instead needful to strengthen words by action. Let God approve His messengers, if, indeed, they be His, as men of truth, and let Him follow them Himself, as they have so often promised; for without Him they can do nothing (John xv. 5). He has sent a servant, and by the servant His staff; but there is neither voice nor breath thereby (2 Kings iv. 29-31). I rise not, I am not lifted up nor brought out of the dust, I do not breathe the free air of hope, unless the Prophet Himself shall come down, unless He shall come to me with the sign of peace.

6. It is farther to be added, that He who declares Himself our Mediator before God, is the Son of God, is Himself God (1 Tim. ii. 5). And what is man that He takes knowledge of him, or the son of man, that He has consideration for him? What ground of confidence have I, that I should dare to trust myself to majesty so great? Wherefore, I repeat, should I, who am but dust and ashes, presume to think that God would take care for me? Between Him and His Father is indeed love; but He has no need of me, nor of my goods. How, then, shall it be made clear to me that He who is my Mediator is impartial? Yet if God has truly determined, as you say, to have mercy upon me, and still meditates greater acts of favour on my behalf, let Him establish a covenant of peace, let Him make a perpetual alliance with me by this sign. In order that the words which proceed out of His Lips be not made of no avail, let Him empty Himself, let Him humble Himself, let Him stoop from His high heaven, and kiss me with the kiss of His Mouth. Let the Son of God, if He will be a Mediator acceptable to both parties, and suspected by neither, become Man, become Son of Man, and establish my trust on a sure ground by this. With assured confidence shall I take the Son of God as Mediator when I perceive that He is also a son of my own human race. I can no longer retain any suspicion of Him, since He is my brother and my flesh. For I hope that He will then not be able to despise me, when He is bone of my bones, and flesh of my flesh.

7. It was thus, then, that the ancient plaint of humanity earnestly begged for that Kiss sacrosanct, that is, the mystery of the Incarnation of the Word; while faith failed, being exhausted with long and weary expectation, and the unbelieving people, abandoning itself to discouragement, murmured against the promises of God. This is not an invention of mine; you will find it for yourselves in the Scriptures. Thence arise those sayings mingled with complaint and blame: *Precept upon precept, line upon line, here a little and there a little* (Is. xxviii. 10). Thence those prayers also, coming from hearts anxious and troubled, yet loyal: *Recompense, O Lord, them that wait*

for Thee, and let Thy prophets be found faithful and true. And again, *Accomplish, O Lord, the predictions of Thy ancient prophets.*[1] From thence also those promises so sweet and full of consolation: *The Lord shall appear, and shall not lie: if He tarry, wait for Him; for He shall surely come, He shall not tarry* (Habak. ii. 3). And again: *His time is near to come, and His days shall not be prolonged* (Is. xiii. 22). And again, in the person of Him who is promised: *Behold I will extend peace to her as a river, and the glory of the nations as a flowing stream* (Is. lxvi. 12). In which words are sufficiently apparent both the persevering constancy of the preachers, and the distrust of the peoples. Thus it was that the mass of men murmured, that faith was tottering, and that, according to the foreboding of Isaiah, *The angels of peace themselves wept bitterly* (Is. xxxiii. 7). Therefore that the whole human race, while Christ so long delayed His coming, might not perish from mere despair, suspecting its feeble and helpless mortality to be contemned and scorned, and distrusting its reconciliation with God by grace, so often promised; the saints, who had been kept firm in faith by the Spirit which animated them, desired earnestly the confirmation of their faith by His presence in the flesh, and urged eagerly, on account of those who were weak and incredulous, the sign of peace to be regained.

8. O Root of Jesse, who standest for an ensign of the peoples, how many prophets and kings have desired to see Thee, yet have not seen! Surely of all the most happy was Simeon, whose old age was rich in mercy! He rejoiced that he saw the sign so greatly desired: he saw it, and was glad: and having received the kiss of peace, departed in peace; yet not before he had declared that Jesus was born, to be a sign; but *a sign which should be spoken against* (Luke ii. 25-35). And thus indeed it was. Opposition arose to the sign of peace, from the time that it appeared; but from those who hate peace. For it was peace to men of good will; but to the evil disposed a stone of stumbling and a rock of offence (Rom. ix. 33). Herod was troubled, and all Jerusalem with him (Matt. ii. 3), so it was that the Lord *came unto His own, and His own received Him not* (John i. 11). Happy were those shepherds in their watch by night, who were deemed worthy to behold that sign in a vision. Even then He was hiding Himself from the wise and prudent, and revealing Himself unto babes. Even Herod wished to behold Him, but he was not found worthy, for his motive was not pure. For this was the sign of peace, and was given only to men of good will; but to Herod, and to those like him shall be given only the sign of Jonas the prophet (Luke xi. 29). To the shepherds, on the contrary, the angel said, 'This shall be a sign *unto you*,' you who are humble, who are obedient, who do not exercise yourselves in high things; you

---

[1] *Precationes.* This was the ancient reading, but the Vulgate reads *prædicationes*, and the LXX. agrees, τὰς προφητείας. Ecclus. xxxvi. 17, 18.—ED.

who are watchful, who meditate day and night in the law of the Lord, *to you*, He says, *this shall be the sign.* What sign? The sign which the angels promised, which the peoples asked for, which the prophets had predicted, this sign the Lord has now brought to pass, and shows it to you; so that in it the unbelieving may obtain faith, those who are fearful hope, and they who are perfect entire security. *This then*, he says, *shall be to you a sign.* Of what is it the sign? Of pardon, of grace, of peace; and of that peace which has no end. This is the sign: *Ye shall find a Babe wrapped in swaddling clothes, lying in a manger.* Yet in Him is God *reconciling the world unto Himself* (2 Cor. v. 19). He shall die for your sins, and rise again for your justification; so that being justified by faith, you may have peace with God (Rom. v. 1). This sign of peace a prophet formerly proposed to King Ahaz, that he should ask it of the Lord his God, either in the heaven above, or in the depth beneath. But the impious king refused (Is. vii. 11, 12), not believing, unhappy man that he was, that in this sign the highest and the lowest should be joined in fellowship and peace: inasmuch as the dwellers in the very depths of the grave should receive the sign of peace, when the Lord descending thither, should salute them with this holy kiss; and the celestial spirits also should share in it, and that with joy everlasting when He should return to heaven.

9. This sermon must be brought to a close. But to sum up in a few words what has been treated of in it. It appears that this holy kiss was necessarily accorded to the world for two reasons: that it might produce faith in the weak, and satisfy the longing desire for it in the perfect, since by this kiss is meant no other than the Mediator between God and men, the Man CHRIST JESUS, who with the FATHER and the HOLY SPIRIT liveth and reigneth, God, for ever and ever. AMEN.

SERMON III.

WHAT IT IS TO KISS THE FEET, THE HAND, AND THE LIPS OF THE LORD.

'*Let Him kiss me with the kisses of His mouth.*'—Cant. i. 1.

WE shall read to-day in the book of experience. Turn your minds inward upon yourselves, and let each of you examine his own conscience in regard to those things which are to be mentioned. I desire to make examination, whether to any of you it has been given to speak out of the deep desire of his heart, these words of the text which we are to consider. Not to all men does it belong to take these words upon their lips with sincere desire; he alone is able to do so, who has received even once only, the spiritual kiss from the lips of Christ; him his own experience incessantly urges to obtain a renewal of that which he found so full of sweetness. It is my strong opinion that no one can comprehend what it is, save he who has experienced it; it is, as it were, a hidden manna; and he who tastes of it, still hungers for it again. It is a fountain sealed, from which no stranger may draw; but he who drinks of it still thirsts to drink again. Listen to one who had experienced that which he again asks for : *Restore unto me the joy of Thy salvation* (Ps. li. 13). Let not a soul then which is laden with sin, and still subject to the passions of the flesh, which has not yet tasted the delights of the Holy Spirit, which is wholly ignorant of, and inexperienced in, inward joys; in short, a soul like mine, make the least pretension to such a degree of grace.

2. Nevertheless, to such a one I will point out the position in regard to this saving grace which is befitting to him. Let him not have the rashness to lift himself so high as to the lips of the Divine Bridegroom, but let him, with holy fear, lie with me at the Feet of that Lord so severe; let him, like the publican, tremble nor dare to lift up his eyes unto heaven (Luke xviii. 13), for fear lest his eyes, accustomed only to earthly gloom, should be dazzled by the light of heaven, should be blinded by its glory; and, being stricken by the unaccustomed splendour of that majesty, should be whelmed anew in a still deeper darkness. It is not for thee, O sinful soul, whosoever thou art, to regard that place and posture, in which the woman that had been a sinner and became a saint, laid down her sins and put on the garment of holiness, as being vile or contemptible. There the Ethiopian changed her skin, and, being restored to a new whiteness, was enabled to respond with as much confidence as truth to those who reproached her: *Daughters of Jerusalem, though black, I am comely* (Cant. i. 4). If you wonder how she was enabled to do this, or by what merits she obtained it, I will answer in a few words. She wept bitterly; she drew long sighs of remorse from the depths of her soul; her frame was convulsed with salutary sobs, and thus the deeply-seated poison was cast forth. The heavenly Physician came promptly to help; for *His Word runneth very swiftly* (Ps. cxlvii. 15). Is not the Word of God a medicine ? It is so in truth, and a medicine strong and powerful, trying the very heart and reins (Ps. vii. 10). *For the Word of God is quick and powerful, and sharper than any two edged sword, piercing even to the dividing asunder of the soul and spirit, and of the joints and marrow, and is a discerner of the thoughts and intents of the heart* (Heb. iv. 12). According to the example of this happy penitent, do thou also, O unhappy soul, prostrate thyself that thou mayst cease to be unhappy; prostrate thyself even to the earth, embrace His Feet, appease them with kisses, bedew them with thy tears; yet not that thou mayest wash them, but thyself; and that thou mayest become one of that flock of sheep newly shorn, which come up from the laver of cleansing (Cant. iv. 2). And do not have the boldness to lift up your countenance suffused

with tears of shame and grief, until you hear, you also, the words of absolution, *Thy sins are forgiven thee* (Luke vii. 36-48); until you hear, *Arise, arise, O captive daughter of Zion; shake thyself from the dust* (Is. lii. 2).

3. Having then imprinted this first kiss upon the Feet, do not presume immediately to lift up thyself to the kiss of His Lips, but let the kiss of His Hand be for thee a gradation or second step by which to reach the higher blessedness. Take notice of the reason for this. If Jesus shall have said to me, *Thy sins are forgiven thee;* what shall even this avail me if I do not cease to commit sin? If I have put off my tunic, and then put it on again, what doth it profit? Or if I wash my feet and then defile them anew, will it avail anything that they were once washed? Long have I lain in the filthy mire, wallowing in every kind of vice; but if, after escaping therefrom, I shall unhappily fall back into it, my state will undoubtedly be worse than it was at first. For I remember how He who healed me spake to me thus: *Behold, thou art made whole: sin no more, lest a worse thing come unto thee* (John v. 14). What is needed, then, is that He who gave me a goodwill to repent for the past, should also add to this another gift of grace, whereby I may abstain from sin for the future, so that I may not again commit crime upon crime, and my last state be worse than the first. Woe to me if He, without whom I can do nothing, shall suddenly withdraw His supporting Hand from me, even in the midst of my penitence! Nothing, I repeat, am I capable of doing without Him; neither to repent of the past, nor to keep myself from fresh sin. I bear in mind the counsel which the Wise Man gives: 'Do not make a vain repetition in thy prayer' (Ecclus. vii. 14). And I tremble at the decree which the Judge has it in mind to pronounce against the tree which bringeth not forth good fruit (Matt. iii. 10); I confess that on this account I shall not be wholly content with the former grace, by which I am enabled to be repentant for my former sins, unless I shall have received a second to make me bring forth fruits worthy of penitence, and thenceforth not to return to my former pollution.

4. This, then, remains for me to ask and to receive before I presume to approach the higher and more sacred degrees of blessedness. I do not desire to reach the highest point suddenly, but to proceed towards it by gradual steps. For inasmuch as the shamelessness of a sinner is displeasing to God, in the same degree is the modesty of a penitent pleasing to Him. Thou mayst the sooner please Him, if thou shalt observe a becoming measure in thy desires, nor seek for thyself the higher degrees of privilege. From the foot to the lips the ascent is long and difficult, and it would be wanting even in reverence to pass from one straight to the other. What! shalt thou, still marked with recent dust-stains, touch those sacred Lips? and having been but yesterday drawn out of the mire, aspire to-day to the glory of His Countenance? For thee there must be a mid-stage of preparation; and that is by His Hand; it shall first cleanse thee from thy stains,

and then it shall lift thee up. But how shall it raise thee up? By bestowing upon thee that which shall be a ground for aspiring higher: the grace of continence, the fruits worthy of penitence, which are works of piety. These shall lift thee from the dunghill, and infuse into thee the hope of higher things. In receiving this gift, then assuredly thou shouldest kiss the Lord's Hand—that is, give the glory to Him, not to thyself. Give it to Him once, and yet again: the first time because of His pardon to your sins; the second, because of the virtues He has bestowed. For otherwise, what reply have you to make to such reproaches as these: *What hast thou that thou hast not received? Now if thou hast received it, why dost thou glory, as though thou hadst not received it?* (1 Cor. iv. 7).

5. After you have, then, made in those two kisses, a double proof of the Divine condescension, perhaps you may be so bold as to enter upon the endeavour to reach still higher and more sacred things. For in proportion as you grow in grace, your confidence also will augment, you will love more fervently, and knock at the door with more assurance of success, to seek that in which you feel you are wanting: for to him who knocks it shall be opened. And to you, when in such a disposition of mind and soul, I believe there will not be refused that kiss, the loftiest and most sacred of all, which contains in itself at once a supreme condescension and a sweetness ineffable. This is the way, and this the order, which must be followed. In the first place, we fall at the feet of the Lord, and lament before Him who has made us, the faults and sins which we ourselves have committed. In the second, we seek His helping Hand to lift us up, and to strengthen our feeble knees that we may stand upright. In the third, when we have, with many prayers and tears, obtained these two former graces, then at length we perhaps venture to lift our eyes to that Countenance full of glory and majesty, for the purpose not only to adore, but (I say it with fear and trembling) to kiss, because the spirit before us is Christ the Lord, to whom, being united in a holy kiss, we are by His marvellous condescension made to be one spirit with Him.

6. Rightly, O Lord Jesus, yea, rightly has my heart declared to Thee: *My face hath sought Thee: Thy face, Lord, will I seek* (Ps. xxvi. 8). Thou hast made me to hear Thy mercy in the morning when I lay prone in the dust, and kissing the prints of Thy sacred steps, Thou didst pardon the evil of my former life. Then, as the day of my life went on, Thou hast rejoiced the soul of Thy servant; since, by the kiss of Thy Hand, Thou hast accorded unto me the grace to live well. And now what remains, O good Lord, unless that in deigning to admit me, in the fulness of Thy Light, in the fervour of my spirit, to the kiss of Thy Divine Lips, Thou shouldest fulfil me with the joy of Thy Countenance? Teach me, O most dear and tranquil One, teach me where Thou dost dwell, and at noonday dost repose. Brethren, it is good for us to be here; but lo! the evil of the day calls us away. They, indeed, who just now announced

an arrival of guests, oblige me to break off, rather than conclude, a subject so agreeable. I go, then, to the care of these guests, lest anything be wanting in the discharge of those duties of charity of which we speak, and lest we should hear those words spoken of us: *They say, and do not* (Matt. xxiii. 3). Do ye in the meantime pray that God will make the free will offerings of my mouth acceptable unto Him, that they may be to your edification, and to the honour and glory of His Name.

SERMON IV.

OF THE THREEFOLD PROGRESS OF THE SOUL, ARISING FROM THE KISS OF THE FOOT, THE HAND, AND THE LIPS OF THE LORD.

'*Let Him kiss me with the kisses of His mouth.*'—Cant. i. 1.

THE sermon of yesterday was occupied in describing the threefold progress of the soul, under the name of three kisses. That, I dare say, is still in your remembrance. In the discussion of to-day I propose to continue the same subject in so far as God in His goodness shall deign to assist my poor powers. I said, if you remember, that those were given severally to the Feet, to the Hand, and to the Lips of Christ our Saviour. In the first are dedicated the first fruits of our conversion; the second shall be accorded to those who are making progress in holiness; but the third is rarely experienced, and by those only who are perfect. From this alone, which is placed last, it is that the Scripture which we have undertaken to expound takes its point of departure, and for that reason I have joined the other two to it. Whether that was needful you will judge; but I think that the very nature of the subject suggested, and indeed required, that course. And I think that you will observe also this, that the Bride desired to indicate a distinction when she said, using a phrase very unusual, '*of His Mouth.*' Why, when it would have sufficed simply to make her request, should she have added expressly and precisely beyond the usual phrase and manner of speaking, words which show that the grace for which she asked was not the only one, but was the highest? When the Evangelist relates how the false Apostle betrayed our Lord with a kiss, he says, 'And he kissed Him' (Mark xiv. 45); nor does he add 'with his mouth,' or 'of his mouth.' It is thus that everyone expresses himself either in writing or speech. There are, then, three states or modes of souls sufficiently well-known at least to those who have experienced them, when, as far as is possible in these weak bodies of ours, they are enabled to take knowledge either of the pardon which they have received for their evil actions, or the grace which has enabled them to do good ones; or lastly, of the very presence of Him who is their patron and benefactor.

2. Let me repeat to you more plainly why I have spoken of the first and the second of these under this name. We all know that a kiss is a sign of peace. Now if, as the Scripture declares, *our iniquities separate between us and our God* (Is. lix. 2), let that be taken away which interposes between us, and then there is peace. When, then, we make satisfaction so that we are reconciled with God by the taking away of the sin which separates us, what else can I call the pardon which we receive except a kiss of peace? Now, *that* kiss cannot be imprinted elsewhere than upon the Feet; for the satisfaction, which is the remedy for a transgression of the law of God, which arose from pride, ought to be humble and shame-faced.

3. But when we are endowed with fuller grace, and in a manner, so to speak, more familiar, and so are enabled to lead a life purer and more worthy of God, we begin to lift up our heads from the dust with greater confidence, in order to kiss, as is usual, the hand of our benefactor, provided that we seek, not our own glory, but that of our Creator, in the good things we have received, and provided also that we ascribe His gifts to Him, and not to ourselves. For otherwise, if instead of glorying in the Lord you glory in yourself, you are plainly shown to be kissing, as it were, your own hand, not the Hand of God; and this, according to the saying of the blessed Job, is a very great iniquity, and the denial of God who is above (Job xxxi. 28). If, then, following the testimony of Scripture, to seek one's own glory is, as it were, to kiss one's own hand, it follows that he who gives glory to God is said, not unfitly, to kiss the Hand of God. We see that it is thus even among men, that slaves are accustomed to kiss the feet of their offended lords when they are asking pardon of them for their faults; and those who are poor kiss the hands of the rich when they have received assistance from them.

4. But as God is a Spirit, a pure Substance, not distinguished into parts or members, there will be, perhaps, someone who cannot at all accept what I have said of Him; but will demand of me that I should show to him the Hands and the Feet of God, and so justify what I have said upon the kiss of the hand or foot. But if I, in my turn, shall become a questioner, what will he reply to me with regard to the mention in Scripture of 'the kiss of His Mouth'? For these [parts of a body] either exist together, or if the one is wanting, the others are wanting also. We say, then, that God has a Mouth, wherewith 'He teaches man knowledge'; and a Hand, wherewith 'He giveth food to all flesh'; and Feet, for which 'the earth is His footstool,' and at which the sinners of the earth 'fall down low upon their knees.' All these, then, God has; but in making that assertion, we reason, as it were, from effects, for it is not by His Nature that He has these. A confession, full of penitence and shame, finds in God that at which [the sinner] may fall down and humble himself, an ardent devotion finds a source of refreshment and renewal, and a joyful contemplation an object of safe repose in its ecstasies. He who governs all things is all things to all His creatures; yet, to speak with accuracy, He is not

any of all these things. If we consider Him as He is in Himself, He *dwelleth in the Light that no man can approach unto* (1 Tim. vi. 16), His '*peace passeth all understanding*' (Phil. iv. 7), His *wisdom is infinite* (Ps. cxlvii. 5), *there is no end of His greatness* (Ps. cxlv. 3), and *no man can see Him and live* (Exod. xxxiii. 20). Not that He is far from everyone of us, for He is the Principle of Being (*Esse*) of all things that exist, and without Him they would fall back into nothingness; but yet, to make a statement still more wonderful, though nothing is more certainly present than He, nothing is more incomprehensible. For what can be more surely present to everything than its own Principle of Being? Yet what can be more incomprehensible to each individual than the Principle of Being of all things? But when I say that God is the Principle of Being to all things, it is not that they are the same being as He; but it is that all things proceed from Him, subsist by Him, and are in Him (Rom. xi. 36). He, then, that has created all things is the Principle of Being to all things created; but with regard to Cause and Principle, not with regard to substance. In such a manner it is that the Divine Majesty condescends to all His creatures. He is assuredly the Principle of Being to them all—He is life to all that live; and, furthermore, He is Light to them who have the use of reason, Virtue to them who use their reason rightly, and, finally, He is Glory to them who triumph [in the probation of this life].

5. Finally, in the creation of all these things, in governing them, administering them, in giving them motion and growth, in renewing and in strengthening them, He has no need of any bodily instruments, since He created all things, both bodies and spirits, by His mere word. Souls have need of bodies and of bodily senses, by which they become known the one to the other, and are enabled to act the one upon the other. But it is not thus with the Almighty God; for from the volition of His Will alone follows promptly the effect He bids, whether it be in the creation of things, or in the ordering of them according as He shall please. What He wills He carries into effect, and to the fullest extent of His good pleasure; nor in performing it has He any need to employ bodily organs. What! do you suppose that to have relation with those things which He has Himself created He requires the assistance of bodily senses? Of all things that exist, nothing hides itself or escapes from His light, which is everywhere present; nor has He any need, in order to take knowledge of anything, to make use of the ministry of any sense. Not only does He have knowledge of all things without Himself having body, but also without body He makes Himself known to those who are of pure heart. I am repeating the same truth in different words that you may understand it the better; but as the little time remaining is insufficient for finishing the subject, it will perhaps be better to defer its farther consideration until the morrow.

SERMON V.

OF THE FOUR ORDERS OF SPIRITS—NAMELY, THE SPIRIT OF GOD, OF THE ANGELS, OF MAN, AND OF THE BEAST.

FOUR orders of spirits are known to you—that of the animals, our own, the angelic, and His who created all these. To each of these a body is necessary, either for its own sake or for the sake of others, or for both of these reasons, excepting only that One to whom every creature, whether corporeal or spiritual, justly bears witness and says: *Thou art my God: my goods are nothing unto Thee* (Ps. xvi. 2). As to the first order, that of animals, it is plain that it has such need of a body that it cannot in any wise exist without one; for when the creature dies, that [class of] spirit ceases at once both to be the source of vivifying power, and itself to live. But *we* live on after the body dies; still, there is no access open to us, except through the body, to those things whereby we live in happiness. He had perceived this who said: *The invisible things of God are clearly seen, being understood by those things which are made* (Rom. i. 20). For, indeed, those things which are made—that is, corporeal and visible things—unless they be perceived by the instrumentality of the body, do not come to our knowledge at all. The spiritual creature, therefore, which we are, must necessarily have a body, without which, indeed, it can by no means obtain that knowledge which is the only means of attaining to those things, to know which constitutes blessedness. If anyone object to me the case of little children who have been made regenerate [in Baptism], that should they go forth from the body without knowledge of things corporeal, they are believed to pass, nevertheless, into a life of blessedness, I reply, briefly, that it is grace, not nature, which confers this upon them. And what have I, now that I am discoursing of things in the course of nature, to do with a miracle of God?

2. Again, that heavenly spirits have need of bodies is proved by that true and plainly Divine declaration: *Are they not ministering spirits, sent forth to minister unto them who shall be heirs of salvation?* (Heb. i. 14). But how can they without bodies fulfil their ministry, especially towards those who are living in bodies? Then, again, it is a property of bodies only to move about, and to pass from one place to another, a thing which angels are shown to do by well known and undoubted authority. Hence it is that they were seen by the patriarchs, that they entered in unto them and ate with them, and washed their feet. Thus spirits both of the higher and the lower order require bodies of their own, but for this reason only, that they may render assistance, not that they may receive it.

3. But the lower animals, though under an obligation by their creation to perform service, are able to help only in matters of a temporal and corporeal kind, and therefore the spirit which is

in an animal passes away with time and dies with the body. He which is but a servant does, indeed, *abide not in the house for ever* (John viii. 35), although those who use him will apply all the profit of his temporal servitude to the gaining of things eternal. But the angel performs these duties of benevolence with an entire freedom of spirit, showing himself to men, as to his future fellow citizens and co-heirs of heavenly blessedness, a prompt and ready minister of good things to come. Both orders, then, without doubt, need bodies, that they may render service; the one [the animal] that he may serve us from obligation, the other [the angel] that he may assist us from benevolence. As for themselves, I do not see what advantage they derive from bodies, at least, with regard to eternity. The irrational spirit participates in the knowledge of things temporal by means of its body, nevertheless its body never assists it to such a point that, by the corporeal and sensible objects with which it is thus brought into connection, it should be led onwards to the knowledge of things spiritual and intelligible. Yet, as we know, it helps, by its service of body and, in time, to the attainment of such things, those who, using this world as though they used it not, transfer every use of temporal things to the profit of things eternal.

4. Moreover, the heavenly spirit, without any help from the body, or perception of those things which are felt by means of the body, is able to apprehend the highest things, and to penetrate the most secret, by its native force and the kinship of its nature to them. Was not this the Apostle's meaning when, having said, '*The invisible things of God are clearly seen, being understood by the things which are made,*' he added forthwith, '*by the creature of the world*'?[1]

Surely because it is not so with the creature of heaven. For what the spirit clothed in flesh and a sojourner upon earth strives laboriously, by slow degrees and by little and little, to attain from the consideration of things presented to his senses, that the dweller in the heavens can most swiftly and easily reach by his natural [*ingenita*] fineness and loftiness of perception, without help from bodily senses or from any limb or organ, nor yet as instructed by the contemplation of any material thing. Why should such a spirit search among corporeal things for spiritual meanings and spiritual truths which he reads in the Book of Life without contradiction, and understands without difficulty? Why should he labour in the sweat of his face to thrash grain, to press wine from grapes and oil from olives, who has enough and to spare of all ready to his hand? Who would beg his food at the houses of others that has abundance of bread in his own? Who would dig a well and seek for veins of water in the

---

[1] Rom. i. 20. This is, of course, a merely fanciful argument, and does not give the meaning of the Greek ἀπὸ κτίσεως κόσμου. But St. Bernard was led to it by the ambiguous rendering of the Vulgate, '*a creaturâ mundi.*' St. Anselm has much the same idea about this passage, though he supposes the *creatura mundi* to be man: '*Hominem, qui dominus est, participium, nodus, et vinculum omnis creaturæ. Homo enim ex seipso, suisque partibus et potentiis tam corporis quam animæ, vel maxime cognoscere potest creatorem suum Deum.*'—ED.

bowels of the earth if a living spring of limpid waters gushed up for him spontaneously? Neither the brutish spirit nor the angelic, therefore, are assisted in any wise by their bodies in the requirement of those things which render a spiritual being blessed; the former because it is unequal by the dulness of its nature even to the comprehension of them, the latter because it so excels in glory and power that it has no need of such help.

5. Now, the spirit of man holds a certain middle place between the highest and the lowest, and it is plain that a body is necessary to it for each of these two purposes, so that without one it can neither help others nor be helped itself. For, to say nothing of the other members of the body and their offices, how, I ask, could you either instruct a hearer if you had not a tongue, or if yourself without ears could you comprehend the words of an instructor?

6. Since, then, without the assistance of a body neither the brutish spirit can perform the duties of its servile condition, nor the angelic and heavenly spirit can discharge its ministry of kindness, nor, again, can the rational soul be of service to his neighbour, nor, indeed, to himself, in regard to his salvation, it is plain that every created spirit has need of a body, whether simply to help others, or at once to help and to be helped. What if there are some animals which, as far as use is concerned, are unprofitable and altogether unadapted to the supplying of human necessities? They are good to look at, if not to use; and are of more advantage to the hearts of those who behold them, than to the bodies of those who make use of them. Though they appear to be injurious, and even dangerous to human safety in this world, still their bodies are not without that which works together for good to those who, according to the Divine purpose, are called to be saints. And although they be not beneficial by affording us good, or by rendering to us service, they are so, assuredly, by affording a subject on which to exercise the intellect, according to that helpful system of mental and spiritual training which is common to all who have the gift of reason, and by which '*the invisible things of God are clearly seen, being understood by the things that are made.*' For both the devil and his satellites, whose intention is always malignant, are ever desirous to do injury; but God forbid that they should succeed against those who are aiming at good, of whom it is said: *Who is he that will harm you, if ye be followers of that which is good?* (1 Peter iii. 13); yea, rather, they are of service to them, though against their will, and work together for good to those who are good.

7. On the other hand, whether the bodies of angels be natural to them, as those of men are to them; and whether they are animal bodies, as [those of] men are, though immortal, which men are not yet; whether, also, they change those bodies, and give to them such form and figure as they choose, when they desire to become visible; rendering them as dense and solid as they will, although they are in reality subtle and impalpable, and imperceptible to our sight, because of the fineness and purity of their nature and substance; or whether,

again, remaining in their simple spiritual substance, they put on bodily forms when they require them, and when their need of them is over suffer them to dissolve again into the same material out of which they were taken: these are points upon which I am unwilling to reply.[1]

The Fathers appear to have held diverse opinions respecting them. I do not see any clear reason for teaching the one or the other, and confess that I do not know. I do not think, moreover, that a knowledge of these things will assist you much in your spiritual progress

8. Know only this one fact, that no created spirit can by itself reach unto our minds—that is, supposing it to have no assistance from either our body or its own. No spirit can so mix with or be poured into us that we should become by the participation of it either learned or more learned, either good or better. No angel, no soul, is capable of possessing itself of me in such a manner; nor am I capable of possessing any other. Nor have the angels themselves any such power with regard to each other [*i.e.*, without bodily organs]. This prerogative is reserved for the supreme Spirit, who is not limited by time or space, and who alone, when He imparts knowledge either to angel or man, does not need that we should have ears to hear, or that He should have a mouth to speak. By His own inherent power He pervades our souls; by His own inherent power He is made manifest; and being Himself a pure Spirit, He is apprehended by the pure. He alone has no need of any person or thing; He alone is sufficient, both to Himself and to all, by His Almighty Power alone.[2]

---

[1] St. Bernard propounds the same doubt in 'De Consideratione,' Bk. v., c 5. Among the Fathers and chief Doctors of the Church there was great difference of opinion upon this point: some affirming that Angels are incorporeal (bodiless); others, and not a few, denying this, so that the Master of the Sentences, Bk. ii., *distinct*. 8, has not ventured to define anything in face of this variety of opinions. I see that St. Augustine has spoken doubtfully upon this matter, but yet rather inclines to the view that Angels have bodies. For as he had been imbued with the Platonic teaching, he elsewhere mentions the opinion of the Platonists respecting the bodies of Angels in such a way as that he appears to agree with it ('De Civitate Dei,' Bk. viii., c. 14-16). And in other passages he frequently calls Angels living beings, and assigns bodies to them. In 'Enchiridion' (c. 59) he says that the question as to the bodies of Angels is a very difficult one. There is not space to point out other passages; Estius has noted a great many in Sentences, Bk. ii., *distinct*. 8.

At the present time it appears certain, and the opinion is approved by all, that Angels are incorporeal; that is to say, have not bodies united to them by their nature. (See St. Thomas, 'Summa,' part i., q. 50, art. 1; and q. 51, art. 1 and 2.) Whether this is a part of the faith or no is a question on which all are not agreed. (See Estius, *loco citato*) Sixtus of Sienna ('Biblioth. Sanct.,' Bk. v., *annot*. 8), commends St. Bernard's modesty in confessing ignorance and not hazarding an opinion on this question.

[2] St. Bernard treats of this question rightly in 'De Consideratione' (Bk. v, cv. 12): 'An Angel is influential by the good thoughts which he suggests in us, not by the good which he works in us; he exhorts us to good, but does not create it in us. God is in us in such a way that He affects our soul expressly, that He pours into it His gifts, or rather is Himself poured into our soul, and causes us to have union and participation with and in Him, in so much that a certain one has not feared to say that He is one Spirit with our spirit (1 Cor. vi. 17). An Angel, then, is with the soul, God is in the soul; the former dwells with it under the same roof, but God is with it as its life.'

9. Yet He works effects unbounded and unnumbered by the creatures corporeal or spiritual which are subject to Him; but as commanding them, not as entreating their aid. For example, He has at this moment employed my tongue to do His work, that is, to instruct you; whereas He could undoubtedly have done it far more easily and sweetly. But this is through His indulgence, not through His indigence. In your spiritual progress He desires not a relief for Himself but the acquiring of merit by me. This every man who is doing any good needs to know, lest he should glory in himself, and not in the Lord, with regard to the good works of the Lord. There are those who do good without intending it, as an evil man or an evil angel. And in this case it is certain that the good which is done by his means is not done on His account, seeing that no good done can be of advantage to an unwilling doer of it. It is then only a dispensation which is entrusted to him. But (I know not how or why) we feel the good done by an evil minister to be more grateful and pleasant; and that is the reason why God sometimes does good to the just by the means of evil men, not that He needs their assistance in doing good.

10. As for those creatures which have neither reason nor sense, who can doubt that God has still less need of them? But when even they concur in the performance of some good work, then it appears how all things serve Him who can justly say, *The world is Mine, and the fulness thereof* (Ps. l. 12). Assuredly, seeing that He knows the means best adapted to ends, He does not in the service of His creatures which are in bodies seek efficacy, but suitability. Suppose, then, that the ministry of such creatures is generally made use of in carrying on the various works of Divine Providence—as, for example, in the showers falling to vivify the seeds, or to increase the crops, or to ripen the fruits—what need of a body, I ask, has He to whom all bodies whatever, whether heavenly or earthly, are known to yield instant obedience? Clearly He, who finds no body alien to Himself, would find a body of His own superfluous. But if I tried to include in the present discourse all that occurs to me to be said upon this subject[1] it would exceed its proper limits, and perhaps would overtax the strength of some of you, therefore I reserve for another occasion what remains unsaid on this.

---

[1] Compare what is said upon the same subject in the treatise *Concerning Grace and Free Will* (c. xiii., *n.* 44, 45).

SERMON VI.

OF THE SUPREME AND INFINITE SPIRIT, WHO IS GOD, AND OF THE SENSE IN WHICH MERCY AND JUDGMENT ARE CALLED THE FEET OF GOD.

IN order that this sermon may be continuous with that which went before it, let me remind you of what was last said, that the Supreme and Infinite Spirit, and He alone, has no need of the help of any body or of the agency of any bodily organ to do whatever He wills to do. We have, then, no difficulty in saying that as God alone is truly immortal, so He alone is truly incorporeal, because He alone, of all spirits, is so raised above the entire nature of a body, and transcends it to such a degree, that He has no need of its ministry in any of His works, but when it so pleases Him, acts by the sole *Fiat* of His Will, and thus performs whatever is His good pleasure. It is that Divine Majesty alone, therefore, which has no need of any bodily organization, neither on its own account nor for the sake of others, because to Its omnipotent bidding obedience is swiftly rendered; every high thing bends before it, every obstacle yields, every created thing submits, and this without the intervention or help of any creature, corporeal or spiritual. He teaches or He warns without a tongue; He gives or withholds without the use of hands; without feet He runs, and comes to the succour of those who perish.

2. Thus He was wont to do with our fathers in former ages. Men felt a continual stream of benefits, but they did not know who was their Benefactor. By His strength He did indeed order all things from the height even unto the depth; but as He at this same time disposed them sweetly and gently, His action, though perpetual, was unfelt by men. In the good gifts of the Lord they rejoiced, but the Lord of Sabaoth was unknown to them, because all His judgments were calm and tranquil. From Him were men, but they were not with Him; by Him they lived, but not for Him; it was from Him that they had any wisdom, but they did not use it to gain the knowledge of Him; they were insensate, ungrateful, and altogether alienated from Him. Thus at length it came about that they no longer attributed their being, their life, their reason, to their Creator, but to nature, or even (which was still more utterly unreasonable) to chance; while there were many who attributed not a few of the good things which came to them to their own labour and skill. How great praise these seducing spirits thus arrogated to themselves! How much was given to the sun and moon! how much attributed to earth and to water! Even things which the hand of man had made, plants, shrubs, and the commonest of seeds, were honoured as divinities

3. Alas! it is thus that men have degraded the object of their worship, and changed their glory into the similitude of a calf that

eateth hay (Ps. cvi. 20). And God had pity upon their errors; He deigned to come forth from the clouds and darkness of His holy mountain, and to set His tabernacle in the light of the sun (Ps. xviii. 6). To those who knew only the flesh, He offered His Flesh, in order to teach them by it to know also the Spirit For whilst He was in the Flesh, He made use of the Flesh indeed, but to do by it, not the works of the flesh, but the works of God; commanding nature, fixing and rendering certain the uncertainty of chance, rendering the wisdom of men foolishness, and breaking down the tyranny of the demons, and thus plainly manifested that it was He by whom the same wonders were worked in earlier ages also. He did, I repeat, in the flesh and by means of the flesh actions of power, plainly miraculous; He spake words of salvation, He endured cruel indignities; and yet He showed evidently that it was He who had created the world by His power, sovereign, though invisible; who ruled it by His wisdom, and protected it in His love and mercy. Lastly, when He preached the Gospel to those ungrateful ones, when He gave signs and wonders to those who were unbelieving, when He prayed even for those who crucified Him, did He not clearly declare Himself to be that High and Lofty One, who, with His Father, makes His sun to shine daily upon the evil and on the good, and sendeth rain upon the just and upon the unjust? (Matt. v. 45). As He Himself said: *If I do not the works of My Father, believe Me not* (John x. 37).

4. Behold Him! He who in a deep adorable silence imparts eternal wisdom to the angels in heaven, He in the Flesh opens His Mouth and teaches His disciples upon the mount. See how the leper is healed at the mere touch of His Hands, how blindness is dispersed, hearing restored, the silent tongue set free, the disciple about to be whelmed in the deep caught by the hand and saved: and can you fail to recognise that great Being to whom David had said long before: *Thou openest Thine Hand and satisfiest the desire of every living thing* (Ps. cxlv. 16); and again, *Thou openest Thine Hand and they all are filled with good* (Ps. civ. 28). See how the woman that was a sinner, now a penitent and upon her knees at His Feet, hears Him say: *Thy sins are forgiven* (Luke vii. 48), and recognises Him of whom she may have read what had been written many ages before: *The devil shall go forth from before His Feet* (Hab. iii. 5, Vulg.). For where sin is remitted, there without doubt, the devil is driven forth from the heart of the sinner. Therefore it is that He speaks in general terms of all true penitents: *Now is the judgment of this world; now shall the Prince of this world be cast out* (John xii. 31), because God forgives sins to him who humbly confesses them; and thus the devil loses the dominion which he had usurped in the sinner's heart.

5. Lastly, He walks with the Feet of His Flesh upon the waves (Matt. xiv. 25); He of whom the Psalmist had sung before as yet He was incarnate: *Thy way is in the sea, and Thy path in the great*

waters (Ps. lxxvii. 19). That is to say, Thou shalt tread under foot the swelling hearts of the proud, and repress the disordered desires of carnal men; shalt render the ungodly righteous, and lower the pride of the arrogant. Yet because He does this invisibly, the carnal man does not recognize whose Hand it is that brings it to pass. Wherefore also it is that the Psalmist adds: *And Thy Footsteps are not known.* Hence also the Almighty Father saith to the Son: *Sit Thou at My Right Hand until I make Thine enemies Thy footstool* (Ps. cx. 1), that is, Until I shall render all those who despise Thee subject to Thy will, whether unwillingly and to their destruction, or gladly and to their happiness. Now, since the flesh was not capable of comprehending this, which is a work of the Spirit (for *the natural man receiveth not the things of the Spirit of God* (1 Cor. ii. 14), it was needful that the sinner should prostrate herself in the body, kneeling upon mortal knees, and with mortal lips imprinting a kiss upon the Feet of the Redeemer, and thus receive the pardon of her sins. Thus is *this change which the Right Hand of the Most High hath wrought* (Ps. lxxvii. 10), by which He marvellously, yet invisibly, justifies the unrighteous, made apparent even to carnal men.

6. But I must not omit to refer to those spiritual Feet of God which it behoves the penitent, first of all, in a spiritual and mystical sense, to kiss. I know the inquiring temper of your minds, which will not, with its own goodwill, pass over the least detail without thorough examination. Nor is it a matter to be neglected as of small importance to know what is meant by the Feet of God so frequently referred to in Scripture. At one time He is represented as *standing*, as in this: *We will worship in the place where His Feet have stood* (Ps. cxxxii. 7); at another as walking, as in the verse: *I will dwell in them and walk in them* (Lev. xxvi. 12, and 2 Cor. vi. 16); at another even as running, as here: *He rejoiceth as a strong man to run a race* (Ps. xix. 5). If it seemed right to the Apostle to speak of the Head of Christ as the Deity (1 Cor. xi. 3), then I think that we may not unfitly speak of His Feet as the Humanity, and call the one mercy, the other judgment. These two words are well known to you, and if you reflect, many passages of Scripture will occur to you in which they are each so employed. That God has taken the Foot of *mercy*, in assuming the Flesh which He united with Himself, is taught in the Epistle to the Hebrews, whence we learn that Christ was tempted in all points like as we are, though without sin, that He might be compassionate and merciful (Heb. iv. 15). And as for that other, which has been named the foot of *judgment*, does not He who is God and Man plainly signify that it belongs to Himself as Incarnate, where He declares that the Father *hath given Him authority to execute judgment also, because He is the Son of Man?* (John v. 27).

7. With these two Feet, then, fitly conjoined under the one Divine Head, it was that the invisible Emmanuel was born of a woman, made under the Law, was seen upon earth, and had converse among men (Baruch iii. 37). It is, again, on these two Feet that He passes

to and fro even now, but spiritually and invisibly, benefiting and
healing all those who are oppressed by the devil. On these, I repeat,
He traverses the souls of those vowed to His service, enlightening
and penetrating constantly the hearts and reins of the faithful. These
are, it may be, the legs of the Bridegroom which are so strikingly
commended by the Bride in a later passage of this book, where she
likens them, if I do not mistake, to pillars of marble, set upon sockets
of fine gold (Cant. v. 15). And this is very beautifully phrased, for
it is in the Incarnate wisdom of God, which is represented as gold,
that *mercy and truth have met together* (Ps. lxxxv. 10), and elsewhere it is said that *all the paths of the Lord are mercy and truth*
(Ps. xxv. 10).

8. Happy is the soul[1] in which the Lord Jesus has once set these
His Feet! There are two signs by which you may recognise the
soul in which this is the case, and such a soul bears of necessity the
prints of those Divine footsteps. These are *fear and hope :* the one
bearing the print of judgment, the other of mercy. With reason it is
that *God taketh pleasure in them that fear Him, in them that hope in
His mercy* (Ps. cxlvii. 11); *since the fear of the Lord is the beginning
of wisdom* (Prov. i. 7); hope, the progress in it; and charity its consummation and perfectness. And since that is the case, the benefit
(*functus*) is of no small value which is derived from that first kiss[2]
which is imprinted upon the Feet of Christ, provided only that
neither the one nor the other of them be neglected. For if you are
deeply touched with grief for your sins and with fear of God's judgment, then you have pressed your lips upon the footprints of truth
and of judgment. If you temper that fear and that grief by a consideration of the Divine goodness, and by a hope of obtaining pardon,
then you may know that you are embracing the foot of mercy. But
to embrace the one without the other is not expedient, for the remembrance of judgment alone precipitates the soul into the abyss of
despair, and a deceptive assurance of mercy wherewith a mind
flatters itself, generates a most pernicious security.

9. It has been given even to me, a miserable sinner, sometimes to
sit at the Feet of the Lord Jesus, and to embrace now the one, now
the other, with a devotion as full and complete as His benignity
deigned to enable me to feel. But if it ever happened that, being
pressed by the reproaches of conscience, I was forgetful of mercy,
and attached myself too long to judgment, I was soon cast down by
incredible fear and pitiable shame, and surrounded by the darkness
of horror, so that trembling in the shadow, I could only cry: *Who
knoweth the power of Thine anger : even according to Thy fear, so is
Thy wrath* (Ps. xc. 11). But if, on the other hand, leaving that, I
had embraced the other, the foot of Mercy, more than was meet,
I was dissolved in negligence and indifference so great that I
speedily became less earnest in prayer, less prompt in action, more
inconsiderate in speech, more given to idle laughter—in short, less

---

[1] *Lit.* mind, *mens.*   [2] See Sermon IV.

steady and stable in every part of my nature, whether of the inward or outward man. Therefore, having learned from that best of teachers, experience, I no longer dwell upon judgment alone, any more than upon mercy alone; but *unto Thee, O Lord, will I sing of mercy and judgment* (Ps. ci. 1). Those two sources of righteousness for ever I will not forget; they shall both equally be my songs in the house of my pilgrimage; until mercy having been exalted high above judgment, my unhappy condition shall cease and come to a full end, and the glory which shall be granted to me shall alone inspire my hymns of praise to Thee, without the least mingling of pain or grief, for ever.

SERMON VII.

OF THE ARDENT LOVE OF THE SOUL FOR GOD; AND OF THE CARE AND ATTENTION THAT OUGHT TO BE GIVEN TO PRAYER AND TO PSALMODY.

I HAVE undertaken a new labour in inviting, of my own accord, your questioning. For, since on the first occasion I took pains to make clear to you, over and above indeed what was needed, the names and the meanings, spiritual and mystical, of the Feet of God, you are proceeding to inquire similarly what is the meaning of the Hand of God, which, as we said, was in the second place to be kissed. Well, I consent; I will meet your wishes—nay, I will do more than you have asked, for I will show you not one Hand only, but two, and each bearing its distinct name. I call the one Liberality, and the other Force; because God gives liberally, and preserves powerfully that which He has given. Now, he who is not ungrateful will, in recognising and confessing that God, as He is the liberal Bestower of all good things, so He is their powerful Preserver, will, I say, kiss each of these. Enough, I think, has been said of these two; let us go on now to speak of the third.

2. *Let Him kiss me with the kisses of His Mouth.* Who is it speaks these words? It is the Bride. Who is the Bride? It is the Soul thirsting for God. But I first specify the dispositions of men in various relations to each other, so that those which belong properly to a bride may appear more clearly. If a man is a slave, he fears the face of his lord; if he is a hireling, he looks for wages from his lord's hand; if a disciple, he gives attention to his teacher; if a son, he renders honour to his father; but she who asks this is held by the bond of love to him from whom she asks it. Of all the sentiments of nature, this of love is the most excellent, especially when it is rendered back to Him who is the principle and fountain of it— that is, God. Nor are there found any expressions equally sweet to signify the mutual affection between the Word of God and the soul

as those of Bridegroom and of Bride; inasmuch as between individuals who stand in such a relation to each other, all things are in common, and they possess nothing separate or divided. They have one inheritance, one dwelling-place, one table; and they are, in fact, one flesh. On this account it is that a man shall leave his father and his mother, and shall cleave unto his wife, and they shall be two in one flesh (Gen. ii. 24). A woman also on her part is bidden to forget her own people and her father's house, that her husband may have pleasure in her beauty (Ps. xlv. 11, 12). If, then, mutual love is especially befitting to a bride and bridegroom, it is not unfitly that the name of Bride is given to a soul which loves. It is a sign of her love that she makes this request. She asks neither for liberty, nor for wages, nor for an heritage, nor, finally, for knowledge, but only for this; and she does this as a chaste and modest bride, who does not deny or dissimulate the sacred affection which she feels. Notice how abruptly she breaks into her discourse. She has a great favour to ask of one who is great, yet she does not have recourse, as is too often the case, to caresses or flatteries; she does not wind her way to her request by gradual approaches. She employs no preface, nor makes any attempt to win goodwill or favour; but her request bursts forth openly and abruptly out of the abundance of her heart, and, even, as it were, with a sort of effrontery.

3. Does it not appear to you that she wished to say: *Whom have I in heaven but Thee, and there is none upon earth that I desire in comparison of Thee* (Ps. lxxiii. 25)? Without doubt the love is chaste which seeks the object of its love alone, without care for anything he may possess. And that love is sacred which dwells not in fleshly concupiscence, but in purity of the spirit. That love is ardent which is so absorbed and, as it were, inebriated with its own affection that it loses all thought of the greatness of its object. What! *He looketh upon the earth, and it trembleth* (Ps. civ. 32), and from Him she presumes to ask this? Is she inebriated? Undoubtedly it is so with her; and perhaps, when she burst forth thus passionately, she had come forth from the banqueting-house, into which, at a later time, she gloried so greatly to have been led (Cant. i. 3, and ii. 4). For this is what David also said of certain saints in addressing the Holy One: *They shall be inebriated with the fatness of Thy House: and Thou shalt make them to drink of the rushing river of Thy pleasures* (Ps. xxxvi. 8). Oh, how great is the power of love! how perfect the confidence which is felt under the influence of the Spirit of liberty. How abundantly manifest it is that *perfect love casteth out fear* (1 John iv. 18)!

4. It is, nevertheless, from a feeling of modesty and timidity that she directs her address, not to the Bridegroom Himself, but to others, as if He were not present. It is, indeed, a great thing that is asked, and there is every need that the petition should be accompanied with modesty, and that the petitioner should be recommended. That is wherefore she seeks, through the friends of her

well-beloved and the dwellers in His house, to commend herself to Him. But who are these friends? I believe that they are the holy angels who are present with human beings who pray, and offer to God their prayers and vows, since they are known to lift up pure hands unto heaven without anger or variance. This is shown by the angel of Tobias, who said to Tobit: *When thou didst pray, I did bring the remembrance of thy prayers before the Holy One · and when thou didst bury the dead, I was with thee likewise* (Tobit xii. 12, 15). I think you are sufficiently persuaded of that truth from other testimonies of the Scriptures also. Furthermore, that the angels deign to be present, and to associate themselves with the praises of those who sing Psalms, is shown with great plainness by the Psalmist: 'The chiefs (*principes*) went before, and with them were joined the players upon stringed instruments: in the midst were the maidens who played the timbrel' (Ps. lxviii. 25, Vulg.). Wherefore he says also: 'In the presence of the angels will I sing praise unto Thee' (Ps. cxxxviii. 1, Vulg). On this account, I greatly regret that some of you are weighed down by heavy sleep during the sacred vigils. Such persons do not pay due reverence to the citizens of heaven, but, in the presence of the 'chiefs,' appear as men dead; whereas they are, on the other hand, touched by your vigilance when you are awake, and delight to assist at your solemn services. I fear lest, revolted by your sloth, they will some time or other withdraw with indignation,[1] and that then each of you should begin thus late to say to God with a lamentable voice: *Thou hast put away mine acquaintance far from me: Thou hast made me an abomination unto them;* and again: *Lover and friend hast Thou put far from me, and mine acquaintance into darkness* (Ps. lxxxviii. 8, 18); and again: *My lovers and my friends stand aloof from my sore, and they that seek after my life lay snares for me* (Ps. xxxviii. 11, 12). For if the good spirits thus depart from us, who will be able to sustain the attacks of evil spirits? I say, then, to those who are in the habit of thus giving way to sleep: *Cursed be he that doeth the work of the Lord negligently* (Jer. xlviii. 10, Vulg.). To them also saith, not I, but the Lord: *I would thou wert cold or hot: so then, because thou art lukewarm, I will spew thee out of My Mouth* (Apoc. iii. 15, 16). When, then, you are engaged (*statis*) in prayer, or the chanting of the Psalms, have some thought of your chiefs; perform that in which you are occupied with reverence and according to the Rule, and you may glory in the thought that *your angels always*

---

[1] Sixtus of Sienna ('Biblioth.,' Bk. v., *annot.* 216) makes the following observations upon this passage: 'Divines are in the habit of referring to words of St. Bernard in Sermon VII. *in Cantic.* to show that guardian Angels do sometimes abandon the charge of those of whom they have been given the care.' Albertus Magnus, in the first volume of his 'Summa,' quæs. 1-8, expounding this passage, says: 'Men are deserted by their Angel guardians, not as regards place or local guardianship, but only as regards power and efficacy; but this is not because of any sloth on the part of the Angel, but is the fault of the man.' The Saint was accustomed to say in a similar manner, that a sinner departs from God [and abides in] a region of unlikeness to Him, by distance not of place, but of merit!

behold the Face of the Father (Matt. xviii. 10). They are, in fact, sent to perform their ministry for our benefit, who shall be heirs of salvation (Heb. i. 14); they bear to heaven our devotion, and bring back grace to us from thence. Let us take part in the functions of those with whom we are to be sharers in glory, that as in the mouth of babes and sucklings praise may be perfected (Ps. viii. 2). To them let us say: *Sing praises unto our God, sing praises;* and let us hear their answering response: *Sing praises, sing praises unto our King* (Ps. xlvii. 6).

5. Associate yourselves, then, with the sweet singers of heaven to chant in common the praises of God, since you are yourselves *fellow-citizens of the saints, and of the household of God;* and *Sing praises with understanding* (Ps. xlvii. 7). As food is sweet in the mouth, so are Psalms in the heart. Only let the soul that is faithful and prudent grind them, as it were, between the teeth of his intelligence, for fear lest if they be swallowed in great fragments, and not masticated, the palate be defrauded of their sweetness, which is above honey and the honeycomb. Let us offer a honeycomb, as did the Apostles at the banquet of heaven, at the Table of the Lord (Luke xxiv. 42). Honey in the comb—that is, spiritual devotion in the letter of Scripture. *The letter*, says an Apostle elsewhere, *killeth* if it be swallowed down without the seasoning of the Spirit (2 Cor. iii. 6). If, then, with the Apostle, thou wilt sing with the Spirit, sing with the understanding also (1 Cor. xiv. 15), and then you, too, shall know the truth of that saying of Jesus: *The words which I speak unto you, they are spirit, and they are life* (John vi. 63); and also of that which we read as from the mouth of wisdom: *My Spirit is sweeter than honey* (Ecclus. xxiv. 20, Vulg.).

6. Thus thy soul shall delight itself in fatness; thy burnt offering shall be fat and perfect. Thus thou wilt placate the King; thus thou wilt give pleasure to the chiefs of the heavenly hosts, and render all the dwellers above favourable to thee. At the sweet odours of thy devotion, they shall say of thee: *Who is this that cometh up out of the wilderness like pillars of smoke, perfumed with myrrh and frankincense, and with all powders of the merchant?* (Cant. iii. 6). Replies the Psalmist: *The princes of Juda are their leaders, the princes of Zabulon and the princes of Naphthali* (Ps. lxviii. 27)—that is, the princes of those who praise God, who observe continence, and who love contemplation. For our princes know well that the praises of those who sing Psalms, the firmness of those who observe continence, and the purity of those who delight in contemplation, are accepted by their King; and they have it much at heart to require from us the first-fruits of the Spirit, which are no other than the first and purest fruits of wisdom. For you know, brethren, that, in Hebrew, *Juda* signifies 'praising' or 'confessing,' *Zabulon* 'a settled or strong dwelling,' and *Naphthali* 'a hind let loose' (Gen. xlix. 21); for its leaps and bounds well typify the ecstasies of the speculative mind, and it is able to thread the closest thickets of forests, as those [of that disposition can penetrate] the greatest difficulties of meaning. We know, also, who

it was that said: *Whoso offereth the sacrifice of praise shall honour Me* (Ps. l. 23).

7. But since 'praise is not seemly in the mouth of a sinner' (Ecclus. xv. 9), have you not extreme need of the virtue of continence, so that sin may not reign in your mortal body? But continence has no merit before God when it seeks glory from man. Wherefore there is especial need of a pure intention, so that the mind craves to please God only, and is able to attach itself simply to Him. For to cleave to God is nothing else than to behold God; and this is a singular felicity, and it is bestowed upon those only who are of a pure heart (Matt. v. 8). David had this pure heart, for he said to God, *My soul has attached itself closely to Thee* (Ps. lxiii. 8); and also, *It is good for me to draw near to God* (Ps. lxxiii. 28). In beholding God he was drawn near to Him; and in drawing near to God he beheld Him. When, therefore, souls are in the continual exercise of these lofty virtues, the heavenly messengers converse frequently and familiarly with them, especially if they shall have perceived them to be frequent in prayer. Who shall accord unto me, O kindly chiefs of the heavenly hosts, the privilege of making known my requests before God by your means? I do not say to God, for to Him the thoughts of man lie open, but before, and in the presence of, God; that is to say, to those who are with God, the archangels (*virtutibus*), and those blessed ones who are delivered from the burden of the flesh. Who shall raise out of the dust, and free from the dunghill, a being as poor and as helpless as I am, that I may have a place among the princes, and sit upon a throne of glory? I do not doubt that they receive with joy and affection in the palace him whom they have deigned to visit in a filthy hovel. After all, how can they, after having rejoiced in the conversion of a sinner, fail to acknowledge him in his exaltation?

8. That is why I think that it is to them, who are the attendants and the companions of the Bridegroom, that the Bride communicates her prayer, and makes known the desire of her heart, in these words. And see with what familiarity and confidence the soul, sighing under the burden of the flesh, converses with the heavenly powers. She desires earnestly the affection of her Spouse; she asks for that which she desires; but she does not name Him whom she loves, inasmuch as she does not doubt of their knowledge, because she converses with them frequently of Him; just as Mary Magdalene does not mention by name Him whom she sought, but said to Him whom she thought was the gardener, *Sir, if thou have borne Him hence* (John xx. 15). Of whom does she say *Him*? It is not stated, because she believes that everyone knows Who it is that is not for one moment absent from her heart. So it is with the Bride. Speaking with the companions of her Spouse, as to her confidants, to whom she is aware that every thought of her heart is known, she does not mention the name of her Beloved, but bursts forth in these words. What is meant by this kiss I will not keep you longer to explain;

but you shall hear in the sermon of to-morrow what (in response to your prayers) shall be suggested to me by the goodness of Him who teacheth all things. For flesh and blood does not reveal this secret, but only He who searcheth the deep things of God; that is, the Holy Ghost, who proceedeth from the Father and Son, with whom He liveth and reigneth for ever and ever. AMEN.

SERMON VIII.

THAT THE KISS OF GOD IS THE HOLY SPIRIT; AND THAT THE CHURCH ASKS FOR THIS KISS THAT SHE MAY HAVE THE KNOWLEDGE OF THE HOLY TRINITY.

TO-DAY, in discharge of the promise made yesterday, I propose to consider the third and highest of these sacred mysteries. Listen very attentively to this hallowed secret, which is indeed of consummate sweetness, but which is rarely experienced, and is comprehended with difficulty. It seems to me (to go a little farther back still) that He who saith, *No man knoweth the Son, but the Father; neither knoweth any man the Father but the Son, and he to whomsoever the Son will reveal Him* (Matt. xi. 27), has here designated a certain kiss ineffable and unknown to any created being. For the Father loves the Son, and embraces Him with a love which is unlike every other—the Supreme embracing His Equal, the Eternal His Co-eternal, the One Being His Sole One. But He is united to the Son by an affection not less, proceeding from the Son, as He Himself attests when He says, *That the world may know that I love the Father, arise, let us go hence* (John xiv. 31); that is, without doubt, to His Passion. Now, this cognition of mutual love between Him who Begets and Him who is Begotten, what is it but a kiss, as deeply mysterious as it is sweet?

2. I hold it for a thing certain that even the angelic creation is not admitted to the knowledge of that *arcanum* of Divine Love, which is at once so august and so sacred. And, in fact, St. Paul, knowing this, speaks of that *peace which passeth all understanding* (Phil. iv. 7), even that of angels. On this account even the Bride, although she may be so bold as to ask much, does not dare to ask for this, which is reserved for the Father only; her request is a lesser one. Behold the newly-made Bride receiving a new proof of the affection of her Bridegroom; yet not that mentioned above. *He breathed on them,* says St. John, speaking of Jesus breathing upon His Apostles, that is, the primitive Church; *and said unto them, Receive ye the Holy Ghost* (John xx. 22). That was, without doubt, a kiss which He gave to them. What? that physical breath? Nay, but the invisible Spirit, who was thus communicated by the breathing of the Lord, so

that by this very action it might be understood that He proceeds from the Son equally as from the Father. It is sufficient for the Bride if she receive the gift of grace from her Bridegroom, though it be not that highest grace of all. Let no one suppose that this is a small favour, or of little value; for this signifies nothing else than to receive the inpouring of the Holy Spirit. For if the Father is rightly understood as bestowing the kiss, and the Son as receiving it, we shall not err in understanding by the kiss the Holy Spirit, inasmuch as He is the peace unalterable, the bond indissoluble, the indivisible love, the inviolable unity, between the Father and the Son.

3. It is, therefore, by the influence of the Holy Spirit, that the Bride has the boldness to ask trustingly, under this name or figure, that the inpouring of the Holy Spirit may be granted to her. She does indeed hold, as it were, a pledge, which deprives her request of any shadow of presumption. I mean the declaration of the Son, when He said: *No man knoweth the Son but the Father; neither knoweth any man the Father but the Son;* and then added, *and he to whomsoever the Son will reveal Him* (Matt. xi. 27). But the Bride has no doubt that if He wills to grant this knowledge to any, it will be to her. Therefore, she prays boldly that this may be given to her; that is, that Holy Spirit, in whom both the Son is revealed, and the Father. For the One is not made known without the Other; according to that saying: *He that hath seen Me, hath seen My Father also* (John xiv. 9). *Whosoever denieth the Son, the same hath not the Father. But he that acknowledgeth the Son hath the Father also* (1 John ii. 23), from which it appears plainly that neither is the Father known without the Son, nor the Son without the Father. And it follows from this that he who said: *This is life eternal, to know Thee, the only True God, and Jesus Christ whom Thou hast sent* (John xvii. 3), placed the highest blessedness in the knowledge, not of either Divine Person, but of Each. Finally, we read that those who follow the Lamb have *His Name, and the Name of His Father, written in their foreheads;*[1] that is to say, that their knowledge of Each Divine Person is a glory to them.

4. But someone perhaps says: The knowledge of the Holy Spirit, then, is not necessary, since, when it is declared that life eternal consists in knowing both the Father and the Son, no mention is made of the Holy Spirit. That is true; but how can anyone who knows perfectly the Father and the Son be ignorant of the Goodness of the One and of the Other? And this Goodness is the Holy Spirit. For a man does not wholly know another man, as long as he is ignorant, whether the will of that other is good or evil. And we may add to this, that when it is said: *This is life eternal, that they might know Thee,*

---

[1] Rev. xiv. 1, according to the Vulgate. Codd. Sinaiticus and Alexandrinus have this reading; but others, which are followed by the English A.V., omit 'His Name and.' The R.V. restores the words, and there can be little doubt that it does so rightly.—ED.

the only true God, and Jesus Christ, whom Thou hast sent; if mention be made of that mission as showing the goodness and benignity of the Father in deigning to send the Son, and that of the Son in willingly obeying, that proves that the speaker is not wholly silent respecting the Holy Ghost, since the goodness and grace of the Father and the Son are referred to, and Their Love and Goodness is the Holy Ghost.

5. When, therefore, the Bride is praying that this gift may be conferred upon her, her entreaty is for the inpouring of the grace of this threefold knowledge, as far as it can be experienced in this mortal body. But it is the Son of whom she entreats it, since it is the function of the Son to reveal it to whom He will. The Son reveals Himself then to whom He will, and He reveals also the Father. This revealing is doubtless made by the Holy Ghost; for such is the sense of the words spoken by the Apostle: *For God hath revealed* [them] *unto us by His Spirit* (1 Cor. ii. 10). But in giving the Spirit by whom He reveals this knowledge, He reveals also the Spirit Himself; in giving He reveals Him, and in revealing gives. Now, that revelation which is made by the Holy Ghost not only enlightens [the soul] to knowledge, but also enkindles it to love, as St. Paul says: *The Love of God is shed abroad in our hearts by the Holy Ghost which is given unto us* (Rom. v. 5). And therefore also perhaps it is not said of those who, when they knew God, glorified Him not as God, that their knowledge was an effect of the revealing of the Spirit, because when they had knowledge of God, they did not love Him (Rom. i. 21). It is true that you have: *God hath showed it unto them* (i. 19); but it is not added: 'By His Spirit,' lest those impious minds who were contented with the knowledge which puffeth up, and cared not for that which edifieth, should arrogate to themselves the having received the kiss which belongs to the Bride. Finally, the Apostle states by what means they had this knowledge: *The invisible things of God are clearly seen, being understood by the things which are made* (1. 20), whence it appears that they have not perfectly known Him for whom they had no love. For if they had known Him completely, they could not have overlooked that goodness which impelled Him to be born in the Flesh, and to die for our redemption. Listen, then, and learn what it was that had been revealed to them of God: *His Eternal Power and Godhead* (Ibid.). You see that, exalting themselves in the presumption of their own spirit, and not under the influence of the Spirit of God, they wished to peer into those things which were great and sublime in God, and have failed to discern that God [Incarnate] was meek and lowly of heart. Nor is this wonderful, for we read that Behemoth, who is their head, scorns to cast his eye upon what is humble and low; but *beholdeth all high things* (Job xli. 34). Whereas, on the contrary, David did not *exercise himself in great matters,* nor *in things too high for him* (Ps. cxxxi. 1), lest the searcher out of glory should be overwhelmed with glory (Prov. xxv. 27, VULG.).

6. And do you also, brethren, that you may conduct yourselves with prudence while searching out Divine mysteries, bear in mind the warning of the wise man: *Seek not out the things that are too hard for thee, neither search the things that are above thy strength* (Ecclus. iii. 21). Walk among those exalted subjects in the Spirit, and not in thy own judgment. The teaching of the Holy Spirit does not sharpen curiosity, but kindles charity. Rightly thus does the Bride, when seeking Him whom her soul loveth, not trust herself to the judgment of the flesh, nor follow the futile reasonings of human curiosity, but, as here, prays for this Gift, that is, she invokes the Holy Spirit, so that through Him she may receive at once the love for knowledge, and the seasoning of grace to accompany it. Well is it said that the knowledge thus given is accompanied with love, since a kiss is the sign of love. But the knowledge which puffeth up, being without love, is not thus conveyed. Nor can they who have a zeal for God, but not according to knowledge, arrogate this to themselves at all; but this gift conveys both the one and the other of these graces; both the light of knowledge and the unction of piety. For He is a Spirit of wisdom and knowledge; and as a bee bears honey and wax, so He has in Himself both that which enkindles the light of knowledge, and that which infuses the savour of grace. Let not him who has understanding of the truth, but without love, nor him who loves, without understanding the truth, think that he has received that gift, for in it there is no place either for error or for lukewarmness. That is the reason why the Bride, in order to receive this twofold grace, presents her two lips; I mean the reason full of intelligence, and the will full of love for heavenly wisdom; so that, being full of joy at having received an embrace so full and so perfect, she may have the happiness to hear: *Grace is poured upon thy lips, therefore God hath blessed thee for ever* (Ps. xlv. 3). Therefore the Father, in His Kiss to the Son, communicates to Him the depths of His Divinity in their fulness, and breathes [upon Him] the sweetness of His Love. And Scripture intimates this, where it is said: *Day unto day uttereth speech* (Ps. xix. 2). In this Embrace, eternal, unique, and blessed, it is not given to any created being to have part; the Spirit alone, who is both of the One and of the other, is conscious of that mutual Recognition and Love, and is a Witness of it. For who hath known the Mind of the Lord? or who hath been His Counsellor? (Rom. xi. 34).

7. But someone will perhaps say to me: 'How, then, have you come to a knowledge of that which you say is hid from the ken of every creature?' Undoubtedly *the Only Begotten Son, which is in the Bosom of the Father, He hath declared Him* (John i. 18). Yes, it is He who hath declared Him, not to me, a miserable man, unworthy of such an honour, but to the friend of the Bridegroom, to John, whose words these are; and not only to him, but to John the Evangelist, as the disciple whom Jesus loved. For his soul was pleasing to God, truly worthy of the name and of the dowry of the

Bride, worthy of the embraces of the Bridegroom, worthy, finally, to
recline upon the Breast of the Lord. In the Bosom of the only
Begotten Son John drank in that which He had from the Bosom of
the Father. Yet it was not He alone who received that great grace,
but all those also to whom the same, who is the Angel of great
counsel, said: *I have called you friends, for all things that I have
heard of My Father I have made known unto you* (John xv. 15).
This also did Paul drink in, who had received his Gospel neither
from man, nor by man, but by the revelation of Jesus Christ
(Gal. i. 11, 12). Assuredly all these holy men can say as truly as
happily, 'The Only Begotten Son, who is in the Bosom of the
Father, hath declared Him unto us.' And that revelation, what
was it but the bestowal of this embrace sacred and eternal; as it
is said: *I and My Father are One.* And again: *The Father is in
Me, and I in Him* (John x. 30, 38). That is, indeed, as it were,
a kiss, but one to which no creature draws near. A kiss it is of
love and of peace, but the love surpasses all knowledge, and the
peace all understanding. But that which eye hath not seen, nor ear
heard, nor hath it entered into the heart of man to conceive, God
revealed to Paul by His Spirit, that is, by the Kiss of His Mouth.
Therefore the relation of the Father to the Son, and of the Son to
the Father, is, so to speak, a kiss by the mouth. But that [relation]
of which we read: *We have received, not the spirit of this world,
but the Spirit which is of God, that we may know those things
which are freely given unto us by God* (1 Cor. ii. 12), is of and from
this.

8. Now, to distinguish more clearly between these two, he who receives the fulness itself has the one, but he who receives only of
the fulness has but the other. Paul was indeed a great man, but
how high soever he might lift his head (*os*), and even though it
should reach unto the third heaven, he must of necessity remain far
below the Countenance of the Most High (*os Altissimi*), and must
resign himself to remain within the limits of his condition. And
since he will not be able to attain to that Countenance of glory, he
must humbly entreat that God will condescend to him, and send to
him a gift from on high. But He who thought it not robbery to be
equal with God (Phil. ii. 6), so that He could say without fear *I and
My Father are One*, because He is united to [His Father] as to an
equal, and is embraced by Him as by an equal, He does not, from a
lower station, beg for a gift, but is joined in an embrace with equality
of rank, and by a privilege which is the right of Him alone. To
Christ, therefore, the kiss is fulness, to Paul it is participation.

9. Happy, nevertheless, is the sign by which comes not only the
knowledge of God, but also the love of Him as our Father, who
cannot be fully known unless He be at the same time perfectly loved.
What soul among you has ever felt in the depths of his conscience
the Spirit of the Son crying, Abba, Father? (Gal. iv. 6). That soul
which feels itself animated by the same Spirit as the Son, that soul,

I say, may believe that it is the object of the affection of the Father. Trust in Him, O soul, whosoever thou art, that hast the happiness to be in that condition; trust in Him, doubting nothing. In the Spirit of the Son recognise that thou art a daughter of the Father, the sister, or the Bride, of the Son. Such a soul is, in fact, you will find, called by one or by the other name. The proof of this is at hand; it will not be difficult to produce it. For what is the voice of the Bridegroom to her? Is it not, *Come into My garden, My sister, My spouse?* (Cant. v. 1). She is sister because she has the same Father; she is spouse because she is in the same Spirit. And if a marriage in the flesh makes of two persons one flesh, shall not a spiritual bond much more join two into one Spirit? And, in fact, the Apostle declares that he who is joined unto the Lord is one Spirit (1 Cor. vi. 17). But hear also with what affection and what condescension the Father names her His daughter, and as His daughter-in-law invites her to the kind embrace of His Son: *Hearken, O daughter, and consider, incline thine ear; forget also thine own people and thy father's house; so shall the King greatly desire thy beauty* (Ps. xlv. 10, 11). It is from Him that she makes this request. But, O holy soul, maintain the deepest reverence, for He is the Lord thy God; not to be embraced, perhaps; but rather to be adored, with the Father and the Holy Spirit, for ever and ever. AMEN.

SERMON IX.

OF THE BREASTS OF THE BRIDEGROOM—THAT IS, CHRIST: WHEREOF THE ONE IS PATIENCE IN WAITING FOR THE CONVERSION OF SINNERS; THE OTHER, BENIGNITY OR WILLINGNESS TO RECEIVE THEM.

LET us come now to the exposition of the book, and give the reason for the words of the Bridegroom, as well as the result which follows from them. For without a commencement, they seem to hang in mid-air, and then abruptness, as it were, renders their sense obscure. Therefore it will be well, in the first place, to ascertain upon what previous facts or truths they rest. Suppose, then, that those whom we have called the companions of the Bridegroom now approach the Bride, as yesterday and the day before, to visit and to salute her. They find her plunged in sadness, uttering sighs and groans; their surprise is excited, and they question her thus: What has occurred? Why do we find you more sad than usual? What is the cause of these unexpected sighs? When, alienated and turned away from the path of right, you were following your earthly companions, you saw yourself obliged, by the sad condition to which their cruelties had brought you, to return at length to your true Lord, did you not entreat with many prayers and tears to be permitted but once to touch his feet? 'I remember it,' she replies. 'Very well, then,' they continue, 'after having obtained that grace and received pardon for your offences in the permission to kiss His Feet, did you not again become impatient; and not content with such a condescension, but desiring still greater favour, you asked with the same eagerness, and obtained the second grace, that you should kiss His Hand, and by that grace have obtained virtues neither few nor small?' 'I do not deny it,' she replies again. But they still continue: 'Were you not accustomed to protest and declare with an oath, that if ever it were granted to you to attain to kiss His Hand, that favour would suffice for you, and that you would ask for nothing more?' 'It was even so.' 'What then? Do you complain that anything has been taken away of what has been bestowed upon you?' 'Nothing.' 'Then, do you fear that you will fall again under condemnation for those offences of your past life which you believed had been pardoned?' 'No, not at all.'

2. 'Come, then, say in what way we can satisfy your need.' 'I shall not be at rest,' she replies, 'unless He complete His goodness to me.' I am thankful that I have been permitted to kiss His Feet; it is still more a cause of gratitude to me to kiss His Hand; but if He has any care for me at all, let Him grant unto me the third and crowning grace. I am not ungrateful, but I love. I have received, I confess it, favours which are far above my merits, but yet they are far below my desires. It is not reason which bears me on, but the vehement yearning of my soul. Do not, I entreat, complain of my presumption, which is but the effect of my ardent love. It is true that shame would withhold me, but love overcomes shame. I am not unmindful that *the King's honour loveth judgment* (Ps. xcix. 4), but the violence of love does not wait for judgment; it is not moderated by advice, nor restrained by shame, nor controlled by reason. I beg, I supplicate, I entreat again and again that He grant unto me this my request. Lo, in His grace for many years now I strive to live chastely and soberly, I apply myself to reading, I resist all manner of vices, I occupy myself continually in prayer, I keep watch against temptations, I reflect upon my past years in bitterness of my soul, I study to conduct myself among my brethren as far as in me lies peacefully and without quarrel, I submit myself to the higher powers, going forth and coming in at the command of my elders; I desire not the goods of any other—on the contrary, I have given up all that I have, and my own self also; in the sweat of my face I eat my bread. But yet I go through all these practices of piety from mere custom, and not for the sweetness felt in them. What else am I, to borrow the language of a Prophet, than as *Ephraim, an heifer that is taught to tread out the corn?* (Hos. x. 11). And is it not said in the Gospel, that he who does only that which it is his duty to do is *an unprofitable servant?* (Luke xvii. 10). I fulfil perhaps my appointed tasks as best I can, but throughout them

all my soul does not cease to be as a land without water. That my offering may be a perfect one, let Him, I entreat, grant the grace for which I pray.

3. I remember that many of you also were accustomed in their private confessions[1] to complain of a similar languor and dryness of soul, and of a kind of heaviness and stupor of mind which rendered them incapable of entering into high or refined thoughts, so that they felt little sweetness of spirit, or none at all. What do those souls yearn for, if not for this? Yes, they long and sigh for the Spirit of wisdom and of understanding; of understanding that they may reach knowledge; of wisdom that they may love and take delight in that which they grasp with the understanding. I suppose that the Psalmist was referring to this disposition of mind when he uttered the prayer: *Let my soul be satisfied as with marrow and fatness, and my mouth shall praise Thee with joyful lips* (Ps. lxiii. 5). He sought certainly for this mystical kiss, which, after having spread upon his lips the unction of special[2] grace, should be followed by the effect which in another prayer he asks for: *Let my mouth be filled with Thy praise, that I may sing of Thy glory and honour all the day long* (Ps. lxx. 8). Lastly, when he has tasted that heavenly sweetness, he bursts forth: *Oh, how great is Thy goodness, O Lord, which Thou hast laid up for them that fear Thee!* (Ps. xxxi. 19). We have, however, lingered over [the explanation of] this, yet I have not, I fear, even yet expounded it as it deserves. But let us pass now to the rest, for that great truth is better known by the impression it makes [for itself], than by the expressions which are used of it.

4. The text goes on to say: *Thy breasts are better than wine, and their fragrance than the choicest perfumes* (Cant. i. 1, 2, Vulg.). Whose are these words, the author does not say, and thus leaves us at liberty to assign them freely to the person they best befit. There seem to me to be reasons for attributing them not unsuitably to the Bride, or to the Bridegroom, or even to the Bridegroom's companions. First I will state those in favour of attributing them to the Bride. While she is conversing with the friends of the Bridegroom, He draws near who is the subject of their discourse. He is wont to approach those willingly who are speaking of Him. It was thus that He joined Himself to those who were going to Emmaus, and discoursing of Him by the way, and to them He showed Himself a pleasant and conversible companion (Luke xxiv. 15). It is this very thing which is promised in the Gospel: *Where two or three are gathered together in My Name, there am I in the midst of them*

---

[1] The monks under the charge of St. Bernard were in the habit of revealing to him their faults of negligence (as the Saint calls them in Sermon I. for the Day of the Circumcision, *n.* 5); and they did this in private. Guy, the fifth Prior of the Chartreuse, gives this name to confessions made in private cells; those which were made on Saturday, though in private, he calls common or public. See 'Life,' Bk. i., *n.* 28.

[2] *Specialis.* Another reading is *spiritualis.*

(Matt. xviii. 20); and by the prophet: *Before they call, I will answer, and while they are yet speaking, I will hear* (Is. lxv. 24). So also in this instance, though not called, He is present; and delighting in the words spoken, He anticipates the petitions offered. And I judge that sometimes He does not wait for the spoken words, but appears in response to thoughts alone. Thus speaks the man who was found to be after God's own heart: *Lord, Thou hast heard the desire of the humble: Thine ear has heard the preparation of their heart* (Ps. x. 17, Vulg.). Do you also, brethren, keep watch over yourselves whereever you are, bearing in mind that God knoweth all your thoughts, that He trieth the very heart and reins, that He has fashioned the heart of each of you individually, and understands all your actions. The Bride, then, feeling that the Bridegroom is present, stops short. She is ashamed of the presumption in which she finds herself surprised. In her modesty, she had thought to make her attempt by means of intermediaries, but now she turns suddenly to Him, and endeavours to excuse her temerity as best she can: *Thy breasts are better than wine*, she says, *and their fragrance than the choicest perfumes*. As if she said: 'If I seem to raise my desire too high, it is Thou, O my Bridegroom, who art the cause of this, in that Thou hast deigned to nourish me with the sweetness of Thy breasts, and thus I have laid aside all fear, not because of my boldness, but of Thy lovingkindness, and am more bold in my requests than is fitting. This confidence renders me mindful only of Thy kindness to me, but unmindful of Thy Majesty.' All this is said to make clear the connection of the words which follow.

5. Now, let us consider after what manner the breasts of the Bridegroom are thus praised. These are the two evidences of His goodness by nature, that He patiently waits for the sinner, and receives the penitent with clemency. It is the very essence of sweetness,[1] I repeat, that abounds in the Breast of the Lord Jesus, and it is twofold: patience in waiting for the sinner, and freeness in granting pardon to him when penitent. This is not a discovery of my own; you may read of it in the Scripture, as with regard to His patience: *Despisest thou the riches of His goodness and forbearance and longsuffering?* And again, *Knowest thou not that the goodness of God leadeth thee to repentance?* (Rom. ii. 4). To this end, indeed, it is that He long suspends the execution of His vengeance against the despisers, in order that He may show the grace of remission to the penitent. For He desireth not the death of a sinner, but rather that he should be converted and live. Let us give also some examples respecting [what I have called] the other breast—that is, of willingness to pardon. Of this you read, *In the hour when the sinner shall lament for his sin, it shall be remitted unto him* (Ezek. xxxiii. 11, 12); and again, *Let the wicked forsake his way, and the unrighteous man his thoughts, and let him return unto the Lord, and He will have mercy upon him; and to our God, for He will abundantly pardon* (Is. lv. 7). David sums

---

[1] *Dulcedo suavitatis.*

both these attributes beautifully in few words: *The Lord is merciful and gracious; slow to anger, and plenteous in mercy* (Ps. ciii. 8). It is just because the Spouse has made proof of this double goodness that she is emboldened, as she confesses, even to venture to ask of Him this grace. 'What wonder is it,' she says, 'O my Spouse, if I presume to ask so much of Thee, since I have had experience of such abundance of sweetness from Thy breast? It is the sweetness of Thy breast, not any confidence in my own merits, which encourages me to be so bold in my request.'

6. Of that further saying, *Thy Breasts are better than wine*, the meaning is this: The unction of grace, which flows from Thy Breasts, is more efficacious to me for my spiritual advancement than the severe reprimand of those set over me. Not only *better than wine*, but *their fragrance than the choicest perfumes*, because, not content with nourishing those who are present with the milk of inward sweetness, you sprinkle over those who are absent the pleasant odour of a good reputation, and make them to have a good report both from those who are within and from those who are without. You have, I say, milk within and perfumes without, since there will be none for you to nourish with milk, if you do not first attract them to you by the sweet odour of your perfume. We shall see later on whether those perfumes contain any meaning worthy of consideration when we come to that passage, *We will run after the odour of Thy perfumes* (i. 3). Now let us consider, as I promised, whether the words which hitherto we have attributed to the Bride have any fitness for the Bridegroom also.

7. The Bride is speaking of the Bridegroom; suddenly, as I have before explained, He is present; He gives assent to her petition; He gives her the embrace asked, and fulfils in her the Scripture, which says: *Thou hast given him his heart's desire, and hast not withholden the request of his lips* (Ps xxi. 2), of which the fulness of breasts is a witness. For so great is the efficacy of it, that the Bride, on receiving it, becomes fruitful, and thus gives testimony to its power. Those whose desire and endeavour it is to pray frequently, they have made proof of what I say. Often we approach the altar and begin to pray with a heart lukewarm and dry. But if we steadily persist, grace comes suddenly in a flood upon us, our breast grows full of increase, a wave of piety fills our inward heart; and if we press on, the milk of sweetness conceived in us will spread over us in fruitful flood. The Bridegroom then speaks thus: 'Thou hast, O my Spouse, that which thou prayedst for; and this is a sign to thee that thy breasts have become more precious than wine. Thence shalt thou know that thou hast received it because thou hast become fruitful. Therefore have thy breasts filled with abundance of milk better than the wine of worldly knowledge, which inebriates indeed, but with curiosity, not with charity, which fills but does not nourish; which puffs up instead of edifying; which gluts but strengthens not.'

8. But, again, let us attribute these words to the attendants. Unjustly it is, they say, that you murmur against the Bridegroom, because

that which He has already granted to you is of more value than that which you ask for. For that is, indeed, for your own delight and gladness; but the breasts from which you nourish the children you bring forth are better—that is, more necessary, than the wine of contemplation. The one is that which maketh glad the heart of one man alone; but the other that which edifies many. For, although Rachel be the fairer, Leah is the more fruitful. Do not, therefore, linger too much over the sweetness of contemplation, for the fruits of preaching are the better.

9. There occurs to me still another sense, which I had not thought of, but I cannot pass it over. Why should we not say that the words befit those who are as little children, and are the first care, as little children are to their mother or their nurse? For souls still young, as it were, and tender, do not bear patiently to see those whose duty it is to instruct them fully in the faith, and to train them by their own examples, giving themselves wholly to the repose of contemplation. And is it not just such souls as these who become the prey of distress and inquietude of mind at a later time, when they are forbidden with solemn charges to disturb the repose of the Beloved until she please (ii. 7)? Seeing that the Bride sighs for the grace of her Beloved, that she seeks retreat, that she flies from the world, that she avoids crowds, and prefers her own repose to the care which she ought to take of others, they cry, Do not thus, do not thus; for in the helpfulness [of preaching] there is more fruit than in all the sweetness [of solitude]: for it is by the former that you deliver us from the desires of the flesh which war against the soul, that you take us from the world and gain us for God. It is this that they express in these words: *Thy breasts are better than wine.* The spiritual delights which thy breasts distil upon us are better than all the pleasures of the flesh, with which we were formerly enthralled and intoxicated as with wine.

10. It is with great beauty and fitness that they compare carnal desires to wine. For as the grape once pressed has nothing more to yield, but is condemned to lasting dryness, so the flesh, under the pressure of death, is exhausted of all its delights, and never after revives to the enjoyment of its passions. Wherefore the Prophet saith: *All flesh is grass, and all the goodliness thereof is as the flower of the field: the grass withereth, the flower fadeth* (Is. xl. 6, 7); and the Apostle: *He that soweth to his flesh shall of the flesh reap corruption* (Gal. vi. 8); and again, *Meats for the belly, and the belly for meats: but God shall destroy both it and them* (1 Cor. vi. 13). But see how that comparison suits, not only the flesh, but also the world. For the world, too, passeth away, and the lust thereof; all things that are in the world have an end, and their end is unending. But not so with those things of which the Breasts are the type. For when they are exhausted they are renewed from the fount of the maternal breast, to nourish those who draw sweetness from them. Rightly, therefore, is it said that the breasts of the Bride are better than the love of the

flesh or of the world, since they are never drawn dry by the number of those who receive of them, but are fed from the deep fount of Charity, and so flow ever new. Truly these streams come forth from the body of Charity, and [in him who receives them] become a well of water springing up into everlasting life (John vii. 38 and iv. 14). The praise of them far surpasses that of the choicest perfumes, because they are nourished not only with the taste and the savour of words, but they exhale the sweet fragrance which good deeds send forth. What remains to be said of them, with what milk it is that they are expanding, with what sweet odours they are perfumed, these things I will, Christ helping me, treat of in another sermon. Who with the Father and the Holy Ghost liveth and reigneth, ever one God, world without end. AMEN.

SERMON X.

OF THE THREE SPIRITUAL PERFUMES—NAMELY, PENITENCE, DEVOTION, AND PIETY.

I HAVE neither such depth of knowledge, nor such brilliancy of genius, as to discover of myself anything new. But the mouth of St. Paul is a great and unfailing fountain which is open to us. From him it is that I draw what I am about to say on the subject of the bosom of the Bride, as, indeed, I am accustomed frequently to do. *Rejoice*, he says, *with them that do rejoice, and weep with them that weep* (Rom. xii. 15). He here expresses, in a few words, the affections of a mother's heart, because little children cannot either be in pain and grief, or in health and gladness, without the close sympathy of their mother in either case, nor can she fail to feel with them. Thus, following the opinion of St. Paul, I shall assign those two affections to the breasts of the Bride—to the one compassion, to the other congratulation. If it were otherwise, if she had not these as yet—that is, if she had not learned to be quick in congratulating others, nor to be ready to condole with them in their grief—she would be but a child, and not of a marriageable age. If a person of such character as this is taken to discharge the oversight of souls, or to preach, he does not profit others, and to himself he does very great harm. And if he should thrust himself into these ministries, what a shameless action is that!

2. But let us return to these thus typified, to the differences between them, and to the graces they yield. Congratulation pours forth the milk of exhortation, and compassion that of consolation. Our spiritual mother[1] feels her pious bosom abundantly supplied from above with both the one and the other of these as often as she is fulfilled

---

[1] *I.e.*, apparently the Church Catholic.—ED.

with the love of God. You see her occupied in nourishing her little children out of her abundance; to one she gives consolation, to another exhortation, according as each seems to have need. For instance, if she sees that one of her children in the Gospel has been taken unawares by some violent temptation so that he is rendered troubled and sorrowful, doubting and fearful, and is no longer able to bear up against the force of the temptation, how she condoles with him and soothes him! how she sorrows for him and gives him comfort, and finds many a pious reason to enable him to rise out of his state of depression! If, on the contrary, she sees one active, energetic, and making good progress in the spiritual life, she rejoices greatly, she plies him with beneficial advice, she animates him to advance still further, instructs him in that which is requisite to perseverance, and exhorts him so that he may go on from strength to strength. To all she adapts herself, in her own heart she reflects the feelings and the dispositions of all, and, lastly, she shows herself the mother no less of the feeble and failing soul than of the strong and progressive.

3. How many are there at the present day—I mean of those who have taken upon them the cure of souls—who are animated by sentiments the very reverse of these? It is a fact not to be spoken of without groaning and tears; they forge, so to speak, in the furnace of avarice, and make merchandise of, the very instruments of Christ's Passion—the scourge, the spitting, the nails, the lance, and, in fine, the Cross and the Death of Christ. They squander all these things for the making of shameful gains; they hasten to huddle into their own pouches the price of the Redemption of the world. The only difference which distinguishes them from Judas Iscariot is that he, for the price of all these things, received but, comparatively speaking, a few pence; while they, with a greed much more insatiable, exact uncounted sums of money as their gains. They have for riches a thirst which is insatiable; well-nigh their sole fear is lest they may lose these; and if they should do so they grieve. Upon the love of them they brood in satisfaction, if, perchance, there be a moment left free from the task of keeping what they have or of gaining more. As for the salvation of souls, or their loss, they think of it not at all No maternal care for souls assuredly have they who, being too well nourished, having fattened and grown great upon the patrimony of the Crucified, *are not grieved for the affliction of Joseph* (Amos vi. 6). A true mother is unmistakably to be known (*non dissimulat*); she is never void of nourishment for her children. She ceases not to rejoice with them that do rejoice, and to weep with them that weep; to press from her bosom the life-giving milk—from that of congratulation the milk of exhortation; from that of compassion, of consolation. I need not say more of these, and of what they contain.

4. I have also to point out what are the perfumes with which the same are fragrant, provided that I am assisted by your prayers, so that by their means that which it is given me to think may also be spoken

worthily, and to the profit of my hearers. The perfumes of the Bride differ from those of the Bridegroom, as they are different the one from the other. What was to be said of those of the Bridegroom is contained in a former discourse. Let us consider just now only the perfumes of the Bride; and that with the greater care, because Scripture commends them particularly to our attention in calling them not only good, but best of all. I mention several kinds, so that out of many those most befitting the Bride may be chosen. There is the perfume of contrition, the perfume of devotion, and that of piety. The first is pungent, and causes pain; the second is soothing, and relieves pain; the third is curative, and removes disease. Now we will speak of these separately.

5. There is, then, a perfume or unguent which the soul—that is, if it be ensnared and entangled with many crimes—compounds for itself, if, when it begins to reflect upon its ways, it collects, heaps together, and pounds in the mortar of conscience its sins of many different kinds, and, putting them into the caldron, as it were, of a heart that heaves and boils [with distress], cooks them together over a kind of fire of grief and repentance, so that the man may be able to say, with the Psalmist: *My heart was hot within me: while I was musing the fire burned* (Ps. xxxix. 3). Here, then, is one unguent which the sinful soul ought to prepare for itself at the commencement of its conversion, and to apply to its still fresh wounds; for the first sacrifice to be made to God is a troubled and contrite heart (Ps. li. 17). Although the sinner is poor and needy, and therefore unable to compound for himself an unguent better and more valuable, yet let him not neglect to prepare this, though of poor materials and of no value, for a broken and contrite heart God will not despise (*ibid.*); and it shall appear so much the less vile in the sight of God, as by remembrance of his sins it becomes the more so to the sinner himself.

6. Yet if we say that this invisible and spiritual unguent was designated in type by that visible ointment wherewith the Feet of God manifest in the Flesh were anointed by the woman who was a sinner, we shall not be able to regard it as being altogether worthless. For what do we read of it in the Scripture? That *the house was filled with the odour of the ointment* (John xii. 3). It was poured by the hands of a sinful woman,[1] and poured upon the extremities of the body—that is, upon the feet; yet it was not so vile and so con-

---

[1] In this passage, as in several others, and particularly in Sermon III. on the Assumption, 'the woman who was a sinner,' mentioned in Luke vii. 37, is confounded with Mary, sister of Lazarus and of Martha, who poured precious ointment upon the feet of the Lord Jesus in the village of Bethany (John xii. 3), on which occasion, it is said, '*the house was filled with the odour of the ointment.*' But most ancient writers before Gregory the Great, and not a few since, distinguish, with exceedingly cogent arguments, between one of these persons and the other, and both from Mary Magdalene, out of whom Christ had cast seven devils (Mark xvi. 9); who, according to Luke (viii. 2, 3), followed Christ with other holy women, even (as it seems) before the conversion of her who was a sinner. Compare Sermon XII., *n.* 6.

temptible that the power and the sweetness of its perfume could not fill the whole house. And if we consider with what fragrance the Church is perfumed by the conversion of one sinner, and how powerful an odour of life unto life each penitent becomes if his repentance is perfect and public, we shall be able to pronounce, without the least doubt, that *the house was filled with the odour of the ointment.* Assuredly the odour of penitence extends even as far as the mansions of the blessed in heaven, so that, as the Truth Himself declares, there is joy among the angels of God over one sinner that repenteth (Luke xv. 10). Rejoice, O penitents; be strengthened, ye that are weak of heart. To you I speak who are but lately converted from the world and from your evil ways, who are feeling the bitterness and confusion of a mind touched with repentance, and in whom the excessive pain of wounds, as it were, yet recent, still throbs and torments. Your hands may with safety drop the bitterness of myrrh into this salutary ointment, for a broken and contrite heart God will not despise. Nor is such an ointment as this to be despised or counted vile, of which the odour not only draws men to conversion, but moves the Angels to joy.

7. Yet there is a perfume as much more precious than this, as the materials of which it is composed are of more excellent kinds. For the materials of the former do not require to be sought from far; we find them without difficulty within ourselves, and in our own little garden-plots gather them easily in great plenty, as often as necessity requires. For who is there who [does not know himself to] have sins and iniquities of his own, enough and too many, always at his hand, unless he desires to deceive himself upon this point? But these are, as you recognise, the materials of the former ointment, which I have described. But as for the sweet spices which compose the second, our earth does not produce them at all; we must seek them in a land very far off. For is not every good gift, and every perfect gift from above, and does it not come down from the Father of Lights? (James i. 17). For this perfume is compounded of the benefits which Divine goodness has bestowed upon the human race. Happy is he who with care and pains collects them for himself, and sets them before the eyes of his mind with acts of thanksgiving proportioned to their greatness. Assuredly when these shall have been bruised and pounded in the mortar of our breast, with the pestle of frequent meditation, then boiled together on the fire of holy desire, and finally enriched with the oil of joy, there will be as the result a perfume far more precious and more excellent than the former. Sufficient as proof of this is the testimony of Him who says: *Whoso offereth praise glorifieth Me* (Ps. l. 23). Nor can we doubt that the remembrance of benefits is an incitement to praise of our benefactor.

8. Furthermore, while Scripture, when speaking of the former, testifies only that it is not despised by God (Ps. li. 17), of this latter it is plain that it is the more commended, in that it is said to *glorify* God. Besides, the former is poured upon the Lord's Feet; the latter

upon His Head. For if in Christ the Head is to be referred to His Divinity, as St. Paul declares the Head of Christ *is God* (1 Cor. xi. 3), then, without doubt, he anoints the Head, who renders thanks; for this is addressed (*tangit*) to God, not to man. Not that He who is God is not Man also, for God and Man is one Christ, but because every good gift, even that which is ministered through man, comes from God, not from man. For *it is the Spirit which quickeneth; the flesh profiteth nothing* (John vi. 63). And we know that *Cursed is the man that trusteth in man* (Jer. xvii. 5); although all our hope rests rightly upon Him who is the God-Man, yet this is not because He is Man, but because He is God. Therefore, the former perfume is poured upon His Feet; but this upon His Head, because the humiliation of a contrite heart is befitting to the humility of the flesh, but praise and glory to the [Divine] Majesty. See, then, of what a nature is this perfume which I have been describing to you, with which that Head, so august even to the Principalities and Powers of Heaven, does not disdain to be touched; nay, rather regards it as an honour to Him, as He Himself declares: *Whoso offereth praise glorifieth Me* (Ps. l. 23).

9. Wherefore it does not belong to him who is poor and needy and of small courage to compound such a perfume as this, inasmuch as it is confidence alone which commands the sweet spices which are its materials, but a confidence which is born of freedom of spirit and purity of heart. For the soul which is of small courage and of little faith is hampered by the consciousness of the little which it possesses; its poverty does not permit it to occupy itself in the praises of God, or in the contemplation of those benefits which produce the praises. And if ever it has the wish to rise to that point, immediately it is recalled to the consciousness of its cares and uneasiness about its necessities at home, and is straitened in itself by the miseries which press it hard. If you ask of me the cause of that misery, I reply that you are, or have been, conscious in your own selves (if I do not mistake) of that which I refer to. It seems to me that this depression of mind and want of joyful trust usually comes from one of two causes. Either, that is to say, it is from newness of conversion, or, especially if the conversion is not recent, from lukewarmness of conduct. Both the one and the other cause humiliates and casts down the conscience, and throws it into trouble and inquietude, since it feels that its former passions are not yet dead in it, either because of the shortness of the time since its conversion, or because of the feebleness and want of zeal in its efforts, and thus it is obliged to occupy itself entirely with rooting up from the garden of the heart the thorns of iniquity and briers of evil desires, nor is it able to divert any thoughts from itself. What then? how can one, who is wearily occupied in sighing and groaning [over such a task as this], at the same time rejoice in the praises of God? How can *thanksgiving and the voice of melody*, to borrow the phrase of the prophet Isaiah (li. 3), sound forth from the mouth of one that is groaning and lamenting?

For, as the Wise Man teaches us, *Music in mourning is a tale out of season* (Ecclus. xxii. 6, Vulg.). And the giving of thanks follows the benefit, not precedes it. But the soul that is still in sadness needs to receive the benefit, and does not rejoice in having obtained it. It has a great reason to offer its prayers, but not to offer its thanksgiving. How is it to acknowledge a blessing which it has not, in fact, received? It was correct, therefore, for me to say that it was not the privilege of a soul that is poor and needy and of small courage to compound this precious perfume, which requires to be composed of remembered benefits of God; nor is such a one able to behold the light, as long as its gaze is fixed upon the darkness. For it is in bitterness—the sorrowful remembrance of past sins occupies it; nor can it admit any thought of joy. It is to such that the prophetic spirit bears testimony, saying: *It is vain for you to rise up early* (Ps. cxxvii. 2); as if he would remind them: It is in vain for you to rise up that you may behold bounties to be a delight to your soul, unless you have first received the light which shall comfort it with regard to the stains of sin which trouble it. This perfume, therefore, is not for the soul which is still in a state of spiritual poverty.

10. But see who they are who may rightly take the glory of having it in abundance. The Apostles *departed from the presence of the council, rejoicing that they were counted worthy to suffer shame for the Name of* JESUS (Acts v. 41). Assuredly those men were well filled with that unction of the Spirit, whose cheerfulness did not abandon them, I do not say, because of words, but not even because of blows. They were indeed rich in charity, in whom it was exhausted by no spending, and who were enabled to offer themselves as a complete and worthy burnt sacrifice to God. Their hearts poured forth everywhere that holy unction, with which they had been imbued in plenitude, when they spake in various tongues the wonderful works of God as the Spirit gave them utterance (Acts ii. 4, 11). Nor can it be doubted that they abounded in the same perfumes of whom the Apostle thus speaks: *I thank my God always on your behalf, for the grace of God which is given you by Jesus Christ: that in everything ye are enriched by Him, in all utterance, and in all knowledge; even as the testimony of Christ was confirmed in you, so that ye come behind in no gift* (1 Cor. i. 4-7). Would that I too might be able to render the same thanksgivings on your account, and to see you rich in virtue, ready and prompt to praise God, and superabounding in this spiritual fatness in JESUS CHRIST OUR LORD.

SERMON XI.

OF TWO PRINCIPAL FACTS IN THE REDEMPTION OF THE HUMAN RACE; THE MANNER IN WHICH IT IS ACCOMPLISHED, AND THE BENEFITS WHICH WE DERIVE FROM IT.

I SAID at the end of the last sermon, and I willingly repeat it now, that I desire to see you all become sharers in that sacred unction, by which a holy devotion acknowledges the benefits of God with joy and thanksgiving. For this is extremely beneficial, inasmuch as it lightens the troubles of this present life, which become more supportable when we rejoice in the praises of God, and also because nothing represents so perfectly on earth the state of the blessed in heaven as the gladness of those who are occupied in praising God; as the Scripture declares: *Blessed are they that dwell in Thy House: they will for ever be praising Thee* (Ps. lxxxiv. 5). I think it was this perfume that the Psalmist had particularly in view when he said: *Behold, how good and how pleasant it is for brethren to dwell together in unity; it is like precious ointment upon the head* (Ps cxxxiii. 1, 2). This does not seem to be a description of the former kind. For though that be good, it is far from being pleasant, because the remembrance of sins causes bitterness, not pleasure. Nor do those who are compounding it dwell together, since each is occupied in separately lamenting his own sins. But as for those who are wholly occupied in praising God, they regard God only, and think but of Him; and on this account, it is truly said that they dwell together in unity. Again, that which they are engaged in doing is not only good because they are ascribing glory to Him to whom it most justly belongs, but also pleasant, because they take delight in doing it.

2. On this account I counsel you, my friends, to turn yourselves away sometimes from the anxious and painful retracing of your past erring lives, and to pursue paths which are easier and afford more pleasant thoughts in the recalling of God's benefits, so that by fixing your thoughts and your eyes upon Him, you may obtain some relief from the shame and confusion of face which are caused by thinking of yourself. I would that you should make trial of the advice which the holy Psalmist gives when he says: *Delight thou in the Lord, and He shall give thee thy heart's desire* (Ps xxxvii. 4). Sorrow for sin is indeed necessary, but it ought not to be continual; and there should be mingled with it the more joyful remembrance of the Divine goodness, lest the heart should be burdened because of the sorrow it feels, and despair should bring about the actual loss of it. With wormwood let us mix honey, so that the draught thus tempered with moderate sweetness may be able to be drunk, and that its bitter may be salutary. Listen how God Himself tempers the bitterness of a

contrite heart, so as to draw back from the abyss of desperation him who is in fear and discouragement; to console the sorrowful by the honey of a sweet and faithful promise; to raise up him who is of little faith. He says by the prophet: *With my praise will I restrain thee as with a bridle, that thou perish not* (Is. xlviii. 9, Vulg.); that is to say, 'For fear lest the sight of your sins should cast you into excessive sorrow, and that, carried away by despair, like a horse without rein, you should fall down a precipice and perish, I will rein you back (He says) by the bridle, as it were, of My mercy; I will raise you up by My praises; you shall breathe again at the sight of My benefits, instead of being confounded at the sense of your own demerits; and the more blamable you find yourself to be, the more shall you find Me kind and forgiving.' If Cain had been restrained by this bridle, he would not have said: *My iniquity is too great to obtain pardon* (Gen. iv. 13, Vulg.). God forbid! God forbid! For His goodness is greater than any iniquity whatsoever. That is why the just man is not his own accuser always, but only in the beginning of his discourse,[1] for his custom was to close his discourse with praises of God. Notice in what order a just man proceeds: *I thought on my ways, and turned my feet unto Thy testimonies* (Ps. cxix. 59); so that after having endured contrition and unhappiness in his own ways, he takes delight in the way of the testimonies of God, as in all manner of riches. Do you also, after the example of the righteous, if you have feelings of humility about yourselves, be assured also of the goodness of the Lord. For so you read in the words of the Wise Man: *Think of the Lord in goodness, and in simplicity of heart seek Him* (Wisd. i. 1). The frequent, or, I should say, the continual, remembrance of the Divine liberality will easily bring the mind to a firm belief in this. Otherwise, how can that precept of the Apostle be carried out, *In everything give thanks* (1 Thess. v. 18), if those benefits for which thanks are owed are suffered to fade from the heart? I would not that you should be open to that opprobrium which was deserved by the Jews, of whom Scripture testifies that they were not mindful of His benefits, nor of the wonderful works that He had showed them (Ps. lxxviii 11).

3. But as it is impossible for any man to recount and enumerate all the blessings which our merciful and compassionate Lord does not cease to pour upon the children of men (for *who can utter the mighty acts of the Lord, or who can show forth all His praise?* (Ps. cvi. 2), at least that which is the chief and the greatest of His benefits, I mean the work of our redemption, ought never to depart for a moment from the memory of those whom He has redeemed. And in this

---

[1] Prov. xviii. 17. St. Bernard quotes, not the Vulgate: '*Justus prior est accusator sui*,' but either a translation ('*Justus accusator est sui in principio sermonis*') of the LXX. text of the passage, Δίκαιος ἑαυτοῦ κατήγορος ἐν πρωτολογίᾳ, which would be an unusual thing with him; or, more probably, from his recollection of the reading made use of by one of the Fathers, perhaps St. Ambrose ('De Offic. Ministror.,' Bk. i., c. 25), '*Justus in exordio sermonis accusator est sui*'; or St. Cyril (Bk. ii., in Joan. c. 14).—ED.

work there are two principal things which occur to my mind at this time, which I will commend to your meditation and study. This I will do in as few words as possible, being mindful of that saying: *Give instruction to a wise man, and he will be yet wiser* (Prov. ix. 9). These two things are: the manner in which it was accomplished, and the benefits which we derive from it. As for the manner, it was the self-emptying (*exinanitio*) of God; as for the benefit derived by us, it is that we should be filled with Him. Meditation upon the former great mystery is the seed-ground of holy hope; upon the latter, the incentive to the most exalted and ardent love. Both the one and the other are necessary to our spiritual progress; to ensure, on the one hand, that our hope be not unaccompanied by love, and therefore mercenary; and, on the other, that our love be not lukewarm, and so become unfruitful.

4. The fruit and final reward of our love which we await, shall be such as He, whom we love, has promised: *Good measure, pressed down, and shaken together, and running over, they shall give into your bosom* (Luke vi. 38). That measure, as I hear, shall be without measure. But that which I long to know is what that is which shall be bestowed without measure, or rather, that eternal blessedness (*immensitas*) which is promised to us. But *eye hath not seen, O Lord, except Thee, what Thou hast prepared for them that love Thee* (Is. lxiv. 4, and 1 Cor. ii. 9). O tell us what good things Thou dost prepare, O Thou who art preparing them! We believe, we hope in absolute confidence, as Thou hast in fact promised, that *we shall be satisfied with the goodness of Thy House* (Ps. lxv. 4). But with what good things, I pray, and of what nature? Shall it be with corn and wine and oil that we shall be satisfied, or, perchance, with gold and silver and precious gems? But these things we have known and seen; we have seen and have even contemned. That which we seek, eye hath not seen, nor ear heard, nor hath the heart of any man risen to imagine it. This, of whatsoever nature it be, is what we choose and we desire; and this it delights us still to seek. *They shall all be taught of God*, He saith (John vi. 45), and *God shall be all in all* (1. Cor. xv. 28). As I apprehend it, then, the fulness [of blessedness] which we await from God shall be derived from no other than God Himself.

5. But who can comprehend how great a variety of blessedness and sweetness is comprehended in this brief saying, *God shall be all in all?* Not to speak of the body, there are in the soul three faculties—the reason, the will, and the memory—and these three are, in fact, the soul itself. Everyone who walks in the Spirit feels how greatly each of these faculties is wanting in him during this present life. Wherefore is this the case, except that God is not yet all in all? Hence it is that the reason very often errs in its judgments, the will is agitated by manifold (*quadruplici*) troubles and passions, and the memory is confused by the multitude of things which it has let slip. To this threefold power of vanity a creature so noble is subjected,

though against its will, yet it hopes one day to be delivered. For He who satisfieth with good things the longing desire of the soul, shall Himself be to the reason fulness of Light, to the will the completeness (*multitudo*) of peace, to the memory an eternal continuity. O Truth, O Charity, O Eternity! O Trinity, blessed and blessing! To Thee the trinity of my unhappy being aspires in its unhappiness, caused by its grievous separation from Thee. In how many errors, sorrows and fears, has not that separation involved it? Woe is me! what a trinity have I accepted in exchange for Thee! *My heart panteth*, and thence my pain; *my strength faileth me*, and thence my fear; *the light of my eyes is also gone from me* (Ps. xxxviii. 11), and therefore my error and wandering. O trinity of my soul, how different a trinity hast thou found in the place of exile [from the Trinity of my God].

6. *Yet, why art thou cast down, O my soul? and why art thou disquieted in me? Hope thou in God, for I shall yet praise Him* (Ps. xlii. 5) when error shall have passed away from my reason, the pain of wavering from my will, and every kind of fear from my memory; and to those troubles a marvellous peace, a perfect blessedness, an eternal security, shall have succeeded. God as Truth shall perform the first: God as Charity, the second; and God as Supreme Power, the third: and thus God shall be all in all, the reason receiving a light which shall never be extinguished, the will obtaining a state of peace which cannot be disturbed, and the memory eternally inhering in the unfailing Source of being and of fact. You will consider whether you should not rightly assign the first of these to the Son, the second to the Holy Ghost, the third to the Father; yet so as not to withdraw either of these from either the Father, or the Son, or the Holy Ghost, lest with regard to either of the Divine Persons, either distinction should lessen the Plenitude, or Perfection take away from that which in each is Proper and Particular. Consider also that there is a similar threefold division in that which the children of this world make their own—namely, the allurements of the flesh, the vain shows of the world, and the pomps of the devil; and, nevertheless, it is by all this that the present world seduces those unhappy ones who are lovers of it, as St. John declares: *All that is in the world, the lust of the flesh, and the lust of the eyes, and the pride of life* (1 John ii. 16). So much with regard to the benefits of redemption.

7. As for the *manner* of redemption which I defined, if you remember, to be the self-emptying of God, there are three chief points which I propose for your consideration. For this is not a simple inanition, or one which is only limited or partial; but the Lord emptied Himself so far as to assume flesh, to undergo death, to endure the Cross (Phil. ii. 7, 8). Who can possibly be able to form a just idea of the greatness of the humility, of the condescension, of the goodness, shown by the Lord of Glory in clothing Himself with Flesh, in suffering death, in bearing the ignominy of the Cross?

Someone will perhaps say: 'Could not the Creator repair His work without such difficulty?' He could have done so, but He preferred to do it by the way of suffering, so that man might thenceforth find no ground for that worst and most odious vice of ingratitude. Unquestionably He endured many labours and pains that He might render man the debtor for much love, and that the difficulty of Redemption might carry gratitude to a much greater height in those whom the comparative ease of their Creation[1] had so little inspired. For what did man, created and ungrateful, say in his own behalf? ' I was of free grace brought into existence, but my Creator had no difficulty or labour in forming me; for He spake, and I was made, as were all other works of His Hands. What great gift is it that you have bestowed at no greater cost than a word spoken?' Thus did human impiety depreciate the benefit of creation, and draw a reason for ingratitude from that which ought to have been a ground for love, and for excuses, which themselves needed excuse, on behalf of human sins. But the mouth of those who spoke those evil words has now been stopped. It appears more clearly than light at what vast cost [God] has accomplished thy salvation, O man; for He has not disdained from being Lord to become a servant, from being rich to become poor, from being Son of God to become the Son of Man. Remember, then, that though thou wert created out of nothing, thou wert not redeemed for nothing. It was in six days that He created all things, and thee among the rest. But it occupied more than thirty years of life upon the earth to accomplish thy salvation. How great were [thy Saviour's] exertions, and how great His sufferings! Did He not endure the wants and infirmities of the flesh, the temptations of the devil, and the ignominy of the Cross; and was there not heaped upon them all the horror of His Death? And all these were necessarily endured. Thus it was, thus, that Thou, O Lord, hast saved men and beasts; how excellent is Thy loving kindness, O God! (Ps. xxxvi. 6, 7).

8. Meditate upon these things, revolve them continually in your minds. With such precious perfumes steep your hearts, that you may dissipate the evil odour of your sins which has long troubled them, and that you may abound in their odours, as salutary as they are sweet. Yet do not suppose that you possess the best of those which are upon the bosom of the Bride. The want of time, and the necessity of bringing this sermon to a close, forbids my beginning to speak of these now. What has been said of the others, retain in your memory, approve your possession of them by your life; and finally, assist me by your prayers, that I may be enabled to speak worthily worthy words concerning these joys of the Bride which are so great; and may build up your souls in the love of the Bridegroom, our Lord Jesus Christ. AMEN.

---

[1] *Conditionis.* But probably we should read *creationis;* otherwise *conditio* is used in the sense of *founding* or *bringing into existence.* But see the next sentence.—ED.

SERMON XII.

OF THE PERFUME OF PIETY, WHICH IS THE MOST EXCELLENT OF ALL; AND OF THE RESPECT WHICH THOSE UNDER AUTHORITY OUGHT TO HAVE FOR THOSE SET OVER THEM.

I REMEMBER that I spoke to you of two perfumes: the one, of penitence, which comprehends many sins; the other, of devotion, which contains many benefits—both of them salutary, but not both agreeable. The first has a stinging power which makes itself felt, because the bitter remembrance of sins moves the soul to compunction, and causes pain, whereas the power of the other is soothing; it gives consolation and relieves spiritual distress by bringing into view the goodness of God. But there is a perfume which far excels both of these; I have called it the perfume of piety, because it is that which results from the necessities of the poor, the cares of the oppressed, the disquiets of the sorrowful, the faults of sinners, and finally, from all the misfortunes of those who are unhappy, even though they be our enemies. Those materials seem to be despicable, but the perfume which is distilled from them surpasses all other sweet odours. It is a perfume which cures, because *blessed are the merciful, for they shall obtain mercy* (Matt. v. 7). Many miseries, therefore, collected together, and regarded with an eye of compassionate goodness, are the materials from which is composed the best of all perfumes, worthy of the bosom of the Bride, and agreeable to the senses of the Bridegroom. Happy is the soul which has had the care to anoint and to enrich itself with these perfumes, pouring upon them the oil of mercy, and heating them with the fire of charity. Who, think you, is that happy man who has pity and lendeth (Ps. cxii. 5), but he that is wont to compassionate others, who is quick to help them, judging it better to give than to receive; to whom it is easy to forgive, hard to be angry, and almost impossible to take revenge; and who in all things regards the interests of his neighbours even as his own? O happy soul, whosoever thou art, who art of such a disposition, so imbued with the dew of mercy, so endued with charitable affections, so rendering thyself all things to all men, so regarding thyself as but a broken vessel, that thou mayest be at the service of others, and assist them in their need, whensoever and wheresoever it may be; and who, finally, art dead to thyself, that thou mayst live to the benefit of all. O happy soul, thou plainly possessest this third and best of perfumes, and from thy hands have dropped all its sweetness. In the worst of times it shall not dry up, nor shall the fire of persecution exhaust it; God shall be ever mindful of every sacrifice thou hast made, and shall render perfect thy burnt-offering.

2. There are men in the city of the Lord who are rich in virtues; are there any among them who possess this perfume? The first who

occurs to me, and who is met everywhere in the way of goodness, is Paul—that vessel of election, yea, in truth a vessel of odour and sweetness, filled with every kind of fragrant powder. For he was to God a sweet savour of Christ in every place (2 Cor. ii. 14). Assuredly that generous heart, which took so great care of all the Churches, scattered far and wide fragrance of surpassing sweetness. See of what nature those were which he has amassed for himself. *I die daily*, he says, *through your glory* (1 Cor. xv. 31, Vulg.); and again, *Who is weak, and I am not weak? who is offended, and I burn not?* (2 Cor. xi. 29). And in many such passages, which are well known to you, that good man shows how he abounded in preparing these precious perfumes. It was fitly thus, that the bosom which nourished the members of Christ should be redolent of the rarest and most precious perfumes, for Paul was assuredly a mother to them, travailing in birth as it were, once and again, until Christ were formed in them (Gal. iv. 19), and the members reformed in the likeness of their Head.

3. Let me tell you also of another, who was rich in this respect, who possessed materials carefully chosen for the compounding of precious balms. What does he himself say? *The stranger did not lodge in the street, but I opened my doors to the traveller* (Job. xxxi. 32). And again: *I was eyes to the blind, and feet was I to the lame. I was a father to the poor. . . . I brake the jaws of the wicked, and plucked the spoil out of his teeth* (xxix. 15-17). *If I have withheld the poor from their desire, or have caused the eyes of the widow to fail; Or have eaten my morsel myself alone, and the fatherless hath not eaten thereof; If I have seen any perish*[1] *for want of clothing; If his loins have not blessed me, and if he were not warmed with the fleece of my sheep* (xxxi. 16-20). With what a sweet odour must that good man have blessed the earth by these works of charity! Each of such actions is a separate perfume, and with these he had stored his conscience, so as to counteract the exhalations of his noisome flesh by the sweet odour exhaled from his soul.

4. Joseph, after he had drawn in his train the whole of Egypt through the sweet odour yielded by his good deeds, afforded the same fragrance even to those who had sold him into slavery. He did, indeed, reproach them with an angry countenance; but his tears burst forth from the fulness of his heart; nor were they signs of his wrath, but betrayed the strength of his emotion (Gen. xliii. 30, and xlv. 2). Samuel mourned for Saul, who sought to kill him (1 Sam. xv. 35, and xvi. 2), and the unction of his kindliness coming from within him, and warmed in his breast by the fire of charity, found issue by his eyes. And it was because of the sweet odour which his reputation spread throughout all the land that the Scripture says of him, *All Israel, from Dan even to Beersheba, knew that Samuel was established to be a prophet of the Lord* (1 Sam. iii. 20). What

---

[1] St. Bernard, it is well to say, quotes '*despexi prætereuntem*' (the ancient version), 'I despised the passer-by,' and varies from the Vulgate, which is rare with him, especially in a passage of some length.—ED.

shall I say of Moses? With what rich perfume had he too filled his heart! That rebellious house, in the midst of which he was for a time occupied, was never able, with all its murmurs, or its angry passions, to make him lose that unction of spirit with which he had once been imbued, or to hinder his retaining his gentleness of temper among their constant strifes and daily quarrels. Well deserved, therefore, was the witness which the Holy Spirit bore to him, that 'he was the meekest of all men who were upon the face of the earth' (Num. xii. 3, Vulg.). Even with those who hated peace, he was peacefully disposed, insomuch that he not only did not indulge anger against an ungrateful and rebellious people, but even interceded for them, so that the Divine anger was softened at his mediation; as it is written, *He said that He would destroy them, had not Moses His chosen stood before Him in the gap, to turn away His wrath, lest He should destroy them* (Ps. cvi. 23). And lastly, he said: *Forgive, if Thou wilt, their sin · but if not, blot me out of the book which Thou hast written* (Exod. xxxii. 32). A man truly filled with the unction of mercy! He obviously speaks with the feeling of a father, whom no happiness can delight apart from his children. It is as if a rich man should say to some poor woman who is a mother, 'Enter, and dine with me, but leave without the infant you carry in your arms, for fear that it should cry, and be a trouble to us.' What would that mother answer, do you suppose? Would she not rather choose to remain without food, than to dine with the rich man alone, after having abandoned her dear pledge of affection? So also Moses did not choose to be admitted alone, even into the joy of his Lord, while his people remained without; for although they were restless and ungrateful, he retained for them the affection, as he held the place, of a mother. The bowels of his affection suffer, but he prefers to bear the suffering that they cause, rather than they should be torn from him.

5. What again can be a proof of greater kindness of heart than the lament of David over the death of that man, who had always thirsted for his death (2 Sam. i. 11), and that he bore with so much regret the death of him, whom he succeeded in the kingdom? How hard it was to console him for the death of a son, even though he was [in intention] a parricide! (2 Sam. xix. 4). Assuredly a kindliness of heart so great was an infallible mark of an abundant measure of this best of perfumes; therefore, also, he addressed with confidence his prayer to God: Lord remember David and all his kindness of heart (Ps. cxxxii. 1, Vulg.). All these holy persons had then this best of perfumes, of which the fragrant odours are spread through all the Churches even at the present day. And not only they, but all those also who, during this life, have shown themselves benevolent and charitable, who have striven so to live humanely among men as not to keep for their own advantage, but to use for the common benefit of all, every grace which they possessed, regarding themselves as debtors, alike to enemies and to friends, to the wise and to the

unwise. As they were useful to all, humble in all circumstances, and before all things showed themselves to be dear to God and to men; so their fragrance is held in pious memory. As many, I repeat, of those who have gone before, who have been in character such as this, were of good report as of sweet perfume in their own days, and their sweetness remains at the present time. Thus also with you, my brother, whosoever you are, if you shall willingly share with us, who are your companions, the gift which you have received from on high; if you show yourself always helpful, sympathetic, kindly, tractable, humble, you, too, will have from all of us a similar testimony that you are fragrant with the richest perfumes. Everyone among you who not only patiently bears with the infirmities, whether of body or of mind, of his brethren, but also if it is permitted him, and if he has the ability to do it, to assist them by his services, to strengthen them by his exhortations, to train them by his wise counsels; and if discipline does not permit him to do this, at least he does not cease to assist them in their weakness by his earnest prayers; everyone, I say, who among you acts in this manner, exercises a precious influence among his brethren, sprinkles over them, so to speak, the costliest perfumes. Like sweet balm in the mouth, is such a brother as this in a community; he is pointed out with the finger as a wonder, and all say of him: This is a lover of the brethren, who prayeth much for the people, and for the Holy City.[1]

6. But let us now turn to the Gospel, and look if there be anything in it having reference to these perfumes. [And we so find that] *Mary Magdalene, and Mary the mother of James, had bought sweet spices that they might come and anoint Jesus* (Mark xvi. 1). Now, what were these perfumes so precious that they were purchased and brought to anoint the Body of Christ, so abundant also that they suffice to anoint it completely? For neither of the two former was either purchased[2] or made for the service of the Lord, nor do we read that they were poured over His whole body. But suddenly a woman is brought before us, who kissed His feet; and in another place, either she, or another, having an alabaster box of ointment, brake it, and poured the ointment upon His Head (Luke vii. 38; John xii. 3; Mark xiv. 3). But in the instance we are considering, it is said, *They bought sweet spices, that they might come and anoint Jesus.* They bought, not ointments, but sweet spices; the ointment for embalming is not taken ready-made, it is newly compounded; and that to anoint, not a part only of the Lord's Body, as His Head, or His Feet, but in the phrase used by Scripture, 'to anoint *Jesus*,' that is to say, His entire Body.

7. Do you also [who hear me, whosoever you may be], who art putting on bowels of mercies, show yourself liberal and kindly, not to your relatives or connexions only, or to those who you think have helped you in the past, or, as you hope, may help you in the future; for this even the Gentiles do (Matt. v. 46, 47); but, according to

---
[1] 2 Macc. xv. 14. The Vulgate adds '*et populi Israel*' after '*fratrum*.'—ED.
[2] Many MSS. omit *purchased*.

St. Paul's precept, study to do good unto all men (Gal. vi. 10). So your constant principle should be that for the sake of God, the offices of humanity, whether corporal or spiritual, are not to be denied even to an enemy; and if you act upon this rule, you will abound in these most precious perfumes, and will have undertaken to anoint, not the Lord's Head or Feet only, but (as far as in you lies) His whole Body, that is, the Church. And perhaps it was for this very reason that the Lord Jesus would not have the sweet spices which had been prepared expended upon His Body dead, in order that they might be reserved for His Body living; for the Church is living, and subsists upon the Living Bread, which came down from heaven. It is that Body of Christ which is the more dear to Him, because it did not taste of death; whereas the other, as no Christian is ignorant, He gave over unto death. It is this that He wishes to be cherished, to be anointed, and that its weak members should be restored to health by careful and salutary treatment. For this His Body, then, it was that He reserved those sweet spices, when anticipating the hour, and hastening His glory, He instructed, rather than avoided, the devotion of the holy women. He declined to be anointed, not as despising the ointment, but as sparing it; not as refusing that pious service, but as reserving the usefulness of it to a later time. I say 'the usefulness,' not as referring to the material ointment, but evidently to the spiritual, which was designated or typified by it. In those sweet spices, therefore, the Master of piety reserved for use those choicest perfumes of piety, which He earnestly desired should be employed for the needs of His members, whether those needs be bodily or spiritual. When, only a little while before, a sweet perfume, and costly, was poured upon His Head, or even upon His Feet, did He forbid it? Not at all, but, on the contrary, reproved those who did so. To Simon, who was indignant that He should permit Himself to be touched by a woman who was a sinner, He addressed a long parable of reproof; and to others, who complained of the pecuniary loss sustained by the expending of the perfume, He said: *Why trouble ye the woman?* (Matt. xxvi. 10).

8. If I may make here a little digression, it has sometimes happened to me when, for my own good, I was sitting at the Feet of Jesus in great affliction, and offering to Him the sacrifice of a spirit troubled and afflicted at the remembrance of my sins; and I might, as in rare instances has been the case, stand up and rejoice in the remembrance of His mercies, I, too, have heard those that said: *To what purpose is this waste?* That is, they complained that I was spending life to my own profit alone, while, as they thought, I might make myself useful to many. And they, too, said: *This might be sold for much, and given to the poor.* But it would not be a profitable transaction for me, even though I should gain the whole world, to lose my own self and work my own destruction. And therefore I regarded such scoffs as realizing what Scripture says of dead flies, which corrupt the sweetness of perfumes (Eccles. x. 1); and I be-

thought myself of that utterance of Divine wisdom: *My people, they which lead thee cause thee to err* (Is. iii. 12). But let those who accuse me, as if I were slothful, listen to the Lord replying for me, and making my excuse: *Why trouble ye the woman?* That is to say, you see only the surface of things, and judge according to what you see. This is not a man, as you suppose, who is able to set his hand to heavy tasks, but [one who is in his weakness] a woman. Why do you attempt to lay upon him a yoke which I perceive that he is not able to bear? He hath done a good work upon Me. Let him remain in that which is good, as long as he has not strength to go on to that which is better. If ever, by progress in the spiritual life, from a woman he shall have become a man, and a perfect man, then he may take upon him the task of performing the work of perfection.

9. Brethren, let us revere Bishops, but let us have a dread of the labours in which it is the duty of their charge to engage. If we consider those labours, we shall not be desirous of the honours [which belong to them]. Let us recognise that our powers are unequal to these, and that the weak and delicate shoulders of women can have no call to support burdens which task men; we ought to honour, but not to seek to obtain them. Now, there would be a want of good manners in criticising the actions of those, the burden of whose labours we shun. What rashness is it of the woman who spins in the house to reproach her husband when returning from the field of battle! I say, then, that if one who dwells in the cloister remarks that [a prelate], whose daily duty lies among the people, conducts himself with less discretion and self-restraint than he should, for example, in speech, in his food, in length of slumber, in freedom of laughter, in indulging anger, or allowing himself liberty of judgment, let him not jump immediately to a conclusion, and that unfavourable, but let him remember that it is written: Better is the iniquity of a man than a woman who doeth good (Ecclus. xliv. 14), for you indeed do well in guarding yourself with vigilance; but he who is of assistance to many does even better, and leads a more manly life. If such an one does not succeed in fulfilling this function without the commission of some faults, that is, without some want of uniform observance of rule in life and conversation, we must remember that *charity covereth a multitude of sins* (1 Pet. iv. 8). These warnings are given against a twofold temptation, by which men in religion are frequently assailed, that either they should be induced to seek for themselves by ambition the dignity of the Episcopate, or, by the instigation of the devil, rashly to condemn the actions of Bishops.

10. But let us return to the perfumes of the Bride. Do you not see how vastly to be preferred to the others is that perfume of piety which alone must not, under any circumstances, be lost? So highly is it valued, indeed, that not even the gift of a cup of cold water is suffered to go unrewarded (Matt. x. 42). Nevertheless, that of contrition and penitence, which is composed of the remembrance of past sins, and is cast at the Lord's Feet, is good also; for a broken and

contrite heart God will not despise (Ps. li. 17). But I judge that which is called of devotion, and made of the remembrance of the benefits of God, to be far better, inasmuch as it is thought worthy of being used for the Head, and that God speaks of it thus: *Whoso offereth praise glorifieth Me* (Ps. l. 23). But the unction of piety and charity, which comes from a regard to those who are miserable, and is diffused over the whole of the Body of Christ, vastly surpasses both the one and the other; and when I say the Body of Christ, I mean not that which was crucified in His Passion, but that which was obtained by the suffering of the former. That perfume is, in truth, the best, of which He who says: *I will have mercy and not sacrifice* (Matt. ix. 13)—declares that He does not regard others in comparison with it. I think, then, that, among all the virtues, the bosom of the Bride exhales most of all the perfume of that, since she strives in all things to conform herself to the will of her Spouse. Was it not that odour of mercy which Tabitha exhaled even in death? And if she was raised speedily to life again, it was because that odour of life in her overcame the odour of death.

11. Let me give you now, in conclusion, a brief abstract of the whole subject: Whosoever in words is full of fervour and stimulating strength (*inebriat*), and by benefits done to others gains a name of which the good report is fragrant, may claim the words: *Thy breasts are better than wine, and their fragrance than the choicest perfumes.* But who is it whom these words truly describe? Who is there among us who possesses fully and perfectly even one of these two qualities in such a manner that he is not sometimes either unfruitful in his teaching or without earnestness in his actions? But there is one who, with good right and without hesitation, may be praised as possessing both. It is the Church which, though the number of her children be so great, is never wanting in teaching to arouse and to stimulate them, or in good deeds of which the fragrance excites their admiration; for that which is wanting in one, she finds in another [of her children], according to the measure of the gift of Christ, and of the good pleasure of the Holy Ghost dividing unto everyone severally as He will (Eph. iv. 7, and 1 Cor. xii. 11). The Church gives forth a fragrant odour of good report in those her children who make to themselves friends of the mammon of unrighteousness; and she gives forth teaching to arouse and to stimulate, in the ministers of the Word, who pour forth upon the earth the wine of spiritual joy, which, so to speak, inebriates it, and who bring forth fruit in patience. With safety and confidence she names herself Spouse, since her breasts are truly better than wine, and their fragrance than the choicest perfumes. And though none of us would presume so far as to venture to say that his soul was the Spouse of the Lord, yet, since we are members of the Church which justly glories in that name, and in the fact which the name signifies. we may claim, not unjustly, a participation in that glory; for that which the whole body of us possess, fully and entirely, each of us, as individuals, must surely have our part in. Thanks be

to Thee, O Lord Jesus, for that Thou hast deigned to join us to Thy Church, which is to Thee so dear, that we might be not only of the number of Thy faithful, but also [that our souls] might be united to Thee, as Spouse, in embraces blissful, chaste, and eternal, when, with face unveiled, we shall behold Thy glory—the glory which Thou hast, equally and in common with the Father and the Holy Ghost, for ever and ever. AMEN.

SERMON XIII.

THAT PRAISE AND GLORY IS ALWAYS TO BE RENDERED UNTO GOD, FOR ALL THE GOOD GIFTS WHICH WE RECEIVE OF HIM.

THE sea is the source of fountains and rivers; the Lord Jesus Christ is the source of every kind of virtue and knowledge. For who but He who is the King of glory is the Lord of every virtue? So He, too, according to the song of Hannah (1 Sam. ii. 3), is *a God of knowledge*. Continence in the body, diligence of heart, rectitude of will, flow from that Divine source. Nor is this all; for if anyone is of skilled and able intellect, or of striking and powerful speech, or of winning and saintly character, it is from hence that this ability comes. Whatever discourse is wise and full of knowledge has its origin from Him, for *in Him are hid all the treasures of wisdom and knowledge* (Col. ii. 3). What? are not pure purposes, just judgments, holy aspirations, one and all streams from that same source? If all waters seek incessantly to return to the sea, making their way thither sometimes by hidden and subterranean channels, so that they may go forth from it again in continual and untiring circuit, becoming visible once more to man and available for his service, why are not those spiritual streams rendered back constantly and without reserve to their legitimate source, that they may not cease to water the fields of our hearts? Let the rivers of divers graces return from whence they came, that they may flow forth anew. Let the heavenly shower rise again to its heavenly source, that it may be poured anew and still more plentifully upon the earth. In what manner, do you ask? In the manner prescribed by the Apostle St. Paul: *In everything give thanks* (1 Thess. v. 18). Whatever you think you have of wisdom and of virtue, attribute it to Him who is the Power of God and the Wisdom of God—that is, to Christ.

2. Who is so actuated by folly, you say, as to presume to think otherwise? No one, truly; even the Pharisee returned thanks to God (Luke xviii. 11). Nevertheless, he had not praise from God for righteousness; and that thanksgiving of his, if you remember well the Gospel, did not render him more acceptable to God. Wherefore? Because an outward show in word of devotion does not suffice to excuse the pride of heart in the man before Him who from afar off

recogniseth the proud (Ps. cxxxviii. 6). God, O Pharisee, is not mocked. Do you suppose for a moment that you possess anything which you have not received from Him? No, you reply; and therefore I render thanks to my liberal benefactor. If you do not possess anything at all of your own, then there was in you no antecedent merit on account of which you received those things upon the possession of which you boast yourself. If you confess this to be the case, then, in the first place, it is with unjustifiable presumption that you exalt yourself above the Publican who does not possess the same [merits] as you, only because he has not received them as you have. Farther, take care lest, by not attributing to God wholly and entirely the gifts which He has bestowed, but diverting to yourself some portion of the glory and honour of them, you may not justly be accused of fraud, and fraud towards God. For if you attribute to yourself somewhat of those merits of which you boast, I should suppose that it is because you are yourself deceived rather than that you desire to do an injustice; and it is that error that I would correct. But now, since, by the act of returning thanks, you show that you arrogate nothing to yourself, and that you prudently recognise your merits to be the gifts of God, it is evident that, in despising others, you betray yourself, and show that you speak with a double heart—on the one hand, lending your tongue to a falsehood; on the other, usurping the glory of the truth. For you would not consider the Publican to be an object of scorn in comparison of yourself if you did not suppose that you were worthy of praise in comparison of him. But what do you reply to the Apostle who lays down this rule: *To God alone be honour and glory* (1 Tim. i. 17, Vulg.)? Or what to the angel who declares and distinguishes what it pleases God to reserve to Himself, and what He deigns to share with men? For he says: *Glory to God in the highest, and on earth peace to men of goodwill* (Luke ii. 14). Do you not see how the Pharisee, in giving thanks—with his lips, indeed—honours God, but in the thought of his heart gives honour to himself? And we see many persons act thus: in their mouths resound words of thanksgiving. But this is by a kind of habit rather than by their true impulse or intention; insomuch that men, even of the most abandoned class, are in the habit of giving thanks to God for their good success, as they think it, in the carrying out of this or that crime or outrage. You hear, for example, a robber, after having carried out an evil plan, and deprived someone of his portmanteau (*manipulum*), exulting secretly, and saying: 'Thank God, I have not made fruitless watches, nor spent my night to no profit!' Similarly, he who has killed a man, does he not boast of it, and offer his thanksgiving that he has prevailed against his adversary, or avenged himself of his enemy? Even an adulterer, exulting in his success, thanks God that he has obtained his long-hoped-for pleasure.

3. Not every offering of thanks, therefore, is acceptable to God, but that only which proceeds from a pure and sincere heart. I say *pure*, because of those who boast themselves of their bad actions, and

even offer thanks to God for them. Let anyone who is of this character listen to these terrible words: *Thou thoughtest that I was altogether such an one as thyself, but I will reprove thee, and set them in order before thine eyes* (Ps. l. 21). And I have added *sincere*, because of hypocrites, who, indeed, glorify God for their good works, but only with their lips; while in heart they keep back all praise for themselves; and since they act deceitfully in His presence, their iniquity is hateful. The former, in their impiety, attribute to God their own bad actions; the latter fraudulently arrogate to themselves the good things which they have received from Him. As regards the former of these offences, it is so full of folly and worldliness, and, I might even say, is, in a certain sense, so brutal, that I need hardly warn you to avoid it. But the latter is, above all, a besetting temptation to those who are religious and spiritually minded men. It is without doubt a great and rare virtue to have no consciousness of greatness, although performing great actions; and that the sanctity of a man, while it is manifest to all others, should be hidden from himself. To appear admirable to others, and to think humbly of yourself, this I judge to be the most marvellous among the virtues themselves. You are truly a faithful servant if you suffer nothing to remain with yourself (*tuis manibus adhaerere*) of all the glory of your Lord, when that glory, though it does not come from you, yet passes through you or by your means. It is then that, according to the saying of the Prophet (Is. xxxiii. 15), you cast from you gains acquired by falseness, and keep your hands clean from every bribe. Then it is that, as the Lord commands, you let your light shine before men, that they may glorify, not you, but your Father which is in heaven (Matt. v. 16). Thus, too, you are an imitator of St. Paul and of faithful preachers, who preach, not themselves, but Christ Jesus the Lord (2 Cor. iv. 5); nor seek their own interests, but those of Jesus Christ (Phil. ii. 21). And on that account you, too, as they, shall hear the greeting: *Well done, thou good and faithful servant; thou hast been faithful over a few things, I will make thee ruler over many things* (Matt. xxv. 21).

4. If Joseph, in Egypt, knew that the house and all the goods of his master had been entrusted to him, he was not ignorant at the same time that his mistress was an exception; and because of this, he would not consent to her, saying: *My master hath committed all that he hath to my hand, neither hath he kept back anything from me but thee, because thou art his wife* (Gen. xxxix. 9). He knew that the wife is the glory of her husband, and regarded it as a great injustice and a shameful ingratitude to dishonour one who had loaded him with so many honours. That man, prudent with the wisdom of God, knew that a husband is jealous of his wife as being his own honour, and that she is to be sacredly reserved to him, not passed on to another; nor did he presume to stretch out his hand to that which was not given to him. What then? Shall a man be jealous of his glory, and yet dare to wish to defraud God of His, as if He had no care for it? But hear what God Himself says: *I will not give My*

glory unto another (Is. xlviii. 11). What, then, wilt Thou give, O Lord; what wilt Thou bestow upon us? *Peace*, He replies, *I leave with you; My peace I give unto you* (John xiv. 27). That is sufficient for me; I gratefully receive that which Thou leavest to me, nor do I grasp at that which Thou reservest. With this [partition] I am satisfied and I do not doubt that it is for my advantage. Glory I wholly renounce, lest perchance in usurping what is not granted to me, I justly lose that which is bestowed. Peace I desire; peace I long for, and nothing more. The soul for which peace does not suffice will not find even Thee sufficient. For Thou art our Peace, who hast made both one (Eph. ii. 14). That I should be reconciled with Thee, that I should be reconciled with myself, this is necessary for me; and this is enough. For from the moment that I am set in contrariety to Thee, I am a burden to myself (Job vii. 20). I am on my guard, and do not desire to be either ungrateful for the peace Thou hast bestowed upon me, or a sacrilegious usurper of Thy glory. Let Thy glory, O Lord, remain undiminished to Thee; with me all will be well if I possess peace.

5. When Goliath was overthrown the people rejoiced that they had recovered peace; but to David alone fell the great glory. Joshua, Jephtha, Gideon, Samson, Judith also, though a woman, triumphed gloriously in their day over their enemies; but though the people had the enjoyment of the peace that these heroes had achieved, they did not share with them the glory. Judas Maccabæus also, a man illustrious by many victories, because he had so often fought valiantly, and thus given peace to his people, did he ever share with them his glory also? 'There was,' it is said, not great glory, but 'very great gladness among the people' (1 Macc. iv. 58). Are the works which the Creator of all things has done less than those due to the great men named, that He should have less ground for a glory all His own and unshared by others? Alone He created all things that exist; alone He triumphed over the enemy; alone He freed the captives, and shall He have a companion in His glory? *Mine own Arm*, He says, *brought salvation unto Me;* and again: *I have trodden the winepress alone; and of the people there was none with Me* (Is. lxiii. 5, 3). What share can I, then, pretend to in the victory, when I had none in the battle? It would be the extremest effrontery in me to claim either glory without victory, or victory without combat. But do ye, O mountains, bring peace unto the people (Ps. lxxii. 3); peace unto us, not glory; reserving that to Him alone who alone has fought the battle and gained the victory. Thus, I entreat, thus let it be: *Glory to God in the Highest, and on earth peace to men of goodwill.* He, however, is not a man of good will, but evidently of very evil will, who is not at all content with peace, but restlessly aspires also to the glory which belongs to God, with an eye of pride and a heart never satisfied; and such a man neither retains peace nor attains glory. Who would believe the wall if it should lay claim to produce the ray of light which is thrown upon it through the window? or who would not laugh to

scorn the clouds if they pretended that the showers which they let fall were engendered in them? I am well assured that the rivers of water have not their source from the channel in which they run, nor words of prudence from the lips and the teeth which give utterance to them, even though my bodily senses do not[1] enable me to reach this conclusion.

6. If, then, I discern something in the saints which is worthy of praise and admiration when I examine it in the clear light of truth, I find that though they appear to be admirable and praiseworthy it is another than they who is really so, and I praise God in His saints. Take, for example, Elisha, or that great prophet Elijah, each of whom restored the dead to life. It was not by any power of their own, but in the discharge of a ministry committed to them, that they achieved those new and unprecedented marvels; it was God who abode in them and performed those marvellous works. He is invisible and unapproachable by His own Nature, but renders Himself visible and admirable in His saints, and alone admirable, since He *alone doth wonderful things* (Ps. lxxi. 19). Painting and writing are both arts worthy of praise, yet it is not the pen [or the brush] that is to be praised; nor is the glory of an eloquent discourse given to the tongue or the lips which pronounce it. It is time that the Prophet should speak. *Shall the axe*, he says, *boast itself against him that cutteth with it? or shall the saw exalt itself against him by whom it is drawn? as if a rod should lift itself up against him that lifteth it up, and a staff exalt itself, which is but wood* (Is. x. 15); so is everyone who glorieth against the Lord, unless he glory in the Lord (2 Cor. x 17). If it be needful for a man to glory, St. Paul teaches us in whom, and in regard to what it should be done. *Our glory*, he says, *is this, the testimony of our conscience* (2 Cor. i. 12). I may glory without fear if my conscience bears me witness that I am usurping nothing of the glory of my Creator; assuredly without fear, because I do it not against the Lord but in the Lord. This kind of glorying is not only not forbidden to us, but we are persuaded to employ it, for it is said: *Ye receive glory one from another, and the glory which is from God alone you do not seek* (John v. 44). In fact, the ability to glory in God alone comes but from God alone. Nor is this glory small, since it hath the Truth for its object, and is therefore true; and, in truth, is so rare that even of the small number of those who are perfect there are but few who possess it perfectly. Leave, then, the sons of men, who are vain, who are untruthful: leave them by vanity to deceive each other (Ps. lxi. 10). For he who glories wisely will strictly prove his work, to examine it diligently by the light of truth; and so he shall have glory in himself, and not in the mouth of another. Foolish am I if I shall have confided my glory to the vessel of your lips, and so be obliged to beg it of you when I would obtain it. For thus it would be in your power to approve or to disapprove of me at your will. But in retaining [this] in my own power I preserve it for myself

---

[1] In some MSS. *not* is wanting.

more faithfully. Or, rather, I do not trust it to myself at all, but commit it in preference to Him for safe keeping who is able to keep that which is committed unto Him until that day (2 Tim. i. 12), for He is both watchful in keeping and faithful in rendering up His charge. Then shall every one have sure praise from God, but those only who have contemned the praises of men. For the glory of those whose taste is only for earthly things ends in confusion, as it is declared even by David : *Those that please men have been confounded, because God hath despised them* (Ps. lii. 6).

7. Brethren, if you know and feel these truths let none of you desire to be praised in this world, because every honour which you reach after and obtain in this life, and which you do not refer to God, is a theft from Him of which you are guilty. What ground have you for glorying, what ground, I repeat, you who art decaying dust ? Is it the sanctity of your life ? But it is *the Spirit that sanctifieth ;* and when I say 'spirit' I mean not your spirit, but the Spirit of God. Even though you should be renowned for signs and wonders, they are performed by your hand indeed, but by the power of God only. Or does the popular favour attend you, because you have, perhaps, spoken something good in itself, or elegantly worded ? But it was Christ who bestowed upon you a mouth and wisdom. For what is your tongue but as the pen of the writer ? And this very thing you have received only as a loan ; it is a talent entrusted to you to be returned with usury. If you are found untiring in the work committed to you, faithful in bringing forth fruit [of the grace of God], you shall receive a reward for your labour. But if it be otherwise the talent shall be taken from you—its interest being required, nevertheless—and you shall be called a wicked and slothful servant. Every praise, therefore, on account of good actions, and of the manifold graces which are made apparent in you, is to be referred to Him who is the Author and Giver of all that is good and laudable. And these must be referred to Him, not in appearance only, as is the wont of hypocrites, or as a matter of form and custom, as by those who are worldly [*secularibus*, people in the world], nor even by a kind of necessity, as beasts of burden are obliged to bear their loads, but as it becometh saints, with faithful sincerity, with careful devotion, with grateful but restrained and moderated cheerfulness. Therefore, while offering to Him the sacrifice of praise, and performing our vows from day to day, let us endeavour, with all the watchfulness in our power, to join intelligence to our accustomed service, fervour to our intelligence, gladness to our fervour, gravity to our gladness, humility to our gravity, freedom of spirit to our humility, so that in the meantime we may go forward with the free steps of a mind purified from evil passions, and pass, in a sense, out of ourselves by the extraordinary fervour of our desires and affections, to feel spiritual joys and gladsome delights, to dwell in the light of God, in the ineffable sweetness of the Holy Ghost, and may show that we are of those whom the Prophet had in view when he said : *They shall walk, O Lord, in the*

light of Thy countenance, in Thy Name they shall rejoice all the day, and in Thy justice they shall be exalted (Ps lxxxviii 16, 17)

8. But perhaps someone will say to me What you say is good, but it would be still better, that you should continue to speak of your precise subject. Wait a little, I reply ; I am not unmindful of it. Have we not taken in hand to expound these words *Thy Name is as oil poured forth ?* This is our subject, this our endeavour [1] I leave you to judge whether the preliminary observations which I have made were necessary. Now, listen to these few words, in which I will show that they are not unconnected with the subject Do you not remember that in treating of the bosom of the Spouse, the last thing referred to was the sweetness of the perfumes it exhaled? What, then, follows more clearly than that the Spouse should recognise that this same fragrance is to be attributed to the gift of her Bridegroom, that she may not be thought to arrogate it to herself? Now, you know well that all I have said tends towards that object. 'The fragrance,' she says, 'which is exhaled from me, and which renders my perfume pleasing, I ascribe not to my own efforts, or my own merits, but acknowledge that it is due to Thy bounty, O my Bridegroom, Thou whose adorable Name is as oil poured out' Thus much for the sense of the text

9. As to the explanation of the verse, which has given me the occasion to speak to you at such length on the detestable vice of ingratitude, it requires another occasion, and the commencement of another sermon At present it is sufficient for me to suggest to you one reflection. If the Bride does not venture to attribute anything to herself of all her virtues, and of all her graces, how much less should maidens young and untried ? and with these we may, so to speak, compare ourselves. Let us, then, in conclusion, follow the footprints of the Bride, and say with her · *Not unto us, O Lord, not unto us, but unto Thy Name give glory* (Ps. cxv 1). Let us say it, not with tongue and in word only, but in deed and in truth, lest (which I greatly fear) those words should be spoken of us also · *They loved Him with their mouth, and with their heart they lied unto Him · but their heart was not right with Him, nor were they counted faithful in His covenant* (Ps lxxvii. 36, 37). Let us say it, then, let us say it, with a voice that comes rather from the depths of the heart, than merely from the lips : *Save us, O Lord our God, and gather us from among the nations, that we may give thanks to Thy Holy Name* (not, observe, to our own), *and may glory* (not in our own praise, but) *in Thy praise* (Ps. cv. 47) for ever and ever. AMEN.

---

[1] *Cf.* Virgil, Æneid, Bk vi 129. But the coincidence of phrase is perhaps unintended and fortuitous —ED

SERMON XIV.

OF THE CHURCH OF FAITHFUL CHRISTIANS, AND OF THE SYNAGOGUE OF PERFIDIOUS JEWS.

*I*N *Judah is God known: His Name is great in Israel* (Ps. lxxv. 1.). *The people* (of the Gentiles) *who walked in darkness have seen a great light* (Is. ix. 2), which was in Judah and in Israel, and have desired to approach it, and be enlightened; so that those who once were not a people, now became the people of God (1 Pet. ii. 10); and one corner-stone united together the two walls which came from different sides, so that, thenceforth, the place of his abode was a place of peace. That which inspired [the nation] with confidence was the voice of invitation which it had heard: *Rejoice, ye Gentiles, with His people* (Rom. xv. 10). Therefore He desired them to draw near; but the Synagogue forbade them, asserting the Church gathered out of the nations to be unclean, and unworthy of a favour so great. Then, reproaching it as a sink of idolatry, and blaming the blindness of its ignorance, said [the Jew]: In what way have you merited this favour? Touch me not. To which the other replied: Why must I not do so? *Is He the God of the Jews only? Is He not also of the Gentiles?* (Rom. iii. 29). And if merit is wanting in me, yet assuredly pity and compassion is not wanting in Him. He is not only righteous, but also compassionate *O Lord, let Thy tender mercies come unto me, and I shall live;* and again she says: *Many, O Lord, are Thy mercies: quicken me according to Thy judgment* (Ps. cxix. 77, 156), which, inasmuch as it is moderated and restrained, is itself mercy. What, then, will the Lord so just and so merciful do, if there be one who glories in the Law, and proudly attributes righteousness to himself; who supposes that he does not need mercy, and despises another who does need it; and, again, another who is aware of his offences, who confesses his unworthiness, who prays God not to deal with him according unto judgment, but to extend to him the Divine mercy? What, I say, will the Judge do, and that Judge one to whom judgment and mercy are equally familiar, so that neither of the two belongs to Him more than the other? What can possibly be more appropriate, than that He should deal with each according to his prayer, and dispense judgment to the one and to the other mercy? The Jew seeks judgment; let him be judged; but let the Gentiles honour God for His mercy. And it is judgment that those who despise the merciful righteousness of God, and desire to set up their own righteousness (which assuredly accuses, not justifies, them), should be left to that same righteousness of their own, to be overthrown rather than justified.

2. For the Law, which has never rendered anyone perfect, is a yoke which neither their fathers nor they have ever been able to

bear. But the Synagogue is strong; it cares not for an easy yoke, nor for a light burden. It is in health; it has no need of a physician, nor of the anointing of the Spirit. It trusts in the Law; let the Law deliver it, if the Law has the power. But there has been no Law bestowed which is able to give life; nay, moreover, it is death that the Law gives: *for the letter killeth* (2 Cor. iii. 6). *Therefore* (said the Lord) *I say unto you, that ye shall die in your sins* (John viii. 24). This, then, O Synagogue, is the judgment which you, in your error, are clamouring for. O blinded and obstinate! you shall be left to your error, until the fulness of the Gentiles, which you proudly despise, and reject by envy, shall come in, and you shall acknowledge as God Him who is known in Judæa, whose Name is great in Israel. For the rendering of this judgment it is that Jesus has come unto this world, that they who see not might see, and that they who see may become blind (John ix. 39). Yet this judgment is but in part, for the Lord will not cast off His people (Ps. xciv. 14) altogether; He preserves to Himself as a seed His Apostles, and the multitude of the believers, who were of one heart and of one soul. He will not reject them to the end, but will save a remnant. He will again take to Himself Israel His servant, remembering His mercy (Luke i. 54), so that mercy shall not fail to accompany judgment, even there where it finds no place. Otherwise, if He had treated them according to their merits, He would inflict judgment without mercy upon those who show no mercy (James ii. 13). For Judah hath in abundance the oil of the knowledge of God, and keeps it jealously to herself, as a miser, as it were in a closely-sealed vessel. I ask for it, and she does not take pity upon me; nor will she even lend it. She desires to possess alone the worship, the knowledge, the great Name of God, not because she is jealous for her own happiness, but because she is envious of mine.

3. Therefore do Thou, O Lord, give judgment in my cause that Thy great Name may be henceforth magnified, and thy oil Divine be multiplied still more. Let it rise, let it bubble up, let it be poured forth and roll among the nations, and let all flesh have part in the salvation of God. Wherefore, as the ungrateful Jew desires, should the unction of salvation remain upon the beard of Aaron alone? It is not for the beard, but for the head. Nor does the head exist for the beard alone, but for the whole body. Let it receive first, but not exclusively. Let that [unction] which it has received from on high be poured upon the lower limbs also. Let the heavenly fluid descend— descend upon the breast also of the Church. She does not disdain —she eagerly receives—that which falls upon her from the beard [of her High Priest]; and when saturated with the dew of grace, that she may not show herself ungrateful, she cries: *Thy Name is as ointment poured forth* (Cant. i. 2). Let it roll farther yet, I entreat; let it reach even to the skirt of her clothing—that is to say, let it extend even to me, the last and lowest of all, and the most unworthy, yet still belonging, as it were, to that clothing. I earnestly entreat, appealing to the

goodness [of my God], that this stream of grace may come to me, as it were, from the bosom of my mother [Church], for I am as a babe in Christ. And if any man whose eye is evil because of Thy goodness should murmur, do Thou, O Lord, answer for me; let judgment come forth from Thy Countenance, not from the arrogance of Israel. Nay, more, do Thou reply on Thy own behalf, and say to the slanderer—for it is of Thee that he utters slanders, because of Thy free grace Thou dost bestow Thy good gifts—declare, I say, to him: *I will give unto this last even as unto thee* (Matt. xx. 14). That displeases the Pharisee; but why, O Pharisee, dost thou murmur? My right is the will of the Judge. Is He not as just in discerning merit as He is rich in rewarding it? May He not do as He will [with His own]? To me, I confess, mercy is shown; but to thee no injury whatever is done. Take what thine is, and go thy way. If He has decreed to bestow upon me also the gift of salvation, what dost thou lose by His so doing?

4. Exaggerate your merits to any degree you will, and extol your labours, the mercy of the Lord is better than life (Ps. lxiii. 3). I have not, I confess it, endured the burden and heat of the day, but I bear an easy yoke and a light burden according to the good pleasure of our Father. My task has been of scarcely an hour long, and if it had been longer, love would have prevented me from perceiving it. Let the Jew busy himself in his own strength; but as for me, my only care is to make proof what is the good and acceptable and perfect Will of the Lord. It is from it that I repair the losses in time and in labour which I have sustained. He trusts to the letter of an agreement; I to the decree of God's good pleasure; yea, I believe, nor shall I be confounded in my faith, for my life depends upon His Will. That grace reconciles the Father to me, that restores to me my lost inheritance, and with even a greater weight of grace delights me with sweet melody, delicious viands, and all the delightful joys of all His rejoicing family. If that elder brother of mine is indignant, and prefers to make merry with his friends upon a kid without the doors rather than with me in our Father's House upon the fatted calf, the answer shall be returned to him: *It was meet that we should make merry and be glad; for this thy brother was dead, and is alive again; and was lost, and is found* (Luke xv. 32). The Synagogue still feasts without, and with demons for friends, whom it delights to see that she is still so blind as to devour the kid [so to speak] of sin—to swallow, and, as it were, to hide it in the stomach of her folly and ignorance; while, in her scorn of the righteousness of God and desire to establish her own righteousness, she declares that she has no sin, and no need of the death of the fatted calf, because she supposes herself to be pure and righteous by the works of the Law. But the Church, after having rent asunder, by the death of the Word crucified, the veil of the letter which killeth, is led by the Spirit of liberty to advance boldly into His secret things—to recognise and take delight in them, to be chosen into the place of her rival, to become the Bride, to enjoy the graces

of which the other is deprived; and, being everywhere bedewed and anointed with the oil of her gladness, clinging closely to the Lord Christ, and receiving the vital warmth of the Holy Spirit, she obtains this happiness beyond her fellows (Ps. xlv. 7), and says: *Thy Name is as ointment poured forth.* What wonder if she who embraces Him who is filled with this sacred unction should herself be anointed therewith!

5. The Church, then, reposes within, but as yet the Church of those who are perfect; yet for us also there is hope. Let us who fall short of this perfection rest without, and rejoice in the hope which is given to us. In the meantime, the Bridegroom and the Bride are alone within; they enjoy mutual and ineffable delights, untroubled by any tumult of carnal desires, or by the fleeting images of earthly things. Without await them the company of virgin souls, who cannot be as yet free from such disquietudes; but they wait in assured peace, knowing that of them it has been said: *The virgins, her companions that follow her, shall be brought [unto the King]* (Ps. xlv. 14). And that each of them may know of what spirit they are, I call those virgin souls who, having been covenanted to Christ before they were defiled by the embraces of the world, persevere constantly in the love of Him to whom they have devoted themselves, and are so much the more happy the earlier they did so. And I call those 'their companions' (*proximas*) who, after having shamefully given themselves over in bondage to the princes of this world—that is, to impure spirits—yet, at length, being ashamed of their own defilement in which they were once conformed to this world, came forth from it, and hasten to put on the likeness of the new man, and that with the greater sincerity the later they were in their reformation. Both the one and the other class go forward together; they do not fail, nor are they wearied, even though they do not feel as yet in full that inward consolation which moves souls to say: *Thy Name is as ointment poured forth.* For these souls do not venture to address themselves directly to the Bridegroom, yet their endeavour is to press closely in the footsteps of her who leads them on (*magistræ*); they will enjoy the delightful perfume of the oil poured forth, and will be incited by it to desire and to seek for still higher and better things.

6. I am not ashamed to confess that often, and particularly at the commencement of my conversion, I myself experienced extreme coldness and hardness of heart. I sought after Him whom my soul was desirous to love; for it was not then able to love one whom it had not yet found, or, at least, it loved Him less than it wished to do, and on that account was seeking Him that it might love Him with an increased affection, though assuredly it would not have sought Him without having some degree of love for Him previously. While, then, I was seeking Him in whom my frozen and languid spirit might find warmth and repose, and no one came from any side to my help, to dissolve the icy torpor of my spiritual senses and to bring back the sweetness and fruitfulness of the spring—at that time, I say, my soul languished and drooped in torpor, a prey to hard and hopeless depression and dull

discontent. At such times it would murmur to itself: *Who is able to abide the rigour of His frost?* (Ps. cxlvii. 17). Then, on a sudden, at a word, at the sight of some holy or piously-minded person, or at the mere remembrance of one dead or absent, the Holy Spirit would breathe upon [my frozen soul], and the waters would flow; then tears were my food day and night. What was that but the perfume exhaled by that anointing with which that holy one was endued? It was not the anointing itself, for that did not reach me except through the medium of some man; and though the gift caused me joy, yet I was confounded and humiliated to know that I enjoyed but a passing gust of sweetness, and that the unction from which it arose was not vouchsafed to me. And having only the pleasure to perceive it at a distance, but not to draw near and touch it, I understood that I was unworthy that God should communicate to me its sweetness directly (*per se ipsum*). And if now the same thing occurs to me, I receive, indeed, eagerly the favour accorded to me, and I feel thankful; but I am touched with extreme grief not to have merited it by myself, nor received it, so to speak, from hand to hand, as I earnestly entreated that I might do I am ashamed to be moved more at the remembrance of man than at that of God. And then I cry with groaning: *When shall I come and appear before God?* (Ps. xlii. 2). I think, too, that some of you have gone through the same experience, and do so sometimes even now. What are we to think of this, except that God permits it either to warn us of pride, to preserve our humility, to nourish brotherly charity, or to increase our desire for holiness? One and the same kind of food serves both as medicine for the sick, and as diet for the sickly (*aegrotativis*). Even more, it strengthens the weak, and delights those who are in health; it both heals disease, and preserves health; nourishes the body, and, at the same time, is agreeable to the taste.

7. But let us return to the words of the Bridegroom; let us be careful to listen to what He says, and to delight in that which delights Him. The Bride, as I have said, is the Church. She it is to whom more has been forgiven, and who loves the more. That with which her rival hastens to reproach her, she herself turns to her profit. Thus she is the more gentle for chiding, more patient to endure, more ardent in love, more prudent in self control; thus she becomes the humbler for the consciousness of her faults, more acceptable by her modesty, more prepared to obey, more earnest and devoted in thanksgiving. Finally, while the Synagogue, as has been said, murmurs, recalls her merits, her labours, and the burden and heat of the day which she has borne, the Church, on the contrary, recounts but the benefits which she has received, and cries: *Thy Name is as ointment poured forth.*

8. This is evidently the testimony which Israel gives to celebrate the Name of the Lord; yet not the Israel which is according to the flesh, but that which is according to the Spirit. For how could the former speak thus? It is not that he has not oil, but that he has it

not poured forth. He has it, but it is hidden; he has it in his books, but not in his heart. He attaches himself to the outward letter; he clasps in his hands a vase filled with fragrant oil, but it is closed, and he opens it not that he may be anointed therewith. The anointing of the Spirit is inward—yea, it is inward; open, then, and be anointed, and no longer shalt thou be a rebellious house. Of what avail is oil in thy vases, if thou hast it not to anoint thy limbs? What does it profit thee to read the life-giving Name of the Saviour in books, and not to have faith in Him in thy heart and obedience in thy life? Thou hast oil; pour it forth, and thou shalt feel its threefold virtue. But the Jew disdains these things; do you, then, listen. I wish to tell you what I have not yet mentioned, why the Name of the Bridegroom is compared to oil. Now, for this there are three reasons. But since He is called by many names, inasmuch as that which is proper to Him is known to none (for it is *Ineffable*), we must first of all invoke the Holy Spirit that He will deign, by His Divine wisdom, to reveal to us, since it has not pleased Him to declare it in the Word written, that Name, out of all those which have been given to Him, which He would have us to understand in this passage; but of this also at another time. For although I am quite prepared to speak of all these things, yet that neither you should be burdened, nor I wearied with speaking, the hour warns us to make an end. Keep in mind what I have drawn your attention to, that it may not be needful to repeat it to-morrow. This is what I have in hand and propose to speak of next; namely, why the Name of the Bridegroom is compared to oil; and what is that special Name among the many given to Him. And since I am able to speak nothing of myself, let your prayer be offered that the Bridegroom Himself, Jesus Christ our Lord, may by His Spirit reveal it to us. To Him be honour and glory, for ever and ever. AMEN.

SERMON XV.

IN WHAT MANNER THE NAME OF JESUS IS A SALUTARY MEDICINE TO FAITHFUL CHRISTIANS IN ALL ADVERSITIES.

THE Spirit of wisdom is benevolent,[1] and He is not accustomed to show Himself unapproachable to those who invoke Him, since often, before even He is called upon, He saith, *Lo, I am here* (Is. lxv. 24). Listen, now, to what at your prayer He has deigned to make known by means of me upon that subject, of which we treated yesterday, and receive in due season the fruit of your prayers. Behold, I show you a Name which is rightly compared to oil, and I will explain to you by what right it is thus compared. You read, upon

---

[1] Wisd. i. 6, Vulgate and Douay version.

every page of the Divine Scripture, many Names given to the Bridegroom, but these I will sum up in two only. None of these you will, in my judgment, find, which do not express, either the grace of His beneficence, or the power of His majesty. The Holy Spirit thus instructs by the mouth of one through whom He frequently speaks: *These two things have I heard, that power belongeth to God, and mercy to Thee, O Lord.*[1] Again, as to His Majesty, we read: *Holy and terrible is His Name* (Ps. cx. 9). As to His goodness towards men, *There is none other Name under heaven given among men whereby we must be saved* (Acts iv. 12). Let me render this still more clear by examples. *This is His Name, whereby He shall be called, The Lord our Righteousness* (Jer. xxiii. 6). It is here a name of *power*. Again: *And his Name shall be called Immanuel* (Is. vii. 14), here implying His goodness to men. Also He speaks thus of Himself: *Ye call Me Master and Lord* (John xiii. 13)—the former a name of grace, the latter of greatness. For it is no less a deed of beneficence to bestow knowledge upon the mind than to give food to the body. Again, the Prophet says: His Name shall be called *Wonderful, Counsellor, the Mighty One, God, the Everlasting Father, the Prince of Peace* (Is. ix. 6). The first, the third, and the fourth attributes, express His majesty; the others, His goodness to men. Which, then, of these is 'as oil poured forth?' Evidently the Name of His Majesty and Power is in some mysterious manner transfused into that which is the Name of His Goodness and Grace; and this last is poured forth abundantly through Jesus Christ our Saviour. For example, does not the Name of 'God' pass into and become transfused in that which is '*God with us*,' that is, in '*Immanuel*'? So the name of '*Wonderful*' into that of '*Counsellor*'; 'God, the Mighty One' into those of '*the Everlasting Father*' and '*the Prince of Peace*'; and '*The Lord our Righteousness*' into '*the Lord gracious and full of compassion*' (Ps. cxi. 4). In this I say nothing new, for Abram also was, in an earlier age, changed into Abraham, and Sarai into Sarah; and in those cases also we find that a mystery of beneficence was prefigured and celebrated.

2. Where, now, is that Voice of thunder which made itself heard so frequently and so terribly by the people of old time: *I am the Lord! I am the Lord!* (Exod. xx. 2). In its place there is dictated to me a prayer, which commences with the sweet name of *Father*, and thus affords good ground for confidence that the petitions which follow will be granted. Those who were servants are now called friends; and the Resurrection of Jesus is announced, not even[2] to disciples only, but to those who are named brethren. And I do not wonder that this pouring forth of the Holy Name was made when the fulness of time came; for God thus fulfilled what He had promised by Joel (ii. 28), and poured out His Spirit upon all flesh; and I read that something similar had taken place among the Hebrews in ancient

---

[1] Ps. lxi. 12, Vulgate and Douay version.
[2] *Saltem.* So in MS., but another reading is *tantum.*

times. Your minds, I dare say, outstrip my words, and you already know what I am about to mention. For of what nature was the answer, I would ask, which was given to Moses when he inquired at first who was speaking to him? I AM THAT I AM ? and I AM *hath sent me unto you?* (Exod. iii. 14). I know not whether Moses himself would have understood it thus if the Name had not been already poured forth. But that was done, and it was understood; not only poured (*fusum*), but poured forth (*effusum*); for the inpouring (*infusum*) was already achieved. Already the heavens possessed it; already it had been made known to the angels. But it is [now] sent forth abroad ; and the Name which had been so infused into the angels that it was become even familiar to them, was sent forth among men also, so that thenceforth the cry of joy should be with justice raised from earth, *Thy Name is as oil poured forth*, if the odious obstinacy of an ungrateful people had not hindered. For He says : *I am the God of Abraham, the God of Isaac, and the God of Jacob* (Exod. iii. 6, 15).

3. Approach, ye nations ; your salvation is at hand. That Name is poured forth which whosoever calls upon shall be saved. The God of angels names Himself the God of men also. He has shed forth oil upon Jacob and it has fallen upon Israel. Say, then, to your brethren. *Give us of your oil* (Matt. xxv. 8). But if they will not, pray ye the Lord for oil, that He may send it unto you also. Say ye unto Him, *Take away our reproach* (Is. iv. 1). Permit not, I entreat, an evil tongue to insult Thy beloved, whom Thou hast been pleased to call from the ends of the earth, and that with so much the greater bounty as he was less worthy [of Thy goodness]. Is it fitting, I beseech Thee, that a wicked servant should shut out those whom their kind Father has invited? *I am*, Thou sayest, *the God of Abraham, the God of Isaac, and the God of Jacob.* And are there no more [than these]? Pour forth, pour forth ; open still wider Thy Hand, and fill with blessing every living thing. Let them come from the east and from the west, and sit down with Abraham, Isaac, and Jacob in the kingdom of heaven (Matt. viii. 11). Let the tribes, the tribes of the Lord come, let them come ; unto the testimony of Israel. to give thanks unto the Name of the Lord (Ps. cxxii. 4). Let them come, and take the seats of guests ; let them feast in gladness of great joy ; let there everywhere be heard but one great chorus of thanksgivings and praises, one song of them that feast (Ps. xlii. 4): *Thy Name is as oil poured forth.* Of one thing I am sure, that if we have Philip and Andrew for porters at the gate of heaven, whosoever among us seeks for this celestial oil, whosoever of us desires to see Jesus, will encounter no repulse. At once Philip cometh and telleth Andrew, and again Andrew and Philip tell Jesus. But what will Jesus say ? Without doubt what He has already said : *Except a corn of wheat fall into the ground and die, it abideth alone : but if it die it bringeth forth much fruit* (John xii. 22-25). Let the grain, then, die, and let there rise from it the harvest of the Gentiles. It is needful that Christ should suffer,

that He should rise from the dead, and that repentance and remission of sins should be preached in His Name, not only in Judæa, but among all nations (John xxiv. 46, 47); insomuch that from one Name, which is Christ, thousands of thousands of believers shall be called Christians, and shall say: *Thy Name is as oil poured forth.*

4. I recognise that Name also in that which I have read in Isaiah: *The Lord God shall call His servants by another Name, in which he that is blessed in the earth shall be blessed in God.*[1] Amen. O Blessed Name! O oil everywhere poured forth! How far does it penetrate? It spreads from Heaven to Judæa, and thence over the whole earth; and from every part of the earth rises the adoring cry of the Church: *Thy Name is as oil poured forth.* Yes, that is indeed poured forth, with which not only the heavens and the earth are steeped, but even the abodes of the dead besprinkled; so that in the adorable Name of Jesus every knee shall bow and every tongue confess (Phil. ii. 10, 11), and say, *Thy Name is as oil poured forth.* Behold the Christ, behold Jesus, whether infused into angels, or effused upon men—yea, upon men who had defiled themselves as beasts upon their dunghill, saving both men and beasts, in like manner as God has multiplied His mercy. How dear is that Name, but how common (*vile*)!—common, but precious in its power to heal! If it were not common it would not have been poured out upon a sinner such as I; and if it had no power of healing it would have profited me nothing. I am a sharer in that Name—a sharer, too, in its heavenly inheritance. I am a Christian; I am even the brother of Christ; and if I be truly that which I am thus called, I am an heir of God, and a joint heir with Christ (Rom. viii. 17). What wonder is it if the Name of the Bridegroom be thus poured forth, when He Himself is poured forth likewise? For when He emptied Himself did He not take upon Him the form of a servant (Philipp. ii. 7)? Therefore He says: I am poured out like water (Ps. xxii. 14). The plenitude of His Divinity was poured forth when He dwelt in bodily form upon the earth; so that we all who bear about a mortal body should participate in that plenitude, and, being filled with an odour of life, should say: *Thy Name is as oil poured forth.* I go on to say, *What* is that Name which is poured forth, in what manner, and in what degree?

5. First, why is it called *oil?*—for this I have not as yet explained. I had begun to do so in a former sermon, but another subject suddenly presented itself which seemed to me to require to be treated of. But I have deferred to speak of this longer than I supposed, for which I see no other reason than this, that Wisdom is as the virtuous woman in the Book of Proverbs (xxxi. 10), who layeth her hands to the spindle, and her hands hold the distaff. For she knows how out of a little wool or flax to draw out the thread and to broaden the web with the shuttle, and so to clothe all her servants in garments both of linen and of wool. There is no doubt that oil has its points of

---

[1] St. Bernard quotes the Vulg. inexactly—'*In Domino. Amen,*' instead of '*In Deo. Amen.*' The Septuagint renders ' In the true God.'—ED.

resemblance to the Name of the Bridegroom, and that not without reason has the Holy Spirit compared the one to the other. Perhaps you may discern better than I the reasons for this; but, as far as I am able to judge, the reasons are three. that it gives light, it gives nourishment, and it anoints. It maintains flame, it nourishes the flesh, it relieves pain; it is light, it is food, and it is medicine. Notice now that the same thing can be said of the Name of the Bridegroom: for when preached it enlightens the mind, when it is meditated upon it is food to the mind, and when invoked it softens and alleviates the wounds of mind and soul. Let us examine each of these qualities separately.

6. Whence do you suppose so bright and so sudden a light of faith has been kindled in the whole world, except by the preaching of the Name of Jesus? Is it not by the light of this sacred Name that God has called us into His marvellous light, so that when we had been enlightened by it, and in that light we had seen light, St. Paul was enabled to say to us: *Ye were sometimes darkness, but now are ye light in the Lord* (Eph. v. 8). This Name, in conclusion, it was that the same Apostle was bidden to bear before the Gentiles, and Kings, and the children of Israel (Acts ix. 15); this Name he bore as a lamp to enlighten his country and his people, crying everywhere: *The night is far spent, the day is at hand · let us, therefore, cast off the works of darkness, and put upon us the armour of light let us walk honestly, as in the day* (Rom. xiii. 12, 13). To all he displayed a lamp shining upon its pillar, when in every place he preached Jesus Christ, and Him crucified. How resplendent was that Light, how it dazzled the eyes of all beholders, when, coming forth as a lightning flash from the mouth of Peter, it set the lame man upon sound and strong limbs; when it restored to sight many who were spiritually blind! Did it not shoot forth a light of fire, when he said, *In the Name of Jesus Christ of Nazareth rise up and walk?* (Acts iii. 6). But the Name of Jesus is not only light, it is also nourishment Do you not feel spiritually strengthened as often as you meditate upon it? What enriches the mind of the thinker as does the Name of Jesus? What so restores exhausted powers, strengthens the soul in all virtues, animates it to good and honourable conduct, fosters in it pure and pious dispositions? Dry and tasteless is every kind of spiritual food, if this sweet oil be not poured into it; and insipid, if it be not seasoned with this salt. A book or writing has no single point of goodness for me if I do not read therein the Name of Jesus; nor has a conference any interest for me, unless the Name of Jesus be heard in it [1] As honey to the mouth, as melody in the ear, as a

---

[1] St Augustine, in his 'Confessions,' makes a similar declaration about himself (Bk iii., c 4) with respect to reading a book of Hortensius : 'There was only one thing in all that eloquent language which distressed me ; it was that the name of Christ was not to be found there . . . and any writing in which that Name was wanting, however learned, polished, and veracious it might be, would not wholly satisfy me.'

song of gladness to the heart, is the Name of Jesus.[1] But it is also a medicine. Is any of you sad? Let Jesus come into your heart; let His Name leap thence to your lips, and behold, when that blessed Name arises [as a sun], its light disperses the clouds of sadness, and brings back serenity and peace. Is any falling into crime? or even, in his despair, rushing upon death? Let him call upon that life-giving Name; does he not speedily begin to breathe again and revive? In the presence of that saving Name, who has ever remained fast bound (as is the case with some of us) by hardness of heart, ignoble sloth, rancour of mind, or cold indifference? Who has not known the fountain of his tears, which seemed dried up, to burst forth anew, and with added abundance and sweetness, at the calling upon the Name of Jesus? Who, when in fear and trembling in the midst of dangers, has called upon that Name of power, and has not found a calm assurance of safety, and his apprehensions at once driven away? Where is the man who, when labouring under doubt and uncertainty, has not had the clear shining of faith restored to him by the influence of the Name of Jesus? Or who has not found new vigour and resolution given to him at the sound of that Name full of help, when he was discouraged by adversities, and almost ready to give way to them? Those are the diseases and ailments of the soul, and for them this is the remedy. And what I say is proved by these words: *Call upon Me in the day of trouble: I will deliver thee, and thou shalt glorify Me* (Ps. l. 15). Nothing is so powerful as the Name of Jesus to restrain the impulse of anger, to repress the swelling of pride, to cure the wound of envy, to bridle the impulse of luxury, and extinguish the flame of fleshly desire; to temper avarice, and put to flight ignoble and impure thoughts. For, when I utter the Name of Jesus, I set before my mind, not only a Man meek and humble in heart, moderate, pure, benign, merciful, and, in short, conspicuous for every honourable and saintly quality, but also in the same individual the Almighty God, who both restores me to spiritual health by His example, and renders me strong by His assistance. All these things are said to me when the Name of JESUS is pronounced. From Him, inasmuch as He is Man, I derive an example; inasmuch as He is the Mighty One, I obtain assistance.

[1] See 'Jubilus Rhythmicus De Nomine Jesu,' verses 1-8:

> '*Jesu dulcis memoria,*
> *Dans vera cordi gaudia;*
> *Sed super mel et omnia,*
> *Ejus dulcis memoria.*
> *Nil canitur suavius,*
> *Nil auditur jucundius,*
> *Nil cogitatur dulcius,*
> *Quam Jesus Dei Filius.*'

M. Hauréau ('Des Poèmes Latins attribués à St. Bernard,' Paris, 1890) declares positively (pp. 63 68) that this poem is not from the hand of St. Bernard. The passage above shows, however, and that incontestably, that the writer of it, if not the Saint, had borrowed his very words.—ED.

Of His example I make, as it were, medicinal and salutary herbs, and His help is an instrument to prepare them; thus I obtain a remedy of power, such as none among physicians is able to compound.

7. In this sacred Name, O my soul, hidden in the Name of Jesus as in a vase, thou hast a saving antidote (*electuarium*), which shall never be found without efficacy against any disease or infection. Let it be always in thy bosom, always in thy hand, so that all thy affections, and all thy actions may be directed towards Jesus. To this you are invited, where it is said: *Set Me as a seal upon thine heart, as a seal upon thine arm* (Cant. viii. 6). But of this at another time. You have here (let us now consider) a sure remedy both for your heart and for your arm. You have, I say, in the Name of Jesus a means of correcting those actions in you which are bad, and of perfecting those that are defective; of protecting your feelings and affections from being defiled; or if defiled, of restoring them to health and purity.

8. There were in Judæa certain [others] named Jesus, in whom she glories; but these are but empty names; they render neither light, nor nourishment, nor healing. Therefore it is that the Synagogue is even to this day in darkness, weak with hunger, and languishing from disease. Nor will its hunger be satisfied, nor its disease healed, till it comes to know that it is our Jesus who rules in Jacob and unto the ends of the world [until then], *at evening let them return, grin* [for famine] *like dogs, and go about the city* (Ps. lix. 14, 7), They, indeed, were sent on before, as the staff was sent before him by the Prophet to the presence of the dead child (2 Kings iv. 29-35); nor could they read a meaning in those names of theirs, for they were void of power. The staff was laid upon the face of the child; but there was neither voice nor hearing, because it was but a staff. He came who sent the staff; He descended and came unto His people; and ere long He saved them from their sins, proving that to be the fact which was said of Him: *Who is this that forgiveth sins also?* (Luke vii. 49). No doubt He is that One who saith, *I am the salvation* of My people (Ps. xxxv. 3). Now there is voice; now there is hearing; it is manifest that He does not, like those who came before Him, bear an empty name. The life and salvation poured into the soul is felt; nor is so great a benefit passed over in silence. Within there is hearing; without there is speech. I am touched with penitence; I make confession [of my sins]; and to confess shows spiritual life: *Thanksgiving perisheth from the dead, as from one that is not* (Ecclus. xvii. 28).[1] Here is the proof of life, and of feeling. I am raised perfectly from the dead; my resurrection is complete. What is the death of the body, but the depriving it of feeling and of life? Sin, which is the death of the soul, had left

---

[1] The word in the Vulgate is *confessio*, which may mean either acknowledgment of sin, or thanks for benefits. But the word here seems to be intended in the former sense. For a third sense of the word see Rom. x. 10.—ED.

unto me neither any feeling of compunction, nor utterance of confession, and I was dead. Then He came who taketh away sins, and He restored to me each of these powers, saying unto my soul, *I am thy salvation* (Ps. xxxv. 3). What wonder if death gives place, where Life descends from heaven? Now with the heart the man believes unto righteousness, and with the mouth makes confession unto salvation (Rom. x. 10). As the child opened widely his mouth, even seven times, so the man saith, *Seven times a day do I praise Thee, O Lord* (Ps. cxix. 164). Note the number of seven. It is a sacred number, not without a mystical meaning. But it will be better to reserve this for another sermon; so that we may draw near with keen appetite, not with distaste, to this repast so excellent, to which we are invited by the Spouse of the Church, our Lord Jesus Christ, who is above all, GOD blessed for ever. AMEN.

SERMON XVI.

OF CONTRITION OF HEART, AND OF THE THREE KINDS OF TRUE CONFESSION.

WHAT, then, is intended by that number seven? For I suppose that none among us is so undiscerning as to suppose that the seven times which the child yawned was a number fortuitously reached, and without meaning. Nor do I think the fact is without signification that the prophet Elisha stretched himself upon the dead body of the child, setting mouth upon its mouth, eyes upon its eyes, and hands upon its hands (2 Kings xxxiv. 34). The Holy Spirit has willed all these circumstances to take place thus, and thus to be recorded, for the instruction without doubt of those spirits whom the treacherous companionship of their body of corruption has led astray, and whom the wisdom of this world, which is foolishness, has taught to be without understanding. For the corruptible body presseth down the soul; and the earthly tabernacle weigheth down the mind, that museth upon many things (Wisd. ix 15). Let no one, then, wonder or take it ill, if I seem to be minutely curious in searching into such things as these, which are, if I may say so, the treasure-houses of the Holy Spirit; since I know that to do thus is truly to live, and that in such things is the life of my spirit. Yet I say to those who outstrip me by the quickness of their apprehension, and in every sermon are anxious to arrive at the end, almost before they have heard the beginning, that I have a duty towards those of slower minds as well, and that, indeed, it is much greater towards them than towards others; nor is it nearly as much my object and my care to explain words as it is to touch and to influence hearts. It is my duty (so to speak) to draw water, and to give it to others to drink; and this duty is not discharged by rushing through subjects in great haste, but rather by treating them with leisurely care, and making them frequently the occasion for exhortation. It is true that the discussion of these mysteries (*sacramentorum*) has detained us longer than I could have supposed. I thought, I must confess, that one sermon would suffice for all of those subjects, that we should quickly traverse that forest, sombre and shady with allegories, and arrive, in a journey of perhaps one day, at the open plain of the moral meanings of our subject; but it has proved otherwise. We have been occupied in their consideration two days already, and we have still some distance to go. The eye of an observer at a distance traverses in a moment the tops of great masses of verdure, and marks the mountain peaks; but it cannot pierce into the vast depths of the low-lying valleys, or penetrate the obscure coverts of the thickets. How could I foresee, for instance, that when treating of the calling of the Gentiles and the rejection of the Jews, the miracle of Elisha would present itself of a sudden to my mind? But now, since we have fallen upon that incident, let us linger upon it for a little while, and we will return afterwards to the subject we have left; and, in fact, this, as well as the other, has in it food for souls. Does it not happen to hunters also and their hounds often to leave the quarry they had started, and to follow another, which they rouse unexpectedly?

2. It is a fact which gives me no little confidence to reflect upon, that this great Prophet, mighty in word and deed, has deigned to descend from the height of heaven, and to visit me, who am but dust and ashes; to have pity upon me in my state of death, to bend down to me as I lay prostrate, to be narrowed and made equal to my littleness, to share the light of His eyes with me in my darkness, to unloose the dumbness of my mouth with a kiss from His own, to strengthen my weak hands by the touch of His own in their strength. I meditate upon these benefits with sweetness unspeakable; my heart is filled with joy, my soul receives new vigour, and all that is within me; and my bones render praise to God. This He has once done for all the world; this each of us feels to be in process of doing daily in us; so that to his heart is given the light of intelligence, to his mouth the word of edification, to his hands the work of righteousness. It is He who gives us the power to think good and faithful thoughts, to express them usefully, to carry them out efficaciously in our life. In this is a threefold cable not easily broken, to draw souls out of the prison of the devil, and to draw them after one's self into the kingdom of heaven: it consists of three things; to think rightly, to speak worthily, to conform also our life to that which we speak. He has touched my eyes with His own, thus adorning the forehead, as it were, of my inner man with two bright luminaries, faith and intelligence. With His Mouth He has touched mine, and has pressed upon one who was dead the sign of peace, since, when we were still sinners and dead to righteousness, He has reconciled us to

God. He has, I say, with His sacred Mouth touched mine, thereby breathing a second time upon my face the breath of Life, and that life more holy than at first. For in the first place He created me to be a living soul; but in the second, reformed me to be a quickening spirit (1 Cor. xv. 45). His Hands upon mine He placed, affording me an example of good works, a model of obedience. Or, at least, He has set His Hands to great and noble deeds, that He might teach my hands to war, and my fingers to fight.

3. And *the child*, it is said, *yawned seven times*. It would have been enough to manifest the glory of the miracle had the child yawned but once; but the multiplicity, and the number itself being so noble, warn us of a mystery. If you consider that corpse as the type of the whole human race, which was spiritually dead, you will see that the universal Church, from the time of its receiving life from the Prophet stretched upon it, yawned, so to speak, seven times; for it has been the custom of the Church to sing praises to God seven times a day. And if you yourself consider, you will perceive that you are living a spiritual life, and fulfilling this mystical number, if you hold in subjection your five organs of sense to a twofold charity, and, according to the Apostle's precept, make your members the instruments of righteousness unto sanctification, as you formerly yielded them as instruments of unrighteousness unto sin (Rom. vi. 13); or if you use those five senses for the salvation of your neighbours, and make up the number of seven by adding these two things—viz., the praising God for His mercy, and for His justice.

4. Seven other yawnings I have to consider, which are seven experiences, without which a soul cannot be assured that it has truly regained life. Four of these have reference to the feeling of penitence for sin; three to the outward sound of confession of it. If you are living, if you have a voice and spiritual consciousness, you recognise the same in yourself. That is to say, you know that you have entirely recovered spiritual sensibility if you feel your conscience keenly grieved by a fourfold penitence; namely, a twofold shame, and a twofold fear. With the threefold confession, of which we will speak afterwards, the number seven is made up, and these are an unfailing proof of life regained. Does not the holy prophet Jeremiah also observe this number in his Lamentations? And do you also, in that which you make for yourself, observe the form which the Prophet has prescribed, think of God as your Creator, your Benefactor, your Father, your Lord. You are a criminal before Him in regard to each of these His characters; be, then, penitent as you think of each. To the first and the last of these let your fear respond; to the second and third your shame. A father, just because he is a father, is, indeed, not the object of fear, because it is the nature of a father always to pity and to spare. Even when he punishes, it is with a rod that he strikes, not with a heavy staff, and Himself heals the wounds which he has made. It is a father's voice which says: *I will strike, and I will heal* (Deut. xxxii. 39). You have, then, no

cause for extreme terror of God your Father; since though He sometimes strikes that He may bring about correction in you, He never strikes to avenge Himself. But when I consider that I have offended that heavenly Father, there is good reason for my feeling shame, though there be none for fear. He has begotten me of His own will by the Word of Truth, not urged by the spur of any necessity. Then, also, He did not spare His only begotten Son for me, who was thus begotten. Thus He, indeed, treated me with all the affection of a Father; but I have not behaved in turn with the obedience of a son. With what assurance, I ask, can a son so evil venture to raise even his eyes towards the Countenance of a Father so good? I am ashamed to have done actions so little worthy of my parentage; I am ashamed to have degenerated from a Father so exalted. O my eyes, do ye cause streams of tears to flow; let my face be covered with shame and confusion, and let shadow fall upon it. May my life be worn away in grief, and my years in mourning. Shame upon me! What profit have I of those things of which I am now ashamed? If I have sown unto the flesh, from the flesh I shall reap only corruption (Gal. vi. 8); if to the world, both it and the lust thereof passes away (1 John ii. 17). Yet I, unhappy and devoid of reason, have not blushed to prefer such perishing and vain advantages as these, which are almost nothing, and of which the end is death, to the love and to the honour which I owe to the Eternal Father! Well may I be covered with confusion to hear these words: *If I be a Father, where is Mine honour?* (Mal. 1. 6).

5. But even if He were not a Father, has He not overwhelmed me with benefits? Without speaking of innumerable other blessings, He brings forward against me, as witnesses of my ingratitude, the sustaining of this my mortal body, the use of a lengthened time in this world, and, above all, the Blood of His dear Son, which cries out against me from the ground. My ingratitude puts me to shame, and to complete my confusion, I stand convicted also of having rendered evil for good, and hatred for love. It is true that, from a Benefactor, as from a Father, I have nothing to fear; for He is truly beneficent, giving to all men liberally, and upbraiding not (James i 5) [for what He has given]. He does not upbraid us for His gifts, because they are truly gifts; nor does He sell His benefits, but bestows them. And, lastly, His gifts are without repentance. But the more benign and liberal I am obliged to think Him, the more unworthy I must consider myself to be. Blush with shame, O my soul, and be dissolved with grief; since, although it is according to the goodness of God to give without reproaching me or reclaiming what He has given, yet it is a disgrace to me to show myself ungrateful, and unmindful of these gifts. Alas! what shall I, even now, and thus late, render unto the Lord for all the benefits which He hath done unto me?

6. Let me, if I am not affected, as I ought, with shame and regret, at least be open to feelings of fear, and let the fear come to the help

of the regret; let it be aroused, that it may arouse me. Put aside for a moment the tender names of Benefactor and Father, and turn to other Names more austere; for He of whom we read as *the Father of mercies, and the God of all consolation* (2 Cor. i. 3), we read of also as *the Lord God, to whom vengeance belongeth* (Ps. xciv. 1); as *God the Judge righteous and powerful* (Ps. vii. 12); as *terrible in His doings toward the children of men* (Ps. lxvi. 5); as *a jealous God* (Exod. xx. 5). It is for you that He is Father and Benefactor, for Himself He is Creator and Lord; for, as Scripture declares, He *hath made all things for Himself* (Prov. xvi. 4). He, then, who defends and preserves with so much care that which is yours, will He not ever be jealous, think you, for Himself? will He not require the honour due to His sovereignty? Because of this it is that *the wicked hath provoked God; for he hath said in his heart, He will not require it* (Ps. ix. 13, Vulg.). And what is it to say in his heart, *He will not require it,* except to be without fear of His requiring it? But He *will* require it, and that to the last farthing; He will require it, and will abundantly recompense the proud doer (Ps. xxxi. 23). He will require service from him whom He hath redeemed; He will expect honour and glory from His creature.

7. Let it be granted that as Father He will pass over offences, and as Benefactor forgive, yet not as Creator and as Lord; and He who will spare a son will not spare an evil servant, the work of His Hands. Consider what a fearful and terrible thing it is to have despised Him who is your Creator, and the Creator of all things—to have offended the Lord of glory! It is the prerogative of Majesty, of Lordship, to be feared, and especially of this Lord and of this Majesty; for if the laws of man punish with the supreme penalty one who shall be guilty of high treason against the royal majesty, though it be that of a man, what shall be the end of those who despise the Omnipotence of God? If He do but *touch the mountains, they shall smoke* (Ps. cxliv. 5); and shall a mere petty mass of vile dust that a puff of wind may scatter in a moment, not to be brought together again, dare to arouse the anger of a Being of Majesty so awful? HE, HE is to be feared, who, after He hath killed the body, hath power even to cast into hell (Luke xii. 5). Hell it is I fear; the Face of my Judge, before whom the angels veil their faces in fear—at this I fear and tremble. At the mere thought of the anger of the Almighty, of the beholding of His Face in wrath, of the crash of a perishing world, of the roar of the elemental fires bursting forth, of the tumultuous conflict of the powers of nature, of the voice of the Archangel, of the awful word of the Judge's doom— at the mere thought of these I tremble and shake. Terrible to me is the mere idea of the teeth of the monster of hell, of the lions roaring for their prey, of the abyss which contains and which hides them. I shudder at the gnawing of the never-dying worm, at the ever-burning lake of fire, at the smoke, the sulphur, the livid clouds, the whirlwinds of flame, and, lastly, at the outer darkness which broods over all. Who shall make my head to be a river, mine eyes a fountain of tears (Jer. ix. 1), so that by my weeping day and night I might anticipate and so

avoid the weeping and gnashing of teeth, the hard fetters upon hands and feet, the weighty and cramping chains, which strangle, which burn to the bone, and yet are never consumed? Alas, my mother! why hast thou borne me to be a son of sorrow, a child of wrath, reserved for fiery indignation and everlasting lamentings? Why didst thou nurse upon thy knees, why didst thou nourish from thy breast, one born but to be consumed, to become food for the everlasting fire?

8. He who is affected deeply with these thoughts has, without doubt, recovered spiritual sensibility—that twofold fear, accompanied by that twofold shame, constitute, as it were, the four yawnings of the child raised up. The three which remain refer to the voice of confession [of sin], and of him [who makes use of this] it cannot be said that he has neither voice nor feeling, provided that his confession comes from a humble, simple, and faithful heart. Confess humbly, purely, and faithfully, therefore, whatever gives you remorse of conscience, and you have fulfilled your duty in this respect. There are those who boast themselves in doing evil, and delight in the worst crimes (Prov. ii. 14), of whom the Prophet speaks when he says: *They declare their sin as Sodom* (Is. iii. 9). But I put these out of the question at present—they are people of the world; and what have we to do with them who are without?

9. It happens to us, nevertheless, sometimes to hear men even who have professed the religious life, and wear its garb, recall their past bad actions, and boast of them most impudently—as, for example, of the bravery they have shown in duels, or the cleverness in a dispute of words, or of similar things, which the vanity, indeed, of the world estimates highly, but which are hurtful, pernicious, and even dangerous to the salvation of the soul. This is an indication of a worldly mind, and the habit of humility which such persons wear is not a proof of the renewing of their mind in holiness, but a screen which hides their former temper still persisted in. Some recall such things as if they grieved over and repented of them; but as they still glory inwardly in them, they do not efface the fault of them, but merely deceive their own selves, for *God is not mocked* (Gal. vi. 7). They have not put off the old man, but merely covered it with the new. The old leaven is not acknowledged nor abandoned by such a confession as that; but is, on the contrary, established the more, according to the saying of the Psalmist: *My bones grew old: whilst I cried out all the day long* (Ps. xxxi. 3). I am ashamed to recall the extreme effrontery of others who have not scrupled to recount with pride things for which they ought to weep, as that, even after they received the sacred habit, they cunningly overthrew someone, or over-reached some brother in a matter of business, or that they took revenge on one who had done them injury by word or deed—that is, they boldly rendered evil for evil, and railing for railing.

10. There is a kind of confession so much the more perilous, as it conceals vanity in a manner more subtle. I mean that in which we do not hesitate to reveal discreditable and shameful faults; not because

we are really humble, but that we may be thought to be so. Now, to seek praise for humility is the reverse of humility, not the virtue itself. The man who is truly humble wishes to be held in slight esteem, not to be proclaimed and praised as being humble. He rejoices to be contemned, and is proud only on this one point—that he despises praises. What can be more perverse and unworthy conduct than to make confession, which is the guardian of humility, contribute to the satisfaction of pride, and so wish to appear the better for the very reason that he seems to appear worse? Oh, prodigy of boasting, to have no other means of being thought a saint than to be thought the wickedest of sinners! But such a confession, having only the appearance, not the reality, of humility, not only does not deserve forgiveness, but even calls down anger. What did it profit Saul that, when chidden by Samuel, he confessed that he had sinned (1 Sam. xv. 30)? No doubt that confession was itself criminal which did not blot out the crime confessed. Whenever did the Master of humility, whose natural desire assuredly is to give grace unto the humble, despise a really humble confession? It would assuredly be a thing impossible that He should not be reconciled if the humility which the words express be manifested also in the heart. This is why I have said that confession of sin should be humble.

11. It must also be made *with simplicity*. Let not a soul (if it be guilty) delight in making excuse for its intention (under the pretext, perhaps, that it is not known to men), nor to pare down and diminish a grave fault, nor to ascribe it to the advice of another person, since no one is obliged to act against his own will. The first of these is not a confession, but a defence; nor does it appease, but rather provokes, the wrath of God. The second is a mark of ingratitude; for the less a fault is regarded as being, the more is the glory diminished of him who forgives it. To this must be added that a benefit will be accorded so much less willingly, as it is known that he who receives it will be less thankful for it, as supposing it to be less necessary to him. That person renders himself unworthy of pardon who depreciates the value of the grace he hopes to receive, and this is what everyone does who endeavours to make light of his offence in the words which he uses [to confess it]. As for the third, the example of the first man may serve to dissuade us from it (Gen. iii. 2); for though he did not deny his fault, yet he did not obtain pardon for it; and this, doubtless, was because he mixed up with it the fault of his wife. It is a form of excuse to inculpate another when you are yourself accused. Holy David teaches us that the desire to make excuses for yourself, when censured, is not only useless, but exceedingly harmful; for he calls *to make excuses* for *sins 'evil words'* (Ps. cxl. 4, Vulg. and Douay), and entreats God not to incline His heart to them. Assuredly he was very right; for a person sins against his own soul who excuses himself, repelling thereby from him the remedy of leniency, and with his own lips preventing the entrance of life. What perverseness can be greater than to take arms against his own salvation, and to transfix himself

with his own tongue as with a sword? He that is evil to himself, to whom will he be good (Ecclus. xiv. 5)?

12. Finally, confession must be made in faith—that is to say, it must be filled with hope, free from distrust of obtaining pardon of our offences, or of fear lest by making it you should be rather condemning yourself than justifying. Judas, who betrayed our Lord, and Cain, who slew his brother, confessed their crime, but each despaired of God's mercy. The one said: *I have sinned, in that I have betrayed the innocent Blood* (Matt. xxvii. 4); the other: *My iniquity is greater than that I may deserve pardon* (Gen. iv. 13, Vulg.). Their confession was truthful; but because it was made without faith, it profited them nothing. These three conditions of confession of sin, then, joined to the four formerly named of penitence for it, make up the number seven.

13. When you have thus been touched with heartfelt sorrow for your sins, when you have thus confessed them, and you thenceforth feel good assurance that the gift of life has been conferred upon you, you will be no less assured, I think, that the Name of JESUS is not empty nor fruitless, since He has been able and willing to perform such great works in your soul; and that it was not in vain that He followed in person the staff which He had sent before. He has not come in vain, because He has not come empty.[1] How, in fact, could He have been empty in Whom dwells the fulness of the Godhead? (Col. i. 19; ii. 9). For God giveth not the Spirit by measure unto Him (John iii. 34). So, also, He came in the fulness of time (Gal. iv. 4), as if to indicate that in every way He was full [of power]. Truly He was full, whom the Father hath anointed with the oil of gladness above His fellows (Ps. xlv. 7); whom He hath anointed and sent into the world full of grace and truth (John i. 14). He has anointed Him, that He may anoint others; and all those have been anointed by Him who have been found worthy to receive of His fulness. Therefore He saith: *The Spirit of the Lord God is upon Me, because the Lord hath anointed Me to preach good tidings unto the meek, He hath sent Me to bind up the broken-hearted, to proclaim liberty to the captives, and the opening of the prison to them that are bound; to proclaim the acceptable year of the Lord* (Is. lxi. 1). He came, as you hear, to anoint with the oil of salvation our contritions, and to soothe our griefs; therefore it was that He came filled with a Divine anointing—He came meek and lowly in heart, and full of an infinite pity for all those who call upon Him for aid. He knew well that it was to people crippled and helpless that He was coming down from heaven, and He showed Himself in that capacity which their need required. And that wise and foreseeing Physician, because He had many maladies to cure, provided Himself beforehand with many remedies. He brought with Him the Spirit of wisdom and understanding, the Spirit of counsel and ghostly strength, the Spirit of knowledge and true godliness, and the Spirit of the fear of the Lord.

14. Do you see how many vials full of heavenly balms the

---

[1] *Vacue, vacuus.*

Celestial Physician has prepared for the healing of the wounds of that unhappy man who fell among thieves? Seven they are in number, seven suited, perhaps, to excite the seven yawnings of which we have spoken, for in each was the Spirit of life. From these He pours oil upon my wounds, and wine also, but in less quantity than the oil; for it was in accordance with my infirmities that mercy should be exalted above judgment, as oil rises in a vessel above wine. He brought, therefore, five vessels of oil, but of wine two only; for it is strength only and fear that are typified by wine; the remaining five signify oil, because of its softness and healing qualities. In the spirit of strength it was that, like a mighty man that shouteth by reason of wine (Ps. lxxviii. 65), He descended into hell, shattered the gates of brass, and brake asunder the bars of iron; that He bound the strong man, and delivered them who were subject to bondage. Nevertheless, He descended also in the spirit of fear; but it was to inspire fear, not to feel it.

15. O Wisdom! with what healing skill dost Thou re-establish the health of my soul by this wine and this oil, mingling strength with sweetness, and sweetness with strength. Strong Thou art on my behalf, yet towards me Thou art sweet. From one end of the world to the other Thy Almighty power extendest, and Thou dost dispose all things with sweetness, driving far away my enemy, and sustaining me when weak. Heal me, O Lord, and my healing shall be complete; I will sing and give praises unto Thy Name, and say: *Thy Name is as oil poured forth.* Not as wine poured forth (for I do not desire that Thou shouldest enter into judgment with Thy servant), but as oil, because Thou crownest me with lovingkindness and tender mercies (Ps. ciii. 4). Yes, it is as oil, for oil rises above all other liquids with which it may be mixed, and thus is an apt type of that Name which is above every name. O Name, infinitely dear and sweet! O Name, glorious beyond all words; fore-ordained and fore-ennobled, and of supremest exaltation for all ages! This is truly the oil which maketh glad the face of man, which anoints the head of him that fasteth, so that he regardeth not the oil of the sinner. This is *the new Name which the Mouth of the Lord hath named* (Is. lxii. 2, Vulg.); *which was so named of the Angel before He was conceived in the womb* (Luke ii. 21). Not only the Jew, but whosoever shall call upon this Name shall be delivered (Joel ii. 32), wheresoever it is poured forth, far and wide. This Name the Father has bestowed upon the Son, the Bridegroom of the Church, our LORD JESUS CHRIST, who is above all, GOD blessed for ever. AMEN.

SERMON XVII.

THAT IT IS NEEDFUL TO OBSERVE WITH CARE THE APPROACH AND THE DEPARTURE OF THE HOLY SPIRIT; AND OF THE ENVY OF THE DEVIL TOWARDS THE HUMAN RACE.

DO you think that we have made sufficient advance in the sanctuary of God to venture to examine an admirable mystery? or, rather, to follow the Holy Spirit into the deeper recesses of truth, and to search out that which still remains unknown to us? For that Spirit searcheth, not the hearts and reins of men only, but also the deep things of God; and I follow Him with safety whithersoever He shall lead, whether it be into the heights[1] or into the depths of our own nature. Only, may He guard our hearts and our intellects that we may not believe Him to be present when He, perhaps, shall be absent, and be led into error by following the impulses of our own mind or senses in the belief that they are from Him. For He comes and goes according to His own will; nor is it easy for any to know whence He cometh or whither He goeth (John iii. 8). But it is possible to be ignorant upon those points without risk to our salvation; but not to know when the Holy Spirit comes to us, or when He goes from us, is manifestly full of peril. For when these comings of the Spirit, in His dealings with the soul, and His goings, are not sedulously observed, it follows that you do not ardently desire His coming when He is absent, nor give Him glory when He is present. Indeed, He retires from the soul for the very reason that He may be sought for the more eagerly again; and how can He be sought for if He is not known to be absent? And, again, when He deigns to return in order to console the soul, how shall He be received with the reverence due to His Majesty if His presence is not even perceived? The soul, then, which is unaware of His departure lies open to be seduced, and that which is not aware of his return will be unthankful for the honour done to it in His coming.

2. Once, when the prophet Elisha had learned that the departure from the earth of his master [Elijah] was about to take place, he made a certain request of him, and he obtained it, as you know, upon this condition only: that Elisha should behold him at the moment of his departure (2 Kings ii. 9, 10). This happened unto them in figure, and was recorded on account of us. We are taught and warned by the prophet's example to be watchful and careful in the work of our salvation, which the Holy Spirit is incessantly carrying on in the depths of our souls with all the wonderful resource and sweetness of His Divine skill. Let that sacred and directing unction

---

[1] *Alta* is the uniform reading of the MSS., not *alia*.

which teaches all things never be taken away from us, if we do not wish to be deprived of a twofold gift. Never, when He comes to us, let Him find us unprepared; but rather let Him find us with countenance uplifted, and hands spread out to receive an abundant benediction from God. What does the Lord require that we should be? *Like unto men that wait for their Lord, when He shall return from the wedding* (Luke xii. 36); and assuredly He never returns with empty hands from the abundant delicacies of the table of heaven. It behoves us, then, to watch, and to watch without intermission, since we know not when the Holy Spirit may come, or when He may again depart. He cometh and goeth; and the soul which, while it has the advantage of His presence, is able to stand upright, cannot fail to fall when deserted by him; yet it shall not be so cast down as to be injured, for the Lord upholdeth it with His Hand. These two conditions do not cease to occur alternately in all those who are spiritual; or, rather, the Spirit visits those who are spiritual at daybreak, and suddenly puts them to proof [by His departure], in order that He may train and build them up in goodness. *The just man falleth seven times and riseth up again* (Prov. xxiv. 16), yet if he falls *in the day* it is to be understood that he sees that he falls, and, knowing that he has fallen, seeks the Hand of Him who is able to raise him up, saying, *O Lord, in Thy favour Thou gavest strength to my beauty. Thou turnedst away Thy Face from me and I became troubled* (Ps. xxix. 8, Vulg. and Douay).

3. To doubt respecting the truth is another danger, which it is necessary to endure when the breathing of the Spirit is not granted to us; and still another is that of embracing erroneous opinions, but this latter is easily avoided by keeping in mind our ignorance, so as to say also: *Be it indeed that I have erred, mine error remaineth with myself* (Job xix. 4). That is the declaration of holy Job; recognise it. Ignorance is the worst of mothers, and she has two daughters as evil—falsehood and doubt; the one the more miserable, the other the more pitiable; the former more hurtful, the latter more full of discomfort. When the Spirit speaks, both the one and the other of these give place; and not only to truth, but to assured truth. For that is the very Spirit of truth, to whom falsehood is absolutely contrary. And He is also the Spirit of wisdom, since He is the very Light of eternal life; and reaching everywhere, because of His purity, He suffers neither obscurity nor the uncertainty of doubt. When that Spirit does not speak, there is great need to beware, if not of unhappy doubt, assuredly of harbouring that which is completely false. There is a great difference between being in a state of uncertainty whether to think this or that, and rashly affirming as true that of which you are ignorant. Either, then, let the Holy Spirit always speak, though that, indeed, does not at all depend upon our will; or when it pleases Him to be silent, let His silence at least have a significance to us, and point out to us this one fact; lest, falsely supposing that He goes before us, we should follow in place of Him

our own error, with a false and dangerous confidence. And if He holds our spirit in suspense, let it, at all events, not be left to fall into falsehood. There are those who doubtfully advance a statement which is untrue, yet these do not lie ; and there are others who affirm for truth that of which they know nothing, and these do lie. For the one class do not affirm that which is not the case, but that which they believe to be the case, and they speak truthfully, even though that which they believe be not true ; whereas the other class declare themselves certain of a thing of which they are not certain, and these do not speak truthfully, even though the thing which they assert should be true.

4. Having said thus much by way of caution to those who have no experience in such things, I shall now follow the Spirit, who is, as I have a good trust, leading me on ; yet observing, as far as I can, the same rule of caution of which I have spoken, and endeavouring to practise myself that which I have urged upon others, that it may not be said of me too, *Thou that teachest another, teachest thou not thyself* (Rom. ii. 21)? The distinction is carefully to be observed between things which are manifest and others which are doubtful ; and as the one class are not to be brought into doubt, so the other are not rashly to be affirmed. Which, indeed, is to be hoped for from the authoritative guidance (*magisterio*) of the Spirit; for our own care and pains will not suffice to obtain it. What man is there who knows, for example, whether the judgment, of which I spoke in a former sermon (the third before this, if I recollect rightly[1]), as pronounced by the Lord between men, was preceded by a judgment pronounced in the heavens ?[2]

5. A thought which occurs to my mind is this : Do you suppose that Lucifer, son of the morning, who lifted himself up by a presumptuous pride, that he, too, envied the human race this outpouring of the oil of Divine grace before he was cast forth into outer darkness; and that in his indignation and jealousy he murmured in a manner to himself, saying, 'To what purpose is this waste ?' I do not assert that the Spirit says this, but neither would I assert the contrary ; I simply do not know. It may have been the case (nor does it seem incredible) that, being filled with wisdom and raised to a high degree of glory, he may have foreseen the creation of men, and that some of them would attain to an equal degree of glory with that he then held. But if he foresaw this he saw, without doubt, that [it would come to pass] in God the Word ; and in his malice he envied men, and, scorning to have them as companions, determined to render them subject to himself. 'They are,' he said, 'weaker than I, and inferior by nature ; it is not fitting that they should be fellow-citizens with me, and equals in glory.' Perhaps that ascension which he presumed

---

[1] Sermon XIV.
[2] In most MSS. the words '*præcesserit, utrumnam videlicet Lucifer, qui,*' etc. (as in *n.* 5), are read here in a parenthesis ; and the first printed edition also has them.

to attempt to make, and the seating himself, signifying mastery, of which he said, *I will ascend above the heights of the clouds; I will sit also upon the mount of the congregation, in the sides of the north* (Is. xiv. 13, 14), was intended that he might obtain some kind of resemblance to the Most High, and that as God, sitting upon the Cherubin, governs the whole race of angels, so he might sit upon a lofty seat and thence govern the whole human race. But God forbid! He has meditated iniquity upon his bed, and iniquity has deceived itself. We recognise no other as our ruler than Him who created us. The Lord, not the devil, shall judge the whole world. He shall be our God for ever and ever, and shall eternally rule over us.

6. Therefore, as even in heaven he conceived sullen anger, so in Paradise he brought forth iniquity, the offspring of malice, the mother of miseries and of death; and of all these the first parent was pride. For, although through the envy of the devil came death into the world (Wisd. ii. 24), yet of every sin pride is the beginning (Ecclus. x. 13). But what has it profited him? None the less art Thou in us, O Lord, and upon us is Thy Name invoked; none the less does the people whom Thou hast gathered, the Church of Thy redeemed, thankfully say, *Thy Name is as oil poured forth.* When I am cast forth [for my sin], this oil [of consolation] Thou dost pour around and upon me, since even in Thy anger Thou didst remember mercy. Yet Satan received dominion over all the sons of pride; he has become prince of the darkness of this world, so that even pride should strive in favour of the kingdom of the humble, and whilst his temporal and proud dominion exists, should establish many humble persons in a sovereignty exalted and eternal   Joyful will be the judgment to see that proud persecutor of those who are humble preparing for them, without knowing it, everlasting crowns, and while he attacks all, succumbing to the efforts of all.   For the Lord shall judge the peoples everywhere and for ever: He shall save the children of the poor, and shall cast down him who treats them wrongfully. Everywhere and always He will protect His own; He will put to flight the persecutors, nor suffer the rod of sinners to come into the lot of the righteous lest the righteous put forth their hands unto iniquity (Ps. cxxv. 3). There shall come even a time when He shall destroy the bow, and break the weapons, and the shields He shall burn in the fire (Ps. xlv. 10, Vulg. and Douay). As for thee, unhappy one, thou settest a seat for thyself in the north, a place of cloud and cold; and lo! the poor are raised out of the dust, and the needy out of the dunghill, that they may sit with princes, and occupy a throne of glory, whilst thou shalt lament to see those words accomplished: *The poor and needy shall praise Thy Name* (Ps. lxxiv. 21).

7. Thanks be to Thee, O Father of orphans and Judge of the helpless, a mountain fat and fertile has communicated to us its warmth; the heavens have dropped dew from the presence of the God of Sinai, a saving oil is poured forth, a Name is spread abroad, a Name which the enemy envied for us and for himself; it is spread abroad, I say,

even into the hearts and into the mouths of children, and in the mouths of babes and sucklings is perfected praise. These things the sinner shall behold in useless anger; and as his wrath shall be implacable, so the fire shall be inextinguishable which is prepared for him and for his angels. The zeal of the Lord of Hosts shall perform this. How great is the love, O my God, the object of my deepest affection (*amor meus*), wherewith Thou dost love me! Everywhere Thou hast been mindful of me; everywhere earnestly desiring the salvation of one poor and needy, and that in opposition not only to proud men, but also to proud and rebellious angels! In heaven and on earth Thou, O Lord, dost judge those who do me harm, and repulse those who take arms to attack me. Everywhere Thou dost help and assist me; and Thou art ever at my side, O Lord, that I may not be overwhelmed. These blessings I will celebrate in praises unto the Lord as long as I live; I will praise my God while I have my being. These are His wonders; these the mighty works which He hath done. This, the first and greatest of His judgments, it is which the [B.] Virgin Mary, conscious of His secret works, has revealed unto me in the words: *He hath put down the mighty from their seat, and hath exalted the humble and meek. He hath filled the hungry with good things, and the rich He hath sent empty away* (Luke i. 52, 53). The second also, which you have already heard, is similar to the first: *That they which see not might see: and that they which see might be made blind* (John ix. 39). In these two judgments let the poor be comforted, and let him say: *I remembered Thy judgments of old, O Lord; and have comforted myself* (Ps. cxix. 52).

8. But let us return to ourselves, and let us examine our ways. And that we may be enabled to do this in truth, let us invoke the Spirit of Truth; let us recall Him from that height of heaven whither He has led us [in thought], so that He may guide us thither to go ourselves; for without Him we can do nothing. We need not fear that He will disdain to condescend to us, since, on the contrary, He would have reason to be indignant with us if we should endeavour to accomplish even the least spiritual work without His assistance. He is not a Spirit which departs and does not return; He leads, and continues to lead us on from glory to glory as being the Spirit of the Lord. Sometimes He draws us to Himself, and into the sphere of His own Light; sometimes, accommodating Himself to our capacities, He enlightens our darkness, so that whether He is above us, or whether He is in us, we should be always in the light, and walk as children of light. We have passed out of types and shadows; we have reached the region of moral truths. Our faith has been built up, let our life and conduct be ruled and directed; and as the understanding has been trained, let the actions be prescribed by it. Since *a good understanding have all they that do the commandments of God* (Ps. cxi. 10), let our acts and our understanding also be directed to the praise and glory of our Lord Jesus Christ, who is above all, GOD blessed for ever. AMEN.

SERMON XVIII.

OF THE TWO OPERATIONS OF THE HOLY SPIRIT, OF WHICH THE ONE IS CALLED *EFFUSION*, AND THE OTHER *INFUSION*.

THY Name is as oil poured forth. What is it which the Holy Spirit reveals to us in this text, as assuredly brought to pass in us? It appears to me, in the first place, that it is the fact of His operation in us being twofold. There is one operation, by which He first establishes us inwardly in virtues, in order to our salvation; and then the other, by which He adorns us outwardly with His gifts, to our profit and to the good of others. The former grace we receive for ourselves; the latter for our neighbours. For example, faith, hope, and charity are given us for ourselves; for without these we cannot be saved. But words of knowledge or of wisdom, the gift of healing the sick, of prophecy, and similar powers, in which we may be wanting without any detriment to our own salvation, these assuredly are bestowed upon us only that they may be used for the benefit, bodily and spiritual, of our fellow-creatures. And these two operations of the Spirit, which we experience either in ourselves, or in others, have names corresponding to the effects they produce; let us name them, if you please, *infusion* and *effusion*. To which of these two, then, have the words, *Thy Name is as oil poured forth*, reference? Is it not to *effusion*? For if He had desired rather to refer to *infusion*, He would have said 'inpoured,' instead of 'poured forth.'[1] Besides, it is because of this fragrance poured forth upon her Bosom that the Bride says, *Thy Name is as oil poured forth*, ascribing that fragrance to the Name of her Spouse, as it were oil poured upon it. And whosoever feels himself endued with a gift of outward graces, which he is able in turn to pour forth upon others, is also enabled to say to the Lord: *Thy Name is as oil poured forth.*

2. But here we must take good heed of two dangers: that of giving to others what is meant for ourselves, and of keeping for ourselves what is given to us for others. You certainly are retaining for yourself that which belongs to your neighbour, if, for example, being not only full of virtues, but also outwardly adorned with the gifts of knowledge and of eloquence, fear perhaps, or sloth, or an ill-judged humility, restrains your good gift of speech, which might be of service to many people, in a useless, or, rather, blamable silence; and thus

---

[1] In the edition of Horst, and in others, the following sentence is inserted here: 'Besides, it is of the fragrance exhaled outwardly by the Bosom of the Bride, not of her inward virtues, that this is spoken *Thy Name is as oil poured forth*. Besides, it is because of this fragrance,' etc. ; but most MSS., and also the first printed edition omit it. It is true that it is found in the St. Evroul Codex, but that omits the following sentence: 'Besides, it is because,' etc. And in fact one or the other is superfluous.

you are evil spoken of, because you withhold corn from the people (Prov. xi. 26). On the contrary, you dissipate and lose that which is your own if, before you have received a complete inpouring from God, and while you are, so to speak, but half filled, you hasten to pour yourself forth, and thus violate the law not to plough with the firstling of thy cow, or to shear the firstling of thy sheep (Deut. xv. 19). You defraud yourself both of life and of salvation when, without rightfulness of intention, but puffed up by a wind of vain glory, or infected by the poison of worldly cupidity, you thus impart yourself to another; indeed, what you thus communicate is but the mortal imposthume which is swelling within yourself.

3. If, then, you are wise, you will show yourself rather as a reservoir than as a canal. For a canal spreads abroad water as it receives it, but a reservoir waits until it is filled before overflowing, and thus communicates, without loss to itself, its superabundant water, knowing that there is blame to one who deteriorates that which he receives; and that you may not regard my counsel as to be despised, hear a wiser than I: *A fool uttereth all his mind, but a wise man keepeth it in till afterwards* (Prov. xxix. 11). But in the Church at the present day we have many canals, few reservoirs. Those by whom the dew of heaven distils upon us are of charity so great that they desire to pour it forth before they are themselves filled with it; they are more prepared to speak than to hear, are quick to teach that which they have not learned, and long to preside over others, while they do not as yet know how to govern themselves. For my part, I think there is no degree of piety more helpful to salvation than that of which the Wise Man speaks: Have pity on thy own soul, pleasing God, and contain thyself (Ecclus. xxx. 24, Vulg. and Douay). If I have but a little oil for my own anointing, why dost thou think that I ought to give it to thee and remain empty? That is for my own need; nor do I bring it forth publicly, except at the order of a Prophet. If any of those who have perhaps an opinion of me above anything which they behold in me, or who hear somewhat concerning me, shall press me too hard with their requests, they will be answered thus: *Lest there be not enough for us and you, go ye rather to them that sell, and buy for yourselves* (Luke xxv. 9). But *charity*, you reply, *seeketh not her own* (1 Cor. xiii. 5). And do you know for what reason she doth not? It is because she is in want of nothing. For who seeks that which he already possesses? Charity is never without those things which are hers; that is, those which are necessary for salvation; and these she not only possesses, but possesses them in abundance. In these she desires to abound for herself, that she may abound for all others also; she desires to have sufficient for herself, that she may be wanting in nothing for any others. In other words, she is imperfect if she is not full.

4. But you, my brother, whose own salvation is not yet sufficiently assured, who have as yet no charity, or a charity so light and weak, that it is like a reed, believing every spirit, and blown about with

every wind of doctrine; or, rather, whose charity is so great, that going even beyond the commandment, you love your neighbour more than yourself; or again, who have so little, that going against the commandment, it dissolves under the influence of inclination, disappears under fear, is troubled by sadness, is reduced by avarice, narrowed by ambition, disquieted by suspicions, set aside by reproaches, racked by cares, puffed up by honours, and by envy made to pine away; you, I say, who have such sentiments in matters which relate to yourself, by what folly do you desire, or consent, to busy yourself in those which relate to others? Listen to the advice which a cautious and watchful charity gives: *Not that other men be eased, and ye burdened; but by an equality* (2 Cor. viii. 13). *Be not righteous over much* (Eccles. vii. 16). It suffices that you should love your neighbour as yourself; that is the equality of which the Apostle speaks. David says: *My soul shall praise Thee as with marrow and fatness: and my mouth shall praise Thee with joyful lips* (Ps. lxiii. 5), showing his desire first to be filled with the inpouring of grace, and then to begin to pour it forth: not merely to receive it, but to be filled with it, that he might give forth easily out of his fulness, and not gasp in the effort to do so out of an empty heart. In this he displayed caution, lest in doing good to others, he should do wrong to himself, and yet [acted] with a pure motive, as imitating Him, of whose fulness we have all received. Do you also learn not to attempt to give forth except out of a full [heart and mind], nor to desire to be more liberal than God. Let the reservoir imitate its source, for that does not flow into a river, nor spread itself into a lake, until it is brimming over with its own waters. The reservoir must not be ashamed not to be more profuse than its source. Lastly, even He who is the Fountain of life, who is full in Himself, and full of Himself, did He not begin by leaping forth [as it were a fountain] into the secret recesses of the Heavens, which were nearest to Him, and filled them all with His bounty; and then, at length, when He had filled those loftier and more secret regions, burst forth upon the earth, and multiplying His mercy by a gratuitous and superabundant overflowing of it, brought salvation both to men and beasts? First He filled those inner regions; and, then, thus bursting forth, as it were, with the multitude of His mercies, He visited the earth and made it glad (*inebriavit*); He enriched it and made it fruitful with every kind of good. Therefore do thou do likewise. Be thou first filled, then pour forth with care and judgment of thy fulness. The charity which is liberal, yet prudent, usually wastes not, but increases. *My son*, says Solomon, *squander not;* and an Apostle declares, *Therefore we ought to give the more earnest heed to the things which we have heard, lest at any time we should let them slip* (Heb. ii. 1). What then? art thou more holy than Paul? or wiser than Solomon? Furthermore, be it far from me to grow rich by thy impoverishment. For if to thyself thou art evil, to whom shalt thou be good? Assist me, if thou art able, of thy abundance; but if otherwise, be sparing for thy own good.

5. But now listen while I state how great things are necessary for our own salvation, and what they are; how great and manifold is the infusion of grace, which we need, before we presume to give forth to others. I shall try to put them before you as briefly as I can. For the sun (*hora*) is mounting high in the heavens, and presses me to reach the end of my discourse. The Physician draws near to the wounded man; the Divine Spirit to our soul. For what soul is there which does not feel itself wounded by the sword of the devil, even after the wound of original sin was healed by the saving medicine of Baptism? When, then, the Spirit draws near to that soul which says, *My wounds stink and are corrupt because of my foolishness* (Ps. xxxviii. 5), what is it that it is needful He should first do? Before all things, the ulcerous tumour which may have grown in and over the wound, and hinders its cure, must be removed. The ulcer of inveterate evil custom must be cut away with the sharp blade of a sincere repentance. But this cannot be done without severe pain; let that, then, be alleviated with the healing ointment of devotion, which is, in fact, the comfort caused by the hope of forgiveness. Of that hope is born the mastery which is acquired over our passions, and the victory over sin. For we find the Psalmist giving thanks, and saying: *Thou hast loosed my bonds, I will offer to Thee the sacrifice of thanksgiving* (Ps. cxvi. 16). Then are applied the remedy of penitence, the apparatus[1] of fasts, of vigils, or prayers, and of other exercises of the repentant. Let him be nourished in labour with the food of good works, that he fail not. That good works are nourishment to the soul, you may learn from these words of the Lord Himself: *My meat is to do the will of Him that sent Me* (John iv. 34). Therefore let works of piety accompany the labours of penitence which strengthen the soul. *Alms*, says Tobit, shall be a great confidence before the Most High God (Tob. iv. 12, Vulg. and Douay). Now, food arouses thirst, and drink is needed. To the nourishment of good works let there be added, therefore, the draught of prayer, blending works well done in the stomach, as it were, of conscience, and rendering them acceptable to God. Prayer is as wine which maketh glad the heart of man; it is the wine of the Holy Spirit, a draught of which brings not only the gladness [of heaven], but entire forgetfulness of the pleasures of earth (*carnalium voluptatum*). It moistens the dry soil of the conscience, it brings about the perfect absorption of the food of good actions, and distributes them into all the members of the soul; strengthening faith, giving vigour to hope, rendering charity active and yet methodical, and shedding an admirable unction over the whole character.

6. When a sick man shall have partaken of food and of drink, what, then, remains for him to do but to repose, and in the quiet of contemplation to recover himself after the toils of busy life? When he is thus in a holy slumber, he beholds God in a vision; yet, as it were, in a glass and darkly, and not as yet face to face. Nevertheless, though it be true that he knows God rather by inference and

---

[1] *Malagma* = an emollient poultice.

surmise (*conjectati*) than by distinct view, and beholds Him but as He passes by, and by a flash of glory which disappears in a moment, yet that momentary and passing vision does not fail to arouse in him an ardent and burning love, and he says: *With my soul have I desired Thee in the night; yea, with my spirit within me will I seek Thee early* (Is. xxvi. 9). Such a love is full of zeal; it is worthy of a friend of the Bridegroom, and with that love a faithful and prudent servant, whom his Lord hath set over His household, ought to feel himself animated and glowing. It fills and warms the soul, it boils over and spreads itself fearlessly, it bursts forth in vehement waves, and it says: *Who is weak, and I am not weak? who is offended, and I burn not?* (2 Cor. xi. 29). Let him who is possessed by that love preach, and bear fruit; let him do marvels, let him even work miracles; vanity will find no place in him who is wholly occupied by charity. For charity, if only it be perfect, is the fulfilling of the law (Rom. xiii. 10), and the perfectness of the heart. In truth, God is charity (1 John iv. 16); and there is nothing which is able to fill and satisfy a creature made in the image of God, except God, who is Himself charity, and who alone is greater than that creature. It is very full of peril to promote [to ecclesiastical functions] one who has not yet attained this perfect charity, however great be the talents which, in other respects, he may appear to possess. Though he have all knowledge, though he have bestowed all his goods to feed the poor, though he even give his body to be burned—without charity, he is nothing Behold with how many and great graces it behoves us to be previously filled, that we may venture to impart to others, so that we may bestow out of fulness, not out of poverty. In the first place, we ought to have repentance; secondly, devotion; thirdly, a laborious penitence; fourthly, works of piety; fifthly, earnestness in prayer; sixthly, the repose of contemplation; and in the seventh place, the fulness of charity. All these things worketh in us one and the same Spirit, according to that operation which is called *infusion;* thus and so far may the other, which is called *effusion*, be exercised safely, and with pure intention to the praise and glory of our Lord Jesus Christ, who with the Father and the Holy Ghost liveth and reigneth, God, for ever and ever. AMEN.

SERMON XIX.

OF THE NATURE, MANNER, AND PROPERTIES OF THE ANGELICAL LOVE TOWARDS GOD, ACCORDING TO THE SEVERAL ORDERS OF ANGELS.

THE loving Bride still continues to speak. She continues still to celebrate the praises of her Spouse, and to invite new graces from Him, while showing that those she has already received are not unfruitful. For hear what words she adds: *Therefore do the virgins love Thee.* As if she would say: 'Not in vain nor uselessly is it, O my Spouse, that Thy Name is poured forth upon my bosom, nor is Thy Name without effect : for therefore do the virgins love Thee.' Wherefore do they love ? Because of this outpouring of His Name. It is that which has aroused their love for the Spouse; they have taken of that grace, and therefore do they love Him. When the Bride has received that gift of infused grace, they who cannot be far from their mother's side have speedily discerned the fragrance of it, and, being filled with its sweetness, say : *The Love of God is shed abroad in our hearts by the Holy Ghost which is given unto us* (Rom. v. 5). Then the Bride, taking notice with joy of their devotion, says : 'Thou seest, O my Spouse, the fruit of Thy Name poured forth; for because of it the virgins love Thee.' They feel it when poured forth, though they were not capable of receiving it wholly; therefore they have loved Thee. Thus the effusion of that Name renders it capable of being received, and when received it cannot but be lovable; but this applies to virgins only. Those who are of greater capacity rejoice in it as a whole, nor do they need the effusion of it.

2. The angelic race behold in fixed contemplation the profound abyss of the judgments of God. They take supreme pleasure, and experience an unspeakable happiness, in the exalted righteousness of these, and, furthermore, regard it as their glory that it is by their ministry these are carried into execution and are made known, and because of this they deservedly love the Lord Jesus Christ. *Are they not all*, it is said, *ministering spirits, sent forth to minister for them who shall be heirs of salvation?* (Heb. i. 14). I believe that Archangels (for we must, doubtless, consider them as differing in some respect from those who are simply Angels) delight in a wonderful manner, because they are admitted more nearly into the counsels of the Eternal Wisdom, and that the same counsels are also carried out by them with the greatest wisdom and judgment as to time and place. And this is the cause why they, too, love the Lord Jesus. There are other blessed spirits, which are called Virtues; perhaps for this reason, that they are ordained by God to examine with a happy curiosity, and, at the same time, to admire, the secret and permanent causes of miracles and wonders, and that they cause these signs of power to take place in the world when and where they please, having command over all the elements; and on this account they, too, most justly have an ardent love for the Lord of all power, and for Christ who is the Power of God. For it is an employment full of sweetness and grace to contemplate the hidden and uncertain truths of wisdom in Wisdom itself, and it is none the less full of honour and glory that God deigns to make use of their ministry in order that the effects, of which the causes are hidden in His WORD, may be known and admired by men.

3. There are other spirits, who are named Powers, since they delight in beholding and magnifying the Almighty power of our Crucified Lord, which extends everywhere with invincible force; and they receive power to defeat and to put to flight the opposing powers of demons and of men, for the good of those who are to be heirs of salvation.

And have not these, too, a most well-founded cause for loving the Lord Jesus? Above these, again, are Principalities, who, beholding Him from a position more elevated, and discerning clearly that He is the Firstbegotten of all Creation, and the Principle of existence to the whole universe, receive a degree of dignity so great and exalted that it extends over the whole earth; and that from the lofty and sublime eminence on which they are, they are able to change and vary kingdoms and dignities at their will—to dispose of men and of things, making the last to be first, and the first last; putting down the mighty from their seat, and exalting the humble and meek. And this is to them a reason for loving the Lord Christ. But the Dominations also love Him. Wherefore? Because they are led by a certain praise-worthy presumption to trace out and find something, I know not what, that is deeper and more sublime in the Dominion of Christ, which is bounded by no limit, and can be checked by no resistance. They consider that He fills all the world, not only by His power, but also by His Presence—that all things, from the height of heaven to the depth of the abyss, are obedient to His righteous and holy Will, which directs, and that in an admirable order, the revolutions of the seasons, the movements of bodies, and even the impulses and ideas of minds; and that He does all this with a care and vigilance so exact that not one of all these things is able to fail in performing its functions even by (as the phrase is) one point or one iota, and yet with a facility so great that He who governs all feels no inquietude or anxiety whatever. These Angels, then, seeing that the Lord of Sabaoth judges all things with a tranquillity so complete, are, as it were, transported out of themselves, in their trance of sweet and intense contemplation, and rapt into that vast ocean (so to speak) of the Divine splendour; they come to themselves again in a calm so wonderful and pervading, and in which they enjoy so great peace and security, that in their quiescence all the other spirits seem to serve and to defend them, as if, by a singular prerogative, they were, in truth, Dominations.

4. Upon the Thrones God is seated. And I suppose that this order of spirits have a cause more just, and reason more abundant, for loving, than have all the others who have been already mentioned. For even if you enter the palace of some human king, do you not find his royal seat in a place of high honour—among the benches, chairs, and seats of various kinds with which it is filled? Nor is it necessary to inquire where the king is accustomed to sit, since his royal seat or throne presents itself at once to the eye, and is more lofty and more richly adorned than others. So, also, are we to understand that those spirits whom the Divine Majesty, by a singular and astonishing favour, has deigned to select for the Throne on which to sit, surpass all others in beauty and magnificence. To be seated (*sessio*) signifies authority; and I think that He, who in heaven and in earth is our only Master and Teacher, Christ the Wisdom of God, though He indeed reaches everywhere because of His perfect purity,

enlightens particularly and principally, by His presence, those blessed spirits as being His throne, and that from thence, as from a solemn *auditorium*, He teaches knowledge to angels and to men. Thence it is that the *Angels* derive their knowledge of the Divine judgments, and the *Archangels* theirs of the Divine counsels; there the *Virtues* hear when and where they are to work signs, and of what nature these are to be. There, in short, all the Angels, whether *Powers*, or *Principalities*, or *Dominations*, learn what are the duties of the offices they bear, and what are their honours and dignities; and especially how (which is the caution given to all) they should use the power bestowed upon them without abusing it, either by acting according to their own will, or for the sake of their own glory.

5. As for those heavenly bands which are called Cherubin, I am inclined to think, following even the signification of the word, that they have nothing which they derive either from, or by means of, the Thrones, since it is permitted them to drink to the full from the Fountain itself, the Lord Jesus, who deigns Himself, and by Himself, to introduce them into all the fulness of truth, and to reveal to them abundantly all the treasures of wisdom and knowledge which are hidden in Him. Neither do those who are called Seraphin [require to learn from the Thrones], since God, who is Himself Love, has so drawn them to, and absorbed them in, Him, and raised them to the same ardour of holy affection, that they appear to be of one Spirit with Him, just as the fire which enkindles air, and impresses upon it heat and colour like its own, so that it is manifestly not merely ignited, but itself become fire. They love, then, above all things, to contemplate in God, the former, that knowledge which is in Him without measure or limit; the latter, the love which is never absent from Him. It is from this that they have obtained names which express that which in each is pre-eminent. For the word Cherubin signifies *fulness of knowledge;* and Seraphin, *inflaming* or *inflamed*.

6. God is, then, loved by the Angels because of the supreme righteousness of His judgments; by the Archangels because of the supreme wisdom of His purposes; by the Virtues on account of the most blessed showing forth of miracles and wonders by which He deigns to draw the unbelieving to faith; but by the Powers on account of that power, equally just and prevailing, by which He is wont to defeat the cruelty of the wicked, and to defend the good against them; by the Principalities on account of that eternal and primordial power which bestows the principle of existence, and existence itself, upon every creature, whether of higher rank or lower, spiritual and corporeal, extending with prevailing strength from one extremity of the universe to the other; by the Dominations, also, because of the calm and untroubled Will which, though it everywhere dominates with irresistible strength, disposes all things with sweetness according to the goodness belonging to its nature, and with a tranquillity which nothing can disturb. He is loved also by the Thrones because of the benevolence of His supreme Wisdom, which communicates itself without

envy, and of the unction of grace, which teaches all things freely. Furthermore, He is loved by the Cherubin because He is God, the Lord of all knowledge, and as He knows what each has need of for salvation, so He distributes His gifts with judgment and providence, according to the necessity of the individual, to those who worthily make request for them; and, lastly, by the Seraphin, inasmuch as He is Himself Love, that He hateth nothing that He has made, and wills that all men should come to the knowledge of the Truth and be saved.

7. All these spirits, then, love God according to the degree of knowledge they have of Him. But there are souls which are childlike (*adolescentulæ* = young girls), which, as they know less, so they comprehend less, and are not adequate to these sublime heights of attainment; and these are little children in Christ, to be nourished with milk and with oil. These it is who have need to draw from the bosom of the Spouse the nourishment for their love. The Spouse hath oil poured forth; and from the fragrance which it exhales they are aroused to taste and know how gracious the Lord is. And when she sees and feels their ardent love she turns to her Lord, and saith: *Thy Name is as oil poured forth, therefore have young maidens loved Thee beyond measure* (*nimis*, Vulg.). What is 'beyond measure'? Greatly, vehemently, ardently. Or, rather, this spiritual discourse is addressed indirectly to you who have but lately come hither; and it reproves that indiscreet fervour and immoderate zeal which you follow with too great obstinacy, and which we have so frequently endeavoured to repress. You are not willing to be contented with the common life. The appointed fasts, the solemn vigils, the ordinary Rule, the measure fixed as to food and to dress, in which we all share, does not suffice for you. You prefer your own private rules to those which are common to all. You who have once entrusted to me the care of your souls, why do you again interfere with it? See, then, you have for a guide not me, but your own will once more, which, as you know, has so often caused you to offend against God.[1] It is that which teaches you not to show any forbearance towards your nature, not to listen to reason, not to yield to the advice or example of your seniors, not to obey me. Do you not know that *obedience is better than sacrifice* (1 Sam. xv. 22)? Have you not read in your Rule, that whatsoever is done without the will or consent of your spiritual father, shall be imputed to vainglory, and not as deserving any recompense (Rule of S. Benedict, c. 49). Have you not read in the Gospel that Jesus, when a Boy, left to holy youth a pattern how to obey? For when He had remained in Jerusalem, though He had said that it behoved Him to be about His Father's business, yet as His parents did not acquiesce in His words He did not disdain to follow them to Nazareth: the Master to follow His disciples, the Son of God to follow human beings, the Divine Word and Wisdom to follow a carpenter and his wife! What does the sacred history even add? *And He was subject unto them* (Luke ii. 43-51). How long will ye be wise

---

[1] See Sermon XXXIII., *n.* 1, and 'Sermon on the Death of Humbert,' *n.* 1.

in your own eyes? God entrusts Himself and submits Himself to mortal men, and will you still walk in your own ways? You had received a good intention, but you do not carry it out wisely. I fear lest, instead of a good spirit, you have harboured one who, under an appearance of good, will overthrow you, and that you who have begun in the Spirit, will complete your course in the flesh. Do you not know that Satan himself is often transformed into an angel of light (2 Cor. xi. 14)? God is Wisdom, and He desires to be loved, not only to our own delight, but also wisely. Wherefore the Apostle says: *Yours is a reasonable service* (Rom. xii. 1). Otherwise, if you neglect knowledge, the spirit of error will with great ease lead you astray by means of your zeal; nor has our cunning enemy any device more effectual in eliminating love from the heart than that of inducing us, if he can, to act without due prudence and caution. Wherefore I intend to give you certain rules, which it is necessary for those who love God to observe. But as it is time for me to bring my sermon to a close, I will endeavour to explain them to you to-morrow, if God shall continue to me life and the leisure to address you. For then we shall assemble in new vigour after the repose of the night, and (which is the chief thing) shall be rendered more willing and ardent by the preceding prayers to hear the discourse respecting love; in dependence on the grace of our Lord Jesus Christ, to whom be honour and glory for ever and ever. AMEN.

SERMON XX.

OF THE THREE WAYS IN WHICH WE LOVE GOD.

LET this sermon take for a beginning the words of a master in the spiritual life: *If anyone love not the Lord Jesus Christ, let him be Anathema* (1 Cor. xvi 22). Without doubt He is altogether to be loved by whom I have my very existence, my life, and my reason; and I cannot be ungrateful without being unworthy of all these. He is plainly worthy of death who refuses to live for Thee, O Lord Jesus; and he is, in fact, dead, as he who does not devote his reason to Thy service is unreasonable, and he who cares to be anything except for Thee is good for nothing, and is nothing. Indeed, what is man, except that Thou hast taken knowledge of him (Ps. cxliv. 3)? It is for Thine own self, O my God, that Thou hast created all things; and he who desires to exist for himself, and not for Thee, begins to be as nothing among all things that are. What is it that the wise man says: *Fear God, and keep His commandments: for this is the whole [duty of] man* (Eccles. xii. 13). If, then, this is the whole man, without this man is nothing. Incline towards Thyself, O my God, what Thou hast deigned to enable me to be, humble as it is; take wholly to Thyself, I entreat, the brief remainder of the years which pertain to my poor life; and for all the years which I have lost, because I have occupied them in losing myself, despise not, I entreat, an humble and contrite heart. My days have declined as a shadow, they have perished without fruit. It is impossible for me to recall them; make me, in Thy goodness, at least to meditate upon them before Thee in the bitterness of my soul. Thou seest that wisdom is the whole desire and purpose of my heart: if there were any in me it is in Thy service I would employ it. But, O God, Thou knowest my simpleness; unless it be perhaps a beginning of wisdom to recognise my ignorance; and, indeed, this is by Thy gift. Augment it in me, I pray; I shall not be ungrateful for the least of Thy gifts, but shall strive to supply that which is lacking in me. It is, then, for these Thy benefits that I love Thee with all my feeble powers.

2. But there is a fact which moves, and excites, and fires me much more than this. Above all things, it is the cup which Thou didst drink, O Jesu, merciful and kind, the great task of our redemption undertaken by Thee, which is a stronger motive than any other for love to Thee. It is this which easily draws to itself all the love I have to give, which attracts my affection more sweetly, which requires it more justly, which retains it by closer ties and a more vehement force. To this end the Saviour endured many and great things, nor in the making of the whole world did its Creator take upon Himself a task so laborious. For in that earlier work *He spake, and it was done: He commanded, and it stood fast* (Ps. xxxiii. 9). But in the later one He had to bear with men who contradicted His words, met His actions with ill-natured criticism, insulted His sufferings and even revived His Death. Behold, then, how He loved us! Add to this that He loved us thus of His free gift, not to make return for any love which we had for Him. *For who hath first given to Him, and it shall be recompensed unto him again* (Rom. xi. 35)? And St. John Evangelist says expressly: *Not that we loved God, but that He* [previously] *loved us* (2 John iv. 10). Indeed, He loved us while as yet we did not exist; He did even more, for He loved us when we were opposed to, and were resisting, Him, as St. Paul testifies: *When we were enemies, we were reconciled to God by the death of His Son* (Rom. v. 10). In other words, if He had not loved us when enemies, He would not now have us for friends; just as, if He had not loved those who did not as yet exist, they would not be existing now for Him to love.

3. In the next place, His love is tender, wise, and strong. I say that it is tender, since He has taken upon Him our flesh; wise, since He has held Himself free of all sin; and strong, since it reached to the point of enduring death. For those whom He visited in the flesh yet He loved not in the flesh, but in the foreseeing wisdom of the Spirit. For the Lord Christ is a Spirit who hath made Himself visible to us[1] (Lam. iv. 10), being moved towards us with a zeal of God, not

---

[1] The reading of the Vulgate here is very remarkable: '*Spiritus oris nostri Christus Dominus captus est.*'—ED.

of man, and with a love wiser assuredly than the first Adam felt for his Eve. Therefore those whom He sought out in the flesh He loved in the spirit, and redeemed in His power and courage. It is a thing full of ineffable sweetness to behold the Creator of man as a Man. But while by His wisdom He separated [human] nature from sin, by His power He banished death from [that] nature. In taking flesh He condescended to me; in separating it from all stain of sin He consulted His own dignity; in submitting to death He made satisfaction to His Father, and thus showed Himself at once the kindest of Friends, a prudent Counsellor, and a powerful Helper. In Him with full confidence I trust, who was willing to save me, who knew the means, who had the power to carry them out. The soul whom He sought out, whom He also called by His grace, will He cast out when it comes to Him? But I do not fear that any violence or fraud will have the power to pluck me out of His Hand; for in vanquishing death He vanquished all enemies, and in deluding the old Serpent, the seducer of the world, by an artifice more holy than that he had employed, He was at once wiser than the one and more powerful than the other. He took upon Him human flesh in truth, but only the likeness of sin; in the former giving sweet consolation to weak and ailing man, and in the latter prudently concealing from the devil the snare by which he was deceived. Furthermore, that He might reconcile us with His Father, He bravely underwent death and overcame it, pouring forth His Blood as the price of our Redemption. If, then, that Sovereign Majesty had not tenderly loved me, He would not have sought for me in my prison. But to this affection He joined wisdom to circumvent our tyrant, and patience to placate the just wrath of God His Father. These are the ways of loving which I promised to give you, but I have set them before you first as shown forth in Christ, that you might hold them in greater esteem.

4. Learn, O Christian, from the example of Christ the manner in which you ought to love Christ. Learn to love Him tenderly, to love Him wisely, to love Him with a mighty love. Tenderly, that you be not enticed away from Him; wisely, that you be not deceived and so drawn away; and strongly, that you be not separated from Him by any force. Delight yourself in Christ, who is Wisdom, beyond all else, in order that worldly glory or fleshly pleasures may not withdraw you from Him; and let Christ, who is the Truth, enlighten you, so that you may not be led away by the spirit of falsehood and error. That you may not be overcome by adversities, let Christ, who is the Power of God, strengthen you. Let charity render your zeal ardent, wisdom rule and direct it; let constancy make it enduring. Let it be free from lukewarmness, not timid, nor wanting in discretion. Are not those the three things prescribed to thee in the Law, when God said: *Thou shalt love the Lord thy God with all thy heart, with all thy soul, and with all thy strength* (Deut. vi. 5)? It seems to me, if no other sense occurs to you better to give to that threefold distinction, that the love of the heart answers to the earnestness of affection;

the love of the soul to the purpose or judgment of the reason; and love with the strength to the constancy and vigour of the mind. Love, then, the Lord thy God with the entire and full affection of the heart; love Him with all the vigilance and all the foresight of the reason; love Him with the full strength and vigour of the soul, so that for His love you would not fear even to die; as it is written in a later verse of this Canticle: *Love is strong as death, jealousy as hard as hell* (Cant. viii. 6, Vulg. and Douay). Let the Lord Jesus be to your heart sweet and pleasant, so as to destroy the false attractiveness of the carnal life; let His sweetness overcome the other, as one nail drives out another. To your understanding and your reason let Him be a wise leader and a guiding light, not only to enable you to avoid the snares of heretical fraud, and to preserve the purity of your faith from their cunning devices, but also to make you cautious to avoid excessive or indiscreet vehemence in your conduct. Let your love be intrepid and constant, neither yielding to fear nor exhausted by sufferings. Finally, let us love tenderly, wisely, ardently, knowing that the love of the heart, which we call tender, is indeed sweet, but easily led astray[1]—at least, if it be not accompanied by the love of the soul; while the latter, again, though it be rational, yet is apt to be weak, unless courage and ardour go with it to strengthen it.

5. And recognise in clear examples that what I say is true. When the disciples had heard with dismay their Master, shortly before His Ascension, speaking of His departure from them, they heard from Him: *If ye loved me, ye would rejoice, because I said I go unto the Father* (John xiv. 28). What then? Did they not love Him for whose departure they were grieving? In a certain sense they loved Him, and yet they did not really love Him. That is, they loved Him tenderly, but not wisely; they loved in a carnal way, not reasonably; finally, they loved with all their heart, but not with all their soul. Their love was against the interests of their salvation; wherefore He said to them also, *It is expedient for you that I go away* (John xvi. 7), blaming their deficiency in wisdom, not in affection. When, again, He was speaking of His coming death, Peter, as you remember, who loved Him, and desired to retain Him, replied, endeavouring to hinder Him; to whom He made answer, so reproving him as to show that it was his want of prudence only that He blamed. For what is the force of the words following, *Thou savourest not the things which be of God* (Mark viii. 33), but, Thou lovest not wisely, as following the impulse of human affection against the design of God? And He even called him Satan, inasmuch as in seeking to hinder the Saviour from dying he was an adversary of salvation, though unknowingly. And, therefore, having been thus corrected, he no longer opposed himself to the Saviour's death when the sad prophecy of it was again made by Him, but declared that he would die with Him. But that promise He did

---

[1] *Seducibilem;* a word which does not appear to occur elsewhere, even in Low Latin: it is not to be found in Forcellini's Lexicon, or Du Cange's Glossary, I. q. *seductilis.* See 'Confessions of St. Augustine,' Bk. ii., c. 3.—ED.

not fulfil, because he had not yet attained to the third degree of love, which consists in loving God with all our strength. He had learned to love [God] with all his soul, but he was still weak; he knew well what he ought to do, but was without the help which would enable him to perform it; he was not ignorant of the mystery [of salvation] but he shrank from martyrdom. That love was plainly not strong as death, which yielded to [the fear of] death; but afterwards it became so, when being, according to the promise of Jesus Christ, endued with power from on high, he began to love with courage so great that, having been forbidden in the council of the Jews to preach the adorable Name of Jesus, he replied firmly to those who forbade him, *We ought to obey God rather than men* (Acts v. 29). Then, indeed, he loved God at length with all his power, since he did not spare his own life for that love. For *greater love hath no man than this, that a man lay down his life for his friends* (John xv. 13); and he laid down his life at that time, though he did not actually give it up. To be not drawn away by flattery, nor seduced by artifices, nor violently removed from it by injuries and outrages, that is to love God with all the mind, with all the soul, and with all the strength.

6. And notice, that that love of the heart is in a manner carnal, with which the heart of man is affected towards Christ according to the flesh, and towards the actions which He did or commanded while in the flesh. A person who is filled with that love is easily touched with any discourse which dwells on that subject. There is nothing he listens to more willingly, reads more attentively, recalls oftener to memory, meditates upon with greater enjoyment. His sacrifices of prayer receive from it a new perfection, and resemble, as it were, victims as fat as they are beautiful. As often as he prays, the image of the GOD MAN arises before him, either in His Birth or His Infancy, either in His teaching or His Death, His Resurrection, or His Ascension; and all these, or similar images, necessarily animate the soul to the love of holiness, drive away fleshly vices, put to flight temptations, and calm desires. I consider that a principal cause why God, who is invisible, willed to render Himself visible in the Flesh, and to dwell as a Man among men, was to draw, in the first place, to the salutary love of His sacred Flesh all the affections of carnal men who were unable to love otherwise than in a carnal manner, and so by degrees to draw them to a pure and spiritual affection. Were not those, for instance, who said to Jesus, *Behold, we have left all and followed Thee* (Matt. xix. 27), still in this [first] degree of love? They had left all things for the sole love of the bodily Presence of Jesus, so that they were not able even to listen with equanimity to the announcement of His salutary Passion and Death as near at hand, and even afterwards it touched them with a profound sadness to look up to[1] the glory of His Ascension. For this reason it was that He said to them: *Because I have said these things unto you, sorrow hath filled your heart* (John xvi. 6). Thus in

---

[1] *Suspicere.* Another reading is *suscipere.*

the meantime He had drawn them away, and kept them, from every carnal affection by the grace of His personal Presence in the Flesh.

7. But He afterwards pointed out to them a higher degree of love, when He said: *It is the Spirit that quickeneth, the flesh profiteth nothing* (John vi. 64). I think that he who said, *Though we have known Christ after the Flesh, yet now henceforth know we Him no more* (2 Cor. v. 16), and perhaps the Prophet also, notwithstanding [that he lived before Christ], when he said, *The Spirit before our face was Christ the Lord*,[1] stood upon this higher ground; for that which he adds, *Under Thy shadow shall we live among the Gentiles*, it seems that he speaks in the name of those who are beginning to rest at least in the shadow, since they do not feel themselves to be capable of sustaining the heat of the sun; and being nourished with the sweetness of the flesh, are not as yet capable of perceiving the things which are of the Spirit of God. By the shadow of Christ I suppose to be meant His Flesh, with which Mary was overshadowed[2] (Luke i. 35), so that it was to her as a veil to temper the heat and light of the Spirit. Let him be consoled then, with the devotion of the flesh who has not as yet the life-giving Spirit, or, at least, who has Him not in the manner of those who say: *The Spirit before our face was Christ the Lord*, and, *Though we have known Christ after the Flesh, yet now henceforth know we Him no more.* For it is assuredly not without the Spirit that Christ is loved, even in the Flesh, though He be not loved in His fulness [thus]. And of this devotion the measure is this, that the sweetness of it occupies the whole heart; draws it entirely to itself from all love of the flesh or of carnal things, and frees it from their temptations; this it is to love with all the heart. Otherwise, if I prefer to the Flesh of my Lord any ties of relationship, or any pleasure that I may receive—I mean in such a way as to be able to perform fewer of those good works which He has taught me by word and by example while He abode in the Flesh—does it not plainly appear that I do not love Him with all my heart, since it is divided, and I seem to have given a part to the love of Him, and a part to the love of myself? For He Himself says: *He that loveth father or mother more than Me is not worthy of Me; and he that loveth son or daughter more than Me is not worthy of Me* (Matt. x. 37). Therefore, to express it briefly, to love Jesus with the whole heart is to prefer the love of His most sacred Flesh to all things which engage our affections or our vanity, either in our own self, or that of another; in which I equally comprehend the glory of the world also, because it is essentially carnal; and those who delight in it are, without doubt, carnally minded.

8. But yet such devotion towards the Flesh of Christ is a gift of the Holy Spirit, and a great gift; yet I must call such love carnal, at least in comparison with that other affection, which has regard, not so much to the Word as Flesh, as to the Word as Wisdom, as

---

[1] Lam. iv. 20, but apparently quoted from memory and inexactly.—ED.
[2] See Sermon XXXI., *n.* 9.

Righteousness, as Truth, as Holiness, Goodness, Virtue, and all other Perfections of whatever kind. For Christ is all these, inasmuch as by God *He is made unto us wisdom, and righteousness, and sanctification, and redemption* (1 Cor. i. 30). Does it appear to you that two persons have equal and similar love towards Christ, of whom the one sympathizes indeed piously with His sufferings, is moved to a lively sorrow by them, and easily softened by the memory of all that He endured: who feeds upon the sweetness of that devotion, and is strengthened thereby to all salutary, honourable, and pious actions; while the other, being always fired by a zeal for righteousness, having everywhere an ardent passion for truth, and earnestly desiring wisdom, prefers above all things sanctity of life, and a perfectly disciplined character; who is ashamed of ostentation, abhors detraction, knows not what it is to be envious, detests pride, and not only avoids, but dislikes and despises every kind of worldly glory; who vehemently hates and perseveres in destroying in himself every impurity of the heart and of the flesh; and lastly, who rejects, as if it were naturally, all that is evil, and embraces all that is good? If you compare these two types of affection, does it not appear to you that the second is plainly the superior? and that in comparison with it the former is in a manner carnal?

9. Yet that love, by which a carnal life is shut out, and the world is contemned and overcome, is good, though it be carnal. In that type of affection it becomes *rational* as it makes progress, and it is perfected when it becomes *spiritual*. It is called rational when in all the sentiments cherished regarding Christ the proportion of the faith (*ratio fidei*) is so carefully observed that no deviation is made from the pure doctrine of the Church by any apparent similarity to truth, nor by any snare of heretical or diabolical deception. As also in our personal conduct this caution must be observed, that the bounds of discretion be not exceeded through the influence of superstition, or of levity, or of the zeal of an unregulated disposition. And this it is to love God with all the soul, as I have already said. If to this be added force so great, and an assistance so powerful, as that of the Holy Spirit, so that neither troubles nor sufferings, however violent, nor even the fear of death, can ever cause the desertion of righteousness, then God is loved with all the strength, and that is *spiritual* love. And I think this name peculiarly suitable to such love, because of the fulness of the Spirit which so particularly distinguishes it. But I think that these observations may suffice with regard to that saying of the Bride: *Therefore have the virgins loved Thee beyond measure.* May our Lord Jesus Christ, who is our Guardian, deign to open to us the treasures of His mercy, that we may be able to expound the words which follow. Who liveth and reigneth with the Father, in the Unity of the Holy Spirit, one God for ever and ever. AMEN.

SERMON XXI.

IN WHAT MANNER THE BRIDE, THAT IS, THE CHURCH, ASKS THAT SHE MAY BE DRAWN TO FOLLOW AFTER HER SPOUSE, WHO IS CHRIST.

DRAW me after Thee: we will run in the odour of Thy perfumes.[1] What? is it needful that the Bride should be drawn to follow, and to follow after such a Spouse, as if she followed Him unwillingly, and not of her own impulse and wish? But not everyone who is caused by force to move is thus moved against his will. For example, one who is infirm or weak, and is not able to walk alone, is not otherwise than glad to be drawn to the bath or to the table, though a criminal doubtless is reluctant to be brought to the judgment or to the place of punishment. Now, she who here speaks desires and entreats to be drawn; but she would not do this if she were able to follow her beloved by her own strength, according to her wish. But wherefore is she unable? Must we allow that the Spouse, too, is weak and infirm? If it were one of her maidens who declared herself so, and entreated to be helped forward, we should in nowise wonder. But of the Spouse, who seemed to be able even to help others forward, so strong and perfect was she; who is there who does not find it strange, that she needs to be drawn forward herself, as if she were weak or languishing? Of what soul shall we feel any confidence, that it is strong and healthful, if we shall consent for her to be called weak, who for her singular perfection, and more excellent virtue, is named the Spouse of the Lord? Is it the Church, perhaps, who spake thus, when she beheld her Beloved ascending up on high, and earnestly desired to follow Him, and be assumed with Him into glory? For, to whatever degree of perfection a soul may have attained, as long as it groans under the body of this death, and is held captive in the prison of this evil world, as long as it is constrained by necessities, tortured by faults and wrong doings, it arises of necessity more slowly and sluggishly than it would desire to the contemplation of heavenly things, nor is it altogether free to follow the Bridegroom [who is the Lamb, Rev. xiv. 4] whithersoever He goeth. It was this which drew that lamentable cry from him who said: *O miserable man that I am, who shall deliver me from the body of this death?* (Rom. vii. 24). It was this which inspired the suppliant entreaty: *Bring my soul out*

---

[1] Such is the reading of the old MSS., and of the first editions, instead of 'to the odour' of Thy perfumes, as we have elsewhere observed. Thus we run 'aroused by that odour' (*nn.* 4, 9, 11) and not in the confidence of our own merits.' And again a little further on: 'As for Thee, O my Spouse, Thou wilt run in the unction itself, but I in the fragrance which it exhales. Thou in the fulness of the perfume: but I in its fragrance' (*n.* 11).

of prison (Ps. cxlii. 7). And so also the Bride says, and says as it were with a groan, *Draw me, and I will run after Thee :* because the corruptible body presseth down the soul, and the earthly tabernacle weigheth down the mind, that museth upon many things (Wisd. ix. 15). Or perhaps she speaks thus in her desire to depart and be with Christ; especially when she sees those souls, on account of which it seemed needful that she should remain in the flesh, making good progress, already having love for the Bridegroom, and remaining in the safe refuge of charity. This, indeed, she had referred to before: *Wherefore the maidens have loved Thee exceedingly.* Now, it seems as if she would say : 'Lo the maidens have loved Thee, and by that love are firmly united to Thee ; they have no need of me any longer ; there is no reason for my delaying still in this life; therefore, *Draw me, and I will run after Thee.*

2. This I should have considered to be her thought, if she had said, 'Draw me *to Thee.*' But as she says, '*after Thee,*' that phrase seems to me rather to make request that she might have grace to follow the footsteps of His life, to be able to emulate His virtue, to hold fast, and by, His rule of life, to attain the perfection of His character. In these especially [the soul] has the greatest need of assistance, to be enabled to deny herself, to take up her cross, and thus to follow after Christ. In order to attain this, the Bride has great need to be drawn onward ; and by none other than He who says : *Without Me ye can do nothing* (John xv. 5). 'I know well,' she says, 'that I am not able to reach Thee, except by following after Thee ; nor can I follow after Thee, except I am helped by Thee to do so : and, therefore, I pray that Thou wouldest draw me after Thee.' In truth, *Blessed is the man whose help is from Thee : in his heart he hath set steps in the valley of tears* (Ps. lxxxiv. 5) in order one day to reach Thee upon the mountains of everlasting joy. How few there are, O Lord Jesus, who are willing to follow after Thee ! and yet there is no one who does not wish to reach Thy Presence, since it is known to all that *at Thy Right Hand there are pleasures for evermore* (Ps. xvi. 11). On that account, all desire to obtain happiness from Thee, but they have not a similar desire to imitate Thee ; they wish to reign with Thee, but not to suffer with Thee. Such was he who said : *Let me die the death of the righteous, and let my last end be like his* (Num. xxiii. 10) ; he desired that the closing of his life might be similar to that of the righteous, but not that its beginnings might be so. Even carnal men desire for themselves the death of men who are spiritual, and yet shudder at the idea of leading their life. For they know that precious in the sight of the Lord is the death of His saints ; since, *when He giveth to His beloved sleep, lo ! the heritage of the Lord* (Ps. cxxvii. 2, 3), and because *Blessed are the dead which die in the Lord* (Rev. xiv. 13) ; while, on the contrary, according to the declaration of the prophet, *The death of the wicked is very evil* (Ps. xxxiii. 22, Vulg. and Douay). They do not care to seek Him, whom they yet desire to find ; they wish to reach

Him, but to do so without following Him. Not such were they, of whom He said: *Ye are they which have continued with Me in My temptations* (Luke xxii. 28). Blessed are they who were found worthy to receive such a testimony from Thee, O good Jesus! They did in truth come after Thee, both with their feet, and in the affections of their hearts. Thou hast made known to them the ways of life, in calling them after Thee, who art the Way, and the Life; Thou sayest unto them, *Follow Me, I will make you fishers of men* (Matt. iv. 19); and again, *If any man serve Me, let him follow me: and where I am, there shall also My servant be* (John xii. 26). Therefore they congratulated themselves, saying: *Behold, we have forsaken all and followed Thee* (Matt. xix. 27).

3. It is thus, then, that Thy Beloved, leaving all things for Thy sake, desires always to follow after Thee, to walk closely in Thy footsteps always, and to follow Thee whithersoever Thou goest, knowing that Thy ways are ways of blessedness, and all Thy paths are peace, and that therefore he who followeth Thee walks not in darkness. If she prays that she may be drawn onward, it is because Thy righteousness is as the mountains of God, and that in her own strength she is not able to attain unto it. She prays, as she is wont, that she may be drawn onward, because no man can come to Thee unless Thy Father shall have drawn him (John vi. 44); and those whom The Father draweth, Thou dost draw also; for the works which the Father doeth, those also doeth the Son likewise. But the suppliant is more familiar with the Son, and makes this request to be drawn of Him, as of her own Bridegroom,[1] whom the Father hath sent to be her Leader and her Guide, to go before her in the way of righteousness, to prepare for her the path of virtues, to train her up even as His own self, to teach her the way of wisdom, to bestow upon her the law of life and of discipline; and to bring her to such perfection that He may justly take pleasure in her beauty.

4. *Draw me after Thee: we will run in the fragrance of Thy perfumes.* I have need to be drawn for this reason, because the fire of Thy love has grown somewhat cold in us; nor are we, on account of that coldness, able to run as we did yesterday and in former days. But we shall run when Thou shalt have restored to us the joy of Thy salvation, when the warmth of grace shall have returned to us, when the Sun of Righteousness shall have warmed us anew, and the cloud of temptation shall have passed away, which at this moment hides Him from us; and at the gentle breath of a softer breeze, the perfumes have begun to dissolve and flow, and give forth their fragrance. Then, and in that fragrance, shall we run [on the way of righteousness]. We shall run, I say, when the perfumes are breathed upon us, for the torpor in which we now are shall be dissipated, and devotion shall be reawakened in us, so that we shall have no need to be drawn on, but under the influence of that sweet fragrance shall advance of our own accord. But now, and until that happy change,

[1] Some MSS. add 'Who hath pleasure in her beauty.'

draw me, and I will run after Thee. Do you perceive that he who walks in the Spirit does not remain always in one state, nor make progress always with the same ease, because the way of man, as the Scripture declares, is not in his own power; but that he forgets the things which are behind, and presses forward to those which are before, now with more energy, and now with less, according as the Holy Spirit, who is the Dispenser of all graces, bestows them upon him with greater or less liberality? I believe that if you well examine your own selves, you will find what I have said confirmed by your own inward experience.

5. When, therefore, you feel yourself affected with torpor, luke warmness, and weariness, do not on that account give way to unbelief, nor desist from spiritual exercises, but seek the Hand of Him who is able to help, and, after the example of the Bride, entreat that you may be drawn after Him, until you are reawakened and reanimated by grace, and thus you become more cheerful and vigorous; you are enabled to run [the race that is set before you], and you say, *I have run the way of Thy Commandments, since Thou hast set my heart at liberty* (Ps. cxix. 32). But though you should rejoice in the grace of God, as long as it is present, do not, nevertheless, count upon that gift as if you held it by a right of inheritance, and be as secure of it as if you could not possibly lose it, lest suddenly God should draw back His Hand and withdraw His grace, and you should fall into excessive discouragement and sorrow. Do not ever say in your abundance, *I shall never be moved* (Ps. xxx. 6), for fear lest you should also be obliged to make use with grief of the words which follow: *Thou didst hide Thy Face, and I was troubled.* You will be cured rather, if you are wise, by following the counsel of the Wise—to be not unmindful of good things in the day of evil, nor of evil things in the day of good (Ecclus. xi. 25).

6. Do not, then, in your day of strength, suffer yourself to feel secure, but lift up your voice towards God with the prophet, and say: *Forsake me not when my strength faileth me* (Ps. lxxi. 9). On the other hand, be consoled in time of temptation, and say with the Bride: *Draw me, and I will run after Thee: we will run in the fragrance of Thy perfumes.* Thus hope will not desert you in the evil day, nor Providence be wanting to you in the day of prosperity; you will retain, among the changeableness of earthly conditions, [which are] at one time prosperous, at another adverse, as it were an image of eternity; I mean to say that you will maintain this equableness of spirit, and a constancy not to be shaken by any event; you will at all times bless God, and will thus make good for yourself a position, so to speak, of immovable stability among the changing events and certain disappointments of this inconstant world, until you shall begin to be renewed, and to take upon you once more that ancient and glorious likeness of God, who is eternal, *with whom is no changeableness, neither shadow of turning* (James i. 17). Thus as He is so shalt thou be, even in this world; neither cast down in adversity nor in prosperity

made careless. It is in this, I say, that man, that creature so noble, made in the image and likeness of God who created him, indicates that he is even now on the point of regaining the dignity of his ancient honour, when he regards it as unworthy of him to be conformed to this perishing world; and chooses rather, according to the precept of St. Paul, to be transformed by the renewing of his mind (Rom. xii. 2) into that likeness in which he knows that he was first created. And in this way he even compels the things of this world, which were, in fact, created on his account, to conform themselves to him, as it is becoming they should do; and thus all things begin to work together for good, and to regain, as it were, the form which is theirs, and natural to them, rejecting that [present one] which is degraded, and recognising their Lord, for whose service they were created.

7. On this account I think that the saying which the Only Begotten Son of God uttered of Himself, that He, if He were lifted up from the earth would draw all things unto Him (John xii. 32), may be applied also to all His brethren—that is, to those whom the Father has foreknown and predestinated to be conformed to the image of His Son, that He might be the Firstborn among many brethren. I, then, even I, my brethren, am able boldly to say, 'If I be lifted up from the earth, I will draw all things unto me.' Nor is it a rash thing of me to make use of the words of Him of whom I put on the likeness. If it be thus, then the rich of this world ought not to think that the brethren of Christ, because they hear Christ saying, *Blessed are the poor in spirit, for theirs is the kingdom of heaven* (Matt. v. 3), possess heavenly things alone, because those only seem to be mentioned in the promise. They possess earthly things also; and having indeed nothing, yet possess all things. They do not beg for them, as those who are poor and miserable, but possess them as masters; and are so much the more the masters of them as they are less desirous to obtain them. For the whole world is a store of riches to the man who has faith. Evidently the whole world; for whether he be in prosperity or in adversity, all things serve him equally, and work together for his good.

8. Thus, then, the man who is avaricious hungers for the things of this world like a beggar, while he who has faith despises them as their lord. The one, while he possesses them, is their servant; the other, while despising them, uses them for good. Ask some one of those who pant with an insatiable heart for earthly riches, what is his opinion of those who sold all their goods and gave to the poor, and whether they did wisely or no. Doubtless he will reply that they did wisely. Ask him again why he does not himself practise what he approves in others. 'I cannot,' he will reply. Wherefore? Plainly because avarice is the mistress of his heart, and will not permit him; because he is not free; because the things which he seems to possess are not his; nor is he himself his own master. If they are truly yours, try to put them to profitable use; and in exchange for earthly possessions obtain heavenly. If you are not able to do this, then confess that

you are not the master but the servant of your money—only the keeper of it, not the possessor. In short, you suit yourself to your purse as a slave to his mistress; and just as such an one is obliged of necessity to be glad or to be sorrowful according to the mood of his mistress, so you: when your pouch is swelling with gain, your spirits rise; and they fall similarly when it shrinks. For you are stricken with sorrow when that is exhausted, and when it is replenished are filled with joy, or, rather, puffed up with pride. Such is the man who is avaricious. But as for us, let us strive to imitate the freedom and the constancy of the Bride, who, being well instructed in all things, and preserving in her heart the teaching of Wisdom, knows how to endure both abundance and penury. When she entreats that she may be drawn onward, she shows that what she needs is, not money, but spiritual strength; and, on the other hand, when she consoles herself with the hope of the return of grace, she proves that even in privations she holds fast her faith.

9. She says then: *Draw me, we will run after Thee: we will run in the fragrance of Thy perfumes.* And what wonder is it that she needs to be drawn onward when she is following the footsteps of a giant? Who is able to come up with Him who strides upon the mountains, who leaps over the hills? *His Word,* saith the Psalmist, *runneth very swiftly* (Ps. cxlvii. 15). She is not capable of keeping pace with, or of rivalling the speed of, one who *rejoiceth as a giant to run His course* (Ps. xix. 5); that is not possible to her powers, and therefore it is that she prays to be drawn onward. 'I am weary,' she says; 'I am sinking from fatigue; desert me not, but *draw me after Thee,* that I may not begin to wander after other companions, or to run hither and thither, as in uncertainty. *Draw me after Thee;* for it were better for me that Thou shouldest keep me close to Thee, even by the use of a measure of violence, by making me afraid with Thy threatenings, or causing me to smart with chastisements, than that Thou shouldest spare me in my evil and slothful security, and leave me to myself. Draw me after Thee, even if it be in some sort against my will, that Thou mayst make me willing; draw me, even in my sloth and slowness, that Thou mayst make me ready and swift. A time may come when I shall no longer need one to draw me onward, since we shall run voluntarily and with all willingness. But now I am not able to run alone, though alone I make my petition to be helped forward; let the maidens also run with me. Let us run together, let us run with equal pace; I, aroused by the fragrance of Thy perfumes; they by my example and my exhortation: and thus let us all run in the fragrance of Thy perfumes.' The Bride has her imitators, as she herself is the imitator of Jesus Christ. And, therefore, she does not say, as of one person only, 'I will run,' but 'We will run.'

10. But the question arises, wherefore the Bride, in imploring to be drawn onward, does not similarly join the maidens with herself, but says, *Draw me,* and not 'Draw us.' What then? Does the Bride need to be drawn, and the maidens, do they not need? O thou

who art beautiful, and happy, and blessed, explain to me the reason for this distinction. Wherefore dost thou say *Draw me*, and not *us?* Is it that thou enviest them this honour? God forbid. Nor wouldst thou (if that were the case) have added that they with thee would follow after the Bridegroom if thou hadst wished to follow Him alone. Why, then, shouldst thou have added in the plural, 'we will run,' when thy request was in the singular, 'draw me'? Charity, she replies, would have it thus. Learn from me by this word to hope for a twofold blessing from on high in spiritual exercises; that is, for correction and consolation. The one has its sphere of action without, the other visits us within. The former represses presumption, the latter raises up the heart and bestows confidence; the one worketh humility, the other consoles in discouragement; the one gives prudence, the other devotion. The former teaches the fear of the Lord; the latter tempers that very fear with an infusion of salutary joy, as it is written: *Let my heart rejoice, that it may fear Thy Name* (Ps. lxxxv. 11, Vulg. and Douay). And again: *Serve the Lord with fear, and rejoice with trembling* (Ps. ii. 11).

11. Now we are drawn onward when we are exercised by trials and tribulations; but we run forward when we are visited with inward consolations and secret inspirations, and breathe, as it were, an atmosphere of perfume and fragrance. That, then, which appears hard and austere I reserve for myself, as to one who is strong, and healthy, and perfect; and I say, speaking for myself alone, *Draw me*. That which is sweet and pleasant I share with you, as with one who is weak, and I say, *We will run*. I know that young souls (*adolescentulas*) are tender and delicate, and unfitted to sustain temptations, and, therefore, I desire that they should run with me, but not that they should be drawn with me; I wish to have them for companions of my consolation, not of my labour and trouble. Wherefore? Because they are weak, and I fear lest they should fail and fall by the way. But as for me, O my Spouse, take me, train me, try me, draw me after Thee, for I am prepared to suffer all chastisements, and I am strong to endure them. But as for the rest, let us run together; alone I will be drawn onward, but together let us run. Yea, let us run, but in the fragrance of thy perfumes, not in any confidence of our own merits. We have not the presumption to believe that we can run in the greatness of our own strength, but we trust in the multitude of Thy mercies. For if ever we have run, and have been able to will voluntarily to do so, yet it was not of man that willeth, nor of man that runneth, but of God that showeth mercy (Rom. ix. 16). Let that mercy be turned towards us and we shall run. Thou, indeed, O Lord, dost run in the greatness of Thy strength, rejoicing in it as a giant; but we cannot run at all unless we derive strength from the breathing of Thy perfumes. Thou, whom the Father has anointed with the oil of gladness above Thy fellows (Ps. xlv. 7), dost run in [the strength of] that unction itself, but we only in the fragrance which it exhales. Thine is the fulness of it, but ours its fragrance. This

would be the time to discharge the promise which I remember to have made long ago, to speak to you of the perfumes of the Bridegroom, if the length to which this sermon has already extended did not forbid it. I will defer that, then, to another time, for the importance of the subject does not allow it to be confined within inadequate limits. Pray the Lord of Divine unction that He will deign to render acceptable the freewill offering of my lips, and that I may be able, at your desire, to recall to your minds the remembrance of the sweetness of His abundant grace; of the grace, I say, which is in Him who is the Bridegroom of His Church, Jesus Christ our Lord. AMEN.

SERMON XXII.

OF THE FOUR PERFUMES OF THE BRIDEGROOM, AND OF THE FOUR CARDINAL VIRTUES

IF the perfumes of the Bride are so precious and so distinguished as they were found to be when they were treated of in your hearing, of what value must be those of the Bridegroom? And if I am not capable of expounding these in a manner worthy of their great excellence, yet that their virtue is surpassingly great, and their grace efficacious, is shown, without doubt, by this fact alone, that their fragrance arouses not the young maidens alone, but the Bride herself, to run [in the way of righteousness]. If you take notice, you will see that she does not venture to promise anything of this kind, as to follow from her own perfumes. She does indeed rejoice in thinking that they are most excellent, yet she does not say that in them she has run, or would run; this she only promises to do in the perfumes of the Bridegroom. What would she have said, had she felt the outpouring upon her of that unction itself, of which even the fragrance alone, however slight it were, had such influence upon her as to cause her to run forward [in the way of godliness]? It would be wonderful if she did not even fly. But someone, perhaps, says in himself: 'Cease your commendations; it will sufficiently appear what they are when you have begun to define them.' But no. I do not at all promise that. Believe me when I confess that I do not as yet know whether those ideas which are presented to my mind are well founded. I suppose that the Bridegroom has not a few kinds of perfumes and balms, that these are different in nature, that some of these are more a delight to the Bride than others, as being nearer and in closer relation to Him, and that they delight her only; but that there are others which reach as far as the maidens, and some which find their way even to those who are most distant and most entirely strangers to Him, so that there are none hid from his life-giving heat. But although the Lord is good and kind to all, He is most markedly so to those of His own house; and the more nearly anyone draws to Him by the influence of a pure mind and holy life, the more also, as I believe, He perceives the fragrance of newer perfumes and of a sweeter anointing.

2. But these things the intelligence does not comprehend any farther than it is led by experience. That is why I would not rashly arrogate to myself a prerogative which is given only to the Bride. The Bridegroom alone knows the delights which it is given to His Beloved to taste by the Holy Spirit, by what inspirations He marvellously revives her spiritual senses, and by what odours He soothes them. Let her be for thee, then, a fountain proper to Him alone, in which no stranger shares, nor does any unworthy drink thereof; that is to say, *a spring shut up, a fountain sealed* (Cant. iv. 12); but thence do streams flow into the streets. These, I confess, are at my disposal, provided that no one finds fault or is ungrateful if I drink of them and draw from them for the good of all. For, that I may commend a little my ministry in this respect, it is not without some labour and fatigue that I go forth day by day to draw from the open streams of the Scriptures, in order to distribute to each one according to his need; so that without his own labour every one of you may have a supply of the spiritual waters for his various necessities; as, for example, to drink, and for cleansing, as for cooking his food. For the Divine Word is the saving water of wisdom, not only to drink, but also for cleansing, as the Lord hath said: *Now ye are clean through the word which I have spoken unto you* (John xv. 2). The Divine Word cooks, so to speak, over the fire which the Holy Spirit kindles, the crude reflections of the carnal mind, and turns them into spiritual teachings, which are nourishment for the soul, so that you may say: *My heart was hot within me, and while I was musing the fire burned* (Ps. xxxix. 3).

3. Those who, being of a spirit perfectly pure, are capable of apprehending by their own selves truths more lofty than those which have been brought forward by me, I congratulate upon the fact, and I do not dispute their right; but at the same time, they must allow me to bring forward simpler truths for simpler people. Would that it might be granted unto me that all might exercise the gift of teaching (*prophetent*), and that it might not be needful for me to occupy myself in it! Would that this care might fall upon some other, or at least, which I would prefer, that there were no one among you who had need of it; and that you were also open to the teachings of God Himself, that I might be able to remain in a profound repose, and contemplate the Bridegroom, who is God! For now it is the case (and I do not say it without tears), that it is not permitted to me, I do not say to contemplate, but even to seek after the King in His glory, sitting upon the Cherubin, sitting upon His Throne, high and lifted up, in that Form in which He was begotten, Equal to His Father, in the splendour of His Saints, before the morning star [was created], in which also the Angels always desire to behold Him, God

of God. That which remains to me, who am but a man, is to speak of Him to men as Man, and in that Form in which, that He might in His exceeding condescension and love manifest Himself unto men, He was made a little lower than the angels, He who hath set in the sun His tabernacle, whence He cometh forth as a bridegroom out of His chamber (Ps. xix. 5). I speak of Him to you rather in His sweetness, than in His loftiness; as the Anointed One, rather than the High and Lofty One, who inhabiteth Eternity; of Him, that is, whom the Spirit of the Lord hath anointed, and sent forth to *preach the Gospel to the poor, to bind up the broken-hearted, to proclaim liberty to the captives, and the opening of the prison to them that are bound, to proclaim the acceptable year of the Lord* (Is. lxi. 1, 2).

4. Leaving, then, to each individual whatever of more sublime and profound truth it has been granted to him by God's special grace to feel and experience regarding the perfumes of the Bridegroom, I offer for the common good what I have drawn from a source common to all. For He is the fountain of life, a Fountain sealed, springing forth from a walled garden, by the mouth of St. Paul, who made of himself a canal for that precious stream. He is truly that Wisdom which, according to the expression of holy Job, *is drawn from secret places* (Job xxviii. 21); which divides itself into four streams, and flows into the open ways of men; in which the Apostle declares to us the great truth that God hath made Him to be to us *wisdom, and righteousness, and sanctification, and redemption* (1 Cor. i. 30). From these four streams, then, as it were of most precious perfumes—for it matters little whether we consider them as of water or of precious perfume, of water which cleanses, or of oil which perfumes—from these four, I say, as from precious ointments, composed of celestial balms upon the mountains of sweet spices, so great a sweetness and fragrance has filled the nostrils of the Church, that, being drawn from the four quarters of the earth by that perfume, [her people] hastened to the heavenly Bridegroom, as that queen of the East came from the ends of the earth to hear the wisdom of Solomon, being attracted by the good odour of his reputation (1 Kings x. 1-7).

5. Now, the Church was before not able to run towards the odour of her Solomon, until He, who was from all eternity Wisdom from the Father, was made by the Father to be for her benefit Wisdom also in time; for it was from that time that she began to perceive the Divine odour which proceeded forth from Him. Thus He was made for her in the same way righteousness, and sanctification, and redemption, so that she might be able to follow after the odour of these also, which were in Him before the beginning of all things. For *in the Beginning was the Word* (John i. 1); but the shepherds made haste to come to see Him, only then at length when His Birth was announced to them. Then it was that they said the one to the other: *Let us now go even to Bethlehem and see this thing which is come to pass, which the Lord hath made known to us* (Luke ii. 15, 16). *And,* it goes on, *they came with haste.* Before, when the Word was

with God, they did not stir; but when it came to pass that the Word was made [Flesh] and shown unto men, then they came with haste—they ran. Just as the Word was in the beginning, but the Word was with God; and yet the Word was made [Flesh] when He began to be among men also; so He was Wisdom in the beginning, He was righteousness, He was sanctification and redemption. But to the angels, and in order that He might be these to men also, the Father has made Him all these things, and He has done so because He is the Father. For, says the Apostle, *of God He is made unto us wisdom*. He does not say simply *is made*, but *is made unto us;* since that which He was unto the angels He is made unto us also.

6. But I do not perceive, you will say, how He was Redemption unto the Angels. For in no passage of the Scriptures does it appear that they were ever captives of sin, or subject unto death, so that they had need of redemption; those only excepted, who, falling by the irremediable lapse of pride, have never deserved to be redeemed. If, then, the Angels have never been redeemed, some having no need to be, and others not deserving it; the one class, because they have not fallen; the other, because their fall was irrevocable: for what reason do you say that the Lord Jesus Christ has been to them redemption? Listen, while I briefly declare it. He who has raised up man who had fallen granted to the Angel, who was upright, the grace not to fall; thus, as He delivered the one from his bondage, so He protected the other from becoming subject to that bondage. And in this manner He was Redemption equally to each class, delivering the one from its fall, and preserving the other from falling. It appears, then, clearly that the Lord Christ was to the holy Angels redemption, as He was righteousness, wisdom, and sanctification; and that, nevertheless, He was made to be these four blessings on account of men, who are able to behold the invisible things of God only by the beholding of the things that are made (Rom. i. 20). So, then, all that He was unto the Angels, He was made to be unto us; that is to say, wisdom, righteousness, sanctification, and redemption— wisdom in preaching, righteousness in the remission of sins, sanctification in the close relation which He had with sinners by His Life; and redemption by His Passion, which He endured on behalf of sinners. It is then when He was made by God to be all these things; that the Church has perceived His fragrance, and has followed, nay, has run, after Him.

7. Recognise, then, this fourfold anointing; recognise the abundant and inestimable sweetness of Him, whom the Father hath anointed with the oil of gladness above His fellows (Ps. xlv. 7). Thou, O man, wast sitting in the gloomy[1] shadows of death through ignorance of the truth; thou wast sitting bound by the chains of thy sins. He descended to thee in thy prison, not to torment thee, but to deliver thee from the power of darkness. In the first place, that Teacher of truth dissipated by His wisdom the darkness of thy ignorance.

[1] *Tenebrosis;* another reading is *tenebris.*

Then, by the righteousness which is of faith, He broke the bonds of thy sins, freely justifying the sinner. By that twofold benefit, He accomplished that word of the holy David: *The Lord looseth the prisoners; the Lord giveth sight to the blind* (Ps. cxlvi. 7, 8). More than this He did, by living a holy life among sinners, and so provided for thee a pattern of life, as a road whereby thou mightest return to thy own fatherland. Lastly, as it were to heap upon thee His goodness, He gave over His soul to death, and drew from His own side the price of thy redemption, and thus rendered satisfaction to the Father. In all this He plainly realized the verse: *With the Lord there is mercy, and with Him is plenteous redemption* (Ps. cxxx. 7). Truly it was *plenteous:* for it was not a drop, but a flood that poured forth plenteously, of His Precious Blood, from five parts of His Body.

8. What ought He to have done for thee, that He has not done? He has restored sight to one blind, broken the chains of a captive, led back a wanderer, reconciled the guilty. Who will not run with ardour, with rapidity, after Him who delivers from error, and forgives offences; who by His Life bestows merits, and by His Death acquires [for thee] rewards? What excuse can there be for him who does not eagerly run in the fragrance of these perfumes, except perchance that their sweetness has not reached him? But the odour of life has gone forth into the whole world; for the whole earth is full of the mercy of the Lord, and His goodness is over all His works. Therefore he who has no perception of that fragrance, sweet, life giving, and everywhere diffused, and because of this does not run after Christ, is either dead, or he is corrupt.[1] That fragrance is the renown of His Name. The fragrance of faith in Him extends[2] everywhere; it arouses to run the Christian course; it brings to trial of His anointing, to the vision of Him for reward. All who attain it chant with one accord: *Like us we have heard, so have we seen, in the city of the Lord of Hosts, in the city of our God* (Ps. xlviii. 8). We follow after Thee, O Lord Jesus, because of the goodness and kindness which we are fully assured of finding in Thee; because we learn that Thou dost not despise the poor, nor abhor the sinner. Thou didst not abhor the thief when he confessed, the sinful woman who wept tears of penitence, the Canaanite mother who came to Thee with her supplication, nor her who was taken in adultery, nor him who sat at the receipt of custom, nor the publican who implored pardon, nor the disciple who denied Thee, the persecutor of Thy disciples, nor Thy very crucifiers themselves. In the fragrance of these Divine virtues we run. Again, we perceive the fragrance of Thy wisdom from that word which we have heard, that if any lack wisdom, let him ask it of Thee, and Thou wilt give it to him; for Thou givest to all liberally, and upbraidest not (James i. 5). And the great fragrance of Thy righteousness is spread abroad upon every side, inasmuch as Thou art not only Righteous, but also Righteousness itself — yea, a

---

[1] *Putidus,* or *putridus.*   [2] *Pervenit,* or *prævenit.*

Righteousness which renders righteous him who is unrighteous. And as powerful as Thou art to justify, so bountiful art Thou also to forgive. Wherefore, let whosoever is touched with a sincere sorrow for his sins, who hungers and thirsts after righteousness, believe without hesitation in Thee, who justifiest the ungodly; and being justified by faith alone, he shall have peace with God. Of Thy holiness, also, the fragrance most sweet and full is spread abroad by Thy Conception, as by Thy Life. Sin, therefore, Thou hast neither committed nor contracted. Let those, then, who have been justified from their sins, who desire and propose to follow after holiness, *without which no man shall see the Lord*, let them attend to Thy voice: *Be ye holy, for I am holy* (Lev. xix. 2). Let them consider Thy ways and learn from Thee, for Thou art righteous in all Thy ways, and holy in all Thy works (Ps. cxlv. 17) And the fragrance of Thy Redemption, what numbers does it arouse to follow Thee! When Thou wert lifted up from the earth, Thou didst draw all men unto Thee. Thy Passion is the last refuge for men, and their only remedy. When wisdom is wanting, righteousness proves insufficient, and the merits of sanctity fail, Thy Passion comes to the rescue. For who can have the presumption to think his own wisdom, righteousness, or holiness sufficient for his salvation? As says the Apostle: *Not that we are sufficient of ourselves to think anything as of ourselves; but our sufficiency is of God* (2 Cor. iii. 5). Therefore, when my own strength shall have failed me, I am not troubled, I do not lose heart. I know what I have to do: I will take the cup of salvation and call upon the Name of the Lord (Ps. cxvi. 13). Enlighten mine eyes, O Lord, that I may know what is accepted before Thee at all times (Wisd. ix. 10); and thus I am wise. Remember not the sins of my youth, nor my transgressions (Ps. xxv. 7); and [thus] I am righteous. Teach me Thy way, O Lord (Ps. lxxxvi. 11); and I [thus] am holy. But yet, unless Thy Blood interpose for me, I am not saved. It is to obtain all these graces that we follow—nay, we run after Thee; send us away [satisfied], for we cry after Thee.

9. But we do not all run with equal attraction towards all these perfumes, for you will see that some are more ardently affected by the love of wisdom; others are more carried towards penitence by the hope of obtaining pardon; others, again, are more animated to the practice of virtues by the example of His life and conversation; and others, still, are more fired with ardour for piety by the remembrance of His Passion. I think that we may be able to find examples of each of these classes. Those who had been sent by the Pharisees, for instance, were attracted by the fragrance of His *wisdom*, when they returned and said: *Never man spake like this man* (John vii. 46), for they admired His teaching, and confessed His wisdom. The holy Nicodemus did the same, when he came to Jesus by night (iii. 2), drawn by the great light of His wisdom, and returned, enlightened and instructed in many things. But Mary Magdalene came attracted by the fragrance of His *righteousness;* she, to whom

many sins were forgiven, for she loved much (Luke vii. 47). Doubtless, she was no longer a sinner, as the Pharisee reproached her with being, but righteous and holy; he knew not that righteousness and holiness are the gift of God, not the work of man; and that he to whom the Lord will not impute sin, is not only righteous, but also blessed. Had he forgotten the manner in which [the Lord] in touching his [the Pharisee's] own bodily leprosy, or that of some other sufferer, had not contracted it Himself, but had cured it? Thus that Righteous One, being touched by the woman who was a sinner, imparted righteousness, and did not part with it; nor was He defiled with the stain of sin, of which He cleansed her. The Publican also followed after Christ, who, when he humbly implored pardon for his sins, *went down to his house*, as He who was Himself Justice declared, *justified* (Luke xviii. 14). Peter followed [Christ], he who *wept bitterly* for his fall (xxii. 62), so as to wash away his sin and regain righteousness. And David, who, acknowledging and confessing his crime, was found deserving to hear: *The Lord also hath put away thy sin* (2 Sam. xii. 13). Then again Paul bears witness that he followed Christ, when he boasts that he was His follower, and says to his disciples: *Be ye followers of me, as I also am of Christ* (1 Cor. xi 1). They also did so who said: *Behold, we have left all and followed Thee* (Matt. xix. 27). That is, they had left all things for the desire to follow Christ. This precept exhorts all people in general to follow after the same fragrance: *He that saith he abideth in Christ ought himself also so to walk, even as He walked* (1 John ii. 6). If you wish to hear who they are who have run in the fragrance of the Passion of Christ, I will tell you: they are all the martyrs. You have, then, four kinds of odours: the first of wisdom, the second of righteousness, the third of sanctification, the fourth of redemption. Keep them in memory, avail yourself of the good of them, and do not institute any inquiry as to how they are composed, of what materials, or how mingled. For these things are not so easily to be ascertained with respect to the perfumes of the Bridegroom, as with regard to those of the Bride, which were previously considered. For in Christ all things are with a fulness which has neither measure nor limit. For *His wisdom is infinite* (Ps. cxlvii. 5); His *righteousness is like the great mountains* (Ps. xxxvi. 6), the mountains of God; His holiness so great as to be unequalled by any other, and His redemption is a mystery that cannot be discovered.

10. This also must be said, that it is to no purpose that the wise men of this world have disputed at such great length concerning the four great virtues, which they are in no wise able to attain, since they knew not Him, who of God is made unto us wisdom to teach us prudence, righteousness to remit offences, sanctification to give an example of living temperately and chastely, and redemption for a perfect pattern of patience in His Death bravely endured. Someone will perhaps say: The other qualities are very fitting for the virtues named; but sanctification seems to have no proper relation to

temperance. To which I reply, first, that temperance is the same as continence, for it is usual in the Scriptures for continence or purity to be spoken of as sanctification. In fact, what did those sanctifications so frequent under the Law of Moses consist of but certain purifications of those who abstained from food, from drink, from indulgence, and such-like? But notice especially the Apostle himself, who commonly uses, or adapts, the word 'sanctification' to, or in, this sense. *This is*, he says, *the will of God, even your sanctification . . . that every one of you should know how to possess his vessel in sanctification and honour; not in the lust of concupiscence.* And, again. *For God hath not called us to uncleanness, but unto holiness* (1 Thess. iv. 3-7). It is plain that in such passages he puts sanctification for temperance.

11. After having made clear what seemed a little obscure, I return to the point whence I digressed. What have you to do with virtues who know not the power (*virtutem*) of God, which is Jesus Christ? Where, I ask you, is true prudence, if not in the teaching of Christ? or true righteousness, if not in His mercy? Where is true temperance, if not in the Life of Christ? or true fortitude, if not in the Passion of Christ? Those only, therefore, who are imbued with His teaching are to be called prudent; those alone to be regarded as righteous who from His mercy have attained the pardon of their sins; those alone as temperate who study to imitate His Life; and those alone as courageous who in adversities follow with constancy the example of His patience. That man labours in vain to acquire virtues who looks elsewhere than to the Lord in the hope of obtaining them; for it is His teaching which is the seed-plot of prudence; His mercy is a work of righteousness; His Life a mirror of temperance; and His Death a glorious pattern of courage. To Him be honour and glory for ever and ever. AMEN.

SERMON XXIII.

OF THREE WAYS OF CONTEMPLATING GOD, REPRESENTED UNDER THE FIGURE OF THREE STOREROOMS.

THE King hath brought me into His storerooms (Cant. i. 3, Douay). Lo, here is the source of fragrance; here is the point towards which we run. The Bride had said that we must press forward, and in what strength; but whither our course was to be directed, she had not said. Now, then, she declares that it is towards the Lord's storerooms, and in the strength of the fragrance which is exhaled from them. This she presses with her characteristic eagerness, and desires to be introduced into His fulness. But, in the first place, what is to be understood by these storehouses? Let us, to begin with, imagine that in the dwelling of the Bridegroom there are chambers fragrant with perfumes, and filled with all kinds of delights. It is in these that, as in a treasury,[1] is stored and kept in reserve whatever is most rare and valuable of the products of garden and of field. Hither, then, do all those who run direct their steps; but who are they that run? These are the souls who are fervent in the Spirit, the Bride, the maidens in her train; but she whose love is most ardent runs more swiftly, and arrives sooner. When she arrives, she suffers no repulse, and not even any delay. Forthwith the portals are opened to her, as to an inmate of the house, as to one greatly beloved, who is specially dear and welcome. But what as to her maidens? They follow afar off; they are still weak; they cannot press forward with devotion equal to that of the Bride; they cannot experience fervour and earnest desire such as hers; therefore they arrive later, and they remain without. But the charity of the Bride does not rest, nor does she pride herself, as is frequently the case, upon her happy successes so as to be forgetful of them. On the contrary, she consoles them the more assiduously, and exhorts them to endure patiently and calmly the repulse they have received, and her absence. Then she declares to them the joy which she has attained, and that for the very reason that they may rejoice with her, in the hope of one day attaining to a share in the graces and blessings of their mother. For she does not so pursue her own [spiritual] advantage as to neglect the care of them, nor desires that her benefit should be hurtful or prejudicial to them. However far removed from them she is by superior merits, it is of necessity that her charity and tender care for them keep her with them always. It is her duty, moreover, to follow the example of her Bridegroom, both, on the one hand, in seeking the heavens, and, on the other, in promising to be ever upon earth with His people, even to the consummation of all things. So also the Bride, whatever progress she may make, and whatever advancement she may attain, is prevented by her care, her deep interest and affection for those whom she has begotten in the Gospel, from ever leaving them or forgetting them in the depths of her heart.

2. Let her say, then, to them: Take courage and rejoice. *The King has brought me into His storerooms:* regard yourselves as having been thereby brought in also. I alone seem to have entered in, but the advantage is not to me alone. Every advancement of mine is virtually yours; it is for you that I make profit; and I share with you the graces which more than you I have deserved. Do you wish for an unquestionable proof that her words are to be taken in this sense and intention? Then listen to the reply which they make: *We will be glad and rejoice in thee;* we do not deserve to do so in ourselves, but *in thee.* And they add: *We are mindful of thy bosom* (Cant. i. 4); that is, we shall endure patiently until

---

[1] *Officina:* but the earlier sense is 'a workshop.' This usage is later: *e.g.,* '*Denique Cellario cunctisque similibus Monasterii officinis laicales præfecit personas,*' etc. 'Ratpertus Monachus de Casibus St. Galli,' cap. 6, ap., Du Cange.—ED.

thou come, knowing that thou wilt return to us with thy bosom filled with graces. We confidently hope, then, to rejoice and be glad; meanwhile we are mindful of thee. The words which he adds, *more than wine*, signify that they are still touched with the remembrance of the desires of the flesh, which are spoken of as wine, and that, nevertheless, those desires are overcome by the thought of that abounding sweetness which, as they have experienced, flows from her. I should speak of this now, if I did not remember that I have done so above.[1] But now you see what confidence they have with regard to their mother, how they look upon all her advantages and all her joys as belonging to themselves, and console themselves for their own repulse by her admission. They would not have so great confidence, if they did not recognise her as their mother. Let prelates, who like better to make themselves feared by those committed to their charge, than to be useful to them, take this to heart. Be ye learned, O ye that are judges of the earth. Learn from this that you ought to be as mothers, not masters, to your subjects; study to make yourselves loved rather than feared; and if there be need sometimes of severity, let it be that of a father, not of a tyrant. Show yourselves mothers in affection, fathers in reproof. Be gentle, not harsh; be not forward to inflict stripes; let the view of the maternal bosom promise indulgence; let the hearts [of those under you] grow fat with milk, not swell with anger. Why do you lay your heavy yoke upon those whose burden it is rather your duty to bear? Why does the young son, who has been bitten by a serpent, avoid displaying his wound to the priest, to whom he ought rather to resort as to the bosom of a mother? *If ye are spiritual, restore such an one in the spirit of meekness; considering thyself, lest thou also be tempted* (Gal. vi. 1). For otherwise *he shall die in his sin . . . but his blood will I require at thine hand* (Ezek. iii. 20). But of this at another season.

3. Now, since the context is clear by what I have said above, let us see what is the mystical meaning of 'the storehouse.' Later on mention is made of the garden also and the chamber, and I take these three for the subject of our present discussion; for when treated together, they throw light mutually on each other. Let us seek, then, if you please, these three words in the Holy Scriptures: the storehouse, the garden, and the chamber. For a soul that is athirst for God willingly occupies itself with, and lingers in, these, knowing that in them it will assuredly find Him whom it thirsts for. Let, then, the *garden* represent the plain and simple historical sense of the Scripture; the *storehouse* the moral sense of it; and the *chamber* the secret and mystical truth, reached by Divine contemplation.

4. In the first place, I think that the historic sense is not unfitly referred to the *garden*, because in the history are found men of many virtues, as it were fruitful trees in the garden of the Bridegroom and

[1] Sermon IX.

in the Paradise of God; and from their conduct and their actions you may take examples, as from a tree you gather fruit. Who can question that a good man is, as it were, a plant of God? Hear what holy David sings concerning a good man: *He shall be like a tree planted by the rivers of water, that bringeth forth his fruit in his season; his leaf also shall not wither* (Ps. i. 3). Jeremiah also expresses himself to the same effect, and in almost the same words: *He shall be as a tree planted by the waters, and that spreadeth out her roots by the river, and shall not see when heat cometh; but her leaf shall be green* (Jer. xvii. 8). And the Psalmist: *The righteous shall flourish like the palm-tree; he shall grow like a cedar in Lebanon* (Ps. xcii 12). And of himself he says: *I am like a green olive-tree in the house of God* (Ps. lii. 8). History is, then, as it were, a garden, and it is threefold; for it contains the creation, the reconciliation, and the reparation of heaven and of earth. *Creation*, that is like the sowing or planting of a garden. *Reconciliation* is, as it were, the germination of that which is sown or planted. For at the due time the heavens have distilled dew from above, the clouds have poured down righteousness. the earth has opened and brought forth the Saviour (Is. xlv. 8), by whom was brought about the reconciliation of heaven and earth. For He is our peace, who hath made both one (Eph. ii. 14), reconciling by His blood all things, whether in earth or heaven (Col. i. 20). *Reparation*, again, is to come to pass at the ending of the dispensation. For there shall be a new heaven and a new earth; the good shall be gathered from among the evil, to be set in safety in the storehouse of God, as fruits from a garden. *In that day, it is said, shall the branch of the Lord be beautiful and glorious, and the fruit of the earth shall be excellent and comely* (Is. iv. 2). In this garden of the historic sense, then, you have three periods included.

5. In the *Moral* sense, secondly, you have a threefold discipline: three cells, as it were, in one storehouse. Therefore it is, perhaps, that they are spoken of in the plural as 'storerooms' (*cellaria*), in contemplation of this number of cells. A little farther on, the Bride felicitates herself on having been brought into 'the cellar of wine' (ii. 4, 'banqueting house,' A.V.). We, then, because we read, '*Give an occasion to a wise man, and he will be wiser*' (Prov. ix. 9), take occasion from this name, which the Holy Spirit has thought fit to give to this cell, to give it also to the two others; to call one the cell of *perfumes*. the other that of *unguents*. We shall explain presently the reasons for these names. But in the meantime notice that all which surrounds the Bridegroom is sweet, as all is salutary—wine, perfumes, and unguents. *Wine*, the Scripture declares, *maketh glad the heart of man* (Ps. civ. 15). We read also that oil maketh his face cheerful (*Ibid.*, Douay), and it is with oil and medicinal powders that ointments or unguents are compounded. Lastly, perfumes are not only agreeable by their odour, but are useful because of their medicinal virtue. It is, then, with good reason that the Bride

rejoices at having been brought into a spot where graces are so great and so abundant.

6. But I have other names also for them, for which, as I consider, a still greater probability may be shown. To name them in their order, I take the first cell to be that of *discipline*, the second that of *nature*, the last that of *grace*. In the first you learn, following the rule of Christian ethics, to be the last of all; but in the second to be equal to all, and in the last to be superior to all; that is to say, you learn how to act as an inferior, how to act as an equal, and how to act as a superior; or, again, to be below, to be beside, to be above others.[1] In the first you learn to be a disciple, in the second to be a companion, in the third to be a master. Nature has, indeed, made all men equal;[2] but that natural order having been corrupted by pride, men have become impatient of that equality, desirous to elevate themselves above others, and full of efforts to do so; greedy of vainglory, envying and provoking one another. Thus, first of all, insolence of character requires to be restrained by the yoke of discipline, until the stubborn[3] will, worn down by observance of the severe and constantly repeated rules of the elders, may be humbled and cured, and regain by its obedience that good of nature which it had lost by the indulgence of pride, until the man shall have learned to possess his soul in patience, and to live peacefully and kindly, as far as in him lies, with his fellow creatures; that is to say, with all men; and that not by fear of punishment, but by the spontaneous impulse of the will. Then he will pass on into the cell of nature, and will make proof of that which is written: *Behold how good and how pleasant it is for brethren to dwell together in unity! It is like the precious ointment upon the head* (Ps. cxxxiii. 1, 2). For characters thus disciplined, are, as it were, sweet spices pounded together, from which is composed the oil of joy, which is the good of *nature*, and a sweet and excellent unguent is produced from it. The man who is, so to speak, anointed with this becomes peaceful and amiable; one who provokes no quarrel, who deceives no one, who attacks no one, who offends no one; who does not set himself above others, or prefer himself to everyone else, but, on the contrary, maintains with those around him a continual interchange of kindnesses given and received.

7. I think that if you have clearly understood the leading characteristics of the two former cells, you will be of opinion that I have not unfitly named the one that of *perfumes*, the other that of *unguents*. For in the former, as the forcible pounding of a pestle forces forth and extracts the strength and fragrance of spices, so the pressure of the rule and the rigour of discipline expresses, so to speak, and draws

---

[1] The terseness of the original, *subesse, coesse, praeesse*, may be admired, but hardly equalled.—ED.

[2] It is curious to find this phrase, which Thomas Jefferson made so famous in his 'Declaration of Independence' [of the United States], written in 1776, employed *totidem verbis* more than six hundred years earlier.—ED.

[3] *Cervicosa;* not a common word.—ED.

forth the natural force of the characters of those who are ruled. And in the latter the agreeable sweetness of a voluntary and, so to speak, innate affection runs eagerly of its own accord, like, as it were, the fragrant oil which is upon the head, and which at the slightest touch of warmth rolls downward and is diffused over the whole body. Thus in the cell of discipline are enclosed, as it were, the simple materials of perfumes in a dry state, and thus I have thought it ought to be called 'of perfume.' But in that which is said to be of nature, the unguents compounded of these are found and are stored, and therefore it is called ' of unguents.' As for the wine-cellar, I suppose that the reason for the name is no other than that in it is stored the wine of a zeal fervent with charity. One who has not as yet deserved to be brought into this cell should assuredly not be set in authority over others. For it is essential that one who has the direction of others should be fervent with this wine, in like manner as was the great Doctor of the Gentiles, when he said: *Who is weak, and I am not weak? Who is offended, and I burn not?* (2 Cor. xi. 29). Otherwise, it is altogether wrong that you should aspire to rule over those to whom you have no desire to be of service, and should claim for yourself, with excessive ambition, the subjection of those whose salvation you are not earnestly desirous to forward. This cell I have named that of grace, not because it is possible to obtain even the two others without grace, but because of the fulness of grace which is reached in this alone. For *love is the fulfilling of the law*, and *He that loveth another hath fulfilled the law* (Rom. xiii. 10, 8).

8. You have seen the reason of the names, see now the different characters of the cells; for it is one thing to repress by fear, and by the rigid rule of discipline, the wanton and wandering senses and the irregular appetites of the flesh, and another to preserve a kindly agreement with brethren by a spontaneous disposition to do so. These differ in difficulty, and, indeed, in the faculties which effect them; and so also to live a regulated life under the authority of another, and to do so with our own will for the only constraining influence, are altogether distinct things. In the same way, no one will declare the living in peace and on good terms with others, and the ruling over them for their benefit, to be actions of equal merit and requiring the same powers. How many are there who live in peace under the direction of an intelligent guide, whom, if they were set free from the obligation to obey, you would speedily perceive not to be able to remain even peaceful and harmless to their neighbours? And similarly there are very many who are seen to conduct themselves simply and without offence among their brethren who, if they were set over them, would behave themselves so as to be not only useless, but even unwise and harmful. Such persons ought to content themselves within the bounds of a mediocrity which is advantageous to them, following the measure of the grace which God has bestowed upon them; not having, indeed, any great need of a master, but yet being unfitted to be masters themselves. These,

indeed, are of a more excellent character than the former class; but such as know how to govern well are superior both to the one and to the other. Those, too, who are faithful and wise in ruling over the Lord's household have it in promise from Him that He will make them rulers over all His goods (Matt. xxiv. 48). But as there are few who rule wholly to the advantage of others, so there are fewer still who do so with humility. Yet both the one and the other duty are easily fulfilled by him who has attained perfect discretion, the mother of all the virtues, and has drunk of the wine of charity to the point of contemning his own glory, and of entire forgetfulness of himself, so that he seeketh not his own; and this state is reached only in the cell called of wine, and under the wonderful guidance of the Holy Spirit. The virtue of discretion lies prone and helpless without the fervour of charity, while the vehement fervour of charity without the moderating influence of discretion hurries on to the precipice. Therefore he is to be praised to whom neither is wanting, insomuch that fervour animates his discretion, and discretion regulates his fervour. So it behoves him to be constituted who rules over others. But I should regard him as the highest in character, and as having learned perfectly the sum of this discipline, upon whom has been bestowed the power to pass through and around all these cellars without stumbling; who in no respect whatever either resists his superiors, envies his equals, or towards his inferiors commits either the error of being wanting in care for them, or ruling them in pride; who is obedient to those who are above him, to his companions obliging, to those under him kindly condescending for their good; which high degree of perfection, indeed, I have no hesitation in attributing to the Bride. This is intimated in the statement she has made, that *The King hath brought me into His storehouses*, since she mentions not some one only, but speaks in the plural, '*His storehouses.*'

9. Now let us pass to the bedchamber. What is that chamber? Have I the presumption to think that I know what it is? By no means do I arrogate to myself any experience of so exalted a subject, nor do I boast of a prerogative, which is reserved to the happy Bride alone, being careful, according to that proverb of the Greeks, to 'know myself,'[1] and to know, as did the Psalmist [in a similar case], that *such knowledge is too wonderful for me; it is high, I cannot attain unto it* (Ps. cxxxix. 6). If I had no knowledge whatever, I should say nothing. What little I do know I will not enviously keep back from you; what I do not know, may He, *who teacheth man*

---

[1] Γνῶθι σεαυτὸν, 'Know thyself.' This precept was inscribed in letters of gold over the portico of the Temple of Apollo at Delphi. It was attributed to Thales, one of the Seven Wise Men of Greece; and indeed to Pythagoras, Chilo, Cleobulus, Bias, and Socrates, as well as to Phemonœ, a (mythical) Greek poetess of the ante-Homeric period, said to have been the daughter of Apollo. Juvenal (Sat. XI., verse 27), says:

E caelo descendit γνῶθι σεαυτόν.

See also Cicero, 'Tusculan. Disputat.,' I., 1, 22, 52.—ED.

knowledge (Ps. xciv. 10), vouchsafe to impart to you. I have already said, and I dare say that you remember, that the chamber of the King is to be sought in the secret and mystical truth reached by Divine contemplation.[1] But, as in speaking of perfumes, I said that the Bridegroom has many, and of different kinds, and that all of these are not bestowed upon everyone, but that each has part in them, according to the various character of his discernings, so I think of the chamber of the King also, that it is not one, but many. Nor has He one queen also, but assuredly very many; He has many woman friends,[2] and of maidens the number is uncounted. Each of these has her secret confidence with the Bridegroom, and says: *My secret is for myself, my secret is for myself* (Is. xxiv. 16). It is not granted to all to enjoy in the same degree the dear and secret Presence of the Bridegroom, but it is given to whomsoever it has been prepared by the Father. For we have not chosen Him, but He has chosen us, and established us in our place; and wheresoever any soul has been placed by Him, there is He with that soul. One woman, moved with penitence, found her place at the Feet of the Lord Jesus (Luke vii. 38); another, if it were really another,[3] found the fruit of her devotion at the Head of Jesus (Matt. xxvi. 7). St. Thomas attained the grace of that secret [favour] at His Side; St.

[1] C. 3.
[2] There is apparently a reminiscence of 1 Kings xi. 3.
[3] St. Augustine expresses himself in a similar manner (in Joannem Tract. ix. *n.* 3) Whether Mary, who anointed our Lord, as we read in several passages of the Gospel, and Mary, the sister of Martha, were the same, or different persons, has been a subject of much controversy among old writers. Jansenius Gandavensis ('Concordiae Evang.,' c. 48) treats the question with his usual solidity. There are some writers, especially among the Greeks, for example, Origen and Theophylact, who think that there were three distinct women named Mary mentioned in the Gospels. The first was the 'woman who was a sinner,' mentioned, but not named, by St. Luke (vii. 37). The second is also mentioned, but not named, by St. Matthew (xxvi. 7), and St. Mark (xiv. 3). The third was the sister of Martha (John xii. 3). St. John Chrysostom, on the contrary (Hom 81), thinks that there were only two Marys—one who poured the perfume on the Head of Jesus, and that on two different occasions; the other the sister of Martha. St. Jerome again (in Matt. xxvi.) would identify her who poured the perfume on the Head of Jesus with the sister of Martha; and regards her who poured perfume on His feet, in the house of a Pharisee, as a different person; St. Ambrose, in his Commentary on St. Luke, seems of the same opinion. St. Gregory the Great admits only one Mary, and many writers are of his opinion. St. Ambrose (*loc. cit.*), though he is not unwilling to believe that these were different persons, writes sometimes as if they appeared to him to be the same, 'who was changed through change of time and of character,' so that she who began by being the 'sinner' of the Gospel, in the end became holy. 'For although,' he says, 'the Church does not change the person, as for the soul, it changes as it makes progress towards good.' However that may be, St. Bernard expresses the same doubt in his Sermon XII. *in Cantica*, but in Sermon III. *in Assumptione, n.* 2, he asserts, and that at much length, that she who is referred to in Luke vii. is the same with her of whom mention is made in Matt. xxvi., Mark xiv., and John xii. He speaks thus: 'See the prerogative of Mary, and what an advocate she has in every circumstance. If the Pharisee is indignant (Luke vii.), if her sister complains (John xii.), if even the disciples murmur (Matt. xxvi., Mark xiv.), in every case Mary keeps silence, and Christ speaks for her.'

John leaning upon His Breast; St. Peter in the Bosom of the Father; and St. Paul in the third heaven.

10. Who of us can worthily distinguish between these varieties of merits, or rather of rewards? Nevertheless, that I may not seem to pass over in silence that which is within our knowledge, notice that the former of the women mentioned sought her safety under the shelter of humility; the latter in the seat of hope; St. Thomas in firmness of faith; St. John in breadth of charity; St. Paul in the depth of wisdom; St. Peter in the light of truth. If, then, in the [home of the] Bridegroom there are many mansions, each, whether Queen, or friend, and even she who is only of the number of the maidens, finds place and lodgment there proportioned to her merits, and is permitted to remain there until she passes beyond it by inspiring contemplation, enters into the joy of her Lord, and of the sweet secrets of the Bridegroom explores the utmost depths. This I will endeavour to make more clear in its place, as far as the Lord shall vouchsafe to enable me. But now it is sufficient to know that to none, whether of the maidens, or of the friends, or even of the Queens, is access opened to that secret of the inner chamber of the Bridegroom, which He reserves for Her who is His dove, His undefiled, His only and perfect one. On that account I am not troubled or surprised if access to it is not given unto me, especially because it is to my mind quite clear that not even the Bride attains to the knowledge of all the secret things into which she desires to be admitted. For does she not earnestly ask the Bridegroom where He feeds His flock, and where He rests at noon (Cant. i. 6)?

11. But let me tell you to what point I have arrived, or rather that I think I have reached; for you will not impute vanity to that which I say in the hope of serving you. There is, then, in the dwelling of the Bridegroom a chosen spot in which the Sovereign Ruler of the universe decrees His laws and shapes His designs, setting laws in weight, and measure, and number, to all things created. That place is lofty and secret, but it is by no means noiseless. For though He, as far as regards Himself, disposes all things with sweetness, yet He disposes them, and does not permit that one who has reached that point by contemplation should remain in quiescence; but He wearies, and by a course, marvellous and yet delightful, renders full of unrest and lassitude the soul that searches out and admires these deep things. The Bride expresses beautifully, in a later part of this Canticle, each of these feelings, that is, the delight and, at the same time, the inquietude of this contemplation, as where she says: *I sleep, but my heart waketh* (v. 2). For in speaking of sleep she signifies that she tastes the repose of a trance most sweet, and the stillness of complete admiration; but when of waking, that she endures the weariness of a restless curiosity and laborious research. Thus the holy Job says: *When I lie down I say, When shall I arise and the night be gone?* (Job vii. 4). Do you not understand by these words that a holy soul desires to escape from a repose which, in a

certain sense, troubles it, and to seek again the same employment, troublous, and yet sweet? For he would not have said, *When shall I arise?* if that repose of contemplation had been entirely pleasing to him; nor, on the other hand, if it had been wholly displeasing, would he have awaited with impatience the hour of repose, that is to say, *the evening*.[1] That, therefore, where entire rest is not attained, is not the bedchamber of the Bridegroom.

12. There is still another place, in which the vengeance, most severe and most secret, of God the Judge, just and terrible in His dealings with the children of men, watches ceaselessly over His creatures, gifted with reason, but doomed on account of sin. The awestricken beholder, I repeat, here regards God, who by a just and secret judgment neither washes away the evil actions of those who are reprobate, nor accepts their good actions; and, moreover, He hardens their hearts, lest they should perchance repent and return, and be converted, and He should heal them. Nor is this without a sure and eternal reason, which is manifestly so much the more awful, as it is, in fact, immovable and eternal. That is a very fearful saying upon this subject which we read in the Prophet, where God, speaking to His Angels, says: *Let us have pity on the wicked* (Is. xxvi. 10). And when they are stricken with terror, and inquire: *Will he, then, not learn to do righteousness?* No, He replies; and he adds the reason: *In the land of righteousness will he deal unjustly, and will not behold the majesty of the Lord.* Let ecclesiastics, let the ministers of the Church, be seized with fear who commit so many wrongs in the lands of the Saints of which they have possession, and who, far from being content with the stipends which ought to suffice for them, keep for themselves, with wicked and sacrilegious greed, the overplus, which ought to go to nourish the poor; who are not ashamed to consume for their own pride and luxury the sustenance of the needy, and thus are guilty of a double crime; inasmuch as they seize upon what is not their own, and abuse holy things to the service of their vanities and lusts.

13. Who, then, in seeing that He, whose judgments are like the great deep, spares and pities such persons in this life, in order not to spare them in eternity, will seek rest in this place? This vision is filled with the tremor[2] of judgment, not with the peace and security of the bedchamber of the King. Terrible is that place, and wholly devoid of calm and rest. When brought into it, I shudder to the very heart, and revolve in my mind with fear that saying: *Who knoweth whether he be worthy of love or of hatred?* (Eccles. ix. 1). Nor is it wonderful if I (who am but as a leaf driven to and fro, or as the dry stubble, Job xiii. 25) should totter in that place, where that great man who contemplated with such marvellous insight [the doings of the Creator] declares that his feet were almost gone, and his treadings had well nigh slipped, saying: *I was envious of the foolish, when I saw the prosperity of the wicked.* Where-

---

[1] Job vii. 4, Vulg. and Douay.
[2] *Tremorem*, otherwise *terrorem*.

fore? Because *they are not in trouble as other men, neither are they plagued like other men; therefore pride compasseth them about as a chain* (Ps. lxxiii. 3-6), that they should not be humbled and made penitent, but be condemned, because of their pride, with the devil, who is proud, and with his angels. For those who have no part in the trouble of men shall assuredly have part in that of demons, and shall hear that terrible sentence from the Mouth of the Judge: *Depart from Me, ye cursed, into everlasting fire, prepared for the devil and his angels* (Matt. xxv. 41). And yet this, too, is a habitation of God; it is plainly no other than the house of God and the gate of Heaven. It is here that God is feared; here is His Name [beheld as] holy and terrible; it is, as it were, the entering in of His glory; for *the fear of the Lord is the beginning of wisdom* (Ps. cxi. 10).

14. Let it not astonish you that I have set down the beginning of wisdom as belonging to this, and not to the earlier place. For as in the earlier we listen to Wisdom teaching of all things as a professor in his lecture-hall, so in this we receive these teachings in ourselves; there we are indeed instructed, but here we are touched and influenced. Instruction renders men learned, but feeling[1] makes them wise. The sun does not render all things warm upon which its light falls, so Wisdom also instructs many persons what they ought to do, without going on to give the earnestness and ardour needful to do it. It is one thing to know of the existence of great treasures, another to possess them; and it is the possession, not the knowledge, which renders a man rich. Similarly, there is a difference between the knowledge of God and the fear of God, and it is not the knowledge, but the fear of Him, which renders a man truly wise, provided it be a fear which makes [a durable] impression on the soul. Would you call a person wise whom his own acquirements render vain? It is only the most foolish of persons who would call those wise who, when they had known God, glorified Him not as God, nor rendered thanks to Him. For my part I am rather of the Apostle's opinion, when he says that their heart was manifestly foolish (Rom. i. 21, 22). And truly *the fear of the Lord is the beginning of wisdom*, because the soul begins to have discernment of, and inclination for, God when He has stricken it with fear, not when He has communicated to it knowledge. If you fear the righteousness of God, if you fear His power, then, inasmuch as He is righteous and powerful, you incline to Him with preference and choice; for fear is a kind of preference. It (preference) renders one wise (*sapor sapientem facit*), as knowledge makes one knowing. and riches render one rich. To what purpose, then, is the former place? It serves only to prepare us for wisdom. There you are prepared for it, that here you may enter upon its possession. The preparation for it is the attainment of a certain degree of knowledge. But this is followed only too easily by the elation of vanity, unless this be repressed by fear; and therefore it is rightly said, *The fear of the Lord is the beginning of wisdom*, since this

---

[1] *Affectio* = sentiment.

fear first opposes itself to that which the Apostle declares is foolishness. The former, then, gives a certain approach, as it were, to wisdom, but the latter an entrance into it. Nevertheless, the beholder finds perfect rest neither in the one nor in the other, because in the one God appears, as it were, full of care, in the other full of trouble. Seek not, then, the bedchamber of the Bridegroom in these spots, whereof the one resembles rather the audience chamber of a professor, the other the tribunal of a judge.

15. But there is a place where God is beheld as truly tranquil and in repose; it is, in fact, the place, not of a judge, not of a teacher, but of a Bridegroom. I do not know how it may be with regard to others, but as far as concerns myself, that is for me a chamber into which entrance has sometimes been granted unto me; but, alas! how rarely that has happened, and for how short a time it has lasted! It is there that is clearly recognised the mercy of the Lord from everlasting and to everlasting upon them that fear Him. Happy is he who can say: *I am a companion of all them that fear Thee, and of them that keep Thy precepts* (Ps. cxix. 63). The decree of the Lord standeth fast; His purpose of peace endureth upon them who fear Him, forgiving the evil actions and rewarding the good which they have done, and, by a marvellous method of His mercy, making, not only those things which are good, but also those which are evil, work together for their good. O truly blessed, and, indeed, the only blessed one is he, *unto whom the Lord will not impute iniquity!* (Ps. xxxii. 2). For there is none without sin, no not one; for *all have sinned and come short of the glory of God* (Rom. iii. 23). But *who shall lay anything to the charge of God's elect?* (Rom. viii. 33). It is sufficient for all righteousness to me to have Him upon my side, against whom alone I have offended. Everything which He has decreed not to impute unto me is as though it had not been. Not to sin is the righteousness of God, but the forgiveness of God is the righteousness of man. I have seen these things, and can bear witness to the truth of that saying: *Whosoever is born of God doth not commit sin, for His seed abideth in him* (1 John iii. 9). Now, the heavenly seed is the eternal predestination, wherewith God hath loved His elect, and bestowed graces upon them in His Beloved Son, before the foundation of the world; beholding them in Him with favour, that they might be rendered worthy to see His power and His glory, and be made sharers in the inheritance of Him, to whose image and likeness they were to be conformed. These, then, I have looked upon as having never sinned, because, even though they are seen to have sinned in time, their offences do not appear in eternity, because the charity of their Father covers the multitude of sins.[1] He calls them blessed, then, *whose iniquities are forgiven, and whose sins are covered*

---

[1] It is in the same sense that in the treatise upon 'Grace and Freewill,' *n.* 29, the sins of the predestinate are said 'to be hidden in the charity,' that is to say, of God. Compare Sermon IV., *De Diversis*, *n.* 5, and Sermon I. for Septuagesima, with notes.

(Ps. xxxii. 1). Then I have felt on a sudden so great a joy and confidence arising in me, that it surpassed the fear which had gone before it in the place of horror—I mean in that of the second vision—and it seemed to me as if I were one of those blessed ones. O that it had lasted longer! Again and again do Thou visit me, O Lord, with Thy salvation, *that I may see the good of Thy chosen, that I may rejoice in the gladness of Thy nation* (Ps. cvi. 4, 5).

16. O place of true repose, and which I may not unfitly call by the name of chamber! O place in which God is beheld, not, as it were, aroused and in wrath, nor as distracted with care [of all His great creation], but in which is experienced the influence of His good, and favourable, and perfect will! That vision does not terrify, but soothes; it does not arouse an unjust curiosity, but allays it; and tranquillizes the spirit in place of wearying it. Here true rest is felt. The God of peace renders all things peaceful, and the soul, looking up with fixed gaze at His ineffable stillness, is itself awed into quiescence. It is as if one beheld some king or great judge, who, after the hearing of causes in his court all the day long, dismisses his crowds of attendants, puts an end to the labours of his office, returns with night to his peaceful palace, enters into his chamber with those few companions whom he condescends to honour with his intimacy in private, and there enjoys his repose with the more confidence because it is in such complete retirement, and because, as he looks peacefully around, he sees only the faces of those who are dear to him. If it should ever be the happy lot of any of you to be caught up and withdrawn for awhile into that hidden and mysterious sanctuary of God, and not to be called away from it either by the needs of the body, by the sting of some care, or, it may be, by the haunting pang of some sin, or, at least, by the inrushing flood of ideas and images belonging to this world, which are very difficult indeed to banish, such an one will be able in truth, when he returns to us again, to lift up his head and say: *The King hath brought me into His chamber.* And yet I would not rashly affirm that this would have been that very chamber into which the Bride rejoices to have entered. It is indeed a chamber, and the chamber of the King; but of the three that we have pointed out as included in the threefold vision, there is that one alone in repose and peace. For, as we have already shown, in the first chamber there is but a brief and fleeting repose, and in the second none whatever; because in the first God is beheld as wonderful and admirable, and the curiosity is violently excited to search out the numerous instances of His glory; while in the second He is beheld as terrible, and human weakness is thrown into terror at the sight of Him. But in the third He is beheld not as terrible, and He even deigns to appear not so much admirable, as lovable, serene and peaceful, sweet and gentle, and full of mercy towards them who look unto Him.[1]

---

[1] *Intuentibus*, otherwise *invocantibus se* = towards them who call upon Him. See Ps. lxxxvi. 5.—ED.

17. Now that you may retain in memory a brief summary of what I have said to you about the cellar, the garden, and the chamber of the Bridegroom, at unusual length in this sermon, remember that there are three times, three merits, and three kinds of reward. In the garden, take note of the *times*; in the cellar, of the *merits*; and in the bedchamber, of the *rewards*, in that threefold contemplation of the soul that is seeking and searching for the chamber of the King. As for the cellar, we have spoken of it sufficiently. But with regard to the garden and the chamber, if there should appear to be something to be added or further explained, I will not pass over an opportunity of doing so. If not, let what has been said suffice, without repetition, so that I may not weary you (which God forbid!) by my words, which are spoken to the praise and glory of the Bridegroom of the Church, our Lord Jesus Christ, who is above all, God blessed for ever. AMEN.

SERMON XXIV.[1]

PRINCIPALLY AGAINST THE DETESTABLE VICE OF DETRACTION: AND IN WHAT RECTITUDE IN A MAN CHIEFLY CONSISTS.

NOW at length for the third time, dear brethren, the eye of Providence has looked favourably from heaven upon my return to you from Rome, and a more peaceful aspect of affairs has smiled upon us at length. The furious anger of the faction of Peter Leonis has cooled, their schism has come to an end, the Church has regained peace. That wicked one who for eight years almost has troubled it by a terrible schism, has been brought to nothing in the sight of all. Shall it be in vain that I have been restored to you after perils so great? Since I have been granted to your desires, let it be for your spiritual advancement also; the life which I owe to your merits, I desire to devote to cares for you and your salvation. Since then you wish that I should continue, what I began long since, my comment on the Song of Songs, I willingly do so, and I think it better to resume the discourse which was interrupted, than to commence something new. But I fear lest, my mind being at all times unequal to that duty, and having been for so long a time unused to the discharge of it, and distracted by matters very different, my thoughts should be too weak and unworthy for a subject so sublime. But that which I have, I give unto you; and it may be that God, having regard to my faithful endeavour to serve Him, may enable me to give even that which I have not. If it be

---

[1] Delivered in the year 1138, on his return from Italy, after the schism of Peter Leonis was at length brought to an end.

otherwise, then let not my will, but my want of ability be blamed for it.

2. Now, the place where we ought to commence, I think, is at this passage: *The upright love thee* (i. 4). But before we begin to explain it, let us see who it is speaks thus. For we ought to supply what the author does not say. Perhaps, then, we may attribute these words to the young maidens, whose are the sentences which precede them.[1] For after they had said to her, 'We will rejoice *and be glad in thee, remembering thy bosom, which is better than wine*' (and there is no doubt that there they speak to their mother); they continue with the words which follow: *The upright love thee*. I believe that they added this on account of some of their number who had not the same sentiments, although they seemed to run equally well; who sought their own advantage, not walking sincerely and in simplicity, but taking occasion to murmur against her, because she entered alone into the storehouses of the Bridegroom. Which is no other than that the Apostle makes mention of: *Perils from false brethren* (2 Cor. xi. 26). These are they, against whose taunts the Bride herself, later on, is obliged to defend herself, replying to them: *I am black, but comely, O ye daughters of Jerusalem* (i. 5). It is then to console her because of those who murmur and blaspheme, that it is said by those others who are souls good, simple, humble, and gentle: *The upright love thee*. 'Have no care,' they say, 'for the unjust blame of those blasphemers, when it is quite clear that *The upright love thee*.' It is a goodly consolation, in truth, when we do good and are spoken ill of by the evil, if the righteous love us. The esteem of the good, with the approving testimony of conscience, is sufficient for us against the tongues that speak evil. *My soul shall make her boast in the Lord: the humble shall hear thereof, and be glad;* yes, *shall be glad* (Ps xxxiv. 2). Let me be pleasing to those who are gentle, and I shall endure with equanimity whatsoever the envy of the abandoned (*perditarum*) shall be desirous to utter against me.

3. It is, then, in this sense, that I understand what is here said: *The upright love Thee*. Not unfitly, as I think, since everywhere,

---

[1] From the commencement of the sermon on to this point there is a great diversity of reading in the MSS. In some of them the entire exordium is omitted, and the sermon begins thus: 'The upright love Thee. Whom are we to suppose are they who speak these words? If the young maidens, then without doubt they say this to their mother, in like manner as they had said to her "We will rejoice and be glad in thee, remembering thy bosom, which is better than wine"; and continue "the upright love thee," etc. Other MSS. have our reading. From this variety arises great confusion in most editions, in which both introductions are reproduced, but wrongly. The explanation of this confusion is that St. Bernard preached the same sermon twice—the first time with the shorter introduction, in the year 1137, before he went to Rome for the third time; the second time in 1138, when he returned thence, and then he prefixed the longer introduction, in order to take up the interrupted work where he had left it in the previous sermon. One MS. in the Royal Library, No. 4,511, reproduces the sermon with the *two* introductions; and one Colbertine has it once here with the one introduction, and again after Sermon LX. with the other.

even in the choir of maidens, such are found who watch closely the actions of the Bride, not to imitate them, but to detract from their merit. By the good deeds of their elders they are tormented, but upon the evil they gloat and feed. You see them walking apart, drawing together, and making little knots, where they indulge themselves without restraint in insolent words and scurrilous whispers. They are joined close one to the other, so that not a breath can escape, so great is their eagerness to detract from others and to listen to detraction. They associate themselves together in order to speak ill of their neighbour, and are united to cause disunion. They form among themselves friendships full of unfriendliness, combine under a common impulse of malignity, and make odious cabals. It was thus that Herod and Pilate formerly acted, of whom the Gospel relates that *in that day were they made friends together* (Luke xxiii. 12), that is, on the day of the Passion of Our Lord. When they assemble together in such a spirit, it is not to eat the Lord's Supper, but rather to give to others, and to drink themselves, of the cup of demons; while some bear on their tongues the poison that slays the souls of others, and others willingly receive the mortal venom which enters their heart through their ears. That is how, according to the Prophet, *death enters in through our windows* (Jer. ix. 21), when with [slavering] mouths and itching ears we give to, and receive from, each other in turn the mortal cup of scandal and detraction. Let not my soul come into their meeting, for they are hated by God, as the Apostle bears witness: *Detractors* [are] hateful to God (Rom. i. 30, Vulg. and Douay). Listen in what terms God Himself, speaking in a Psalm, confirms that statement: *Whoso privily slandereth his neighbour, him will I destroy* (Ps. ci. 5).

4. Nor is that wonderful to us when we perceive that this vice conflicts with, and persecutes, more even than others, charity, which is [the nature of] God Himself, as you yourselves can easily discern. For everyone who slanders his neighbour gives proof, in the first place, that he is wholly void of charity. In the second place, what other object can he have in uttering the slander than to induce others to hate or despise those of whom the slander is spoken? The slanderous tongue strikes, therefore, a deadly blow at charity in all those who hear the calumny, and, as far as its power extends, entirely destroys and extinguishes it; and not only in them, but in all those who are absent, but to whom the calumny is, perhaps, repeated, as words fly from lip to lip by those who have heard it. You see, then, how a malicious report may in a brief space of time easily infect with the plague of its malice a great number of souls. Wherefore the prophetic spirit says of such: *Their mouth is full of cursing and bitterness; their feet are swift to shed blood* (Ps. xiii. 3, Vulg. and Douay). And speech speeds as rapidly as the feet of a swift runner. If there be one only who speaks, and he speaks but one sole word, yet that one word enters into the ears of a multitude of hearers, and in one moment slays their souls; for a heart full of the venom of envy

can scatter bitter words only through its bitter instrument of the tongue, according to the saying of the Lord: *Out of the abundance of the heart the mouth speaketh* (Luke vi. 45). There are different varieties of this pest. There are some persons who vomit forth the poison of detraction, nakedly and without discrimination, as it comes into their heads. And again, there are others who take pains to conceal the malice they have conceived, and which they are no longer able to keep to themselves, with the cloak of an affected reserve. Before the slander is uttered, you see the man heaving deep sighs, putting on a grave look and a pretended sadness, casting his eyes down to the ground, speaking slowly, and uttering his slanders with a plaintive voice. Thus they produce so much the greater effect, as those who hear them believe that they are spoken with regret, and rather with reluctance than with malice. 'I regret it very much,' he protests, 'on his account, because I have great love for him; but I have never been able to correct him in this respect.' 'I knew well,' says another, 'that he was subject to that vice, though I should never have made it known. But since the fact has been declared by someone else, I am no longer able to deny the truth. I do it with regret, but it is true, nevertheless.' And he adds: 'It is a great pity, for he has good qualities in other respects; but in that matter he is, to speak the truth, inexcusable.'

5. Having said these few words respecting a vice so full of malignity, let me return to my orderly exposition, and show who are they who are spoken of here as *the upright*. I suppose that there is no one of right intelligence who imagines that it is 'uprightness' in a bodily sense that is predicated of those who love the Bride, therefore it is to be explained of spiritual uprightness, that is, rectitude of heart and of mind. It is the Spirit who speaks, comparing spiritual things with spiritual. Therefore God 'made man upright' according to the mind, not according to the earthy and material body. For He created him in His own image and similitude (Gen. i. 27), and as you sing in the Psalms, *The Lord our God is upright, and there is no unrighteousness in Him* (Ps. xcii. 15). God, then, who is upright, made man upright and similar to Himself, that is to say, without unrighteousness, even as there is no unrighteousness in Him. Now, unrighteousness is a vice of the heart, not of the flesh, and from this you know that the likeness of God which you have is to be preserved, or to be restored, in the spiritual part of your nature, and not in its earthy and clayey part. For God is Spirit, and it behoves those who desire to become like Him, or to persevere in His likeness, to enter into their heart, and to employ themselves in the spirit in that blessed work; so that with open face, beholding as in a glass the glory of the Lord, they may be changed into the same image from glory to glory, even as by the Spirit of the Lord (2 Cor. iii. 18).

6. Perhaps it may be said, again, that God has bestowed upon man an upright stature in body also, so that this exterior and bodily uprightness, though of a lower kind, may admonish the inner man to

preserve his spiritual uprightness, and the beauty of the perishable clay may rebuke the deformity of the mind; for what can be more indecent than to bear a bent and deformed mind in an upright body? It is a thing unfitting and shameful that a frame of clay, which is what our earthly body really is, should have its eyes raised on high, directed freely towards heaven, and taking pleasure to contemplate the great lights of the heavens; but that the being of spiritual and heavenly nature should, on the contrary, have its eyes, that is, its inward senses and affections, drawn downwards towards the earth, and that which ought to be nourished upon golden and precious sustenance should be clinging to the soil, wallowing in filth, like an unclean swine. Blush with shame, O my soul, to have changed the Divine likeness for that of the brute; and being of the heavens, to be wallowing in the mire. Blush with shame, O my soul, says our body, when you consider yourself and me. You were created upright and similar to your Creator, and you received me for a helper like unto yourself, at least, as far as the lineaments of bodily uprightness were concerned. Whithersoever you turn, whether it be to God above or to me below (for no man ever hated his own flesh), on every side meet you the various kinds of your own excellence; everywhere you have the familiar teachings of wisdom, bidding you preserve the nobleness and dignity of the state in which you have been placed. Why, then, are you not stricken with shame for having lost your glorious prerogative, while I have preserved and retained mine, which I only received in order to be a companion and helper to you? Why shall the Creator have to behold His likeness obliterated in you, while He preserves yours in me, and it is always a representation of you? But now you have turned that companionship and assistance, which was due to you from me, into a cause of confusion and shame; you abuse the service which I render you; and, as if you had become a brute and bestial spirit, treat unworthily the noble human body which you inhabit

7. Souls which are thus bent and deformed are not capable of loving the Bride, because those who are lovers of the world are not of the Bridegroom. *Whosoever will be a friend of the world is, it is said, the enemy of God* (James iv. 4). Therefore, to seek and to have a love for things which are on the earth is to bend down and deform the soul; while, on the contrary, to think of, and to long for, the things which are above is its uprightness. And in order that this rectitude may be perfect, it must exist first in the mind, and then pass into the life (*in sensu et consensu*).[1] I should, in fact, call you upright if you

[1] In this passage, again, and for a similar reason to that given above, the discrepancy in the old MSS. has thrown the early editions into confusion. In those in which the lengthy introduction here given is wanting, we find the following reading: 'And this uprightness, that it may be perfect in all respects, must be first in the mind, then in the life. I should say that he is upright in heart who has right sentiments in all things, and whose actions differ in no respect from the right sentiments which he has felt. See of whom it is said to the Bride, "The upright love thee": that is to say, those who know in all things what is right, and practise it accord-

think aright in all things, and your actions accord with your thoughts. Let your faith and your actions declare the condition of your mind, which is invisible. Consider as upright him whom you have ascertained to be Catholic in faith and righteous in actions. If one of these two be wanting, do not hesitate to conclude that he is deficient in uprightness; for you have in the Scripture: *If thou offerest rightly, but dost not rightly divide, thou hast sinned* (Gen. iv. 7). Whichsoever, indeed, of these two, faith and works, you offer to God, you do rightly; but you do not rightly to divide either from the other. Since you are right in offering, be not wrong in dividing. Why do you divide works from faith? Wrongly are you dividing, and the division destroys your faith; for *faith without works is dead* (James ii. 20). Will you offer to God a service that is dead? For if devotion is as a kind of soul to faith, what is faith which does not work by love but a dead corpse? Do you think to honour God with a gift that is fœtid? Do you think to please Him by being the murderer of your faith? How can the offering be a cause of peace in which there is a discord so cruel? It is not astonishing that Cain should have used murderous violence against his brother, when he had first slain faith in himself. Why do you wonder, O Cain, if He who despises you has no respect unto your offerings? (Gen. iv. 5). Nor is it matter for surprise that He has no respect unto you who are so divided against yourself. If you give your hand to the duties of religion, why do you give your heart as a sacrifice to jealousy? While you are at discord with yourself, you cannot be at peace with God; and so far from winning His favour, you offend against Him anew; not, indeed, as yet by offering violence to your brother, but by wrongly dividing your own offering. Though not yet guilty of the death of your brother, you are of the death of your faith (*fratricida, fideicida*). Can you possibly suppose yourself to be upright, when, even while you stretch your hand to God, jealousy and hatred of your brother are bending your heart down to the earth? while your faith is dead, while your works are but death, while your heart is without devotion, but filled with bitterness? Faith there was indeed in his offering, but no love in his faith; a right oblation, but a cruel division of it.

8. Separation from charity is the death of faith. Do you believe in Christ? do, then, His works, that your faith may continue living. Let love animate your faith, and action prove its reality. Let not him be bowed to the earth by the works of earth, whom faith lifts up towards heavenly things. You who declare that you are abiding in Christ ought even so to walk as He walked. But if you seek your own glory, if you envy the prosperous, if you slander the absent, if

---

ingly.' Then the sermon is concluded in these words: 'May God grant that we may be of those, and numbered with those who are loved by the Bridegroom, by the grace of the same Jesus Christ our Lord, who, with the Father and the Holy Ghost, liveth and reigneth, God for ever and ever. Amen.' But other MSS. prefer our reading.

you render back evil for evil, you act quite otherwise than Christ acted. You confess that you know God, but in words you deny Him. You have acted not uprightly, but impiously, in thus giving your tongue to Christ, but your heart to the devil. Listen to the Saviour's words : *This man honoureth me with his lips, but his heart is far from Me* (Is. xxix. 13, and Matt. xv. 7). Assuredly you are not upright, who are so far from right in dividing your offering. You cannot lift up your head, for it is pressed down under the yoke of the devil. Iniquity rules over you, so that you cannot raise yourself, and stand upright. Your iniquities have gone over your head, as an heavy burden they are too heavy for thee (Ps. xxxviii. 4). As says the Prophet, Wickedness sits upon a talent of lead (Zech. v. 7). You see, then, that faith, which worketh not by love, even though it be right, does not make a man upright. But he who is without love is not able to love the Bride. Again, neither do works, however upright they be, suffice, without faith, to render the heart upright. For who can call a man upright, who is not pleasing to God ? *But without faith it is impossible to please God* (Heb. xi. 6). And he who does not please God is not able to find pleasure in God. But on the contrary, he who does please God cannot fail to find pleasure in Him. Furthermore, he who finds no pleasure in God can find no pleasure either in [the Church, which is] His Bride. How, then, can a man be upright who loves neither God, nor the Church of God, of which it is said, *The upright love thee ?* If, then, neither faith without works, nor works without faith, are sufficient for uprightness of soul, let us, brethren, who believe in Christ, study to make the works of our hands and the desires of our hearts alike upright. Let us lift up our hearts with our hands to God, that we may be found upright wholly ; approving by right actions the rectitude of our faith, that we may be lovers of the Bride, and beloved by the Bridegroom, our Lord Jesus Christ, who is God blessed for ever. AMEN.

SERMON XXV.

THAT THE BRIDE, NAMELY, THE CHURCH, IS BLACK, YET COMELY.

I HAD already said in a former sermon that the Bride is obliged to reply to the attacks and reproaches of those who are envious of her glory, and who, while in the body they appear to be of the number of her maidens, are yet far removed from her in spirit. To them it is that she says : *I am black, but comely, O ye daughters of Jerusalem* (i. 5). It is evident that they speak disparagingly of her, accusing her of being black. But consider her patience and gentleness. For not only has she not rendered railing for railing, but contrariwise has returned to them a blessing, calling them daughters of Jerusalem, who had deserved for their wickedness to be called daughters of Babylon, or daughters of Baal, or whatever other name of reproach had come to her mind. Surely she had learned of the prophet, or rather from that anointing which teaches gentleness, not to break the bruised reed, nor to quench the smoking flax (Is. xlii. 3). Therefore she considered that those who were already angry should not be still farther irritated by her, nor anything added to the stings of envy, by which they were tormented. On the contrary, she strove the more to be pacific with those who were enemies unto peace, knowing that she was debtor, even unto the unwise. She preferred, then, to soothe them by a courteous word, because it was her care rather to labour for the salvation of those weak ones, than for the gratification of her own vengeance.

2. That perfection is indeed to be desired for all; but especially does it befit those who would be good rulers in spiritual things. For those who are good and faithful pastors know that they are set over others in order to care for weak and languishing souls, not to live in pride and state. And when some of those committed to their charge utter murmurs, and perhaps even burst out into threats and violent words against them, they remember that they are not masters, but physicians of the soul; and oppose at once to that spiritual madness, remedial and healing treatment, not harshness and punishment. This, then, is the reason why the Bride calls those 'daughters of Jerusalem' whose ill-will and insulting words she is enduring, so as to soothe their murmurs by words full of sweetness, to compose their excitement, to heal their envy. It is written: *A peaceful tongue appeaseth strife* (Prov. xv. 18). Also these were, in fact, daughters of Jerusalem in a certain sense, nor does the Bride speak falsely in so naming them. For whether it be on account of the Sacraments of the Church, which they receive indifferently with the good; or on account of their profession of a common Creed and Faith; or the companionship which they have at least according to the body with the faithful; or even because of the hope of their future salvation, which ought not to be altogether abandoned, even with regard to those who live in so abandoned a manner, as long as life is continued to them they are called, with good reason, daughters of Jerusalem.

3. Let us examine now that which is said: *I am black, but comely.* Is not this a contradiction in terms? By no means. I speak for the unlearned, who are unable to distinguish between colour and form—form is inherent in the composition of the thing spoken of; colour is but a quality of it. Not everything, then, which is black, is necessarily on that account ill-favoured. For instance, blackness in the pupil of the eye is not unbecoming; there are black gems which are highly prized in ornaments; while black hair contrasted with a pale complexion augments the beauty and charm of a face. You will easily notice the same thing in a great number of instances, and will find many things which are not otherwise than graceful in form, but of which the colour is not agreeable. That is perhaps the

case with the Bride, who is beautiful in form and features, though of dark, even black, complexion; but, then, she is in the place of her pilgrimage. It shall be quite otherwise when the exalted Bridegroom shall present her to Himself *a glorious Church, not having spot, or wrinkle, or any such thing* (Eph. v. 27). But if she should say at the present time that she has no blackness of hue, she would deceive herself, nor would there be truth in her. Therefore do not wonder that when she has said *I am black*, she adds with words of modest confidence, *but comely*. How is it possible that she should not be beautiful, to whom it is said: *Rise up, my fair one, and come away* (ii. 10). But she to whom it was said '*Come*' had not yet arrived; lest perhaps any should suppose that this was spoken, not to her while still toiling on her way, her countenance darkened with the fierce rays of the sun; but to her already in blessedness, reigning in glory, having left behind every trace of blackness or stain.

4. In the next place, why does she say that, though black, she is at the same time beautiful? She is black, perhaps on account of the life that she led formerly in the shadow, under the control of the prince of this world, in which she still bore the image of the earthly; while she is beautiful with the image of the heavenly, with which, when afterwards she walked in newness of life, she was thenceforth invested. But if this is the case, why should she not say, as speaking of the past, 'I was black,' rather than, 'I am black?' But if anyone is pleased with this sense of the words, then those which follow, *as the tents of Kedar, as the curtains of Solomon*, ought to be understood as referring, ' Kedar,' to the former life, and ' the curtains of Solomon' to the new. It is of the skins, or tents, of Kedar that the prophet speaks, when he declares: *Suddenly are my tents spoiled, and my curtains in a moment* (Jer. iv. 20). The former word, *black*, describes the mean and ignoble tents of Kedar; the latter, *comely*, the curtains of the King of glory.

5. But let us see if both the one and the other do not refer better to the condition of the higher life. If we consider the exterior of those who are holy, how humble and abject it is, how vile and neglected in outward appearance; and yet, at the very same time they are inwardly contemplating with unveiled face the glory of the Lord, they are being transformed into the same image from glory to glory, as by the Spirit of the Lord (2 Cor. iii. 18), does it not seem to you that each of these souls will be able to reply to those who reproach him with his blackness: *I am black, but comely?* Would you that I should show you a soul which was at the same time black and yet beautiful? *His letters, say they, are weighty and powerful; but his bodily presence is weak, and his speech contemptible* (2 Cor. x. 10). This was Paul. So you, O daughters of Jerusalem, form your judgment of Paul from his bodily presence, and you despise him as being black and repulsive because you perceive him to be a man of small stature, afflicted by *hunger and thirst, by cold and nakedness, by many perils, by stripes above measure, by deaths oft* (2 Cor. xi. 27, 23)? These are the things which

[in your estimation] blacken Paul. For reasons like this the Doctor of the Gentiles is reputed inglorious and ignoble, obscure, black, and in one word, as it were, the offscouring of this world. Nevertheless, is it not he who was caught up into Paradise, who, in his pureness of soul, passed through the first and the second heaven, and penetrated even to the third ? O soul truly most beautiful ! which, though inhabiting a body so weak and ailing, the heavenly glory did not scorn to admit, the highest angels did not reject, even the Divine splendour did not repulse. This soul do you style 'black'? Black it is, but beautiful, O daughters of Jerusalem. Black according to your judgment, but beautiful in the judgment of God and of His angels. Even though it be black, it is only outwardly. But to him it is a very small thing that he should be judged by you, or by those who judge according to the outward appearance. For man indeed *looketh on the outward appearance, but the Lord looketh on the heart* (1 Sam. xvi. 7). If it be black without, it is, therefore, beautiful within, and pleasing to Him whom it has desired to please. It does not devote itself to be pleasing to you, knowing that if it did so it would not be the servant of Christ. Happy is the blackness which produces whiteness of soul, the light of knowledge, purity of conscience.

6. Hear now what God promises by His prophet to those who are black after this fashion, whom either the humility of penitence or the zeal of charity, as it were the burning rays of the sun, seem to have robbed of outward fairness. *Though your sins be as scarlet*, saith the Lord, *they shall be as white as snow : though they be red like crimson, they shall be as wool* (Is. i. 18). That outward blackness and disfigurement which appears in holy men is not to be contemned, for it produces inward whiteness, and prepares the soul to make wisdom its seat. For *wisdom is the brightness of eternal life*[1] as the Wise man defines it ; and it is needful that the soul which it has chosen for its seat should be clear and white. But if the soul of the righteous is the seat of wisdom, then I may assert without hesitation that the soul of the righteous is clear and white ; perhaps even righteousness consists in this whiteness of soul. For Paul, for whom *was laid up the crown of righteousness* (2 Tim. iv. 8), was undoubtedly righteous. His soul, then, was white and clear ; in it wisdom dwelt, so that he spoke wisdom in a mystery among them that are perfect — the hidden wisdom, which none of the princes of this world knew (1 Cor. ii. 7, 8). Moreover, it was that outward blackness and ruggedness, caused by a weak constitution of body, by many troubles and trials, by frequent watchings and fastings, which either produced in him, or rendered him deserving of, that brightness of wisdom and of righteousness. Therefore, that which was black in St. Paul was, in fact, a richer ornament to him than any degree of outward splendour, and than even royal magnificence. Not to be compared with him in essential

---

[1] Wisd. vii. 26, '*vitæ æternæ.*' But St. Bernard no doubt quoted from memory, for the passage cited reads '*æternæ lucis*' = ' of eternal light '—and I cannot discover any trace of a reading '*vitæ.*'—ED.

comeliness are the greatest physical beauty, not the fair and polished skin, not the rose-tinted complexion, which must ere long be the prey of corruption, not the splendid dress, which grows old and tattered with time, nor the sparkle of gems, nor any things of that kind, which are, one and all, subject to corruption.

7. It is, then, with good reason that the saints, despising all unnecessary care and adorning of the outward man, which is corruptible, devote all their care and pains to cultivate and render fair that inward man which is in the likeness of God, and is being renewed from day to day. For they are well assured that nothing can be more acceptable to God than His own image if it be restored to its original beauty. It is for that reason that all their glory is inward, not outward: that is to say, it consists not in the flower of the field, or in the praises of the people, but in the Lord. Therefore they say, *Our rejoicing is this, the testimony of our conscience* (2 Cor. i. 12); and of their conscience the sole judge is God, whom alone they desire to please; and to please Him is, in their eyes, the true, and only, and highest glory. Nor, certainly, is this inward glory small, since the Lord of glory deigns thus to be glorified, as it is said in the Psalm, *The King's daughter is all glorious within* (Ps. xlv. 13). It is also safer than any other glory, since each person has it in himself and not in another. And it may be that not the inward brightness only, but the outward blackness also, is a reason for glory, since there is nothing useless in the saints, but all things work together for their good. They glory, therefore, not only in hope, but also in tribulations. *Most gladly, therefore*, says the Apostle, *will I rather glory in my infirmities, that the power of Christ may rest upon me* (2 Cor. xii. 9). That infirmity is, in truth, to be desired which is compensated for by the power of Christ. Who will grant unto me, not merely to have infirmities, but even to fall into extreme weakness and helplessness, that I may be recovered and made strong by the strength of Him who is the Lord of all power and strength? For *His strength is made perfect in weakness. For*, he continues, *when I am weak, then am I strong* (2 Cor. xii. 9, 10).

8. This being so, the Bride has good ground for counting that as a glory to herself which by her envious rivals is blamed as a deformity, and to boast not only of her beauty, but also of her blackness. She does not blush for that blackness, which she knows that her Spouse in former days likewise bore, for it makes her like unto Him; and what glory can be so great? For she assuredly regards no distinction as being so high as this, to bear the reproach of Christ. And this makes her say with joy and gladness: *God forbid that I should glory, save in the Cross of Our Lord Jesus Christ* (Gal. vi. 14). The very reproach of the Cross is welcome to him who is not ungrateful to the Crucified. It is, so to speak, a blackness, but a blackness which is the form and likeness of the Lord Jesus. Go to holy Isaiah, and he will describe to you the form and spirit in which you are to view Him. For is it not He of whom the Prophet says: *He is a Man of*

Sorrows, and acquainted with grief; and that *He hath no form nor comeliness?* And he has added: *We did esteem Him as one who is a leper, as smitten of God and afflicted.* But *He was wounded for our transgressions, He was bruised for our iniquities; and with His stripes we are healed* (Is. liii. 3-5, Vulg.). See what has rendered Him black. Add to this what David has said: *Thou art fairer than the children of men* (Ps. xlv. 2), and you will find in the Bridegroom all that the Bride has declared of Him in this passage.

9. Does it not seem to you that, according to what has been said, He was able to reply rightly to the envious Jews: 'I am black, but comely, O ye sons of Jerusalem?' He was truly black, who *had no form nor comeliness;* black, because *He was a worm and no man, a reproach of men, and despised of the people* (Ps. xxii. 6). Lastly, He even caused Himself to be *made sin* [for us] (2 Cor. v. 21), and shall I fear to say that He is black? Behold Him! covered with rags, livid with stripes, defiled with spitting, pale with the pallor of death; can you even then hesitate to confess that He is black? But ask of the Apostles how they saw Him on the mount [of Transfiguration]; learn of the angels [all the perfection of Him] upon whom they yearn to look, and you will declare in wonder and admiration that He is indeed *beautiful*. He is, then, beautiful in Himself; His blackness is on thy account. O Lord Jesus, how perfect and adorable, even though Thou art clad in my human form, is Thy beauty to me! Not only because of the wonders of Divine power with which Thou dost shine on every side, but because of Thy righteousness, Thy kindness, and Thy truth. Blessed is he who, considering diligently Thy life and actions as a Man dwelling among men, sets himself with all his endeavours to imitate Thee to the utmost. This blessed gift, the first-fruits of her dowry, she [Thy Church] who is Thy fairest and best beloved, has already received; nor is she either slow to imitate that which is most beautiful in Thee, or ashamed to endure those sufferings of which the blackness is upon Thee. Therefore, it was that she said: *I am black, but comely, O ye daughters of Jerusalem.* Therefore, also, she adds the comparison, *As the tents of Kedar, as the curtains of Solomon.* But that is a saying difficult and obscure, and not to be even attempted by those who are wearied. You have time to knock hereafter at that door. If you do so with sincere hearts, He who is the Revealer of mysteries will appear: nor will He who invites you to knock delay to open. For it is He who openeth, and no man shutteth--the Bridegroom of the Church, Jesus Christ Our Lord, who is blessed for ever and ever. AMEN.

SERMON XXVI.[1]

ST. BERNARD LAMENTS THE DEATH OF HIS BROTHER GERARD.

*A*S *the tents of Kedar, as the curtains of Solomon.* We must begin from this point, since it was here that we left off in the last Sermon. I know that you are expecting to hear what these words signify, and what relation they have to those which precede them, since they are used by way of comparison ; for it may be said that they are so connected, that the two parts of the comparison refer only to the first half of the sentence which precedes it : '*I am black*,' or, again, that the two parts of the comparison refer respectively to the two sentences which precede them, each to each. The former sense is the more simple, the latter the more obscure. But let us try each of them, and that which is the more difficult first , for it is not in the two former, but in the two latter words of each clause that there is any difficulty. For 'Kedar,' which means 'darkness,' seems to agree sufficiently clearly with the idea of blackness,[2] but 'curtains of Solomon' not so well with that of fairness or beauty. Then, who does not see that 'tents' falls, nevertheless, into the same interpretation ? What are these tents, in fact, but the bodies in which we perform our pilgrimage ? For *we have here no continuing city, but we seek one to come* (Heb. xiii. 14). Furthermore, we have a warfare to carry on in them, as soldiers have in tents ; for we have, as men violent, to take the kingdom of heaven by force (Matt. xi. 12). For the life of man upon earth is a warfare (Job vii. 1, Vulg. and Douay), and as long as we combat in this body, we are exiled from the presence of the Lord, that is, from the light ; for the Lord is Light, and insomuch as anyone is not with Him, he is in darkness, that is, in Kedar. Let him recognise as his that lamentable exclamation : *Woe is me ! that I sojourn in Mesech, that I dwell in the tents of Kedar ! My soul hath long dwelt with him that hateth peace* (Ps. cxx. 5, 6). This, then, is the abode which we have in the body ; not the home of a citizen, or the domicile of one native-born, but either the tent of a soldier, or the temporary lodging of a traveller. This body, I repeat, is a tent, the tent of Kedar, because it surrounds the soul, and deprives it now for awhile of the enjoyment of the infinite Light, nor suffers it even to behold that Light, except, as it were, in a glass and darkly, but not face to face (1 Cor. xiii. 12).

---

[1] Preached in A.D. 1138.
[2] It is not often that arguments from the derivation of words are understated by our author ; but such is apparently the case here. Kedar (קדר) means, according to Gesenius, 'black skin,' or 'black-skinned man ' (it is the collective patronymic of the Arabs), and therefore answers literally to the appellation of 'black' in verse 4.—ED.

2. Do you see whence comes the blackness which is upon the Church, and how it is that some stains of rust and mould are upon even the fairest souls? It is from the tents of Kedar, from the pursuit of a laborious warfare, from the long duration of an unhappy existence, from the hardships of a suffering and calamitous exile, from the body, in fact, which is both burdensome and weak; for the corruptible body presseth down the soul, and the earthy tabernacle weigheth down the mind that museth upon many things (Wisd. ix. 15). Wherefore souls desire to be dissolved, that, being delivered from the body, they may depart (*avolent*) into the embrace of Christ. Therefore one of these unhappy souls, lamenting, said: *O miserable man that I am! who shall deliver me from the body of this death?* (Rom. vii. 24). For such a soul is aware that in the tents of Kedar it is not possible to be entirely exempt from spot and wrinkle, or from some degree of blackness, and therefore it desires to go forth from the body that it may be free from all these defects. And this is why the Bride has said that she is black *as the tents of Kedar*. But how is she beautiful *as the curtains of Solomon?* There is somewhat sublime and sacred wrapped up in the veil of these words, but I know not what it is, and scarcely dare to approach it at all, except at the good pleasure of Him who has hidden and sealed the mystery. I have, in fact, read that 'he who is a searcher of [the Divine] majesty shall be overwhelmed with its glory' (Prov. xxv. 27, Vulg.). This, therefore, I pass over and defer to another time. Let it be your care in the meantime to obtain for me this grace by your prayers, as you are accustomed to do, so that I may return more willingly, because with a greater degree of confidence, to that subject which needs the greatest attention. And perhaps one who knocks piously at the door will attain what the rash theorist can never reach. And besides, my grief, and the pain which I am enduring, compels me to come to an end.

3. For how long shall I dissemble and hide the fire which is within me, which consumes my sad heart, which feeds upon my vitals?[1]

---

[1] Here begins the funeral oration made by St. Bernard for his brother Gerard. Berengarius, that impudent disciple of Abaelard, reproaches the writer for it unjustly, declaring that 'he made an unsuitable mingling of sorrow with joy.' Again, he objects that St. Bernard 'had borrowed, word for word, certain lines of the funeral oration made by St. Ambrose upon the death of his brother Satyrus.' Now, those lines are not found at all in that oration; nor if they were, would the fact furnish any charge against St. Bernard. It will be well to cite the two passages referred to by him. This is the first: 'My brother has quitted this life; or, to speak more correctly, has quitted death for life. Yes, my brother, who was the standard of conscience, the mirror of a holy character, the bond of religion, has left us. Who will show more ardour in labour? Who will comfort better the affliction of those in trouble?' The other is this: 'The ox seeks for his companion ox, and when he finds himself alone, gives proof, by his frequent lowing, of the tender attachment which he feels. Yes, even the ox requires the companion with whom he is accustomed to draw the plough with laborious neck.' The latter passage is, in fact, found at the end of the opening of the oration in St. Ambrose; neither the one nor the other in Bernard. It is true that, in order to escape the charge of falsehood or deception, Berengarius prefixes the words 'if I do not mistake.'

Though closely concealed, it rages the more fiercely, and does not cease to spread. What have I to do with this song of joy, who am myself in bitterness of soul? The vehement power of grief interrupts my purpose, and the indignation of the Lord drinks up my spirit; for he, by whose means my studies in the [ways of the] Lord were wont to be wholly free, has been taken away, and with him my very heart has left me. But hitherto I have put constraint upon my soul, and have concealed my feelings, lest affection should seem to overcome faith. While others are weeping, I, as you may have observed, followed with dry eyes[1] the sad funeral train, and with dry eyes stood at the grave, until all the funeral services were performed. With my own lips I, clad in my priestly robes, completed the customary prayers for him, and with my own hands cast the earth, according to custom, upon the body, soon to become earth, of my beloved. Those who beheld me wept, and wondered that I did not weep also, since all commiserated, not him indeed, but me who had lost him ; for whose heart, though it were of iron, would not be moved at my condition, at seeing me surviving my Gerard? The loss was common to all, but, in comparison with my individual trouble, it was not considered. But as for me, I resisted my feelings, with whatever force of faith I could command, striving not to be moved uselessly by this allotment of nature, this payment of the common debt due by all men, this customary incident of our mortal condition, brought about by the will of the Almighty, by the judgment of the Just One, by the stroke of Him who is to be feared, in a word, by the will of the Lord. In this way I then, and afterwards, constrained myself to refrain from the indulgence of much weeping, however sorrowful I was and full of trouble. I was able to command my tears, but not my sorrow, and, as it is written: *I was so troubled that I could not speak* (Ps. lxxvii. 4). But my grief, thus suppressed, shot deeper roots into my heart, and became, as I feel, the more bitter, because it was allowed no expression. I am overcome, I confess, and what I suffer inwardly must come forth to the light. Let it come forth, then, to the eyes of my children, who, knowing the greatness of my loss, will pardon the excess of my grief, and be the more moved kindly to console me.

4. You know, my children, how well founded is my grief, how great and how painful my wound ; for you are well aware how faithful a companion was he who has now left my side, in the way wherein I was walking, how vigilant, laborious, cheerful, and agreeable. Who was so peculiarly necessary to me? By whom was I equally beloved? He was my brother by blood, but still more closely related to me in religion. Mourn for my sad lot, I entreat you, to whom these things are known. I was weak in body, and he sustained me ; I was of feeble spirit, and he strengthened me ; I was slothful and negligent, and he urged me on ; improvident and forgetful, and he reminded me of my duty. Wherefore art thou thus torn from me?

---

[1] According to Geoffrey ('Life,' Bk. iii., c. 21), Bernard scarcely ever rendered the last duties to any Religious without weeping.

Why art thou thus snatched from my hands, O man of one mind with me, man after my own heart? We loved each other in life; why in death are we separated? A most bitter separation indeed, which Death only could have wrought! For when did he living ever desert me? It is a terrible sundering, the work of Death alone! Who would not have spared the sweet tie of our mutual affection, except Death, the enemy of all that is sweet? Ah, that is truly called death which, by snatching away one of us, has slain two at one blow! Is not his death mine also? It is, in fact, death for me even more than for him, since that which remains to me of life is more painful to me than all the deaths in the world. I live that I may endure a living death; and shall I call that life? You would have treated me more mercifully, O cruel Death, in depriving me of the use of life, than of the only fruit to be derived from it; for life without fruit is more bitter than death. A twofold doom is preparing for the barren tree; the axe and the fire (Matt. iii. 10). Thou wert envious of my labours, and hast withdrawn from me my nearest relative and my friend, whose care was the principal cause of the fruit (if any) which followed them. It would have been far better for me to be deprived of my life, than of thy presence, my dear Gerard, who by thy zeal urged me on in my labours for the Lord, who wert a faithful[1] helper and a cautious adviser. Why, I ask, have we loved, or have we lost? It is a hard condition, but my lot, not his, is the one to be pitied. For thou, dear brother, if thou hast lost those who are dear to thee, hast regained those who are dearer still. But what consolation remains for me, unhappy, after the loss of thee, my only (*unicum*) comfort? The society in the body which was between us was agreeable equally to each of us, because of the union of our hearts; but I alone feel the wound of our separation. That which was peaceful and sweet in our friendship belonged to us both; that which is sad and sorrowful has fallen to me alone; upon me has the wrath of God fallen, upon me is His anger weighing. To both of us equally were the welcome presence, the sweet companionship, the interesting conversation; but I alone have wholly lost these delights; you have but exchanged them for others still better, and assuredly you have gained much by the change.

5. How great, then, is the recompense of joys and blessings uncounted which thou, O dearest brother, hast received for the loss of me! You have assuredly, in exchange for me who am of so little worth, the everlasting Presence of Christ; nor do you feel any loss in your absence from me, since you are blended with the Choirs of Angels. You have, then, no reason to complain that my presence has been taken from you, since the Lord of Glory has deigned to give unto you abundantly of His Presence, and of that of His blessed ones. But what have I in exchange for thee? How greatly could I wish to know what feeling thou hast now for me, once the object of thy dearest affection, now wavering under cares and pains, and deprived

---

[1] *Fidelis;* otherwise, *fortis.*

of thy support which used to sustain my weakness; if it is permitted to thee still to give any thought to us unhappy ones, now that thou hast entered into the depth of light, and art absorbed in that great ocean of everlasting felicity! For perhaps, even though thou hast known me according to the flesh, thou knowest me no more now; and because thou hast entered into the sphere of the power and majesty of the Lord, thou art conscious of His righteousness only, and art unmindful of me. But he that is joined unto the Lord is one spirit (1 Cor. vi. 17) with Him, and is wholly transformed into a certain feeling of the Divine presence; he can no longer have thought or taste but for God only, and that which he thinks of, or desires, is God alone—he is, in fact, filled with God. But God is Love; and the more closely anyone is united to God, the more filled is he with love. Although God is impassible, He is not incapable of compassion; and it is His especial attribute always to have pity and to spare. Therefore it must necessarily be that you, my dear brother, should be pitiful, because you are joined unto Him who is Pity itself. Although you can no longer feel any unhappiness, although you can no longer suffer, yet you can still feel for the sufferings of others. Your affection, then, is not diminished, but changed; nor, in putting on God, have you put off all sympathy for us,[1] for He, too, careth for us (1 Peter v. 7). You have put off all that was weak, but not all that was charitable, for Charity never faileth (1 Cor. xiii. 8), and you will not forget me for ever.

6. I seem to hear my brother, as it were, saying: *Can a mother forget . . . the son of her womb? yea, they may forget, yet will I not forget thee* (Is. xlix. 15). I have much need that it should be so. You know in what state you left me, how I totter even to falling; I have none to give me a helping hand. In every new need which occurs, I look to Gerard, as I had been accustomed to do, and he is not here. Then, unhappy as I am, I sigh and groan, as one without help. Whom shall I consult in difficult matters? to whom have recourse in troubles? Who will bear my burdens? who put to flight dangers? Were not the eyes of my Gerard wont to direct[2] my steps everywhere? Was not your breast, my brother, more familiar with my cares than even my own, you who bore them more than I, and felt them more acutely?[3] Was there not upon your lips speech so winning and persuasive that you were constantly able to relieve me from the burden of worldly conversation, and to restore me to my beloved silence? The Lord had bestowed upon him judgment and discretion, so that he knew when and how to speak. He gave such satisfaction by the prudence of his replies, through the grace given unto him from above, both to those of the house and to strangers, that if anyone had conferred with

---

[1] In connection with this assertion, reference may be made to the two appearances of Gerard after his death, related in the 'Life of St. Bernard,' Bk. iv., c. 2, n. 10; and Bk. v, c. 3, n. 18.

[2] *Anteibant;* otherwise, *animabant.*

[3] This is shown by his warning Bernard against pride on account of the miracles performed by him ('Life,' Bk. i., c. 9, n. 43).

Gerard, he had scarcely anything to ask of me. He did, indeed, go
to meet new-comers, and put himself in their way, that they might
not break in suddenly upon my leisure. If he was unable to satisfy
any by himself, those he conducted to me, and the others he sent
away. O man of marvellous industry! O faithful friend! He sought
to please his friend, and he was not wanting, at the same time, in the
duties of charity. Who departed from him with empty hands? If it
were a rich man, he carried away advice; if a poor, substantial help.
Nor could he, who burdened himself with so many cares that I might
be free from them, be said to seek the things which were his own.
For he, being, in truth, the most humble of men, hoped that my leisure
would be of more value to the house than his would be. Yet sometimes he required that he might be released from his task, and give
way to another, as if someone else would perform it better than he.
But where was such an one to be found? Nor was he kept in office,
as is often the case, by an impatient and restless disposition, but by
the mere impulse of charity. For he used to labour more than all
others, and to receive less than any; so that often while he ministered
things necessary—for example, food and clothing—to others, he himself was in many respects in need of them. Lastly, when he felt that
he was drawing near his departure, lifting up his voice to God, he
said: 'Thou knowest, O God, that as in me lay, I always longed for
quiet, for the care of my own soul, and to be occupied with Thee
only. But I have been retained in the cares of duties by the fear of
displeasing Thee, by the will of the brethren, by the desire to obey,
and, above all, by the brotherly affection which I bore to him who is
at once my abbot and my brother.' So it is. I render thanks, then,
to thee, O my brother, for every result of my studies in Divine truth,
if they have produced any. If I have made any progress in them,
if I have been of service to any, it is to thee I owe it. Thou didst
charge thyself with the care of the affairs of the house; and I, thanks
to thee, was able to sit at leisure, or, at least, to occupy myself more
sacredly with the duties to which God called me, or to devote myself
more usefully to my sons [in the faith] with their instruction and
training. For how could I be otherwise than in peace of mind within,
while I knew that thou wert busied without—thou who wert my right
hand, the light of my eyes, my heart, and my tongue? And, indeed,
thy hand was tireless, thine eye candid and straightforward, thine
heart full of wisdom, and thy tongue gave wise counsel, as it is written:
*The mouth of the righteous speaketh wisdom, and his tongue talketh of
judgment* (Ps. xxxvii. 30).

7. But why have I said that Gerard was busied without, as if he
were unacquainted with the inner life, and a stranger to spiritual gifts?
Those spiritually-minded persons who knew him, knew that his words
were full of the Holy Spirit. Those of his chamber knew that his
mind and his affections savoured not of the flesh, but were warmed
by the fire of the Spirit. Who more rigid than he in the observance
of the Rule? who more strict in the mastery (*castigando*) of his body,

more absorbed and elevated in contemplation, or more keen and penetrating in discourse? How often, in discussion with him, I have learned things which I knew not! and I, who had come to instruct others, have returned myself instructed. Nor is it wonderful that this was the case with me, since eminent and learned men have testified to me that the very same thing had taken place with them also when with him. Though he had not acquired human learning, he had sound and powerful intelligence, enabling him to divine many of its truths; and he had also the illuminating Spirit. Nor was he very accomplished in the greatest things alone, but also in the smallest. What was there which escaped his skill and knowledge—for example, in all that relates to buildings, in the culture of land and of gardens, in works for water, and in all the other arts and labours of country people? He was easily the director of masons, of smiths, of agriculturists, of gardeners, of shoemakers, and even of weavers. Whilst in the judgment of all he was wiser than any, in his own eyes alone he was not wise. Would that the malediction which we find in Scripture, *Woe unto them that are wise in their own eyes* (Is. v. 21), did not touch many far less wise than he more than it touched him! Those to whom I speak know that what I say of him is true, and even much more than I have said. But I pass over many things, because he is my brother and my flesh. Yet this one thing I add in entire assurance: he was useful to me in all things, and beyond all other men; he was of use in small things and great, in private affairs and public, in the monastery and out of it. It was with good reason that I was wholly attached to him, who was everything to me. He left to me the honour and name of Superior, and but little beyond, for the labours of that office he used to discharge. I was called Abbot, but he was so in effect, for he took upon him all the cares of that charge. Rightly did I rest upon him, by whose means it was that I was able to rejoice in the Lord, to preach and to pray with greater freedom and security from interruption. It was by thy means, O my brother, I repeat, that my mind was less disturbed, my rest more agreeable, my discourse more efficacious, my preaching fuller of edification, my reading more frequent, and the affections of my heart more fervent.

8. Alas! thou hast been taken from me, and all these things with thee. With thee have passed away all the joys, and all the gladness, of my life. Already cares are breaking in upon me, already anxieties, hitherto unknown, press upon me on all sides, difficulties and annoyances from every quarter seek me, because I am alone; in going from me, these are all thou hast left me, and under this burden I groan without a companion. I must of necessity lay it down, or be crushed under it, since you have withdrawn your shoulders from its support. Who will grant unto me speedily, after thee, to die? For to die instead of thee, and so to deprive thee of the glory which thou art now enjoying, this I should not wish to have done. I shall live, as long as I live, in bitterness and in sorrow; and let this be my only consolation, to mourn and to be afflicted. I will not spare myself;

I will assist the Lord's Hand; for it is the Hand of the Lord that hath touched me. It is I, I say, whom He hath touched, whom He hath wounded; not him whom He hath called into rest: for He hath slain me in cutting short the days of my brother. For who could say that the Lord hath slain him, whom He hath caused to enter into life? But that which has been to him the gate of life has manifestly been to me the gate of death; and by that death I should say that I am the person dead, not he who has fallen asleep in the Lord. Flow forth, flow forth, ye tears, long since brimming over; flow forth, since he who would have hindered your course has himself gone forth from this life! Let the torrents of my suffering head be opened, and the fountains of waters burst forth, if perchance they may suffice to wash away the stains of those sins by which I have deserved the wrath of God! When the Lord shall have had compassion upon me, then perhaps I, too, shall deserve to be consoled, provided that I do not spare to afflict myself; for they that mourn shall be comforted (Matt. v. 4). Therefore let every good man condescend to me, and let him who is spiritual uphold me in my sorrow, in the spirit of sympathy and gentleness. Let my grief be regarded, I entreat, with compassion, and not after the manner of men. For we see day by day that those who are dead lament for their dead; but in what manner? There is with them much weeping, but no fruit. We do not blame their distress and grief, unless it be excessive, but the cause of it. Affection is from nature, and the distress which it causes us is a part of the penalty of sin; but the cause is vanity and sin. For in the world what is lamented, if I do not mistake, is the deadly injury inflicted [by death] upon carnal glory, and upon the advantages of the present life. And those who weep thus are themselves to be wept for. Surely that is not the case with me? My grief is similar to theirs, but the cause is different, and the intention of it quite unlike their intention. I do not complain at all of the loss of the things of this world. What I grieve for is only that I have lost faithful help and salutary counsel in those things which belong to God. It is my Gerard for whom I mourn—Gerard, my brother according to the flesh, nearer still to me in the spirit, and in the work and purpose of my life ever my companion and associate.

9. My soul clung closely to his, and it was rather unity of sentiment than unity of blood which made us two to be one. Our nearness of blood counted, no doubt, for something; but it was companionship of mind and will, conformity of character and inclination, which united us more closely still. Since we were of one heart and of one soul, the sword [of death] has passed through my soul equally as through his; but having severed them, it has placed one part in heaven, but left the other in the mire of earth. It is I, it is I, who am that unhappy portion which is left prostrate in the clay, mutilated by the loss of the better part of itself; and yet people say to me: 'Do not weep.' My very bowels are torn away; and it is

said to me, 'Do not feel any pain.' But I do feel pain, and that in spite of myself; I have not the insensibility of a stone, nor is my flesh of bronze; I have feeling assuredly, and sharp pain, and my trouble is ever in my sight. He who has stricken me will not be able to accuse me of hardness and want of sensibility, as those of whom He said: *I have stricken them, but they have not grieved* (Jer. v. 3, but quoted inexactly). I have confessed my great affliction, and denied it not. Someone has called this carnal; I do not deny that it is human, just as I do not deny that I am a man. If that does not suffice, then I shall not deny that it is carnal. For I also am carnal, and one sold under sin, destined to death, and justly deserving of punishments and pains. Far from being insensible to penalties, I shudder at death, I confess, for myself and for those who are dear to me. And Gerard was not only mine, but was very dear. Was he not plainly mine, who by blood was my brother, by profession my son [in the faith], my father for the care he had of me, my companion and colleague in character and wishes, as in affection he was most intimate and dear? He has departed from my side: and I feel that his death has inflicted upon me a deep and terrible wound.

10. Forgive me, my sons; or rather, if you are my sons, lament for the trouble of your father. Pity me, pity me, you at least who are my friends, who take notice how heavy is the stroke which I have received from the hand of the Lord for my sins. He has stricken me with the rod of His indignation: justly, in regard of my deserts; but severely, in regard of my power to bear it. Who, except one who is ignorant by what bonds of affection Gerard and I were united, would suppose it a light thing to me to live without Gerard? Nevertheless, I do not desire to oppose at all the decrees (*sermonibus*) of the Holy One; I do not call in question His judgment, by which each one is caused to receive that which he deserves: Gerard, the crown which he has merited; and I, the punishment which is due to me. Is it reasonable to declare that I call in question the sentence because I feel the penalty keenly? To feel is human, but to repine would be impious. It is human, I repeat, and unavoidable, that we should not be indifferent to those who are our friends; that we should enjoy their presence, and lament its being taken from us. Social intercourse, particularly among friends, will not be tedious; the reluctance to separate, and the pain which is felt by each when separated, shows plainly the effect that their mutual affection has had upon those who live together. I grieve on thy account, my dearest Gerard, not because thy condition is to be regretted, but because thou art taken away. And, therefore, perhaps it is my condition rather, I who drink the cup of bitterness, which calls for regret; and still more, because I drink it alone. For thou hast no part in it, and I endure alone what those who have a mutual affection are accustomed to endure equally when deprived of the presence of each other.

11. May God grant that thou mayst not be lost to me, but only have gone before me, and that I may one day, whether soon or late, follow thee whithersoever thou hast gone I do not doubt at all that thou hast gone to join those whom in the midst of thy last night on earth thou didst invite to praise God, when with a serene countenance and a voice of joy thou didst burst forth on a sudden, to the great astonishment of all, into that Psalm of David: *Praise ye the Lord from the heavens, praise Him in the heights* (Ps. cxlviii. 1). While it was still midnight, my brother, the day was dawning[1] for thee, and the night was as clear as the day. Assuredly that night was full of delights for thee, and it brought thee into the Light. I was summoned to witness that miracle, to see a man exulting in the hour of death, and scorning its approach. O Death, where is thy victory? O Death, where is thy sting? (1 Cor. xv. 55). Thou hast no sting any longer, but a song of praise and victory. For a man dies while singing, and sings while dying. Thou who art the mother of sorrow art taken as a subject for joy; thou, the enemy of glory, as an occasion for glory; thou, who art the gate of hell and the gulf of perdition, as the portal of the kingdom of God and the entrance into salvation; and all this by a man who is a sinner. This, too, is justly done, since thou hast rashly and unjustly usurped dominion over One who is a Righteous Man and Blameless. O Death, thou art thyself dead, and pierced with the hook which thou hast incautiously swallowed, of which thus speaks the Prophet: *O Death, I will be thy death; O grave, I will be thy destruction* (*morsus*) (Hosea xiii. 14). Pierced, I say, with that hook, thou shalt open a broad and joyful passage into life for those faithful ones who pass through thee. Gerard does not fear thee, O shadowy phantom! Gerard passes through thy jaws to his heavenly fatherland, not merely with security, but with joy and thanksgiving. When, then, I had come to him, and he had finished in my hearing, with a loud voice, the last verses of the Psalm which he had begun, looking up to heaven, he said: *Father, into Thy Hands I commend My spirit* (Luke xxiii. 46). And repeating often the same sentence, and pronouncing again and again *Father, Father*, he turned unto me and said, with a joyful countenance: 'How great is the condescension of God in being the Father of men! and how great the glory of men to be the sons and the heirs of God! For if they are sons, they are also heirs.' So he whom we are lamenting sang when about to die: and I confess that he changed my grief almost into a song of joy, because, my mind being fixed upon the glory which was before his vision, I almost forgot my own unhappiness.

12. But the sharp pang of my grief recalls me to myself, and the pressure of care arouses me from the thought of that sweet and peaceful spectacle, as one rises from a light slumber. Let me mourn, then, but for myself, for reason forbids that I should mourn on his account. I believe, indeed, that, were occasion afforded him, he

---

[1] *Diescebat*: not a classical word.—ED.

would say to us now. 'Weep not for me, but for yourselves.' David was right to weep over his parricidal son (2 Sam xix. 1), because he knew that, on account of the enormity of his crime, his issue from the power of death was for ever hindered. He was right to mourn over Saul and over Jonathan (2 Sam i. 17), because, when they were once swallowed up by death, that they should emerge from it was not then within the bounds of hope.[1] And certainly they shall rise again, but not to life; or if to life, then in order that living they should die by a death still more calamitous. It is true that, with regard to Jonathan, there may be ground for a doubt; but in my case I have still a reason for my grief, though it be not the same reason. I grieve, first, for my own trouble, and for the loss which this house has sustained; secondly, I grieve on account of the necessities of the poor, of whom Gerard was the father. I grieve on account of our whole Order, and of our profession, which derived no small strength from thy example of zeal and wisdom, O Gerard, and lastly, I grieve, not indeed for thee, but for the loss of thee. Yes, this—this is what wounds me so deeply, because I love thee so devotedly. And let no one trouble me by saying that I am wrong thus to afflict myself, since the kind-hearted Samuel mourned without restraint over his abandoned King, and the devout David over his parricidal son, and that without wronging their faith, or calling in question the Divine judgment. '*Absalom, my son, my son Absalom!*' said holy David (2 Sam xviii. 33), and is not my brother more than Absalom? The Saviour, too, when looking upon the city of Jerusalem, of which He foresaw the destruction, *wept over it* (Luke xix. 41). And shall I have no feeling of my own bereavement, and that so recent? Shall I not groan over a wound so fresh and so deep? He wept over the sorrows of others, and shall I not dare to weep over my own? Assuredly He did not at the sepulchre of Lazarus either rebuke those who were weeping, or forbid them to weep, and even more than this, He wept with them, for it is said, *Jesus wept* (John xi. 35). Those tears were, it is certain, the evidences of His Humanity, not the signs of his disapproval (*diffidentiæ* = distrust). Moreover, at His Voice the dead man came forth from the tomb; so that you must not imagine that a person cannot yield to grief without prejudice to his faith

13. It is thus with my tears also. They are not a sign of unbelief, but an indication of our human condition, nor because, when stricken, I moan, do I therefore accuse Him who strikes; I rather call upon His goodness, and endeavour to turn aside His severity. Thus, though my words are full of grief, there is no murmuring in them Have I not expressed a feeling full of righteousness in acknowledging that in one most equitable sentence He hath both punished one who deserved punishment, and crowned one who was

---

[1] St Bernard appears here to express some doubt of the salvation of Jonathan. But other fathers and commentators assert that he is in blessedness There is a slight variation here between the MSS. and editions. See Horst's note.

worthy of reward? Yes, the Lord is kind and righteous, and He has done everything well. I will sing to Thee, O Lord of mercy and judgment. Let the mercy which Thou hast shown unto Thy servant Gerard sing to Thee and praise Thee, and let the judgment also sing, which we ourselves are bearing. In the one Thou shalt be praised because Thou art good, in the other because Thou art righteous. Is praise due to Thee for Thy goodness alone? It is due also for Thy righteousness. *Righteous art Thou, O Lord, and upright are Thy judgments* (Ps. cxix. 137). Thou hast given Gerard; Thou hast taken Gerard away; and though we grieve for the loss of him, we are not forgetful that he was given to us; we render thanks that we have been deemed worthy to possess him, and our reluctance to be without his presence is wholly in submission to Thy Divine will.

14. I call to mind, O Lord, my covenant with Thee, and the pity Thou hadst upon me, that Thou mightest be the more justified in Thy saying, and clear when Thou art judged. For when I was at Viterbo[1] last year on the business of the Church my brother Gerard was taken with serious illness, and the attack increased upon him until it seemed as if God were about to call him to Himself. I was unable to bear the thought of losing my travelling companion and being left alone in a strange land, nor, again, of not being able to restore him safe to those who had entrusted him to me; for he was so engaging, that he was loved by all. In this distress I betook myself to prayer with tears and sobs. 'Lord,' I cried, 'wait until my return. If Thou willest to take him away from me, let it be when he is restored to his friends, and I will not complain.' And Thou didst hear my prayer, O Lord: he recovered; we accomplished the work that Thou hadst given us to do, and we returned with joy, bringing with us the sheaves of peace. And then I became almost entirely forgetful of the compact which I had made with Thee, but so wast not Thou. I am ashamed of these sobs of grief, which accuse me of going from my word. What can be added to this? Thou hast required again the treasure which was Thine, which Thou hadst committed to us for awhile, and hast received it. But tears again put an end to my words. Do Thou, O Lord, impose a limit to my tears, and bring them to an end.

[1] St. Bernard sojourned at Viterbo on two occasions: the former time in 1133, as we learn from his Letter 151 (vol. ii., p. 479, of Eng. Ed.), the latter in 1137; and it is that which is mentioned here.

SERMON XXVII.

OF THE ADORNMENT OF THE BRIDE: AND IN WHAT SENSE THE HOLY SOUL IS CALLED *HEAVEN*.

NOW that we have rendered the last offices of affection to our dear friend on his return to his [heavenly] country, I resume, brethren, the purpose of edification which was thus interrupted: for it is incongruous to continue long lamenting one who is in joy and gladness, and out of place to trouble with many tears one who is sitting at a banquet; and although we may, with weeping, deplore our own loss, it behoves us to do even that with moderation, so that it may not seem to be the case that it is not so much the loss of our friend as of his service to us that we deplore. The grief of those who are bereaved should be tempered by the joy of the beloved one who is its object, and that he is with God should make it more easy to bear the fact that he is no longer with us. I desire, then, relying on the support of your prayers, to bring to light, if I am able, the sense which is hidden under those passages of our Song in which the beauty and adornments of the Bride are spoken of. This, if you remember, was touched upon, but left undiscussed; all that was examined and concluded having been the sense in which she was said to be *black as the tents of Kedar*. In what way, then, is she *comely as the curtains of Solomon?* as if Solomon, in all his glory, had had anything of equal worthiness to the beauty of the Bride, and the magnificence of her ornaments! And, indeed, if we should say that those 'curtains' refer rather to the blackness than to the beauty of the Bride, the same as the *tents of Kedar*, I do not know that we should be wrong; nor would there be wanting reasons to support that reference, as we shall see in the sequel. But if we think that the beauty of curtains, however splendid they may be, is to be compared to the glorious beauty of the Bride, we have need to obtain the help of Him at whose door you have knocked in order to be able worthily to unfold a mystery so great. For what beauty is there in those things which are perceived by the outward senses which is to be compared with the inward beauty of a holy soul, or which, to a just judge, can appear other than common and defiled? What is there, I ask, in the spectacle of this world which passeth away that is capable of equalling the fairness and beauty of a soul which has put off its former vesture of earthly and soiled humanity, and clothed itself anew in that which came from heaven, and is in every respect fair? For gems, it is adorned with virtues; it is purer and loftier than the air itself, and more brilliant than the sun. Do not, then, look back to [the curtains of] Solomon for a comparison when you desire to understand what is the degree of beauty and splendour to which the Bride declares herself to be like.

2. What means she, then, by these words: *I am beautiful as the*

curtains of Solomon? These words, as I think, contain a great and wonderful mystery—if we apply them, that is to say, not to the king who ruled over Israel, but to Him of whom it was said: *Behold, a greater than Solomon is here* (Matt. xii. 42). He is so truly Solomon, that He is called not only 'Peaceful' (as the word Solomon signifies in Hebrew[1]), but Peace itself, as St. Paul declares: *He is our Peace* (Eph. ii. 14); and with this Solomon we shall no doubt find something worthy to be compared with the beauty of the Bride. Notice especially with regard to the curtains what is said in one of the Psalms: *Who stretchest out the heavens like a curtain* (Ps. civ. 2). Now, the earlier Solomon, very wise though he were and powerful, assuredly did not stretch out the heavens like a curtain, but rather He who is not merely wise, but Wisdom itself—yes, it is He who hath founded them and stretched them out. Thus, also, it was He, not the former Solomon, who speaks these words: *When He* (that is, doubtless, God the Father) *prepared the heavens I was there.* His Power, no doubt, and His Wisdom, was there with Him who prepared the heavens. Nor must it be supposed that it was inactive, and, as it were, a spectator only, because it is said, 'I was there,' and not also, 'I was preparing.' Look a little farther on, and you will find the express assertion: *I was with Him forming all things* (Prov. viii. 27 and 30, Vulg. and Douay). Lastly, He says: *What things soever the Father doeth, these also doeth the Son likewise* (John v. 19). So, then, it is He also who stretches out the heavens like a curtain. A beautiful curtain indeed is that great expanse which, as a tent, covers the entire surface of the earth, and rejoices the eyes of men by the variety and beauty of sun, moon, and stars which adorn it! What is there more beautiful than this curtain, or more splendid than the heavens? Yet it is not worthy to be even compared to the glory and beauty of the Bride even in this respect—that the beauty of the former, as being of a corporeal nature and apprehended by the bodily senses, is temporary and passing: *For the things which are seen are temporal; but the things which are not seen are eternal* (2 Cor. iv. 18).

3. But the beauty of the Bride is of an intellectual kind; it is spiritual and eternal, for it is the image of eternity. Her beauty, for example, consists in charity; and charity, as you read, *never faileth* (1 Cor. xiii. 8). It is also in righteousness, and *His righteousness endureth for ever* (Ps. cxii. 3). It is also in patience, and we learn that the *patient abiding of the poor shall not perish for ever* (Ps. ix. 18). What is to be said of voluntary poverty? and of humility? Has not the one the promise of the kingdom of heaven (Matt. v. 3), and the other of an everlasting exaltation (Luke xiv. 11)? It is the same with the fear of the Lord; it is holy, and endureth for ever (Ps. xix. 9). So, also, with respect to prudence, to temperance, and to fortitude, and to any other virtues, if such there be, what are they but, as it were, pearls in the Coronet of the Bride, which glitter with constant lustre for ever? For ever, I say, because they are the base and the

---

[1] שְׁלֹמֹה = Shĕlômôh, the 'Peaceful One.'—ED.

foundation of immortality. Nor is there any place whatever in the soul for the life of immortal blessedness except that which is provided by the means and the interposition of virtues. It is on that account that the Psalmist says to God, in whom, without doubt, is this life of blessedness: *Justice and judgment are the habitation of Thy throne* (Ps. lxxxix. 14). And the Apostle says that Christ dwells in our hearts, not in every way, but, as he states expressly, *in our hearts by faith* (Eph. iii. 17). When our Lord was about to sit upon the ass, His disciples cast their mantles upon the animal to form His seat; and this signifies that the Saviour and that salvation cannot rest upon souls that are unclad and bare—that is to say, which are not clad in the doctrine and in the virtues of the Apostles. And therefore the Church, having promise of happiness to come, is careful in the meantime to prepare and adorn herself with a vesture enriched with gold, and decked with a variety of graces and virtues,[1] so as to be found capable and worthy of the fulness of grace.

4. But I could in no way compare in beauty this visible and physical heaven, although most fair of its kind, and adorned with a bright galaxy of stars, with that other splendour of varying colours, spiritual and surpassingly beautiful, which sparkles even now on the robe of sanctification which the Bride has received. But there is a heaven of heaven of which the Psalmist says: *Sing praises unto the Lord, who ascends above the heaven of heavens* (Ps. lxviii. 32, 33). This heaven is intellectual and spiritual; and He who *by His wisdom made the heavens* (Ps. cxxxvi. 5) has created this and established it for ever, and it is this in which He dwells. Do not suppose, then, that the devotion of the Bride allows her to stop short of this heaven, in which, as she knows, her Beloved dwells; for where her treasure is, there is her heart also (Matt. vi. 21). She has a holy jealousy of those who are before that Countenance, for [the sight of] which she sighs, and studies to render her life conformed to theirs with whom she is not as yet associated in that happy vision. She cries by her life more than by words: *Lord, I have loved the habitation of Thy house, and the place where Thine honour dwelleth* (Ps. xxvi. 8).

5. She does not hold it at all unworthy of her to be compared to that heaven. It is stretched out as a curtain, if not extending over plains of space, yet over the affections and longings of souls. It has Divisions also, not of colours,[2] but of degrees of beatitude attained. For [God] has created some Angels, others Archangels, but others Virtues, Dominations, Principalities, Powers, Thrones; others, again, Cherubin, and others Seraphin. These are the stars with which His heaven is studded; these are the bright and glorious colours which adorn the curtains of this Solomon. This is one out of very many which are His, and the chief among them, which are each of them

---

[1] Horst adds: 'Such as we have described in their place'; which words are wanting in the earliest editions and in all our MSS.—MABILLON.

[2] All our MSS. have 'of colours,' except that of Jumièges, which has 'of places' (*locorum*). The editions have 'of heavens' (*caelorum*).

blessed and glorious, though there be a great variety in the conditions of their glory. They are benign, moreover, and of a charity so far reaching, that it extends even to us; so that far from being jealous of the glory they enjoy, they desire that we should obtain it. And in order to attain that end, some of them do not think it burdensome to remain among us, to be actively employed in watching over us and doing us good; they are, in truth, ministering spirits, sent forth to minister unto them who shall be heirs of salvation (Heb. i. 14). Wherefore, as the whole multitude of the blessed are collected together, as it were, into one, they are called, in the singular, 'the heaven of heaven'; and, again, as each of them separately is, in a sense, heaven, they are called 'the heaven of heavens.' It is of each of them that it is said: *He stretcheth out the heavens like a curtain* (Ps. civ. 2). So that you now perceive, I think, what are those curtains which the Bride takes pride in resembling, and to what Solomon they belong.

6. Contemplate, then, the glory of her who compares herself even to the heaven; and to that heaven which is so much the more glorious as its origin is divine. Not unfitly does she select to be a point of comparison for herself *that* from whence she draws her origin.[1] For if, on account of the body she has from the earth, she compares herself to the tents of Kedar, why should she not equally glorify herself as having a likeness to heaven, because her soul is from heaven; especially when her life bears witness to her origin, to the dignity of her nature, and to the land to which she belongs? She worships and adores one God, as do the angels; she loves, as they do, Jesus Christ above all; she is chaste as the angels, and that in a weak body of sinful flesh, as the angels are not; lastly, she desires and

---

[1] Berengar, the disciple of Abaelard, in his treatise, *Apologeticum*, which he put forth on behalf of his preceptor, against the Council of Sens, and against St. Bernard himself, takes hold of these words, and tries to draw from them a proof that St. Bernard supposed souls to be created in heaven, and sent thence into the bodies they are to occupy. That writer thus rudely addresses the holy man: 'You have certainly erred in asserting that souls have their origin from heaven. It will be useful and easy for the intelligent reader to understand by what arguments you support that position; and I will recount them throughout. There is a book named in Hebrew *Firasirim* (*Schirbaschirim*), and in Latin *Canticum Canticorum*, of which the sense hidden under the text reveals Divine mysteries to those who diligently watch for them.' Then, further on, he adds: 'These words of yours, if carefully considered, savour of heresy to every Christian palate. For if you argue that souls draw their origin from heaven upon this ground, that they are one day to return to heaven in order to be happy there, you must say the same of the body, since it, too, is to be happy in heaven. Or, if you write that the soul is celestial as to its origin, because it originated, that is, was created, in the heavens (which, indeed, seems to be the sense of your words), you fall into the error of Origen.' Thus rashly writes the apologist. But, after all, why should not the soul be said to be celestial, seeing that it has a Father in heaven, that its conversation ought to be in heaven, that its own country is in heaven, and that, in the same way, its nature transcends all earthly things? Wherefore St. Augustine says, in arguing against Julianus: 'Since we have a body which is from the earth, and a spirit which is from heaven, we ourselves are at the same time earth and heaven' (Bk. ii., *contra Julian.*). But enough as to Berengar, the unscrupulous calumniator of our saint.—MABILLON.

seeks those things which are with the angels, not those which are upon earth. What can be a plainer proof of her celestial origin than that she preserves an inborn resemblance to the angelic spirits, and that in a region of unlikeness [to them], than to claim for herself on earth the glory of a life solitary and exiled [from heaven]; and, lastly, to live as an angel in a body almost that of a beast? Those actions are the signs of heavenly powers, not of earthly; and they show clearly that the soul, which is able thus to act, draws, without a question, its origin from heaven. Yet listen to words which are unmistakable: *I saw the Holy City, new Jerusalem, coming down from God out of heaven, prepared as a Bride adorned for her husband.* And the Apostle has added, *And I heard a great voice out of heaven saying, Behold the tabernacle of God is with men, and He will dwell with them* (Rev. xxi. 2, 3). To what end? It was, as I believe, that He might obtain for Himself from among the children of men [the Church which is] His Bride. O wonderful mystery! He came for His Bride, and yet not without a Bride He came. He was seeking out His Bride, and yet His Bride was then with Him. Were there, then, two Brides? By no means. For He says: *My dove, My undefiled, is but one* (Cant. vi. 9). But just as He desired out of diverse flocks of sheep to make one, so that there should be *one Fold, and one Shepherd* (John x. 16); so, having from the beginning of the world one Bride, with whom He was closely united—I mean the multitude of the angels—it pleased Him to call together a Church out of men also, and with this to unite that which is from heaven, so that there shall be one Bridegroom and one Bride. The one has been perfected, not multiplied, by the union of the other with itself; and she is aware that this is spoken of her: *She who is Mine is one, she is perfect* (vi. 8). Yes, their conformity [to the likeness of the Lord] makes them one; and if for the moment the conformity is only in the same fervour of devotion, it shall hereafter be realized in the same glory.

7. Thus, then, each of them is from heaven—the Bridegroom, who is Jesus, and the Bride, the heavenly Jerusalem [which is the Church]. As for the Bridegroom, in order that He might be made manifest upon earth, *He emptied Himself, taking upon Him the form of a servant, and being made in the likeness of men, was found in fashion as a Man* (Philip. ii. 7, 8). But as to the Bride: in what form or appearance, or with what degree of beauty think you was she beheld when she came down out of heaven? Was it, perhaps, in the company of the angels whom St. John saw *ascending and descending upon the Son of Man* (John i. 51)? But it were better to say that he saw the Bride when he saw the WORD made Flesh, and recognised two Natures in His one Person. For when He, our holy Emmanuel, brought to earth the rules of heavenly culture and training, when the visible form and image of the beauty of the heavenly Jerusalem, which is our mother, is expressed in Him and made known to us by His means, what have we beheld, except in the Bridegroom the Bride, and, gazing with admiration and reverence, have divined in one and the

same Lord of Glory both the Bridegroom, decked with His Crown, and the Bride, adorned with her necklaces of precious jewels? He, therefore, who descended is also He who ascended; for no one can ascend into heaven but He who descended from heaven, who is one and the same Lord, both Bridegroom and the Head, as also Bride and the Body. Nor is it in vain that this celestial Man has appeared upon earth, since He has made many denizens of earth similar to Himself, and citizens of heaven, as it is said by the Apostle: As is the Man who is heavenly, such are they also who are made like unto Him, and therefore heavenly (1 Cor. xv. 48). A beginning is, then, already made by living on the earth in the manner of those who live in heaven, when, after the example of that heavenly and blessed creation, she who comes from the ends of the earth to hear the wisdom of Solomon, is, nevertheless, attached with chaste love to her heavenly Spouse; and, although not yet united to Him by outward sight, is yet betrothed to Him by faith, according to the promise of God speaking by the prophet: *I will betroth thee unto Me in mercies: I will even betroth thee unto Me in faithfulness* (Hosea ii. 19, 20). Therefore, she strives to be more and more conformed to the pattern which came from heaven: learning to be modest and temperate, chaste and holy, patient and compassionate, meek and humble of heart. And it is by these virtues that she endeavours, far removed as she is, to please Him upon whom the angels desire to look, so that, by sharing the same desire with which they are fired, she may approve herself as being a fellow-citizen with the saints, and of the household of God, that she may show herself His beloved and His Bride.

8. I think that every soul which is such as I have described is not only heavenly because of its origin, but may be not unfitly said to be itself heaven, because of its resemblance to heaven, which is thus brought about. And it is then that such a soul plainly shows that its origin is from heaven, because its conversation is in heaven. A holy soul is, then, a heaven, having understanding for a *sun*, faith for a *moon*, and for *stars* countless virtues. Or we may say that its sun is zeal for righteousness or fervent charity, and its moon is continence. For as the brightness of the moon is said to be wholly from the sun, so there is no merit in continence without charity or justice. Hence the Wise man says: How beautiful is a generation which joins continence to charity (Wisdom iv. 1).[1] As for the stars of this sky, I do not regret having called the virtues by this name when I consider the fitness of the similitude. For as the stars shine by night, and in the day are unseen, so true virtue, which often in prosperity is not apparent, shines out brightly in time of adversity. It is a matter of prudence to hide it in the one case, but in the other it is of necessity rendered visible. A virtue is, then, as a star, and a man of many virtues as a heaven of such stars, unless, perhaps, that which the Lord has spoken by the Prophet, *Heaven is My Throne* (Is. lxvi. 1), is to be

---

[1] Vulgate. The rendering of the Vulgate is but a paraphrase of the Greek text here.—ED.

understood of this visible heaven which rolls around us, and not rather in the sense which the Scripture elsewhere expresses more plainly: The soul of the righteous is the throne of wisdom.[1] But whoso has learned from the teaching of the Saviour that God is a Spirit, and is to be worshipped in the spirit (John iv. 24), will not hesitate to believe that His throne is spiritual. I should confidently affirm this, and not less with regard to the spirit of a righteous man than of the angels. Most of all I am confirmed in that opinion by that faithful promise of the Son of God: *I and My Father will come to him* (that is, to a righteous man), *and make our abode with him* (John xiv. 23). The Psalmist also seems to me to have spoken of no other heaven than this in the words: *Thou dwellest in the holy place, the praise of Israel* (Ps. xxi. 4, Vulg. and Douay). And again, the Apostle speaks unmistakably: *That Christ may dwell in your hearts by faith* (Eph. iii. 17).

9. And it is not wonderful that the Lord Jesus should dwell in this, as in heaven, since not only, as in the case of other living beings, did He speak the word and it came into existence, but He has striven in order to acquire it; He has died to redeem it. Therefore, having after many sufferings and efforts made it His own according to His wish, He says: *This is My rest for ever: here will I dwell, for I have desired it* (Ps. cxxxii. 14). Blessed is that soul to whom it is said: 'Come, Mine elect one, and upon thee will I place My Throne. Why art thou so heavy, O my soul, and why art thou disquieted within me?' Dost thou think that not within thee canst thou find a place for the Lord? What place is there, in truth, in us that is fit for the presence of a glory so great, or sufficient to receive so high a Majesty? Would that I were worthy even to offer adoration in the place where His Feet have stood! Who will grant unto me the grace to be able to follow closely in the footsteps of some holy soul which He has chosen for His habitation? Yet if He shall deign only to pour into my soul the unction of His mercy, and to expand it, as a curtain is extended when anointed, then I may be able to say: *I have run the way of Thy commandments, when Thou didst enlarge my heart* (Ps. cxix. 32, Vulg. and Douay). Perhaps I shall be able to show in my soul, if not an upper chamber sufficiently large for Him to sit with His disciples, at least a pillow where He may lay His Head. At least, I may from afar look up to those blessed ones, of whom it is said: *I will dwell in them, and walk in them* (2 Cor. vi. 16).

10. O how broad the confines of that soul and how commanding its merits, which is found worthy to receive in itself that Divine Presence; and not only worthy to receive it, but capable of so doing!

---

[1] The same passage is cited in Sermon I., for the Purification, *n.* 4; in Sermon V, for November 1, *n.* 5; and in Sermon XXV., *n.* 6. Others of the Fathers, as St. Augustine (*Enarr. in* Ps. xlvi. 9, and Sermon CC., *n.* 1) and St. Gregory the Great (29 Moral., c. 15; and Hom. 38, in Evang.), quote it as Scripture. But it is apparently not found in the Vulgate. Compare Ps. xxxvii. 30, and Prov. x. 31. —Ed.

What, again, shall I say of that soul, which affords, as it were, spacious avenues in which the grace of God may move without constraint? Assuredly, it is not tunnelled with the windings of worldly interests and secular cares, nor occupied with luxuries and sensual pleasures; nor with curiosity about the affairs of others; nor is it filled with tumid pride, nor the desire to rule. For it is essential in the first place that a soul should be free from all things like this, that it may become a heaven, and be the dwelling-place of God. For otherwise how would it be able to contemplate God in peace, or even to see Him as He is? Again, it must be free from all hatred, all jealousy, and all bitterness, for into a malicious soul wisdom shall not enter (Wisd. i. 4). Then it is necessary that it should grow in breadth and volume that it may be capable of receiving God. Now, the growth and extension of the soul is charity, according to the saying of the Apostle: Be ye enlarged in charity (2 Cor. vi. 13). For although the soul, being of a spiritual nature, does not admit of material extension, nevertheless grace confers upon it what is denied by nature. It has growth and is extended, but in a spiritual manner; it increases, not in substance, but in power and in glory; it grows even into a temple holy to the Lord; and attains unto a perfect man, unto the measure of the stature of the fulness of Christ (Ephes. iv. 13). Thus the amplitude of a soul is estimated by the measure of the charity which it possesses; so that, for example, the soul which has much charity is great, and that which possesses little, is itself little; while that which has none at all, is simply nothing, as St. Paul declares, *If I have not charity, I am nothing* (1 Cor. xiii. 2). If a soul has begun to have ever so little charity, so that at least it is careful to love those who love it, and to salute the brethren, and those who offer salutation, then I should say that that soul is something, however little, since it has at least the charity of society, which consists in the natural interchange of courtesy given and received. But as our Lord inquires, What does it more than others? (Matt. v. 47). And I should regard a soul as being not of liberal, or even of moderate dimensions, but as being plainly narrow, small, and petty, which had no more charity than this strictly limited amount.

11. If, however, it progresses and grows greater, so as to overpass the limits of a love so petty and so narrow, let it, in the full liberty of the Spirit, reach the broad confines of a charity and kindness which is wholly free and gratuitous; insomuch as out of the large-heartedness of its good-will, to extend its kindly cares to all men, and to love all and everyone as it loves its own self. And then the reproach could not be addressed to it: 'What doest thou more than is of obligation?' in face of a charity so capacious. The charity, I repeat, which embraces all persons, even those with whom it has no bond of social relation, which is not allured by any hope of personal advantage, nor repelled by any feeling of dislike, which again is constrained by no obligation, except indeed by that of which it is said:

Owe no man anything, but to love one another (Rom. xiii. 8); that is indeed great. But if in addition to this you take by violence the realm of charity, and, like a pious invader, occupy it even to its farthest bounds, then you will regard the bowels of charity as not to be shut up even to enemies; you will do good even to those who hate you, you will pray for those who despitefully use you and persecute you, and strive to be peaceful even with those who are hateis of peace; then the breadth, and height, and beauty of your soul, will be as the breadth, and height, and beauty of heaven. Then will be fulfilled in it that which is spoken: *He stretcheth forth the heavens like a curtain* (Ps. civ. 2); and in it He in whom greatness, immensity, and glory are equally without bound will deign not only to dwell, but to go to and fro at His pleasure in a heaven so extended and so fair.

12. You see, then, what are the heavens which the Church includes, without ceasing to be in her universality, as a vast heaven, extending from sea even to sea and from the River unto the world's end. Consider also as a consequence, to what you can, in this respect, compare it; provided that you have not forgotten what was said a little while ago with regard to 'the heaven of heaven, and the heavens of heavens' (*n*. 9). Our mother [the Church], though she be here below in a place of exile, has, even while she is performing her pilgrimage, heavens of her own, spiritual men, illustrious in their faith and by their life, pure in faith, unshaken in hope, of wide charity, of deep and lofty contemplation. And these heavens let fall the rain of the word of salvation, thunder by their rebukes, lighten by their wonderful works (*miraculis*). They declare the glory of God; they are spread, like a curtain, over all the earth; they show in themselves the law of life and conduct written as by the Finger of God, to give the knowledge of salvation unto their people; they also teach the Gospel of peace, because they are the 'curtains of Solomon.'

13. We must discern also upon these curtains the likenesses of things heavenly, which were described above when we spoke of the ornaments of the Bridegroom (*n*. 3). We must discern similarly the Queen standing on His right hand, decked with ornaments similar, if not equal, to His (Ps. xlv. 9). For although she has no little splendour and beauty for her portion, in the righteousness of the Saints, both in the place of her pilgrimage and in the day of her power, yet there is a difference between His crown of virtues and the consummation of the glory of the blessed. Yet I may say that the Bride is perfect and blessed, though it be in part. For in part she is as the tents of Kedar. Yet she is beautiful, whether in that part which is already blessed and reigns in heaven; or in that, even while she is in the night of this world, she is adorned with men who are illustrious by their wisdom and their virtues, even as the midnight sky is adorned with its stars. Wherefore the Prophet says: *They that be wise shall shine as the brightness of the firmament: and they*

that turn many to righteousness as the stars for ever and ever (Dan. xii. 3).

14. What humility is there here, and yet what sublimity! It is to be at once the tents of Kedar, and the sanctuary of God; at once a habitation on earth, and a palace in heaven; a hut of clay, and a royal hall; a body of death, and a temple of light; an object of contempt to the proud, and yet the Bride of Christ. *She is black, but comely, O ye daughters of Jerusalem;* and although labour and the sorrow of a prolonged exile have darkened her face, yet she is fair with the beauty of heaven, as the curtains of Solomon. If you are displeased with her blackness, yet you cannot but admire her beauty; if you despise her as humble, yet look up to her as sublime. Yet in this condition in which she is, how remarkable a proof of wisdom, of discretion, of fitness, is to be gathered from the fact that this abasement and this elevation, are each so tempered, according to time, in the Bride, that among all the changes and chances of this world, this loftiness raises her up in adversities, so that she does not fail; and this humbleness represses the tendency to pride, so that even in prosperity she does not grow forgetful of her Lord. These two results are each of them most beautiful, but are exactly contrary to each other; nevertheless, they both work together for good to the Bride, and are helpful to her salvation.

15. So much with regard to the comparison which the Bride makes between herself and the curtains of Solomon. Yet there remains still to be treated another sense, which I referred to at the beginning, and promised to explain, namely, that which refers the whole comparison to the blackness of the Bride only. This promise I am fully intending to keep, but it must be deferred to the beginning of another sermon, as well because this is already sufficiently long, as also that the prayer prevents, which, according to our custom, we offer to the praise and glory of the Bridegroom of the Church, Jesus Christ our Lord, who is God blessed for ever. AMEN.

SERMON XXVIII.

OF THE BLACKNESS, YET BEAUTY, OF THE BRIDE: AND IN WHAT MANNER HEARING, RATHER THAN SIGHT, AVAILS IN MATTERS OF FAITH, AND TO THE KNOWLEDGE OF THE TRUTH.

YOU remember, I doubt not, what were 'the curtains of Solomon,' to which the beauty of the Bride was compared, and who was meant by Solomon, provided that the whole comparison is intended to be with the Bride's beauty. If, however, it be referred wholly to her blackness, as that of the tents of Kedar, then I have nothing more to say to you on the subject of those curtains of Solomon, except that they were, perhaps, those of which that King was accustomed to make use as a tent or screen when he thought fit to live under canvas, and which (if that were the case) would no doubt be stained and blackened by their exposure every day to the rays of the sun and the violence of weather. Yet that was not uselessly done,[1] but in order that the costly furniture which was within might be preserved unsoiled and beautiful. In this point of view the Bride does not deny her blackness, but makes excuse for it; nor does she regard as blameworthy such a condition, which charity excuses, and which the judgment of the Truth does not disapprove. For does not an Apostle ask, *Who is weak, and I am not weak? who is offended, and I burn not?* (2 Cor. xi. 29). She takes upon her the blemish (*nævum*) of compassion, in order to lighten or to cure the malady of passion in another; she allows herself to gather blackness, on account of her zeal for whiteness, and obtains fairness and beauty as her reward.

2. The blackening of One renders many white and fair; not that He is tinged with their faults, but that He is touched by their sufferings. *It is expedient*, it was said, *that one man should die for the people, and that the whole nation perish not* (John xi. 50). It is expedient that One, for the sake of all, should be blackened by the likeness of sinful flesh, and that the whole [human] race should not be condemned by the blackness of sin. Let the brightness and the image of the Divine Nature be obscured by the form of a servant, for the life of a servant. Let the radiance of eternal life gather blackness in the flesh, in order that the flesh may by it be purified. Let the Form that was fairer than all the sons of men be obscured in the darkness of the Passion, in order that the sons of men might see a great light and be enlightened by it; let It be defiled upon the Cross; let It grow pale[2] in death; let It have no form or comeliness, that the Divine Bridegroom may obtain for the Church His Bride to be altogether beautiful and glorious, without spot or· wrinkle, or any such thing. I recognise the curtain of Solomon—nay, rather, I embrace the monarch Solomon himself under his covering of black. He, too, has blackness, but it is of the skin alone; it is an external blackness, not extending within; for the King's daughter is all glorious within (Ps. xlv. 13). Within is the brightness of Divinity, the beauty of His virtues, the shining of His glory, [otherwise *gratiæ*], and the white lustre of His innocence; but the appearance of infirmity conceals all these, and renders Him open to scorn from the beholders; His countenance is, as it were, hidden, and He is despised, since He is tempted in all ways like unto [His brethren], yet without sin. I recognise the image and likeness of a defiled and blackened human

---

[1] Three MSS. vary slightly here, and make the preacher say: 'It is needful to recall to you the curtains with which Solomon used once to cover his pavilion. These were no doubt black, by their exposure every day to the rays of the sun, and the violence of weather. Yet that,' etc.

[2] *Totus versus in pallorem* ('Jubilus Rhythmicus de Nomine Jesu').—ED.

nature; I recognise those coats of skins,[1] the coverings granted to our first parents, after they had sinned against God (Gen. iii. 21). For He has accepted blackness for Himself in taking upon Him the form of a servant, in being made in the likeness of men, and in being found in fashion as a man (Phil. ii. 7). I recognise under the covering of goatskin, which is the symbol of sin, both the Hands which did no wrong, and the neck (Gen. xxvii. 16) through which thought of evil never passed ; and on that account no guile was found in His Mouth (Is. liii. 9). I know, O Jesus, that Thou art of mild nature, meek and humble of heart, of benign look and kindly spirit, and that Thou art indeed anointed with the oil of gladness above Thy fellows (Ps. xlv. 7). Whence, then, is it that Thou art rough and shaggy like Esau ? Wherefore is Thy Countenance wrinkled and blackened, and whence this shaggy growth of hair ? Mine, mine they are, and these Hands are rendered bristly with the likeness of me, a sinner. I acknowledge as mine this shaggy growth, and in my flesh I behold God my Saviour.

3. Nevertheless, it was not Rebekah, but Mary, who invested Him in this garment of flesh; and He who accepted the benediction [of His Father] was so much the worthier as she who bore Him was the more holy. Well is it for me that He is found in my likeness, since the benediction is reserved by Him for me, since it is for me that the heritage is claimed. It was, in fact, said to Him : *Ask of Me, and I shall give Thee the heathen for Thine inheritance, and the utmost parts of the earth for Thy possession* (Ps. ii. 8). *Thine inheritance*, He says, *Thy possession, I will give to Thee.* How wilt Thou give it to Him if it be His? And why dost Thou warn Him to ask for it ? or how can it be His if it be necessary that He should ask ? It is, then, for me that He asks it; and it is in order that He may undertake my cause that He puts on my nature. Wherefore, says the Prophet, *The chastisement of our peace was upon Him ;* and, *The Lord hath laid on Him the iniquity of us all* (Is. liii. 5, 6). And the Apostle explains, *In all things it behoved Him to be made like unto His brethren, that He might be merciful* (Heb. ii. 17). So that His voice is truly *the voice of Jacob*, but the hands the *hands of Esau* (Gen. xxvii. 22). That which we hear from His Lips is His ; but what we see in Him, that comes from us. The words which He speaks, they are spirit, and they are life ; but the Form upon which the eye rests is subject to death, and is death. One thing is beheld, another believed. The senses declare that He is black ; but faith protests assuredly that He is fair as the lily (Cant. ii. 1), and altogether beautiful. He is, indeed, black, but only to the eyes of those void of understanding ; for in the judg-

---

[1] *Pelliceas.* The preacher is playing upon the word *pelles*=skins, though rendered 'curtains' throughout, in deference to A.V. and Douay V. Tents, though normally covered with curtains of the black fabric woven out of goats' hair, at all events, in historic times, were no doubt frequently covered with the skins themselves. Both kinds of coverings were combined in the construction of the Tabernacle. See Exod. xxvi. 7-14.—ED.

ment of the faithful He is wholly beautiful; *black yet comely;* black in the opinion of Herod, but by the confession of the penitent Thief, as in the faith of the Centurion, beautiful altogether.

4. How beautiful the man who exclaimed, *Truly this Man was the Son of God,* had surely perceived. But into what he perceived it is for us to examine. For if the Centurion had considered only that which was apparent in the Man before him, on what ground could he have pronounced Him the Son of God, or beautiful? What was there in Him to the eyes of the spectators, other than tortured and uncomely, when nailed upon the Cross with outstretched Hands, and between two malefactors, He was the subject of laughter to the malignant, of weeping to the faithful? He alone was an object of laughter, who alone had the right to be the object of respect and of terror. Whence, then, did he learn the charm of the Crucified One? Whence did he know that the Man who was numbered with the transgressors was in truth the Son of God? To reply to that question is not for me; nor is there need, for the care of the Evangelist has not failed to supply the answer. These are his words: *When the Centurion, who stood over against Him, saw that He so cried out, and gave up the ghost, he said: Truly this Man was the Son of God* (Mark xv. 39). Therefore, he believed at [the hearing of] the Voice; he recognised the Son of God by His Voice, not by His appearance. Was he not, then, perhaps one of the sheep of Him who said, *My sheep hear My voice* (John x. 14)?[1]

5. By the hearing is discovered a truth which the sight was unable to reach; appearance has deceived the eye, and the truth has entered by the ear. The eye declared Him weak, defiled, miserable, condemned to the most ignominious of deaths; while the ear gained the knowledge that He was Son of God, that He was beautiful altogether; but not the ear of the Jews, who were uncircumcised in [heart and] ears. It was not without reason that St. Peter cut off the ear of the high priest's servant, as if to open an entrance for the truth, and that the truth should free him, that is, make him free. The centurion was a man uncircumcised, but not as to his ears, since he recognised the Lord, under so many marks of feebleness, and at the single voice of a dying Man. He did not despise that which he saw, because he believed that which he did not see. Nor did he believe because of what he saw, but, on the contrary, because, without doubt, of what he heard; for *faith cometh by hearing* (Rom. x. 17). It would have been indeed worthy of the truth that it should enter the soul by the eyes, which are its windows, and because sight is the worthier sense; but that is reserved for us, O my soul, to the time when we shall see face to face. In the meantime, it is well that the remedy should enter where the disease entered, that life should follow death, and tread close upon its footsteps; that Light should follow darkness, and

---

[1] This is the reading of two MSS. One other, with the printed editions, adds: 'and I know Mine, and My [sheep] know Me.' The Colbertine MS. adds merely, 'and My [sheep] know Me.'

that the venom of the serpent should be succeeded by the Truth, the remedy for it; so that the eye, which was sick, might be cured, and, being cured, might calmly behold Him whom in its sickness it was unable to discern. The ear was the first portal by which death entered, let it now be the first inlet opened to life; and let the hearing, which took away the power of sight, now restore it; for, unless we have believed [mysteries], we shall not comprehend them. Therefore, hearing has relation to the merit, and sight to the recompense [of belief]. Wherefore the Psalmist says: *Thou wilt give to my hearing joy and gladness* (Ps. li. 8); because the recompense of faithful hearing is the Blessed Vision, and the merit [deserving] of that Blessed Vision is faithful hearing. *Blessed are those who are pure in heart*, saith Our Lord, *for they shall see God* (Matt. v. 8). And it is necessary that the eye which is to see God should be purified by faith, according to that which is written: *Purifying their hearts by faith* (Acts xv. 9).

6. In the meantime, then, and while [that] sight is not as yet prepared, let the sense of hearing be aroused, let it be exercised,[1] and receive the truth. Happy is he to whom the Truth bears witness, saying: *At the hearing of the ear he obeyed Me* (Ps. xviii. 45). I shall be worthy to behold Him if before I have beheld I shall be found to have obeyed Him; I shall behold with confidence Him who has received the sacrifice of my obedience. How blessed is the man who says: *The Lord God hath opened mine ear, and I was not rebellious, neither turned away back* (Is. l. 5.). There you have a model of voluntary obedience, an example of perseverance. For he who does not contradict works voluntarily, and he who has not turned back perseveres. Both one and the other are necessary, because God loveth a cheerful giver (2 Cor. ix. 7), and *he that endureth unto the end shall be saved* (Matt. x. 22). May the Lord deign to open mine ear also, may the word of truth enter into my heart, may He purify mine eyes, and prepare them for the joyful vision [of Himself], so that I too may say to Him: *Thine ear has heard the preparation of my heart* (Ps. x. 17), and that I may be enabled also, with all that are obedient to Him, to hear from His Mouth: *Now ye are clean through the word which I have spoken unto you* (John xv. 3). Not all who listen to His words are cleansed, but those only who obey them: *Blessed are they that hear the Word of God and keep it* (Luke xi. 28). Such an hearing it is which He requires who gives command, saying, *Hear, O Israel* (Deut. vi. 3); such a hearing it is that he offers who says: *Speak, Lord, for Thy servant heareth* (1 Sam. iii. 9); such, again, it is that he promises who speaks thus: *I will hear what God the Lord will speak* (Ps. lxxxv. 8).

7. But in order that you may know that the Holy Spirit observes this order in the spiritual advancement of the soul—that is to say, that He forms the practice of hearing before He makes the soul glad

---

[1] In some editions, 'let it be exercised' is wanting. Perhaps the copyist, being doubtful whether the text were '*excitetur*' or '*exercitetur*,' wrote them both down.

with sight—notice what is said in a Psalm: Hearken, O daughter, and see (Ps. xlv. 11, Vulg. and Douay). Why dost thou open thine eyes? Open rather thine ears. Dost thou greatly desire to see Christ? It is necessary that you should first hear what He says, that you should hear what is said of Him, that you may say when you shall see Him: *As we have heard, so have we seen* (Ps. xlviii. 9). That brightness is without measure, and your vision is feeble; you cannot attain unto it. You may, perhaps, be able to hear His words; to behold Him you are not able. When I had become a sinner I heard God calling in the garden, *Adam, where art thou?* (Gen. iii. 9), but behold Him I did not. But the hearing, if it be pious, watchful, and faithful, brings back the sight. Faith shall purify the eye which impiety has rendered diseased; and though disobedience had closed it fast, obedience shall open it again. Lastly, it is, as says the Psalmist, *through Thy precepts I get understanding* (Ps. cxix. 104); because the observance of the commandments of God restores the intelligence, which transgression has taken away. Consider that good man Isaac, how, when he was already very aged, his hearing retained its vigour beyond the other senses. The eyes of the Patriarch were obscured, his taste was led away, his hands were deceived, but not his ears. What is there wonderful in his ear perceiving the truth, since faith cometh by hearing, hearing by the Word of God (Rom. x. 17), and the Word of God is truth? *The voice*, he said, *is Jacob's voice*, and nothing was truer than this; but, he went on, *the hands are the hands of Esau* (Gen. xxvii. 22); and nothing was more false. You are wrong; the mere likeness of a hand has deceived you. Taste is not a reliable test of truth, though it discern that which is agreeable. Is it to know the truth to suppose that you are eating venison when, in truth, it is the flesh of a tame kid? Much less is there dependence on the eye which sees nothing; in it there is neither truth nor wisdom. *Woe unto those*, says the Prophet, *that are wise in their own eyes* (Is. v. 21). It is not a good wisdom which is thus condemned. It is but the *wisdom of this world which is foolishness with God* (1 Cor. iii. 19).

8. The true wisdom is within, and is hidden (Job xxviii. 13), as holy Job knew. Why do you seek it without, and from the bodily senses? Taste has its seat in the palate, but wisdom in the heart. Do not seek for wisdom with the fleshly eye, for flesh and blood doth not reveal it, but the Spirit (Matt. xvi. 17). Nor is it found in the taste, *for it is not found in the land of the living* (Job xxviii. 13); nor in the touch of the hand, for Job says again: *If my mouth has kissed my hand, this also were an iniquity to be punished by the judge, for I should have denied the God that is above* (xxxii. 27, 28). This, I consider, is the case when the gift of God—that is, wisdom—is attributed not to God, but to the merits of [human] actions. Isaac was a wise man; nevertheless, his senses led him into error. Has hearing alone the truth? It is because hearing perceives the word. Rightly was it forbidden to the woman in the Gospel, who had only carnal wisdom,

to touch the Flesh of the Risen Word, because she trusted more to her eyes than to the Divine oracles—that is, to the carnal senses rather than to the Word of God; for she did not believe that He whom she saw dead was raised again,[1] although He had Himself promised that this should be so. Thus her eyes had no rest until they were satisfied by seeing, because she found no consolation in faith, nor in the promise given by God. Are not heaven and earth, and whatsoever is capable of being reached by the bodily eye, to pass away and perish before one jot or tittle out of all that God has spoken shall fail? And yet she who was unwilling to be consoled by the Word of the Lord ceased to weep immediately upon the sight of Him, because she attached greater weight to the experience of her senses than to the certitude of faith. But that experience is deceptive.

9. We are thrown back, on that account, upon the surer cognition of faith, which comprehends that which sense is unable to reach, and which is not included in past experience. *Touch Me not*, says the Saviour—that is to say, Cease to rely upon this [carnal] sense, which is easily deceived;[2] rest upon My Word; accustom yourselves to the exercise of faith. Faith cannot be deceived; it does not feel the poverty which belongs to the senses, but comprehends things which are invisible—indeed, it passes beyond the boundaries even of human reason, of the course of nature, of the limits of experience. Why do you ask of the eye that which it is not capable of knowing? and why does the hand endeavour to examine that which is beyond its range? Whatever these two senses bring you information upon is of subordinate importance. But faith reveals to you truths respecting Me, from the greatness of which nothing can detract. Learn to hold with firmer grasp, and to follow with greater confidence, that which it recommends to you. *Touch Me not, for I am not yet ascended unto My Father* (John xx. 17). As if it were only when He were ascended that He either could be, or desired to be, touched by her! Yes, doubtless, He could be touched, but by the heart, not by the hand; by prayers, not by the eyes; by faith, and not by the bodily senses. 'Why,' He says, 'do you wish to touch Me now, you who judge of the glory of My Resurrection only by the bodily senses? Do you not remember that, even while I was yet mortal, the eyes of My disciples were not able to sustain for a moment the glory of My Body, though it were about to die? (Matt. xvii. 6). I am still, indeed, in a certain relation to your senses, while I bear this form of a servant, which you are able to recognise through habit. But My glory is wonderful, and raised wholly above you, so that you cannot in any wise attain unto it.' Defer, then, your judgment, suspend your belief, and do not trust at all to your senses for the determination of a matter so great, and which is reserved to faith. Faith will define it more worthily and more surely, inasmuch as faith comprehends it more fully, and, in its deep and mystical intelligence, apprehends the height and the depth,

---

[1] *Resuscitatum;* otherwise, *resurrecturum.*
[2] *Seducibili.* See previous note upon this rare word (p. 112).—ED.

the length and the breadth of that mystery. That which the eye hath not seen, nor the ear heard, nor hath it entered into the heart of man [even to imagine], faith bears in itself—concealed, as it were, by an impenetrable covering, and safely sealed.

10. That faculty, then, can alone touch Me worthily, which shall contemplate Me sitting at the Right Hand of My Father, no longer in humble guise, but in celestial glory; in My very Flesh, but in quite other semblance than aforetime. Why do you desire to touch It in Its disfigurement? Wait till It be glorified, and you shall do so. For that which is now disfigured shall then be beautiful; and disfigured it is, to touch and to sight, even to you, who are yourself disfigured, as relying rather upon your senses than upon faith. But take to yourself [spiritual] beauty, and then the touch of Me will be possible to you; for if you have faith, then you have this beauty also, and can touch Him who has it both more worthily and more happily. Touch Him with the hand of faith, with the finger of earnest desire, with the clasp of devotion, with the fixed gaze of the intellect. But will He still be black, Him whom you touch thus? By no means. Thy *Beloved is white and ruddy* (Cant. v. 10). He is beautiful altogether, and is surrounded with the Roses of Sharon, with lilies of the valleys—that is, with the noble bands of Martyrs, and the choirs of Virgins. I who sit in the midst am akin to each, for I, too, am both Virgin and Martyr. How can I but belong to the white-robed choirs of Virgins, I who am a virgin, the Son of a Virgin, the Spouse of a virgin-bride? How, again, can I but have a place among the empurpled ranks of the Martyrs, I who am the cause and the strength of martyrdom, the pattern and the reward of Martyrs? Be thou like this, and touch thus Him who is thus described,[1] and then say: *My Beloved is white and ruddy, the chiefest among ten thousand.* Thousands of thousands are with Him—ten thousand times ten thousand are around Him; but there is none of all these to whom He can be compared. Do you fear lest you should fall into some error while seeking Him whom you love in the midst of a multitude so great? You will assuredly not hesitate in your choice; you will easily distinguish Him who is chiefest among all those thousands, since He is more majestic than all, and you will say: *He that is glorious in His apparel, travelling in the greatness of His strength* (Is. lxiii. 1). Then He will not be in that complexion blackened by trouble and hardship in which, up to that time, He had presented Himself before the eyes of His persecutors that they might despise and put Him to death, as also before the eyes of His friends that they might recognise Him when He was risen again. No, I repeat, He will then appear no longer in that sable garb, but in a robe of white, and with a beauty which surpasses not only that of the sons of men, but also that of angels. Why [He says] do you wish to touch Me when I am in a state so humble, in the form of a servant, and without form or comeli-

---

[1] The vigorous compression of the original can hardly be approached: '*Talem talis taliterque tange.*'—ED.

ness? Touch Me rather when I shall be adorned with heavenly beauty, crowned with glory and honour—inspiring fear, indeed, by My Divine Majesty, but full of the winning serenity and gentleness which is Mine by nature.

11. At this point we ought to notice the prudence of the Bride, and the marvellous profundity of her sayings, inasmuch as under the figure of the curtains of Solomon, that is, in the flesh, she has sought out God, and in death has discovered the Life, supreme glory and honour among unnumbered disgraces and shames, and under the dark and poor exterior of the Crucified One, the whiteness of innocence, and the splendour of all virtues; just as under those tent-curtains, however black and despised, the ornaments and treasures of a great and rich king are hidden and preserved. Rightly, then, a person does not scorn the blackness of the curtains, who divines and reflects upon the beauty which they conceal. Therefore it is that some have despised the one because they did not know of the existence of the other; for *if they had known, they would not have crucified the Lord of Glory* (1 Cor. ii. 8). Herod knew it not, and therefore despised Him; nor did the rulers of the Synagogue, since they reproached the gloom and infirmity of His Passion, saying: *He saved others, Himself He cannot save. Let Christ the King of Israel descend now from the Cross, that we may see and believe* (Mark xv. 31, 22). But the thief knew Him from the cross where he was hanging, though He was upon the Cross too, and acknowledged His innocence: *This Man hath done nothing amiss.*[1] And then at the same time he declared his belief in His royal Majesty and Glory: *Lord, remember me when Thou comest into Thy Kingdom* (Luke xxiii. 42). The Centurion knew Him, who cried out that He was the Son of God (Matt. xxvii. 54); and the Church knows Him now, and emulates His blackness in order to share in His glory and beauty. She is not confounded at appearing black or being called black, as she says to her beloved: *The reproaches of them that reproached Thee are fallen upon me* (Ps. lxix. 9). For she is black as the curtains of Solomon, but without, and not within; for my Solomon has no inward blackness. Also, she does not say, 'I am black as Solomon,' but 'as the curtains of Solomon'; because the blackness of Him who is truly *the Peaceful* is only on the surface. The blackness caused by sin is inward, and sin defiles the soul before it appears to the eyes of men. Thus it is out of the heart that proceed evil thoughts, murders, adulteries, fornications, thefts, false witnesses, blasphemies, and it is these which defile a man (Matt. xv. 19, 20); but that is not the case (God forbid!) with our Solomon. You will assuredly not find any such defilements in Him who is truly *the Peaceful;* for it must absolutely be the case that He who taketh away the sins of the world is Himself without sin, that He may be found fit to bring peace to sinners, and have a right to claim for Himself justly the name of *the Peaceful*.

---

[1] Luke xxiii. 41; but not quite *verbatim*. See verse 22.

12. But there is also a blackness of repentance which gathers upon one who makes lamentation for his sins. Perhaps He who is my Solomon will not abhor this in me, if I clothe myself with it of my own accord for my sins; because a broken and contrite heart God does not despise (Ps. li. 17). There is also that of compassion, with which one is affected who condoles with some other who is afflicted, and it darkens you with the suffering of a brother. Our Peacemaker has without doubt considered that He ought not to reject this blackness of sympathy, since He has deigned Himself to be indued with it for us, and has borne our sins in His own Body on the Tree (1 Peter ii. 24). There is also the blackness of persecution, which is counted as a rich and exalted ornament, when it is endured for the sake of righteousness and truth. Wherefore it is said of the Apostles that *they departed from the presence of the Council, rejoicing that they were counted worthy to suffer shame for His Name* (Acts v. 41); and again: *Blessed are they which are persecuted for righteousness' sake* (Matt. v. 10). It is, I consider, principally in this blackness that the Church takes glory to herself, and of all the dark coverings of the Bridegroom it is that which she imitates most willingly. Also, it is that which has been promised to her by the Saviour: *If they have persecuted Me, they will also persecute you* (John xv. 20).

13. On this account the Bride adds: *Look not upon me because I am black, because the sun hath looked upon me* (i. 6), that is, Do not consider me as repulsive, because it is the violence of persecution which renders me less attractive, and less glorious according to the glory of the world. Why do you impute as a blemish to me the blackness which the heat of persecution, and not any fault in my behaviour, has caused? Or perhaps she intends by 'the sun' the warm zeal for righteousness with which she is fired and consumed against the ungodly, saying to God: *The zeal of Thine house hath eaten me up* (Ps. lxix. 9); and again, *My zeal hath consumed me, because mine enemies have forgotten Thy words;* and again, *Horror hath taken hold upon me, because of the wicked that forsake Thy law* (Ps. cxix. 139, 53); and again, *Do I not hate them, O Lord, that hate Thee? and am I not grieved with them that rise up against Thee?* (Ps. cxxxix. 21). She observes with care also that saying of the Wise Man: Hast thou daughters? show not thyself cheerful towards them (Ecclus. vii. 24); so that when they are slothful and luxurious, and backward in observance of rule, she shows towards them, not the serenity of satisfaction, but the troubled look of severity. Or, again, 'to be blackened by the sun' means, perhaps, to her to burn with ardent charity towards the brethren, to weep with them that weep, to be weak with the weak, to feel acutely when another is affected with scandal. Or it may be read thus: It is Christ, the Sun of Righteousness, for whose love I languish, whose beams have looked upon me. That languishing draws the colour from the countenance, and that paleness arises from the violence of the soul's desire; wherefore also the Psalmist says: *I remembered God, and*

was delighted, and was exercised, and my spirit swooned away (Ps. lxxvi. 4, Vulg. and Douay). Therefore the ardour of its desire, like a burning sun, makes pale the countenance, while the soul is making its pilgrimage here below, and sighing for the glorious vision of its Lord; the repulse that it receives makes it impatient, and the delay that it experiences gives it pain that is great according to the greatness of its love. Who is there among us who glows with a love so sacred, that the desire which he has to see Jesus Christ inspires him with distaste and scorn for all the varieties of glory, and all the joy, of this present life; so that he says to God, with the Prophet, *I have not desired the day of man, Thou knowest* (Jer. xvii. 16, Douay), and also with holy David, *My soul refused to be comforted* (Ps. lxxvii. 2), that is, scorns to be flushed with the empty joy of present good. Or, lastly, 'the sun hath discoloured me' may mean, in comparison with His own splendour, because when I draw near to Him I find myself to be dusky, even black, and despise myself as disfigured and foul. But otherwise I am indeed beautiful; and why do you call me black, when I yield in fairness only to the sun? But the words which follow seem to agree better with the former sense, for she adds: *My mother's children were angry with me*, which plainly signifies that she has suffered persecution; but that shall be the subject of another discourse. For the present this, which we have received by the gift of our Lord Jesus Christ, Bridegroom of His Church, will suffice, and may it be to His glory, who is God blessed for ever. AMEN.

SERMON XXIX.

OF THE COMPLAINT OF THE CHURCH AGAINST HER PERSECUTORS; THAT IS TO SAY, AGAINST THOSE WHO SOW DIVISION AMONGST BRETHREN.

MY mother's children [sons] *were angry with me* (i. 6). Annas and Caiaphas, and Judas Iscariot, were sons of the Synagogue; and these fought most cruelly and bitterly against the Church at her very beginning, though she was equally a daughter of the Synagogue, inasmuch as they hung upon the Cross Jesus, who united her members into one body. At that time, and by means of them, God fulfilled what He had predicted long before by His Prophet, saying: *I will smite the Shepherd, and the sheep shall be scattered* (Zech. xiii. 7). And perhaps in these words from the canticle of Hezekiah: *My life is cut off, as by a weaver: whilst I was yet but beginning, He cut me off* (Is. xxxviii. 12, Douay). It is, then, of these and others from that race who are known to have opposed themselves to the Christian name that we must consider it to have been said by the Bride: *The sons of my mother were angry with me.* And it is with great propriety that she calls them 'sons of my mother,' not 'of my father,' inasmuch as they had not God for their father, but were of their father the devil, and were murderers, as he was a murderer from the beginning (John viii. 44). Wherefore she does not say 'my brethren,' or 'the sons of my father,' but 'the sons of my mother were angry with me.' Otherwise, if she did not distinguish thus, it would seem that even the Apostle Paul was included in those of whom she complains, since he too at one time persecuted the Church of God (1 Cor. xv. 9); but he obtained mercy, because he did it ignorantly and in unbelief (1 Tim. i. 13), and made proof that he had God for his Father, and thus by father, as by mother, had to the Church the relation of a brother.

2. But remark that she names none in her accusation except the sons of her mother, and accuses them alone, as if they only were in fault. Yet how many things has she endured from strangers? According to the Psalmist, *Many a time have they afflicted me from my youth;* and *The plowers plowed upon my back* (Ps. cxxix. 1-3). Why, then, do you accuse in particular the children of your mother, since you are well aware that you have been very often persecuted by many others also? Now, it is said, *When thou sittest at meat with a ruler, consider diligently what is before thee* (Prov. xxiii. 1). Brethren, we are sitting at the table of Solomon, and who is a greater ruler, or richer, than he? I do not speak of earthly riches, though Solomon abounded even in these; but look upon the board which is before us, and see how it is loaded with heavenly dainties. Now, these that are set before us are spiritual and divine. And he continues: *Consider diligently what is before thee, knowing that it behoves thee to prepare the like.*[1] On that account I consider as diligently as I am able that which is provided for me in these words of the Bride; and it is doubtless for my instruction that she speaks only of the persecution which she endured from those of her own house, and passes over in silence so many and severe sufferings which she has endured in every part of the world, from every nation which is under heaven, as is well known, from infidels, heretics, and schismatics. I know too well the prudence of the Bride to suppose that it is by chance or by forgetfulness that these are passed over without mention. But without doubt she laments more particularly that which she feels more keenly, and thinks it needful for us to avoid with special care. What, then, is that? Evidently it is domestic and intestine discord. That is plainly referred to in the Gospel by the mouth of the Saviour Himself, when He says: *A man's enemies shall be they of his own household* (Matt. x. 36). And by the Psalmist: *Mine own familiar friend, in whom I trusted, who did also eat of my bread, hath lifted up his heel against me* (Ps. xli. 9). And again, *It was not an enemy that reproached me: then I could have borne it: neither was it he that hated me that did magnify himself*

---

[1] Prov. xxiii. 2. The latter clause is not in the Hebrew or the Vulgate, but is an addition of the LXX., which appears to be quite alone in this reading.—ED.

against me; then I would have hid myself from him. But it was thou, a man mine equal, my guide, and mine acquaintance: we took sweet counsel together (Ps. lv. 12-14). That is to say, What you who are my companion at table and chamber make me suffer I feel more keenly, and endure with greater reluctance. You know whose complaint this is, and of whom it is made.

3. Recognise, then, that the Bride complains of '*the sons of my mother*' with the same wounded feelings, and in the same spirit, when she says that they '*were angry with me.*' So she speaks in another place: *My lovers and my friends stand aloof from my sore: and my kinsmen stand afar off* (Ps. xxxviii. 11). Keep far away from you always, I entreat, this evil which is so greatly to be hated and detested; you, who have experienced, and experience daily, how good and how pleasant it is for brethren to dwell together in unity (Ps. cxxxiii. 1); and if in unity, then assuredly not in a habit of scandal. For otherwise, instead of being good and pleasant, it is of all things the worst and most deplorable. Woe to that man who is the cause that the sweet bond of unity is broken! Whosoever it is shall assuredly bear the penalty. May it be mine rather to die than to hear any one among you crying out with good reason: *The sons of my mother were angry with me.* Are not you all sons of one community, and, as it were, of one mother, and, therefore, brethren one of the other? What is there coming from without, which should be able to trouble or distress you if all is well with you within, if you rejoice in brotherly love? *Who is he that will harm you*, it is said, *if ye be followers of that which is good* (1 Pet. iii. 13)? Wherefore do ye *covet earnestly the best gifts* (1 Cor. xii. 31), and you shall prove yourselves to be followers of the good. Now, the best gift of all is charity; there is assuredly no other to be compared with that, which the heavenly Bridegroom of a new Bride took occasion so often to inculcate, once saying, indeed: *By this shall all men know that ye are My disciples, if ye have love one to another;* and again, *A new commandment I give you, that ye love one another;* and, *This is My commandment, that ye love one another* (John xiii. 34, 35; xv. 12); also praying that they might be one, as He and the Father are One (xvii. 11). See also if St. Paul himself, who invites you to seek the best gifts, does not place charity above all the others; both when he says that it is greater than faith and than hope, and far above knowledge; as also when, after having enumerated many and wonderful gifts of grace, he leads us at length to *a more excellent way*, and explains that this is no other than the gift of charity. Lastly, what can we regard as comparable to a virtue which is preferred to martyrdom itself, and to faith, which removes mountains (1 Cor. xii. 31; xiii. 2, 3)? This, then, is what I say to you: Let peace be yours and come from you; then no danger which may seem to threaten you from without will appal you, for it will have no power to injure you. And, on the contrary, nothing that seems to allure you from outside will have any attraction for you if (which may God forbid!) the seeds of discord have begun their growth within you.

4. Therefore, dear brethren, let there be peace among you; do not harm or give pain to each other by word, by action, or even by any sign, for fear lest any one among you, being embittered and preoccupied by his own weakness of spirit, and by the persecution he endures, should be driven to appeal to God to come to his aid against those who injure or distress him, and it should come to pass that he break forth into that grave complaint: *The children of my mother were angry with me.* For in thus sinning against your brother, you sin against Christ, who has said: *That which you have done to the least of My brethren, you have done to Me* (Matt. xxv. 40, 45). Nor is it enough merely to abstain from graver offences—for example, from open insult or abuse; but also from secret and envenomed whispers against any. No, I repeat, it is not sufficient to guard our lips against these and other faults of a similar kind; even slight injuries to others ought to be avoided, if, indeed, we can call any fault slight which is done with the intent of injuring a brother, since, according to the word of our Saviour, if any is angry with his brother without a cause, for this alone he shall be in danger of the judgment (Matt. v. 22). And rightly so, for that which you think a little thing, and for that reason do it with too little hesitation, the person against whom it is done views in quite a different light—as a man who looks upon the surface of things, and judges of them according to their appearance, is prepared to think a mote to be a beam, and a single spark a blazing fire. For that charity, which believes all things, is not in the hearts of all. But the spirit of man, and the thoughts of his heart, are disposed rather to suspect evil than to believe good; especially when the Rule of silence neither permits you, whose conduct is in question, to excuse yourself, nor him who suspects you, to declare the wound which his sense of right feels, that it may be cured. Thus he burns inly, even unto death, and groans within himself, being wholly occupied with anger and irritation, and unable to occupy his mind with any other subject than the injury he has sustained. He cannot pray, he cannot read, nor meditate upon any holy or spiritual subject; and while this soul, for which Christ died, is thus going on the way which leads to death, being cut off from the influence of the life-giving Spirit, and deprived of His benefits, what is the condition, I ask you, of your mind? What pleasure can you take in prayer, or work, or any occupation that you may have in the meantime, you against whom Christ cries out in anxiety for your brother whose heart you have made sad? The Son of My mother, He says, is fighting against Me, and he who partakes at My table of its sweet sustenance has filled Me with bitterness.

5. If you say that [your brother] ought not to trouble himself so deeply for so slight a cause, I reply that the slighter the cause of offence is, the easier it is for you to abstain from giving it. However, I know not how you can call any cause whatsoever slight (as I have said) that is more than the occasion of anger, since even this, as you have learned from the lips of the Judge Himself, renders the offender

liable to the judgment. Do you call that a light thing at which Christ is offended, and for which you are to be brought to judgment, since *it is a fearful thing to fall into the Hands of the living God?* (Heb. x. 31). When, then, you have received an injury, as may be the case sometimes (for it is a difficult thing to prevent this from happening in communities such as this), do not, after the manner of those in the world, hasten to strike back your brother again with a hostile response. Do not ever venture to retort, under the pretext of reply, with cutting and ironical words, and thus pierce deeply a soul for which Christ deigned to be crucified; do not make surly answer, nor grumble under your breath, nor take a sneering air, nor laugh mockingly, nor knit your brows, as if in wrath or threatening. Let your anger die away where it is born—do not permit it even to show itself, for it brings death with it, and it may slay some soul—that you may be able to say with the Psalmist: *I was troubled, and I spoke not* (Ps. lxxvi. 5, Douay).

6. I have understood that there are some who interpret these words in a more mysterious manner, and regard them as having been spoken of the devil and his angels, who were also sons of the heavenly Jerusalem, which is our mother, from which they have fallen, and who do not cease to make war upon their sister—that is, the Church. Again, if anyone should take these words in a good signification, and as referring to spiritually-minded men who are in the Church, and who strike with the sword of the Spirit, which is the Word of God, against carnal brethren wounding them for their salvation, and bringing them by this warfare to a love for spiritual things, against this explanation I should not contend. Would that the Just One would reprove me in mercy, would correct me, striking that He may cure, slaying that He may give life, so that I, too, may dare to say: *I live: yet not I, but Christ liveth in me* (Gal. ii. 20). *Agree*, it is said, *with thine adversary quickly, whiles thou art in the way with him; lest he deliver thee to the judge, and the judge to the officer* (Matt. v. 25). A good adversary with whom, if I shall live in peace, there shall be no ground for the judge to speak against me, or deliver me to the torturer. For my part, I do not regret it if it has ever been my lot to make any among you sorry after this fashion, for you have been made sorry unto salvation. I do not know that I have ever done that without great sorrow to myself, according to that which is said: *A woman, when she is in travail, hath sorrow* (John xvi. 21). But God forbid that I should keep in memory that sorrow now that I have fruit of my pain, inasmuch as I see Christ formed in you who are my offspring. I know not how it is, but I have even more tender sentiments towards those who have been, after and by means of my loving corrections, enabled to rise above some weakness or failing than towards those who have been strong from the beginning, and have had no need of such means of remedy.

7. It is, then, in this sense that the Church, or the soul that loves God, is enabled to say that 'the sun hath altered her colour'—

namely, in sending forth and arming certain men of the children of her mother to carry on against her a war for her salvation; to make her a captive to the faith and love of Him, after having pierced her with many of those arrows of which it is written: *The arrows of the Mighty are sharp* (Ps. cxx. 4); and again: *Thine arrows stick fast in me* (Ps. xxxviii. 2). That is why the Psalmist goes on to say: *There is no soundness in my flesh.* But as for the soul, it is thus rendered more healthy and more strong, and says: *The spirit indeed is willing, but the flesh is weak* (Matt. xxvi. 41); and with the Apostle: *When I am weak, then am I strong* (2 Cor. xii. 10). Do you see how the weakness of the flesh strengthens the spirit, and increases its powers, while, on the contrary, the strength of the flesh is a cause of weakness to the spirit? What wonder is it that you should be made stronger by the weakness of your enemy? Unless, perhaps, you should, with excessive foolishness, regard that which is for ever lusting against the spirit (Gal. v. 17) as your friend. See, then, if the prayer was not wise and well founded which was made by that holy man who asked of God: *Pierce Thou my flesh with Thy fear* (Ps. cxix. 120, Douay). That fear is the best of all arrows which pierces and slays the desires of the flesh, that the spirit may be saved alive. And does it not seem to you that he who keeps under his body and brings it into subjection (1 Cor. ix. 27) is himself aiding the Hand of Him who is carrying on the combat with it?

8. There is yet one other arrow: it is the Word of God, which is living, powerful, and sharper than any two-edged sword (Heb. iv. 12), of which the Saviour says: *I came not to send peace, but a sword* (Matt. x. 34). There is still another, a chosen arrow: it is the love of Christ, which not only pierced the soul of Mary, but transfixed it from side to side, so that it left no part of that virgin heart empty of this love, but she loved with all her heart, all her soul, and all her strength, and was full of grace. Or perhaps it may be thus, that it transpierced her, in order to penetrate even to us, and that we might all receive of that fulness; that she might be the mother of charity, of which God, who is Love, is the Father; that she might bring forth and might set her tabernacle in the Sun, that the Scripture might be fulfilled, which says: *I will give thee for a light to the Gentiles, that thou mayest be My salvation to the ends of the earth* (Is. xlix. 6). For this was fullfiled by means of Mary, who brought forth and rendered visible in the flesh Him who was invisible, and whom she had conceived, but not of the flesh, nor with the flesh. As for her, she received through all her being a wound of Love, deep, sweet, and wide. How happy should I consider myself if I could only feel myself touched with the point of the weapon which gave that wound, and if my soul, being touched with that light wound of love, might be able to say: *I am wounded with love* (ii. 5). Oh that I might be not only in that manner wounded, but also stricken to the entire extermination of that colour and warmth of the flesh, which war against the soul!

9. If the daughters of this world remark disdainfully upon such a soul as this, calling it pallid and bloodless, does it not seem to you that it might fitly reply : *Look not upon me because I am black, because the sun hath looked upon me?* And if it bears in mind that it has reached its present state through the exhortations or chidings of some servants of God, who were jealous over it with a godly jealousy, may it not therefore go on to say, and truly : *My mother's children were angry with me?* The sense, then, of these words, according to what has been said, will be, that the Church, or any pious soul, speaks them, not by way of grief or complaint, but in a feeling of joy, of thankfulness, and even of a sacred pride ; that for the Name of Christ, and for His Love, she has been deemed worthy to be swarthy and dusk, and to be reproached with it for His sake ; and this honour the Church attributes, not to her own merit, but to the grace and mercy which have prevented and followed her to bring this about. For who can believe without a preacher? and how shall they preach, except they be sent? (Rom. x. 14, 15). She mentions that her mother's children have been angry with her, not in a spirit of anger, but rather of gratitude. On that account she adds : *They made me the keeper of the vineyards.* For this saying, if examined as to its spiritual sense, does not, in my opinion, appear to breathe any feeling of complaint or bitterness, but rather of satisfaction. But before we take in hand to explain that passage (which is a sacred one), let us endeavour, by our accustomed prayers, to call to our aid that Holy Spirit, who searches the deep things of God, or certainly the Only Begotten Son, who is in the Bosom of the Father, Jesus Christ Our Lord, the Bridegroom of the Church, who is above all, God blessed for ever. AMEN.

SERMON XXX.

THAT THE FAITHFUL PEOPLE, OR THE SOULS OF THE ELECT, ARE SIGNIFIED BY THE VINEYARDS, OF WHICH THE CHURCH IS CALLED THE GUARDIAN: AND THAT THE PRUDENCE OF THE FLESH IS DEATH.

THEY made me the keeper of the vineyards. Who did this? Are they your adversaries, of whom you spoke last? Listen and understand, if she does not confess that she has been entrusted with this charge by those very persons at whose hands she suffered. Nor is this strange, if the purpose of correction was the motive of the attack. For who does not know that opposition is frequently offered to many persons with a friendly intention, and with excellent results? How many do we know of daily who are led on to a higher standard and to a far stricter mode of living by the pious rebukes of their superiors? Let us therefore show, if we are able, how a contest against the Church may be carried on by her children in a spirit of hostility, and yet how the harm which they inflict may be for her good; for there is nothing more agreeable than that those who intend to do harm should do good even against their will. The former interpretation given of the words covers either sense, because the Church has never been without those who have been well disposed towards her, or without others who have been ill disposed; and each of these classes of people have attacked her, though from precisely opposite motives; yet each kind of attacks have been to her profit. In fact, she is able so to glory in having profited by the trials which she has endured at the hand of her rivals, that for one vineyard, which they have seemed to have taken away from her, she rejoices in having been set over many. This, she says, is the benefit that they have done in contending against me and my vineyard, those, I mean, who say, *Rase it, rase it, even to the foundation thereof* (Ps. cxxxvii. 7), namely, that instead of one, I can number many vineyards as mine. It is that she says in effect, when she continues, *My own vineyard I have not kept*, as if she would explain the reason why she is no longer the keeper of one vineyard, but of many; and that is, indeed, the literal sense of the words.

2. But if we follow it simply, and are contented with the most obvious meaning which occurs to us, we shall consider that the Holy Scripture intends to speak here of those earthly and material vineyards, which, as we see daily, receive from the dew of heaven and the fatness of the earth the elements from which they pour forth wine, in which is excess and riot (*luxuria*); and thus we draw out no sense befitting and worthy, I do not say of the Bride of the Lord merely, but of any modest and retiring matron, from the words of the Scripture. For what sort of fitness is there in married women to undertake the custody of vineyards? And even if that were otherwise, what reason have we for supposing that the Church was ever destined to such an office? Does God take a particular care of earthly vineyards? But if we interpret in a spiritual manner, and understand by the vineyards Churches, that is, faithful nations, according to the thought of the Prophet, when he says, *The vineyard of the Lord of Hosts is the house of Israel* (Is. v. 7), then we shall, perhaps, begin to perceive how it is by no means unworthy of the Bride to become keeper of the vineyards.

3. Furthermore, I think that we shall find in this a veritable prerogative, and one of no small value, if anyone takes the trouble to consider carefully how greatly she has extended her bounds in vineyards of this kind in every part of the world since the day when she was attacked in Jerusalem, and driven forth by the children of her mother, with those who were of that her new plantation, I mean the multitude of them who believed, of whom we read that they were *of one heart and of one soul* (Acts iv. 32). And it is that vineyard which she here confesses that she had not kept, but that did not turn to her discredit; for that was not in the persecution so torn up thence

that it could not be planted elsewhere, and let out to other husbandmen, who should render up its fruits in their seasons. No, indeed, it did not perish; it was but planted in other grounds, where it grew and waxed great, as the Lord gave it His blessing. And now lift up your eyes and see if *the hills are not covered with the shadow of it, and the boughs thereof like the goodly cedars;* if it has not *sent out her boughs unto the sea, and her branches unto the river* (Ps. lxxx. 10, 11). Nor is that wonderful, for it is God's husbandry, it is God's building (1 Cor. iii. 9). It is He who makes it fertile, who extends it, who trains and who prunes it, so that it may bring forth more fruit. When has the care and labour of Him, whose Right Hand planted it, ever been wanting to it? Assuredly that vine, which is the Lord Himself, of which the Apostles are the branches, and the Father the Husbandman (John xv. 1, 2, 5), cannot be neglected. In faith it is planted, and rooted in charity; the soil in which it grows is stirred with the hoe of discipline, manured with the tears of penitents, watered with the exhortations of preachers; and thus it gives wine in abundance, wine which makes glad, but does not inebriate; wine which is full of sweetness, void of impurity. This wine not only renders glad the heart of man, but of it the angels drink with joy; for they rejoice in the penitence and conversion of sinners, they thirst for the salvation of men. The tears of penitents are to them a wine which has the odour of life, the savour of grace, the taste of forgiveness, the joyfulness of reconciliation, the wholesomeness of returning innocence, the sweetness of a conscience rendered peaceful.

4. Then, again, from this single vine, which the violence of a cruel persecution seemed to have destroyed, how many shoots have been planted and have flourished in every part of the world? And over all these the Bride has been set as guardian, that she might not sorrow, because her first vineyard she did not keep. Be consoled, O daughter of Sion; if blindness in part has happened unto Israel, what hast thou lost by this? Reverence in silence the mystery; do not lament it as a loss. Rather make broad thy bosom, and gather in the fulness of the Gentiles. Say to the cities of Judah: *It was necessary that the word of God should first have been spoken to you: but seeing ye put it from you, and judge yourselves unworthy of everlasting life, lo, we turn to the Gentiles* (Acts xiii. 46). The offer was made by God to Moses, that if he would give up a people which had quickly turned aside out of the way of God's commandments, and abandon it to the Divine vengeance, that he himself should become a great nation; but he refused. Wherefore? Because he felt for that people an exceeding love, which held him in close attachment to them; and because he did not seek to advance his own interests but the honour of God, nor cared for that which should profit himself, but for that which should be to the good of many. That was his great desire.

5. For my part I think that in this was a secret design of Providence, and that this gift, so great and so excellent, was reserved to the Bride, so that she, and not Moses, should be developed into a

great nation. For it was not expedient that a friend of the Bridegroom should prematurely snatch from the Bride her benediction. Therefore it was not Moses, but the new-made Bride to whom it was said: *Go ye into all the world, and preach the Gospel to every creature* (Mark xvi. 15); it was she, I say, who was sent forth [to grow] into a great nation. For can any nation be greater than all the world? And all the world easily yielded to her who offered grace and brought with her peace. That grace was far different to the Law. In how strong a contrast did the sweetness of the one and the austerity of the other present themselves to every conscience? Who could look with the same eye upon her who condemned and her who consoled, her who punished and her who forgave, her who struck with revenging hand and her who embraced with gentle arms?[1] It was not possible to receive with the same ardour the darkness and the light, war and peace, judgment and mercy, the shadow and the reality, the rod of punishment and the heritage of reward, the restraining bridle and the joy-giving kiss Heavy were the hands of Moses, as Aaron and Hur experienced (Exod. xvii. 12); heavy was the yoke of the Law, as the Apostles themselves bore witness when they declared that neither their fathers nor they were able to bear it (Acts xv. 10); in truth, a heavy yoke; and the reward to be earned by bearing it was but a paltry one, for it did not extend beyond the earth. It was for these reasons that Moses was not sent forth [to grow] into a great nation. But thou, O holy Church, who art our mother, who hast the promise, not only of the life that now is, but of that which is to come (1 Tim. iv. 8), shalt obtain an easy and willing welcome from all, because of the double grace which thou bearest, that thy yoke is light and easy, and the realm of glory assured to thee is great and illustrious. If thou wert driven from a single city thou hast been welcomed by the whole world; as well because thy promises are engaging as because thy commandments are not alarming or grievous. Why dost thou still mourn the loss of one vineyard, when it has been repaid to thee with so great usury? As a recompense to thee because thou hast been abandoned, and hated, so that none passed through thee, it is said: *I will make thee an eternal excellency, a joy of many generations: thou shalt also suck the milk of the Gentiles, and shalt suck the breast of kings; and thou shalt know that I the Lord am thy Saviour and thy Redeemer, the Mighty One of Jacob* (Is. lx. 15, 16). In such a sense as this, then, it is that the Bride speaks of herself as having been made keeper of the vineyards, and having failed to keep her own.

6. I am accustomed, when occasion is given to me by these words, and understanding souls to be meant by vines, I am accustomed to blame myself for having undertaken the cure of souls when I am not sufficient to guard and keep my own soul. And if you approve of this interpretation, notice also, that we may go on to call faith the root of the vine; the various virtues the branches; good works the bunch or cluster of grapes which it bears; and devotion the wine they

[1] *Plectentem et amplectentem.*

yield. For as there can be no branch without the root, so without faith there is no virtue. For *without faith it is impossible to please God* (Heb. xi. 6); nay, it will be perhaps impossible to be otherwise than displeasing to Him, since *whatever is not of faith is sin* (Rom. xiv. 23). It behoved those persons, then, who set me as keeper in their vineyards, to have considered previously whether I had kept my own. Yet, alas! how long did that remain untilled and desert, and became a mere solitude! Upon it the vine had failed, and the vigorous shoots of the virtues had been dried up because its faith was sterile. There was, indeed, faith, but it was dead. For how could it be otherwise than dead without good works? And that, indeed, was the case with me during my life in the world. It is true that afterwards, when I was converted unto the Lord, I began to keep my vineyard better, by a very little, yet not as I ought to have done. And who is, in fact, capable of doing this? Not such was the holy Psalmist, who said: *Except the Lord keep the city, the watchman waketh but in vain* (Ps. cxxvii. 1). To what snares of him who shooteth his arrows from his lurking-places against the innocent do I remember that I was then exposed! How many times, O my vineyard, hast thou been robbed, and by unnumbered subtle devices, and that at the very time when I was endeavouring with increased vigilance and care to guard thee! How many and how precious were the clusters of grapes—that is to say, the good works, which either were choked by anger, or borne away by feelings of pride, or trodden under foot and defiled by vainglory! How great the ravages which carnal greediness, or lukewarmness of spirit, or weakness and timidity of disposition, or sudden temptation, have worked in my soul! In such a state was I, and yet they set me as keeper of the vineyards, not considering what I had done, and was doing, with my own; not listening to the accusations and warnings of that master in the spiritual life who said: *If a man know not how to rule his own house, how shall he take care of the Church of God?* (1 Tim. iii. 5).

7. I wonder at the rash boldness of very many people who do not gather anything from their own vineyards, unless it be briers and thorns, and yet do not fear to obtrude themselves as keepers even over the vineyards of the Lord. Robbers they are, and thieves, not faithful guardians, nor laborious vine-dressers. But let us not occupy ourselves longer with these. Woe to me also for the peril in which the vineyard of my soul is even now—indeed, even more now than heretofore, inasmuch as being engrossed with the care of many, it is impossible but that I should become less careful, less occupied in loving thoughtfulness for that one. No opportunity is given to me to surround it by a protecting hedge, or to dig out the [place for] the wine-press. Alas! the enclosing wall of it is broken down, so that all they who pass by pluck her grapes (Ps. lxxx. 12). It lies open and exposed on all sides to sadness, to wrath, to impatience. Certain little foxes of pressing necessities, which are, so to speak, constantly gnawing, demolish and lay it waste; it is overrun in all

quarters with anxieties, suspicions, cares, and there is scarcely an hour that is free from the crowd of discordant applicants, from the trouble and care of business. I have no power to stop their coming, and no possibility of refusing to receive them; and they do not leave me even the time to pray. What shower of tears that I could hope to pour forth would suffice to moisten and melt away the *sterility of my soul?* (Ps. xxxv. 12). I wished to say 'of my vineyard'; but I followed the words of the Psalm from habit, and the meaning is the same. Nor do I regret an error which draws my attention to the analogy between the two; for the subject of the discourse is not the vineyard, but the soul. Therefore he is thinking of the soul when he speaks of the vineyard, and by the name and under the figure of the one, he deplores the sterility of the other. With what tears, then, can I water my vineyard, which is so barren? All its branches are dried up for want of moisture; they lie on the ground, and bear no fruit, for want of the life-giving sap which should sustain them. O good Lord JESUS! Thou knowest what bundles of these twigs [of dried and perished good works] the fire of contrition which burns in my heart consumes every day in the burnt-sacrifice which I offer to Thee! Receive, I entreat, the sacrifice of a broken spirit; a broken and a contrite heart, O God, Thou wilt not despise (Ps. li. 17).

8. It is thus, then, that I apply, in my imperfect manner, the present passage to myself. But perfect will be everyone who is enabled in another sense to say, *My own vineyard I have not kept;* namely, in that sense in which the Saviour says in the Gospel, *He that loseth his life for My sake shall find it* (Matt. x. 39). The person is evidently fit and worthy to be set as keeper over the vineyards, who is not prevented from, or even hindered in, the care of his own vineyard, by all the diligence and carefulness which he gives to watching over others committed to his charge; while at the same time he seeks not the advancement of his own interests, or that which is of advantage to himself, but that which is useful and beneficial to many. Without doubt, if the care of so many vineyards (that is, souls belonging to the circumcision) was confined to St. Peter, it was because he was *ready to go both into prison, and to death* (Luke xxii. 33), so little was he restrained by the love of his own vineyard, that is, of his soul, from the care of those intrusted to his charge It was also on a similar ground that so great a space of vineyards among the nations was confided to St. Paul; because, so far from being too much engrossed in the care of his own, he was ready not to be bound only, but also to die at Jerusalem for the Name of the Lord Jesus (Acts xxii. 33). He said, in fact, *None of these things move me, neither count I my life dear unto myself* (xx. 24). It was to form a right estimate of things, to regard nothing that belonged to him as to be preferred to his own self.

9. How many persons there are who have preferred even the meanest of things, a little money, to their salvation! But St. Paul

did not prefer to it even his life. *I count not my life*, he said, *dearer than myself* (*pretiosiorem quam me*, Vulg.) Do you, then, O Apostle, make a difference between yourself and your life? (*animam* = soul; Douay 'life'). You are prudent in regarding yourself as of more value than anything that is yours. But in what sense is your life not yourself? I suppose that because St. Paul was then walking in the Spirit, and in mind consenting to the law of God, that it was good (Rom. vii. 16); he therefore regarded this, his mind, as the principal and supreme entity in himself, and thought it more proper to call it [himself], than to give that name to any other element whatsoever in his nature. As for the remainder, which is plainly of an inferior character, and to be attached to an inferior and commoner essence (which is the body), to which belongs, not only the function of life and sensibility, but also of self preservation and self support; the spiritual man, considering it, I say, an unworthy thing to give to this sensuous and carnal nature the name of himself, judged it more fitting to rank it in the class of things appertaining to him, than to call his entire personality by the name of it When I speak of 'myself,' he says, understand that which is more excellent in me; that in which also I stand by the grace of God, that is to say, my mind and my reason. When I speak of 'my life' or 'my soul,' understand that lower principle which animates my flesh and which participates in its concupiscence. That was 'me,' indeed, once, but it is so no longer; inasmuch as I *walk not after the flesh, but after the spirit* (Rom. viii. 4). For *I live, yet not I, but Christ liveth in me* (Gal. ii. 20). It is I, according to the spirit (*mentem*), but not I, according to the flesh. For what, if even now my soul shares in carnal desires? *It is no more I that do it, but sin that dwelleth in me* (Rom. vii. 17). And therefore it is I said that it was not indeed I, but that which is carnal in me; and that is no other than my [fleshly] soul (*anima*). For in truth the carnal affections make a portion of the soul, as does that life, which it communicates to the body. This, then, is the life (or soul) which St. Paul held of little value in comparison with himself, prepared as he was, not only to be bound, but also to die at Jerusalem for the Lord, and thus to lose his life, according to the Lord's precept (Matt. x. 39).

10. You also, if you abandon your own will; if you perfectly renounce the pleasures of the body; if you crucify the flesh, with its desires and lusts, and mortify your members which are upon the earth, you will show yourself to be an imitator of St. Paul, in that you do not regard your life as dearer than yourself; you will show yourself also a disciple of Christ, by even losing it, unto salvation. And indeed you will act more prudently by losing it in order to preserve it, than by so preserving it as to lose it. For *whosoever will save his life shall lose it* (Matt. xvi. 25). What do you say to this, you who are close observers of the quality of your provisions,[1] but negligent of your own characters? Hippocrates and his followers teach how

---

[1] See notes to Ep. 345.

to preserve [our] lives in this world; but Christ and His disciples teach us how to lose them. Which of the two do you elect to follow as your master? But that person makes it very clear which he has chosen whose discourse is all of his ailments, of this complaint in eyes or head, or that in chest or stomach. Each of them, without doubt, speaks what he has learned from the master he has preferred. Have you read these minute symptoms in the Gospel, or in the Prophets, or in the writings of the Apostles? Flesh and blood have certainly revealed to you this wisdom, not the Spirit of the Father; for this wisdom is of the flesh. And hear what they who are *our* physicians think of it: *The wisdom of the flesh,* they say, *is death* (Rom. viii. 5, 7), and again, *The wisdom of the flesh is enmity against God.* Do you think that I ought to propose to you the opinion of Hippocrates or Galen, or, forsooth, that of the school of Epicurus? I am a disciple of Jesus Christ, and I speak to the disciples of Jesus Christ. If I had brought before you teaching other than His, I should have done very wrongly. Epicurus strives for the pleasure of the body, Hippocrates for its health; but my Master bids us to contemn both the one object and the other. Hippocrates uses all his efforts to sustain the life of the soul in the body; Epicurus seeks out, and teaches others to seek out, whatever can afford pleasure and delight during this life; but the Saviour warns us to lose this life [so that we may gain it].

11. What other advice have you ever heard in the school of Jesus Christ than this which was just now repeated: *He that loveth his life shall lose it* (John xii. 25)? *Shall lose it,* He says, whether by laying it down as a martyr, or by afflicting it as a penitent. Although to mortify the deeds of the flesh by the Spirit is a kind of martyrdom, and it is done with a spiritual weapon which does not, indeed, excite so much horror as that with which the limbs of the body are cut and carved, but is not less painful, since its action continues much longer. Do you see how, by this saying of the Master, the wisdom of the flesh is condemned—that wisdom, I mean, which either ministers to the desire for bodily pleasure, or which cares for the good health of the body beyond what is needful? To show us that the true wisdom does not expend itself upon pleasures, a wise man teaches (Job xxviii. 13, Douay) that it is not even found in the land of them who live in delights. While he who has found it cries: I have loved it [wisdom] more than health and beauty (Wisd. vii. 10). But if above health and beauty, how much more above pleasure and shameful enjoyment? But even though a man has severed himself from pleasures, what does this profit if he expends his cares and thoughts every day in investigating differences of constitution, or in devising variations in the cooking of food? 'Beans,' gravely reflects such a person as this, 'produce wind; cheese is heavy upon the stomach; milk causes headache; the chest will not bear the drinking of water; cabbages nourish melancholy; leeks inflame the bile; fishes from ponds, or from stagnant and muddy water, do not at all agree with

my constitution.' What then? Is there nothing to be found in the rivers, in the fields, in the gardens, in the cellars, which you can eat?

12. Consider, I pray you, that you are a monk, not a physician; and that it is not your business to make a study of constitutions, but to obey your rule. Have consideration, I entreat, first for your own quiet, then for the labour of those who minister to your wants; do not increase the charges upon the house—have some regard to conscience. To conscience, I say, not your own, but his who, sitting opposite you, eats what is set before him, and murmurs at your unaccountable abstinence. For he is scandalized, either at your hateful superstition, or at what he perhaps thinks the hardheartedness of him whose duty it is to make needful provision for you. Your brother, I repeat, is scandalized at your singularity; he thinks you superstitious in that you require superfluities, or he accuses me of being unfeeling in that I do not seek out and provide the food necessary for you. It is to no purpose that some people flatter themselves that they have precedent in their favour by the example of St. Paul, who bade his disciple drink no longer water, but *use a little wine for thy stomach's sake and thine often infirmities* (1 Tim. v. 23). They ought to notice, in the first place, that it was not to himself that the Apostle gave that direction; and, in the next, that the disciple did not make this request on his own behalf. Then, it was not to a monk that this direction was given, but to a Bishop, whose life was of great importance to the nascent and still tender Church. This was Timothy. Give me another Timothy, and I will feed him even upon gold if you wish it, and give him precious cordial to drink. But it is you who make these dispensations, for your own self, and that through tenderness for your own feelings. That dispensation of yours, granted to yourself, is, I confess, a matter for suspicion to me, and I strongly suspect that carnal prudence is deceiving you under the cover and by the name of discretion. And I desire, at least, to admonish you if you allege the authority of the Apostle for drinking wine, that you do not overlook the limitation which he adds of '*a little*.' And so enough of that subject. Let us return to the Bride, and let us learn from her not to keep our vineyards merely for our own good,[1] especially we who seem to have been made keepers of the vineyards of JESUS CHRIST our Lord, the Bridegroom of the Church, who is above all, God blessed for ever. AMEN.

[1] *Utiliter;* that is, to our own good. So the oldest MSS., and printed editions. Horst and others read: '*Proprias utiliter nos custodire.*'

SERMON XXXI.

THE EXCELLENCY OF THE VISION OF GOD. HOW AT THE PRESENT TIME THE DELIGHT IN THE DIVINE PRESENCE FELT BY HOLY MEN VARIES ACCORDING TO THE VARYING DESIRES OF THEIR SOUL.

TELL me, O Thou whom my soul loveth, where Thou feedest, where Thou makest Thy flock to rest at noon (i. 7). The WORD, who is the Bridegroom, frequently appears to zealous souls, and not under one appearance only. Why is that? Doubtless, because we are not yet able to see Him as He is (1 John iii. 2). Also, that vision which we shall have of Him in Heaven is abiding, because the Form in which we shall then behold Him shall always abide. For He IS, and He receives no change or alteration from anything which is, or has been, or shall be. Take away the Past and the Future, and where, then, is any place for change or vicissitude? Everything which, passing from the condition of that which has been, does not cease to tend towards the condition of that which shall be, passes through the point of *being*, but it is not. For how can we say that a thing *is* which never remains in the same state? Thus, that alone truly *is* which is neither cut off from its past, nor blotted out from its future, but alone remains without change. Because He [*i.e.*, God] has not been, therefore He IS from all eternity; and because He will not be, therefore He IS to all eternity. On this account, therefore, He is the veritable Existence, Uncreated, Illimitable, Unchangeable. When, then, He who is thus, or, rather, is not thus or thus,[1] is beheld as He is, that vision, as I have said, endures, since it is not mingled with, or altered by, any change. He, then, is that one and the same denarius which, as we read in the Gospel, is given to all (Matt. xx. 9) who behold Him thus, because He is presented to them only in this appearance. For as that which He appears is unchangeable in Itself, so It is present without change to those who behold It; and those who behold It neither desire, nor are capable of beholding, anything more delightful or more to be desired. When, then, can the eagerness of their gaze be satiated, the sweetness in which they delight be withdrawn, or the truth be exhausted—in one word, when can eternity come to an end? For if both the will to behold, and the full ability of beholding, be equally enlarged to all eternity, what can be wanting to complete felicity? What, I ask, remains to be experienced, or even to be wished for, by those whose desire is always to behold Him, and in whom that desire is being eternally satisfied?

2. But such a Beatific Vision is not for the present life, but is reserved for the final state of existence; to those, at least, who are able to say: *We know that when He shall appear we shall be like*

---

[1] *I.e.* (apparently) is not in this or that mode of existence.—ED.

Him: for we shall see Him as He is (1 John iii. 2). Even in the present life He appears to whom He wills; but in the manner that He wills, not as He is. There is no man, however wise or holy, there is no prophet, who is able, or ever was able, to see Him, in this mortal body, as He is;[1] yet those who shall be found worthy shall do so when their body shall be immortal. Therefore He is indeed seen, but in the manner that seems good unto Him, and not as He is. For though you have seen that great luminary (I mean that Sun, which you behold every day), you have never seen it as it really is, but only as it lights up other things; for example, the air, or a wall, or a mountain. Nor would you be able to behold it even in a certain degree, if the light of your body, that is, the eye, did not resemble in some degree the light of heaven in its inborn clearness and serenity. For no other member of the body is capable of taking cognizance of light, on account of the essential unlikeness between it and them. Nor is the eye itself, when it is troubled, capable of receiving the light, and that is because it has lost its resemblance to light. Thus as the eye which is disturbed and confused cannot behold the sun, which is peaceful, because of its unlikeness to it, so it beholds the sun when clear and untroubled, on account of a certain similarity between the two. If the eye enjoyed an equal degree of purity with the object on which it gazes, it would behold that object without being dazzled, and as it is, because of the full similarity existing between them. So also he that is enlightened by that Sun of Righteousness, which lightens every man that comes into the world, is able to behold Him in the degree that he is enlightened by Him, and as being like Him in some degree; but still, as he is not perfectly like Him, he is not able to see Him as He is. Wherefore the Psalmist says: *They looked unto Him and were lightened, and their faces were not ashamed* (Ps. xxxiv. 5). Thus it is in truth; provided that we are enlightened as far as we have need, so that *with open face, beholding as in a glass the glory of the Lord, we are changed into the same image from glory to glory, even as by the Spirit of the Lord* (2 Cor. iii. 18).

3. It is therefore necessary not to approach Him rashly and irreverently, but with respect and awe, lest the irreverent observer of His Majesty be crushed and destroyed by His glory. He is not to be approached by a change of places, but by an increase of excellences; and those not bodily, but spiritual, since the Spirit of the Lord is our guide to Him. I say that it is by the Spirit of the Lord that we draw near to Him, and not by [the power of] our own spirit, although it is in our own spirit that this takes place. Thus the more pure and virtuous a spirit is, the nearer it is to God, and to have attained absolute purity and virtue is to have come into the very Presence of God. For to be in His Presence is to see Him as He is; and to do this is nothing else than to be as He is, and so not to be dazzled and confounded by being unlike Him. But that, as I have said, will be only in Heaven.

[1] On this subject, compare Sermon IX., *De Diversis;* and, further on, with regard to Moses, Sermon XXXIII., *n.* 6, and Sermon XXXIV., *n.* 1.

But in the present sphere of existence what are that great variety of forms, and that vast number of different species among created things, but, as it were, rays from the Sun of the Divine Nature, showing indeed that He from Whom they derive their being truly exists, but not explaining in full what He is? Therefore you discern somewhat concerning Him, but Himself you do not discern. But when you behold something relating to Him, though without beholding Him, you are assured, nevertheless, of the fact of His existence, and that ought to lead you to seek for Him. Nor will grace be wanting to him who seeks, while he who neglects to seek will not have the excuse of ignorance. Now, this mode of beholding is common to all rational creatures. For it is easy, as we are taught by the Apostle, for all those who have the use of reason clearly to see the invisible things of God, as they are understood by the things which are made (Rom. i. 20).

4. It was, without doubt, in another manner that God deigned formerly to manifest Himself to the Patriarchs, granting to them a frequent and familiar communion with His Presence, although even to them He was not visible as He is, but as He deigned to make Himself known. Nor was it in one manner only that He was made known to all; but, as the Apostle declares, *at sundry times and in divers manners* (Heb. i. 1), though in Himself He is one, as He declared to Israel, *The Lord Thy God is one Lord* (Deut. vi. 4). Nor was that manifestation common to all; yet it was made from without, by appearances visible to the senses, or words heard by the ears. But there was still another manner in which God was discerned, differing from those, inasmuch as it was inward: when God deigned of His own accord to make Himself known to a soul that sought for Him, and lavished on that seeking the entire love and ardour of its affections. And this is the sign of His coming thus to a soul, as we are taught by one who had experienced it: *A fire goeth before Him, and burneth up His enemies round about* (Ps. xcvii. 3). For it is needful that in every soul in which He is about to appear such an ardour of sanctified longing should go before His Face, as to consume every impurity of evil thoughts and works, and so to prepare a place for the Lord. And then the soul perceives that the Lord is at hand, when it feels itself consumed in that fiery longing, and it says with the Prophet: *From above hath He sent fire into my bones, and it prevaileth against them* (Lam. i. 13); and again: *My heart was hot within me, and while I was musing the fire burned* (Ps. xxxix. 3).

5. After a soul has been thus pressed by frequent aspirations towards God, or rather by continual prayer, and is afflicted by the violence of its longings, it is sometimes the case that He, who is so earnestly desired and longed for, has pity on that soul and makes Himself manifest to it; and I think that, led by its own experience, it will be able to say with the prophet Jeremiah: *The Lord is good to them that wait for Him, to the soul that seeketh Him* (Lam. iii. 25). His Angel, too, who is one of the companions of the Bridegroom, who

has been commissioned to [watch over] that individual soul, to be the minister and the witness of that secret and mutual communion, how greatly, I say, does that Angel rejoice; how is he transported with joy, so that turning to the Lord he says: 'I thank Thee, O God of infinite majesty, for that Thou hast granted the earnest desires of that soul, and hast not denied to him the request of his lips!' It is that Angel which is the untiring attendant everywhere of the soul confided to his care, and does not cease to entreat and warn it by frequent suggestions, saying: *Delight thyself in the Lord, and He shall give thee thy heart's desire;* and again: *Wait on the Lord, and keep His way* (Ps. xxxvii. 4, 34); and again: *Though he tarry, wait for Him; for He shall surely come, He shall not tarry* (Hab. ii. 3, Vulg.). Then, addressing himself to the Lord, he says: *As the hart panteth after the water brooks, so longeth that soul after Thee, O God* (Ps. xlii. 1). It has desired Thee in the night, its spirit within it has sought Thee early (Is. xxvi. 9). And again: Daily he has stretched out his hands unto Thee (Ps. lxxxviii. 9); send her away, for she crieth after Thee (Matt. xv. 23); Return, O Lord, how long, and be entreated in favour of Thy servant (Ps. lxxxix. 13, Douay). Look down from heaven, and see, and visit that desolate soul. Faithful is the paranymph;[1] he is conscious of that mutual love, but without being jealous of it; and far from seeking his own interest, seeks only that of his Lord. He goes and comes between the Bridegroom and the Bride, presenting the prayers of the one, bringing back the gifts of the other. The one he arouses, the Other he placates. And sometimes, though rarely, leading on and conducting, he introduces the one to the Other; for he is a servant of God and of His House; every day he beholds the Face of the Father, nor does he fear to be refused any request.

6. But be most careful not to allow yourself to think that there is anything imaginary, on the one hand, or corporeal, on the other hand, in this mingling of the Word with the soul of the believer. I am saying only that which the Apostle says, that *he that is joined unto the Lord is one spirit* (1 Cor. vi. 17). I go on to express, in what words I am able, the absorption of a pure soul into God, or the hallowed and blessed descent of God into the soul, comparing spiritual things with spiritual. That union, then, is made in the spirit, because God is a Spirit, and is moved with love for the beauty of that soul which He may have seen to be walking according to the Spirit, and to have no desire to fulfil the lusts of the flesh, especially as He knows that it is filled with ardent love for Himself. A soul in this condition, with such feelings and so beloved, will be far from content that her Bridegroom should manifest Himself to her in the manner which is common to all; that is, by the things which are made, or even in the manner peculiar to a few, namely, by dreams and visions; such a soul desires that by a special privilege He should descend from on high into her,

---

[1] *Paranymphus*, the friend and attendant of a bridegroom. The word παράνυμφος does not occur in the N. T., but is expressed by a synonym in John iii. 29: ὁ φίλος τοῦ νυμφίου.—ED.

and pervade her wholly in the deepest affections, and to the very ground of the heart. She desires that He whom she loves should not show Himself to her in an outward shape, but should be, as it were, inpoured into her; that He should not merely appear to her, but should enter into and dominate her; nor is it doubtful that her happiness is so much the greater, as He is within rather than without. For He is the Word; He does not sound in the ears, but penetrates the heart; He is not full of words, but full of power; nor does He come to the ears with a sound, but to the affections with sweetness ineffable. The features of His countenance are not formed and defined, but exercise a formative power; they do not strike upon the vision of the eye, but they rejoice the heart, not with charm of form and colour, but with the affection they excite.

7. I am not, however, able to describe the manner in which God manifests Himself *as He is*, although in this manner of manifestation He declares Himself no other than as He is. For however full of reverence and devotion souls may be, He will not continue His Presence in them permanently and precisely thus, nor with complete uniformity to all individuals. For, according as the desires of a soul vary, so the delight felt in the Divine Presence must needs vary also; and that heavenly sweetness strikes in divers ways upon the palate of the soul, according to the variation of its desires and longings. Also, you have noticed in this Song of love how often He has changed His countenance, and in how great a number of winning forms He has deigned to appear before His beloved; and how, like a modest spouse, at one time he seeks to enjoy in secret communion with a holy soul, and to take pleasure in its devotion; at another He seems to conduct Himself as a physician, with oils and unguents—doubtless on account of weak and tender souls, which have still need of remedies and consolations, and therefore are called by the name of maidens to signify their delicacy. If anyone murmurs, let him recall that *they that be whole need not a physician, but they that are sick* (Matt. ix. 12). Sometimes, again, He presents Himself as some traveller, joining Himself to the Bride and the young maidens who are walking with her, and solaces all that company during the fatigues of their way by His pleasant discourses, so that they say when He departs, *Did not our hearts burn within us while He talked with us* of Jesus, *by the way* (Luke xxiv. 32)? How delightful a companion is He who by the sweetness of His manners and His discourse, as by the delightful odours which He breathes around Him, draws all to follow after Him; and therefore they say, *We will run in the odour of Thy perfumes* (i. 4). Again, there are times when He appears as some opulent head of a family, in whose house are abundant provisions for all; or, rather, as a King powerful and splendid, who appears to exalt the poverty of his timid bride, to display to her the treasures of his glory, and excite in her a desire for them; to show to her his richly-stored winepresses and granaries, the produce of his gardens and his fields, and, finally, to bring her into his inner chamber. For the heart of

her husband doth safely trust in her, and he thinks that none of all these things should be hidden from her whom he hath raised out of poverty, whom he embraces as amiable and beloved, and whom he has proved to be faithful. And He does not cease to manifest Himself from above in this or that inward and spiritual manner to those who seek for Him, so that the word may be accomplished which He spake: *Lo, I am with you always, even unto the end of the world* (Matt. xxviii. 20).

8. In all these manifestations He is kind and gentle, and of tender mercy. For as in His embrace He shows Himself loving and tender, so the oil and perfumes and other remedies of which He makes use prove Him forgiving, and rich in pity and compassion. Then in the road He is found to be cheerful, affable, full of help and comfort; in the showing forth His riches and possessions bountiful, and one who gives recompenses proportionate to His royal liberality. It is thus that you will find the WORD shadowed forth under a great variety of figures all through this Song of Songs. It is that, I think, which is signified by the Prophet where He says: *Christ the Lord is a Spirit before our face: under His shadow shall we live among the Gentiles* (Lam. iv. 20); which, however, we see now only in a glass, and darkly, and not yet face to face. But that endures only while we live among the nations [of this world]; for when we are among the angels it shall be otherwise; then we shall enjoy a felicity similar to theirs; then we shall see Him, no longer in types and shadows, but as He is —that is, in the form of God. For just as there were only types and shadows to make Him known to those of the elder dispensation, as I have said, but to us, through the grace of Christ present among us in the Flesh, the truth shines forth by its own light; so also it cannot be denied that we ourselves, in comparison with the life to come, live now in, as it were, a shadow of the truth. Unless we shall contradict the Apostle when He says: *We know in part, and we prophesy in part* (1 Cor. xiii. 9); and again: *I count not myself to have apprehended* (Philip. iii. 13). Is not that the precise difference between him who walks by faith and him who walks by sight of the object aimed at? Therefore *the just lives by faith* (Hab. ii. 4), but the blessed rejoice in beholding [Him whom they love]; and so, also, while the man who is holy lives here below in the shadow of Christ, the angel, likewise holy, glories in the splendour and light of His countenance.

9. And if faith be a shadow yet it is good, for it tempers the Light to our weak and darkened eyes, and prepares them for its brilliance; for it is written: *Purifying their hearts by faith* (Acts xv. 9). Faith, then, does not extinguish the light, but preserves it Whatever that be, and however great, which is open to the vision of an angel, the shadow of faith preserves for me; wraps it, as it were, in an ample and trusty bosom, to be revealed to me in due time. Is it not better for you to possess, though in a shrouded and hidden state, that which if uncovered and bare you would not be capable of grasping? Even the Mother of the Lord lived in the shadow of faith, for of her it was

said: *Blessed is she that believed* (Luke i. 35 and 45). She lived also in the shadow cast by the Body of Christ, according to the words of the angel: *The power of the Highest shall overshadow thee.* Nor is this a shadow to be lightly thought of, which is cast by the power of the Highest. There was assuredly power in the Flesh of Christ which overshadowed the Virgin, and that which was impossible to a mortal woman, to sustain the Presence and the unapproachable Light of the Divine Majesty, she was enabled to endure by the sheltering shadow or envelope of that vivifying Body. A strength, indeed, by which all opposing power was subdued. As strength it puts demons to flight; as shadow it provides a safe shelter for men; a strength which gives vigour, a shelter providing pleasant coolness.

10. We, then, who walk by faith and are nourished with the Flesh of Christ, that we may live the life Divine, we live in the shadow of Christ. For His Flesh is meat indeed (John vi. 55). And perhaps it is for that very reason that in the passage quoted at first we have Him described under the figure of a shepherd or pastor, where the Bride seems to address Him as if He were some one of the shepherds, saying: *Tell me where Thou feedest, where Thou makest Thy flock to rest at noon.* He is the Good Shepherd, who giveth His Life for His sheep (John x. 11); His Life He spends for them to redeem them; His Flesh He gives to them to nourish them. A marvellous thing, indeed; He the Pastor, the Pasturage, and the Price of redemption! But this discourse is growing long, inasmuch as the passage is so extensive, and contains truths so great that it cannot be expounded in a few words; and I see that this necessity obliges me to break off rather than to finish. It is needful, then, as the subject is not exhausted, that we should keep it still in mind, so that I may resume it where it has been dropped, and complete it, as far as I may be enabled to do by the Lord Jesus Christ, the Bridegroom of the Church, who is over all, God, blessed for ever. AMEN.

SERMON XXXII.

CHRIST COMMUNICATES HIMSELF TO THE HOLY SOUL AS *BRIDEGROOM*, AND TO THE SOUL THAT IS WEAK AND IMPERFECT AS *PHYSICIAN*. OF THE MOODS OF THE SOUL—HOW THEY DIFFER FROM EACH OTHER, AND FROM WHAT CAUSES.

TELL me where Thou feedest, where Thou makest Thy flock to rest at noon (i. 7). This is the point where we are; from hence we proceed with our subject. But before commencing to speak of that vision and interview, I think it well to recapitulate, in a few words, the other modes of vision already treated of, and to show how they may be spiritually applied by us according to the prayers and merits of each; so that having fully grasped them, if God give us the grace so to do, we may follow more easily, and with fuller understanding, what remains to be said upon the subject. But that is very difficult indeed; for although the words in which those visions or similitudes are described are corporeal, and describe objects in the physical sphere, yet they are intended to suggest things spiritual to our minds, and for this reason the causes and meanings of them are to be searched by the spiritual faculty. And who is competent to understand or to sound so many different affections and modes of progress in the spirit by which the manifold grace of the Divine Bridegroom is manifested? Yet if we enter into ourselves, and the Holy Spirit deigns to show us by His light that which by His continual working in us He does not disdain to bring about in our souls, I think we shall not remain entirely without understanding of these deep things; for I trust that we have received, not the spirit of this world, but the Spirit which is of God, that we may know the things which are freely given to us by God (1 Cor. ii. 12).

2. If, then, any of us finds it, with the Psalmist, good for him to draw near to God (Ps. lxxiii. 28), and to speak more plainly, if any among us is so filled with an earnest longing [for those things that are above] that he desires to be dissolved and be with Christ; but desires it vehemently, thirsts for it ardently, and, without ceasing, dwells upon the hope of it: he shall, without doubt, receive the Word, and in no other form than that of the Bridegroom in the time of visitation; that is to say, in the hour when he shall feel himself inwardly embraced, as it were, by the arms of wisdom, and shall receive a sweet inpouring of the Divine Love. For the desire of his heart shall be granted unto him, though he is still in the body as in a place of pilgrimage, and though only in part for a time, and that a short time. For when [the Lord] has been sought in watching and prayers, with strenuous effort,[1] with showers of tears, He will at length present Himself to the soul; but suddenly, when it supposes that it has gained His Presence, He will glide away. Again He comes to the soul that follows after Him with tears; He allows Himself to be regained, but not to be retained, and anon He passes away out of its very hands. Yet if the devout soul shall persist in prayers and tears, He will at length return to it; He will not deprive it of the desire of its lips, but will speedily disappear again, and not return unless He be sought again with the whole desire of the heart. Thus, then, even in this body the joy of the Presence of the Bridegroom is frequently felt; but not the fulness of His Presence, because though His appearance renders the heart glad, the alternation of His absence affects it with sadness. And this the Beloved must of necessity endure, until, having laid down the burden of an earthly body, she shall be borne up upon the pinions, so to speak, of her earnest desires, and fly away, passing freely over the plains of contemplation as a bird through the air, and following in spirit her Beloved, whithersoever He goeth, without anything to hinder or retard.

---

[1] *Labore* is wanting in many MSS.

3. Nevertheless, He will not present Himself, even in passing, to every soul; but to that soul only which is shown by great devotion, vehement desire, and tender affection, to be His Bride, and to be worthy that the Word in all His beauty should visit her as a Bridegroom. For he who is not as yet in that state, but still is touched with repentance at the remembrance of his sins, and, speaking in the bitterness of his soul, says unto God: *Do not condemn me* (Job x. 2); or who perhaps suffers still from violent temptations, being drawn away and enticed by his own concupiscence—such a soul as this needs not a Bridegroom, but a Physician; and on this account receives, not, indeed, approval and tenderness, but only remedies, oil and unguents, for the cure of its wounds. Is not this the condition in which we often find ourselves in our prayers, we who are every day either tried by the passions which are in us now, or touched with remorse for those which were in us formerly? From what a degree of bitter sorrow hast Thou often delivered me by Thy appearance in my soul, O good Lord Jesus! How many times, after having poured forth tears of distress, sobs and groans, untold, Thou hast anointed my wounded conscience with the unction of Thy mercy, and with the oil of gladness hast besprinkled me! How often have I betaken myself to prayer, despairing almost of my salvation, and it has sent me back full of joy and confidence of pardon! Those who are similarly afflicted know well that the Lord Jesus is indeed a Physician who healeth those that are of contrite heart, and giveth medicine to heal their sickness (Ps. cxlvii. 3). And those who have not had this experience, let them believe what He says of Himself: *The Spirit of the Lord hath anointed Me, to preach good tidings unto the meek, to bind up the broken-hearted* (Is. lxi. 2; Luke iv. 17-21). If they still doubt, let them draw near and make trial of Him, and so learn in their own persons the meaning of that saying: *I will have mercy, and not sacrifice* (Matt. ix. 13). But let us continue the subject.

4. There are those who, being wearied with spiritual exercises, and fallen into lukewarmness, are in a kind of faintness of spirit, and walk in sadness along the ways of the Lord. Their heart is full of dryness and weariness in doing what is enjoined upon them, and their murmurs are frequent. They complain that their days and their nights are long, and they say, with holy Job: *When I lie down, I say, When shall I arise, and the night be gone? and I am full of tossings to and fro until the dawning of the day* (Job vii. 4). When a soul is in such a state as that, if the Lord, touched with compassion, draws near to it upon the road on which we walk, and He who is from heaven begins to speak of heavenly things, or to sing to us some sweet canticle from among the songs of Sion, to relate also somewhat of the City of God, the peace of that City, the eternity of that peace, of the fixedness of that eternity—I declare to you that the pleasantness of that narrative will be as a soft couch to that wearied and slumbering soul; it will drive away every trace of aversion from the mind, and of weariness from the body, of the hearer. Does it not seem to

you that he who wrote: *My soul hath slumbered through heaviness: strengthen Thou me in Thy words* (Ps. cxix. 28, Douay), must have experienced this trial, and have prayed for this very succour? And when he has obtained it, will he not cry out: *O how love I Thy Law! it is my meditation all the day* (Ps. cxix. 97)? For our meditations on the Word who is the Bridegroom, on His glory, His greatness, His power, His grace, are so many words spoken by Him to our souls. And not only when He speaks, but when we meditate upon and revolve in our minds with eagerness His testimonies and the judgments of His mouth, when we meditate in His Law night and day, let us know for certain that the Bridegroom is present, and is speaking to us, so that the sweetness of His discourse may prevent our being wearied by our labours.

5. Do you, then, when you feel yourself to be dwelling upon such thoughts as these, not suppose that these thoughts are from yourself, but recognise that they are spoken within you by Him who says by the Prophet: *I who speak righteousness* (Is. lxiii. 1). For the thoughts of our own mind have a great resemblance to the words of the Truth speaking within us; nor is it easy to distinguish what the heart produces of itself from within, from that which it hears spoken; unless a man bears carefully in mind what the Lord says in the Gospel: *Out of the heart proceed evil thoughts* (Matt. xv. 9); and again, *Wherefore think ye evil in your hearts?* (Matt. ix. 4); and again, *When he* [the devil] *speaketh a lie, he speaketh of his own* (John ix. 44). And the Apostle remarks, *We are not sufficient of ourselves* to think anything as of ourselves (that is to say, anything good[1]); *but our sufficiency is of God* (2 Cor. iii. 5). When, then, we dwell in thought upon things evil, the thought is of ourselves; but if upon good, it is by the inspiration of God. In the one kind of thoughts our heart speaks; but to the other it listens. *I*, says the Psalmist, *will hear what the Lord God will speak in me: for He will speak peace unto His people* (Ps. lxxxv. 9, Douay). Therefore it is God who speaks within us thoughts of peace, piety, righteousness; nor do we think those things of ourselves, but hear them spoken with us. Out of the heart there come murders, adulteries, fornications, thefts, false witness, blasphemies (Matt. xv. 19); these we do not hear, but they are the utterance of our own hearts. For *the fool hath said in his heart, There is no God* (Ps. xiv. 1). And because of this *the wicked hath contemned God:* because *he hath said in his heart, Thou wilt not require it* (Ps. x. 13). But there is still another kind of thoughts which are felt in the heart, but are not the utterance of the heart itself. For that does not come out of the heart, as do our thoughts. Nor is it that word of which we have been speaking, namely, that which is spoken by God the Word: since this other kind of words is evil. It is sent forth by powers which are hostile to us, and consists of thoughts suggested to us by evil angels; such as, for instance, was that which, as we read, the devil sent into the heart

---

[1] *Subaudis*, but *subaudi* is the reading of Tiraquellius.

of Judas Iscariot, the son of Simon, that he should betray his Lord (John xiii. 2).

6. But who is so skilled and watchful an observer either of the movements of his thoughts within, or of those that come to him from without, that in each forbidden desire he is able to distinguish between the malady of his own, or the wound inflicted by the serpent? To no mortal do I think this to be possible, except to him who has been enlightened by the Holy Spirit, and has thus received that special gift of grace which the Apostle, in enumerating it among other *charismata*, calls *the discerning of spirits* (1 Cor. xii. 10). Yet how greatly does it behove a man, as Solomon reminds us, to keep his heart with all diligence (Prov. iv. 23), and to observe all the movements within it with the most vigilant attention! Even when you are well skilled in this by long experience and frequent trial, yet you may not be able to discern and distinguish with unerring correctness between the evil that is inborn, and the evil that is introduced from without. For *who can understand sins?* (Ps. xviii. 13, Douay). Nor, after all, is it of great consequence to us to know *whence* an evil has come to us; that which is really of importance is to know that it is in us, if that be the fact; and from wheresoever it comes, our wisdom is to watch and pray, that we may not give the consent of our will unto it. From both one and the other kind of evil the prayer of the Psalmist asks deliverance: *Cleanse Thou me from my secret faults, O Lord, and from those of others spare Thy servant* (Ps. xviii. 13, 14, Douay). As for me, I am unable to impart to you that which I have not received. I can give you no precise rule, I confess, whereby to distinguish between the ideas emanating from your own heart, and those sown in it by the enemy. Both one and the other are evils; each of them comes from an evil cause; each of them is in the heart, yet they do not both come from the heart. I am sure that they are in me, though I am not sure which to attribute to my own heart, and which to an enemy. But from that inability arises, as I have said, no danger.

7. But there is another point in which it would be not only dangerous, but even fatal, to be deceived; and deservedly so, inasmuch as a plain rule is laid down for us, not to attribute to ourselves that which is of God in us, or to think the visit of the WORD to us to be only the working of our own thoughts. For as far as good is different from evil, so far different are these two from each other; since evil cannot possibly come from the WORD, nor good come from the human heart, unless it has been first conceived there by the WORD; because a good tree cannot bring forth evil fruit, neither can a corrupt tree bring forth good fruit (Matt. vii. 18). But I believe it has been sufficiently stated what is of God in our heart, and what is of ourselves; nor was that, I think, without need; and that it will serve to show those who are enemies to grace,[1] that without grace

---

[1] This is, I think, an allusion to Abaelard, who reduced the grace of Christ to little more than the giving of reason to man, and to the good example given by the Saviour. See on the Eleventh Treatise of St. Bernard.

the heart of man is not capable of thinking good thoughts, but that the capacity of doing so comes from God ; and that the good things which it thinks are due to the voice of God in it, and are not its own offspring. Do you, then, if you hear His Voice, be no longer as if ignorant whence it cometh, or whither it goeth ; but recognise that It comes forth from God, and into your heart. Only, take care that the word which comes forth from the Mouth of God does not return unto Him void, but prosper and accomplish all things for which He sent it, so that you, too, may be able to say, *His grace which was bestowed upon me was not in vain* (1 Cor. xv. 10). Happy the soul of which the WORD is the inseparable companion, showing Himself accessible at all times ; and who, being kept in continual delight by the sweetness of His companionship, frees himself without ceasing from every vice and tyranny of the flesh, *redeeming the time, because the days are evil* (Eph. v. 16). He shall not be cast down, he shall not be rendered weary ; as says the Scripture, *There shall no evil happen to the just* (Prov. xii. 21).

8. But I think that the Lord [also] appears as a great Father of a family, or as a Sovereign of royal splendour, to those who, drawing near[1] to Him with heart exalted, with greater liberty of spirit, and purity of conscience, and rendered more noble and courageous thereby, are accustomed to lift up their hearts to higher things. These are restless and eager to penetrate deeper mysteries, to attempt loftier achievements, to attain greater perfection, not in sensible things, but in sanctity. These, for the grandeur of their faith, are found worthy to be led forward into all fulness ; and there is nothing so rare in all the treasure houses of wisdom that the Lord, who is the God of all knowledge, thinks fit to withdraw it from those heroic souls who thirst for truth, and are devoid of vanity. Such was Moses, who dared to say to God : *If I have found grace in Thy sight . . . show me Thy glory* (Exod. xxxiii. 17, 18). Such was Philip, who, for himself and his co-disciples, asked of the Lord that He would show them the Father (John xiv. 8) ; such, too, was Thomas, who refused to believe unless he should touch with his hand the wounds [of the nails], and the pierced Side of his Master (xx. 25). That was a want of faith, but it came from a greatness of soul which was wonderful in its way.[2] Such also was David, who himself said to God : *My heart said unto Thee, Thy Face, Lord, will I seek* (Ps. xxvii. 8). Such souls aspire to great things because they are great ; and because they aspire to them, they attain them, according to the word of promise made to them : *Every place whereon the soles of your feet shall tread, shall be yours* (Deut. xi. 24). For great faith merits great rewards ; and you

---

[1] *Accedentes*, otherwise *ascendentes*.

[2] How could it be from greatness of soul, if it came from weakness of faith ? St. Bernard distinguishes two things : one, that he refused to believe, which showed a weakness of faith ; the other, the condition he named, and this evinced a greatness of mind, the sign of which is to dare great things. See Sermon CLXII, in the Appendix to the works of St. Augustine, and William, Abbot of St. Thierry, 'De Contemplando Deo,' chap i., *n*. 3.

shall obtain the good things of the Lord, in proportion as you shall attain to set upon them the foot of an assured confidence.

9. Thus God speaks to Moses face to face, and it is his eminent reward to behold the Lord openly, not by types and figures, whilst to other Prophets He is said to make Himself known only in vision, and to speak to them in a dream (Numb. xii. 6-8). To Philip, again, according to his heartfelt petition, was shown the Father in the Son, from whom he received, without doubt, the instant reply: *Philip, he who hath seen Me, hath seen the Father:* and, *I am in the Father, and the Father in Me* (John xiv. 9, 10). Thomas He permitted to touch Him, according to the desire of his heart, and did not refuse him the request of his lips (xx. 27). What shall I say of David? Does it not signify that he was not left wholly without the granting of his prayer, where he says that he *will not give sleep to his eyes, nor slumber to his eyelids, until he find out a place for the Lord* (Ps. cxxxii. 4, 5). A great Bridegroom, then, will present Himself thus to great souls; and He will treat them magnificently, sending them His Light and His Truth; leading them on and conducting them at length to His holy mountain and into its tabernacles, so that one thus blessed may say: *He that is Mighty hath done to me great things* (Luke i. 49). His *eyes shall see the King in His beauty* (Is. xxxiii. 17); going before him towards oases in the desert, in which bloom the fragrant roses, and the lilies of the valleys, where are the pleasant shades of gardens, the gushing of silver fountains, the storehouses filled with all good things, the odours of perfumes, and lastly, the hidden precincts of the chamber of the King.

10. These are the treasures of wisdom and knowledge which are hidden in the Bridegroom; these are the life-giving sustenance prepared for the refreshment of holy souls. Blessed is the man whose longing for them has been satisfied to the full! Of this only let him be warned, that he ought not to wish to possess alone gifts which would suffice for the needs of many. For if, after all these things, the Bridegroom is described as appearing in the character of a pastor, it is perhaps to warn him who has obtained such great gifts that his duty is to feed the simpler ones of the flock, who are not able to attain by their own efforts to the knowledge of these good things; just as sheep do not dare to go forth without their shepherd to seek the green pastures. Of this fact the Bride prudently takes note, and that is why she desires to be told where the Bridegroom feeds [His flock], and takes shelter during the mid-day heat; being prepared (as may easily be understood from her words) to be nourished and to feed her flock with Him, and under His protection. She does not consider it safe for the flock to stray far from their Chief Pastor, because of the attacks of wolves upon them; and especially of those who come to us in sheep's clothing; it is for that reason that she desires to feed in the same pastures, and repose in the same shades, as He. And she gives her motive in the words, *Why should I be as one that turneth aside by the flocks of Thy companions?* (i. 7). These

are they who wish to appear as friends of the Bridegroom, and are not; their care is to feed their own flocks, not His; they are those who go about insidiously, saying: *Lo, here is Christ; or, lo, He is there* (Mark xiii. 21), so that they may lead away many, may withdraw them from the flock of Christ, and add them to their own. So far as relates to the letter of the text. As for the spiritual sense hidden in it, I propose to defer the consideration of it to another discourse, which, by the intercession of your prayers, and in the fulness of His mercy, may He deign to grant unto me to deliver, Who is the Bridegroom of the Church, JESUS CHRIST our Lord, who is above all, God blessed for ever. AMEN.

SERMON XXXIII.

OF THOSE THINGS WHICH A DEVOUT SOUL OUGHT TO SEEK WITHOUT CEASING. WHAT IS TO BE UNDERSTOOD BY THE WORD '*NOON*,' AND OF FOUR CLASSES OF TEMPTATIONS TO BE SEDULOUSLY AVOIDED.

TELL me, O Thou whom my soul loveth, where Thou feedest, where Thou makest Thy flock to rest at noon (i. 7). And another voice speaks thus: *Tell me why Thou judgest me thus* (Job x. 2, Douay). Where he does not blame the sentence upon him, but examines the cause of it, and asks to be instructed by his afflictions, not destroyed by them. And still another prays in the same sense, saying: *Show me Thy ways, O Lord; teach me thy paths* (Ps. xxv. 4). What he means by 'ways' and 'paths' he shows elsewhere: *He leadeth me in the paths of righteousness* (Ps. xxiii. 3). Every soul, therefore, that is full of care to serve God does not cease to seek for these three things: righteousness, and judgment, and the place where dwelleth the glory of the Lord; or, as it were, the *path* in which to walk, the *precaution* with which to walk, and the *dwelling* whither to direct our course. Of this dwelling the Psalmist speaks thus: *One thing have I desired unto the Lord, that will I seek after: that I may dwell in the House of the Lord all the days of my life* (Ps. xxvii. 4); and, again: *Lord, I have loved the habitation of Thy House, and the place where Thine Honour dwelleth* (xxvi. 8); while of the two others he says: *Justice and judgment are the habitation of Thy Throne* (lxxxix. 14). It is with reason that the devoted soul seeks these three things, as being the throne of God, and the basis (*præparationem*) of His Throne. Beautiful it is to see how, by the peculiar prerogative of the Bride, all these things concur equally to the consummation of her virtues, so that she is *beautiful* by the form of righteousness, *prudent* by knowledge of judgments, and *chaste* by her desire for the presence and glory of her Bridegroom. Such it becomes well the Spouse of the Lord to be: beautiful, prudent, and chaste. Therefore the petition, which I have placed last, has reference to place: she seeks that He, whom her soul loves, will tell her where He feedeth, where He makes His flock to rest at noon.

2. And first remark with what beauty she distinguishes the love of the Spirit from that of the flesh, when, wishing to express her beloved more by her very affection than by His Name, she does not say simply, 'Him whom I love,' but, *O Thou whom my soul loveth*, indicating thereby that her affection is of the soul. Next, consider with attention what it is she finds so desirable in the place where He pastures His flock. Nor let it escape you that she speaks of the midday hour, and inquires especially respecting the place in which He who feeds His flock also reposes, which is a sign of great security. For I suppose that this word 'reposes' was added because in that land it is not necessary at all to be on foot and wakeful in order to keep the flock in safety; since even when the shepherd is inactive and reclining under the trees, his flock go to and fro upon the meadows as they please. Happy the region where the sheep go in and out at pleasure, and none make them afraid. Who will grant unto me to behold you, and myself with you, feeding upon the mountains with the ninety and nine, which, as we read in the Gospel (Matt. xviii. 12), the Shepherd of all had left there, while He deigned to go to seek that one which had strayed and was lost? He, without doubt, reposes securely when He is beside His sheep, who did not hesitate to depart and go far from them, knowing that He left them in safety. Rightly does the Bride seek and sigh for that spot which is one both of pasturage and of peace, of repose and of security, of joy, of admiration—yea, of wonderment. But, alas! how unhappy am I to be so far distant from it, to salute it only from afar! The mention only of it makes me break into tears, excites my heart to affection, and my tongue to use the words of those who said: *By the rivers of Babylon there we sat down, yea, we wept, when we remembered Zion* (Ps. cxxxvii. 1). Our desire is to cry out with the Bride and with the Psalmist: *Praise Thy God, O Sion, for He hath strengthened the bars of thy gates; He hath blessed thy children within thee. He maketh peace in thy borders, and filleth thee with the finest of the wheat* (Ps. cxlvii. 13, 14). Who would not wish to be fed from thence for peace, and for fatness, and for satiety? No fear is there, nor distaste, nor deficiency. Paradise is a safe dwelling-place, the WORD a sweet nourishment, eternity abundance without limit.

3. I have the WORD also here below, but in the Flesh; the Truth also is set before me for nourishment, but in the Sacrament. An Angel is rendered fat with the finest of the wheat, and filled with the pure grain; but it behoves me to be content during this life with the Sacrament, as with a husk; with the flesh, as with bran; with the letter, as with chaff; with faith, as with a veil [upon the truth]. And such things as these bring death in the tasting (Rom. viii. 6-13), unless they be seasoned in some degree with the firstfruits of the Spirit.

Assuredly, I can find only death in the pottage, unless it be rendered sweet with the meal of the Prophet (2 Kings iv. 41). Indeed, without the Spirit even the Sacrament is received only to condemnation; the flesh profiteth nothing (John vi. 63); the letter killeth (2 Cor. iii. 6); and faith itself is dead. But it is the Spirit that quickeneth these [means of grace], that I may live in them. But with whatever abundance of the Spirit those things may be enriched, it is not possible to find the same sweetness in the husk of the Sacrament, and in the fatness of the wheat; in faith as in vision; in remembrance as in presence; in time as in eternity; in the reflection in a mirror as in the countenance itself that is reflected; in the form of a servant as in the Image of God. Evidently, in all these things, faith is rich for me, but intelligence is poor. Is there not a great disparity between the degree of appreciation and enjoyment experienced by the understanding, and that by the faith, since the one is for a merit, the other for a reward? You see, then, that there is as much difference between the nature of the nourishment as there is between the places referred to; and as the heavens are exalted high above the earth, so do those who dwell in them abound far more, and in gifts which are far better, than those below.

4. Let us hasten, then, my children, let us hasten to reach a safer dwelling-place, a sweeter pasturage, a richer and more fruitful field. Let us hasten to attain a land where we may dwell without fear, have abundance that cannot be exhausted, and can be enjoyed without distaste. Thou, O Lord of Sabaoth, who judgest all things in an awful calm, Thou dost also support all things with justice and in security. THOU art at once the Lord of armies and the Shepherd of the sheep. Therefore Thou dost both pasture Thy sheep and, at the same time, remain in a Sabbath rest; but not here. Therefore it was that Thou didst remain quiescent when Thou sawest from heaven one of Thy sheep (I speak of Stephen) beset with wolves upon the earth (Acts vii. 55). And, therefore, I entreat, *tell me where Thou feedest, where Thou makest Thy flock to rest at noon;* for that noonday is the whole day, a day which knows no evening. And, therefore, that *day in Thy courts is better than a thousand* (Ps. lxxxiv. 10), because it knows no set of sun. It has had perhaps a morning, namely, when *the dayspring from on high hath visited us, through the tender mercy of our God, to give light to them that sit in darkness* (Luke i. 78, 79). Then in truth *we have received Thy mercy, O God, in the midst of Thy Temple* (Ps. xlvii. 10, Douay); when [the Lord] rose from the midst of the shadow of death, and the morning light broke upon us, and in the morning we beheld the glory of the Lord. How many kings and prophets have desired to see it, and have not seen it? Wherefore? Because it was still the night, and that the morning, so long awaited, and to which mercy was promised, had not yet come. Wherefore, also, one thus prayed: *Cause me to hear Thy lovingkindness in the morning, for in Thee is my trust* (Ps. cxliii. 8).

5. For that day was heralded by an aurora lasting from the moment

in which the [rising of the] Sun of Righteousness was announced to the earth by the Archangel Gabriel, and that a Virgin had conceived by the operation of the Holy Ghost [Him who was] God, and that a Virgin had brought forth; and onwards, until He was beheld upon the earth, and lived among men. For up to that time only a feeble light, as it were, the light of an aurora, was visible, so that almost all the earth was ignorant that the Day was among men. And, in truth, if they had known they would not have crucified the Lord of glory (1 Cor. ii. 8). To His few disciples He said: *Yet a little while ye have the Light with you*[1] (John xii. 35), inasmuch as it was the aurora, the beginning, or rather the indication of the day, while the Sun still concealed His beams, and scattered them but little upon the earth. St. Paul also said that the night was far spent, the day was at hand (Rom. xiii. 12), signifying that though the light was still dim, the day was approaching rather than was already come. But when did he say this? It was when the Sun of Righteousness, having returned from the depths, had already mounted into the height of heaven. How much more would he have spoken thus when the likeness of a body of sin—as it were a thick cloud—veiled that dawning; a body, I say, like ours in all its capabilities of suffering, so that neither the bitterness of death nor the shame of the Cross were wanting to it! How much more dim and feeble was the light at that season than when the presence of the Sun was plain and evident!

6. All the Life of Christ upon the earth was, then, as it were, an aurora, or dawning, and even that somewhat indistinct, until, after His Death and Resurrection, He caused the dawning to disappear in the clearer light of His Presence, as it were, the sun full risen; then the morning broke, and the night was swallowed up in victory. Thus we read in the Gospel: *Very early in the morning, the first day of the week, they came unto the sepulchre at the rising of the sun* (Mark xvi. 2). Was it not the morning when the Sun was risen? But that morning drew from the Resurrection of Christ a new beauty, a purer and more steadfast light than was its wont, since even though we have known Him after the Flesh, yet now henceforth know we Him no more (2 Cor. v. 16). And the Psalmist writes: *The Lord hath girded Himself, He is clothed with beauty and strength* (Ps. xcii. 1, Douay); because He hath thrown off from Him as a cloud the infirmities of the flesh, and hath put on Him the robe of His glory. Just so is it with the sun: when he is risen above the horizon, and pours forth his rays upon the earth, he begins to increase by degrees in brightness to the sight and in warmth to the feeling. But though he increase ever so much in strength and in heat, though he multiply his rays in number and power, throughout the whole course of this mortal life of ours (for He shall be with us even unto the end of the world—Matt. xxviii. 20), yet He shall not attain unto His midday light, nor be beheld here below in that fulness of glory in which He shall hereafter reveal Him-

---

[1] St. Bernard understands '*adhuc modicum lumen in vobis*' as 'a little light is still with you.'—ED.

self, but to those alone to whom He shall deign to accord that vision. O true noontide, fulness of warmth and of light, abiding-place of the sun, which exterminates all shadows, dries up marshes, and drives forth pestilential odours! O perpetual solstice, and day that declines not! O mid-day light, enjoying at once the freshness of spring, the beauty of summer, the fruitfulness and abundance of autumn, and, not to omit anything, the deep rest and unbroken quiet of winter! Or, at least, if you prefer it so, it is the winter only that disappears and is wanting. 'Show to me' (says the Bride) 'this spot of brightness, peace, and abundance so great, that, like as Jacob, still abiding in his mortal body, saw the Lord face to face, and his life was preserved (Gen. xxxii. 30); or as Moses beheld Him, not in types and figures, nor through dreams, as did other Prophets, but in a manner transcendent and known to no others but to God and himself (Num. xii. 6-8); or as Isaiah, who, after the eyes of his heart had been opened, saw the Lord upon His Throne high and lifted up (Is. vi. 1); or even in the manner of St. Paul, who was caught up into Paradise, and heard unspeakable words (2 Cor. xii. 4), and saw with his eyes Jesus Christ his Lord: so may I, too, be found worthy to contemplate Thee in Thy light and Thy beauty by means of a transport and rapture of soul; and to behold Thee feeding Thy flock with fuller abundance and more complete security than now.'

7. For here, too, Thou dost feed Thy flock, but not to the full; nor is it permitted to Thee to repose, but it is needful to stand and watch over them because of terrors of the night. Alas! [here] the light is not clear, nor the nourishment full, nor the dwelling safe; therefore *tell me where Thou feedest, where Thou makest Thy flock to rest at noon.* Blessed dost Thou call me when I hunger and thirst after righteousness (Matt. v. 6). What is this in comparison with the happiness of those who are satisfied with the goodness of Thy House (Ps. lxv. 4), who eat and rejoice in the sight of God, yea, who exceedingly rejoice? (Ps. lxviii. 3) But, and if I suffer anything for righteousness' sake, Thou sayest again that I am none the less blessed (1 Pet. iii. 14). And it is certain that to have nourishment where you apprehend suffering is to experience enjoyment, but not security. To have nourishment and suffering together, what is that but a grievous joy? All things that I possess here fall short of being perfect; many are beyond my prayer, nor is any safe. When wilt Thou fill me with joy with Thy Countenance? (Ps. xv 11, *Douay*) *Thy Face, Lord, will I seek* (Ps. xxvii. 8). Thy Countenance is a noonday to me. *Tell me where Thou feedest, where Thou makest Thy flock to rest at noon.* I know sufficiently where thou feedest without resting; tell me where Thou doest both the one and the other. I am not ignorant where at other times Thou doest this, but I would know where Thou doest this at noon. For during the time of my mortal life, and in the place of my pilgrimage, I have been accustomed to be spiritually fed, and to feed others, with nourishment from Thee, in the Law, in the Prophets, in the Psalms. Thou dost feed us also

in the pastures of the Gospels, and with the Apostles I have rested. Often, also, I have sought, and have been able to find, spiritual nourishment for me and mine in the actions, the words, and the writings of the Saints. Still more frequently (because it was very close at hand to me) I have eaten the bread of sorrow, and drunk of the wine of regret ; *my tears have been my meat day and night, while they daily say unto me, Where is now thy God?* (Ps. xlii. 3.) I have, indeed, been nourished from Thy Table : for Thou hast prepared a Table before me against them that trouble me (Ps. xxiii. 5), and from it, I repeat, I receive somewhat by the gift of Thy mercy, which imparts comfort and consolation, as often as my soul is sorrowful and disquieted within me. Those pastures I know, and following Thee, my Shepherd, have often sought them ; but tell me, I entreat, those which I know not.

8. There are, however, other shepherds who call themselves companions of Thine, but are not so; and these have their flocks, and their fields of pasture filled with deadly things ; to these they lead their followers, but not with Thee, nor by Thy bidding ; these I have not entered, nor drawn near to them. These are they who say : *Lo! here is Christ, or lo! He is there* (Mark xiii. 21), promising pastures fertile with wisdom and knowledge ; and the promise is believed, so that many hearers flock together to them ; and these they make twofold more the children of hell than themselves (Matt. xxiii. 15). Why is this, except that there is not there the clear and noonday light, so that the pure truth should become known to them ; and thus they easily accept falsehood on account of a resemblance to the truth, from which, in the dim light, it is not easily distinguished, and especially also because *stolen waters are sweet, and bread eaten in secret is pleasant* (Prov. ix. 17). And for this reason I entreat that Thou wouldest tell me *where Thou feedest, where Thou makest Thy flock to rest at noon*, that is to say, in the clear light, that I may not be seduced, and begin to wander after the crowds of those who follow these [so-called] "companions of Thine"[1] who are themselves but unsteady wanderers, having no certitude or steady grasp of true doctrine, who are ever learning, and never able to come to the knowledge of the truth (2 Tim. iii. 7). This the Bride [that is, the Church] declares on account of the varying and vain dogmas of philosophers and heretics.

9. It seems to me that we ought to desire this noonday of Christ, not only on this account, but also on account of the wiles of invisible powers, of seducing spirits who hold themselves in ambush, and make ready their arrows within the quiver, that they may secretly shoot at those who are of a right heart, so that in clear light we may be able to discover the stratagems of the devil, and easily to discern, with the help of our good angel, that angel of Satan, who is able to

---

[1] The preacher was not improbably referring to some special heretical sect, who called themselves 'Companions of Christ.' But it is not possible now, apparently, to verify the reference.—ED.

transform himself into an angel of light (2 Cor. xi. 14). For we are not able otherwise to guard ourselves sufficiently from the attack of the demon of noonday (Ps. xci. 6) unless we walk also in noonday light. And I think that demon is so called because there are of the number of the evil some who, abiding although they do in a night which is perpetual on account of their will being gloomy and hardened in wickedness, yet know how to simulate the day, and even the mid-day, in order to deceive; in the same way that their chief is not content to be equal with God, but opposeth and exalteth himself above all that is called God or that is worshipped (2 Thess. ii. 4). That is why, unless the heart of one whom a demon of this nature is endeavouring to tempt be enlightened by the true light of noonday, which shines from heaven, which detects and convicts that which is false, he will not be able adequately to protect himself, but the demon will doubtless tempt and subvert him by an appearance of good, persuading the soul which is incautious and unprepared, to accept evil for good. And then the mid day—that is, the clearness—appears the greater, tempting since it offers a greater show of good.

10. How often, for example, has it suggested to anticipate the watches [of the night] in order to turn to derision some sleeper at the Offices of the brethren? How often to prolong fasts in order to render an individual powerless, and therefore useless, in Divine service? How often, envying those who were making good progress in communities, has it suggested to them, under the pretence of attaining greater perfection, to seek the solitude [of an hermitage]? And those unhappy ones have learned at length the truth of that maxim which they had read to no purpose: *Woe to him that is alone when he falleth, for he hath not another to lift him up* (Eccles. iv. 10). How often has it urged a man to greater manual labour than he has strength to perform, and thus exhausting his powers has rendered him incapable of discharging his regular duties? How often urged one to immoderate bodily exercise—which, according to the Apostle, *profiteth little* (1 Tim. iv. 8)—and so withdrawn him from practices of piety? Lastly, have not some of you experienced—I say it to their shame—how at first they could not be restrained, with such ardour they were filled, and then after a time fell back into such a degree of remissness that, in the phrase of the Apostle, having begun in the Spirit, they were made perfect by the flesh (Gal. iii. 3), and have made a shameful alliance with the body after having entered upon an unrelenting conflict with it? You see such persons—shame it is to say—demanding importunately things which are superfluous after having obstinately refused those which were necessary. Although I know not whether those who remain stiffly determined in their own will, making abstinences which are unwise and indiscreet, and gravely troubling by their marked singularity those to whom they ought to conform their conduct, as they dwell with them in one house; I know not, I say, whether they are abiding by the rule of piety: they seem to me to have by thus acting, departed far from it. Let those

who are wise in their own eyes, and have determined to abide by no advice nor command but their own, let them see to it how they shall give account, not to me, but to Him who says: *Rebellion is as the sin of witchcraft, and stubbornness is as iniquity and idolatry.* And He had declared before that *obedience is better than sacrifice, and to hearken than the fat of rams* (1 Sam. xv. 23, 22); that is to say, than an abstinence which is disobedient and contumacious. That is why the Lord says by the Psalmist: *Will I eat the flesh of bulls or drink the blood of goats?* (Ps. l. 13), in order to show that the fastings of those who are proud or impure are far from being acceptable in His sight.

11. But here I fear, lest in condemning those who push their fasts beyond measure, I may seem to give licence to the gluttonous, and that they may hear to their peril what is spoken for a remedy to the others. Wherefore let both the one class and the other listen. There are four kinds of temptations, and they are thus described by the Psalmist: *His Truth shall be thy shield and buckler. Thou shalt not be afraid for the terror by night; nor for the arrow that flieth by day; for the pestilence that walketh in darkness; nor for the destruction that wasteth at noonday* (Ps. xci. 4-6). And do ye all attend also, for I hope that you may all find profit in these words. All among us who have been converted to the Lord feel in ourselves the truth of what the Holy Scripture says: My son, if thou come to serve the Lord, prepare thy soul for temptation, set thy heart aright, and constantly endure (Ecclus. ii. 1). Therefore, according to the order of common experience, it is fear which first disturbs and troubles us at the beginning of our conversion; and that fear is caused by the frightful image which we form to ourselves of the extremely strict life we are about to embrace, and of the austerity of an unwonted discipline. And this is called 'the terror by night,' either because 'night' in Scripture means usually 'adversities,' or because the recompense, on account of which we are preparing to endure adversities, is not yet revealed, but hidden from us as in a shroud of gloom. For if that day should shine in whose light we should discern equally both the trials and the recompenses, the desire of the recompense which would be clearly visible to us would render the fear of any trials whatever as nothing in comparison with the desire to obtain it. For *the sufferings of this present time are not worthy to be compared with the glory which shall be revealed in us* (Rom. viii. 18). But now, since these things are concealed from our eyes and all is night around us, we suffer from the terrors of the night, and are a prey to fears of those evils which are present to us in place of the good things to come which are not visible. Those, then, who are newcomers ought to watch and pray against this first temptation, lest, being suddenly overcome by weakness of the spirit and by the difficulty of the moment, they fall back (which may God forbid!) from the good work they had begun.

12. But after having overcome that temptation, let us arm ourselves moreover against the praises of men who find occasion for praise in the laudable life we lead; for otherwise we shall be exposed

to be wounded by *the arrow which flieth by day*—that is, by vainglory. For fame is said to fly, and during the day, because it is born of the works of the light. If this is puffed aside as being empty air, there still remains to be feared something more solid—that is, the richest honours of this world; for one who cares not for praises may desire place and dignity. And see if it was not this order of temptation that was observed towards Our Lord, to whom, after the suggestion was made that He should throw Himself from the pinnacle of the Temple from a motive of vanity alone, all the kingdoms of the world were shown and offered (Matt iv. 6, 8). Do you, then, also reject these after the example of the Saviour? otherwise you will inevitably be surprised by *the pestilence which walketh in darkness*, which is hypocrisy. For that descends from ambition, and has its dwelling in darkness; there it hides what it really is, and pretends to be what it is not. At all times it has some secret object, and, retaining an appearance of piety to conceal itself, it is prepared to put even virtue up to sale[1] in order to obtain honours.

13. The last temptation is *the destruction that wasteth at noonday*, which usually besets those who are perfect—namely, those brave and lofty souls who have overcome other temptations, whether pleasures, flatteries, or honours. For what remains to the tempter, or what means has he left to attack souls like these? He approaches, then, in disguise, since he dares not do so openly, and attempts to overthrow, by a false pretence of good, the man whom he has found by experience to hold in horror that which is openly evil. For those who are able to say with the Apostle: *We are not ignorant of his devices* (2 Cor. ii. 11), the more advanced they are in virtue, the more careful are they to guard against this snare. Thus it was that Mary was troubled at the angelic salutation (Luke i. 29), suspecting (if I do not mistake) some snare of the enemy; and Joshua does not receive the angel as a friend before he knew that he was really a friend. In fact, he inquires whether the angel were for them or for their adversaries (Josh. v. 13-15), as one who had had experience of the cunning devices of the demon of the noonday. The Apostles also, when they were once toiling in rowing, the wind being contrary, and the boat labouring in the sea, seeing the Lord walking on the sea, thought He was a phantom, and cried out for fear. Does not that show clearly that they suspected a delusion of the demon of the noon? For you remember that the Scripture says that *in the fourth watch of the night Jesus went unto them, walking on the sea* (Matt. xiv. 24-27). Let, then, this fourth temptation, which is the last to be tried, be feared by us: and the higher anyone seems to have attained, the more careful and watchful let him learn to be against the attacks of the demon of noonday. But the true Noonday, the Lord Jesus, manifested Himself to the disciples in that He said: *It is I: be not afraid;* and their unfounded suspicion was at once dispelled. May God grant that as often as the cloaked falsehood endeavours to creep upon us, the true

---

[1] *Vindicans*, but read *vendicans.*—ED.

Noonday, rising from on high, may send forth His light and His truth to put it to flight—to separate the light from the darkness, so that we may not fall under the censure of the Prophet as putting *darkness for light, and light for darkness* (Is. v. 20).

14. If the length of this discourse does not weary you, I will now try to assign these four temptations, in their order, to the Body of Christ, which is the Church. And I will endeavour to do this as briefly as possible. Consider the Primitive Church. Was it not at first pervaded in an extraordinary degree with the *terror that walketh by night?* For it was then, as it were, a night, when everyone who slew the saints thought that he was thus doing God service. But after that temptation was overcome, and that tempest stilled, she became glorious and illustrious, and, according to the promise made to her, was speedily placed in a position of worldly distinction. Then the enemy, vexed to have been frustrated, turned cunningly from the 'nightly terror' to the 'arrow that flieth by day,' and with it wounded certain members of the Church. Vain and ambitious men rose up, greedy of reputation, and desired to make for themselves a name; and, going forth from the Church, their mother, they long afflicted her with various and perverse teachings. But this evil plague also was vanquished by the wisdom of the saints, as the former had been by the patience of the martyrs.

15. At the present time, by the mercy of God, the Church is free from each of these evils; but evidently it is still contaminated by *the pestilence that walketh in darkness.* Woe to this generation [which is corrupted] by the leaven of the Pharisees, which is hypocrisy! If, indeed, that ought to be called hypocrisy which is so prevailing that it cannot be hidden, and so devoid of shame that it does not try to hide. At the present day a contagious corruption is creeping through the whole body of the Church, the more desperate of cure as it is universal, and the more dangerous because so deeply seated. If an heretic arose to wage against her an open war, she would exclude him from her bounds, and he would dry up and wither away; or if one attacked her with violence, she would peradventure hide herself from him. But at the present time whom shall she exclude, or from whom shall she hide herself? All are her friends, and all her enemies; all are her intimates, and all her adversaries; all are of her own household, and none at peace with her; all are very nearly related to her, and yet all are seeking their own interests. They are Ministers of Christ, and they are serving Antichrist. They are advanced to honour upon the goods of the Lord, and to the Lord they render no honour at all. From this proceeds that meretricious splendour, that habit fit for a comedian, that magnificence almost royal which you see every day. Because of this you see gold upon the bits of their horses, upon their saddles, and even upon their spurs; yes, their spurs shine more brightly than their altars. Because of this you see fine tables loaded with splendid services of plate, chased goblets, and, also, with viands correspondingly costly; then follow merrymakings and drunkenness,

the guitar, the lyre, and the flute. Thence come groaning winepresses and storehouses full and overflowing with all manner of good things. Thence come vases of rich perfumes, and coffers filled with immense treasures. It is for the attainment of such objects that they desire to be, and are, Provosts of churches, Deans, Archdeacons, Bishops, Archbishops. For these dignities are not given for merit, but are disposed of in that infamous traffic which walketh in darkness.

16. It was once predicted [of the Church], and now the time of its fulfilment draws near: *Behold, in peace is my bitterness most bitter* (Is. xxxviii. 17, Douay). It was bitter at first in the death of the martyrs; more bitter afterwards in the conflict with heretics; but most bitter of all now in the [evil] lives of her members. She cannot drive them away, and she cannot flee from them, so strongly established are they, and so multiplied are they above measure. The plague of the Church is inward; it is incurable. It is that which makes its bitterness most bitter, even in the midst of peace. But in what a peace! Peace it is, and yet it is not peace. There is peace from heathens, and from heretics; but not from her own sons. At this time is heard the voice of her complaining: *I have nourished and brought forth children, and they have rebelled against me* (Is. i. 2). They have rebelled; they have dishonoured me by their evil lives, by their shameful gains, by their shameful trafficking, by, in short, their many works which walk in darkness. There remains only one thing—that the demon of noonday should appear, to seduce those who remain still in Christ, and in the simplicity which is in Him. He has, without question, swallowed up the rivers of the learned, and the torrents of those who are powerful, and (as says the Scripture) *he trusteth that he can draw up Jordan into his mouth* (Job xl. 23)—that is to say, those simple and humble ones who are in the Church. For this is he who is Antichrist, who counterfeits not only the day, but also the noonday; who exalts himself above all that is called God or worshipped—whom the Lord Jesus shall consume with the Spirit of His Mouth, and destroy with the brightness of His Coming (2 Thess. ii. 4, 8); for He is the true and eternal Noonday: the Bridegroom, and Defender of the Church, Who is above all, God blessed for ever. AMEN.

SERMON XXXIV.

OF HUMILITY AND OF PATIENCE.

*I*F *thou know not, O thou fairest among women, go thy way forth by the footsteps of the flock, and feed thy kids beside the shepherds' tents* (i. 8). Once holy Moses, presuming much on the grace and familiarity into which he had entered by the goodness of God, ventured to aspire to a certain great vision, so as to say to God: *If I have found grace in Thy sight, show me Thy glory* (Exod. xxxiii. 13-

23). But in place of that vision which he had desired he obtained one of a far lower kind, by means of which, nevertheless, he might one day reach that which he wished for. The sons of Zebedee also, walking in the simplicity of their hearts, dared also to ask a great thing, but were, notwithstanding, relegated to a lower step, from which their course upwards must be made (Matt. xx. 21-23). So it is also here with the Bride. She seems to be asking for some great thing, and is repressed with a reply austere indeed, but faithful and helpful. For it behoves one who aspires to things lofty to have lowly thoughts of himself, lest while he exalts himself above his measure he fall below himself, not being steadied and rendered firm by sincere humility. And because very great graces are not to be obtained except with the merit of humility, it is essential that he who is to receive them should be humbled by reproof, that he may deserve them by humility. Do you, then, when you see yourself humbled, take it as a sign, and even as a certain proof, that some grace from God is drawing near to thee. For as *pride goes before destruction* (Prov. xvi. 18), so before honour comes humility. Each of these truths is expressed in that which you read, that God resisteth the proud and giveth grace to the humble (James iv. 6). And, lastly, did He not think fit to recompense with abundant blessing His servant Job, after the great victory which he won over the demon, and after the eminent trial of his remarkable patience? But note that He took care previously to humble him by many and severe trials, and so to prepare the way for that blessing.

2. But it is little that we endure willingly the humiliation which God of His own accord sends to us, if we do not welcome with a similar willingness that which He puts upon us by the agency of some other person. Wherefore receive a remarkable instance of this from holy David. He was once reviled, and that by one of his servants, but he did not even feel the insults which were heaped upon him, because his mind was preoccupied by Divine grace. *What have I to do with you*, he said, *ye sons of Zeruiah?* (2 Sam. xvi. 10). O man truly 'after God's own Heart,' who thought that it behoved him to be angry rather with him who would have avenged the repeated insults, than with him who offered them! Hence he could say with a quiet conscience: *If I have rendered to them that repaid me evils, let me deservedly fall empty before my enemies* (Ps. vii. 5, Douay). He forbade, then, [his servants] to hinder the man who was attacking him with insolence, regarding his curses as a gain. And he added: *It is the Lord that hath said unto him, Curse David.* Truly he was a man 'after God's own Heart,' since he knew so well the intention in the Heart of God. The tongue of an evil speaker was raging against him, but his concern was only to divine the secret purpose of God in permitting it. The voice of the reviler was in his ears; but his heart was preparing itself in humility for the Divine benediction. Was God, then, in the mouth of the blasphemer? By no means. But God used it for the humbling of David. Nor was that hidden from the Psalmist, for God had made known to him the hidden secrets of

His wisdom; therefore he says: *It is good for me that Thou hast humbled me, that I may learn Thy justifications* (Ps. cxix. 71, Douay).

3. Do you see that humility justifies us? I say humility, not humiliation. How many are humiliated who are not humble? Some are bitter and grudging because they are humiliated; others bear it with patience; some even with willingness. The first are blameworthy; the second blameless; but the last righteous. Although innocence is a part of righteousness, yet its perfection is to the humble. He who is able to say: *It is good for me that Thou hast humbled me*, is the truly humble. He who bears humiliation unwillingly cannot say this, much less he who murmurs at it. To neither of these do we promise grace merely because he is humiliated; although indeed the two differ widely from each other, since while the one possesses his soul in patience, the other perishes in his murmuring. But although only one of these is deserving of anger, to neither is there a promise of grace, since it is not to those who are humiliated, but to the humble that God giveth grace (James iv. 6). He, therefore, is humble who turns humiliation into humility of soul, and it is he who says to God: *It is good for me that Thou hast humbled me.* To no one at all is that good which is endured merely with patience, for we know that *God loveth a cheerful giver* (2 Cor. ix. 7). Wherefore also when we fast we are bidden to anoint our head with oil, and to wash the face (Matt. vi. 17), so that our good work may be seasoned, as it were, with spiritual joy, and our burnt-offering be fat and without blemish. For it is a perfect and joyful humility which alone deserves the grace of God, of which it is a sign beforehand. That which is constrained or forced, such as he feels who possesses his soul in patience, although it obtains life because of the patience, yet will not have grace,[1] on account of the sorrow and regret mingled with it. For such a person does not answer to the description given in this saying of Scripture: *Let the brother of low degree*[2] *rejoice in that he is exalted* (James i. 9), because his humiliation is not endured willingly or gladly.

4. But do you wish to look upon one who glories in the right way, and is truly worthy of glory? *Most gladly*, says the Apostle, *will I glory in my infirmities, that the power of Christ may rest upon me* (2 Cor. xii. 9). He does not say that he patiently endures his infirmities, but that he even glories, and that *most gladly*, in them, and thus he shows that it was good for him that he was humbled; nor was it sufficient for him to possess his soul in patience when humiliated, unless he could accept it, as it were, by his own will, and thereby receive grace. Listen to that which is the general rule upon this question: *He that humbleth himself shall be exalted* (Luke xiv. 11). The Lord here signifies that not every kind of humility shall be exalted, but that only which is willingly accepted, not of necessity, nor with sorrow

---

[1] That is, the special grace promised to the humble, which is not only inward, but also outward, and consists in exaltation even in this life.
[2] *Humilis.*

and reluctance. So, also, on the other hand, it is not everyone who is exalted that shall be abased; but those only who exalt themselves of their own accord and through vanity. Thus, then, it is not he who merely is humiliated that shall be exalted, but he who willingly and cheerfully accepts humiliation, and that because his willingness is a merit. For grant that the material part of humility is supplied to you by another person, for example, by reproaches, losses, or sufferings, yet a person cannot be rightly said to be rendered humble by another in the same sense in which he is rendered humble by himself, when he is resolved to suffer all these things quietly and with a joyful mind, because it is the will of God that he should undergo them.

5. But whither am I being borne? Very patiently, as I feel, are you enduring the excessive length of this discourse, though it be of humility and patience; but let us return to the point whence we have digressed. For all this was suggested to us by the reply made by the Bridegroom to the Bride, who needed to be cautioned and repressed when aspiring to great things. For Him to do this was not to offer her reproaches, but to afford her an opportunity for a greater and more complete degree of humility, and to render her more capable and worthy of those loftier privileges and attainments which she sought. But since we are only, as it were, at the portals of the present chapter, we will resume the consideration of the subject, if you please, at the beginning of another discourse; especially lest the words of the Bridegroom should be treated of with strength exhausted, or should fall on weary ears. Which may He avert from His servants, who is JESUS CHRIST our Lord; above all, God blessed for ever. AMEN.

SERMON XXXV.

OF THE SHARP REPROOF WHICH THE BRIDEGROOM GIVES TO THE BRIDE, AND OF TWO KINDS OF IGNORANCE WHICH ARE ESPECIALLY TO BE FEARED AND AVOIDED.

*I*F *thou knowest not, He says, go forth.* This is a harsh and severe reproof; since He says, *go forth.* This is the phrase which servants are wont to hear from their lords when displeased and angry, or maidens from their mistresses, whom they may have deeply offended. 'Go forth,' they say, 'leave me, depart out of my sight and out of this house.' With this speech, severe and bitter, and having so sharp an edge of blame, it is that the Bridegroom addresses His beloved; but all the blame is under the express condition 'if thou knowest not.' He could say nothing stronger or more effectual to affright her, than to threaten her that she shall be sent away from Him. This you may easily realize, if you take notice whence she is bidden to go, and whither. What is she to leave, do you think, and for what exchange? Is it not to go from the Spirit to the flesh, from the blessings of the soul to worldly desires, from the inward rest, in which the mind is at peace, to the din and bustle of the world, and the inquietude of outward cares? All of these are things in which is nothing but labour, sorrow, and distress of spirit. For the soul which has once learned of the Lord, and received from Him the power to enter into itself, and in its inmost depths to sigh for the Presence of God, and at all times to seek His Face; for God is a Spirit, and those who seek Him must walk in the Spirit, not in the flesh, to walk after the flesh; such a soul, I say, would think it less horrible and less insupportable to endure for a time even hell itself, than, after having once experienced the sweetness of that spiritual life, to go forth from it and leave it, in order to be exposed to the enticements, or rather to the troublous claims of the flesh, to be cast again upon the insatiable desire (*curiositatem*) of the senses, of which it is said in Ecclesiastes: *The eye is not satisfied with seeing, nor the ear filled with hearing* (Eccles. i. 8). Listen to a man who had experienced that of which I speak: *The Lord is good unto them that wait for Him, to the soul that seeketh Him* (Lam. iii. 25). If anyone should try to turn away from this supreme happiness that holy soul, I verily believe that it would feel as if torn away from Paradise, and from the portal of glory. Listen, again, to another and a similar soul: *My heart said unto Thee, Thy Face, Lord, will I seek* (Ps. xxvii. 8). Wherefore it was his wont to say: It is good for me [*i.e.*, it is for me the highest good] *to draw near to God* (Ps. lxxiii. 28); and again, speaking to his soul, he declares: *Return unto thy rest, O my soul: for the Lord hath dealt bountifully with thee* (Ps. cxvi. 7). I say, then, to you: There is nothing which he who has once received this blessing so greatly fears, as that he should be abandoned by grace, and find himself obliged to go forth to the consolations, or rather the desolations, of the flesh, and to support again the tumultuous assaults of the carnal senses.

2. Terrible, then, and greatly to be feared, is that threatening command: *Go forth, and pasture thy kids.* For it is as if He said: 'Know yourself to be unworthy of that sweet and familiar contemplation of things heavenly, intellectual, and Divine, which you now enjoy. Wherefore go forth from My sanctuary, which is your heart, in which you were accustomed to drink with pleasure such deep draughts of the hidden and sacred meanings of truth and wisdom; be as one of those in the world; entangle yourself again with the delights of the flesh, and feed upon them.' These are what He speaks of as 'kids' (these signify *sins*, and are said to be collected, in the Last Judgment, on the left hand of the Judge), the wandering and wanton senses and desires of the flesh, by which, as by windows, death has entered into the soul. To these well apply the words which follow in the text: *beside the shepherds' tents.* For kids are pastured, not as lambs, above the tents of the shepherds, but beside them. Now, those shepherds (*pastores*) who are true pastors, although they have tabernacles com-

posed of earth, and set upon the earth, that is to say, their bodies, in these days of their service here below, yet are wont to feed their Lord's flocks, not with things of earth, but from celestial pastures; nor do they preach to them according to their own will, but to that of their Lord. But kids, that is, the senses of the body, do not seek for, nor desire, heavenly food, but feed beside the tents of the pastors; that is to say, among the good things cognizable by the senses of the present world, which is the region of material bodies, and with these they do not indeed satisfy their desires, because these grow with habit, but indulge them.

3. A sad and shocking change of pursuits! After having made it his endeavour to nourish the soul during the time of its exile and wandering here with holy meditations, as it were with food from heaven, to seek out the good pleasure of God and the mysteries of His will, to reach up to heaven by the fervency of his devotion, after having saluted Patriarchs and Apostles, and the choirs of Prophets, marked with admiration the triumphs of Martyrs, and viewed with wonder the glorious ranks of the Angels, now, to lay all these occupations aside, to subject himself in disgraceful servitude to the body, unto obedience to the flesh, to become a slave to gluttony or intemperance, and to seek throughout the world for means to satisfy, in some degree, or at least to soothe their imperious, yet insatiable, desires, by the resources of this world which passes away! My eyes let fall a torrent of tears over such a soul as that, which, after being brought up in scarlet, embraces dunghills (Lam. iv. 5). *He evil entreateth the barren which beareth not, and doeth not good to the widow* (Job xxiv. 21). For notice, it is not merely said, *Go forth,* but *go forth by the flocks of thy companions, and feed thy kids,* in which, as it seems to me, a warning is given to us of no small importance. What is it? Alas! that a creature so fair, once made a member of the [Lord's] flock, but now rushing miserably to destruction, is not permitted even to remain among the flocks, but is bidden to fall behind them. How is that, do you ask? It is in that manner of which we read in the Psalms: *Man, when he was in honour, did not understand; he hath been compared unto senseless beasts, and is become like unto them* (Ps. xlviii. 13, Douay). See how this creature, so beautiful, came to belong unto the general body of the animals. And I think that these would say, if they were able to speak: Behold, Adam is become as one of us (Gen. iii. 22, Douay). Says the Psalmist: *When he was in honour.* If you ask, In what honour? he dwelt in Paradise; his life was passed in a place of entire pleasure; he suffered no manner of pain or of privation; his steps were among trees loaded with fragrant fruits; he reposed upon a bed of flowers; he was crowned with glory and honour, and set over all the works which the Hands of His Creator had made; but above all, he excelled in glory, because he bore the Divine image and likeness; he ranked with, and enjoyed the society of, the Angels, and all the powers of the army of heaven.

4. But he changed that glory of God into 'the similitude of a calf

that eateth hay.' Thence it is that the Bread of Angels is made to be, as it were, hay laid in the manger, and set before us as before the beasts in the stable. Indeed, the *Word was made Flesh* (John i. 14); and, according to the Prophet, *All flesh is but grass.* But that grass is not dried up, nor has its flower fallen, because the Spirit of the Lord hath rested upon it. And when once the end of all flesh came [by the Flood], it was for this reason, namely, that the Spirit of life had left it; for God said: 'My Spirit shall not remain in man for ever, because he is flesh (Gen. vi. 3, Douay). By the name of 'flesh' in this passage it is man's sin that is specified, not his nature; for it is sin, not nature, that drives away the Spirit. Because of sin it is, then, that *all flesh is grass, and the glory thereof as the flower of grass.* *The grass withereth,* he goes on, *the flower fadeth,* but not that Flower which springs out of the stem and root of Jesse, inasmuch as the Spirit of the Lord has rested upon Him (Is. xi. 2); not that grass which *the Word was made,* since the Prophet continues, *But the Word of our God shall stand for ever* (Is. xl. 6-8). For if the Word is made [Flesh, that is] grass, and the Word abides for ever, then [that] grass abides for ever. Otherwise, how shall He bestow eternal life, if He Himself does not live eternally? for He says: *If any man eat of this bread, he shall live for ever.* And of what bread He speaks He explains in adding: *And the Bread that I will give is My Flesh, which I will give for the life of the world* (John vi. 51). How, then, can He, by whom eternal life is bestowed, be other Himself than eternal?

5. But recall now with me, if you please, the declaration of the Son to the Father in the Psalm: *Thou wilt not suffer Thy Holy One to see corruption* (Ps. xvi. 10). Doubtless, He refers here only to His Body, which lay for a time dead in the sepulchre. This is that Holy Thing of which the Angel declared to the Virgin: *That Holy Thing which shall be born of thee shall be called the Son of God* (Luke i. 35). How, then, could that holy Flesh (grass, *fenum*) see corruption which was born of a pure womb, as it were of meadows ever flourishing in perpetual greenness, and which draws upon it without ceasing the gaze of the Angels, who regard it with never-failing delight? It would surely lose its greenness if Mary lost her virginity. The food of man has, then, been changed into that of beasts, since man has changed into a beast. O sad and lamentable transmutation! that man, the dweller in Paradise, the lord of earth, a citizen of heaven, and one of the household of the Lord of Sabaoth, the brother of blessed spirits, and co-heir of celestial Virtues, should have found himself, by a sudden transformation, and through his own weakness, lying in a stable, clamouring for food such as is the lot of beasts, because of his resemblance to their nature, and still more, bound fast to the manger, on account of his savage unruliness, like as those of whom it is written: *With bit and bridle bind fast their jaws, who come not near to thee* (Ps. xxxi. 9, Douay). Yet know, O ox, thy owner, and thou, O ass, thy master's crib, that the Prophets of God may be found faithful

in their predictions of these wonderful works of God. Recognise, now that thou art become a beast, Him whom, when thou wert man, thou didst not recognise; adore in the stable Him whom in Paradise thou didst flee from; honour the Manger of Him whose Throne of authority thou didst contemn; and that Bread—yea, that Bread of Angels, from which thou didst turn in distaste, now that it has become food suited to thy state of animal, take and eat.

6. But what is the cause, you would ask, of such an abasement? It is certainly no other than that *man when he was in honour, did not understand.* What did he not understand? The Psalmist does not explain; but let me explain. He was placed in honour, and took such pleasure in the loftiness of his elevation, that he failed to remember that he was but clay; and he soon experienced in himself the truth of what one of the sons of his captivity, at a period far later, both wisely observed and truly recorded, that '*if a man think himself to be something, when he is nothing, he deceiveth himself*' (Gal. vi. 3). Woe to that unhappy one, who was not then in existence when it was said of him: *Why is earth and ashes proud?* (Ecclus. x. 9). Hence it is that a creature so beautiful[1] is confounded with the herd; hence it is that its likeness to God is changed into the likeness of the brute creation; and in place of the companionship of Angels a fellowship with beasts of burden entered upon. Do you see, then, how great reason we have for fleeing from that ignorance which has been the cause of so many hosts of evils to all our race? For the Psalmist declares that man became like unto the beasts that perish, and are devoid of reason, because he did not understand. Ignorance, then, must at any cost be avoided by us; lest, perhaps, if we are found to be still without understanding, after having been so severely disciplined and punished, evils greater and heavier than the former should find us out, and it be said of us: *We would have healed Babylon, but she is not healed* (Jer. li. 9). And rightly so, since chastening has not enabled us to understand and take heed of what we have heard.

7. Is it not perhaps for this reason also that the Bridegroom, in order to turn His beloved from her ignorance by the thunder of His reprimand, said to her, not 'Go forth with the flocks'; or, 'Go forth to the flocks,' but *Go forth by* [or after] *the footsteps of the flocks.* Why is this? Without doubt to show that a second ignorance is more shameful and more to be feared than the first, because it has rendered man equal to the beasts, or even inferior to them. For men justly deprived of the light of God's countenance (*ignorati*), that is reprobate, because of this ignorance of theirs, both have to endure His terrible judgment, and to be given over to the everlasting fire—a punishment to which beasts are not liable. Without doubt, then, the condition of those who will be in that state is worse than that of those who will not be liable to it at all. *It were*

---

[1] The Bride, *i.e.*, the human soul; or sometimes the word is used in the sense of *the Church*, which is the aggregate of regenerate souls.—ED.

better for him [says the Scripture, of one] *if he had not been born a man* (Mark xiv. 21, Vulg.). Not, you observe, that he had not been born at all, but that he had not been born a man; but (for example) a beast of the field, or some other creature which, not having received the power of judgment, would not have to appear before the judgment of God, nor by consequence be liable to everlasting punishment. Let the rational soul, then, which is full of shame to have, by its former ignorance, made itself a companion of the beasts of the field in the enjoyment of the good things of earth, know that it will not have even them for companions if it incurs the penalty of enduring the torments of hell; that it will be driven away with shame from their company; that it will be no longer with them, but obviously will be after them, since they will have no more evil to endure, while it will be exposed to every kind of suffering; and from these it will not be delivered for ever, because it has added a second ignorance to the first. Therefore man comes forth, and goes away solitary after the bands of his companions, since it is he alone who is to be thrust into the depth of hell. Does it not seem to you that he who is cast, with hands and feet bound, into the outer darkness (Matt. xxii. 13) is found in the lowest place? Assuredly the last state of that man shall be worse than the first; since, instead of being made, as before, like unto the beasts that perish, he is now set below even them.

8. I think, farther, that if you examine the matter closely, you will conclude that even in this life [such a] man takes a place lower than the beasts of the field. Does it not seem to you that the man who is gifted with reason, and does not act according to reason, is in some sense more beastlike than the beasts themselves, which are without reason? For if the beasts of the field do not govern themselves by reason, they have an excuse in their very nature, since the gift of reason has been denied to them; but man, on whom it has been bestowed as his special endowment and prerogative, has no such excuse. Justly, therefore, on this account, ought man to be separated from other living creatures, and ranked after them all, since he alone has degenerated from his condition and violated the laws of his nature; he alone, though gifted with reason, feels and acts similarly to those who are without it. It is shown, then, that man [if in a state of sin] is inferior to all the tribes of the brute creation, both in the present life, by the depraving of his nature, and in the future life, by the extremity of punishment which awaits him.

9. See, then, in what a miserable and accursed condition a man is who is found in ignorance of God. Ignorance of God, or of his own self, ought I to say? Unquestionably both the one and the other—each kind of ignorance is fatal, and each suffices to bring about everlasting perdition. Would you know how this is the case? As regards ignorance of God, you will, I think, have no doubt, if you believe without question that this only is eternal life, to know the true God, and Jesus Christ whom He has sent (John xvii. 3). Listen,

then, to the Bridegroom, who condemns clearly and unmistakably in the soul an ignorance of itself. For what does He say? Not, 'if you know not God,' but *if thou know not thyself,* etc. (Cant. i. 7, Douay). It is plain, then, that [the soul] which is ignorant will be left to be ignorant (1 Cor. xiv. 38), whether it be with regard to God, or with regard to itself. Of these two kinds of ignorance there is much to be said that will be useful, if God shall enable me to say it. I will not, however, say it now, lest you being wearied, and the discourse not having been preceded by your prayers, as is our custom, either I may expound with too little care, or you may listen with too little attention to, a subject of such great importance, and which is not to be entered upon except with a strong and eager desire. For if the food of the body, if taken without appetite, and in a state of repletion, not only does not profit, but even is the cause of much harm, much more will the food of the soul bring, not increase of knowledge, but merely unhappiness of mind, if it be taken without desire, or even with disgust. Which sad effect may He avert from us, who is the Bridegroom of the Church, Jesus Christ our Lord, who is above all, God blessed for ever. AMEN.

SERMON XXXVI.

THE KNOWLEDGE OF LITERATURE IS GOOD FOR OUR INSTRUCTION, BUT THE KNOWLEDGE OF OUR OWN INFIRMITY IS MORE USEFUL TO SALVATION.

I AM here in fulfilment of my promise, in order to comply with your requests, and in discharge of the duty I owe to God. It is a threefold reason, as you see, which urges me on to speak: respect for my promise, brotherly charity, and the fear of the Lord. If I be silent, my own mouth will condemn me. If, on the contrary, I speak, I still fear the same judgment, inasmuch as my mouth will none the less condemn me because I say and do not. Aid me, I entreat you, by your prayers, that I may be able to speak what is true and edifying, and to carry out in my actions that which I preach to others. You are aware that I propose to speak to-day of ignorance, or rather of the various kinds of ignorance; for, if you remember, we distinguished two kinds—the one in regard to ourselves, the other to God —and I warned you that each was to be avoided, because each was a cause of condemnation. What I have to do now is to expound this subject more clearly and at greater length. But I think we must in the first place inquire whether every kind of ignorance be a cause of condemnation? And it seems to me that this is not the case; that it is not every [kind or degree of] ignorance that is blamable, since there are many things—they are, indeed, innumerable—of which we are allowed to be ignorant without peril to our salvation. For example, if you are ignorant of some mechanical art, as that of the wheelwright, or of the mason, or some other of those industries which are carried on by men for the purposes of this present life, would that be an obstacle to your salvation? How many men are there who have been saved, being acceptable to God in character and actions, without having been acquainted even with the liberal arts (though these latter are more honourable and more useful both in learning and in practice)! How many persons does the Apostle enumerate in the Epistle to the Hebrews, who became dear to God, not by their acquaintance with polite literature, but by a pure conscience and by faith unfeigned! (Heb. xi.). Others there were who pleased God in their life by the merits, not of their knowledge, but of their life. Peter and Andrew, and the sons of Zebedee, and all the rest of their fellow-disciples, were not drawn from the school of rhetoric or of philosophy, and yet the Saviour used them as instruments [by which to bring about] salvation throughout the earth. It was not because the wisdom in them was greater than that of all other men (as a certain holy man confesses of himself—Eccles. i. 16), but because of their faith and gentleness, that He saved them; yea, and made them Saints, and even teachers of others. They have made known to the world the ways of life, not by the sublimity of their preaching, or by the learning taught by human wisdom; but after that the world in its wisdom knew not God; it pleased Him to save by the foolishness of their preaching those who believed (1 Cor. ii. 1; i. 17, 21).

2. I may seem to you, perhaps, to speak too severely of knowledge; to blame, as it were, the learned, and to forbid the study of literature. But I would by no means do this. I am not ignorant how great are the services that have been rendered to the Church, and are rendered to her continually, by her learned sons, whether in repulsing the attacks of her enemies or in instructing the simple. Besides, I have read the words of the Prophet: *Because thou hast rejected knowledge I will also reject thee, and thou shalt be no priest to Me* (Hosea iv. 6); and also: *They that be wise shall shine as the brightness of the firmament, and they that turn many to righteousness as the stars for ever and ever* (Dan. xii 3). But I know also where I have read: *Knowledge puffeth up* (1 Cor. viii. 1); and again: *He that increaseth knowledge increaseth sorrow* (Eccles. i. 18). You see that there is a difference between these [kinds of knowledge], for one kind renders [the possessor] vain, and another renders him sad. Now, I would ask you whether of the two is the more conducive to salvation, that which puffs up or that which saddens? But I doubt not that you would prefer the latter, since pain is a means to health, of which tumour and swelling is but a semblance. But he who entreats for salvation is near to gain it, for *he that asketh receiveth* (Luke xi. 10). Also, He who heals the heart that is broken holds in abhorrence that which is swollen with pride, as the highest Wisdom teaches us: *God resisteth the proud, but giveth grace unto the humble* (James iv. 6). And the

Apostle declares: *I say, by the grace given unto me, to every man that is among you, not to think [of himself] more highly than he ought to think, but to think soberly* (Rom. xii. 3). He does not forbid knowledge, but only the knowledge which renders vain. And what does he mean by '*soberly*'? He means to guard with the greatest care that knowledge which is essential before and beyond everything else to our salvation, for the time is short. All knowledge, however, which is founded on the truth is good in itself. But you whom it behoves, on account of the briefness of the time, to hasten to work out with fear and trembling your own salvation, you must take care to acquire first and most carefully what you feel to be of nearer concern to your salvation. Do not the physicians of the body define a part of medicine to consist in the choice among different kinds of food, which should be taken first and which afterwards, and in what manner each should be taken? For although all kinds of food, since God created them, must be good, yet you may certainly render them evil [to you] if you do not observe the proper manner and sequence in partaking of them. Apply, then, what I say of the food of the body to the various kinds of knowledge, which are food to the mind.

3. But it is better to send you at once to the Master, for this teaching comes not from us, but from him; or, rather, it is ours, because it is the word of Truth. *If any man*, he says, *think that he knoweth anything, he knoweth nothing yet as he ought to know* (1 Cor. viii. 2). You see that he does not praise the person who knows many things if he is still ignorant of the right manner to know them, and that it is in that very point he places the fruit and usefulness of knowledge. What, then, does he understand by the manner of knowing? What else can he mean by it than in what order, with what degree of eagerness, and with what intention and object we ought to acquaint ourselves with all things? In what order? that is to say, so as to acquire first that which is more fitted to the work of our salvation. With what degree of eagerness? by which we learn that we ought to apply ourselves with the greatest ardour and vehemence to make progress in that which excites us the most strongly to the love of God. And lastly, with what intention and object? not to learn, that is to say, in order to satisfy vainglory, to indulge curiosity, or any motive like that, but only for our own edification or that of our neighbour. For there are those who wish to learn merely in order that they may know,[1] and such curiosity is blamable There are others who wish to learn for no other reason than that they may be looked upon as learned, which is a ridiculous vanity; and these will not escape the censure which a satiric poet levels against them when he says: 'To know a thing is nothing in your eyes, unless some other person is

---

[1] John of Salisbury writes in a very similar way: 'Some are drawn towards learning by curiosity, others by the desire to be accounted learned, or even by motives of self-interest. There are very few who pursue study in a disposition of charity or humility, to instruct themselves or to be of service to others' ('Polycraticus,' Bk. vii. c. 15).

aware of your knowledge' (Persius, *Satire I.*, 27). And others, again, desire to learn only that they may make merchandise of their knowledge, for example, in order to gain money or honours; and such trafficking is ignoble. But there are those who desire to learn that they may edify others; that is charity. And, lastly, there are some who wish to learn that they may be themselves edified; and that is prudence.

4. Of all these the two last are the only learners who do not fall into an abuse of knowledge; since they wish to know only that they may do good. Says the Psalmist: *A good understanding have all they that do His commandments* (Ps. cxi. 10). But let all the others note what is said by the Apostle: *To him that knoweth to do good, and doeth it not, to him it is sin* (James iv. 17); as if he had said by a metaphor: 'To take food, and not to digest it, is injurious to the health. For food badly cooked and ill-digested generates unhealthy humours, and injures the body instead of nourishing it. So also much knowledge stuffed into the memory, which is, as it were, the stomach of the soul, if it is not digested by the fire of charity, and transfused into the limbs, that is, into the actions and habits, so that it is made the means of good actions through the good that is known, shall not that knowledge be counted for sin, like food turned into bad and injurious humours?' Is not sin, in fact, as a bad humour in the soul? and are not bad tendencies and habits as depraved humours? He who knows the good, and does it not, will his conscience not suffer from inflammations and torturing pains? Will it not return in itself a response of condemnation and death, as often as that Divine saying comes into the memory: *That servant which knew his Lord's will, and prepared not himself, neither did according to His will, shall be beaten with many stripes?* (Luke xii. 47). It is perhaps the cry of such a soul to which the Prophet gives utterance, when he says: *My bowels, my bowels! I am pained at my very heart* (Jer. iv. 19). Except that perhaps the very repetition seems to point to a double sense in the words, and obliges me to look for some other than that I have given. I think that the Prophet may have spoken this in regard to himself, inasmuch as being full of knowledge and of charity, and earnestly desiring to communicate that knowledge, he could find no one who cared to listen to him, and thus his knowledge was, as it were, a burden to him, since he was unable to communicate it. Therefore the pious teacher of the Church laments, both for those who scorned the opportunity of learning their duty, and for those who, knowing it, yet lived evil lives. And on this account he repeats the word.

5. Do you observe with what emphatic truth the Apostle asserts that *knowledge puffeth up*? I wish, then, that the soul should first of all commence by acquiring a knowledge of itself, as is required both by natural order and by that of usefulness. The natural order, because we are to ourselves the first and nearest fact; but also that of usefulness, since the knowledge of ourselves does not puff us up,

but rather humbles us, and prepares us for edification. For certainly the spiritual edifice cannot stand except on the firm foundation of humility. Now, the soul can find no motive more effective or more powerful for humility than a thorough knowledge of itself as it really is, only it must be honest in purpose and without guile, and standing in presence of itself, must ignore nothing that it beholds. When it views itself thus in the clear light of truth, it will find itself far different from what it had believed itself to be; and sighing at the sight of its truly miserable state, will it not cry to the Lord with the Psalmist: *In Thy truth Thou hast humbled me?* (Ps. cxix. 75, Douay). For how can it be otherwise than humbled, in obtaining this true knowledge of itself, when it beholds itself laden with sins, heavily burdened with its mortal body, involved in earthly cares, infected with the corruption of carnal desires, blind, bent earthwards, weak, entangled with many errors, exposed to a thousand perils, trembling with a thousand fears, struggling with a thousand difficulties, the subject of a thousand suspicions and a thousand distressing necessities, prone to vices, but to virtues slow and backward? How, after that revelation of himself to himself, can he lift up his eyes and walk with head erect? Will he not rather be converted at the sight of so many miseries, at the sharp pang of the 'thorn which is fastened' [into it]? (Ps. xxxi. 4, Vulg.). He will be converted, I say, to tears, to sighs and groans; he will be converted to the Lord, and in deep humility will cry to Him: *Heal my soul, for I have sinned against Thee* (Ps. xli. 4). And then, when converted unto the Lord, it shall receive consolation, because He is the Father of mercies, and the God of all consolation.

6. As for me, as long as I look at myself, I see only one subject after another for bitter regret. But if I look up, and lift up my eyes towards the help of the Divine compassion, the joyful sight of God tempers at once the bitter revelation of myself, and I say to Him: *My soul is troubled within me, therefore will I remember Thee* (Ps. xlii. 6). Nor is that vision of God of small avail, in which we have experience of His kindness and readiness to be entreated. For He is in truth good and merciful, so much better than we are evil, as to prevail over our ill (Joel ii. 13). His Nature is goodness, and to Him it belongeth to have mercy always and to spare. Through such an experience, and in such an order of events, then, does God make Himself known to us, and to our great benefit; that is to say, after man has become aware of the deplorable condition in which he is, and has cried unto the Lord, the Lord hears and helps him, declaring: *I will deliver thee, and thou shalt glorify Me* (Ps. l. 15). Thus, the knowledge of thyself will be a step to the knowledge of God: He will become visible in His image, which is renewed in thee; whilst thou, beholding with confidence as in a glass the glory of the Lord, art changed into the same image from glory to glory, even as by the Spirit of the Lord (2 Cor. iii. 18).

7. But now notice, finally, how each of these kinds of knowledge

is necessary to your salvation, so that if you are wanting in one or in the other, you cannot be saved. For if you do not know yourself, you will not have the fear of God in you, and therefore you will have no humility. What ground, then, you can possibly have to hope for salvation, without the fear of God and without humility, you can see for yourself. You have done well to show me by that little murmur that you do not nourish any such vain expectation, or rather that your belief is entirely opposite to it; and therefore we need not linger upon a question which is clear in itself. But listen to what remains— or had we better stop here, on account of those who are weighed down by sleep? I thought that I would include in one sermon what I had promised respecting the two kinds of ignorance, and I would do so, only that I should seem to be excessively lengthy to those whom this sermon wearies and disgusts. For I see some yawning, and others are asleep. Nor is that strange; the Vigils[1] of the preceding night (which were, indeed, very long) are their excuse. But what shall I say to those who slept then, and yet are sleeping now all the same? But I do not wish to put them to shame farther; it is sufficient to have mentioned the fact. I think that henceforth they will keep awake better, and fear to be again remarked. In that hope I pass over the matter for this time, and in consideration for them will divide what remains to be said, and make an ending, where the end really was not. May the indulgence shown to them bring them to render glory with us to the Bridegroom of the Church, JESUS CHRIST our Lord, who is above all, God blessed for ever. AMEN.

SERMON XXXVII.

OF THE TWO KINDS OF KNOWLEDGE AND THE TWO KINDS OF IGNORANCE: THE EVILS OR INJURIES CAUSED BY THESE.

I THINK that there is no need to-day to urge you not to yield to sleep, because the exhortation given to you so recently as yesterday will doubtless be still in your minds, and being addressed to you in a kindly spirit has, I hope, produced a good effect. You remember, then, that you agreed with me in holding that no one is saved without a knowledge of himself, because from that knowledge is born humility, which is the mother of salvation, and the fear of the Lord which, as it is the beginning of wisdom, so it is the beginning of salvation. No one, I say, is saved without that knowledge; at least, no one who is of an age and capability to have it. This exception is made to cover the case of young children and of those wanting in the powers of reason, to whom another principle applies.

---

[1] That office which we call 'Matins' was thus named, according to the intention of St. Benedict (Mabillon's note).

But if you have not the knowledge of God, could there be a hope of salvation for you without that knowledge? No, not even a hope. For you cannot love One whom you do not know, nor have eternal happiness in the possession of One whom you do not love. Attain, then, to the knowledge of yourself, that you may fear God; and attain to the knowledge of Him, that you may love Him also. In the one is the beginning of wisdom, in the other is the consummation of it, because the fear of the Lord is the beginning of wisdom (Ps. cxi. 10), and love is the fulfilling of the law (Rom. xiii. 10). So great reason is there for your guarding against both the one and the other kind of ignorance, since without the fear and the love of God salvation is not possible. Other things are indifferent; the knowledge of them does not ensure salvation, nor does ignorance of them prevent it.

2. Yet I must not be understood to say that the knowledge of literature is either to be neglected or despised, since it both instructs and adorns the soul, and renders it capable of instructing others. But it is needful and expedient that those two things, in which, as we have said above, consist the essentials of salvation, should precede that knowledge. Did not the Prophet have that order in view, and intend to inculcate it, when he said: *Sow to yourselves righteousness, reap the hope of life?* And then, after that, *light for yourselves*, he says: *the light of knowledge*.[1] He has placed knowledge the last, as it were a picture, which cannot be drawn on the empty air; and he has set in the first place the two things which form, so to speak, the solid substance upon which the picture is to be superposed. I may, then, apply myself in all security to gaining knowledge if I have previously received good assurance of life by the blessing of hope. You have, then, sown for yourself to righteousness if you have learned, from a true knowledge of yourself, to fear God; if you have humbled yourself, wept sincerely for your sins, given liberal alms, and done other works of piety; if you have afflicted your body with fasts and vigils and your breast with blows; if, finally, you have wearied heaven with your prayers. This is indeed to sow to righteousness. Good works, pious pursuits, tears of penitence—these are the seeds. *Going, they went,* says the Psalmist, *and wept, casting their seeds.* But what, shall they weep always? By no means. *They shall come with joyfulness, carrying their sheaves* (Ps. cxxvi. 6). Rightly is it said *with joyfulness*, since they bring back fruits of glory, as it were, sheaves of

---

[1] Hós. x. 12; but probably quoted from memory. No version or commentator that I can discover has anything like this reading. The nearest is the LXX.: σπείρατε ἑαυτοῖς εἰς δικαιοσύνην, τρυγήσατε εἰς καρπὸν ζωῆς, φωτίσατε ἑαυτοῖς φῶς γνώσεως, etc. The Vulgate version (and those founded on it) take quite a different turn here. St. Bernard may have had in his mind the following from St. Ambrose (*Comm. in* Ps. cxix., *octon. prim.*): '*Seminate vobis ad justitiam, vindemiate ad fructum vitæ, illuminate vobis lumen cognitionis: non prius illuminate, sed seminate,*' etc. The sentiment is a common and favourite one with St. Bernard. See parallel passages in 'Convers. ad Clericos,' c. 15, and 'Serm. de St. Benedicto.'—ED.

grain. But that, you say, shall be in the resurrection at the last day; and that is a very long time to await. But be not discouraged, do not in mere failure of heart lose hope; in the meantime you have the first-fruits of the Spirit, which, even at the present time, you reap with joy. *Sow to yourselves righteousness; reap the hope of life.* He does not merely put you off to the last day, when the object desired shall be possessed, not hoped for: but he speaks of the present. Our joy, no doubt, and exultation shall be very great indeed when [eternal] life shall come to be in our actual possession.

3. But shall the hope of so great a joy be itself without joy? *Rejoicing in hope*, says the Apostle (Rom. xii. 12). And David said, not that he should rejoice, but that he did rejoice, because he hoped to go into the house of the Lord (Ps. cxxi. 1). He did not yet possess [eternal] life, but he had attained the hope of life; and he experienced in himself the truth of that saying of Scripture that not only the reward, but the *hope* itself, *of the righteous shall be gladness* (Prov. x. 28). That gladness is produced in the soul of him who has sown to himself righteousness, by the assurance that his offences are pardoned, provided that the efficacy of the grace which he has received to live more holily for the future attests for him the certitude of that pardon. Everyone among you who feels this working in himself knows what saith the Spirit, whose words and whose working are never contrary the one to the other. That which is heard outwardly with the ears is felt inwardly by the heart, and therefore it is that the teachings of the Spirit are understood with full sympathy. For it is one and the same Spirit who speaks in us and who works in you, *dividing to every man severally as He will* (1 Cor. xii. 11); giving to some the grace to speak, to others the grace to do that which is good.

4. Whosoever, then, of you, after the first stages (so bitter and full of tears) of his conversion, has the happiness to breathe freely in hope, and to be raised as upon the wings of grace into the peaceful air of heavenly consolations, is even now reaping the harvest and receiving the fruit of the tears which for a time he shed; he has attained to see God, and has had the happiness to hear Him say: *Give to* [him] *of the fruit of his hands* (Prov. xxxi. 31). For how can it be that he who has tasted and seen how sweet the Lord is (Ps. xxxiv. 8) has not seen God? How full, O Lord Jesus, of sweetness and kindness has that soul felt Thee to be who has not only received of Thy bounty pardon for sins, but also the gift of holiness! Nor is even that all, for, as if to load him with blessings, there has been added to it the promise of eternal life. Happy is he who has already reaped as much as this, and who has in the meantime his fruit unto holiness, and in the end eternal life! It was with good ground that he who wept and lamented at the sight of himself as he really was, rejoiced when he had seen the Lord, since to the sight of that marvellous mercy he owed it that he returned home bearing sheaves of glory so great: remission, sanctification, most of all the hope of [eternal] life. How true is the prediction which we read in

the Psalm: *They that sow in tears shall reap in joy* (Ps. cxxvi. 5). In it is briefly referred to each kind of knowledge: the one the knowledge of ourselves, which causes us to sow in tears; the other the knowledge of God, which enables us to reap in joy.

5. If, then, we begin with this twofold experience—the knowledge of God and of ourselves—any knowledge which we may be able afterwards to add to this will not make us vainglorious, inasmuch as any worldly gain or honour which it can possibly bring us is far below the hope which we have conceived and the joy which that hope brings to us, and which is profoundly rooted in the soul. And that *hope maketh not ashamed, because the love of God is shed abroad in our hearts by the Holy Ghost which is given unto us* (Rom. v. 5). It makes us not to be ashamed, because it fills the heart with an assured and settled conviction [of the mercy of God]. By this the *Spirit itself beareth witness with our Spirit that we are the children of God* (Rom. viii. 16). What, then, can come to us from any knowledge of our own, however great it be, which is not far below this glory, to be counted among the sons of God? That is indeed too little to say, for the whole earth and all that it contains, if it were possible to put that into the possession of each one of us, would not deserve to be put into comparison with a gift so precious. But if we be ignorant of God, how is it possible for us to hope in One whom we know not? And if we be ignorant of ourselves, how can we be humble, since we think ourselves to be something, while we are nothing? But we know well that neither those who are proud, nor those who are without hope in God, have any part or lot in the inheritance of the saints.

6. Consider, then, now with me with what care and solicitude we ought to repel from us both these kinds of ignorance, of which the one produces the beginning, the other the consummation, of every kind of sin; just as, on the contrary, of the two corresponding kinds of knowledge, the one is the beginning of wisdom, and the other its perfection—that is to say, the one produces the fear of the Lord, the other the love of Him. But with regard to these two kinds of knowledge, we have explained above; let us now consider the two kinds of ignorance. Now, just as the fear of the Lord is the beginning of wisdom (Ecclus. i. 14), so pride is the beginning of every sin (Ecclus. x. 13); and as the love of God is justly considered as the perfection of wisdom, so despair [of His love and mercy] is both the starting-point and completion of malice. And in like manner, as from the knowledge of thyself is caused in thee the fear of God, and equally from the knowledge of God the love of Him, so, on the contrary, from ignorance of thyself comes pride, and from ignorance of God despair. For ignorance of yourself produces in you pride, inasmuch as your mind, being at the same time deceived and deceiving, causes you to think yourself better than you really are. In this way pride is the beginning of all sin, since you are greater in your own eyes than in the eyes of God, or than you are in fact and reality. And therefore the Scripture, speaking of him who first committed this

great sin (I mean the devil), declares that *he abode not in the truth, but was a liar from the beginning*,[1] inasmuch as he was not in truth what he was in his own imaginations. But suppose that he had erred from truth in thinking himself lesser and lower than he really was, what then? Doubtless ignorance would then have been an excuse for him; he would have escaped the snare of pride, and, instead of being brought into disgrace by [this] his iniquity, would perhaps have been brought back into grace and favour by his humility. For if we could know clearly the condition in which each of us individually is before God, we might have an opinion of ourselves which should be neither too high nor too low, but which should conform in all respects closely to the truth.[2] But since it has pleased God that this should be hidden from us, so that no man knows whether he be worthy of love or of hatred (Eccles. ix. 1), it is assuredly both more fitting and more safe to choose for ourselves the lowest place, according to the advice of the Truth Himself; from this we may afterwards be transferred to a higher, and that with honour, instead of being obliged to cede with shame the higher place to another (Luke xiv. 10).

7. There is, then, no danger, howsoever much you may humble yourself, that you will regard yourself as much less than you really are—that is to say, than truth holds you to be. But it is a great evil and a peril to be guarded against, to exalt yourself even in a small degree more than the truth, or in your own thoughts to prefer yourself even to one person whom, perhaps, the Truth regards as equal to you, or, perhaps, even superior. To explain this by a familiar illustration: when you pass through a low doorway you have nothing to fear from stooping, however low you may stoop; but if you raise your head higher than the doorway, though it were but by the breadth of a finger, you will strike against the frame and injure yourself by the blow. So also with the soul: there is nothing to be feared from humbling yourself, to however great an extent, but much to be apprehended from even the least presumptuous self-exaltation. Therefore beware, O man, of comparing yourself either with those who are greater than you, or those who are less; with many or with one. For how do you know whether that very one, whom you perhaps regard as the vilest and most miserable of mankind, at whose life you shudder as being infamous and defiled with crimes beyond all others; whom you think is to be scorned therefore, not only in comparison with yourself, who are living, as you confidently think, in temperance, righteousness, and piety, but even in comparison with other criminals, as being of all the ungodly the worst; how do you know, I say, whether he may not one day be made, by an exertion of the power of the Most High, to be better than you, and than those whom you prefer to him, or whether he is not so even now in the sight of God? And for these reasons it is that the Lord has willed us to take our place, not in the midmost ranks, not in the lower, nor even among

---

[1] John viii. 44.   [2] See Sermon XX., *De Diversis*.

the lowest, but has said: *Sit down in the lowest place* (Luke xiv. 10)
—that is to say, alone and last of all; and do not presume, I say
not to *prefer* yourself to any, but even to put yourself in comparison
with one. See what great evil is caused by ignorance of ourselves,
since it produces the sin which is that of the devil, and is the beginning of all others—namely, pride. What is produced by ignorance
of God we will see on another occasion. For, as we assembled today a little late, the shortness of the time will not permit of more
now. Let it suffice on this occasion for each of us that he is warned
against ignorance of himself; warned, not merely by this discourse,
but by the condescension and goodness of Him who is the Bridegroom of the Church, JESUS CHRIST our Lord, who is above all, God
blessed for ever. AMEN.

SERMON XXXVIII.

HOW FROM IGNORANCE OF GOD COMES DESPAIR: AND HOW THE BRIDE IS CALLED THE FAIREST AMONG WOMEN.

WHAT, then, comes from ignorance of God? For, as you remember, it was at this point we left off yesterday, and we have to take up our subject here. What, then, comes of it? Despair, as I have already said; but in what manner we have now to consider. A man perhaps, returning to a right frame of mind,[1] and sincerely condemning himself for all the evil actions which he has done, proposes to reform, and to retire from the evil road on which he is, and from his sensual thoughts and actions. But if he is ignorant how good and merciful God is, how gentle and favourable to the penitent, and how willing to forgive, will not his carnal reason accuse him, and say: 'What are you doing? do you wish to lose this life as well as the future life? Your sins are too many and too great. If you were even to cut the skin off your bones,[2] you could not make satisfaction for offences so numerous and aggravated. Your constitution is delicate; you have lived in comfort, and you will not easily alter the habits of a life.' And the unhappy man, rendered desperate by these and similar arguments, returns to his former errors, not knowing how easily the Almighty Goodness, who willeth not that any should perish, would break through all those obstacles [for him]. Then follows [a settled state of] impenitence, which is the worst of all crimes, and is indeed that blasphemy which cannot be forgiven (Matt. xii. 31). He is deeply agitated, and swallowed up by excessive sadness, and by a profound melancholy, so that he refuses to emerge from it, or to receive any consolation. It is with him as it is said in

---

[1] '*Reversus in se.*' This is the phrase in the Vulgate, Luke xv. 17.—ED.
[2] *Excories*, a Low Latin word, not classical.—ED.

Scripture: *The wicked man, when he is come into the depth of sins, contemns* [them] (Prov. xviii. 3). Or, at least, he shuts his eyes to his miserable state, and, flattering himself with some plausible reasoning, throws himself again, and irrevocably, into the business and the pleasure of the world, to enjoy and to profit by all its good things to the utmost of his power. But when he [and those like him] shall say, Peace and safety, then sudden destruction cometh upon them, like travail upon a woman with child : and they shall not escape (1 Thess. v. 3). Thus it is that from ignorance of God comes the consummation of all evil, which is despair.

2. The Apostle says that some have not the knowledge of God (1 Cor. xv. 31) ; but I say that all those who are unwilling to be converted to God are without the knowledge of Him. For, doubtless, they are not reluctant to do so for any other reason except that they imagine Him to be rigorous and severe who is good and kind ; hard and implacable, who is full of mercy ; cruel and terrible, who is most to be loved—and iniquity deceives itself, imagining an idol in place of that which He really is. O ye of little faith, wherefore do ye fear? Because you think He is unwilling to forgive your sins ? But when His Hands were nailed to the Cross He nailed your sins to it also with them. Because you are delicate, and nursed in habits of luxury? But He knoweth the clay of which we are made. Because you are accustomed to evil, and bound by habits of sinning as by iron chains ? But *the Lord looseth them that are fettered* (Ps. cxlvi. 7). Are you perhaps afraid that He is enraged because of the number and greatness of your crimes, and will be slow to extend to you a helping Hand ? But you have the assurance that *where sin abounded, there grace did much more abound* (Rom. v. 20). Are you careful and anxious about food and clothing, and other things necessary for your body, and on that account are reluctant to give up your property? *Your Heavenly Father knoweth that ye have need of all these things* (Matt. vi. 32). What more can you wish ? or what still holds you back from salvation? But this is the very thing I say : you are ignorant of God, and you are not willing to believe that which I tell you of Him. I could wish that you would believe those at all events who tell you what they have themselves experienced ; for unless you believe you will not have true understanding. But that faith is not given to all.

3. May God grant us never to suffer from such ignorance as this, that is to say, respecting God, which the Bride is warned to avoid ; she on whom has been bestowed, not merely knowledge, but friendship and familiarity with Him who is as well her Bridegroom as her God, to whom is the favour of continual communion and conversation with Him, and who asks here with fearless directness : *Tell me where Thou feedest, where Thou makest Thy flock to rest at noon.* In which she asks to be shown to her, not Himself, but the place where His glory dwelleth ; although, in truth, His place and His glory are no other than Himself. But He thinks fit to reprove her for pre-

sumption, and warns her to know her own self, and to consider by what limitations she is restrained, since she has regarded herself as fit for so great a Vision, whether because the excess [of her love] hindered her from considering that she was still in the body, or that she hoped, but fruitlessly, to be able to attain, even while remaining in the body, to that Brightness which is inaccessible. Therefore she is forthwith recalled to herself, is convicted of ignorance, and corrected for presumption. *If thou know not, go forth.* The Bridegroom thunders terribly against His beloved, not as Bridegroom, but as Master; not as being angry, but because He desires to purify her by terror, so that being purified she may be rendered fit for that Vision to which she aspires. For that Vision is reserved for the pure in heart.

4. It is with great beauty that, instead of calling her simply 'beautiful,' He styles her *fairest among women;* that is to say, beautiful, with a qualification, and in this way to humble her still more, that she may learn in what she is deficient. For I think that in this passage, under the name of 'women,' He speaks of carnal and worldly souls, which have in them no manly force, displaying nothing constant or generous in their actions, but of which the whole life and character is soft, remiss, and, in a word, womanish. Now, although the soul that is spiritually minded is already beautiful, inasmuch as it walks, not according to the flesh, but according to the Spirit, yet, because it is still in a mortal body, it still falls short of perfect beauty. Thus, it is not beautiful absolutely, but beautiful 'among women;' that is, among worldly souls, which are not spiritually minded as she; but not among Angelic Beatitudes, not among Virtues, Powers, and Dominations. For as among the Patriarchs one was formerly said to be *just in his generation* (Gen. vi. 9), that is, beyond all of his time and his generation; and as Tamar was asserted to be righteous by Judah, that is to say, beyond Judah (Gen. xxxviii. 26); and as in the Gospel the Publican is declared to have gone down to his house justified, indeed, but justified rather than the Pharisee (Luke xviii. 14); and as that great Saint John [the Baptist] was once commended as having no superior, yet only 'among those who are born of women' (Luke vii. 28), not among the choirs of the blessed and heavenly spirits, so also is it here said of the Bride that she is fairest, but only among women, not among the blessed spirits of heaven.

5. Let the soul, then, desist henceforth, as long as she is on the earth, from searching out with too eager a curiosity the things which are in heaven, lest in seeking to view too nearly the majesty [of God], she should be overwhelmed by His glory. Let her desist, I say, as long as her lot is cast among women, from inquiring into the events which take place among those Powers which are on high, which are intelligible to them alone, and with which, because they are heavenly, it is lawful to heavenly beings alone to concern themselves. 'That Vision,' He declares, 'which you ask, O My Bride, to be permitted to behold, is far above your powers; nor are you now capable of sustaining the blinding splendour of that Glory, as of the noonday

sun, in which I dwell. For you have said: *Tell me where Thou feedest, where Thou makest Thy flock to rest at noon.* But to be borne upon the clouds, to penetrate into the fulness of Light, to burst into the abysses of Glory, to dwell in the Light which none can approach unto, for this the present is not the time, nor is your mortal body capable of sustaining it. That felicity is reserved for you at the last, when I shall have caused you to appear before Me in a condition full of glory, not having spot, or wrinkle, or any such thing. Do you not know that as long as you remain in your present body, you are exiled from the Light? How can you, who have not yet attained the full beauty of heaven, suppose yourself capable of beholding the Source of all beauty? How, finally, can you, who do not yet know yourself, seek to know Me in My Glory? For if you had known yourself more fully, you would be aware that your corruptible body is not capable of lifting its eyes to that blinding Splendour upon which the Angels desire to look, much less of fixing them upon it. The time will come when I shall appear [to judge], and then you shall be wholly fair, even as I am now; then you shall be like Me, inasmuch as you shall see Me as I am (1 John iii. 2). Then you shall hear the words: *Thou art all fair, my love: there is no spot in thee* (Cant. iv. 7). But now, though you are like unto Me in part, yet in part you are still unlike; therefore be content to know [Me] only in part. Have regard to your own powers; seek not things too high for you, nor try to penetrate those that are too hard (Ecclus. iii. 21). Otherwise, *if thou knowest not* [thyself], *O thou fairest among women;* for I do not call you simply 'fairest,' but 'fairest among women,' that is, in part; but when that which is perfect shall have come, then *that which is in part shall be done away* (1 Cor. xiii. 10). If, then, *thou knowest not thyself;* but the words which follow have been noted, and it is not needful that they should be repeated. I had promised myself to say something that might be useful respecting the two kinds of ignorance; if, nevertheless, I seem not to have fulfilled this promise, forgive me; it has not been for want of goodwill. For to will is present with me; but how to perform I find not, except in so far as Our Lord JESUS CHRIST shall of His goodness deign to bestow upon me [grace] for your edification. He is the Bridegroom of the Church, over all things, God blessed for ever. AMEN.

SERMON XXXIX.

OF THE CHARIOTS OF PHARAOH, THAT IS, THE DEVIL; AND OF THE CHIEFS OF HIS ARMY, WHO ARE MALICE, SENSUALITY, AND AVARICE.

I HAVE compared thee, O my love, to my company of horsemen among Pharaoh's chariots (i. 9). In the first place we recognise willingly in these words that the Church has been prefigured in the Patriarchs of the ancient Law, and that the mysteries of our salvation have been foreshown [in them]. In the Exodus of Israel out of Egypt, in that twofold wonder at the Red Sea, the giving passage to the people of God, while at the same time vengeance was executed upon their enemies, the grace of Baptism is clearly typified, inasmuch as it saves men and submerges offences. *All our fathers*, says the Apostle, *were under the cloud, and were all baptized unto Moses in the cloud and in the sea* (1 Cor. x. 1, 2). But it is needful to notice, according to our custom, the succession of words [in our text], and to show the connection between the former ones and those which follow them, and so to draw, if we can, some sweet and profitable lesson from them to bear upon our practice. So, then [the Lord], after having repressed the presumption of the Bride with grave and severe reproof, not wishing that she should remain in too great dejection, recalls to her memory some of the blessings which she has already received, and promises to her others which have not yet been granted; He also gives testimony that she is beautiful, and even calls her 'love.' 'If I,' says the Bridegroom, 'have spoken to thee harshly and severely, O my love, do not suppose that it was from mistrust of thee, from hatred, or bitterness of feeling. For the gifts which I have lavished upon thee are unmistakable proofs of my affection. Nor is it in my mind to take away from thee these honours and adornments, but rather to add more and greater ones.' Or the words may be thus understood: 'Do not take it ill, O my love, that you do not receive instantly all that you ask, for you have already received very great gifts from Me, and shall receive still greater if you walk in My precepts, and persevere in My love.' Thus much with respect to the connection of the words.

2. Now let us see of what nature are the gifts which He mentions that He has given. First of all is this, that He has rendered her like unto His army among the chariots of Pharaoh, in freeing her from the yoke of sin by the destruction of all the works of the flesh, in like manner as the people of Israel was freed from slavery to Egypt, and the chariots of Pharaoh were overturned and submerged in the Red Sea (Exod. xiv. 28). That was indeed a very great mercy, and I shall not be wrong if I desire to glory in having received it. It is a great truth that I declare. I confess, and will confess, that

unless the Lord had been my helper, my soul had almost dwelt in hell (Ps. xciii. 17, Douay). I am not ungrateful; I am not forgetful; *I will sing of the mercies of the Lord for ever* (Ps. lxxxix. 1). Let us leave there the resemblance which the Bride bears to my soul. For the rest, after she has been liberated by that unexampled condescension and goodness, she is taken by Him to be His dear friend, endued with glory and beauty as the Bride of the Lord; but as yet her ornaments are only upon neck and cheeks. For there are promised to her jewelled necklaces for adornment, and golden earrings of price inlaid with silver for an added beauty. Who will not be pleased with the order itself of these gifts? First, she is mercifully freed; then condescendingly loved; thirdly, with kindness cleansed and purified; lastly, she receives the promise of ornaments the richest and most precious.

3. I do not doubt that there are some among you who feel already in themselves the truth of what has been said, and, indeed, anticipate it, because they are forewarned by their own experience. But it is for me to be mindful of that verse of a Psalm: *The entrance of Thy words giveth light: it giveth understanding unto the simple* (Ps. cxix. 130). And for their sakes it is that I think it advisable to explain these things at greater length, for loving is the Spirit of wisdom (Wisd. i. 6). And it pleases Him that a teacher should be loving and diligent, and that, while desirous to satisfy the intelligent and learned, he should so proceed as to make allowance for those who are of slower comprehension. Wisdom herself says: They that explain me shall have life everlasting (Ecclus. xxiv. 31, Douay), and I should be unwilling to be deprived of that recompense. Furthermore, even in those things which appear plain there are often hidden meanings, and those of such a character that it is not superfluous to explain them with great care, even to those of the most capacious and swiftly-apprehensive minds.

4. But consider the comparison drawn from Pharaoh and his army and from the horsemen of the Lord. The comparison is not of the two armies between themselves, but of each with a third thing. For what concord hath light with darkness? or what part hath he that believeth with an infidel? (2 Cor. vi. 15). The Bridegroom compares, no doubt, the holy and spiritual soul to the horsemen of the Lord; and, again, Pharaoh to the devil, and the army of the one to the army of the other. You will not wonder that one soul is likened unto horsemen, who are a multitude, if you consider the array [as it were an army] of virtues which are found in that single soul which is holy. What order and regularity in its affections, what discipline in the use of all its faculties, what an armoury of strength in its prayers, what unshrinking resolution in its actions, how formidable is its zeal, what constancy in the combats it sustains with the enemy of souls himself, and how numerous the triumphs it obtains over him! Therefore, it is that we read of it in a later verse: *Terrible as an army with banners* (Cant. vi. 4). And, again: *What will ye see in the Shulamite?*

As it were, the company of two armies (vii. 1). Or if that explanation does not please you, know that a pious soul is never without a guard of Angels, who vie with each other in watching over it with a care truly Divine, that they may keep it for Him to whom it belongs, and present it as a chaste virgin to Christ. Do not say in your heart: 'Where are they, then; who has seen them?' The prophet Elisha saw them, and obtained at his petition that his servant [Gehazi?] should see them too.[1] If you do not see them it is because you are not a Prophet, nor the servant of a Prophet. The Patriarch Jacob saw them, and said: *This is God's host* (Gen. xxxii. 2). The Apostle and Doctor of the Gentiles saw them too, and said of them: *Are they not all ministering spirits, sent forth to minister for them who shall be heirs of salvation?* (Heb. i. 14).

5. Therefore the Bride, being in all her ways protected by Angelic ministries and attended by a bodyguard of Angels, is rightly compared to the horsemen of the Lord; to that army which on a former occasion, in the midst of the chariots of Pharaoh, triumphed over them by an astonishing miracle of Divine assistance. For if you notice with attention, you will find that all those circumstances in that former incident which you regard with wonder and admiration are to be discovered here, and to be admired no less. Indeed, it may well be thought that here the triumph is more magnificent still, since the former had to do with material things only; but here the type is spiritually fulfilled. Does it not appear to you, in fact, that there is far more of glory as of bravery in overcoming the devil than Pharaoh, and in conquering the powers of the air than in overturning the chariots of Pharaoh? There the combat is against flesh and blood; but here against principalities and powers, against the rulers of the darkness of this world, against spiritual wickedness in high places (Eph. vi. 12). Follow out with me the details of this comparison. There it is a people delivered from Egypt, here man drawn away from the world; there Pharaoh is overcome, here the devil; there the chariots of Pharaoh are overthrown, here carnal and worldly desires which war against the soul are destroyed; those in the billows, these in floods of tears; billows of the sea in one case, floods of bitter regret in the other. I believe that when the demons encounter such a soul as this they cry out, as did the Egyptians of old: *Let us flee from the face of Israel, for the Lord fighteth for them* (Exod. xiv. 25). Do you wish now that I should point out some of the chiefs of Pharaoh's army by their own names, and that I should describe some of his chariots, so that you may in a similar manner find out others for yourselves? Learn, then, that one of the great captains of the spiritual and invisible king of Egypt is Malice, another is Sensuality, and a third is Avarice. These princes each possess under their king provinces bounded by such limits as are assigned to them by him.

---

[1] 2 Kings vi. 17. St. Bernard says 'Gehazi'; but this attendant on the prophet was probably not Gehazi, who had been before this period rendered unfit for service by leprosy (2 Kings v. 27).—ED.

For Malice rules in the region of injuries and crimes; Sensuality presides over all uncleanness of the flesh; and Avarice over the province of rapine and fraud.

6. Listen also and learn of what kind are the chariots which Pharaoh has prepared for his princes that they may pursue the people of God. Malice has a chariot standing on four wheels, and these are cruelty, impatience, presumption, impudence. Swift is that chariot to shed blood; it is not stayed by innocence, nor retarded by patience, nor restrained by fear, nor kept back by shame. It is drawn by two horses extremely vicious, and ready for any injury to others—worldly Power, and temporal Ostentation. This car of Malice advances with great rapidity, since on the one side it has Power to accomplish the malicious designs of its occupier, and on the other, Ostentation to approve and applaud them when completed; so that the saying is fulfilled which is written: *The wicked boasteth of his heart's desire, and blesseth the covetous* (Ps. x. 3); and also another Scripture: *This is your hour, and the power of darkness* (Luke xxii. 52). Over these two rule two drivers: Arrogance urges Pomp, and Jealousy Power. For the heart that is swelling with vanity is borne swiftly to the love of the pomps of the devil; while that, on the contrary, which is restrained by fitting fear, which gravity renders modest, humility sincere, and purity healthy and clearsighted, will certainly not be borne lightly away by the wind of vainglory. In the same way is not the horse of worldly Power directed by Jealousy, and urged on with the two spurs of envy, I mean the apprehension of failing, and the uneasy fear of being surpassed. One of these is felt by him who is successful, the other by him who is trying to succeed; and by one or the other of these the powers of the world are constantly galled. So much as to the car of Malice.

7. The car of Sensuality also rolls upon four wheels: the Gluttony of the belly, the Lust of sexual passion, the Luxury of dress and adornment, and the Languor of sloth. It also is drawn by two steeds, Prosperity in life, and Abundance of goods; and directed by two drivers, Ease shameful and inglorious, and treacherous Security. For an abundance of all things easily produces sloth, and according to Scripture *the prosperity of fools shall destroy them* (Prov. i. 32), and assuredly for no other reason than this, that it infuses into them an unfounded sense of security; for *when they shall say, Peace and safety, then sudden destruction cometh upon them* (1 Thess. v. 3). Now, these have no spurs, nor whip, nor anything of that kind; instead of these they make use of a net of gauze[1] to give them shade, and of a fan to give them a cooling breeze. The gauze net may stand for Dissimulation, which casts a kind of shadow over the soul, and enables it to escape the heat and labour of cares. It is the mark of an effeminate and weak soul to seek to avoid even necessary cares for fear of feeling the anxiety and uneasiness of them; and for that

---

[1] *Conopeum*, used in the sense of 'a sunshade.' In many editions is added '*parvulo papilione*,' which in the MSS. is a marginal note.—ED.

object to conceal itself under the shadow of dissimulation. And the fan is Prodigality, which produces the breeze of adulation. For the luxurious are wont to be prodigal, and to purchase with their gold the breath of the mouth of flatterers; but enough upon this subject.

8. Avarice also is drawn upon a chariot of which the four wheels are: Pusillanimity, Inhumanity, Disregard of God, and Forgetfulness of death. It is drawn by Stubbornness and Rapacity as steeds, and these have but one driver, Eagerness for gain. Avarice is content with one servant only; he is not willing to bear the expense of more. But that servant performs what is commanded him with promptness and unwearied industry; he urges on the steeds which draw his master's car with a whip of double thong—the Craving to acquire, and the Fear to lose.

9. The king of Egypt has other captains besides with their chariots, who serve their master in his wars: as Pride, who is one of his chief princes; Impiety, the enemy of the faith, who holds a chief place in the household and realm of Pharaoh; there are also lords and knights of lower rank in the army, whose number is very great, and I leave it to you to seek out the names and the offices, the arms and the equipment of these, to occupy you in these studies. It is thus that the invisible Pharaoh, full of confidence in the prowess of his captains and the strength of their chariots, charges to and fro, here, there, and everywhere, and as a cruel tyrant, wreaks his rage to the utmost of his power against the whole of the Lord's household, and pursues even at this very day Israel escaping from Egypt. The people of God are indeed neither clad in armour, nor borne onward in chariots; nevertheless [His army] is rendered strong by the Hand of the Lord alone, and sings aloud in cheerful confidence: *I will sing vnto the Lord, for He hath triumphed gloriously; the horse and his rider hath He thrown into the sea* (Exod. xv. 1); and again: *Some put their trust in chariots, and some in horses; but we will remember the Name of the Lord our God* (Ps. xx. 7). All this bears on the comparison of the horsemen of the Lord, and the chariots of Pharaoh.

10. The Bride is called by the Bridegroom *his Love*. For she was beloved by Him, even before she was set free; He would not have set free one whom He did not love. But as for her, she was drawn to love Him, because of the priceless blessing of freedom which He had conferred upon her. Hear, in fact, the confession which she herself makes: We love Him, because He first loved us (1 John v. 19). Now recall to your minds the history of Moses and the Midianite (*Æthiopissæ*) woman, and you will see that in it is prefigured the mystical union of the WORD with the soul of a sinner; and distinguish, if you can, what it is, in the consideration of that most sweet of all mysteries, which gives you most heartfelt consolation and pleasure. Is it the benignant condescension of the WORD, all too great as it is? is it the priceless glory accruing to the soul? or is it the sudden and unhoped for faith of the sinner? But Moses was not able to change the skin of his Midianite wife; while Christ is able to change the

complexion of the soul which He loves and saves. For He goes on to say: *Thy cheeks are beautiful as the turtle dove's* (Cant. i. 9, 10, Douay). But this is reserved for another sermon, so that we may take with eagerness and avidity the viands which are set out for us upon the table of the Bridegroom; and may burst forth (*eructemus*) to His praise and glory who is JESUS CHRIST our Lord, God blessed for ever. AMEN.

SERMON XL.

WHAT IS MEANT BY THE FACE OF THE SOUL; WHAT CONSTITUTES ITS BEAUTY OR ITS DEFORMITY, ITS SOLITUDE AND ITS MODESTY.

THY cheeks are beautiful as the turtle-dove's. Tender and sensitive is the modesty of the Bride, and I think that at the reproof of her Bridegroom her whole face was suffused with one blush, and its beauty made so strikingly apparent as to draw from Him the praise: *Thy cheeks are beautiful as the turtle-dove's.* But, nevertheless, that is not to be understood in an outward and carnal sense, as if He spoke of the flush due to the blood coursing in the veins, mounting into the countenance, and mingling there swiftly with the pearl-white tints of the complexion. That causes, indeed, a beauty momentary and perishable, varying from one moment to another, as the bright colour now flames upon the cheeks, and now sinks into paleness; but it is not of this that He speaks. For the substance of the soul, which is incorporeal and invisible, is neither portioned into limbs and organs, nor shadowed with visible colours. Try, then, to reach, in a spiritual way, the conception of a substance wholly spiritual, and in order to estimate justly the comparison made by the Bridegroom, for the face of the soul understand the intention of the mind. For it is by that you judge of the rectitude of an action, just as it is by the face that you judge of the beauty of the body. Understand, then, by the colour which mounts into the cheeks, modesty, which is, more than any other, the quality which beautifies the soul, and adds grace to it. *Thy cheeks,* then, *are beautiful as the turtle-dove's.* He was able to describe her beauty as that of the face, according to the ordinary phrase, in which one, whose beauty is praised, is said to have 'a sweet or beautiful face'; but I know not what could have been the intention in speaking of 'cheeks' in the plural, yet I do not at all think that it was without an object. For it is the Spirit of wisdom who is speaking, and it is not permissible to attribute to Him a single word spoken in a faulty or even objectless way. There is undoubtedly some reason, then, whatever it may be, wherefore He preferred to speak of 'cheeks' in the plural, rather than of 'face' in the singular; and if you have nothing better to propose, I will explain my idea of what it is.

2. In an intention or purpose, which we have said to be the countenance of the soul, there are two elements necessarily required, namely, the act of the will, and the reason of that act; that is, the thing that you intend, and the reason why you intend it. And it is by these two that you form an opinion of the excellence (that is, the moral beauty) or the defect of that soul. So that one in whom these two things are correct and pure may rightly and truthfully be addressed as here: *Thy cheeks are beautiful as a turtle-dove's.* But if any is wanting in one or the other of these qualities, this cannot be said of her, because of the want of symmetry which that defect causes. Much less is this praise due to her in whom both of these excellences are wanting. This will appear more plainly by examples. If, for instance, a person applies his mind to the discovery of truth, and does that from the love of the truth alone, does it not seem to you that the purpose, and the reason of it, are alike honourable, and that such a soul may rightly apply to itself what is said here: *Thy cheeks are beautiful as a turtle-dove's?* since on neither of them does a speck (*nævus*) of blame appear? But if it seeks the truth, not from a pure desire of truth, but for vainglory, or in order to obtain some temporal advantage, whatever it may be, then, although on one side it may appear fair, yet you will not hesitate, I think, to pronounce that on the other it is deformed, since it is disfigured by the faultiness of the motive. But if you see a man who does not devote himself to any honourable pursuits at all, but is entangled in the nets of sensual pleasures, and given up to gluttony and self-indulgence, such as they are *whose god is their belly, and whose glory is in their shame, who mind earthly things* (Phil. iii. 19), what of that man? will you not declare that he is wholly foul, and evidently condemned for both intention and act?

3. To have not God but the world for the motive and end is then the sign of a worldly mind, and it is to have none at all of this spiritual beauty. But to have a degree of regard for God, yet not to act wholly for the sake of God, is evidently the mark of a soul that is insincere. Although it has a fair appearance on one side, because it has a certain degree of regard and care for God, yet this insincerity not only destroys such beauty as there is in this, but spreads foulness over the whole countenance. If, again, the intention is directed towards God wholly or chiefly because of the necessities of the present life, that is not indeed insincerity, but it is a mark of lowness and poorness of heart which is far from being acceptable to Him. Further, to direct the mind towards some other object than God, though it be for the sake of God, is not the repose of Mary, but the care and trouble of Martha. I would by no means assert that a soul doing this has anything of deformity in it, yet I could not declare that it has reached the perfection of beauty, since, inasmuch as it is careful and troubled about many earthly things, it cannot help being covered, by the continual agitation in which earthly things continually exist, with some grains of the dust they scatter everywhere.

No doubt these will be quickly and easily blown off again in the hour of a holy death by the breath of a pure intention and the answer of a good conscience towards God. Therefore, to seek only God, and that for Himself alone, is to have a countenance perfectly fair upon either side, and that because both of the intention and the act; and this it is which is the special quality and prerogative of the Bride by which she merits these words: *Thy cheeks are beautiful as a turtle-dove's.*

4. But why *as a turtle-dove's?* That bird is modest, and is said to consort not with many companions, but to lead its life with a single mate, so that, if it should lose that mate, it does not seek another, but thenceforth lives solitary. You, then, who listen to these words, and who wish to profit by these things which are written for your behoof, and which we are dwelling on and discussing now for your edification, you, I say, if you feel within you the urgings of the Spirit of God, and are earnestly desiring so to act that you may make your soul to become the Bride of Christ (*Dei*), do you make it your study that the two sides of your intention—the act and the motive of it—should alike be beautiful; be like that bird so modest and chaste; sit alone and keep silence, as says the Prophet, because thou hast laid it upon thee? (Lam. iii. 28). It is indeed an aim altogether above you to be espoused to the Lord of the Angels. Is it not above you to be joined to God, and to be one spirit with Him? Sit, then, solitary as the turtle-dove. Have nothing to do with crowds, nothing to do with the masses of mankind; forget, also, thine own people and thy father's house; so shall the King have pleasure in thy beauty (Ps. xlv. 10, 11). O holy soul, remain alone, so as to preserve thyself for Him alone, whom thou hast chosen to thyself from among all others. Avoid appearing in public, shun even those who dwell in the house with you, withdraw yourself from friends and intimates, yea, even from him who ministers to you. Do you not know that you have a Bridegroom who is diffident, and not willing to honour you with His presence when others are present? Withdraw thyself, therefore; I do not mean in body, but withdraw in mind, in intention, in devotion, in spirit. For the Lord Christ, who presents Himself to you, is a Spirit, and He requires solitude of spirit, not of body, although this last is sometimes not without its uses when you are able to maintain it, and especially in the time of prayer. You thus observe the precept of the Bridegroom and the practice He advises: *Thou, when thou prayest, enter into thy closet, and, when thou hast shut thy door, pray* (Matt. vi. 6). And what He has said, that He Himself did. He would wear away the night alone in prayer, withdrawing Himself not only from the crowds which followed Him, but also from the company of His disciples and familiar friends (Luke vi. 12, 13). He had indeed taken with Him three of His Apostles when He was hastening of His own accord to meet death, yet He withdrew Himself even from them when He desired to pray (Matt. xxvi. 36-39). Do you, then, do likewise when you wish to pray.

5. For the rest, the only solitude prescribed to you is solitude of mind and spirit. You are alone if you are not thinking of common things, if you are not interested in things present to you, if you think little of that which many estimate highly, if you despise what all others desire, if you avoid disputes, do not take to heart losses, nor bear injuries in mind. Otherwise you are not really alone, though there be no one with you.[1] Do you not perceive that it is possible for you to be alone when you are in the company of many persons, and to be in company with many persons when you are alone? However large be the throng of men in which you find yourself, you are alone, if only you take care not to listen eagerly to the conversation around you, nor to judge of it rashly. Even if you are witness of a bad action, do not judge your neighbour, but rather make excuses for him. Excuse the intention if you cannot the action; suppose that it was done in ignorance, or by surprise, or by accident. If the case is so clear that there is no room to palliate it, yet strive to persuade yourself that there was some excuse, and say to yourself: 'The temptation was very strong, and it prevailed. What should I have done if I had been similarly tried?' Now, remember that it is to the Bride I have said all this, not to the friend of the Bridegroom, who has another reason for being careful and observant not to commit sin, as also to examine whether he has failed in his duty, and to amend his conduct if in any respect he has done so. But the Bride is free from any such necessity; she lives for herself alone and for Him whom she loves, who is at once her Bridegroom and her Lord, who is above all, God blessed for ever. AMEN.

SERMON XLI.

OF THE GREAT CONSOLATION WHICH THE BRIDE FEELS FROM THE CONTEMPLATION OF THE DIVINE GLORY BEFORE SHE ATTAINS TO THE CLEAR VISION OF IT.

THY neck is as chains of gold (i. 10). It is the custom to adorn the neck with necklaces, not to compare it to them. But those who load themselves with jewels are they who seek to obtain from external ornaments the beauty which they do not find in themselves. But in the case of the Bride, the neck is so beautiful and becoming in itself, as it was formed by nature, that nothing could be added to it by outward ornaments. For what need is there to adorn with borrowed hues that of which the natural and, as it were, innate beauty suffices, insomuch that it is fully equal to the soft splendour of the pearls which are so sought for in order to adorn

---

[1] Compare this with the Letter to the Monks of Mont Dieu.

it? This is what the Bridegroom desired to intimate in declaring not at all that the Bride has jewelled chains pendant from her neck, as is usually the case, but that it is itself *as chains of gold.* Now, we must invoke the Holy Spirit, so that, as He was pleased to show us what was meant in a spiritual sense by the cheeks of the Bride, so He will deign now to show us what is spiritually meant by her neck. And as far as I have understanding (for I must say to you what I think), no explanation seems more reasonable and probable than to say that the *intelligence* of the soul is intended here by the 'neck' of the Bride. You will agree to this opinion, I think, if you consider the reason for this metaphor. For does not the function of the neck [in the body] seem to you to answer to that of the intelligence, by which the soul transmits the vital nourishment of the spirit, and distributes it throughout all the viscera, that is, the faculties and affections? As, then, the neck of the Bride, that is to say, the intelligence, is sufficiently admirable in its pure and simple truth, it has no need of any extraneous ornament, but itself adorns the soul, as it were a precious necklace; and for that reason is described under the metaphor of golden and jewelled chains. Truth is a good necklace, as is purity and simplicity; and wisdom that is sober and chastened is an ornament that is priceless. The intelligence of philosophers or of heretics has in it none of this pure lustre, none of the splendour of truth; and therefore they take great pains to colour and to veil it with trappings of fine words, with ingenious tricks of logic, lest if it should be suffered to appear unadorned, its essential falseness and meanness should become visible also.

2. *We will make thee borders*[1] *of gold, with studs of silver.* If the speaker had said, in the singular, 'I will make,' and not 'we will make' in the plural, I should have pronounced without hesitation the speaker to be the Bridegroom. But now consider whether we shall not do better, and with greater fitness, to attribute these words to His companions, who are consoling the Bride by such a promise as this, that while she is awaiting the vision of Him whom her soul so earnestly desires, they will fashion for her the beautiful and costly pendants which are wont to be ornaments for the ears. And this for the reason, as I think, that faith cometh by hearing, and that as long as we walk by faith, and not by sight, our efforts must be directed rather to the purifying and building up of [the soul] by means of hearing than to attaining[2] a revelation by the sight. In vain is it that the eye is bent upon the truths of heaven, if it be not purified by faith, since to those alone who are of clean heart is that blessed vision promised (Matt. v. 8). It is written also: *Purifying their hearts by faith* (Acts xv. 9). Since, then, faith cometh by hearing, and from it is the purifying of the spiritual vision, there is good reason for directing endeavours to the adornment of the ears, since the hearing, as we are taught by reason, is the preparation for sight. 'You, O Bride,' they say to her, 'are sighing for the glory of your Beloved;

---

[1] Or *pendants.* [2] *Exserendo,* but otherwise *exercendo.*

but this grace is reserved for another season. For the present we bestow upon you these ornaments, to be both a consolation to you in the meantime, and a preparation for the glory which you crave.' It is as though they spoke to her those words of the Psalmist: *Hearken, O daughter, and consider, incline thine ear* (Ps. xlv. 10). You desire to behold; but first hearken. Hearing is the step by which you reach sight. Therefore listen, and incline thine ear to the ornaments which we devise for thee, so that by the obedience of hearing thou mayest come to the glory of vision. Upon thine hearing we bestow joy and gladness. As for that Vision (in which is fulness of joy, and the fulfilment of all thy desire), it is not ours to give, but His alone whom thy soul loveth. It is for Him to show Himself to thee, so that thy joy may be full; He shall make thy joy perfect with His countenance. In the meantime, do thou receive at our hand these jewelled pendants for a consolation; but in His Right Hand are delights for evermore.

3. We must now consider what are the pendants which they offer. *Pendants of gold,* it is said, *and studs of silver.* Now, gold denotes the splendour of Divinity, and the wisdom which is from above. It is this gold which the celestial workers, to whom that ministry is committed, promise to fashion into glittering signs and tokens (so to speak) of truth, and to insert them into the inward ears of the soul. That signifies, I believe, nothing else than to construct the similitudes of certain spiritual realities, and to bring the purest intuitions of the Divine wisdom before the perception of the soul absorbed in contemplation, so that it may behold, at least darkly and as in a glass, what it is not yet equal to beholding face to face. These things are wholly Divine, and are known only to those who have had experience of them; they alone know how, while yet in this mortal body, while yet in the state of faith, while the real substance of Light perspicuous and lucid is not yet made manifest, it may nevertheless come about that contemplation of the pure truth may sometimes already mark out within us the outline of its form, at least in part, so that he from among us who is so happy as to have received that gift from on high may say with the Apostle: *Now I know in part;* and again: *Now we know in part, and we prophesy in part* (1 Cor. xiii. 12, 9). But when the spirit, coming forth, as it were, out of itself, and rapt in ecstasy, beholds somewhat of the more Divine and sacred Truth, which flashes before its vision with the rapidity of lightning, then, either in order to temper the exceeding brilliance of a light too penetrating to be endured, or to render us capable of communicating the substance of it to others, forthwith, I know not whence, there present themselves to our imagination images and figures of lower (that is, earthly) things, to which the truths revealed from above are accommodated, which veil in a certain sense that most pure and splendid ray of truth, and render it more supportable by the mind, and more able to be communicated to others. These are, I think, formed in our minds by the ministry of good angels, as, on the other hand, there is no doubt

that those other [images] which are evil, are produced by the agency of evil spirits.

4. And perhaps this is that very mirror [of the imagination] through which, as I have said, the Apostle saw darkly (1 Cor. xiii. 12), which is formed, so to speak, by the hands of Angels, and from which come gleams of pure light, beautiful and heavenly ideas and images. This, indeed, gives us the knowledge of God, who is discerned as pure Being, and without any phantasy of bodily semblance, and we must attribute to this Angelic ministry that similitude of supreme excellence which affords to us an idea of Him who is clad in majesty so awful. There is another version which seems to express this more strikingly still: *We [artificers] will make for thee images of gold, with* [badges or] *distinctions of silver.*[1] One says *with badges of silver*, [the other] *with studs of silver*. In which are signified, as it seems to me, not only that the inward images are suggested to our minds by the Angels, but also that the grace and eloquence of their outward clothing [of words] is ministered to us by the Angels also, so that by their fitting and graceful expression they are more easily received, and more fully enjoyed, by the hearers. If you shall say, What relation or likeness is there between words spoken and silver, the Psalmist replies to you: *The words of the Lord are pure words, as silver tried in a furnace* (Ps. xii. 6). Thus, then, it is that those heavenly and ministering spirits fashion for the Bride, while she is a pilgrim here on earth, pendants of gold with studs of silver.

5. But notice how, while desiring one thing, she receives another. She sighs for the repose of contemplation, and the labour of preaching is laid upon her; and while she is thirsting for the presence of the Bridegroom, the care of bringing forth children for Him and of nourishing them is entrusted to her. Nor is this the only occasion when this was so; for once before, as I remember, when she was sighing for the presence and affection of her Bridegroom, the reply to her was: *Thy breasts are better than wine* (i. 1), so that she might recall that she was a mother, and be reminded of her duty to impart milk to her little children and nourishment to her sons. Perhaps you may remark the same thing in other passages of this Canticle if you will take the trouble to seek them out. Was not the same truth once prefigured in the holy patriarch Jacob when he was defrauded of the nuptials with Rachel, which he had desired and long waited for, and instead of a wife who was barren, though beautiful, he received against his will, and even without his knowledge, one who was fertile though dim-eyed? (Gen. xxix. 23-25). So, also, it is now; the Bride, inquiring and longing to know where the Bridegroom feedeth, where He maketh His flock to rest at noon, receives, instead of that knowledge, pendants of gold with studs of silver—that is, wisdom with eloquence, without doubt for the work of preaching.

6. From this we are taught that it is often needful to leave spiritual contemplation, however sweet, for the sake of the practical labours

---

[1] Cant. i. 11 in the LXX. στιγμάτων τοῦ ἀργυρίου.—ED.

which give nourishment, and that no one must live for himself alone, but for the good of all.[1] Woe to those who have received the grace to think and to speak worthily of God, if they make a gain of Godliness; if they turn into a reason for vainglory that which they had received that they might win souls to the glory of God; if, having lofty and noble thoughts, they have not also lowly personal feelings. Let them listen in fear and trembling to that which the Lord speaks by the mouth of His prophet: *I gave her . . . silver and gold, which they have used in the service of Baal* (Hosea ii. 8, Douay). Do you, then, hear what the Bride replies, having received on the one hand a reproof, and on the other a promise; for she is not exalted by promises, not angered by a repulse, but practises that which is written: *Rebuke a wise man, and he will love thee* (Prov. ix. 8); and also that which relates to gifts and promises: The greater thou art, the more humble thyself (Ecclus. iii. 18), which will appear the more clearly in her reply. But the consideration of that we will defer, if you please, to the commencement of another sermon; and for what has been said let us render glory to the Bridegroom of the Church, our Lord JESUS CHRIST, who is above all, God blessed for ever. AMEN.

SERMON XLII.

OF TWO KINDS OF HUMILITY: THE ONE BORN OF TRUTH, THE OTHER WARMED BY CHARITY.

WHEN the King sitteth at His table, my spikenard sendeth forth the smell thereof (i. 12). These are the words of the Bride, which we have deferred till to-day to speak of; this is the reply which she makes when reproved by the Bridegroom; yet it is not made to Him, but to His companions; the words themselves make this clear. For she does not say, as if addressing Him: 'O King, when Thou sittest at Thy table,' but *When the King sitteth;* and it is clear that she speaks not to Him, but of Him. Thus, imagine that the Bridegroom, after having (as it appeared) reproved or repulsed the Bride, seeing by her blushes that she was covered with confusion, retired from the spot, that in His absence she might express her feelings more freely; and that if, as was commonly the case, she yielded too much to depression and grief, the consolations of His companions might raise her up again; which, nevertheless, He does not neglect to do Himself when He considers it the right time. For, to show clearly how much she pleased Him, even during the reproof given to her, because she received it with becoming

---

[1] The first editions read: '*Sed omnes illi qui mortuus est pro omnibus, esse vivendum.*'

humility and submission, He wished, before leaving her, to express the praises of her which burst forth, there is no doubt, from the fulness of the heart, and extolled her as beautiful in cheek and neck. Therefore, those who remain with her, knowing the will of their Lord, speak to her courteously, and offer her gifts. It is to them, therefore, that her reply is addressed. So much as to the purpose and connection of the words of the text.

2. But before beginning to extract the kernel of spiritual meaning from this outer shell (*testa*), I will make one brief reflection. Happy is he by whom reproofs are as well received as those of which we have here a pattern. Would that it were never necessary to reprove anyone, that would be better still! But since in many things we offend all, it is not permitted to me to be silent; my duty obliges me to censure those who do wrong, and charity urges me still more strongly to discharge it. But what if, in the discharge of my duty, I thus censure someone, and the reproof does not effect at all its intended purpose, does not accomplish that wherefor it is sent, but returns to me empty, like a javelin which strikes without piercing and recoils, with what feelings am I affected, do you think, brethren? Am I not pained and angered? And, to press into my service some words of a Master [in Israel], because of my own wisdom I am unequal [to express my meaning as well], *I am in a strait between two, and what I shall choose I know not* (Phil. i. 23, 22): whether to feel any pleasure in what I have said, because I have performed what was my duty, or whether to experience any regret regarding it, inasmuch as I have not attained the result I wished for. For I desired that an enemy should perish and a brother be delivered, and this I have not succeeded in, but the event has been precisely the contrary: I have wounded his soul and increased his fault, since scorn has been added to it. *They will not hearken unto thee*, says the prophet, *for they will not hearken unto Me* (Ezek. iii. 7). You see what Majesty it is that is in this case contemned. You think that it is I only that have been scorned. But it is the Lord that has spoken [unto you through me]; and what He said to the Prophet He said also to His Apostles: *He that despiseth you despiseth Me* (Luke x. 16). I am not a prophet, I am not an apostle, and yet I am bold to say I am fulfilling the duty of both the prophet and the apostle; though I am far from approaching their merits, I am charged and burdened with their cares. Though it be to my great confusion, though it be even to my extreme danger, yet I do, in fact, sit in the seat of Moses, though I am far from claiming that my life is such as his, or the grace committed to me equal to that he enjoyed. But what then? Is not respect to be shown to that seat of authority because it is filled by an unworthy occupant? Even when it was occupied by the Scribes and Pharisees, of them the Lord said: *Whatsoever they bid you observe, that observe and do* (Matt. xxiii. 2, 3).

3. Very often impatience also is joined to disrespect, so that a person, when blamed, does not only take no care to correct himself,

but shows irritation against his reprover, and, like one who is raving in insanity, repels the hand of the physician. Strange is that perversity! He is angry with the man who is anxious to cure his wounds, but for the enemy who pierces him with the shafts of temptation he has no anger! For there is one who shoots his arrows against those who are upright in heart (Ps. xi. 2), who has now wounded you even unto death, and yet against him you are not angry! Your indignation is wholly against me, who desire to see you cured. *Be ye angry and sin not*, says the Apostle (Eph. iv. 26). If you are angry on account of [your own] sin, not only do you commit no sin, but you root out the sin which you had committed. But now you retain the sin in rejecting the remedy, and you heap sin upon sin by being angry without reason; this is indeed to sin beyond measure.

4. Sometimes even impudence is added to this; not only reproof is borne impatiently, but the fault reproved is impudently defended; and this is mere madness. *Thou hadst*, saith the Lord, *a harlot's forehead: thou wouldst not blush* (Jer. iii. 3, Douay); and He says, *My jealousy shall depart from thee, I will be no more angry* (Ezek. xvi. 42). I tremble at the very hearing of the words. Do you feel what a perilous and horrible and fearful thing it is to attempt to defend sin? For He says again: *As many as I love, I rebuke and chasten* (Rev. iii. 19). If, then, the anger [of God] has deserted you, so also has His love; nor can you think yourself worthy of His love, if you do not think yourself worthy of His chastisements. You see, then, that it is when God shows no anger with the wicked that He is the more angry with them. *Let favour be showed to the wicked*, He saith, *yet will he not learn righteousness* (Is. xxvi. 10). May such indulgence be far from me. To be thus spared appears to me more terrible than the most violent anger, because it closes up to me the ways of righteousness. Far better is it for me, according to the counsel of the Psalmist, to embrace the severity of discipline, lest the Lord be sometime angry with me, and so I perish from the right way (Ps. ii. 12). I desire that Thou wouldst be angry with me, O Father of mercies; but with that anger wherewith Thou dost correct one who wanders from the way, not that with which Thou dost exclude such an one from it. That censure of Thine is the utterance of a compassion merciful and blessed for us; but that concealment of Thy wrath is what we have to fear most of all. It is not when Thy wrath is concealed from me, but when it is displayed and felt by me that I have most trust in Thy coming favour; for it is especially in Thy anger that Thou rememberest mercy. *Thou*, says the Psalmist, *wast a God that forgavest them, though Thou tookest vengeance of their inventions* (Ps. xcix. 8). He speaks of Moses and Aaron, and of Samuel, whom He had sent before Him; and he regards it as an instance of God's favour and goodness that He did not spare their faults and failings. After that, will you still go on defending your faults, and showing anger when reproved for them, and thus shutting

against yourself for ever the door of the mercy of God? Is not that, in fact, calling evil good, and good evil? Will not that odious impudence speedily produce impenitence, which is the mother of despair? For who repents for that which he considers not to be wrong? *Woe to them*, says the Prophet. And that woe is eternal. It is one thing for a person to be drawn away from the right and enticed by his own concupiscence; and quite another and very different to seek out evil of free will, as if it were good, and thus in a false confidence to draw near to death as if it were to life. For this very reason, I assure you, I have sometimes preferred to hold my peace, and take no notice in words of an evil which I have observed, rather than to give occasion for so great a mischief in reproving it.

5. You will perhaps say to me that, in such a case, the good of my action would return to me again; that I have delivered my soul, and am clean from the blood of that man to whom I have spoken, and have warned him to turn from his evil way that he may live. But although you should add an infinity of such reasons, they would still be no comfort to me while I am apprehending the spiritual ruin of a soul under my pastoral charge. As if I had sought only my own acquittal from blame in speaking to him, and not rather his good! For what mother is there who, when she has diligently nursed her child, and lavished upon him every care in her power, will be able to restrain her tears if she shall find that all her labours and pains were inefficacious, and that her child was dying in spite of them? And she would feel this only with regard to the death of the body; how much more ought I to weep and lament for the eternal death of a son of mine, even if I am conscious that I have left nothing undone to warn or to help him? You see also from how great evils he escapes himself, and also delivers me, who, when reproved, replies with gentleness, acquiesces with modesty, avows his fault humbly, and obeys with submission. To such a soul I profess myself a debtor in all things; I am his minister and servant, as to a soul which is a most worthy Bride of my Lord, and which is able to say with truth: *When the King sitteth at His table, my spikenard sendeth forth the smell thereof.*

6. The odour of humility is excellent, since, rising up from this vale of tears, it is diffused everywhere around, and fills even the chamber of the King with grateful fragrance. Spikenard is a humble plant, which those who have studied with care the nature of herbs say is of a warm nature; and therefore it may be taken here not unfitly, as it seems to me, to denote that virtue of humility which glows with the ardour of Divine love. I say this because there is a kind of humility which truth produces in us, and which is without warmth, as there is also another kind, which is produced and warmed by charity. The one has its seat in knowledge, the other in the affections. If, in fact, you look into yourself under the light of truth and without dissimulation, and judge unflatteringly of yourself, there is no doubt that you will be humbled, even in your own eyes, and that this true know-

ledge of yourself will render you more vile in your own sight, although, perhaps, you cannot as yet endure that this should be the case in the sight of others. You will then be humble, but as yet only by the working of truth, and not at all by the inpouring of love; for if you had been, in addition to the working of truth, which has shown you to yourself in a manner veracious and salutary, affected equally by love, you would without doubt have wished, as far as in you was, that others should have the same opinion of you as you know that the Truth has. I should say that He is nevertheless in you, for it is often inexpedient that all which we know ourselves should be known to others, and we are forbidden by the love of truth itself, as also by the truth of love, to wish to discover to another that which would do him injury. But if you are restrained by self-love, and induced to keep hidden the judgment which truth has formed of you, who can doubt that your love of the truth is imperfect, since you make it subordinate to your own interest or your own reputation?

7. You see clearly, then, that it is not the same thing whether a man, being constrained by light and knowledge, has a lowly opinion of himself, and whether he is assisted by the grace of charity, and accepts a humble position with willingness; for the one is enforced, the other voluntary. *He emptied Himself,* says the Apostle, *and took upon Him the form of a servant* (Phil. ii. 7), thus giving to us a perfect form and model of humility. He emptied Himself, He humbled Himself, not from any necessity of fact or judgment, but by charity towards us. He was able to appear vile and despicable in the eyes of men without thinking Himself so, because He knew Himself well. He was, then, voluntarily humble, and not because He was judged to deserve so to be; He presented Himself as if He had been such, as He knew Himself not, in fact, to be; but though He was not unmindful that He was the Highest, yet He preferred to be regarded as the least of all. He said, in fact: *Learn of Me, for I am meek and lowly in heart* (Matt. xi. 29). He says 'in heart,' in the feeling of the heart—that is, in the will; and in saying this He excludes all idea of necessity, for although I or you find ourselves, in truth, worthy of disgrace and contempt, worthy of the lowest rank and of the worst treatment, worthy even of stripes and punishment, yet it was not thus, it was far otherwise with Him; yet He endured all these things, and as one humble in heart, because He chose so to do—that is to say, He was humble with the humility which was prompted by the kindness of His heart, not enforced by the verdict of truth.

8. For this reason I have said that this kind of voluntary humility is not produced in us by the logical force of truth, but is created within us by the inpouring of charity, because it comes of the heart, the affections, the will; whether I have spoken rightly you must judge. Consider also whether I have been right in attributing it to the Lord, inasmuch as it is clear that it was charity which led Him to empty Himself, to become a little lower than the Angels, to be subject to [those who were supposed His] parents, to bend His head under the

hands of the Baptist, to endure the weaknesses of the flesh, to submit at length to death, and that the ignominious death of the Cross. I submit to your judgment again, whether I have been right in deciding that this humility, thus warmed by charity, is denoted by spikenard, which is a herb unassuming in appearance and of a warm nature. And if you assent to both these opinions, which I think you will do, as they are supported by very plain reasons, then, if you feel yourself humbled by that forced humility which the Truth, who searcheth the very hearts and reins, produces in the senses of a soul that is watchful, make a virtue of this necessity, and add to your humility a glad and willing acquiescence, since there is no true virtue without the assent of the will.[1] That will be the case if you are unwilling to appear otherwise to the outward eye than you find yourself to be inwardly. Otherwise you may well fear lest that which you read in a psalm should apply to you: *He flattereth himself in his own eyes, until his iniquity be found to be hateful* (Ps. xxxvi. 2). And again: *Divers weights and divers measures, both of them are alike abomination to the Lord* (Prov. xx. 10). What! do you at the bottom of your heart think lowly of yourself because you weigh yourself in the balance of truth, and yet outwardly you wish to deceive, to be regarded as of greater value, and to sell yourself at a higher price than that at which the truth values you? Have regard to the judgment of God; do not by any means commit this most discreditable action of exalting yourself by your own self-love, while the truth requires you to be abased, for this is to resist the truth; this is even to fight against God. Rather acquiesce in the Divine conclusion. Let your will be rendered submissive to truth, and not merely submissive, but willingly and devotedly so. *Shall not my soul*, says the Psalmist, *be subject to God?* (Ps. lxi. 1, Douay).

9. But it is not enough to be subject to God, unless you are subject also to every human creature for the sake of God; whether to the Abbot, as to the superior of all, or to the Priors, as authorities constituted by him. I say even more than this: I say, subject to your equals, and even to those who are inferior to you. For *thus it becometh us,* says the Lord Himself, *to fulfil all righteousness* (Matt. iii. 15). If, then, you wish to be perfect in righteousness, make the first step towards him who is less than you; defer to your inferior, show respect towards your junior. For in doing this you shall make the words of the Bride apply to you: *My spikenard sendeth forth the smell thereof*. That perfume is devotion; it is the holy and saintly reputation which you obtain with all persons, so that you are a good odour of Jesus Christ in every place, visible to all, and by all regarded with affection. He whom truth alone obliges to be humble can never reach this degree of perfection, since his humility is only for himself, and does not flow forth to reach and delight others. It has, in fact, no odour, because it has no devotion, inasmuch as such humility is not voluntary and spontaneous, but enforced. But the humility of the Bride is like sweet perfume, and diffuses its fragrance, warm

---

[1] *Convenientia voluntatis.* Another reading is *conniventia voluntatis.*

with love and devotedness, and redolent of sweetness to all. The humility of the Bride is spontaneous, constant, fruitful, and it is as unaffected by severity as by praises. To her it had been said: *Thy cheeks are beautiful as those of a turtle dove, thy neck as a string of pearls.* She had received also the promise of golden ornaments, and yet she replies with humility; the more she is raised up, the more humble she is in all respects. She does not boast of her merits, nor in the midst of the praises of herself which she receives is she at all forgetful of humility, which, indeed, she frankly avows, speaking of it under the name of spikenard. She speaks in the language of the Blessed Virgin Mary: 'I am conscious of no merit deserving of so great a condescension, except that God *hath regarded the low estate of His handmaiden*' (Luke i. 48). For what is the signification of these words, *My spikenard sendeth forth the smell thereof,* except this, 'My humility hath found favour in His sight'? 'Not my wisdom,' she says, in effect, 'not my nobleness, not my fairness, for these in me were nothing worth, but my humility, the only quality which was mine, it was this which gave forth its odour'; that is to say, that odour which was customary to it. Humility is accustomed to please God, and the Lord, who is high above all, is wont, according to His custom, to regard those things which are humble. Therefore when the King sitteth at His table, that is, when He is in His lofty habitation, the odour of humility ascends thither. *He dwelleth on high,* saith the Psalmist; *He humbleth Himself to behold the things that are in heaven and in the earth* (Ps. cxiii. 5, 6).

10. When, then, the King is in His habitation, the spikenard of the Bride gives forth its odour. The habitation of the King is the Bosom of the FATHER, for the SON is always in the FATHER. Doubt not, then, that this King is ever merciful, since His abiding-place continually is the home of Fatherly goodness. It is no wonder that the cry of the humble, rising up, reaches Him, who dwells always in the fountain-head of mercy, to whom gentleness and goodness are familiar, are natural, yea, are consubstantial with Him, who derives all that He is from the Father, so that the trembling glance of the humble penitent, looking up to Him, sees nothing in Him which is not fatherly. Therefore it is that *for the oppression of the poor, for the sighing of the needy, now will I arise, saith the Lord* (Ps. xii. 6). This the Bride knows, because she is of the household of the Lord and is His beloved; she believes that her poorness in merits will not exclude[1] her from the Bridegroom's grace, and she puts her confidence in humility alone. She calls Him 'the King,' for she is terrified by the reproof she has received, and does not venture to call Him her Bridegroom. Nevertheless, though she confesses that He dwells in a high and lofty place, her humility does not lose confidence.

11. It is possible to apply this discourse, and that with much fitness, to the Primitive Church. If you recall the days in which the

---

[1] *Arcendam,* otherwise *arctandam.*

Lord ascended up where He was before, and sat on the Right Hand of the Father, in His ancient, august, and glorious dwelling-place, you remember how the disciples assembled with one accord in one place, continuing in prayer with the women, and Mary the Mother of Jesus, and with His brethren (Acts i. 13, 14). Does it not seem to you that in truth that was a time when the Bride, though so young and so fearful as yet, gave forth the odour of her spikenard? Again, when suddenly there came a sound from heaven as of a rushing mighty wind, and it filled all the house where they were sitting (Acts ii. 2), could she not, though so poor and undistinguished, have taken into her lips these words: *When the King sitteth at His table, my spikenard sendeth forth the smell thereof?* Assuredly it appeared to all who abode in that place, how sweet and how acceptable was that fragrance of humility which ascended to heaven, since it was immediately replied to with gifts so copious and so magnificent as a response. And she was not ungrateful for such a benefit. For listen how in her fervour of gratitude she shows herself to be prepared to suffer all possible evils for the Name of Jesus, for what words follow? *A bundle of myrrh is my Well-beloved unto me : He shall lie betwixt my breasts.* But my weakness, which you know, does not permit me to go on longer. This only I add, that by the mention of myrrh she denotes that for affection to her Beloved she is prepared to endure bitter trials and persecutions. The rest of the verse we will finish another time; if, that is to say, you obtain for me by your intercessions the assistance of the Holy Spirit, to enable me to understand and to interpret the words of the Bride, which He Himself, by His holy inspiration, has originated, and to grant unto me words befitting the praises of Him of whom He is the Spirit: I mean the Bridegroom of the Church, JESUS CHRIST our LORD, who is above all, GOD blessed for ever. AMEN.

SERMON XLIII.

HOW MEDITATION ON THE SUFFERINGS AND THE PASSION OF JESUS CHRIST ENABLES THE BRIDE, THAT IS, THE FAITHFUL SOUL, TO PASS UNINJURED ALIKE THROUGH THE PROSPERITY AND THE ADVERSITY OF THIS WORLD.

A BUNDLE of myrrh is my well-beloved unto me : He shall lie between my breasts. Before He was called 'the King,' now He is called 'well-beloved'; before he was in His royal banqueting-room, now He is abiding willingly with the Bride. Great is the virtue of humility, since the majesty of Godhead itself so easily condescends to it. A name of reverence is quickly changed into a term of friendship, and he who was afar off was in a brief time brought near. *A bundle of myrrh is my well-beloved unto me.* Myrrh, which is bitter, signifies the hard and rigorous facts of trouble and sorrow. The Bride, foreseeing that she is about to endure these for the sake of her Beloved, says these words with a feeling of gladness, trusting that she will endure bravely all that is laid upon her. As it is said of the Apostles : *They departed from the presence of the Council, rejoicing that they were counted worthy to suffer shame for His Name* (Acts v. 41). Wherefore, also, she speaks of Him, not as a great or weighty mass, but as a small bundle ;[1] in order to convey that whatever labour and grief threatens her, she regards it as light for the sake of His love. She has well called it small and light, for He is a little Child who is born to us (Is. ix. 6). Again, it is a bundle small and light, since *the sufferings of this present time are not worthy to be compared with the glory that shall be revealed in us* (Rom. viii. 18). And the same Apostle says that *our light affliction, which is but for a moment, worketh for us a far more exceeding and eternal weight of glory* (2 Cor. iv. 17). That, then, which is now a little bundle of myrrh shall at some future period be to us a weight of glory exceeding great. Is it not *a little bundle* [we have to bear], since *His yoke is easy and His burden is light?* (Matt. xi. 30). It is not that it is light in itself, since the severity of suffering and the bitterness of death are not light, but that to the loving heart it seems a light thing to endure them. And for that reason the Bride does not say merely : *My Beloved is a bundle of myrrh*, but she adds *unto me*—that is to say, 'to me who love Him.' So, also, she calls Him her 'well-beloved,' meaning to declare that her love has force to overcome the bitterness of all troubles, and that it is strong as death (viii. 6). And that you may know that she does not glory in herself, but in the Lord, and relies, not upon her own strength and bravery, but upon the help of the Lord, she declares that *He shall lie between my breasts*, and on that account she can say to Him in a Psalm with the fullest confidence : *Though I walk through the valley of the shadow of death I will fear no evil, for Thou art with me* (Ps. xxiii. 4).

2. I remember that in one of my former Sermons[2] I explained these as signifying sympathy in joy with others, and sympathy with them also in sorrow, according to the precept of St. Paul : *Rejoice with them that do rejoice, and weep with them that weep* (Rom. xii. 15). But because, as she lives between prosperity and adversity, she is aware that there is danger upon either side, she desires to have her Beloved upon her breast and near her heart, so that by His protection she may be continually strengthened against both the one danger and the other, and neither be unduly lifted up in time of rejoicing nor cast down in time of sorrow. You, also, if you are wise, will imitate the wisdom of the Bride ; you will not allow that bundle of myrrh, which you hold so dear, and which is the fellowship you have with the sufferings of your Master, to be torn away from your heart even for

---

[1] *Fascis, fasciculus.* This fanciful play upon words can hardly be translated.
[2] Sermon X., *n.* 1.

an hour; you will retain always in your memory all the bitter pains which He bore for you, and meditate upon them continually, so that you too may say with the Bride: *A bundle of myrrh is my well-beloved unto me: He shall lie between my breasts.*

3. As regards myself, I, brethren, from the beginning of my conversion, set myself, in place of all the merits in which I knew that I was wanting, to bind up this little bundle of myrrh for my individual needs, collected from all the cares and bitter experiences of my Lord, and to keep it always close upon my breast; in the first place, of the privations of His infant years; then of the labours He underwent in preaching, His fatigues in journeying to and fro, His watchings in prayer, His fastings and temptations, His tears of compassion, the snares laid for Him in discourse; and, lastly, of His perils among false brethren, of insults, spitting, blows, abuse, scorn, piercing by nails, and other such things, which He suffered for the salvation of our race, which in the Gospel history, as in a wood, may abundantly be gathered. And, among so many branches of that fragrant myrrh, I think that cannot be passed over, of which He tasted when upon the Cross, nor that wherewith He was embalmed in the sepulchre. In the first of these He applied to Himself the bitterness of my sins, in the second He pronounced the future incorruption of my body. As long as I live I will proclaim loudly the abundance of the graces which come from these; I will never forget those mercies, since it is by them that I have been restored to life.

4. It was these mercies of which holy David formerly entreated with tears: *Let Thy tender mercies come unto me, that I may live* (Ps. cxix. 77). Of them, too, another saint recalled the remembrance, with weeping: *Great are the mercies of the Lord.* How many kings and prophets have desired to see the things which I see, and have not seen them! They have laboured, and I have entered into their labours; I have reaped the harvest of myrrh which they have planted; it is for me that this salutary bundle has been reserved. No one shall take it from me; it shall lie between my breasts. To meditate on these things I have called wisdom; in these I have placed the perfection of righteousness for me, the fulness of knowledge, the abundance of merits, the riches of salvation. There is among them for me sometimes a draught of salutary bitterness; sometimes, again, a sweet unction of consolation. In adversities they raise me up, and in prosperity repress my exuberant delight, and among the joys on the one hand, and the sorrows of the other, of this present life, they enable me to walk in safety along the royal road which leads to life by defending me from the perils on either hand. These conciliate on my behalf the Judge of all the world, showing to me Him who is so greatly to be feared, as one who is gentle and humble, and not only making Him willing to receive and to pardon, but even more, in giving me Him who is far above all powers, and terrible among the kings of the earth, as a model for me to imitate. It is for these reasons that I have these [sufferings of Jesus] frequently in my mouth, as you know,

and always in my heart, as God knows. These are familiar themes in all my writings, as is well known. In a word, my philosophy is this, and it is the loftiest in the world: to know JESUS, and Him crucified. I do not ask, as does the Bride in this passage, 'where reposes at noon' Him who I embrace with joy and gladness, for He dwells ever upon my breast and in my heart. I do not ask 'where He feeds His flock,' for I behold Him as my Saviour, upon His Cross. The one object is loftier, the other has more of sweetness; the one is bread, the other milk; the one the children's food, the other the nourishment which infants find at their mothers' breasts, and therefore *He shall lie betwixt my breasts.*

5. My dearest brethren, do you also gather for yourselves each a bundle so precious and beloved, give it a place in the depths of your heart, fortify with it the portal of your breast, that it may abide between your breasts also. Let [JESUS] be borne, not behind you and on your shoulders as a burden, but in front of you and before your eyes,[1] lest

---

[1] A curious and interesting incident is connected with these words of the Sermon:

When the Abbey of Clairvaux had been suppressed by the Directory of France, the church and monastic buildings were sold, on the 10th February, 1792, to the 'Sieur Pierre-Claude Cauzon, architecte,' for the sum of 337,500 livres. He proceeded to set up a manufactory of glass there, and in order to carry out this purpose, required of the vendors, according to the conditions of sale, that all the relics of saints, as well as the remains of bishops, monks, and others, of which there were great numbers deposited in the church and its precincts, should be forthwith removed.

The inhabitants of Ville, in which parish Clairvaux is situated, seem to have been shocked and outraged, as well they might be, at the contemplated spoliation and sacrilege. They desired that the relics of St. Bernard and St. Malachi and other holy men, 'for which their veneration is extreme,' should be deposited, if they must be removed, in their parish church of Ville-sous-La Ferte. In order to meet their wishes, which (says the official charged to carry out the affair) 'it might, perhaps, be dangerous to treat with disregard and contempt (*fronder*),' order was given by the Directory of Bar-sur-Aube that this should be done, and that the bones of all the less distinguished persons should be deposited together in the churchyard of that parish. This seems to have been accordingly done in 1793. ('Report of M. Delaine, Administrateur du Directoire.')

The statement of these details was necessary to explain what follows.

In 1855 the Count de Montalembert, the illustrious author of 'The Monks of the West,' was collecting materials for that 'Life of St. Bernard,' which, unfortunately, he did not live to finish. At his instance, M. Guignard, Town Librarian of Dijon, visited this Church of Ville-sous-La Ferte, and from his account of what he found there we extract the following interesting facts:

'In the little sacristy of that church there repose, in an old wooden chest, once used for treasure, the bones removed from the Church of Clairvaux in 1793. Before 1836 or 1837 they were in the shells used for their translation; at or after that date they were thrown *pêle mêle* into this worm-eaten coffer, and the shells were burned. It is half-filled by them.'

After describing the nature and condition of the bones, and other mouldering fragments which were with them, he continues:

'Finally there was a very thin board, nearly 5 inches long, and 3¾ inches high, which was covered with a leaf of parchment turning up at the edges, along which it is fastened by small nails. A wooden link, nailed at its lower part to the board, suggests that it was intended to be hung up, or at all events, to be put in an upright position. This parchment bears four lines of writing; it is entirely eaten away in

if you bear Him and do not perceive His sweetness, you should be oppressed by His weight, without being refreshed by His fragrance rising up before you. Remember how Simeon took Him up in his arms (S. Luke ii. 28), how Mary bore Him in her womb, nursed Him on her bosom, how He who is the Bridegroom was laid upon her breast, and, not to pass over anything, how the word [of prophecy of Him] was spoken by the aged Zacharias (i. 67), and, indeed, by others also. I suppose that Joseph, too, the husband of Mary, must frequently have taken the Child upon his knees to smile upon and to please Him. All these bore Him before them, and by no means behind. Let them be for an example to you. Do ye do likewise; for if you have Him whom you are bearing, always before your eyes, it is certain that, beholding the pains and troubles which the Lord endured, you will more easily and willingly bear your own, by His help, who is the Bridegroom of the Church, above all, God blessed for ever. AMEN.

---

the centre, but the ends of the lines are still legible. The writing is plainly of the twelfth century.' This is a *facsimile* of the inscription:

The presence of this written quotation is a proof (were any needful) that the relics are those of St. Bernard. But it suggests even more than this. When we bear in mind the Saint's own words: '*Habete hunc fasciculum . . . ante præ oculis*,' and observe that we have here a text nailed upon a board, with a hook by which it might be hung up, for instance upon a wall, the inference is surely not a violent one that the Saint had carried into effect his own precept, and that this text was written out, it may be by his own hand, to hang upon the wall of his cell, and thus to be literally 'always before his eyes.' Then his disciples, after his lamented death, would carry out the precept so dear to their master, a step further; they would lay it upon his breast in his tomb, and thus his devout aspiration would be accomplished: '*inter ubera mea commorabitur*.'

It is a pleasant thought, and not at all an improbable one, that we have here some few words in the autograph of the Saint.—ED.

SERMON XLIV.

CORRECTION OUGHT TO BE ADAPTED TO THE CHARACTER OF OFFENDERS, SO THAT THOSE OF HUMBLE AND COMPLYING DISPOSITION SHOULD BE GENTLY DEALT WITH, BUT THE STUBBORN AND OBSTINATE SEVERELY CHASTENED TO OBLIGE THEM TO REFORM.

'*My beloved is to me as a cluster of camphire*[1] *in the vineyards of Engedi.*'— Cant. i. 14.

IF the Bridegroom were beloved in the bitter myrrh, much more will He be so in the sweetness of the grape. Therefore my Lord Jesus Christ is to me in His Death myrrh, in His Resurrection a cluster of grapes; and thus He has given Himself to me as a most salutary draught, though commingled with tears. For our sins He died, for our justification He was raised again from the dead (Rom. iv. 25), so that we, being dead unto sins, should live unto righteousness (1 Peter ii. 24). If, then, you have mourned for sins past, you have tasted the bitterness of the draught; but if you have now entered upon a holier life, and are beginning to breathe in more and more the hope of eternal life, the bitterness of the myrrh is changed for you into wine, which maketh glad the heart of man. And, perhaps, when there was offered to the Saviour upon the Cross wine[2] mingled with myrrh, and He would not drink it, this was signified, that He thirsted only for the former. You, then, after experiencing, as I have said, the bitternesses of the myrrh, and then tasting the wine of gladness, may yourself say without rashness : *My Beloved is to me as a cluster of camphire* [grapes] *in the vineyards of Engedi.* Engedi has a twofold meaning, and each sense tends to teach the same lesson, for it means 'the fountain of the kid' and 'the washing of the nations'; and both the one sense and the other point to the tears of sinners. It signifies also 'the eye of temptation,' which also pours forth tears, and looks onward to temptations, which are never wanting to the life of man upon the earth. But the people of the Gentiles, who walked in darkness, were never able to discover by themselves, nor, on this account, to escape, the snares of temptations, until,

---

[1] כֹּפֶר ; βότρυς τῆς κύπρου (Sept.), the Cyprus flower, or Alhenna (*Lawsonia inermis*, Linn.), which is indigenous to India and probably to Egypt, **and may have been introduced by Solomon into his vineyards at Engedi for the sake of the strong odour of its flowers.** The Henna blossoms are yellowish-white **in colour, and the powder from them is used by Eastern women as a dye for the ends of the fingers and the nails, as well as the blossoms (***Tamar-henna***) for bouquets. They grow** in grape-like clusters. The Greek word βότρυς denotes, in fact, simply a **bunch** of grapes or the grape itself. The Latin derivative, *botrys*, signifies, also, **the strongly** aromatic plant *artemisia*, called also *ambrosia ;* but here it appears **to be used** in the sense of a bunch of grapes. See Cant. iv. 13.—ED.

[2] Some copies omit *vinum.*

by His grace who gives light to the blind, they received the eyes of faith, until they came to the Church which has an eye to discover temptation, until they gave themselves to the instructions of spiritual men, who, having been enlightened by the Spirit of Wisdom, and rendered learned also by their own experience, are able to say truly that *we are not ignorant of the snares of the devil nor of his devices* (2 Cor. ii. 11).

2. It is said that in Engedi grow aromatic shrubs, which the people of the country train in the manner of vines; and thence, perhaps, it is that they are here called vineyards. For otherwise, what would the cluster of camphire do in the vineyards of Engedi? Whoever carried clusters [of grapes] from one vineyard to another? For wine is usually carried to places where there is none, and not whither there is a store of it already. He calls, then, by the name of the vineyards of Engedi the peoples of the Church, which possesses a liquid balm, that is, a spirit of gentle kindness, in which she tenderly cherishes the weakness of those who are still babes in Christ, and consoles the sorrows of penitents. If any brother, then, shall have fallen into some fault, the minister of the Church, who has already received of that Spirit, will at once take measures to restore him, and that in the same spirit of gentleness, considering himself lest he also be tempted (Gal. vi. 1). That material oil, with which the Church is accustomed to anoint all those who are baptized, is a type of this.

3. But as the wounds of that traveller who fell among thieves, and whom the charitable Samaritan took up and carried on his own beast to a hostelry, that is, to the Church, were not healed with oil alone, but with wine and oil together (Luke x. 30-34), so the spiritual physician needs to mix the wine of fervid zeal with the oil of gentleness, since it behoves him not only to console the weak, but also to restrain the unruly. For if he perceives that the wounded man, that is, the sinner, is not at all amended by the gentle and kindly reprimands which he has first employed, but, on the contrary, abuses his forbearance, becomes more negligent by his patience, and sleeps the more securely in his sin, then, the oil of his gentle remonstrances being shown to be of no use, it behoves him to employ more powerful remedies, and so to pour in the wine of penitence—that is, to have recourse to stern accusations and reproofs, and if need be, and the stubbornness of the offender be so great, to smite him with the staff of ecclesiastical censure. But whence shall he obtain that wine? It is not wine, but oil, that is found in the vineyards of Engedi. Let him seek it in the isle of Cyprus, for that isle is fertile in producing wine, and that of the best; let him gather there of those weighty clusters, which the spies of Israel formerly bore upon a strong pole (Numb. xiii. 23) between two, [in which they typified] the prophets who went before, and the Apostles who followed after, and in the midst JESUS in His beauty; let him take unto himself this cluster, and say: *My Beloved is to me a cluster of the grape of Cyprus.*

4. We have spoken, then, of this cluster; let us now see how the wine of fervent zeal is expressed from it. For if a man, being himself

a sinner, does not show anger towards one who offends, but, on the contrary, manifests compassion for him, and, as it were, pours over him the dew of a sweet and healing balsam, we know whence that proceeds; and you have already heard, though perhaps without taking notice, the source of it. For it has been said that everyone, from consideration of himself, should be gentle to all others; and following the wise counsel of St. Paul, should know how to make kindly allowance for such as have been overtaken in a fault, considering himself lest he also be tempted (Gal. vi. 1). Is it not, in fact, from thence that the love of our neighbour, of which it is said in the Law as a commandment: *Thou shalt love thy neighbour as thyself* (Luke x. 27) derives its origin? Brotherly affection has without doubt its first beginnings in the deepest feelings of human nature; and from the deeply-seated principle of love to oneself, as from a terrestrial humour, the love of our neighbour draws without doubt a degree of life and increase by which, if grace from on high be breathed upon it, the fruit of charity is brought forth; so that what the soul naturally desires for itself, it considers is not to be denied to another, who seems to have a right to share in it, as being a participant in the same nature, and by the mere right of humanity, but is, on the contrary, to be willingly and gladly shared, as far as it is possible, or there is need of it. Thus, that anointing of sweetness and kindness of disposition which is natural to man, if it be not decayed and ruined by sin, disposes him more to compassionate the faults and offences of sinners than to treat them with indignation and severity.

5. But since according to the word of the Wise man, *Dying flies spoil the sweetness of the ointment* (Eccles. x. 1, Vulg.), and when that is once lost, nature has no means in itself of repairing the loss; a man feels that a sad change has passed over him, and that he has fallen into that state, of which the Scripture says truly: *The imagination of man's heart is evil from his youth* (Gen. viii. 21). That youth was not well spent or good, of which we read in the Scripture that the younger son made demand that his portion of his father's substance should be given over to him, and began to wish to have in his separate possession that which he had enjoyed so happily in common with others, so as to possess alone that, which though it loses nothing by participation, is lost altogether by partition. For *he spent all his substance*, says the Scripture, *in living riotously with harlots* (Luke xv. 13, 14). Who are these harlots? Are they not those carnal concupiscences which banish and destroy the sweetness of this anointing, and of which the Scripture gives us the salutary warning: Go not after thy lusts (Ecclus. xviii. 30). Truly does the Wise Man describe them as 'about to die'; for *the world passeth away, and the lust thereof* (1 John ii. 17). When, therefore, we desire to indulge these, we deprive ourselves of the sweetness of good which is common and social for the sake of that which is individual and selfish. These are undoubtedly those foul and acrid flies which defile in us the beauty of nature, distract our mind with cares and anxieties, and

destroy the pleasure and charm of the common life. It is for this reason that such a man is figured [in the parable] as the younger son, because his nature is corrupted by the unregulated passions of youth, and is without the ripeness and the gathered wisdom which belong to manhood, so that when he has fallen into distress his mind becomes hardened and loveless, and he has no regard for any but himself.

6. It is, then, from the commencement of such a most wicked and unhappy youth as this that the thoughts and inclinations of man turn easily to evil, and that he is by nature more prompt to anger with his neighbour than to compassion for his faults. Thus it is that a man is divested of almost every sentiment of humanity; and while he still needs and expects the help of others, he is disinclined to render help to others in return. [Such] a man, though himself a sinner, judges others severely who are sinners as himself, and even ridicules and scorns them, not considering himself, lest he also should be tempted. From this evil, nature cannot, as I have said, recover by its own strength, nor regain the oil of that original sweetness and kindness which has once been destroyed in it. But yet, what nature is unable to do is in the power of Divine grace. And he upon whom the Holy Spirit shall in His pity deign to pour the salutary unction of His goodness will at once regain his former feelings of goodness and sympathy, and shall obtain from grace even more than he had at first by the gift of nature. It will render him holy in faith and in goodness, and will bestow upon him, not merely oil, but the balsam gathered in the vineyards of Engedi.

7. For there is no doubt that from the 'Fountain of the kid' flow forth gifts more precious still, the anointing of which transforms kids into sheep, which enables sinners to pass from the left hand to the right, after they have been abundantly steeped in the oil of mercy; and thus, where sins abounded, grace much more abounds (Rom. v. 20). Does it not appear to you that such a man is restored in a sense to his humanity, who, putting off the hardness of the spirit of the world, and recovering, by the help of grace, the abundance of human loving-kindness, which carnal lusts, as it were foul and acrid flies, had well-nigh destroyed in him; so that he derives from the humanity which he bears, or, rather, which is himself, the means and the manner of compassionating other men; and regards as something inhuman[1] and brutal, not merely for a man to do to another that which he would not wish to have done to himself, but also the not doing to others whatsoever he wishes they should do to him?

8. This, then, is the source of the oil. But whence is the wine? Evidently from the cluster of the Cyprus grape. For if you love the Lord Jesus with all your heart, with all your soul, with all your strength, could you possibly see and endure without emotion the injuries inflicted upon Him, and the contempt of which He is the object? Assuredly not; you would be at once actuated by a spirit of

---

[1] Another reading is *ritum exhorreat*.

judgment and of zeal, and would be as a strong man to whom wine has given new powers, and being filled with zeal like Phinehas, would say, in the words of David: *My zeal hath consumed me, because mine enemies have forgotten Thy words* (Ps. cxix. 139); and with the Lord: *The zeal of thine house hath eaten me up* (Ps. lxix. 9; John ii. 17). That most fervent zeal, then, is wine expressed from the cluster of Cyprus, and the love of Christ is as a cup which inebriates. For *our God is a consuming fire* (Deut. iv. 24), and a prophet once declared that a fire from above was sent into his bones (Lam. i. 13), insomuch that he burned with the love of God. When, therefore, the love of your neighbour has given you the oil of kindness, and the love of God has procured you the wine of zeal and emulation, you may safely draw near to heal the wounds of him who has fallen among thieves, and be a perfect imitator of that most charitable Samaritan. Safely also may you too say with the Bride: *My Beloved is to me as a cluster of Cyprus grapes in the vineyards of Engedi:* that is to say, the love of Him who is dear to me imparts unto me a zeal for righteousness in feelings of brotherly kindness. But now enough of this; for my weakness warns me, as it does often, to come to a close, and thus obliges me, as you know is frequently the case, to leave my discourses uncompleted, and to reserve for another day the remainder of the verses. But of what account is that? *For I am ready for scourges* (Ps. xxxvii. 18, Douay), and know that what I have hitherto received of chastisement has been less than I deserved. Strike me, O my God; strike me as a servant who labours ill, and perhaps the stripes may be reckoned to me as merits; perhaps Our Lord Jesus Christ, the Spouse of the Church, who found not in me any good to reward, may yet find in my stripes and my sorrows a reason for exercising His mercy, and have pity upon me. He is above all, God blessed for ever. AMEN.

SERMON XLV.

OF THE TWOFOLD BEAUTY OF THE SOUL: HOW THE SOUL SPEAKS TO GOD THE WORD, AND THE WORD TO THE SOUL, AND WHAT LANGUAGE THEY EMPLOY.

'*Behold, thou art fair, my love; behold, thou art fair; thou hast doves' eyes.*'— Cant. i.

HOW beautifully, how exquisitely is all this spoken! From the love of the Bride comes her presumption, from that of the Bridegroom His anger. This is shown by the issue of the matter; for reproof has followed presumption, amendment reproof, and recompense amendment. The Beloved One only is present, the master is withdrawn, the king disappears, dignity is put off, reverence laid aside; for where affection is perfect and strong, there pride gives way. And as Moses once spake unto the Lord, as a friend to his friend (Exod. xxxiii. 11), and the Lord replied to him, so there is now established between the Word of God and the devout soul a relation and communications as close and familiar as that between two neighbours. Nor is that strange; for their love having but one source, it is reciprocal, and their affection mutually manifested. Therefore, words sweeter than honey are exchanged between them, and they exchange looks full of all sweetness, in token of the sacred love which unites them. Then He calls her His beloved one, pronounces repeatedly that she is fair, and receives from her in return similar tokens of affection. Nor is that a superfluous repetition, which is the confirmation of His love, and which perhaps also has some mystery indicated by it.

2. Let us inquire, then, what is the twofold beauty of the soul; for it is that which seems to me to be referred to here. Now, the beauty of the soul is humility. I do not say this of myself, a prophet has said it before me: *Thou shalt wash me with hyssop, and I shall be clean* (Ps. li. 7); signifying the humility of the heart by that herb, which is lowly and of a purifying nature. The writer, who was both king and prophet, having fallen into a grave offence, expresses in these words his good hope that he shall be cleansed, and thus recover his former whiteness of innocence. But the humility of one who has deeply offended, though it may be loved, yet it cannot be admired. But if one who has preserved innocence joins with it humility, does he not seem to you to possess a twofold beauty of the soul? St. Mary lost not holiness, and yet was not wanting in humility. Therefore it was that '*the King desired her beauty*,' because she joined humility to innocence; for, as she herself says: *He hath regarded the humility of His handmaid* (Luke i. 48, Douay). Blessed are they *who have kept undefiled their vestments* (Rev. iii. 4)—that is to say, their simplicity and their innocence, if they are careful also to be clad in the beauty of humility. Assuredly the soul that is found to be such shall hear the words addressed to her: *Behold, thou art fair, My love; behold, thou art fair.* May I, O Lord Jesus, hear Thee say but once to my soul: *Behold, thou art fair.* Do Thou preserve for me, at least, my humility, for I have ill-kept my first robe [of innocence]. I am Thy servant. I do not dare to profess myself Thy friend, for I do not hear Thy repeated testimony to my spiritual fairness. Even to hear it once is sufficient for me. But what shall I do if even that be in question? I know what I will do: I, being a servant, will venerate Thy friend (*amicam*); being but a man deformed and dwarfish, I will dwell in admiration on her perfect beauty; I will rejoice at the voice of the Bridegroom, who Himself admires a fairness so great. Who knows whether I may not at least find grace in the eyes of that friend, that by her favour even I may be found among the number of His friends? For the friend of the Bridegroom remains in silence, yet rejoices greatly because of the Bridegroom's voice. This is His Voice in the ear of the Beloved; let us hear it

and be glad. They are in each other's presence, they are conversing together; let us, too, pause and listen; let no care of this world, no allurement of the flesh, withdraw us from that sacred colloquy.

3. *Behold, thou art fair, My love; behold, thou art fair.* Behold expresses admiration, the rest praise. It is with reason that she is admired, because she has not adopted humility after the loss of holiness, and on account of it, but has retained it while remaining holy. And rightly, too, is she twice over called beautiful, since neither kind of beauty is wanting to her. It is a rare being (*avis*) upon the earth who has not lost innocence, or in whom sanctity, if retained, does not exclude humility; and therefore happy is she who has retained both the one and the other. That she has done so is proved, inasmuch as though conscious of no fault, she does not reject the reproof of the Bridegroom. We, even when we have committed great faults, scarcely suffer ourselves to be reproved; but she, even when she has done no wrong, listens meekly to bitter words addressed to her. For if she desires to behold the glory of her Bridegroom, that is no fault, but rather a ground for praise. And yet when she is blamed she repents, and says: *A bundle of myrrh is my Beloved unto me; He shall lie between my breasts,* which is as if she said: 'That is sufficient for me: I desire to know none but Jesus, and Him crucified.' How great is this humility! Though innocent in every act, she takes upon her the feeling of the penitent, and though she has nothing to repent of, yet she is able to repent. 'Why, then,' you ask, 'is she chidden, if she has done no wrong?' But now listen to the prudence of the Bridegroom, and the dispensation of His grace. For as formerly the obedience of Abraham was tried and made proof of, so now is it with the humility of the Bride. And just as he, when his obedience was complete, heard these words spoken to him: *Now I know that thou fearest God* (Gen. xxii. 12), so in like manner, though in other words, it is said to the Bride, 'I know now that thou art humble;' for that is the significance of what He says: *Behold, thou art fair.* And He repeats the commendation, to show that the beauty of humility is added to the glory of holiness. 'Now I know that thou art fair, not only by the love which I feel for thee, but also by thy humility. I say not now that thou art fairest among women, I praise not thy beauty of cheeks or of neck, as I did aforetime; but I say simply, not in comparison of others, not in part, or with a qualification, but simply that *thou art fair.*'

4. And He adds: *Thou hast the eyes of doves.* Plainly He is still continuing the praise of humility. For He sees that, being blamed and checked for placing so high her researches, she at once, and without delay, lowers them to things simpler, so as to say: *A bundle of myrrh is my Beloved unto me.* There is no doubt a great difference between a Countenance full of glory and a bundle of myrrh, and therefore it is a great mark of humility to suffer the being recalled from the one and to the other. Thus, to say: *Thou hast the eyes of doves* signifies: 'No longer dost thou hold converse with great matters,

nor inquire into subjects too high for thee; but, like that gentle and artless bird, art content with simpler matters, making thy nest in the hollows of the rock (that is to say), abiding in My wounds, and contemplating of thy own free will, as it were with dove-like gaze, the things only which relate to Me Incarnate, and to My Passion.'

5. Or it may be that, because the Holy Spirit appeared in the form of a dove (Matt. iii. 16), it is rather a spiritual vision than a simplicity of vision that is here commended under the term 'dovelike.' If you approve of this supposition, it will be necessary to refer the verse before us to that which was spoken before by the companions of the Bridegroom, when they promised to her pendants of gold, with no intention, as I warned you at the time, of adorning the ears of the body, but rather of developing and training the spiritual hearing.[1] And by this means it follows that, having the heart more completely purified by faith, which cometh by hearing, she is rendered more capable of discerning that which before was beyond her powers. And as by the receiving of these (symbolical) pendants she has obviously obtained an increased power of vision for the discerning of spiritual things, so she has also become pleasing to the Bridegroom, whose preference it is always (as far as relates to Himself) to be contemplated in a spiritual manner. Therefore He numbers this among her praises, and declares: *Thy eyes are those of doves.* Now thou regardest Me, He says, in the spirit, since Christ the Lord is as a spirit before thy face (Lam. iv. 20). Thou art able to do this, because thou hast dove's eyes. Before thou hadst not this power, and so incurred rebuke; now thou mayst behold me as thou wilt, because thou hast a spiritual vision, the eyes of the Dove. This, indeed, is not the grace for which thou madest petition, for not even now art thou capable of that; but this shall suffice thee for the present. Behold Me now to the utmost of thy powers, and as these augment, thou shalt behold Me more clearly; for assuredly, thou shalt be led on from glory to glory (Ps. lxxxiv. 7).

6. I do not think, brethren—I repeat, I do not think—that this Vision, which alone belongs to the present, is either mediocre or common to all, though it be inferior to that which shall one day be enjoyed. This may be inferred from the words which follow, for she goes on to say: *Behold thou art fair, my Beloved.* Now, consider the greatness and high elevation of a soul which claims the right to call Him, who is the Lord of the whole world, her Beloved. For notice that she does not even say simply *Beloved,* but *my Beloved,* to show that she had a right to call Him hers. Assuredly this Vision of Christ must be august and privileged, which confers upon the soul such confidence and authority that it regards the Lord of all, not as her Lord, but as her Beloved. For I suppose that in this instance there is not at all presented to the soul any defined image of the bodily form of Christ, or of the likeness of our weak flesh, or even of His Cross, for in these respects, according to the prophet, *He hath no form nor come-*

[1] See Serm. XLI., *nn.* 2-4.

liness (Is. liii. 2). But that she, beholding Him, now pronounces Him fair and comely, shows that He appeared to her by means of a nobler vision, for the Bridegroom speaks to the Bride face to face, as once He spake to Moses (Exod. xxxiii. 11), and she beholds God clearly, not by symbols and types. Thus, beholding Him in the spirit, by a vision sweet and sublime, she declares Him to be such as in her vision she sees Him to be. Her eyes have seen the King in His beauty; yet not as King, but as her Beloved. One prophet beheld Him upon His throne, high and lifted up (Isa. vi. 1), and of another it is testified that he saw God face to face, and his life was preserved (Gen. xxxii. 30); yet it seems to me that the Bride surpasses both, in that we read that the Lord was beheld by her, and that He was her Beloved. But He says: *If I be the Lord, where is My fear?* (Mal. i. 6). If, then, to them this revelation was attended with fear, for where the Lord is there fear must be [to those who behold Him], I certainly, if the choice were given to me, would prefer the vision of the Bride, and that with so much more willingness and gladness, as I perceive that it is the occasion of a nobler feeling, that is, love. For fear hath torment, but perfect love casteth out fear (1 John iv. 18). Great is the difference between [the Lord] appearing terrible in His doings toward the children of men (Ps. lxvi. 5) and His appearing fairer than the children of men (Ps. xlv. 2). *Behold Thou art fair, my Beloved, yea, pleasant!* These words express affection, not fear.

7. But perhaps thoughts arise in your heart, and you ask doubtfully: 'By what means can the words of the Word, spoken to the soul, and again those of the soul to the Word, be rendered audible, so that the soul should hear the Voice of Him that speaks to her, and praises her as fair, and should pour forth in turn her tribute to Him who has praised her? How can that take place? For it is not the word which speaks, but we speak by the word. Also the soul has no means of speech, except by the words which the bodily organs articulate for her for that purpose.' A very reasonable inquiry; but consider that it is the spirit which speaks, and that [the speaking as well as] the things spoken are to be spiritually understood. As often, then, as you hear or read that the Word and the soul behold each other or converse together, do not imagine that they behold visible bodily forms, or that audible words pass from one to the other. This is what you ought rather to think. The Word is Spirit; the soul is a spirit also; they have faculties [*linguas*] of their own for indicating their presence, and for communicating the one with the other. The tongue of the Word is the favour of His condescension; that of the soul is the fervour of its devotion. The soul which has no devotion is like an infant and speechless, and to such an one no discourse with the Word is possible. Therefore when the Word wishes to speak to the soul, and thus moves His tongue, the soul cannot but hear, for *the Word of God is quick and powerful, and sharper than any two-edged sword, piercing even to the dividing asunder of soul and spirit* (Heb. iv. 12). And, again, when the soul thus addresses the Word, He

cannot possibly be unconscious of it; not only because He is everywhere present, but still more and especially because the tongue of devotion is never stirred to speak, except by an impulse from Him.

8. Therefore for the Word to call a soul *beloved*, and say to it, *thou art fair*, is to pour upon it the grace which shall enable it to love, and to know itself loved. In like manner, when the soul in turn names the Word her Beloved and speaks of Him as full of beauty, it is that she ascribes to Him, without fiction or disguise, the grace that she has to love Him and to be loved by Him; it is that she admires His condescension, and wonders at the greatness of His grace. Indeed, His fairness consists in His love, and that is the greater because it was the earlier (*præveniens*). For this reason it is that she cries in the depths of her heart, and with all the powers of her strongest affections, that she is bound to love Him, and with so much stronger an affection, because He first loved her. Therefore the speech of the Word is an infusion of grace, and the response of the soul is the giving of thanks and glory. She loves so much the more ardently, because she feels that the affection of her Spouse surpasses her own, and her admiration is the greater, because that affection preceded hers. On that account it is that she is not content with saying once that He is full of beauty; she repeats her praise in order to heighten it by repetition.

9. Or perhaps that double phrase may be explained as applying to the two Natures in Christ—in the one the beauty of nature, in the other that of grace. How beautiful art Thou to Thy Angels, O Lord Jesus, in the Form of God, in Thy Eternal Nature, begotten before the morning star, in the splendour of Thy saints, who art Thyself the Form and Splendour of the Substance of the Father, in whom the glory and brightness of life eternal are resplendent from everlasting! How august art Thou to me also, O my Lord, when I contemplate Thee in that state of glory which is Thine! Even when Thou didst empty Thyself of Thy glory, when Thou layedst down the rays of splendour proper to that unfailing Light, even then Thy kindness shone the more brightly, Thy charity was more conspicuous, Thy grace the more radiant. O Star out of Jacob, how beautiful Thou art unto me in Thy rising (Num. xxiv. 17); O Branch springing out of the stem of Jesse (Is. xi. 1), how bright is Thy Flower; O Dayspring from on High, in what joyful light hast Thou visited me, who sat in darkness! (Luke i. 78). What an object of admiration and wonder is He, even to the heavenly Virtues, in His Conception by the Holy Ghost, in His Birth of the Virgin Mary, in the spotless innocence of His Life, in the flowing streams of His doctrine, in the glistering brightness of His miracles, in the mysteries revealed by His Sacraments! In what blaze of glory dost Thou rise, O Sun of Righteousness, from the heart of the earth, after Thy setting [in death]! In what a resplendent vesture (Is. lxiii. 1), O King of glory, dost Thou enter again the highest heaven! At the sight of all these marvels, how can I do otherwise than cry, *All my bones shall say, Lord, who is like unto thee?* (Ps. xxxv. 10).

10. Believe, then, that the Bride, in beholding her Beloved, saw these and similar excellences in Him when she said: *Behold, Thou art fair, my love; behold, Thou art fair.* Nor is it these only, but without doubt some other wonder of the beauty of the higher nature which she had remarked, which transcends our capacity of knowledge, and lies altogether beyond our experience. That repetition points out, then, the perfection of Jesus in each of His two Natures. Hear also how, transported with the sight and at the words of her Beloved, she leaps, as it were, with joy, and sings before Him a nuptial song, full of tender and loving sentiments: *Our bed is flourishing; the beams of our houses are of cedar, our rafters of cypress* (i. 16, Douay). But let us reserve that song of the Bride for another beginning in a newer day; so that, being rendered more willing and active by repose, we may the more readily be glad and rejoice with her, to the praise and glory of her Bridegroom, JESUS CHRIST our LORD, who is above all, God blessed for ever. AMEN.

SERMON XLVI.

OF THE STATE AND COMPOSITION OF THE WHOLE CHURCH. ALSO OF THE MANNER IN WHICH, BY AN ACTIVE LIFE SPENT UNDER OBEDIENCE, THE LIFE OF CONTEMPLATION MAY BE ATTAINED.

'*Our bed is flourishing; the beams of our houses are of cedar, our rafters of cypress.*'—Cant. i. 16.

THIS is an Epithalamium she is singing; and she describes in graceful phrase the nuptial chamber and bed. She invites the Bridegroom to repose; for, indeed, it is better for her to rest and be with Christ. It is only for the sake of saving souls that it is necessary for her to go forth. But now, believing that she has found a suitable opportunity, she announces that the chamber is decked; she points out the couch, as it were, with the finger; she invites, as I have said, the beloved one to rest there; and, like the Apostles going to Emmaus, not being able to endure the fire of love burning within her heart, she constrains Him to accept the hospitality of mind and soul, to abide with her for the night (Luke xxiv. 29, 32), and says with Peter: *Lord, it is good for us to be here* (Matt. xvii. 4).

2. Let us now inquire what is the spiritual significance of all these things. First, it refers to the Church. And I consider that the 'bed' upon which rest is taken means the monasteries and cloisters in which a quiet and peaceable life is passed, exempt from the cares and inquietudes of the world. That bed is said to be decked or adorned, because the life and appointed course of the brethren is adorned and rendered bright by the examples and precepts of our fathers, as if bedecked with fragrant flowers. By 'houses' we are to

understand the great masses of Christians, which those among them
who are set in offices of power and dignity, such as Princes of the
Church and of the State, bind together, and retain them each
strongly in his place, as the beams and rafters of a house retain the
walls, by the just and firm laws laid upon them; lest, if everyone
lived in his own way and at his own pleasure, they should disunite
from each other like walls that begin to bend and spread, and thus
the entire structure of the edifice falls to pieces and is destroyed.
As for the 'rafters,'[1] which are firmly attached to beams, and are a
striking ornament to the mansions of the great, I take the term to
signify the kindly and regular lives and characters of a clergy properly
taught and ordained, and of the rites of the Church rightly performed
and administered. For how shall the Orders of the clergy be able
to subsist, or the charges of the Church be administered, if Princes
did not, like strong and substantial beams, both protect them by
their power, and maintain them by their munificence?

3. If the beams are said to be of cedar, and the crossing-rafters of
cypress, it is, without doubt, because the nature of each of these
kinds of wood has something which befits the meaning intended.
The cedar being a tree of lofty height, and of which the wood is
fragrant and incapable of decay, denotes with sufficient fitness the
qualities needed in those men who are to hold, as it were, the place
of beams in the Church. For those who are set over others need to
be strong and steadfast, hopeful and patient, that their eyes and their
mind should be lifted up to heavenly things; and that, spreading
abroad everywhere the good odour of their faith and life, they should
be able to say with the Apostle: *We are unto God a sweet savour of
Christ in every place* (2 Cor. ii. 15). The cypress, also, being similarly
a fragrant and incorruptible wood, signifies and declares that every
person, whosoever he may be, that is in Holy Orders ought to be of
right faith and of pure life, that he may be worthy to serve as the
ornament of the house of God, and to be in it, as it were, as its
panelled ceiling, enriched with colours and gold. For what saith
the Psalmist: *Holiness becometh Thine House, O Lord, for ever*
(Ps. xciii. 5). In which words are well expressed both the beauty of
holiness, and the endurance of a never-failing grace. It is obviously
necessary that the man who is chosen to be the ornament and
decoration of that House should be himself adorned with goodness
of life and character; and although he ought always to have the
inward witness (that is, of his own conscience), yet he should also be
such an one as has a good testimony from them who are without.
There are other qualities still in these woods, which have no little
relation to those spiritual truths of which we are treating; but I pass
them over for the sake of brevity.

---

[1] *Laquearia* (Vulg.) originally denoted the hollow spaces or panels formed by
planks crossing each other at regular intervals to compose the ceiling of a room;
but in later times they were painted, gilded, or inlaid with ivory and enamels. See
Cheetham's 'Dictionary of Antiquities,' art. Lacunary Work.—ED.

4. As to the well being of the Church, it is happily expressed in a very few words: the authority of prelates, the good life and good report of the clergy, the disciplined obedience of the people, and the peaceful devotion of monks. When in each of these respects all is well, the holy Church, our mother, rejoices in the contemplation of them, and presents them to the sight of her Beloved; she refers all things to His goodness as their cause, knowing that He is the Author and Giver of all good things; nor does she attribute anything to herself. For she says: *Our bed*, and, *The beams of our houses, and the rafters;* this is a sign of her affection, not of her usurping the ownership of these things; the very abundance of her affection gives her such confidence, that she regards nothing which appertains to Him whom she so loves as unconnected with herself. She believes that she is not to be excluded from the companionship of her Spouse, or from the sharing of His repose; inasmuch as she is accustomed to seek, not her own interests, but His. And it is for that reason that she ventures to speak of, as common to both, the bed and the mansion which are His. She is bold to associate herself in the possession of those things which belong to Him, with whom she knows herself to be associated in love. It is not thus with that soul which has not yet given up her own will, but dwells amid her own possessions, and lies down by herself; or, I should say more accurately, not by herself, but who dwells and associates in disorder and shamelessness with harlots; I speak of the lusts of the flesh, with whom that soul squanders its good things, and wastes its portion of the Father's substance, for which it had made request (Luke xv. 12).

5. But is it the case with you, who hear or read these words of the Holy Spirit, that you think some of these things which are said capable of being applied to yourself; that you recognise in your own soul somewhat of the felicity of the Bride which is chanted in this song of love by the Holy Spirit Himself; and yet it is perhaps said to you also that you hear His Voice, but canst not tell whence it cometh, nor whither it goeth (John iii. 8)? Perhaps you desire also the repose of contemplation; and in this you do well, provided that you do not forget the *flowers* with which, as you read, the couch of the Bride is strewed. Therefore do thou take great care similarly to wreathe around thine the blossoms of good works, and to make the exercise of virtues precede that sacred rest, as the flower goes before the fruit. Otherwise, it would be self-indulgent that you should so earnestly desire to rest before you have earned that rest by labour, and you would be neglecting the fruitfulness of Leah in desiring to enjoy only the society of Rachel. But it would be a reversing of the proper order to ask for the reward before having earned it, and to grasp at the mid-day meal before performing the labour, of which the Apostle says: *If a man will not work, neither shall he eat* (2 Thess. iii. 10). And what says the Psalmist? *Through Thy precepts I get understanding* (Ps. cxix. 104), so to teach you that the taste for contemplation is not due except to obedience to God's commandments. Do

not, then, imagine that the love of your own repose is to be in any wise made a hindrance to works of holy obedience, or to the fulfilment of the traditions of the elders. Do not suppose that you will have the company of the Bridegroom for that bed, which you have strewed, not with the flowers of obedience, but with hemlock, and even with weeds and nettles, by your disobedient conduct. When it is thus with you, this is the reason that He will not hear and answer your prayers, and that when you call Him He will not come; for He who is so great a lover of obedience that He preferred to die rather than not to obey [His Father], will assuredly not bestow His gifts upon one who is disobedient. And how should He approve the inane idleness which you call contemplation? For He says by the prophet: *I have laboured with patience* (Jer. vi. 11), referring to the time when, an exile from the heaven of perfect peace, which is His country, He accomplished salvation for us in the midst of the earth. But I fear the more lest that fearful judgment should involve you also which once thundered against the treachery of the Jews in these words: *Your new moons and sabbaths, the calling of assemblies, I cannot away with;* and again: *Your new moons and your appointed feasts My soul hateth; they are a trouble unto Me* (Is. i. 13, 14). And the prophet will weep over you, and say: *The adversaries saw her, and did mock at her sabbaths* (Lam. i. 7). For why shall not an adversary mock at that which the Beloved rejects?

6. I am extremely surprised at the shamelessness of some among us who, after having troubled us all by their singularity, annoyed us by their impatience, and contemned us by their contumacy and rebellion,[1] have, nevertheless, actually the boldness to invite, and that with importunate prayers, the Lord of all purity to come into the foul resting-place of their conscience. But what does the Lord say to such? *When ye spread forth your hands, I will hide Mine eyes from you; yea, when ye make many prayers, I will not hear* (Is. i. 15). And why? Because your bed, far from being strewed with flowers, is defiled with filth. And do you dare to invite the King of glory thither? Do you think that He will rest there for a moment, or are you doing this to ensure reproof to yourself? The centurion in the Gospel prayed that the Lord would not come under his roof, because of his unworthiness, and yet there was not found such faith as His even in all Israel (Matt. viii. 8, 10); and you would have the Lord to enter your soul, reeking as it is with the foul vestiges of your vices? The Prince of the Apostles cries out: *Depart from me, for I am a sinful man, O Lord* (Luke v. 8); and do you say: 'Come to

---

[1] There is added here in many editions '*sua inobedientia coinquinaverint*'; but this clause is wanting in most MSS., and is a mere repetition of the words which precede. The earliest editions contain them, but omit '*suâ contumaciâ et rebellione contempserint.*' A certain degree of surprise may be felt that in a community of so high a character as that of Clairvaux, any members should be found so insubordinate as those referred to by St. Bernard in this passage. But the fact is shown still more clearly in Serm. LXXXIV., n. 4, and in the 'Life,' Bk. vii. It is evident that the evil are mingled with the good everywhere.

me, Lord, and enter into my heart, for I am holy?' *Be ye all of one mind*, says the same Apostle, *love as brethren* (1 Peter iii. 8). And he who was 'a chosen vessel' says : *Lifting up holy hands without wrath or doubting* (1 Tim. ii. 8). Do you see, then, how the Prince of the Apostles and the Apostle of the Gentiles agree and speak in the same spirit with regard to the peace and tranquillity which the person who prays ought to possess? You may stretch out your hands to God all the day long, you who all the day long are engaged in distressing your brethren, destroying tranquillity, and separating yourself from unity [but it is to no purpose].

7. 'What, then,' you ask, 'would you have me to do?' In the first place, I would have you cleanse your conscience from every defilement of anger, and murmuring, and envy, and dispute; and that you should hasten to banish from the hiding-place of your heart all that evidently conflicts with the peace which ought to reign among brethren, and the obedience due to your elders. In the next place, I should wish you to adorn yourself with the flowers of good works and laudable studies of every kind, and seek the sweet perfumes of all virtues ; or, in other words, *whatsoever things are true, whatsoever things are honest, whatsoever things are just, whatsoever things are pure, whatsoever things are lovely, whatsoever things are of good report, if there be any virtue, if there be any praise of discipline, think on these things* (Phil. iv. 8, Vulg.), and endeavour to employ yourself in them. To that end you shall call upon the Bridegroom, and then with confidence, because when you shall bring Him into your soul you, too, shall be able to declare truthfully, *our bed is adorned ;* because your conscience shall everywhere be fragrant with the perfumes of piety, of peace, of gentleness, of justice, of obedience, of cheerfulness, of humility. Let this suffice as regards the bed.

8. As to the *house.* Each person, provided that he walks, not according to the flesh, but according to the Spirit, ought to regard himself as spiritually a house of God. *The Temple of God is holy*, says the Apostle St. Paul, *which Temple ye are* (1 Cor. iii. 17). Take careful heed, then, brethren, of that spiritual building, which is no other than your own selves, lest, perhaps, when it begins to rise to a loftier height, if the beams of it be not strong, firmly fixed, and well bound and braced together, it should totter and fall; take careful heed, I say, that the beams you use are such as are sound and will not decay, such as are massive and will not bend—that is to say, use *the fear of the Lord, which is clean, and endureth for ever* (Ps. xix. 9); and *patience,* of which it is written, *the patience of the poor shall not perish for ever* (Ps. ix. 18) ; *long-suffering,* also, which perseveres without bending under the weight of the structure laid upon it, whatever it be, and is extended even unto the unending ages of the life of blessedness, according to the saying of our Saviour in the Gospel : *Whosoever endureth unto the end, the same shall be saved* (Matt. x. 22); and, above all, use *charity,* which never faileth (1 Cor. xiii. 8), because, as is said in this Song, it is *as strong as death* (Cant. viii. 6), though

jealousy be cruel as the grave. Lastly, take careful heed to underprop and brace firmly together these, the great beams of the structure, with other timbers equally precious and beautiful, if you have it in your power so to do; they will serve to form the panelled and fretted ceiling, and to render the house beautiful; I mean the utterance and teaching of wisdom or knowledge, prophecy, the gift of healing, interpretation of the Scriptures, and other such gifts, which are known to serve rather to the beautifying and perfecting of the character than to be necessary to the salvation of the soul. Concerning these I have no precept to give you; I have only this advice: that since, as it is abundantly evident, timbers (so to speak) of this kind must be sought with much labour, are found with difficulty, and, if found, are not made fit for use without considerable risk, for our earth, especially in these times, is found to produce but few such; for these reasons my counsel and warning to you is, that such as these should not be too eagerly sought for, but that you should make use of other and humbler woods for the panelling of your roofs, which, though they be less splendid in appearance, are shown by experience to be not less useful and strong, and, moreover, are to be obtained with far greater safety and ease.

9. I earnestly desire, also, that I may be possessed of an abundance of those other woods which grow so freely in the garden of the Bridegroom—that is, the Church—I mean peace, goodness, gentleness, joy in the Holy Ghost, the showing mercy with cheerfulness, the giving with simplicity, the rejoicing with them that do rejoice, and weeping with them that weep. Do you not think that a house is (as far as regards the ceiling) sufficiently well adorned when you perceive that it is panelled with such woods as these, skilfully arranged, and in sufficient quantity? *Lord, I have loved the honour of Thy House* (Ps. xxvi. 8). Bestow upon me always, I entreat, the materials wherewith to adorn the chamber of my own conscience, and of that of others, so that it may be made ready for Thy searching view. With these I shall be content. There will be those also who, following my judgment in this matter, will be content also, because they believe that Thou wilt be so; the other [and higher endowments] I relinquish to holy Apostles and apostolic men. But do you also, my beloved, even though you are without those more precious woods, yet if these others are yours, have no fear; approach with confidence to that chief corner-stone, elect and precious, and be ye also built up, as living stones, upon the foundation of the Apostles and Prophets, into a spiritual house, so that you are [made to be] a holy Priesthood, to offer spiritual sacrifices acceptable to God, by JESUS CHRIST our Lord, the Bridegroom of the Church, who is above all, God blessed for ever. AMEN.

SERMON XLVII.

OF THE THREEFOLD FLOWER [OF HOLINESS], NAMELY, OF VIRGINITY, OF MARTYRDOM, AND OF GOOD WORKS; AND OF THE DEVOTION WITH WHICH WE SHOULD PARTICIPATE IN DIVINE SERVICE.

'*I am the Rose of Sharon, and the Lily of the valleys.*'—Cant. ii. 1.

I SUPPOSE that this recalls what the Bride had said in commendation of their couch, that it was decked with flowers. For, lest she should take to herself the praise of the flowers wherewith the couch is decked and the chamber adorned, the Bridegroom replies that He is Himself the Rose of the plain [of Sharon]; that the flowers do not grow in the chamber, but in the plain, from which is derived their beauty and their fragrance. Lest, then, any should have it in their power to reproach His Bride, and to say to her: *What hast thou which thou didst not receive? now if thou didst receive it, why dost thou glory, as if thou hadst not received it?* (1 Cor. iv. 7) He Himself, as a solicitous lover and kindly censor, deigns to point out benignantly to His beloved to whom she ought to attribute the beauty and the fragrance of her couch in which she was glorying. *I am the Rose of Sharon,* He says; it is to Me you owe that of which you boast. We are here warned, then, to our great benefit, that it behoves us by no means to glorify ourselves; if any glory, *let him glory in the Lord* (2 Cor. x. 17). So much with regard to the letter; let us now examine, with the help of Him who is the subject of it, into the spiritual sense which it contains.

2. In the first place, notice that there are three conditions referred to in which a flower may be—in the plain, in the garden, and on the couch: and then you will more easily understand why the speaker has chosen to call Himself, by preference, the Rose of [the field of] Sharon. Flowers grow and bloom in fields and in gardens, but not in the chamber. There they show their beauty and exhale their fragrance, but not erect upon the stem, as in the place where they have grown: they are severed and prostrate, because they have not grown there, but have been brought. They have to be watered, and to be frequently renewed, because they do not long retain their beauty and freshness. If, as I have foreshown in another discourse, the couch strewn with flowers means the soul stored with good works, then, to maintain the same metaphor, you see clearly that it is not sufficient to do once or twice merely that which is right, but that it is needful to add new deeds of good constantly to the former, so that having sown deeds of blessing, you may reap blessings also. Otherwise the flowers of good works wither and fall, and [the adornment formed of them] speedily loses all beauty and strength, unless they are continually renewed by fresh blossoms of good works piled upon the old. Thus much as regards the *chamber*.

3. In the garden and in the plain it is not so. There flowers once produced are constantly nourished, and so are long maintained in the beauty natural to them. Yet there is this difference between them, that the garden, in order to produce flowers, needs the labour and the skill of man who cultivates it; but the field produces its bloom naturally, and of its own accord, without any aid from the industry of man. Now, do you already perceive what is signified by that field, which, though neither furrowed by the ploughshare, nor broken by the hoe, nor enriched by manure, is yet rendered beautiful by its carpet of flowers, upon which, without doubt, rests a blessing from the Spirit of the Lord? *See*, it is said in the Scripture, *the smell of my son is as the smell of a field which the Lord hath blessed* (Gen. xxvii. 27). That flower of the field was not as yet clad in its full beauty, yet it already exhaled fragrance, which the holy and aged Patriarch, though feeble in body, perceived beforehand in the spirit, as his joyful exclamation shows; for though he was deprived of sight, its sweet scent was very apparent to him. It was not fitting, then, that the Bridegroom should call Himself a flower of the chamber, because He is a flower whose bloom is perpetual; nor yet of the garden, lest He might seem to be engendered by the operation of man. But He says with the fullest fitness and grace: *I am the Rose of the field of Sharon;* for He appeared without any effort or cooperation of man, and when He had appeared He was at no time subject to corruption, according to the saying of the Prophet: *Thou shalt not suffer Thy Holy One to see corruption* (Ps. xvi. 10).

4. But let me, if you please, give you another explanation of this, which seems to me quite worth consideration; for why has the Wise Man said that the Spirit manifests Himself in many forms, unless that He is wont frequently to hide under the bark, as it were, of the same text several and diverse spiritual senses? According, then, to the division which I gave before of the various states of flowers, there are three distinct blooms—virginity, martyrdom, and a holy life.[1] Virginity is the flower in the garden; martyrdom that in the field; a holy life that in the chamber. Rightly is virginity compared to a flower in the garden, inasmuch as it is nearly related to modesty—it flies from publicity, it rejoices in concealment, it is willing to endure rule and discipline. Furthermore, in a garden flowers are enclosed, while in the field they are open to the view of all, and in the chamber they are strewed or scattered. So we read: *A garden enclosed, a fountain sealed* (Cant. iv. 12), which phrase expresses the bulwark of modesty, and the inviolate defence which preserves the sanctity of a virgin soul, provided that its sanctity is both in body and spirit. *Martyrdom*, again, is well said to be a flower of the *field*, since martyrs are exposed to the mockery of all, and made a spectacle both to Angels and men. Is not theirs the pitiable condition which is described in the Psalms?—*We are become a reproach to our neighbours, a scorn and derision to them that are round about us* (Ps. lxxix. 4).

---

[1] *Actio bona.*

The good actions of a holy life, also, are well compared to flowers in a chamber, for they produce the testimony of a quiet and safe conscience. After a good work the repose of quiet contemplation is entered upon more securely; and the more fully a man is conscious of not having been wanting through inertness or love of self in the performance of good works, the more confidence will he have in attempting to view and to investigate deeper and loftier truths.

5. In a certain sense all these things represent to us the Lord JESUS. He is the Flower of the *garden*, the Virgin Birth of a Virgin Mother, herself a shoot [from the stem of David].[1] He is the Flower of the *field*—a martyr, the pattern of martyrdom, and the crown of martyrs. He was led forth out of the city, He suffered 'without the camp,' He was raised upon the Cross to be seen of men, He was made the object of universal scorn. He is the Flower of the *chamber* also; the mirror and the model of every kind of beneficence, as He Himself declared in His protest to the Jews: *Many good works have I showed you from My Father* (John x. 32); and the Scripture also testifies of Him: *He went about doing good, and healing all that were oppressed* (Acts x. 38). If, then, each of these three represents the Lord, for what reason has He preferred to call Himself the Flower *of the field* only? It was doubtless that He might encourage the Church, His Bride, to endure the persecution which He knew was impending over each soul which should desire to live godly in Christ JESUS. He does this that He may make it the better known in what He most desires to find imitators. It is because the Church, as I have said elsewhere, always desires repose and quiet, while He, on the contrary, urges her to earnest effort, forewarning her that *we must through much tribulation enter into the kingdom of God* (Acts xiv. 22). On which account also, when He had espoused to Himself the new Church which He had founded upon the earth, He said [to her members]: *The time cometh that whosoever killeth you will think that he doeth God service* (John xvi. 2); and again: *If they have persecuted Me, they will also persecute you* (xv. 20), and many other similar sayings, which you may easily find for yourselves in the Gospels, in which He warns them to be prepared to endure suffering.

6. *I am the Rose of Sharon and the Lily of the valleys.* She then points to the couch; but He summons her to the plain—that is, He excites her to vigorous effort. He regards it as the most persuasive argument possible to her to enter upon this struggle that He should propose Himself to her either as an example for one engaged in the struggle, or a reward for one that has overcome in it. The words may be understood in either of these two senses. Thou, O Lord JESUS, art to me both a mirror of endurance and the reward of enduring. The one is a powerful incentive; the other a great encouragement. By the example of Thy valour Thou dost teach my hands to war; by the Presence of Thy Majesty Thou dost crown me after the victory. Whether I view Thee as a combatant in the midst

---

[1] The terseness of the Latin here, '*virgo, virgâ, virgine,*' is admirable.—ED.

of the strife [with evil], or regard Thee as at once the Bestower of the crown of victory, and that crown itself; in either case Thou dost attract me wonderfully to Thyself; in either capacity Thou art as a strong cable to draw me after Thee. 'Draw me; we will run after Thee.' Willingly do I follow; more willingly still do I enjoy the fruits [of obedience]. If Thou, O Lord, art so good to those who seek Thee, what shall Thy goodness be to those who find?[1] *I am the Flower of the field.* Let him who loves Me come into the field; let him not refuse to engage in the combat with Me and for Me, that he may have it in his power to say with St. Paul: *I have fought a good fight* (2 Tim. iv. 7).

7. And as it is not the proud and arrogant, but rather the humble, who do not presume that they are able to do anything as of themselves, that are really fit for martyrdom, so the Lord adds: *I am the Lily of the valleys*—that is to say, the crown of the humble, wishing to mark by the commanding height of this flower over others, the special glory of their future exaltation.[2] For there will be a time when *every valley shall be exalted, and every mountain and hill shall be made low* (Is. xl. 4), and then shall appear that splendour of eternal life—the lily, so to speak, not of the hills, but of the valleys. *The righteous*,[3] says the prophet, *shall grow as the lily* (Hos. xiv. 5); and who is righteous except he be humble? Thus, when the Lord bent Himself to the hands of His servant John, and the Baptist was stricken with awe of His Majesty, the Lord said: *Suffer it to be so now, for thus it becometh us to fulfil all righteousness* (Matt. iii. 15), showing that He considered the consummation of righteousness to consist in perfect humility. The righteous man, then, is humble; he is of the valley. And we also, if we are found humble, shall grow as the lily, and bloom for ever before the Lord. Shall he not, then, truly and completely show himself the lily of the valleys, when the Lord shall

---

[1] Comp. the hymn *Jubilus Rhythmicus, De Nomine Jesu:*

'*Quam pius es petentibus
Quam bonus Te quarentibus
Sed quid invenientibus?*'

This is one of the coincidences in thought and expression (of which there are not a few) between the prose works of St. Bernard and some of the hymns which have come down to us under his name, which show without doubt that if the latter were not written by St. Bernard *propriâ manu* (which is, upon the whole, the more probable conclusion) they are, at the least, a *cento* of Bernardine phrases. But see M. Hauréau, 'Des Poèmes Latins attribués a St. Bernard,' p. 63 (Paris, 1890). Compare also Serm. IV., *De Diversis, n.* 1.—ED.

[2] The term 'lily of the valleys' suggests to the English reader the modest clustered stalks of the *Convallaria majalis*, with their white pendent flowers. But this flower is a native of Britain, and, as far as I know, is not found at all in Palestine. There is much difficulty is exactly determining the flower intended here by the word *shûshân*. The white lotus, tulip, or amaryllis, and the 'Crown Imperial,' have been suggested by various commentators as being meant. But the flower which seems best to satisfy the various requirements of this and other passages of Scripture is the scarlet martagon (*Lilium Chalcedonicum*), which grows in profusion throughout the Levant. See Matt. vi. 28, Luke xii. 27.—ED.

[3] 'Israel' in the passage quoted.—ED.

change the body of our humility, and make it like unto the Body of His Glory (Phil. iii. 21)? He does not say 'our body,' but 'the body of our humility'; and thus signifies that it is only those who are humble who shall be rendered glorious with the wonderful and immortal splendour of that Divine Lily. Thus much, then, with regard to the words of the Bridegroom, in which He testifies that He is the Rose of the field of Sharon, and the Lily of the valleys.

8. It would be interesting to go on here without a break to comment on what He says with regard to His Bride most dear; but the time does not permit. For by our Rule (Rule S. Bened., c. 43) nothing must be preferred to 'the Service of God,'[1] which is the name that our father Benedict desired to be given to the solemnities of Divine worship, which are offered day by day in our oratory, thus showing more clearly how desirous he was that we should apply ourselves with all our heart to that holy work. Therefore I warn and entreat you, beloved, always to occupy yourselves in the praises of God with pure hearts and earnest minds. With *earnestness*, so as to present yourselves at the worship of the Lord, as well with willingness and gladness, as with reverence; not with laziness and sleepiness, not yawning, not keeping silence, not cutting your words short, or even passing over some altogether, not chanting through the nose or between the teeth, with broken and lowered voice, in a lazy and effeminate fashion, but pronouncing the words of the Holy Spirit with manly and earnest voices, which correspond with the dignity of the subjects of which they speak. And *purely* also—that is to say, so as to occupy your thoughts while you are chanting with nothing else than the words which you are chanting. I do not refer only to the avoiding vain and idle thoughts; those also should at that hour, and in that place at least, be repressed which relate to the duties and occupations which those brethren who are entrusted with various[2] functions are obliged, at other times, for the common good, and, as it were, of necessity, to employ their thoughts upon. I do not counsel you to carry with you when you go into the choir even those thoughts which you have derived from the books which you have been recently reading while sitting in the cloister, or those which have come to you from my voice, in this lecture-hall (*auditorio*) of the Holy Spirit. They are, indeed, to edification; but they do not edify you when you reflect upon them while you are chanting. For the Holy Spirit does not regard as acceptable that which you allow to obtrude at such an hour, which has no concern with your immediate duty, and occasions the neglect of a part of it. We are always capable, by His holy inspiration, of making our will conformable to His Divine Will; through the grace and mercy of Him who is the Bridegroom of the Church, our Lord JESUS CHRIST, Who is above all, God blessed for ever. AMEN.

[1] *Operi Dei*.
[2] The brethren who were deputed to discharge various exterior duties are distinguished from the cloistered or choir brethren in Serm. IX., *De Diversis*, *n.* 4, and farther on in Serm. LVII., *n.* 11.

SERMON XLVIII.

OF THE PRAISES WHICH THE BRIDE AND THE BRIDEGROOM ADDRESS RECIPROCALLY TO EACH OTHER; AND HOW BY THE SHADOW OF CHRIST IS TO BE UNDERSTOOD HIS FLESH AND FAITH IN HIM.

'*As the lily among thorns,*[1] *so is my love among the daughters.*'—Cant. ii. 2.

THEY are not good daughters who, like thorns, pierce and trouble. Consider the evil race of plants which our earth produces, since it was cursed by sin. *Thorns and thistles,* saith the Scripture, *shall it bring forth to thee* (Gen. iii. 18). As long as the soul is clothed in flesh, its course lies among thorns; nor can it avoid having to bear the inquietude of temptations, and the sharp piercing of troubles. If the Bride is a lily, according to the words of the Bridegroom, let her understand with what vigilance and care she ought to watch over her conduct, surrounded as she is on all sides with thorns, of which the sharp points encounter her everywhere. For the tender substance of a flower is unable to endure the slightest puncture of a thorn without injury. Do you feel, then, with how great need and propriety the Psalmist exhorts us to *serve the Lord with fear* (Ps. ii. 11); and the Apostle also, when he bids us *work out your own salvation with fear and trembling* (Phil. ii. 12)? They had learned the truth of that saying by their own experience as friends of the Bridegroom, whose course was full of difficulty, and believed that it applied truly to their souls: *As a lily among thorns, so is My love among the daughters.* One of them, in fact, says: *I am turned in my anguish, while the thorn is fastened* (Ps. xxxi. 4, Douay). And it was well that he was thus pierced, since by the anguish of the wound he was turned to repentance. The piercing of the thorns is good for you if it brings you to repent. Many correct their fault when they feel the penalty of it; and such may take these words for their own. A fault is a thorn, so also is its punishment; and in like manner a false brother, or an evil neighbour, may be considered as a thorn.

2. *As a lily among thorns, so is My love among the daughters.* O lily, bloom bright, shining and beautiful, but tender and delicate, doubters and subverters are all around thee! Among the thorns, what caution and circumspection you have need of! The world is full of thorns; they are on the earth and in the air, and even in your own flesh. To live among these thorns and

---

[1] Dr. Thomson, 'The Land and the Book,' i. 304, gives an interesting illustration of this phrase in his account of the Hûleh lily: 'It is very large, and the three inner petals meet above and form a gorgeous canopy, such as art never approached, and king never sat under, even in his utmost glory. . . . This flower delights most in the valleys, but is also found on the mountains: it grows among thorns, and I have sadly lacerated my hands in extricating it from them. Nothing can be in higher contrast than the luxuriant velvety softness of this lily and the crabbed, tangled hedge of thorns about it.'—ED.

not to be torn by them, is the effect of Divine power, not of any efforts of your own. But *be of good cheer*, said the Lord, *I have overcome the world* (John xvi. 33). Even though in looking forward you see troubles and trials, as it were the sharp points of thorns threatening you, yet let not your heart be troubled, neither let it be afraid, remembering that *tribulation worketh patience, and patience experience, and experience hope, and hope maketh not ashamed* (Rom. v. 3). Consider the lilies of the field, how they grow and shine bravely even in the midst of thorns. If God so care for the grass of the field, which to-day is, and to-morrow is cast into the oven (Matt. vi. 28-30), how much more shall He care for her who is His very dear and cherished Bride! Assuredly *the Lord preserveth all them that love Him* (Ps. cxlv. 20). *As a lily among thorns, so is My love among the daughters.* It is no small proof of virtue to live a good life among the depraved, to preserve the pureness of innocence, and gentleness of character, among the evil-disposed; it is a still greater one to be peaceful with those who are hostile to peace, and to show yourself a friend to your enemies themselves. That will evidently constitute a special degree of likeness to the lily, which does not cease to adorn and beautify with its own fairness the very thorns which pierce it. Does it not seem to you that this is to become a lily in truth, to fulfil in a certain way the perfection taught in the Gospel, in which we are bidden to pray for those who despitefully use us, to do good to them which hate us? (Luke vi. 27, 28). Do you, then, do likewise, and your soul shall be dear to the Lord, and He shall praise you, and say of you: *As a lily among thorns, so is My love among the daughters.*

3. We read farther on: *As the apple-tree among the trees of the wood, so is my Beloved among the sons* (ii. 3). To the commendations of the Bridegroom the Bride renders her praise in return; to praise Him is to acknowledge and to admire the Being who is truly worthy of all praise, and to be praised by Him is to be rendered deserving of the praises given. And as the Bridegroom has praised her under the figure of a flower of surpassing beauty, so she declares His unmatched glory and eminence by comparing Him to a tree of great excellence. Nevertheless, it seems to me that the tree named is not so beautiful as some others, so that it is not fully worthy to be employed as a comparison, not being able to set forth sufficiently all His praise. Nor, indeed, does the Bride seem to have estimated it very highly, inasmuch as she puts it in comparison only with the trees of the forest,[1] which are sterile, or, at least, unable to produce fruits fit for human food. Why, then, are better and nobler trees omitted, and this of but moderate merit brought forward for the purpose of setting forth the praise of the Bridegroom? Ought He, who has not received the Spirit by measure (John iii. 34), to have this measured praise given to Him? It seems to me that He, who has no equal, is spoken of in the making of this similitude[2] as if there

---

[1] *Inter ligna silvarum.*
[2] Some writers have been desirous to understand here by *malus* (תפוח, μῆλον

might be a superior to Him. What shall we say to these things? I confess that the praise is small; but this is because He who receives it is not considered in His greatness. For He is not spoken of here as the Lord who *is great, and greatly to be praised* (Ps. cxlv. 3), but as He who, though He is the Lord, is a little Child, and is greatly to be loved. For *unto us a Child is born* (Is. ix. 6).

4. Therefore it is not His Majesty that is exalted here, but His Humility that is commended; and this is reasonable and right, because the weakness of God is stronger than men, and the foolishness of God is wiser than men (1 Cor. i. 25). Those [men] are as barren trees of the forest, inasmuch as, according to the Prophet, *they are all gone aside, they are become unprofitable together; there is none that doeth good, no not one* (Ps. xiii. 3, Douay). Alone among the trees of the forest the Lord Jesus is a tree bearing fruit—I mean with respect to His Manhood—and though set above the sons of men He is made a little lower than the Angels (Ps. viii. 5). For by a wonderful mystery He both, in becoming Flesh, made Himself to be a little lower than the Angels, and, remaining God, always retained the Angels in subjection to Him. *Thou shalt see*, says the Scripture, *Angels ascending and descending upon the Son of Man* (John i. 51), because that in one and the same Man, who is Christ Jesus, they both sustain the weakness and humbly adore the Majesty. But as the Bride finds greater sweetness in considering Him in His humility, she extols with greater willingness His grace, she magnifies His mercy, she is lost in wonder at His condescension. Her delight is to admire [in Him] a Man among men, not God among the Angels; just as an apple-tree among the trees of the forest is indisputably superior, but not so evidently among the trees of a garden. Nor does she consider that His praises are diminished when the goodness and kindness of His actions are raised still more highly by the thought of His physical weakness. For if, on the one side, she retrenches somewhat from His praise, on the other she fully supplies it, and forbears to dilate upon the glory of His Greatness that she may extol still more the grace of His condescension. For as the Apostle says that the weakness of God is stronger, and the foolishness of God wiser, than men, but does not say 'than Angels'; and as the Psalmist declares of the Bridegroom: *Thou art fairer than the children of men* (Ps. xlv. 2), but does not say 'fairer than Angels,' so when the Bride speaks here, assuredly by the same Spirit, of the Man-God under the figure of a fruit-bearing tree as compared with forest trees, the intention plainly was to exalt Him above all the favour of men, but not above the excellence of Angels.

5. *As the apple-tree among the trees of the wood, so is my Beloved among the sons.* Most fitly is it said *among the sons*, because, being the Only-Begotten Son of His Father, He has made it His object,

---

Sept.) some nobler fruit-tree than the apple, as, for example, the quince, citron, or orange; but the received rendering seems to be correct.—ED.

and without jealousy, to acquire for Him many sons, whom He is not ashamed to call His brothers, so that He may be the first-born among many brethren. But He, who is the Son by *Nature*, is of right preferred to all those adopted sons, who are children by *grace*. Just, also, is the simile, *as the apple-tree*, to Him who, like a fruitful tree, affords a refreshing shadow as well as valuable fruit. Is not that truly a fruit-bearing tree, whose flowers are the fruit of honour and riches? (Ecclus. xxiv. 17). Assuredly He is a tree of life to them that lay hold upon Him (Prov. iii. 18). All the trees of the forest, however fair and however great they be, shall not be compared unto Him; not even those who seem to be helpful by their prayers and their ministry, by their teaching or their holy example; for Christ alone, the Wisdom of God, is the Tree of Life (Rev. xxii. 2), the Living Bread which came down from heaven and giveth life unto the world (John vi. 41, 33).

6. Therefore it is that she goes on to say: *I sat down under His shadow with great delight, and His fruit was sweet to my taste.* She might well long for the shadow of Him, from whom she has both grateful shelter, and will receive needful nourishment. Other trees of the forest afford, indeed, a shadow from the heat, but they have not the Bread of Life, the immortal fruits of salvation. For there is one Author of Life, and One Mediator between God and men, the Man Christ Jesus (1 Tim. ii. 5), and it is He who says to His Bride: *I am thy salvation* (Ps. xxxv. 3), and, *Moses gave you not that Bread from Heaven, but My Father giveth you the True Bread from Heaven* (John vi. 32). On this account, then, she had desired greatly the shadow of Christ, because it is He alone who shelters her from the hot breath of vices, and also fills her with the refreshment and joy of virtue. His Shadow is His Human Nature, and [that which brings me under the shelter of] His Shadow is faith. The Human Nature of Her Son it was which overshadowed Mary; it is faith in my Lord which overshadows me. I might, indeed, say that His Flesh overshadows me also, since it is eaten by me in a mystery. The Blessed Virgin also experienced that shadow of faith, as is shown by the words spoken of her: *And blessed is she who believed* (Luke i. 45). So a prophet says: *The breath of our mouth, Christ the Lord . . . under His shadow we shall live among the Gentiles.*[1] Under His shadow among the Gentiles, but in His light among the Angels. We are in the shadow as long as we walk by faith, not by sight; and, therefore, the just, who lives by faith, is in the shadow. But he who lives by the understanding, happy is he, because he is not in the shadow but in the light. David was a righteous man, and he walked by faith when he addressed this prayer to God: *Give me understanding, that I may learn Thy commandments, and I shall live* (Ps. cxix. 73, 144). He knew that understanding shall succeed to faith, that the light of life and the life of light shall be revealed to the understand-

[1] Lam. iv. 20, but inexactly quoted. Rouald, Tiraqueau, and Horst, here read *vivimus*.

ing. It is needful to come first to the shadow, and so to attain to that of which it is the shadow; since, as says the Prophet: If ye will not believe me, ye shall not understand (Is. vii. 9, and xliii. 10).

7. You see that faith is both life and the shadow of life. For the life which is spent in enjoyments, since it is not lived by faith, is but death and the shadow of death. For the widow, saith St. Paul, *who liveth in pleasure is dead while she liveth* (1 Tim. v. 6). And *to be carnally minded is death* (Rom. viii. 6). It is also the shadow of death—of that death which torments everlastingly. We, too, have sometime been in the darkness and shadow of death, while we lived according to the flesh and not according to faith; we were, indeed, already dead to righteousness, and soon to be swallowed up by that which is the second death. For it is certain that our life, as it was then, has drawn as near to death as the shadow is near to the body which casts it, and each of us may say with the Psalmist: *Unless the Lord had been my helper, my soul had almost dwelt in hell* (Ps. xciv. 17, Douay). But now we have passed from the shadow of death to the shadow of life, or, rather, *we have passed from death unto life* (1 John iii. 14), and are living in the shadow of Christ; if, that is to say, we are of a truth living and not still dead. For I do not think that a person who has been in the shadow lives in it forthwith, because it is plain that not everyone who has faith lives by faith. But *faith without works is dead* (James ii. 26), and that which itself has not life is incapable of imparting it. That is why, after the Prophet had said: 'Christ the Lord is the Spirit before our face,' he goes on to say: 'under His shadow we shall live among the Gentiles' (Lam. iv. 20). Do you, then, take care, according to the example of the Prophet, to live in His shadow, that hereafter you may reign in His light; for He has not only the shadow, He has also the light. Through the flesh He is the shadow of faith, through the spirit He is the light of knowledge. He is Flesh and He is Spirit. He is Flesh to those who remain in the flesh, and He is 'the Spirit before our face'—that is to say, in the future He shall be, provided that, forgetting those things which are behind and pressing forward to those things which are before, we attain to the experience of the truth in those words: *It is the Spirit that quickeneth, the flesh profiteth nothing* (John vi. 64). Nor do I forget that the Apostle, while still sojourning in the flesh, has said: *Even though we have known Christ after the flesh, yet now henceforth know we Him no more* (2 Cor. v. 16). But this was His peculiar privilege: we who have never been so highly favoured as to be caught up into Paradise and into the third heaven, we still are nourished by the Flesh of Christ, we venerate His sacred Mysteries, we order our lives by His example, we keep the faith, and, without question, we live in His shadow.

8. *I sat down under His shadow with great delight.* Perhaps the Bride is here extolling herself as having a happier experience than the Prophet, inasmuch as she has sat under His shadow, not that she lives in it. For to be seated is to rest. It is more to rest in His

shadow than to live in it, as it is more to live in it than simply to be in it. The Prophet predicates of himself that which is common to many: 'We shall live;' but the Bride, who has a special privilege, states it with pride: 'I sat down.' She does not say (as he has done) 'we' in the plural, but 'I,' to mark that this is peculiar to herself. Where, then, we live with labour, we who serve with fear, being conscious of our offences, there the Bride, loving and devoted, sweetly rests. Fear is followed by a penalty, but love by sweetness; wherefore she says: *His fruit was sweet to my taste*, signifying the heavenly charm of the contemplation which she had obtained when sweetly lifted up by love. Doubtless that is in the shadow, because it takes place, as it were, through a glass and darkly. But a time shall come when the light shall brighten to the dawn, the shadows shall wane until they wholly disappear: and then, in the place of them, shall begin a vision as clear as it is constant; it shall be not only sweetness to the taste, but satisfaction, yet without surfeit, to the whole nature. Where the Bride makes pause, let us pause too; glorifying, for the portion given to us of spiritual dainties delightful to our taste, Him who is the Head of the whole family in heaven and earth (Eph. iii. 15), and the Bridegroom of the Church, Our Lord JESUS CHRIST, who is above all, God blessed for ever. AMEN.

SERMON XLIX.

HOW CHARITY IS REGULATED BY DISCRETION, SO THAT ALL THE MEMBERS OF THE CHURCH, THAT IS, THE ELECT, ARE HELD TOGETHER BY MUTUAL BONDS.

'*He brought me into the banqueting house, and His banner over me was love.*'—Cant. ii. 4.

ACCORDING to the obvious meaning of the text, the Bride, after an interview, as sweet as it was confidential, with her Beloved, according to her prayer, returns, on His departure, to her maidens; to whom she appears so refreshed and excited in word and gesture, that it is as if she were inebriate. They are astonished at this novelty in her, and inquire the cause; to which she replies that it is not at all wonderful she should seem to be excited as if with wine, since she has entered into the banqueting house. So much as to the literal sense. Spiritually understood, she does not deny that she is inebriate, but declares that it is with love, not with wine, unless love be wine. As long as the Bridegroom is present, she directs her discourse to Him. She calls Him her *Bridegroom*, her *Beloved*, or *Him whom my soul loveth;* but when speaking of Him to the maidens, she calls Him *the King.* Why is this? Because, as I think, it is more fitting for the Bride, who is loving and beloved, to use (as far as in her lies) terms of affection to Him whom she loves; while at the same time she imposes respect upon her maidens, who require the bond of discipline, by the use of a term of dignity which inspires reverence.

2. *The King has brought me into His banqueting house.* Of what is meant by the banqueting house I forbear to speak now, because I remember that I have treated of it before. (Sermon XXIII.) But if the term is to be understood of the Church, when the disciples, being filled with the Holy Spirit, were thought by the people to be full of new wine, then we must remember that St. Peter, answering on behalf of the Bride, as a friend of the Bridegroom, declared: *These are not filled with wine, as ye suppose* (Acts ii. 15). Notice that he denied, not that they were inebriated, but that they were inebriated in the manner, and from the cause, that the people supposed. Inebriate they were, yet not with wine, but with the Holy Spirit. And as if they had wished to testify to the people that they had been, in truth, brought into the King's banqueting house, St. Peter, speaking still for them all, went on to say: *This is that which was spoken by the Prophet Joel: And it shall come to pass in the last days, saith God, I will pour out of My Spirit upon all flesh; and your sons and your daughters shall prophesy, and your young men shall see visions, and your old men shall dream dreams.* Does it not seem to you that the banqueting hall was that house in which the disciples were assembled, *when suddenly there came a sound from heaven, as of a rushing mighty wind* (Spiritus), *and it filled all the house where they were sitting*, and thus accomplished the prophecy of Joel? And was not each of them, going forth inebriated with the abundance of good things received in that house, and having, as it were, drunk deep of the rushing torrent of its pleasures, able to say with good reason: *The King hath brought me into His banqueting house?*

3. You also, if you shall enter into the House of prayer in solitude and collectedness of spirit, if your mind be thoughtful and free of worldly cares, and if standing in the Presence of God before some altar, you shall touch, as it were, the portal of heaven with the hand of holy aspiration and longing; if, having been brought among the choirs of the saints by the fervour of your devotion (for the prayer of the righteous soul can scale even the heights of heaven), you deplore before them, in deep humility, your spiritual troubles and miseries, you plead your necessities with frequent sighs and groans too deep for utterance, and entreat earnestly their compassion; if, I say, you act thus, I have full confidence in Him who said: *Ask, and ye shall receive* (Matt. vii. 7), and I believe that if you persevere in knocking earnestly at that door, it shall certainly be opened to you, and you shall not go away empty. And when you shall return to us full of grace and love, and are unable, in the fervency of your spirit, to conceal the gift which you have received, and which you will without jealousy impart to others; thus you will be, not merely acceptable to all, but perhaps even the object of their admiration, on account of

the grace which has been bestowed upon you, and you will be able to declare with truth : *The King hath brought me into His banqueting house.* Only be cautious that you glory, not in yourself, but in the Lord. But I would not assert that every spiritual gift comes forth from this cellar here mentioned. The Bridegroom has also other cellars and storehouses, and in these are laid up divers gifts and graces, according to the riches of His glory. But of these, too, as I remember, I have already spoken. (Sermon XXIII.) *Are not these things stored up with Me,* saith the Lord, *and sealed up in My treasures?* (Deut. xxxii. 34, Douay). Therefore the division of graces is made according to the diversity of storehouses, and the manifestation of the Spirit is given to every man to profit withal. And although to one person is given the word of wisdom, to another the word of knowledge, to another prophecy, to another the gifts of healing, to another divers kinds of tongues, to another the interpretation of tongues, and other gifts similar to these to other persons, yet it does not follow that any one of those who receive gifts of this kind should therefore be able to say that he has been brought into the banqueting house. For it may have been from other storehouses that his gifts have been drawn.

4. But if anyone, while in prayer, should obtain the grace to be drawn out of himself, as it were, and into the sphere of the Divine glory, from whence he returns after a time fired with an ardent love of God, inflamed with a burning zeal for righteousness, and also filled with extreme fervour in the pursuit of all spiritual occupations and studies, so that he can say : *My heart was hot within me, while I was musing the fire burned* (Ps. xxxix. 3), that soul will evidently have a not unfounded claim to say that he has been brought into the banqueting house, because out of the abundance of his charity he has begun to manifest and utter the effects of that inebriation which, unlike every other, is in the highest degree salutary and good. For there are two kinds of ecstasy in holy contemplation : one of the understanding, the other of the heart ; one in the light of the understanding, the other in the fervour of the affections ; the one a blaze of discernment, the other a rapture of devotion ; and the glow of piety, the heart aflame with holy love, the access of sublime adoration, are all derived from the banqueting house of the King, equally with the clear vision of the eager spirit ; and everyone, whosoever he may be, who rises fiom prayer endowed with the fulness of these priceless gifts, may say with truth, *The King hath brought me into His banqueting house.*

5. Then the Bride goes on to say : *He set in order charity in me* (Douay). This was absolutely necessary, because zeal without knowledge is insupportable. Where zeal is eager, there discretion, which is the rule of charity by order, is most of all indispensable. Without knowledge zeal is found to be always less useful and less effectual ; and most often it is even very dangerous. The more fervent is zeal, the more eager the temper, the more profuse the charity ; the more

need is there of a watchful knowledge, which moderates zeal, tempers the warmth of the disposition, and regulates the gushings of charity. That is the reason why the Bride, lest the impetuosity of spirit, brought, as it might appear, from the banqueting house, should be excessive and ungovernable, as she fears especially for the souls of the young, adds here that she has received also the orderly regulation of charity—that is, discretion. For discretion assigns to every virtue its due place; and order produces moderation, due proportion and fitness, and therefore never-failing continuance. Therefore the Scripture saith: By Thine ordinance the day continues (Ps. cxix. 91) calling virtue 'the day.' Discretion, then, is not so much a single virtue, as a certain moderator and conductor of all the virtues, a director of the affections, and a teacher of all the conduct of life. Without it, even virtue degenerates into vice, and the natural impulses themselves are changed into passions which disturb and destroy nature. *He set in order charity in me.* This is what took place in the Church, when [the Lord] gave some Apostles, and some Prophets, and some Evangelists, and some Pastors and Teachers, for the perfecting of the Saints (Eph. iv. 11, 12). But it is necessary that the same charity should bind all these together into the unity of the Body of Christ, which it cannot in anywise do, unless it be guided and regulated. For if each person allows himself to be carried away by the warmth and impetuosity of his spirit to do indifferently everything that occurs to him, following rather his own preference than the dictates of reason, it is plain that there will no longer be unity, but confusion and disorder; for no one will be content with the ministry confided to him, but will be busying himself indiscriminately with that of others.

6. *He set in order charity in me.* Oh that the Lord Jesus would, of His grace, set in order in me somewhat of the charity which He has bestowed, so that I might have such care of all things which are His, and relate to Him, as to put before all other things, to the utmost of my power, the duties of the office entrusted to me, yet so as, though these be put first, I may have a reserve of interest and sympathy for matters which are beyond my especial charge, for it is not always the case that those things should be the most loved which have to be the first cared for, for though they come before others in the care they require, they are frequently far behind them in usefulness, and therefore also in the approval and affection they command. Thus it is frequently the case that the thing which, according to a command binding on us, is preferred to another, should, by the dictate of reason, come after it;[1] and that which in the judgment of truth is of the greater importance, the order of charity, requires to be adopted with the greatest caution. Has there not, for example, been laid upon me by authority the care of you all? Now, whatsoever I might

---

[1] Such is the reading of all the MSS. and of the earliest editions. Later ones read: '*Dei judicio,*' etc., and Horst, '*proinde quod veritas judicat præponitur, de judicio,*' etc.

perhaps set before that task, or which might prevent my acquitting myself of the full discharge of it, according to my powers, even though I might seem to be actuated by a motive of charity to do it, yet the reason of the Order would not allow of its being done Yet if I apply myself wholly to this [my first] work, in preference to all others, as I ought, but do not rejoice still more in greater services to God, which I may perceive to be done, perhaps, by some other person, then it is evident that I observe the order of charity only in part and not wholly. But if I occupy myself chiefly with that which is my particular charge, yet do not omit to show sympathy with other and greater work, then I shall be found to have fulfilled on both sides the order of charity, and there is nothing to hinder my saying: *He has set in order charity in me.*

7. If you say that it is difficult to rejoice more in the good work done by another, though it be great, than in a smaller good brought about by oneself, you will notice the more from this the excellence of the grace bestowed upon the Bride, and how it is not given to every soul to say: *He has set in order charity in me* Wherefore have the countenances of some among you fallen at this discourse? For those deep sighs are a sign of sorrow of soul and depression of conscience. It is because, when we compare ourselves with ourselves, we feel by our own experience our imperfection, and how rare a virtue it is not to envy the good of another, but, on the contrary, to rejoice in it, and to be the more willing to praise another's goodness in preference to our own the more we feel ourselves surpassed in virtue. There is still some light in us, brethren, when we feel thus about ourselves. Let us walk while we have the light, lest darkness come upon us (John xii. 35). To walk is to make progress. The Apostle was making progress when he said: *I count not myself to have apprehended;* and adds: *This one thing I do, forgetting those things which are behind, and, reaching forth unto those things which are before, I press toward the mark* (Phil. iv. 13, 14). What does he mean by *this one thing?* It is to say, There is one thing remaining to me which is at once a remedy, a hope, and a consolation. And what is that? It is the forgetting the past and pressing forward to fresh endeavours in the future. It is a great ground for confidence that even the great man who was 'a chosen vessel' did not regard himself as perfect, but earnestly desired to make a farther advance towards perfection. The danger, then, for us is that we should be surprised by the shadows of death when we are not in progress towards good, but are motionless and inert. And who is thus motionless except he who does not make any effort to advance? Take heed of this, and then, if you shall be surprised by death, you will be in a state of gradual amelioration (*refrigerio*). You will say to God: *Thine eyes did see my substance, yet being imperfect;* nevertheless, continues the Psalmist, *all are written in Thy book* (Ps. cxxxix. 16). Wherefore *all?* Doubtless those who are found in earnest desire for progress in good, for there follows: 'The days shall be formed, and none of

them,' that is to say, shall perish. We must understand by 'the days' those who are making spiritual progress, and these, if they are surprised by death, shall be perfected in those merits which are wanting in them. They shall be rendered wholly complete; not one of them shall be left unformed or imperfect.

8. And how, you ask again, can I make any spiritual progress, seeing that I envy that of my brother? If you lament that you envy him, though you feel the envy, you do not consent to it. It is, so to speak, an illness to be cured, not an action to be condemned. Only you must not allow yourself to settle down into an habitual envy, meditating evil designs upon your bed, nursing, as it were, and fostering your disease, satisfying your evil feelings, persecuting the innocent, speaking evil of his good actions, impeding, perverting, and corrupting them. But that jealousy, if it be not yielded to, does not injure a soul which is in motion and stretching forward to better things, because, then, it is not he that does the wrong, but sin that dwelleth in him (Rom. vii. 20). Condemnation, therefore, is not for him who is far from giving his members as instruments unto iniquity; neither his tongue to detraction, nor any other part of his body to the injury or wrong of his neighbour in any way whatsoever; who, on the contrary, is ashamed to be of an evil disposition, who makes vigorous efforts to expel the deep-seated vice by confessing and bewailing it in prayer: and if he does not succeed in doing so, is on that account more gentle towards others and more humble in himself. Who is the wise man who would condemn a soul like this, which has learned from the Lord to be meek and lowly in heart (Matt. xi. 29)? God forbid that there should be found to come short of salvation anyone who is a follower of the Saviour, the Bridegroom of the Church, our Lord JESUS CHRIST, who is above all, God blessed for ever. AMEN.

SERMON L.

OF TWO KINDS OF CHARITY—NAMELY, THAT OF FEELING AND THAT OF ACTION—AND HOW THEY ARE CO-ORDINATED.

YOU are perhaps expecting, my brethren, that I should go on to treat of the words next following in the Canticle, as the words of the preceding verse were completed in the last Sermon. But I have another object; and there are still some fragments that remain, as it were, of our banquet yesterday, which I had collected that nothing might be lost, and which I mean to set before you now. They will perish if not given to any for food; while, if I keep them for my own use alone, I shall myself perish. I am most unwilling to deprive you of those spiritual dainties, your hunger for which I know so well, especially as they are out of the basket of charity, and the sweeter as they are smaller, and the more savoury as more minutely divided. Otherwise, it would be too much against charity to defraud you of charity itself. Therefore, here is my subject: *He has set in order charity in me* (ii. 4).

2. There is charity in action, and there is charity in feeling. As concerning the first, I think that it is a law and explicit commandment given to men; but, as relates to the other, who can have it in such perfection as is contemplated by the precept? The one, therefore, is ordered as a command, the other given as a reward. We do not deny, however, that with the grace of God it is possible, even in this life, to attain the commencement, and even some degree of progress in the latter; but we maintain that the consummation of it is reserved for the happiness to come. How, then, has that been commanded, which can by no means be fulfilled by us? Or if you prefer to think that the command given has reference to charity in feeling, this I would not contest, provided that you agree with me in allowing that it is not possible for any man perfectly to fulfil it, nor has it ever been possible.[1] For who would dare to arrogate to himself a success which St. Paul himself confesses that he had not attained? (Phil. iii. 13). Nor did our great Teacher conceal that the weight of this precept exceeded the powers of men; but He has considered it useful to call man's attention by means of this fact to his own weakness, and that he might thus learn towards what object of righteousness to direct his efforts as far as his powers permitted. In commanding, then, things which are impossible [to the unaided strength of men], He has made men, not offenders, but humble: that *every mouth may be stopped and all the world may be made subject to God.* Because by the works of *the Law no flesh shall be justified before Him* (Rom. iii. 19, 20, Douay). We, then, receiving the commandment, and feeling ourselves to come short of it, shall raise our cry to Heaven, and our God shall have pity upon us, and we shall learn in that day that *not by works of righteousness which we have done, but according to His mercy He saved us* (Titus iii. 5).

3. This is what I would say, provided that we were all of opinion that the charity of the heart and of the feelings was commanded by a distinct law imposed upon us. But the reason which seems to refer the law rather to charity in act[2] is that when the Lord had said:

---

[1] *Tract. de Diligendo Deo,* x. 29.

[2] The opinion of St. Bernard is, that the precept regarding charity relates rather to charity in act, than in feeling. But by charity in feeling he means that lofty and perfect love which is to be found only in the saints and those who are perfect. Again, by charity in act (*actualem*) he means that which does not consist simply in feeling, but comes forth and shows itself in action; but he did not by any means intend to exclude inward charity from it. 'I do not say,' he declares further on (*n.* 4), 'that we ought to be without feelings of charity'; on the contrary, charity in act should include charity in thought, 'which, although it does not as yet refresh the soul with the sweetness of inward delight, yet it powerfully contributes to fire it with the love of that love itself.' Now it is precisely inward love 'with which charity in act is content' (*n.* 6). See on this subject the Admonition to *De Diligendo Deo,* Bk. ii.

Love your enemies, He at once introduces a precept relating to actions, *do good to them which hate you* (Luke vi. 27). And another Scripture says : *If thine enemy hunger, feed him ; if he thirst, give him drink* (Rom. vi. 20). And these precepts relate to actions, not to affections. Again, hear what the Lord Himself commands with regard to the affection due to Him : *If ye love Me, keep My commandments*[1] (John xiv. 15). Here, also, we are referred by Him to actions in enjoining the observance of His commands. It would have been superfluous for Him to warn us as to the doing of works if charity had consisted wholly in feelings. It is in this way that we should understand that commandment which orders you to '*love thy neighbour as thyself*' (Matt. xxii. 39), although it is not explicitly thus stated. And do you not consider it perfectly clear that, in order to fulfil that command as to the love of one's neighbour, it suffices to observe perfectly that which the law of nature prescribes : 'Do that to no man which thou hatest' (Tobit iv. 15), and which the Lord, in fact, commands : *All things whatsoever ye would that men should do to you, do ye even so to them* (Matt. vii. 12).

4. I do not say that we ought to be without feelings of charity, that the heart should be barren and unmoved, and that all we should do is to raise our hands to actions [of charity]. I have read among the great and grave crimes, which the Apostle writes, that men commit, this enumerated, that they are *without natural affection* (Rom. i. 31). But there is an affection which the flesh produces, there is another which reason rules, and a third which is seasoned by wisdom. The first is that of which the Apostle says, that it is not subject to the law of God, neither indeed can be (Rom. viii. 7) ; the second, on the contrary, because it is good, shows itself consentient to the Divine law, and there is no doubt, therefore, that these two are contrary the one to the other, since the one resists, and the other conforms to [the Divine Will]. As for the third, it is wholly different from each of the former, for it tastes and appreciates fully the sweetness of the Lord (Ps. xxxiv. 8) ; it banishes the first, and rewards the second. The first is attractive indeed, but dishonourable ; the second dry, but steady and strong ; but the third full of unction and sweetness. It is, then, by the second that (good) works are done, and in it charity consists ; not, indeed, that charity of heart and feeling, which is seasoned with the salt of wisdom, and made fat with an unction from above, so as to bring to the soul the abundance of sweetness which is in God ; but rather a certain charity of action, which, though it does not as yet refresh the soul with the sweetness of inward delight, yet powerfully contributes to fire it with the love of that love itself. *Let us not love*, says St. John, *in word, nor in tongue, but in deed and in truth* (1 John iii. 18).

---

[1] 'Where, then, are these to be kept?' says St. Bernard in Sermon V. for Advent, *n.* 2. No doubt in the heart, as he there explains ; but they ought to be to the heart what food is to the body, and 'pass not only into the affections, but also into the character and actions of life.'

5. Do you observe how cautiously he proceeds, between love which is vicious and love which is only in feeling, distinguishing from each of these the real and saving charity? He does not admit in it the feigned love of a false tongue; nor, again, does he demand the lofty and consummate enjoyment of active wisdom. *Let us love*, he says, *in deed and in truth;* that is to say, let us be moved to the doing of good works rather by the powerful impulse of truth and fact than by a feeling of emotional charity. *He has set in order charity in me.* Which of these two kinds of charity? Each of them, in fact, but in a reverse order. For charity in act chooses rather (for its sphere) the lower sphere of life, while that of thought and feeling chooses the higher. There is, for example, no doubt that in a right-thinking soul the love of God is preferred to the love of man, heaven to earth, eternity to time, the soul to the body. And yet in well-regulated action the opposite order is frequently, or almost always, found to prevail. For we are both more frequently occupied, and more busily, with cares for the temporal good of our neighbour, and among our brethren we assist with more diligent assiduity those who are more infirm; we apply ourselves, by the right of humanity and the necessity of the case, more to promote the peace of the earth than the glory of heaven; in our anxiety about temporal interests we scarcely permit ourselves to think anything about those which are eternal; in sickness our bodily pains and weakness occupy us almost without ceasing, and the care of our soul is laid aside; and, lastly, we surround our weaker members, according to the saying of the Apostle, with more abundant honour (1 Cor. xii. 23), and thus we fulfil, after a fashion, that saying of the Lord: *The last shall be first, and the first last* (Matt. xx. 16). Who doubts that a man, when he is in prayer, is speaking with God? and yet how often are we withdrawn, and, so to speak, torn away from prayer, and that at the very dictate of charity, because of those who are in need of our assistance or our advice! How often does holy quiet give place, and that from a pious motive, to the tumult of business affairs! How often do we with a good conscience lay down the manuscript we are reading, to go and perspire over manual labour! How often, in order to carry out our worldly occupations, do we (and that very justly) temporarily supersede even the Celebration of the solemnities of the Holy Eucharist![1] A preposterous order in which to act; but necessity has no law.[2]

[1] Among the Cistercians the Daily Services (*Sacra*) used at one time to be intermitted during the harvest. On which account Philip Augustus, having heard that among the monks of Barbeaux, 'at the period of harvest, the brethren used to sojourn in their farmhouses, and thus on account of their temporal interests the celebration of mass was omitted,' is said to have given an order that thenceforth mass should be celebrated every day, in the morning, for the soul of his father, who was buried there. There are letters on this subject in *De Re Diplomatica*, Bk. vi., p. 603. As to St. Bernard himself, we learn from his 'Life,' by Geoffrey (Bk. v., c. 1), that he scarcely ever omitted to offer the holy sacrifice 'down to his last illness' (Mabillon's note).

[2] *Necessitas non habet legem.* This is said in the dictionaries to be a 'Maxim of Law,' but I have not been able to trace it to any one author.—ED.

Charity in act follows its own order, and commences by the last things, according to the bidding of the Father of all (Matt. xx. 8). At least it is a charity kindly and just, not an acceptor of persons; nor does it consider the relative value of things, but the necessities of men.

6. Not so with charity in feeling; that commences always with the first things. For wisdom sets upon all things the value which is really theirs; thus, for example, that which is in its nature the more valuable receives from it the greater measure of attention; those which have less value receive less, and those which have less still, least of all. It is truth, then, that determines this order of charity; but it is charity that adopts it. For the true charity consists in this, that those whose needs are greatest receive first; and, again, charitable truth is manifest, in preserving in our affections that order which is founded in the reason. If, then, you love the Lord thy God with all thy heart, with all thy soul, with all thy strength (Matt. xxii. 37), rising in the earnestness of that affection above that love of love,[1] with which actual charity is content, and receiving in all its fulness the Divine love (to which that other love serves only as a step), are wholly fired and pervaded by it, assuredly you have a knowledge of God, although you cannot know Him adequately or as He is (which is a thing impossible to any creature), but at least such a knowledge of Him as you are capable of receiving here below. Then you shall have a true knowledge of yourself also, when you attain a perception of the fact that you have nothing whatever in yourself to deserve love, except in so far as you belong to God, and because you have poured out upon Him all the affection you can command. You well know yourself, I repeat, as you really are, when by experience of your own love, and of the affection which you bear to your own self, you find nothing in yourself that merits your love except it is on account of Him without whom you yourself have no existence at all.

7. Now, as to your neighbour, whom you are bidden to love as yourself, you shall know him also as he is, provided that he does not appear to you as other than you appear to yourself; for he is that which you are; he is man, as you. Since, then, you love yourself only because you love God, it follows that you love as yourself all those who love God as you love Him. As for an enemy, he is, as it were, nothing, since he has no love for God; you cannot, therefore, love him as you love yourself, who do love God; but you will love even him that he may learn to love God. For it is not the same thing to love a person so that he may love God, and to love him because he does this. In order, then, that you may know him as he really is, you must consider, not that which he is at the present moment (for he is nothing), but that which he may perhaps some day be, which is next to nothing, as long as the matter is still in doubt. Further-

---

[1] In certain MSS. the word *amoris* is wanting. But it is not at variance with the thought of St. Bernard, who, in treating of charity in act (*n.* 4), says, 'it powerfully contributes to fire the soul with the love of that love itself.'

more, if there be one who will clearly never return to the love of God, you must look upon him, not as almost nothing, but as nothing at all, inasmuch as throughout eternity he is nothing. With the exception, then, of such a person as he, who is not merely not to be loved, but who is, besides this, to be held in hatred, according to that saying of the Psalmist: *Do I not hate them, O Lord, that hate Thee? and am not I grieved with them that rise up against Thee?* (Ps. cxxxix. 21) charity, which is jealous in this respect, does not allow that you should refuse to any man, even to your most bitter enemy, some small measure of affection. Whoso is wise will ponder these things.

8. Give me a man who, before all things, loves God with all his being; who loves both himself and his neighbour in the same degree in which each loves God; who loves his enemy as one who may perhaps at some time in the future turn to the love of God; who loves his relatives according to the flesh very tenderly, on account of nature, but his spiritual parents, that is, those who have instructed him, more abundantly on account of grace, and thus his love for all other things whatsoever is regulated by his love for God; who despises the earth, and looks upward to the heaven; who uses this world as not abusing it, and knows how to distinguish, by a certain inward faculty of soul, between things which are to be chosen and loved, and those to be merely used, so that things transitory are made use of as they pass for temporary need, and as long as the need requires, while things eternally enduring are embraced with lasting joy: show me, I say, a man such as this, and I will boldly pronounce him wise, since he takes things for what they truly are, and is able with truth and confidence to boast: *He hath set in order charity in me.* But where is such an one to be found, and when shall it be thus with him? This I ask weeping: how long shall we perceive this fragrance without tasting it? how long look forward to our heavenly home, without attaining it, sighing for it, while beholding it from afar? O Truth, fatherland of exiled souls, and end of their exile! I descry thee, but am unable to enter in; I am detained in the flesh, I am defiled by my sins, I am not worthy to be admitted. O Wisdom, whose powerful guidance extendest from the beginning to the end of all things, establishing and controlling them; who disposest all with admirable gentleness, ordering, blessing, and gladdening all affections, direct our actions according as our temporal necessities require, and dispose our affections as thy eternal truth demands; so that each of us may be able securely to glory in Thee, and say: *He has set in order charity in me.* For Thou art the Power of God and the Wisdom of God, JESUS CHRIST our Lord, the Bridegroom of the Church, God above all, Blessed for ever. AMEN.

SERMON LI.

HOW THE BRIDE MAKES PETITION THAT THE FRUITS OF GOOD WORKS AND THE PERFUMES OF FAITH MAY BE MADE TO ABOUND WITH HER AS FLOWERS, AND ALSO CONCERNING HOPE AND FEAR.

'*Stay me up with flowers, compass me about with apples: because I languish with love.*'—Cant. ii. 5 (Douay).

THE love [of the Bride] has grown because the incentives to it have been more and greater than heretofore; for you see how precious has been the opportunity granted to her, of not only seeing the Bridegroom, but of conversing with Him. It seems, also, that He has appeared to her with a countenance more serene, that His interview with her was more prolonged, and His words kinder. Nor is she only delighted to have had an interview with her Beloved, but is honoured by the praise He has bestowed upon her. Furthermore, through Him she is refreshed with grateful shade, nourished with His fruit, and has drunk of His cup. For it is not to be supposed that she has come forth thirsty from the banqueting-house, into which she gloried so lately that she had been brought; yet, indeed, she is thirsty still, according to the Scripture: *They that drink me shall yet be thirsty* (Ecclus. xxiv. 21). After all these things, the Bridegroom retires according to His wont, and it is then that the Bride declares herself to languish for love, that is to say, the love which she has for Him. For the more delightful she had found His presence, the keener is the pang she feels afterwards because of his absence. The taking away of what you love increases your desire for it; and the more ardently you desire it, the more you feel the privation arising from its loss. For this reason the Bride entreats that she may be comforted in the meantime with fruits and the odour of flowers, until He shall return to her, whose present delay she endures with impatience. So much as relates to the order and connection of the text.

2. Let us try now, under the guidance of the Spirit of truth, to draw out some fruit of spiritual profit. And if it be taken that the Church, which includes all the saints, is here speaking, *we* are here referred to by flowers and fruits; and not only we, but all those also who have been converted from the world in every age. The flowers mean those who are beginning the life of conversion, in whom it is still new and tender; and the fruits, the strength of those who are farther advanced, and the ripeness of those who are perfect. Surrounded and supported by these in this place of her exile, the Church, our mother, to whom to live is Christ, and to die is gain, endures with less impatience her long trial of deferred hope, since, according to the Scripture, there is given *unto her of the fruit of her*

hands, the firstfruits, so to speak, of the Spirit, and *her own works praise her in the gates* (Prov. xxxi. 31). But if you would that I should follow the moral sense, and show you in the soul flowers and fruits, then flowers denote faith, and fruits works. That explanation will, I think, not seem unsuitable to you, if you consider how, just as the flower necessarily precedes the fruit, faith must of necessity go before good action. For St. Paul bears witness that *without faith it is impossible to please God* (Heb. xi. 6), and he says what is even stronger, that *whatsoever is not of faith is sin* (Rom. xiv. 23). Therefore, as there is not fruit without flowers, so is there no good action without faith. But, again, as faith without works is dead (James ii. 20), so in the same way it is useless for the flower to appear, if it be not followed by fruit. *Stay me up with flowers, compass me about with apples, because I languish with love.* Thus it is that a soul, accustomed to quiet, draws consolation from good works rooted in a faith unfeigned, whenever the light of holy contemplation is withdrawn from it, as is often the case. For who is able to enjoy the light of holy contemplation—I do not say continually, but even for any considerable time—while he remains in this body? But as I have said, as often as he falls from the state of contemplation, he resorts to that of action, as to a convenient refuge, from whence he may be able more easily to return into his former state. For these two things are intimately related; they are chamber companions, and dwell together. Martha is sister to Mary, and although she comes forth from the light of contemplation, she never suffers herself to fall into the darkness of sin, or to subside into ignoble sloth, but remains still in the light of good works. And that you may know that these are also light, remember the Lord's words: *Let your light so shine before men, that they may see your good works* (Matt. v. 16); for it is quite clear that He spoke of actions which were capable of being beheld by men.

3. *Because I languish with love.* When the object of affection is present, love grows and strengthens; but when he is absent, love languishes. This languor is nothing else than the weariness of eager and unsatisfied longing, with which the mind of her who loves is necessarily strongly affected in the absence of her beloved. For as she is always absorbed in watching for his coming, she regards as delay whatever haste he may use. Therefore it is that you see the Bride entreating that she may be surrounded with the fruits of good works and the sweet odours of faith, among which she may rest while her Lord delays His coming. I speak to you of that which I have verified by personal experience. I do assure you, brethren, that if I ever find that any of you have profited by my teaching and warnings, then I do not regret that I have preferred the preaching to you, to my own quiet and ease. For when, for example, after a sermon, someone who is passionate is found to have become gentle, a proud mind to be humble, a timid one brave and strong; or when one already gentle, humble, or brave, is seen to have made progress in those graces, and to have become better than he was before; or

when those who perhaps were lukewarm and languid, sleepy and uninterested in spiritual exercises, are awakened and warmed by the fiery touch of the word of the Lord; and when those who, having deserted the fountain of true wisdom, have hewn out to themselves at their own will cisterns which can hold no water, and because their hearts are dry, and they have in themselves no impulse of devotion, have been wont to murmur at every command laid upon them—when, I say, such persons as these, by the dew of the word, and the plentiful rain, which God has reserved to His inheritance, are shown to have, as it were, flourished anew in works of obedience, and to have become submissive and devoted in all things, I have no ground, I assure you, for feeling sorrow at the interruption of my pursuit of happy contemplation, when I am surrounded with such flowers and fruits of piety. I endure with patience the being torn from the society of an unfruitful Rachel, to obtain from Leah the plentiful fruits of your progress in goodness. It will not trouble me at all, I repeat, to break in upon my quiet for the purpose of preparing to preach to you, when I shall see the seed which I have sown in your souls grow in them, and bring forth the rich increase of your fruits of righteousness. For charity, which *seeketh not her own* (1 Cor. xiii. 5), has long since easily won me to prefer your advantage to all else that I hold most desirable. To pray, to read, to write, to meditate, and all the other advantages of spiritual studies; I have counted them all as loss for your sake, and in comparison with any loss to you.

4. *Stay me up with flowers, compass me about with apples: because I languish with love.* This says the Bride to her maidens in the absence of her Spouse, thus warning them to make progress in faith and good works, until He come, because she believes that this will be both well-pleasing to Him, a consolation to herself, and the means of their salvation. I know that I have explained this passage more fully and in another sense in my book upon the Love of God, and if it shall please any of you to read that, he can decide whether of the two is to be preferred. A prudent person will not, I think, condemn the giving of two senses to the same passage, provided that each appear to be grounded in truth, and that charity, which is the rule in interpreting Scripture, shall edify the more persons, inasmuch as there are a greater number of truthful senses, which each may apply to his own special need. For why should that be found faulty in the interpreting of Scripture, which we see is industriously practised in other things? To how many different bodily uses (only to take one thing for an example) do we put the element of water? In the same way a person is not to be blamed who gives divers senses, fitted to the various needs of souls, to a passage of Scripture.

5. Then follow the words: *His left hand is under my head, and His right hand doth embrace me* (ii. 6). I remember that this also was discussed very elaborately in the treatise which I have mentioned; but let us observe the sequence of the discourse. It appears that

the Bridegroom has at length returned, as I suppose, to encourage by His presence the drooping Bride, and that He is with her. For how could it be otherwise than that she should be revived by His presence, whom His absence had so cast down? He is unable, then, to endure the sadness of His beloved one; He is present; nor when recalled by a desire so ardent is He capable of making delay. And as He had found her during His absence faithful to her labours and earnestly desirous of [spiritual] profit, as was doubtless shown by her direction that flowers and fruits should be gathered together for her, so He returns to her with graces more abundant than heretofore for her reward. Happy the soul which lies on the Breast of Christ, and by the Arms of the WORD is enfolded in rest. *His left hand is under my head, and His right hand shall embrace me.* She does not say, *doth embrace*,[1] but *shall embrace*, to signify that she is so grateful for the former grace, as to anticipate the second by her giving of thanks.

6. Learn not to be slow and slothful in returning thanks to God; learn to render thanksgiving to Him for each of His gifts. *Diligently*, says the Scripture, *consider what is put before thee* (Prov. xxiii. 1), so as not to let pass any gift of God, whether great, or mediocre, or even very small, without rendering due thanks for it. Are we not bidden to gather up the fragments that remain, that nothing be lost (John vi. 12); that is to say, let not the least benefits be forgotten? For is not that *lost* which is bestowed upon an ungrateful receiver? Ingratitude is the enemy of the soul, the starving of merits, the dissipation of virtues, and the loss of the benefits that God has bestowed upon us. Ingratitude is as a burning wind, which dries up for itself the fountain of goodness, the dew of mercy, the flowing stream of grace. On this account it is that the Bride, when she has felt the grace done to her by the left hand of her Spouse, renders her thanks, and does not delay even to receive the farther grace which awaits her from His right hand before so doing. For, after having said, *His left hand is under my head*, does she go on to say similarly, 'With His right He has embraced me'; but *shall embrace me*, she says instead.

7. But in what sense shall we understand that the Word has either right hand or left? Can it be said of the WORD, as it is said of ordinary human beings, that there are in Him bodily parts distinct the one from the other, and separate lineaments, so that distinction can be made between the right hand and the left? Ought we not rather to believe that the Word of God, who is Himself God, does not admit in Himself any such diversity, but *is that which He is* (Exod. iii. 14), that is to say, in His Nature Uncompounded, and therefore without parts, as He is One, and therefore without number? For He is God the WORD, of whom it is written: *Of His Wisdom there is no number* (Ps. cxlvi. 5, Douay). But if that which is unchangeable is incomprehensible, it is therefore incapable of being

---

[1] The Vulgate does not read *amplexatur*, but *amplexabitur*.

expressed in language; where, then, I ask, can you find words in which that Majesty so exalted can either worthily be expressed, competently defined, or even suitably spoken of? Yet, in order to expound, according to our capacity, the little that we know and has been revealed to us by the Holy Spirit, and taught us by the usage of the Holy Scriptures and the authority of the Fathers, let it be permitted to us to make use of analogies from things that we know, and not indeed to find out new terms, but to vary the meaning[1] of some known to us, so as to clothe those analogies sufficiently and suitably. For unless this were done, it would be absurd to attempt to teach things unknown by means of words which are equally unknown.

8 Thus, as by the right hand and the left hand it is the custom to denote prosperity and adversity, so it seems to me that by the left hand of the Word may be meant the threatening of punishment, and by His right hand the promise of the kingdom of heaven. Now, there are times when our soul is servilely oppressed by the fear of punishment, and then we cannot say that the right hand of the Bridegroom is *under our head*, but that it is upon our head; nor can a soul thus affected say with the Bride: *His left hand is under my head.* But if it makes progress, so as to pass out of this spirit of servitude into a nobler disposition of free and willing service, insomuch that it is rather invited by the hope of reward than constrained by the fear of punishments, and especially if it is influenced by the pure love of good, then undoubtedly it will be able to say *His left hand is under my head.* For it has, by a better and more excellent disposition of mind, risen above that slavish fear which is aroused or indicated by the left hand, and by the very power and worthiness of its aspirations has drawn nearer to that which is signified by the Right Hand. And in it, according to the saying of the Psalmist, addressing the Lord, are all the promises: *At Thy Right Hand there are pleasures for evermore* (Ps. xvi. 11). This is why the Bride, speaking in the certitude of her hope, declares: *And His Right Hand shall embrace me.*

9 You will now see with me whether a soul thus disposed, and which has attained a position of such sweetness and happiness, may well appropriate to itself what is said in a Psalm: *I will both lay me down in peace and sleep*, especially as it may go on to give the reason which follows: *For Thou, Lord, only makest me dwell in safety* (Ps. iv. 8). That, in truth, is the case. Whereas he who is oppressed with a spirit of servitude, who has but little of hope and much of fear, dwells not in peace, nor is able to rest, because his conscience fluctuates continually between hoping and fearing, and is so much the more tortured by the predominance of the latter, because fear hath torment. And therefore it is not his happy lot to say, 'I will lay me down in peace and rest,' because none can say that unless he be firmly established in hope. But if, by a progressive growth in grace, the fear diminishes, and the hope grows stronger—then at

---

[1] *Mutuari;* another reading is *transferre.*

length charity comes with all its powers to the assistance of hope, and fear is driven out of the soul—will not hope under those circumstances have made good its ground, and will not that soul be able to rest and sleep in peace?

10. *If you sleep among the midst of lots you shall be as the wings of a dove covered with silver.*[1] What I think, then, is intended here is that there is a medium between fear and security, as between the right wing and the left—namely, hope—on which soul and conscience sweetly repose; that is to say, on the soft and pleasant bed of charity. And perhaps it is this that is referred to in a later passage of this Canticle, where, in a description of the couch of Solomon, among other words you have: The midst thereof being paved with charity for the daughters of Jerusalem (iii. 10). For he who feels himself to be strongly established in hope does not serve in fear, but rests in charity. That is, in fact, the case with the Bride, who rests and even sleeps; wherefore it is said [by the Bridegroom]: *I charge you, O ye daughters of Jerusalem, by the roes and by the hinds of the field, that ye stir not up, nor awake My love until she*[2] *please* (ii. 7). It is a great and surprising condescension that He makes the contemplative soul to repose in His Bosom; that He guards it also from intrusive cares; that He protects it from the inquietudes of action and the embarrassments of business, and does not suffer it to be aroused at all, except at its own will. That, however, is not a subject to be entered upon at the close of a discourse; it will be better to defer it to another occasion, when time will not be wanting for the treatment of a theme so attractive. Not that even then we can be sufficient of ourselves to think anything as of ourselves, especially with regard to a matter so noble, so excellent, and so altogether sublime; but our sufficiency is of God, of the Bridegroom of the Church, JESUS CHRIST our Lord, who is above all, God blessed for ever. AMEN.

[1] Ps. lxviii. 13. A difficult verse;[1] and there are a great number of widely differing interpretations of it. The Vulgate (*inter medios cleros*) follows the LXX. (ἀναμέσον τῶν κλήρων), *i.e.*, in the midst of 'such dangers and persecutions, as if your enemies were casting *lots* for your goods and persons' (Douay, *n.*); but St. Jerome turns it otherwise 'inter medios terminos,' that is, 'upon the very bounds or borders of the dominions of your enemies.' The English A.V., 'among the pots,' is founded on still another reading, '*inter medias ollas*,' which Francois Vatablus thus explains: 'Even if you shall have been lying among vessels covered with blackness, *i.e.*, if you shall have been oppressed with great calamity, you shall be rendered glad and, as it were, white and shining by your liberation.' But it is better, with most modern expositors, to follow the Chaldee Targum, and read, 'among the sheepfolds.' The meaning will then be: '*Even if ye have been lying between the sheepfolds*, far from the battlefield, yet shall ye be enriched with captured gold and jewels, *till ye be as the wings of a dove, silver and gold*' (Littledale, 'Psalms,' ii. 381). Ewald renders thus: 'If ye rest thus between hurdles, doves' wings are covered with silver, and their pinions with green gold-shimmer' ('Psalms,' ii. 204.)—ED.

[2] 'He,' A.V.

---

[1] '*Hunc versiculum fateor obscurissimum esse*,' says Cornelius à Lapide.

SERMON LII.

OF THAT ECSTASY WHICH IS CALLED CONTEMPLATION, IN WHICH THE BRIDEGROOM CAUSES THE HOLY SOUL TO ATTAIN PEACE AND REST, BEING EARNESTLY DESIROUS OF ITS BLESSEDNESS.

'*I charge you, O ye daughters of Jerusalem, by the roes, and by the hinds of the field, that ye stir not up, nor wake my love till she please.*'—Cant. ii. 7.

IT is to the maidens that this prohibition is addressed. By this name, of daughters of Jerusalem, He calls those delicate and weak souls which are, as it were, womanly in affections and actions, but are, nevertheless, attached to the Bride, in the hope of attaining spiritual profit, and making their way to Jerusalem with her. These, then, He forbids to disturb the sleep of the Bride, or to presume to awaken her against her will. For her most sweet Spouse has, as we have before been told, laid His left hand under her head, and made her to rest and sleep. And now, as the text goes on to say, He, in His abounding kindness and condescension, makes Himself her guard, and watches over her, lest, being disquieted by the small but frequent wants of her maidens, she should be awakened. That is the literal sense of the text. But as for that contestation 'by the roes and hinds of the field,' it seems to have no reasonable consequence in the literal sense; it is, therefore, to be explained entirely according to its spiritual meaning. However that may be, we may say here that it is good for us to behold for a little the goodness, the sweetness, the condescension of the Divine Nature. For that which thou, O man, hast ever experienced in human feelings, which is most tender and sweet, it is that which is here predicated to thee of the Heart of the Most High. And He who speaks of it thus is He who searches the deep things of God, and because He is the Spirit of God, cannot but know whatsoever is in Him; nor, since He is the Spirit of truth, can He speak any other thing than that which He has seen in Him.

2. [We must believe that] there are those belonging to our race who have been so happy as to merit to taste this joy, and so to experience in their own selves the effects of a mystery so sweet; for otherwise we should be wanting in faith in this Scripture before us, where the heavenly Bridegroom is plainly brought before us, as feeling a most earnest desire for the peace and rest of a certain soul, which was dear to Him, and so anxious as to hold that soul in His own arms, that the sweetness of its sleep might not be troubled by any care or disquiet. I cannot contain my joy to see that the Sovereign Majesty does not disdain to condescend to the weakness of our nature by entering into a relation to it so familiar and so sweet, and that the Supreme Godhead does not think it below its dignity to

ally itself with the soul, even in its present state of exile, and to show for it the ardent affection of a loving Spouse. Thus, thus, it is in heaven, I do not doubt, as I see it to be on earth; and that the soul will assuredly feel that which is described in the text; except that words are not capable of fully describing that which it will then be able to experience, though it is not now able. What, think you, shall the soul receive on high which even here below is honoured with such near association with God as to feel His Arms around her, to be sheltered in His Bosom, to be watched and guarded by His care, so that when sleeping she shall not be aroused by any until she awaken of her own accord?

3. Let us now, then, consider, and let me explain if I can, what is the nature of that sleep which the Bridegroom desires for His beloved (Ps. cxxvii. 2), and from which He will not have her aroused, except at her own will, lest perhaps someone reading what an Apostle has written: *Now it is high time to awake out of sleep* (Rom. xiii. 11), or the prayer that the Psalmist makes to God to lighten his eyes lest he sleep the sleep of death (Ps. xiii. 3), should be troubled by a misunderstanding of words, and be able to form no worthy idea of the slumber of the Bride which in this passage is referred to. Nor is this sleep at all similar to that other slumber of which the Lord speaks in the Gospel—namely, that of Lazarus: *Our friend Lazarus sleepeth; but I go, that I may awake him out of sleep* (John xi. 11). For this He said of the death of the body, though the disciples thought that He referred to an ordinary sleep. But this repose of the Bride is not the unconsciousness of the body which steeps the bodily senses in deep forgetfulness for the time, however peaceful that may be; nor yet that sleep, deeper and more to be feared, which steals away the life. Much more is it far removed from that other slumber which is the state of him who sleeps in death—that is to say, who perseveres irrevocably in sin which leads to death. This may, on the contrary, be called a sleep of life, and even a vigil; for it illuminates the inward sense—it banishes death, and contributes to everlasting life. Yet that is, in truth, a sleep which, though it does not steep the senses in forgetfulness, ravishes and transports them [into a higher sphere]. It is even a death (as I may say without hesitation), since the Apostle speaks thus, in order to praise certain persons while they were still living the life of the body: *Ye are dead, and your life is hid with Christ in God* (Col. iii. 3).

4. I may, then, without any absurdity, call the ecstasy of the Bride death; but it is a death which, far from depriving her of life, delivers her from the snares [which are dangerous to] life, so that she is able to say: *Our soul is escaped even as a bird out of the snare of the fowlers* (Ps. cxxiv. 7). For in this life we proceed in the midst of snares; and the soul is delivered from the fear of these whenever it is, so to speak, ravished out of itself by intense and holy thought, provided that it is separated from, and elevated above, itself to such a degree as to transcend its usual habit of thinking. For a net is spread in

vain before the eyes of them that have wings (Prov. i. 17, Douay). Where there is no consciousness even of life, what fear is there of impurity? For when the soul is in that state it ceases, not, indeed, to have life, but to have any consciousness of its life, and therefore it does not feel any of the temptations of life. *O that I had wings like a dove; for then would I fly away, and be at rest* (Ps. lv. 6). Would that thus I might die often, so as to avoid the snares of death, to escape the deadly blandishments of a life of pleasure, to be insensible to carnal delights, to the passion of avarice, to the incitements of anger and impatience, to the troubles and disquiets of cares and anxieties! Let my soul die the death of the righteous, that no fraud may ensnare it, nor there be any satisfaction to it in evil-doing. Good, indeed, and to be desired, is that death which does not take away life, but only changes it into a better form, which does not strike down the body, but elevates the soul.

5. Yet this is but the death which belongs to men. May my soul die the death which, if I may so speak, belongs to angels; so that, departing from the remembrance of things present, and being divested not only of desire for, but also of the haunting ideas and images of, things corporeal and inferior, it may enter into pure relations with those in which is the image and likeness of purity. Of this nature, as I consider, is the ecstasy in which contemplation wholly or principally consists. For to be, while still living, delivered from the power of desires for things material is a degree of human virtue; but to be brought out of the sphere of material forms and ideas is a privilege of angelic purity. Yet each of these two is a Divine gift—each of them consists in coming out of yourself, in rising above yourself; but the one carries you only a little way, while the other carries you far indeed. Blessed is he who can say: Lo, I have fled far away, and abode in solitude (Ps. lv. 7). He was not content to go forth unless he could go far away, so as to obtain repose. Have you over-passed the pleasures of the flesh, so that you no longer obey its lusts, nor are subject to its allurements? Then you have made progress; you have separated yourself [from the world]; but you have not yet detached yourself entirely from it as long as you have not the power to banish, by the mere purity of your spirit, and to rise entirely out of the reach of, the inrushing and thronging crowd of material images and ideas. Do not, at the point which you have thus far attained, promise yourself rest of soul. You mistake if you think that the place of repose, the secret of solitude, the habitation of peace, the stillness of serene light, is to be found on this side of your earthly existence. But show me the soul who has attained that point of freedom of which I speak, who can justly say: *Return unto thy rest, O my soul; for the Lord hath dealt bountifully with thee* (Ps. cxvi. 7), and I will at once confess that he has found the rest desired. And this place is truly in a solitude, this dwelling is truly in the light, according to the prophet; a tabernacle for a shadow in the day-time from the heat, and for a place of refuge, and for a covert from storm and from rain (Is. iv. 6);

and of it holy David also says: *In the time of trouble He shall hide me in His pavilion: in the secret of His tabernacle shall He hide me* (Ps. xxvii. 5).

6. Regard this, then, as the solitude into which the Bride has withdrawn, and in which place of delight she sweetly rests in communion with her Spouse, by which we are to understand that she is rapt in ecstasy, from which she is not to be aroused by her maidens until she shall choose. But in what terms is that prohibition stated? They are not forbidden in the usual manner, and with simple and unemphatic terms, but with a new and unexampled adjuration: *by the roes and by the hinds of the field*. And it seems to me that by these two kinds of animals it is intended to designate the holy souls who are delivered from the body, and the Angels who are in the Presence of God, with reference both to the clearness of their sight, and the swiftness of their motions. Now, we know that both the one and the other of these qualities befits these two classes of spirits, for they rise easily to the loftiest truths, and penetrate to the deepest mysteries. The fields or plains, also, over which they are said to roam, evidently denote the lightness and freedom from all restraint with which they expatiate in contemplation. What is the intention, then, of that adjuration by them made by the Spouse? It is doubtless in order that the maidens, restless as they are, may not venture, for any slight cause, to recall His Beloved from a company so august, with whom she assuredly associates, as often as she is rapt out of herself by contemplation. It is, then, with great fitness that they are adjured by respect for those good and holy beings, from whose society the Bride is being torn away by their importunity. These maidens are to consider who it is that they are offending when they importune their mother, and are not to presume so much on her motherly kindness as to have the boldness to burst in upon that celestial assembly when no pressing necessity exists for so doing. Let them clearly understand that this is what they do, as often as they disturb, without real cause, the deep quiet of a soul fixed in contemplation. Evidently it is laid down by these words, that it is to such a soul that the choice is left, whether to employ its leisure to its own spiritual good, or to devote itself to cares for them, that is to say, by the words in which it is forbidden to arouse the Bride, except at her own will. The Bridegroom is well aware how ardent is the affection of His Bride, even towards her neighbours, and that, good mother as she is, she is sufficiently prompted by her own charity anxiously to care for the spiritual interests of her daughters, and that she will not, on any account, deny herself to them, or withdraw herself from them, as often and as much as there is need of her; and therefore He has determined that the question of time can be safely left to her discretion. She is not one such as those whom a prophet subjects to withering reproof, who have taken to themselves that which is fat and strong, but have neglected that which was feeble (Ezek. xxxiv. 3, 4). Does the physician seek those that are healthy, and not rather those

that are sick? If he visits the former, it is as friend, and not as physician. So also, O thou who art a good teacher, if you repel all that are unlearned, whom will you instruct? To whom, I ask, will you administer with care and zeal the rules of discipline, if you either avoid the unruly, or are avoided by them? In whom, I ask, shall your patience find its work and be approved, if you admit those only who are peaceful and submissive, and exclude all others?

7. There are some sitting here from whom I should wish to see a more careful heed to this matter. Let them reflect, at least, what respect is due to those set over them, and that, by disturbing them rashly and without good cause, they are drawing upon themselves the displeasure of even the citizens of heaven. And then, perhaps, they will begin to spare us a little more than they have been accustomed to do, and not to break in upon our leisure so inconsiderately and rashly. Rarely, indeed, as they know, is an hour left to me for resting from the incessant coming of visitors, even when [the brethren] bear with me in all patience. But I reproach myself for making that complaint, lest some timid soul should conceal his spiritual needs longer than his strength holds out, in fear of disturbing me. I say no more on this subject, then, lest I should seem myself to afford to those who are weak an example of impatience. The Lord has little children who yet believe in Him, and I could not bear that I should be an occasion of scandal to such (Matt. xviii. 6). I do not make use of the power that I have over them [as their Abbot]; let them rather make use of me as they will, provided only that they attain salvation. They will really spare me in not sparing me at all, and I shall rest the more freely if they have no fear at all of disturbing me when they have need of anything. I shall comply with their wishes as far as I am able, and as long as I have a breath of life shall serve my God in them with real and unfeigned charity. I seek not my own interests, nor those things which are useful to me, but rather court that which is of use to many, of use also to myself. This only I ask and entreat, that my ministry may be accepted and become fruitful, so that at least I may find mercy in the evil day in the eyes of Him who is their Father, and the Father of our Lord JESUS CHRIST, the Bridegroom of the Church, who is above all, God blessed for ever. AMEN.

SERMON LIII.

BY 'MOUNTAINS' AND 'HILLS' ARE SIGNIFIED THE HEAVENLY SPIRITS, OVER WHOM AND THROUGH WHOM THE BRIDEGROOM PASSES IN HIS COMING TO EARTH, THAT IS TO SAY, IN THE MYSTERY OF HIS INCARNATION.

'*The voice of my beloved.*'—Cant. ii. 8.

THE Bride, noticing the increased modesty of her maidens, and their respectful timidity, shown by their no longer venturing to intrude upon her sacred repose, nor presuming, as they had previously done, to trouble the quiet of her contemplation, recognises that this is the effect of the care and labours of the Bridegroom. Rejoicing, therefore, in spirit, as well because they are advantaged in being restrained from needless and excessive restlessness, as because of the condescension and favour of her Bridegroom, and her own prospect of unbroken quiet in future, she declares that it is the Voice of her Beloved which does this, and His grace that has brought it about, with so much zeal on behalf of her peace, and earnestness in defending the sweetness of her leisure, or, rather, of her fervent religious exercises. For the man who has in charge the rule over others, and discharges it with faithfulness and care, scarcely ever allows himself with a good conscience to enjoy rest, since he is always in fear of not doing sufficient for those under his authority, and of not pleasing God, if he prefers his own quiet, and the sweetness of contemplation, to that which is for the common advantage. But there is sometimes no little joy and security in his mind, while enjoying his interval of peaceful repose, when he perceives, from the degree of awe and reverence for him with which God inspires the hearts of those he governs, that his quiet is pleasing to God, who causes them to endure their wants with a patient mind, rather than venture to disturb the grateful rest of their spiritual father. For the just fear of these his children shows manifestly that they have heard inwardly that complaining and, as it were, threatening voice of Him who speaks by the prophet: *I that speak in righteousness* (Is. lxiii. 1). It is His voice, it is His inspiration, and it impresses upon them a righteous fear.

2. When His Voice, then, is heard, the Bride is glad and rejoices, saying: *The Voice of my Beloved.* She is His chosen, and rejoices with great joy on account of the voice of her Spouse. Then she adds: *Behold, He cometh leaping upon the mountains, skipping upon the hills.* Having recognised by hearing His voice the presence of her chosen, instantly she turns inquiring eyes around in order to see Him whom she had heard. Hearing leads to sight, because *faith cometh by hearing* (Rom. x. 17); and it is faith that purifies hearts,

and renders them capable of beholding God. For we read thus: *Purifying their hearts by faith* (Acts xv. 9). Then she sees Him approaching whom she had heard speaking, thus observing the order indicated by the Holy Spirit, who has spoken thus by the mouth of the Psalmist: *Hearken, O daughter, and see* (Ps. xliv. 11, Douay). And that you may be the more surely convinced that it is not by accident or chance, but of set design and purpose, because of the reason already alleged, that I have here set hearing before sight, notice whether the same order is not observed by holy Job where he speaks thus to God: *I have heard of Thee by the hearing of the ear, but now mine eye seeth Thee* (Job xlii. 5). So, also, when the Scripture relates that the Holy Ghost descended upon the Apostles, is not hearing described as having preceded sight? For it is said: *Suddenly there came a sound from heaven as of a rushing mighty wind;* and, then, in the next verse: *There appeared unto them cloven tongues like as of fire* (Acts ii. 2, 3). Here, then, it is plainly shown that the coming of the Holy Spirit was perceived, first by hearing, and afterwards by sight. But enough has been said upon this subject, for you also, if you will take the trouble to pursue this inquiry further, will perhaps be able to find similar instances in other parts of Scripture.

3. Now let us consider a subject which, because it cannot be approached without difficulty, needs a specially careful examination; in which I confess that I am altogether dependent on the aid of the Holy Spirit, that I may be able clearly to explain what are those mountains and those hills upon which the Church saw with great gladness her Bridegroom leaping, and over which she saw Him pass with rapid steps, when, as I think, He was hastening to come to accomplish her redemption for whose beauty He was filled with love. That this is the case I have confidence in believing, inasmuch as a similar passage of Scripture occurs to me in which the Psalmist evidently spoke prophetically under the guidance of the Spirit, and foretold the coming of the Saviour: *He hath set His tabernacle in the sun, and He, as a Bridegroom coming out of his bridechamber, hath rejoiced as a giant to run the way; His going out is from the end of heaven, and His circuit even to the end thereof* (Ps. xviii. 6, Douay). His going forth, and His return likewise, are here most clear; whence it was undertaken, whither, and to what end, most clear also. What then? When we read these words in the Psalms, or in the Canticle before us, ought we to imagine to ourselves a giant of prodigious stature, who is captivated by the love of some fair one dwelling at a distance from him, and whom we behold on his way to her traversing with great steps, with leaps and bounds, those hills and mountains which we see lifting their lofty mass out of the plain, and that so high that some of their most elevated peaks are lost in the clouds? But it is not becoming to have recourse to material images such as these when treating of a spiritual poem, and to us in particular it is altogether forbidden, for we remember what we have read in the

Gospel, that *God is a Spirit, and they that worship Him must worship Him in spirit and in truth* (John iv. 24).

4. What, then [let us inquire], are these mountains and these hills, spiritually understood, so that we may be able as a consequence to comprehend in what way the Bridegroom (who, as He is God, is therefore also Spirit), and with what kind of bounds, can leap upon them and over them? If we suppose that they are those mountains upon which, as the Gospel declares, the ninety and nine sheep were wandering when their kind Shepherd came to the earth to seek His sheep which had gone astray (Matt. xviii. 12); the matter is still obscure, and the understanding baffled, because it is difficult to find out what are those other mountains on which dwell and feed the heavenly and spiritual beatitudes, which are, without doubt, those who are there spoken of as sheep. But if there were no such [mountains] in truth, then the Truth would not have said this. Nor, again, would the Psalmist have said long before of the heavenly Jerusalem, that her foundations were upon the holy mountains (Ps. lxxxvii. 1), if there were, in fact, no such mountains at all. Lastly, to show that the celestial country has mountains and hills, not only spiritual, but also living, and of a reasonable nature, hear the words of Isaiah: *The mountains and the hills shall break forth before* [God] *into singing* (Is. lv. 12).

5. What, then, are they except those very spirits, dwellers in heaven, whom the Lord, as we have said, calls sheep, and who signify at once sheep and mountains? Unless it should perhaps seem to you absurd that mountains should be said to feed upon mountains and sheep upon sheep. Taken in a literal sense, no doubt, this explanation seems harsh; but to the spiritual understanding it will appear harmonious if we understand it in a deeper sense—viz., that the Shepherd of each flock, Christ the Wisdom of God, administers one and the same food of truth both in heaven and on earth, but in one way to His heavenly flocks and in another to His earthly ones. For we mortal men, while we are in the place of our pilgrimage, have indeed necessarily to eat our bread in the sweat of our brow, and to beg it from without in labour and distress—that is, to gain a knowledge of the invisible things of God, which are understood by the things which are made, either from men who are instructed in holy things or from the Scriptures of God. But the Angels receive it in themselves, though not for themselves, and with as much facility as felicity, which is for them the great happiness of their existence. For they are all (capable of being) taught of God, which blessing it is promised that the elect among men shall assuredly attain at some future time, though this assured felicity it is not granted to them as yet to enjoy.

6. Thus mountains do feed upon mountains, or sheep upon sheep, since those celestial and spiritual beings find abundantly in themselves, by the word of life which they receive, the means to render their blessedness perpetual, and are at the same time (as it were)

mountains and sheep; mountains, because of their exaltation and their fulness; sheep, because of their gentleness and goodness. For they are full of God, raised high by merits, and heaped with virtues, and yet do not fail to bend their heads, however lofty, in complete and humble obedience and submission to the sovereign Majesty of God; as innocent and gentle sheep conduct themselves in all things according to the will of their shepherd, and follow him whithersoever he goeth. And, according to David the Psalmist, upon these mountains truly holy, as upon wisdom created first of all things, the foundations of the City of God are firmly set and stand fast from the beginning (Ps. lxxxvii. 1); and this City is one, both in heaven and on earth, though in part it is militant on earth, and in part reigning in heaven. And, nevertheless, from these mountains, according to the prophet Isaiah, resounds thanksgiving, and the voice of melody (Is. li. 3), as from living and harmonious cymbals, accomplishing thus, with sweet and never-ceasing sound, that word of the same prophet which I quoted before, that *the mountains and the hills shall break forth before* [God] *into singing*, and also this other word which the Psalmist has addressed to the Lord God: *Blessed are they that dwell in Thy House, they will be still praising Thee* (Ps. lxxxiv. 4).

7. So much, then, upon this subject; let us now take up again the thread of our discourse, from which we have digressed a little, but necessarily, as I think: those are the mountains and the hills on which the Church has seen her heavenly Spouse leaping with wonderful alacrity, and even overleaping them, in haste to meet and welcome her. Do you desire that I should show you, out of the writings of the Prophets and Apostles, what is to be mystically understood by these? I do not intend to repeat to you all the testimonies with regard to this which may be found in those writings by those who have leisure to search them (for this would take a long time, and there is no need for it), but only those which appear to confirm clearly and briefly what is said here of the boundings of the Bridegroom. Now, David says of Him that *His going forth is from the end of the heaven* (Ps. xix. 6, already quoted). Lo! what a bound was that, even from the height of heaven down to the earth! For I find not any other spot, but the earth, which can be intended when it is said that He has placed His tabernacle in the sun—that is, He, who dwells in the inaccessible Light, has deigned to manifest His Presence openly and in the light. Then, again, He was seen upon earth, and conversed with men (Baruch iii. 38). Upon the earth, and before the eyes of men, I say, that is, according to the phrase here used, ' in the sun ' hath He set His tabernacle; that is, the Body which He has condescended to take to Himself from the body of a Virgin, so that He, who was invisible in Himself, might become visible in It, and thus all flesh might see the salvation of God, which was made manifest in the flesh.

8. He has bounded, then, upon the mountains; that is, upon the highest spiritual beings, when He descended even to them, and

deigned to reveal to them the great mystery of His goodness, which was a secret hidden from the beginning of the world. But passing over, or overleaping those loftier mountain heights, namely, Cherubin and Seraphin, Dominations, Principalities, Powers, and Virtues, He deigned to descend, as it were, upon the hills—that is, even unto a lower order of Angels But has He remained even with them? Nay, He has overleaped even the hills For *He took not on Him the nature of Angels; but He took on Him the seed of Abraham* (Heb. ii. 16), and this was inferior to that of the Angels, so that thus was accomplished the word of the Psalmist, when he spoke thus to the Father of the Son: *Thou hast made Him a little lower than the Angels* (Ps. viii. 5). Though, indeed, it is possible to explain this passage as spoken in commendation of human nature, inasmuch as man, who is made in the image and likeness of God, and endowed with reason in like manner as an Angel, is yet a little lower than the Angel, because he has a body of earth. Hear what the Apostle Paul says plainly of Jesus Christ: *Who, being in the form of God, thought it not robbery to be equal with God; but made Himself of no reputation, and took upon Him the form of a servant, and was made in the likeness of men, being found in fashion as a man* (Phil. ii. 6-8); and again: *When the fulness of the time was come, God sent forth His Son, made of a woman, made under the Law, to redeem them that were under the Law* (Gal. iv. 4, 5). It is, then, beyond doubt that being made of a woman, and made under the Law, He has passed in descending to the earth, not only the mountains, that is, the higher orders of blessed spirits, but also the lower orders of these, who, in comparison of their superiors, may rightly be called hills. But he who is least in the kingdom of heaven is greater than whosoever bears a body of flesh upon the earth, even though it were that great Saint, John the Baptist (Luke vii. 28). For, although we do truly confess that He who is God and man, even as Man is far above, and incomparably superior to, every Principality and Power, yet it is certain that if H surpasses them in majesty, He falls short of them in respect c physical weakness. Thus, then, it is that He leaps upon the mountains, and leaps over the hills, when by a vast condescension He shows Himself as inferior, not only to spirits of a higher rank, but also to those of a lower. For He was manifested as subject, not only to those heavenly spirits, but also to those who dwelt in bodies of clay, overleaping and overcoming by His humility even the humbleness of men. For when He was at Nazareth, at the age of twelve years, He was subject unto Mary and Joseph (Luke ii. 51, 52); at the river Jordan, being then a young man, He bent Himself under the hands of St. John Baptist (Matt. iii. 13). But now the day is already verging towards evening, nor have we yet been able to descend from these mountains.

9. Yet if we should wish for this once only to satisfy our curiosity by examining what is beautiful, by searching out what is hidden in this mystery, it is to be feared that either the sermon would be weari-

somely long, or that in our haste we should treat with too little care a matter very large and important. Let us, then, stop here for to-day, if you wish, upon these mountains, for it is good for us to be here; and Christ our good Shepherd, having placed us with the holy Angels in a rich pasture, we are able to feed in it at once with pleasure and abundance. And we are indeed the sheep of His pasture. Let us, then, as a pure flock of the good Shepherd, meditate with our best powers (*ruminemus*) upon the spiritual food we have received in the sermon of to-day. We will complete in the next what remains to be said upon this subject; let us try to give our best attention to it, by the grace of Him who is the Bridegroom of the Church, JESUS CHRIST our Lord, who is above all, God blessed for ever. AMEN.

SERMON LIV.

ANOTHER INTERPRETATION; IN WHICH BY *MOUNTAINS* ARE SIGNIFIED ANGELS AND MEN; AND BY *HILLS*, DEMONS. ALSO OF THE THREEFOLD FEAR WITH WHICH EVERYONE OUGHT TO FEEL ANXIETY, LEST HE SHOULD LOSE THE GRACE OF ACTING RIGHTLY, WHICH HE HAS RECEIVED FROM GOD.

UPON the same verse which was treated in the sermon of yesterday I will bring before you another interpretation, differing from that which I gave before: you will choose which of the two is to be preferred. There is no need to repeat what was said before, which I think will not in so short a time have escaped you. But if that be the case, that sermon, like the others, has been written down as it was delivered, except perhaps the exact words,[1] so that whatever has slipped from the memory may easily be recalled. Having said this, let me go on to speak of other things. *Behold*, it is said, *He cometh leaping upon the mountains, skipping over the hills*. She speaks of the Bridegroom. He no doubt leapt over the mountains when, having been sent by the Father to preach the Gospel to the poor, He did not disdain to perform the function of Angels, though He was the Lord of Angels, and to become the Angel of the great purpose of God. He who was wont to depute others to come down to earth descended hither in His own Person; the Lord Himself made known the salvation which He brought, and Himself revealed His Righteousness in the sight of the nations (Ps. xcviii. 2). Since, then, all the angels, according to the Apostle, are *ministering spirits, sent forth to minister for them who shall be heirs of salvation* (Heb. i. 14), He who was above them, passing over the injury done by men, and multiplying upon them His grace, was numbered among

---

[1] *Excepta stilo.*

the angels, becoming as one of them. But hear what He Himself said: *I came, not to be ministered unto, but to minister, and to give My life a ransom for many* (Matt. xx. 28). Which, indeed, no angel was found to have done; so that by the devotion and fidelity of His services to men, He has surpassed all those who had come to serve them before. No minister has shown such self-devotion as He, who has given (*ministravit*) His Flesh for their food, His Blood for their cordial, His very life for their ransom. None, surely, is so good as He who, by the fervour of His spirit, by the ardour of His love, and the devotion of His goodness, has not only leaped upon the mountains, but leaped over the hills; that is to say, He has surpassed and overcome them by the earnest desire which He felt to save men; wherefore God, His God, has anointed Him with the oil of gladness above His fellows (Ps. xlv. 7). It is in this earnestness of His desire that He proceeds with great and rapid steps 'as a giant to run his course.' He overpassed Gabriel, and, according to that Archangel's own testimony, was with the Virgin before him; for did he not say: *Hail, thou that art full of grace, the Lord is with thee?*[1] What? Thou findest Him now in the womb [of the Virgin], whom thou hast just left in heaven. How can that be? He has flown and foreflown on the wings of the winds. Thou art surpassed, O Archangel; the Lord has overleaped and anticipated thee.

2. Or, again, He 'leaped upon the mountains' when He appeared formerly to the Fathers in the person of angels; which seems to agree more closely with the letter of the text. For it is not said 'leaping on to the mountains,' but 'in the mountains,'[2] so that He who causes and enables them to leap, leaps also in them; just as it is He who speaks in the prophets and acts in the righteous, when He enables the one to speak and the other to do good works. Add to this that some of them represented Him, so that whosoever of them spoke, he did so not as angel, but as the Lord. For example, that angel who spoke with Moses did not say 'I am the Angel of the Lord,' but 'I am the Lord'; and repeated that frequently. He, therefore, leaped *in the mountains*—that is, in the angels, in whom He was wont both to speak and to manifest His Presence to men. He did this also upon men, but in the person of angels, not in His own Person; nor in His own Nature, but in that of one of His subject races. For he who leaps passes from one place to another, and this cannot be ascribed to God. Therefore He leaped in the mountains, that is, in the angels, who would do this in His own Person; and He leaped to, or upon, the hills, that is, upon the Patriarchs and Prophets, and other spiritual men who were on the earth. But also, He 'leaped over' the hills, since He deigned to appear to, and to speak with, not only great men and spiritual men, but also to certain of the people, and even to some women, by the same ministry of angels. Or it may be

---

[1] Luke i. 28, *prævenit*. This is the reading in the MSS., not *pervenit*, as in the printed editions. The early edition of Rouald also has *prævenit*.

[2] *Non* '*in montes*' *sed* '*in montibus.*'

that by 'hills' the Scripture understands the powers of the air, which are not now numbered among 'mountains,' because they have fallen by pride from the height of virtue; and yet they are not abased by penitence nor humbled to the lowliness of valleys, or to the valleys of the lowly. I suppose that it was of these that those words were spoken in the Psalms: *The hills melted like wax at the presence of the Lord* (Ps. xcvii. 5). He who leaps in the mountains without doubt leaps over these swollen and sterile hills, which hold, as it were, a middle place between the mountains of the perfect and the valleys of the penitent; these He passes over with scorn, and descends into the valleys, that the valleys may abound with grain. Those others, on the contrary, are condemned to perpetual dryness and sterility, as in that calling down of evil of the Prophet upon such: *Let there be no dew, neither rain upon you.* And that you may know that, under the figure of the mountains of Gilboa, this saying applies to the angels who fell, notice the reason that is given: *For there many wounded have fallen* (2 Sam. i. 21). How many from the army of Israel have fallen upon those accursed mountains from the beginning, and how many still fall at the present! It is of those that the same Psalmist speaks when he says to the Lord: *Like as the dead, that lie in the grave, whom Thou rememberest no more: and they are cut off from Thy Hand* (Ps. lxxxviii. 5).

3. It is not, therefore, wonderful if those spirits, which are not, as it were, mountains of heaven, but hills of the lower air, upon which neither dew nor showers of rain fall, should remain always sterile and unfruitful; since the Author of grace and the Giver of blessings leaps or passes over these, and descends to the valleys, so as to pour forth rain from heaven upon the humble who are on the earth, and to make them to bring forth fruit with patience, some thirtyfold, some sixtyfold, and some an hundredfold (Matt. xiii. 8 and Luke viii. 15). He visits the earth and blesses it; He makes it to be very plenteous (Ps. lxv. 9). But it is the earth, not the air, that He has visited, because *the earth is full of the goodness of the Lord* (Ps. xxxiii. 5). It is declared also that God has *worked salvation in the midst of the earth* (Ps. lxxiv. 12): but does the Psalmist say also 'in the midst of the air'? This [may be taken as] against Origen, who, by a false and impudent theory, crucified the Lord of glory once again in the midst of the air for the sake of demons: whereas St. Paul, being conscious of this mystery, affirms that Christ, *being raised from the dead, dieth no more: death hath no more dominion over Him* (Rom. vi. 9).

4. But He who has passed through the air has visited not only the earth, but also the heaven, as the Scripture declares: *Thy mercy, O Lord, is in the heavens, and Thy faithfulness reacheth unto the clouds* (Ps. xxxvi. 5); that is to say, unto the heaven in which dwell the holy angels, whom the Bridegroom does not pass over, but leaps in them, so that He impresses in them, as it were, the prints of His Feet—mercy, that is, and truth—as to which Footprints of the Lord I remember that I have spoken at greater length in another sermon

(Sermon VI.). But the abode of the demons is below the clouds, and removed from them, in the obscure and gloomy air that is lowest of all; and in them the Bridegroom does not make His beneficent power operative, but passes them wholly over, without leaving in them any trace of His Divine passage. For how can truth be found in the devil, of whom we find in the Gospels the declaration of the Truth Himself, that he abode not in the truth, because there is no truth in him (John viii. 44)? Again, who can say that he is merciful, when the same Truth has testified of him likewise in the Gospel, that he was a murderer from the beginning? Now, such as the head of the family is, such are they of his house also. With great fitness and beauty, then, does the Church, singing of the Bridegroom, declare that He dwelleth on high, and humbleth Himself to behold the things that are in heaven and in the earth (Ps. cxiii. 5, 6), but makes no mention of those spirits of pride which are in the air, because God *resisteth the proud, and giveth grace unto the humble* (James iv. 6).

5. The Church sees Him, then, leaping in the mountains, and passing over the hills, according to the imprecation of David: 'Let the Lord visit all the mountains which are in their circuit'—that is, in the circuit of Gilboa—'but Gilboa let Him not visit.'[1] For there are mountains which the Lord visits, on this side and on that of Gilboa, by which is signified the devil; above there are angels, below there are men. To him, when he fell from heaven, was assigned as punishment an abode in that region of the air (Eph. ii. 2) midway between heaven and earth, that he might see and be envious, and be tortured with the envy which he feels. And this the Scripture describes when it says: *The wicked shall see it, and be grieved: he shall gnash with his teeth, and melt away* (Ps. cxii. 10). How unhappy must he be when he looks up to heaven and descries its mountains innumerable, all illuminated and shining with the Divine glory, all resounding with the praises of God, full and abounding with His glory and grace! How still more unhappy when he looks down upon the earth, and beholds there also many mountains of people, chosen and made the sons of God,[2] who are established in the faith of lofty hope, of wide-extending charity; who are accomplished in virtues, rich in the fruits of good works; upon whom falls day by day the Divine benediction, as it were by the dew from heaven, or, so to speak, from the mystical touch of the Bridegroom's foot in His leaping! With how great grief and jealousy, must we suppose, does that spirit so greedily desirous of glory behold those glorious mountains in their perfect ring, while he and his followers are (as it were) regions rough, gloomy, unfruitful in any good thing, and every way to be despised; so that he who calumniated all that lived is himself become the opprobrium of men and of angels, according to

---

[1] 2 Sam. i. 21   This is not, however, a quotation, but a gloss or paraphrase; and the same remark applies to the citation of this verse on p. 326.—ED.
[2] *Populo acquisitionis.*

that saying in the Psalms: *That dragon whom Thou hast formed to be a derision* (Ps. civ. 26) [1]

6. And the cause of this is that the Bridegroom passes them over on account of their pride, leaping upon the mountains which are around, as the fountain which arises from the midst of Paradise, watering the whole earth, and filling with blessing every living thing. Blessed are those who deserve to drink sometimes, even though it be rarely, of the torrent of this delight, and in whom the water of wisdom and the fountain of life leaps forth from time to time, though it does not flow continuously, so that it becomes in them a fountain of water springing up into everlasting life (John iv. 14). And, indeed, the flowing of this river is perennial and abundant, making glad the city of God (Ps. xlvi. 4). May God vouchsafe, in His condescension, to send upon our mountains on earth some gushings of this stream sometimes, as it were by a kind of inundation, so that they, being sufficiently watered, may be able to distil upon us also, who are valleys, some little rills, though they be few and small, that we may not remain altogether dry and unfruitful. Only misery, and poverty, and biting famine is the lot of that region which is never moistened by plentiful flowings, or even little tricklings, from the fountain of wisdom, but is altogether passed by and passed over. 'They were destroyed,' it is said, 'because they had no wisdom, and perished through their own foolishness' (Baruch iii. 28).

7. *Behold, He cometh leaping upon the mountains, skipping upon the hills.* He leaps so as to overleap (*transiliat*), because it is not His will to extend [His presence] to all; nor is it the good pleasure of God [to do this] in every case. Brethren, if, according to the wise saying of St. Paul, *those things are written for our admonition* (1 Cor. x. 11), let us observe the discretion and circumspection of the mystical bounds of the Bridegroom; let us remark how, as among the angels, so among us, He bounds spiritually upon the humble, and passes over the proud. For though the Lord be highest of all, yet hath He respect unto the lowly; but the proud He knoweth afar off (Ps. cxxxviii. 6). Of this, I say, let us take notice, so that we may be prepared for the saving bounds of the Bridegroom, lest, as He passes over the mountains of Gilboa, so He may pass over us also, if He shall have perceived that we are unworthy of His visitation. Why dost thou, who art but earth and ashes, indulge in pride? The Lord abhors the pride even of angels [who are proud], and passes them over on that account. Therefore let the casting off of angels cause the correction of men; for it has been recorded for our admonition. Let the evil even of the devil co-operate for good to me, and may I wash my hands in the blood of the ungodly. In what manner, do you inquire? As thus: A terrible and fearful malediction has been hurled against that proud one, the devil, the Prophet David speaking in the Spirit

[1] This interpretation is a traditional Eastern one, and seems to be founded on the rendering of the LXX.: δράκων οὗτος ὃν ἔπλασας ἐμπαίζειν αὐτῷ. See Job xli. 5, and Baruch iii. 17.—ED.

of Him under the type of Mount Gilboa, as was related above : ' Let the Lord visit all the mountains which are in his circuit; but Gilboa let Him not visit.'

8. When I read these words, and when, turning my eyes upon myself, I consider myself diligently, I find that I am infected with that very disease which the Lord regarded in an Angel with displeasure so great as to turn away altogether from him, at the same time that He deigned to honour with His visitation all the mountains which are around him, whether of Angels or of men; and I say to myself with fear and trembling : ' If it was thus done with an angel, what shall be done with regard to me, who am but earth and ashes ?' It was in heaven that he indulged in pride ; but I have done so upon a mere dunghill. Who does not find pride more bearable in the rich than in the poor? Woe unto me ! if a spirit so powerful was punished with such severity because his heart was lifted up with pride, and if it availed him nothing that pride is recognised to be congenial to the powerful, what penalty must be exacted from me, who am poor and miserable, and yet am proud ? But I receive already the chastisement ; I am stricken already with many stripes. Not undeservedly has for days past that languor of soul, that mental slothfulness, that unaccustomed inertness of spirit stolen over me. I did run well ; but, lo ! a stone of stumbling was in my path ; I have stumbled against it, and fallen. Pride has been found in me, and the Lord has turned away in wrath from His servant. Hence is that barrenness of my soul and that defect in devotion which I experience. How is it that my heart is thus dried up? soured as it were milk, made like earth in which is no water? Its hardness has become so great that I am not able to shed tears. In the chanting of the Psalms I feel no interest, I do not care to read, I have no delight in prayer, I do not resort to my habitual meditations. Where is my former cheerfulness and delight of soul ? my calm, and peace, and joy in the Holy Ghost ? For the same reason I am slothful in manual labour, drowsy during vigils, hasty in anger, obstinate in hatred, more unguarded in speech, and self-indulgent at the table than I was wont, unobservant and slow of heart during preaching. Alas ! the Lord visits all the mountains which are around me, but to me He draws not near. Am not I that one of all these hills which the Bridegroom passes over ? For of those around me I see one remarkable for abstinence, another for admirable patience, another for consummate humility and gentleness, another for much mercy and kindness; this man I behold spending long hours in contemplation, and that man knocking hard at the doors of heaven by the earnestness of his prayers ; and there are others whom I see to excel in other virtues. I remark (I say) that all these are fervent, all devoted, all of one mind in Christ, all rich in grace and in heavenly gifts, as being, so to speak, in truth spiritual mountains which are visited by the Lord, and receive often in themselves the mystical bounds of the Bridegroom. But I, who find in myself none of all

these things, what else can I suppose myself to be than one of the mountains of Gilboa, which the Saviour, who visits in His great goodness all the others, passes over in His wrath and indignation?

9. My dear children, this reflection takes away the vain glorification of self, attracts to us the gifts of grace, prepares us for the mystical bounds of the Bridegroom. These things I have, for your sakes, transferred to myself, and spoken as if they had taken place in my own person, that you might learn a lesson from them. Be ye then followers of me; I do not say in the exercise of virtues or the discipline of character, or the glory of holiness (for in all these respects I do not set myself up as worthy of imitation), but I would that you should follow me in not sparing yourselves, but on the contrary, accusing your own selves as often as you detect that grace is lessening in you, that zeal is growing cold, and virtue languishing, as you see that I likewise accuse myself. To do this is to act as a man who watches exactly over himself, who examines with care his ways and his desires, and who in everything holds in suspicion the vice of arrogance, for fear that it should creep secretly into his heart. In truth, I have learned by my own experience that there is nothing so efficacious in deserving grace, in preserving it, or in recovering it if lost, as to be found at all times not high-minded before God, but filled with holy fear. *Happy is the man that feareth alway* (Prov. xxviii. 14). Fear, then, when favouring grace is with thee, fear when it has departed; fear also when at length it returns; this it is to fear alway. Let these three kinds of fear succeed each other in your soul, according as you are favoured by the presence of grace, or as it has retired grieved from you, or forgivingly returns. When it is present, let your fear be that you may not act and walk worthily of it; for this is the precept of the Apostle St. Paul: See that *ye receive not the grace of God in vain* (2 Cor vi. 1); and to one of his disciples, *Neglect not the gift that is in thee* (1 Tim. iv. 14); while of himself he said: *The grace* (of God) *which was bestowed upon me was not in vain* (1 Cor. xv. 10). That great man, who knew the counsel of God, was well aware that to neglect the gifts of God, or not to use them to the purpose for which they were given, is to display great disregard, and even contempt, for the giver; and that he considered to be intolerable pride. Therefore it was that he both avoided this wrong-doing with the greatest care himself, and taught others to avoid it also. But there is still another den or hiding-place in which pride is wont to lurk, which I wish to discover to you; and this is the more perilous because it is very closely concealed; as says the Psalmist: *He lieth in wait secretly as a lion in his den* (Ps. x. 9). For if he is not able to hinder [a good] action, he endeavours to tamper with the intention of it, suggesting and persuading you to attribute to yourself that which is the effect of grace. And do not be under any mistake about this kind of pride; it is even far worse than the former. For what can be more hateful than language of this kind, which has been used by some: *Our mighty*

hand, and not the Lord, hath done all these things (Deut. xxxii. 27, Douay).

10. If, then, you ought to fear while grace remains with you, what should you do when it has left you? Ought you not, then, much more to fear? Plainly that is the case, for, where grace fails you, you fail too. Listen to the words of Him who is the sovereign Giver of grace: *Without Me*, He says, *ye can do nothing* (John xv. 5). Fear, then, the withdrawal of grace, as the sure prelude of your speedy fall. Fear and tremble exceedingly because you feel that God's just anger is aroused against you, and that the powerful guardianship which hitherto has kept you safe has abandoned you. Do not hesitate to believe that your pride is the cause of this, even though you are conscious of no pride, and there is none apparent in your actions; for that which you do not know God knows, and it is He who is your Judge. And it is not he that commendeth himself that is approved, but whom the Lord commendeth (2 Cor. x. 18). Now, if the Lord deprives you of grace, is that a sign of His commendation? Or will He who giveth grace unto the humble (James iv. 6) take away from one who is humble that which He has already given? Therefore the taking away of grace is a proof of pride [in him from whom it is taken]. Though it must be added that sometimes grace is taken away or withheld, not on account of pride which is present at the time, but to prevent pride which would follow unless grace were taken away. Of this we have a clear example in the person of the Apostle [St. Paul], who endured reluctantly his thorn in the flesh, not because he was exalted above measure, but in order that he might not be so (2 Cor. xii. 7). But pride, whether existing in the present or to be apprehended in the future, will ever be a cause for the withdrawal of grace.

11. Again, if grace shall have returned with the regaining of God's favour, much more is there reason for fear lest a second fall should happen to us, according to that saying in the Gospel: *Behold, thou art made whole; sin no more, lest a worse thing come unto thee* (John v. 14). You hear, then, that it is worse to fall again into sin than to sin the first time; let your fear, therefore, be greater in proportion as your danger increases. Happy are you if your heart be filled with this threefold fear, so that you fear when you have received grace, still more when that grace is lost, but most of all when it has been regained. Do this, and you will be as the waterpot at that marriage at Cana where Christ was a guest, filled to the very brim, containing, not two measures apiece, but three; and you will deserve the blessing of Christ, which shall turn the water [of your poor nature] into the wine of gladness, until the time when your charity, being perfected, shall cast out all fear (1 John iv. 18).

12. I say, then, that thus it is that fear is typified by water, inasmuch as it tempers the heat of carnal desires. *The fear of the Lord*, saith the Scripture, *is the beginning of wisdom* (Ps. cxi. 10); and again: *The fear of the Lord is a fountain of life* (Prov. xiv. 27;

Ecclus. xv. 3; xix. 18-20). Your mind, then, is as one of those waterpots, containing, says the Scripture, *two or three measures apiece*. Now, the three measures represent the three kinds of fear. *They filled them*, continues the Evangelist, *up to the brim*. So that it is not one kind of fear, nor two, which suffices to fill [your mind] to its utmost extent, but three are needed. Fear God at all times and with all your heart, and then you have filled that measure, which is your mind, up to the brim. God loves that an offering made to Him should be without defect, that love offered to Him should be without reserve; in short, that the sacrifice laid upon His altar should be in every way perfect. Therefore be careful to bring that measure, your mind, filled [with holy fear] to the heavenly marriage feast, so that it may be said of you also: *He shall be filled with the spirit of the fear of the Lord* (Is. xi. 3, Douay). He who fears thus neglects nothing; for how can negligence enter into that which is wholly filled? That which is capable of receiving something more is not absolutely full. For a similar reason it is not possible to fear and at the same time to indulge in thoughts of pride. And there is no place for pride to enter your mind if it be filled with the fear of the Lord. And it is the same with other faults and vices, they are of necessity excluded by the fulness of this gracious fear. Then, when your fear shall be thus full and perfect, love, bringing the benediction of the Lord, shall impart to your water the rich flavour and fragrance of wine. For fear without love is but pain and suffering, and love is that wine *which maketh glad the heart of man* (Ps. civ. 15). For love, when perfected, casteth out fear, so that where there was but water, there begins to be the glow and the sparkle of wine, to the praise and glory of Him who is the Bridegroom of the Church, JESUS CHRIST our Lord, who is above all, God blessed for ever. AMEN.

SERMON LV.

HOW IT IS POSSIBLE, THROUGH A TRUE PENITENCE, TO ESCAPE THE JUDGMENT OF GOD.

'*My Beloved is like a roe or a young hart.*'—Cant. ii. 9.

THIS depends upon the preceding verse. The Bride now compares to a roe or a young hart Him whom she had just described as advancing with rapid leaps. The comparison is an apt one, since those animals are swift of foot and agile in leaping. She speaks, then, of the Bridegroom, and the Bridegroom is the Word. And the Psalmist says of God that *His Word runneth very swiftly* (Ps. cxlvii. 15), which exactly agrees with this passage, in which the Bridegroom, who is the Word of God, is described as leaping and traversing swiftly the mountains in the manner of a roe or young hart. This is the ground of the comparison made. To this add, that not even the smallest ground of similarity may be wanting, that the roebuck is remarkable not only for its headlong swiftness, but also for the keenness of its sight. Which last quality has special reference to this part of the narrative, since the Bridegroom is described as not only *leaping* on some mountains, but as *overleaping* others, and unless His sight were keen and piercing He would not be able to distinguish, especially during the rapid speed of His course, those on which He should alight from those which He should pass over. Otherwise, to mark simply His speed, it would have sufficed to compare Him to a young hart, for that animal is noted for its swiftness. But because the Bridegroom, though the ardour of His affection is carrying Him with exceeding swiftness to the meeting with His beloved, yet does not omit to direct His steps, or rather His bounds, with prudence and circumspection, and to take heed where He ought to set His foot, therefore it was expedient to compare Him to a roe as well as to a young hart, as if to express as well by the one His strong desire to save, as by the other His discerning and careful choice. For Christ is just as well as merciful; He is Judge as well as Saviour. Because He loves men He desires all to be saved and come to the knowledge of the truth (1 Tim. ii. 4), and because He has the office of judgment He *knoweth* them that are His (2 Tim. ii. 19) and whom He hath chosen [from the beginning] (John xiii. 18).

2. Let us, then, in the meantime recognise that these two transcendent attributes of the Bridegroom—namely, mercy and judgment —are commended to us by the Holy Spirit under the types of these two animals, so that for a testimony of the uprightness and perfectness of our faith we may imitate the Psalmist, and sing with him unto the Lord of mercy and judgment (Ps. ci. 1). But I do not doubt that those who are instructed and inquiring in such subjects will be able to point out other points of likeness of a similar kind which may fitly and usefully be applied to the Bridegroom; but these may, I think, suffice here as giving a reason for the comparison. Yet there is one more point of beautiful significance in this similitude here instituted by the Holy Spirit between the Bridegroom and (not a stag, but) a *young hart.* For in that is recalled at once the memory of the Fathers (of whom, according to the flesh, Christ came) and the Infancy of the Saviour. For the Child who unto us is born (Is. ix. 6) came into the world weak and poor, and, as it were, as a young fawn. But thou who desirest the coming of the Saviour, do thou hold in salutary fear the scrutiny of the Judge; fear His piercing glance; fear Him who by the mouth of the prophet declares: *It shall come to pass at that time that I will search Jerusalem with candles*[1] (Zeph. i. 12). Piercing is His sight; His eye shall leave nothing unexamined. He shall try the hearts and reins (Ps. vii. 9), and the

[1] *In lucernis,* Vulgate.

very thoughts of men are open and confessed to Him (Heb. iv. 13). If Jerusalem shall undergo a scrutiny so searching, who shall be safe in Babylon? For I think that in this passage the Prophet refers, under the name of Jerusalem, to those who in this world lead a religious life; who imitate, as far as they are able, by their regulated and honourable conduct, the condition and mode of existence in that heavenly Jerusalem, and who are not as those who belong to Babylon, and whose life is full of disorders and crimes. For their sins are manifest, going before to judgment (1 Tim. v. 24); and require, not examination, but punishment. But as for me, who appear to be a monk and a citizen of Jerusalem, my sins are covered and, as it were, cloaked under the monastic habit and name; and on that account there will be need of strict and exact inquiry (of the bringing of lanterns, so to speak), and throwing light upon what is now in the darkness.

3. I may bring forward something more from one of the Psalms to confirm what is said about the judging of Jerusalem. For the Psalmist, speaking in the Name of God, says: *When I shall take a time, I will judge righteousnesses* (Ps. lxxv. 2). By this He means, if I do not mistake, to say that He will discuss and examine the ways and the actions of the righteous. We have great reason to fear that when subjected to a scrutiny so vigorous, many of our actions which we believe to be praiseworthy will be shown to be veritably sins. But there is one resource: that *if we would judge ourselves, we should not be judged* (1 Cor. xi. 31). Good for me is that judgment, which withdraws me and hides me from the Divine judgment, which is so terribly severe. I fear and tremble to think of falling into the hands of the living God; I would be brought before the countenance of His anger already judged, and not for judgment. *He who is spiritual judgeth all things, yet he himself is judged of no man* (1 Cor. ii. 15). I will judge, then, the evil which is in me, and I will judge also the good. I will take care to correct the evil by better actions, to wash it away by tears, to punish it by fasts and other actions of holy discipline. I will think humbly of any good qualities I have, and, according to the precept of the Lord, will count myself an unprofitable servant, who has done only that which it was his duty to do (Luke xvii. 10). I will make it my endeavour not to offer Him tares for grain, nor yet chaff mingled with the grain. I will examine closely my ways and my purposes, so that He who will search Jerusalem with lanterns may find nothing in me unexamined or unsifted. For He will not judge the same thing twice over.

4. Who will give me grace to find out and search clearly all my defaults to their very lowest grounds, so that I may have no need to fear those keen eyes (*capreæ*), nor to blush when the light of those lanterns is thrown upon me? Now I am seen, but I do not see. The eye of Him to whom all things are open and manifest is present, though He Himself is not visible. There will be a time when I shall know, even as also I am known; but now I know only in part, though

it is not in part, but wholly and entirely that I am known. I fear the sight of that Divine Observer who stands, as it were, behind a wall. For this is what the Scripture adds respecting Him whom, for the keenness of His sight, it has compared to a hart: *Behold, He standeth behind our wall, He looketh forth at the windows, shewing Himself through the lattice* (ii. 9). But we will explain that in its place. Him I fear, the hidden Observer of hidden things. But the Bride fears nothing, because she is conscious of no wrong. What has she, in fact, to fear, who is His beloved one, His dove, His undefiled? (vi. 9). Also you read farther on: *My Beloved spake unto me.* He speaks, and that is why I fear to behold him, because I have not His testimony that I am His. But thou, O Bride, what is it that thou hearest Him say of thee? What to thee dost thy Beloved say? *Rise up*, He says, *My love, My fair one, and come away.* But this we must defer to the beginning of another sermon, so as not to limit too much that which requires to be treated at length, lest perhaps I be found faulty in this matter, if you do not find that you are edified and built up in the knowledge and love of Him who is the Bridegroom of the Church, JESUS CHRIST our Lord, who is above all, God blessed for ever. AMEN.

SERMON LVI

THAT SINS AND VICES ARE AS WALLS INTERPOSING BETWEEN GOD AND THE SINNER.

'*Behold, He standeth behind our wall, He looketh forth at the windows, shewing Himself through the lattice.*'—Cant. ii. 9.

ACCORDING to the letter the Bride seems to say that He whom she descried from afar, approaching with leaps and bounds, has now drawn near to her dwelling, and stands behind the wall gazing earnestly through the windows and other openings, and modestly not presuming to enter. But, according to the Spirit, it is to be understood that He has indeed drawn near, but after another manner worthy to be adopted by that Heavenly Bridegroom, and to be described by the Holy Spirit. For the true and spiritual understanding will admit nothing which is not becoming to Him who is described as acting, or to Him who records what is done. The Bridegroom, then, has drawn near to the wall, because He has united Himself to human flesh. The wall is human nature, and the drawing near of the Bridegroom is the Incarnation of the Word. The windows and the lattices by which He is said to look out are, as I think, the senses of the flesh, and the human affections and feelings by which Christ gained an experimental knowledge of human necessities. For *He hath borne our griefs and carried our sorrows* (Is. liii. 4).

He has, then, made use of the human feelings and bodily senses as windows and openings, so to speak, by which, being a man, He might know by personal experience the miseries of men, and so become compassionate. He no doubt knew them also before, but after another manner. Being the Lord of virtues, He well knew the virtue of obedience; and yet, according to the statement of the Apostle, *He learned obedience by the things which He suffered* (Heb. v. 8). In this manner also He learned mercy, though the mercy of God is from all eternity. The Doctor of the Gentiles also teaches the same thing, when he asserts that the Saviour *was in all points tempted like as we are, yet without sin, that He might be merciful* (Heb. iv. 15). Do you see, then, how that was done which was already the fact, and how He learned that which He already knew; how He sought out for Himself, as it were, windows and openings in our nature by which He might become more intimately acquainted with our troubles and miseries? He has found as many gaps in the walls of our nature, ruinous and full of fissures as they are, as He has had experiences in His own person [during His sojourn upon earth] of our infirmity and our corruption.

2. This, then, is how the Bridegroom, standing behind the wall, looks through the lattices and windows. Well is He represented as *standing*, since He alone who, being in the flesh, yielded in nothing to the sins of the flesh, can be said truly to have *stood*. We may also understand with confidence that, though He took upon Him the weakness of flesh, He stood firm in the power of His Divinity; and we know that He Himself once said [of others]: *The spirit indeed is willing, but the flesh is weak* (Matt. xxvi. 41). I think, also, that this interpretation is supported by what holy David, who was a prophet of the Lord, said of this mystery, speaking prophetically and of the Lord, though the subject he mentioned was Moses. For He is the true Moses, who came indeed by water; and not by water only, but by water and blood. For this is what that Psalmist says: *He said that He would destroy them* (he refers to God the Father): *had not Moses His chosen stood before Him in the breach, to turn away His wrath, lest He should destroy them* (Ps. cvi. 23). But in what manner, let me ask, did Moses stand in the breach? and, similarly, how could he stand, if he were broken down? or, in the other alternative, how could he be broken down if he stood?[1] But I will show you, if you will, who it was that truly stood in the breach. I know of no one who was able to do this except Jesus our Lord, who assuredly lived in death, who, though in Body broken (*fractus*) and shattered; who in His Divinity stood erect with the Father, in the one supplicating, as being one with us; in the other, propitiating, as being one with the Father. He stood, then, behind the wall, since that in Him which was in [the likeness of] fallible flesh (*jacebat*) was manifested in the flesh, and that in Him which stood [and was not fallible], was hidden, as it

---

[1] *In confractione . . . stetit.* The passage is not clear; or, at all events, the ground of the argument not evident.—ED.

were, behind the flesh, so that one and the same Person was to the outward eye a Man, and though His Divinity was concealed, was the Almighty God.

3. To each of us, also, who desire His Coming, He is, as I believe, still standing 'behind the wall,' as long as our body, which is assuredly a body of sin, hides His Face from us, and hinders our perception of His Presence, for a while. And this was the experience of the Apostle: *Whilst we are at home in the body, we are absent from the Lord* (2 Cor. v. 6). Not because we are in a body simply, but in *this* body—namely, a body which is from sin, and is not without sin. And that you may know that it is not our bodies, but our sins, which are the obstacle between God and ourselves, hear the Scripture: *Your iniquities have separated between you and your God* (Is. lix. 2). And would to God that this one wall of the body were the only obstacle; would that the sin which is in the flesh were the single barrier, and that many other walls and enclosures made by my vices did not also rise to shut me off from the Source of goodness. For I greatly fear lest, beside that obstacle which exists in my nature, I have added many others by my own iniquity, which have separated me only too far from the Bridegroom, so that, to speak the truth, I must confess that to me He stands behind many walls, and not behind one only.

4. But this I wish to state more plainly. The Bridegroom is indeed equally and indifferently present everywhere by the Omnipresence of His Divine Majesty, and by the Greatness of His Power. Nevertheless He is said to be, by the showing forth or communication of His Grace, nearer to some among His reasonable creatures—that is to say, of Angels and men, and farther off from others. For *Salvation is far from the wicked* (Ps. cxix. 155). And yet holy David says: *Why standest Thou afar off, O Lord?* (Ps. x. 1). But with the Saints, though He sometimes makes Himself to be, in a sense, at a distance from them, it is only partially and for a time, and even then it is by the dispensation of His goodness. But from sinners, from those of whom it is said in a Psalm: *The tumult of those that rise up against Thee increaseth continually* (Ps. lxxiv. 23); and, again: *Their ways are always grievous* (Ps. x. 5), from them He is always far removed, and that in anger, not in mercy. Wherefore the Psalmist prays to God: *Hide not Thy Face far from me; put not Thy servant away in anger* (Ps. xxvii. 9); knowing that the Lord was able to turn away also in mercy. Therefore the Lord is near to His saints and His elect, even when He seems to be far from them; nor does He draw near equally to all, but to some more, to others less, according to the difference of their merits. For although the Lord is near to all them who call upon Him in truth, and is beside those who are of humble heart, yet perhaps He is not so near to all as to enable them to say with the Bride that *He standeth behind the wall*. To her He is near indeed, for only a single wall separates them. Wherefore she desires to be dissolved, and the wall of division being thus broken through

in the midst, to be with Him, who, as she confidently believes, is behind it.

5. But as for me, because I am a sinner, I am far from desiring to be dissolved, but, on the contrary, fear and tremble, knowing that the death of the wicked is very evil (Ps. xxxiii. 22, Douay). How can that death be otherwise than very evil where the Life does not come to bring His succour? I fear to go forth; I tremble when at the very entrance of my wished-for harbour, as long as I have no confidence that I shall meet Jesus coming forth from it to receive and to help me. Can I in anywise go forth securely [from the body] if the Lord do not guard my passing away? Alas! without His help to rescue and save me, I shall be intercepted by demons and made their sport. Nothing like this was to be feared by the soul of the Apostle Paul, between whom and the sight and embrace of the Beloved, one obstacle only interposed, namely, the law of sin, which he found in his members. This is the very concupiscence of the flesh, which he could not be altogether without, as long as he lived in the flesh. Yet it is certain that he did not wander far from the Lord, for this one wall only was interposed between them, wherefore he earnestly desired its removal, crying, *Who shall deliver me from the body of this death?* (Rom. vii. 24) knowing that by the short way of death he should come at once to life. By this one law, then, only, namely, that of concupiscence, St. Paul confesses himself to be bound; and this he was obliged to endure, however unwillingly, because it was rooted in his flesh; for the rest, he says, *I know nothing by myself* (1 Cor. iv. 4).

6. But who is like unto St. Paul? who, that is to say, does not sometimes consent unto concupiscence, and obey it, even unto sin? Let him who has given the consent of his will to any sin know that in this unlawful and evil consent he has raised up another wall between God and himself. And a person in that condition cannot indulge in the happy thought that for him the Bridegroom standeth but behind the wall; since, not one wall only, but several, intervene between them. Much less can he think this, if the consent of his will has passed into sinful action; for thus a third wall is raised against the approach of the Bridegroom, and that wall is the act of sin. What if repetition should even convert the sin into a habit, and the habit should root itself in defiance and contempt of the law? as it is written: *The wicked man, when he is come into the depth of sins, contemneth* (Prov. xviii. 3, Douay). Is it not true, that if you shall come into that state, you will be devoured a thousand times by the roaring lions which await their prey, and not be able to attain unto the Bridegroom from whom you are cut off by so great a number of walls? Of these the first is concupiscence; the second, consent of the will; the third, the actual fact; the fourth, the habit of sin; the fifth, hardened indifference and contempt. Be careful, then, to resist with all your might the first approach of concupiscence, so that it may not draw you into an inward consent, and then the whole fabric of evil will

disappear; nor is there anything to hinder the drawing near to you of the Lord, who is the Bridegroom, except only the barrier formed by your body, and you will be able to glory with the Bride, and to say of Him : *Behold, He standeth behind our wall.*

7. But this one thing you must look to also with all vigilance, that He may always find open the windows, so to speak, and lattices of your nature—that is, your confessions of sins, so that by these He may look upon the secrets of your heart in His mercy and goodness, for the gaze of God is the advancement of your soul. For lattices (*cancellos*) are explained to be very narrow windows, such as those who are engaged in the writing of books are accustomed to make, so as to let the light fall upon the pages. For this reason it is, I suppose, that those whose charge it is to draw up official documents are called *Chancellors*.[1] Since, then, there are two kinds of compunction, the one from sorrow for our faults, the other from joy for the Divine mercies bestowed upon us, it seems to me that as often as I feel the one, which cannot be without anguish of heart—that is to say, as often as I make confession of my sins, I throw open the lattice, that is, the narrower window of my heart. Nor is there any doubt that He, who is a kind and merciful Searcher of hearts, He who stands behind our wall, will look benignantly through that lattice; for a humble and contrite heart God will not despise (Ps. li. 17). And this He Himself bids us to do, saying by the Prophet : *Declare thou [thy transgressions] that thou mayest be justified* (Is. xliii. 25, 26). But if my heart is sometimes expanded with love and gratitude at the consideration of the condescension and goodness of God, and I desire to pour forth my feelings in the voice of praise and of giving of thanks, then I open, as I think, no longer a narrow aperture, but a broad and ample window to the Bridegroom, who 'standeth behind our wall,' through which, I believe, He gazes with so much the more willingness and satisfaction, as He regards the sacrifice of praise as more to His honour. I have at hand passages out of the Scriptures, showing that He approves both one and the other kind of confession ; but I speak to those who are well instructed in those subjects, and you are not to be burdened with things unnecessary, since you have scarcely time for the investigation of those which are strictly needful. For very great indeed are the mysteries of this marriage song, and the proclamations of praise which are made in it to the honour of the Church, and of Him who is her Bridegroom, JESUS CHRIST our Lord, who is above all, God blessed for ever. AMEN.

---

[1] This derivation is to be noted ; and it seems to be correct, that the official scribes or notaries were so named because they usually sat behind *cancelli*, or latticed barriers.—ED.

SERMON LVII.

THAT THE VISITATIONS OF THE LORD ARE TO BE CAREFULLY AND REVERENTLY OBSERVED, AND BY WHAT SIGNS AND TOKENS THEY MAY BE KNOWN.

'*My beloved spake, and said to me.*'—Cant. ii. 10.

SEE the onward steps of grace, and mark the degrees of the Divine condescension. Notice the devotion and promptness of the Bride, with what a vigilant eye she observes the coming of her Spouse, and then notes very diligently even His smallest actions. He comes, He hastens, He draws near, He is present, He looks at, and then addresses, her; and none of all these actions escapes the notice, or wearies the attention, of the Bride. He comes in the Angels, He hastens in the Patriarchs, He draws near in the Prophets, He is present in the Flesh, He has regard to the Church in miracles, and addresses her in the Apostles. Or we may explain it thus: He comes by the pity which He feels and the desire that He has to show mercy, He hastens by His zeal to bring help, He draws near to us by humbling Himself, He is present to each generation as it is present upon the earth, He has regard to those which are to come, He speaks of the things pertaining to the Kingdom of God (Acts i. 3), teaching and persuading. Of such a nature, then, is the Coming of the Bridegroom. The blessings and the riches of salvation accompany Him; all things which are from Him are full of delights, and abound assuredly in joyful and salutary mysteries (*sacramentis*). She who loves Him watches and observes all these things. And blessed is that servant whom the Lord shall find watching. He shall not pass her by, He shall not pass away from her, He shall stay by her, and shall speak to her loving words, since He is, in truth, Her Beloved. And thus it is that you read here: *My Beloved spake, and said to me.* Well is He called her Beloved, who comes to speak to her, not words of blame, but of comfort and love.

2. For here the question is not of those who are deservedly blamed by the Lord; who know not how to discern the face of the sky, nor know at all the time of His Coming (Matt. xvi. 3). For [the Bride] is so prudent and so full of foresight that she sees Him coming from afar, leaping, as it were, in His haste, and, passing over the proud to draw near to her in her humility, humbling Himself so to do. This she has observed with vigilant care; and when at length He was at hand, yet concealed Himself, as it were, behind the wall, she, nevertheless, did not fail to recognise His Presence, and to discern that He looked in through the windows and lattices. Now, as a reward for her great devotion and religious care, she hears Him speaking; for if He had looked upon her and not spoken, she would have

suspected that the look was one of indignation rather than of love. It was thus that He looked upon Peter without speaking a word to him, and that was perhaps the reason why Peter went out and wept bitterly (Luke xxii. 61, 62), because the Lord had looked upon him in silence. But the Bride, who has deserved not only to behold Him but to hear His voice, is so far from weeping that she rejoices, and cries out in her joy: *My Beloved spake, and said to me.* You see that the look of the Lord, though in itself it remains always the same, is not always of the same effect, but varies according to the deservings of those upon whom He looks, so that, while it strikes some with fear, it imparts unto others consolation and security. On the one hand, He looks upon the earth, and it shaketh (Ps lxxvii. 16-18); on the other, He looks upon Mary, and it is to pour grace upon her. *He hath regarded,* she says, *the low estate of His handmaiden: for behold, from henceforth, all generations shall call me blessed* (Luke i. 48). These are not the words of one who weeps or trembles, but of one who rejoices. Similarly He is described here as looking upon the Bride, and she trembles not nor weeps like Peter, because she was not attached to things earthly, as at that time he was; but He filled her heart with joy, testifying by His words the affection with which He regarded her.

3. Listen to the words which He addresses to her—words, not of anger, but of affection: *Rise up, my love, my fair one, and come away.* Happy is the soul that may deserve to hear such words as these! Is there anyone among us, do you think, who is so wakeful and observant of the time of his visitation, who watches so diligently for the coming of the Bridegroom, as, when He shall come and shall knock, to open the door of the heart unto Him at once? For those words do not so apply unto the whole Church, as that we, who together make up the Church, should not have our individual share in these blessings. All of us are, in fact, called, whether severally or together, to this very end, that we should possess blessings as an heritage. Wherefore also the Psalmist dared to say unto the Lord: *Thy testimonies have I taken as an heritage for ever, for they are the rejoicing of my heart* (Ps. cxix. 111). He speaks, I think, of that heritage on account of which he claimed to be the son of his Father which is in Heaven. And if a son, then an heir—heir of God, and joint-heir with Christ. And in that heritage he glories that he has acquired a thing of great price—the testimonies of the Lord. Would to God that I might be found worthy to possess for myself one testimony only of the Lord! Though he exults not in one only, but in many, and says again: *I have rejoiced in the way of Thy testimonies as much as in all riches* (Ps. cxix. 14). And, in truth, what is it that forms the riches of salvation, the delight of the heart, the true and safe security of the soul, except the testimonies which it has from the Lord? *For not he that commendeth himself is approved, but whom the Lord commendeth* (2 Cor. x. 18).

4. Why, then, do we hitherto defraud ourselves of these Divine

testimonies or commendations, and deprive ourselves of this our paternal heritage? As if the Father had not at all begotten us of His own will with the Word of Truth (James i. 18), so we in no respect keep in remembrance the assurance that has been rendered to us of this, nor His testimonies concerning us. Where is that of which the Apostle says: *The Spirit Itself beareth witness with our spirit that we are the children of God* (Rom. viii. 16). How are we children if we are without the heritage of children? Our poverty itself clearly convicts us of negligence and carelessness of our privileges. For if any of us brings a heart pure and perfect, according to the word of the Wise Man, to seek at daybreak the Lord who created him, and will pray before the Most High (Ecclus. xxxix. 5), and studies in all his petitions to prepare the ways of the Lord—according to the word of the prophet Isaiah (xl. 3), to make straight a highway for our God; in whose power it is to say with the Psalmist: *Mine eyes are ever toward the Lord* (Ps. xxv. 15), and for this reason, that *I have set the Lord always before me* (Ps. xvi. 8), will not he receive *blessing from the Lord and righteousness from the God of his salvation?* (Ps. xxiv. 5). He shall, without doubt, be frequently visited, nor shall he ever be ignorant of the time of his visitation, however secretly and noiselessly his spiritual visitor, in His modest reserve, may come. The soul, then, that is watchful and disengaged from other cares shall see Him coming from afar, and shall discern in due course all the incidents which, as we have said, the Bride has remarked with as much precision as skill in the coming of the Bridegroom, for He says: *Those that seek Me early shall find Me* (Prov. viii. 17). She will recognise the earnestness and rapid approach of her Bridegroom; she will know at once when He is drawing near, or when He is actually present; when He looks upon her she will perceive with a happy eye that Divine gaze, as it were a ray of sunlight penetrating through the windows and the openings of her wall; and at length will hear His accents of joy and of affection, calling her His beloved, His dove, His fair one.

5. Who is wise and will understand these things, so as to be able to distinguish them, to define them each in its turn, and to explain them worthily to make others understand them also? If you hope for that from me, I, for my part, would rather listen to someone who has experience, who is fully conversant with, and accustomed to, such subjects. But since such men as this frequently prefer to hide in a modest silence what they have in silence learned, and judge it the safer course to keep to themselves their secret lore, I, the duty of whose charge obliges me to speak, and to whom it is not permitted to be silent, will declare what I know of these matters, either from my own experience or that of others, keeping to truths which most people may easily verify for themselves, and leaving higher and deeper ones for such as are able to apprehend them. If, then, I have been warned, either from without by a man, or inwardly by the Spirit, to have regard to righteousness, and to observe equity, I must consider

that salutary counsel as a token of the speedy coming of the Bridegroom, and a kind of preparation for the worthy receiving of that heavenly Guest. This is what I am taught by the Psalmist when he says that *Righteousness shall go before Him* (Ps. lxxxv. 14); and again, when addressing God: *Justice and judgment are the preparation of Thy throne* (Ps. lxxxviii. 15, Douay). Nor will the same hope fail if the counsel that I hear be of humility, or of patience, or, again, of brotherly charity and obedience to those set over me, and especially if it be of following holiness and peace, and of seeking pureness of heart, because a Scripture saith: *Holiness becometh the House of the Lord* (Ps. xciii. 5); and again: *His place is in peace* (Ps. lxxv. 3, Douay); and: *The pure in heart shall see God* (Matt. v. 8). Therefore whatsoever shall be suggested to my mind of these or of other virtues shall be to me, as I have said, for an intimation that the Lord of virtues is about to visit my soul.

6. But if a righteous man shall reprove me in loving-kindness, and correct me, I shall draw the same inference, knowing that the zeal of the righteous, and his goodwill, make a way for Him who ascendeth upon the west (Ps. lxvii. 5, Douay). Happy is that fall,[1] since a man rises again, and stands by the correction of one who is righteous; since it is his sin that falls, and the Lord ascends upon it, treading it under His feet, and crushing it so that it rises not again. The reproof of the righteous is therefore not to be scorned; it is the destruction of sin, health to the heart, and, as it were, the path of God towards the soul. Speaking generally, it is not safe to listen negligently to any discourse which tends to edification in piety, in virtues, in a good and holy character, since it is the way by which is shown the salvation of God (Ps. l. 23). If a discourse which we hear be sweet and agreeable to us, if we listen to it without distaste and even with ardour, then we ought to believe, not only that the Bridegroom is coming to us, but that He is hastening—that is, is coming with eager wish [to be received in our soul]. For His wish produces yours, and that you hasten to receive His discourse comes from His eager haste to enter into your soul; for we did not first love Him, but, as St. John declares: *He first loved us* (1 John iv. 10). If, then, you feel that His word is, as it were, a burning flame, and that your conscience is so touched by it as to burn within you at the remembrance of your sin, remember what the Scripture saith—that a *fire goeth before Him* (Ps. xcvii. 3); and do not doubt that He is near you. And, indeed, we know from another Psalm that *the Lord is nigh unto them that are of a broken heart* (Ps. xxxiv. 18).

7. But if you are not only touched with penitence by His Word, but also wholly converted to the Lord, so that you resolve and vow to keep the statutes of His righteousness, know, then, that He is Himself present, and especially if you feel yourself glowing with the love of Him. You meet in Scripture with each of these statements con-

---

[1] *Occasus*; a play upon the double meaning of the word, *i.e.*, the sunset, and a fall, or error.—ED.

cerning Him—namely, that fire goeth before Him, and that He Himself is a fire. For Moses says of Him expressly that He *is a consuming fire* (Deut. iv. 24). But there is a difference between these two: for that fire which precedes the Lord has ardour, but not love; it burns, but it does not dissolve; it moves that which it touches, but does not carry it wholly away. It is sent before Him by God only to arouse and prepare you, and also to make you aware of what you are in yourself, so that you may taste with the greater pleasure what you shall be hereafter by the grace of God. But that Fire which is God Himself consumes indeed, but causes no pain; it burns that which it takes possession of, but with a sweetness wonderful and indescribable; it destroys, and in destroying confers the supreme felicity. For it is truly a consuming fire; but though as a fire it burns up vices, yet in the soul it acts as a healing unction. Recognise, then, the presence of the Lord in the virtue which changes your heart, and in the love which fires it. For the Right Hand of the Lord worketh virtue (Ps. cxviii. 16). But this change worked by the Right Hand of the Most High takes place only in fervour of spirit, and in charity unfeigned, so that he who experiences it may say: *My heart was hot within me, and while I was thus musing the fire burned* (Ps. xxxix. 3).

8. When, then, by this fire has been consumed every taint of sin and all the stains of past vices, when the conscience is purified and calmed,[1] there follows a sudden and unusual extension of the mind, an infusion of light which illuminates the intellect either to the knowledge of the Scriptures, or to the comprehension of mysteries; whereof the one is bestowed, I think, for our own satisfaction, the other for the edification of our neighbour; that is, doubtless, the effect of the Divine Eye looking upon us, bringing forth *thy righteousness as the light, and thy judgment as the noonday* (Ps. xxxvii. 6), according to that prophecy of Isaiah: *Then shall thy light break forth as the morning* (Is. lviii. 8). But, in truth, that ray of brightness so great shall penetrate not as through open doors, but through small and narrow apertures, at least, as long as that ruinous and tottering wall, that is, thy body, shall endure. You mistake if you think that it shall be otherwise, to whatever degree of purity of heart you may attain, since he who had meditated so deeply upon heavenly things says: *Now we see through a glass, darkly: but then face to face* (1 Cor. xi. 12).

9. After this Divine look, so full of condescension and goodness, comes a Voice, gently and sweetly presenting to the mind the Will of God; and this is no other than Love itself, nor can it be without effect in soliciting and persuading to the fulfilment of those things which God requires. Thus the Bride hears that she is to arise and hasten, no doubt to work for the good of souls. This is indeed a property of true and pure contemplation that it sometimes fills the mind, which is warmed with Divine fire, with a fervent zeal and desire to gain for God those who are of a like mind in loving Him, and to that end it very willingly lays aside the calm and rest of

[1] *Senerata;* a somewhat unusual sense of the word.—Ed.

meditation for the labour of preaching; and again, when it has attained the object desired, to a certain extent, returns with increased eagerness to that contemplation, which it remembers that it laid aside for the purpose of gaining more fruit. Then, when it has tasted again the delights of contemplation, it recurs with increased power, and with its accustomed willingness, to its labours for the good of souls. But the soul frequently hesitates between these continual changes, being profoundly anxious and fearful, lest when drawn to one or the other of these alternatives by the attractions and advantages which it discerns in each it should deviate ever so little from the Divine will. It was perhaps something of this kind that holy Job suffered, when he said : *When I lie down, I say, when shall I arise? and again, I shall look for the evening* (Job vii. 4, Douay); that is to say, when I am in repose I accuse myself of having neglected some work; and when busied in work, of having disturbed my repose. You see that even a holy man feels grave uncertainty between the claims of fruitful labour and of restful contemplation; and although he is always occupied about good things, yet he always feels a sense of regret as if he had been doing that which is wrong, and from one moment to another intreats with tears and sighing to be shown the Will of God. In these uncertainties, the one and only remedy is prayer and frequent upliftings of the soul to God, that He would deign to make continually known to us what we ought to do, and when, how, and in what manner we should do it. You have, as I think, these three things pointed out and commended in these three words of the Bridegroom—namely, preaching, prayer, and contemplation. For the Bride is fitly called *My love*, since she faithfully studies [to bring about] those objects which are dear to Him, by preaching, by advising, by ministering. Fitly also *My dove*, since she sighs and plains continually in prayer, entreating the Divine mercy without ceasing for her sins. And fitly, again, *My fair one*, since she is all bright and shining with heavenly desires, and devotes herself to celestial contemplation at all times that it is proper and opportune to do so; thus she enfolds herself more and more in their glory and beauty.

10. Let us see, however, if these three words describing that threefold blessing, which may be attained by one and the same soul, can be set in relation with those three persons spoken of in the Gospel, who dwelt in the same house, who were friends, and indeed very intimate friends of the Saviour. I refer to Martha, Mary, and Lazarus. For Martha served, Mary remained quiescent in contemplation, and Lazarus groaned, as it were, under the weight of death and of the stone that shut close his grave, and earnestly begged for the grace of the Resurrection (Luke x. 38-42, and John xi.). These things have been said on this account, because the Bride is described as being so watchful and so skilful in observing the paths of the Bridegroom that it cannot be concealed from her at what time, and with what degree of haste He will come to her. Whether He be

afar off, or be drawing near, or be present, by no degree of suddenness can she be taken by surprise; and on that account she has merited. not only to be looked upon with favour, but that her Spouse should deign to make her glad with accents of love, and to give her great joy because of His Voice.

11. I have added, somewhat boldly perhaps, to this that every soul (as, for example, among ourselves) which shall watch with the Bride, shall with her be saluted as *well-beloved*, consoled as *dove*, embraced as *fair*. Every man shall be counted as perfect in whose soul these three things shall be united with all fitness and propriety, so that he shall know how to repent for his own faults and failings, to rejoice in God, and at the same time to assist his neighbours with all his power; and thus to show himself pleasing to God, circumspect with regard to himself, and useful to others. But who is capable of uniting these three? Would that even after long years they might be found united among us; I do not say all together in each of us, but at least each of them in some of us! We have indeed among us a Martha, the friend, so to speak, of the Saviour, in those who faithfully administer our external affairs. We have a Lazarus (as it were), a mourning and plaining dove, in our novices, who, lately dead in trespasses and sins, labour and mourn under wounds yet recent, and from fear of the Divine judgment, and as those who, wounded unto the death, sleep in the tomb, and are out of the remembrance of all, as they themselves no longer believe that they are borne in mind, until at the bidding of Christ the fear which pressed them down as a heavy stone upon the mouth of a tomb is rolled away, and they are able to breathe in the hope of pardon. We have also a contemplative Mary in those who, in the course of a longer time, and by the co-operation of grace, have been able to attain unto a better and happier state, to presume already that the Divine pardon will be extended to them, and instead of anxiously reflecting upon their offences, to meditate day and night with delight upon the law of God, and never to grow weary of it. Sometimes, even, as they contemplate with ineffable joy the glory of the Lord the Bridegroom, they are changed into the same image, from glory to glory, even as by the Spirit of the Lord (2 Cor. iii. 18). Now, to what purpose He bids the Bride to rise and come away, while but a little before He had forbidden that she should be aroused from her sleep, we must examine in another sermon. May He be present with us in the inquiry, and deign to reveal to us the reason of that mystery; He, I mean, who is the Bridegroom of the Church, JESUS CHRIST our Lord, who is above all, God blessed for ever. AMEN.

SERMON LVIII.

HOW THE BRIDEGROOM BIDS THE BRIDE, THAT IS TO SAY, THOSE MEN WHO ARE PERFECTED, TO UNDERTAKE THE RULE AND TRAINING OF SOULS LESS PERFECT. ALSO OF THE CUTTING DOWN OF VICES IN THEM THAT VIRTUES MAY GROW AND INCREASE.

'*Rise up, my love, my fair one, and come away.*'—Cant. ii. 10.

WHO says this? Without doubt it is the Bridegroom. But is it not He who, a little time before, so strongly forbade that His beloved should be aroused? How, then, is it that now He bids her not only rise up, but 'come away?' Something like this comes into my mind from the Gospel. In the night on which Our Lord was betrayed, after having bidden His disciples who were with Him, and who were fatigued with long watchings, at length to sleep and take their rest, in the very same hour[1] He said to them, *Rise, let us be going; behold, he is at hand that doth betray Me* (Matt. xxvi. 46). Now, also, He similarly, almost at the same moment, forbids the Bride to be aroused, and arouses her. *Rise up*, He says, *and come away*. What, then, is the object of so sudden a change of will, or of plan? Must we suppose that the Bridegroom acted with levity, and desired something at first, which immediately afterwards He desired not? By no means. But recognise in this what I have said to you more than once, if you remember, about the two alternatives of sacred repose and of necessary action,' and that there is not in this life space for lengthened contemplation, or prolonged repose, because the duties of office and the usefulness of work press upon us more urgently, and are more immediately necessary. The Bridegroom, therefore, as is His wont, when His beloved has been for a while reposing in sacred communion with Him, does not delay to summon her to duties which seem to be more needful. Not as if this were against her will, for what He forbade to be done by others (ii. 7) He would not Himself do; but for the Bride to know a wish of her Bridegroom is for her at once to feel the desire to be enabled to fulfil it (i. 4), the desire for good works, the desire to bear fruit to the honour and glory of Him; since for her to live is Christ, and to die is gain.

2. And that desire is vehement; it bids her not only rise, but rise in all haste, for we read: *Rise up, and come away*. Nor is it a small comfort and strength to her that she hears: *Come*, and not 'Go.' because she understands by this that she is not so much sent, as led,

---

[1] Some recent editions add the words *surgere cogit*, which words are wanting in most MSS., and in the earliest editions. And, indeed, the text is smoother and more compact without them.

and that the Bridegroom will be with her. What task can she think difficult with such a companion? *Set me beside Thee*, she says, *and let any man's hand fight against me* (Job xvii. 3, Douay). And again: *Though I walk through the valley of the shadow of death I will fear no evil, for Thou art with me* (Ps. xxiii. 4). She is not, then, aroused against her will, since her Lord bestows upon her previously the will to be aroused; nor is this anything else than an ardent desire to grow and increase in all that is good. She is also animated and rendered more prompt to do that which is enjoined upon her, by the opportunity of the time. 'It is now the time to act, O My Bride,' the Bridegroom seems to say, 'for *lo, the winter is past*, during which no one was able to work. The *rain, too, is over and gone*; the rain, which covered the earth with its floods, hindered the culture of the soil, and either destroyed the corn sown, or prevented the harvests being reaped; the rain, I say, has departed, it *is over and gone; the flowers appear on the earth*,' and this is a sign that the season of spring has come, that toil out of doors is safe and convenient, and that fruits and harvests are near. Then He adds, where this toil should begin, and to what end it should be directed: *The time of pruning is come* (ii. 12, Douay). She is then led to the cultivation of the vines, and in order that these may respond to the hope of the vine-dressers by an increased abundance of fruit, it is before all things necessary that the barren boughs should be cut out, the hurtful ones lopped, and those which are unnecessary pruned. This, then, is the literal sense.

3. Let us now see what is the spiritual meaning hidden, as it were, under this narrative of an historical kind. I have already said to you, and you took note of it, so that you do not need to hear it again, that vines signify souls, or Churches; and I gave also at the same time the reason for this. The more perfect soul is then invited to examine these, to correct them, and to instruct them, to the end that they may be saved; yet this ministry is allotted to it, not undertaken as a matter of ambition, but because called to it by God, as was Aaron. Furthermore, what is this invitation but a certain inward movement of charity, leading us piously to care for the salvation of our brethren, for the beauty of the house of the Lord, for its increase in spiritual gains and in the fruits of righteousness, and for the praise and glory of His Name? As often, then, as one whose duty calls upon him to take the direction of souls, or to instruct them by the delivery of sermons, feels his inner man thus touched with religious sentiments towards God, so often he may understand certainly that the Bridegroom is present with him, and is inviting him to the care and culture of His vines. But to what end? That he may root up and destroy, that he may plant and edify.

4. But since for this task, as for every task under heaven, not every time, or every kind of weather, is fit and suitable, so He who gives the invitation adds also 'the time of pruning is come.' He knew well that this time was come who said: *Behold, now is the accepted time; behold, now is the day of salvation; giving no offence in anything,*

that the ministry be not blamed (2 Cor. vi. 2). His warning, without doubt, was to prune, and even to cut off, everything faulty and superfluous and that was able to give even the least offence, and to hinder the fruit of salvation, because he knew that the time of pruning had come. That was why he said to the faithful cultivator of these vines, *Reprove, rebuke, exhort* (2 Tim. iv. 2), indicating by the first and second of these words the practice of pruning or even cutting off, and by the third that of planting. And this, indeed, is said by the Bridegroom through the mouth of St. Paul, as to the time of working. But listen to what He has Himself said as to the proper discrimination of times and seasons, to those souls which were, so to speak, new Brides, though this was spoken under another metaphor : *Say not ye, There are yet four months, and then cometh harvest? behold, I say unto you, Lift up your eyes, and look on the fields ; for they are white already to harvest* (John iv. 35) ; and again : *The harvest truly is plenteous, but the labourers are few; pray ye therefore the Lord of the harvest, that He will send forth labourers into His harvest* (Matt. ix. 37). Just as then He pointed out that it was time to reap the harvest of souls, so here He declares that it is the time to prune and to cultivate these spiritual vines, that is, souls or Churches, wishing, perhaps, by the difference of the names of which He makes use that we should understand by harvests, peoples, and by vines, societies of saints dwelling together.

5. Now, the time of winter, which He says has passed, seems to me to signify that period during which the Lord Jesus did not walk openly, because the Jews conspired against Him, and sought to kill Him. Wherefore He said to certain of them, *My time has not yet come ; but your time is always ready ;* and again : *I go not up yet unto this feast ; for My time is not yet full come* (John vii. 6-8). Yet He afterwards went up, though not openly, but, as it were, in secret. The winter, then, endured from that time until the coming of the Holy Spirit, who aroused into warmth the torpid hearts of the faithful, and was, as it were, that fire which the Lord came to send upon the earth (Luke xii. 49) for this very end. Would you deny that it was then winter when Peter sat beside the fire of coals, being ice-cold in heart as well as in body ? The Scripture says expressly, *It was cold* (John xviii. 18). Great, in truth, was the cold which lay at the heart of him who denied his Master, cramping its throbs with deadly grasp. Nor was this strange, since the fire had been taken away from it. A little time before he was aflame with fervent zeal, being then beside Him who is the Fire, so that, in order not to lose Him, he drew his sword and cut off a servant's ear. But that was not the time for pruning, and therefore the Saviour said, *Put up thy sword into the sheath* (John xviii. 11). For that was the hour and the power of darkness ; and whosoever of His disciples had then lifted up the sword, whether of steel or of the Word, would either have perished by the sword, and thus have been of service to no one, and have borne no fruit, or at least have been constrained to apostasy by the fear of the sword, and thus to perish

the more surely himself, according to the word of the Lord spoken immediately afterwards : *All they that take the sword shall perish with the sword* (Matt. xxvi. 51). For which of the others could have stood undismayed before the terrible image of death, when their prince himself, whom the great Leader of their salvation had forearmed with His puissant Voice, and forewarned to strengthen his brethren, when even he trembled and fled ?

6. But neither he nor they had as yet been filled with power from on high ; and for this reason it was not safe for them to go forth among the vines, to make use of the spiritual hoe and pruning-knife —that is, the inspired tongue and the sword of the Spirit—to prune the boughs and cut back the young shoots so that they may bear more fruit. And, lastly, the Lord Himself was silent during His Passion, and when interrogated about many things, answered not (Matt. xxvii. 12), *being made,* as says the Psalmist, *as a man that heareth not, and in whose mouth are no reproofs* (Ps. xxxviii. 14). And indeed He said : *If I tell you, ye will not believe : and if I also answer you, ye will not answer Me* (Luke xxii. 67, 68), knowing that the time of pruning had not yet come, and that His vine would not respond at all to labours bestowed upon it, that is to say, would not produce the fruit either of faith or of good works. Wherefore ? Because it was winter in the hearts of the perfidious, and the winter rains of malice and evil had overspread the earth, more calculated to drown than to foster the seeds of the Word that were sown ; and these would render profitless any labour that was undertaken for the culture of the vines.

7. Of what rains, do you think, am I now speaking ? Of those which we see that are carried hither and thither by strong winds, and which the clouds at length let fall upon the earth ? By no means. I speak of those which men of a turbulent spirit cause to rise from the earth into the air, when they open their mouth against the heaven, and with their tongue go through the world ; and thus, like sour and bitter showers, make the earth marshy and barren, useless for cultivated plants, though not, indeed, for that wild herbage, visible and exuberant, which is bestowed by God for bodily uses, and of which He takes care only for the beasts of the field. For what plants, then, does God care ? For those assuredly which His Hand, and not that of man, has sown and planted, which can germinate and take root in faith and charity, and bring forth fruits unto salvation, if they be watered by good and seasonable rains. They are, in fact, souls for which Christ died. Unhappy are the clouds which let fall upon these rains such as I have described, which cause only mud, and do not help on fertility. For as there are good trees which bear good fruits, and evil trees which bear evil fruits, the difference in the fruits corresponding to that in the trees which bear them, so, as I think, there may be clouds which are good, and let fall benign showers, and others which are evil, and let fall injurious ones. Perhaps it may have been to indicate this

difference in the character of clouds, and of the showers they let fall, that a Prophet has these words as spoken by the Lord: *I will command My clouds that they rain no rain upon it* (that is, upon His vineyard) (Is. v. 6). For why, do you think, does He add so significantly *My clouds*, unless there were also evil clouds which are not His? *Away with Him! away with Him! Crucify Him!* cry the Jews (John xix. 15). O clouds full of violence and storm! O rain laden with tempests! O torrent of iniquity, fitter to ravage the earth than to make it fat! Not less evil nor less bitter, though it did not fall with equal violence, was that which followed: *He saved others; Himself He cannot save. If He be the King of Israel, let Him now come down from the Cross, and we will believe Him* (Matt. xxvii. 40). Nor was the windy loquacity of the philosophers a shower of good, for it brought barrenness, rather than fertility, upon the lands. Much more are the evil doctrines of heretics evil rains, producing thorns and thistles instead of harvests of good grain. Evil rains also were the traditions of the Pharisees, which the Saviour condemned; and they themselves were as injurious clouds. And do not suppose that I do injustice to Moses (who must himself be regarded as a beneficent cloud) when I say that not every shower that fell from him can be called good; for, otherwise, I should contradict Him who says: *I gave them also* (that is, to the Jews) *statutes that were not good, and judgments* (and doubtless this refers to those given by Moses) *whereby they should not live* (Ezek. xx. 25). Such was, for example, that literal observance of the Sabbath which, though the word signifies rest, did not bring them rest; the rigid system of offering sacrifices, the prohibition to eat the flesh of swine, and of other animals, which were similarly pronounced unclean by Moses; all these were showers, so to speak, falling from the same cloud; but I would not that they should fall upon any field or garden of mine. They were doubtless good in their time; but that time having passed, I do not hold them to be good now. For every shower, however soft, or however gently it falls, is injurious if it be unseasonable.

8. Thus, as long as such harmful rains had flooded and occupied the land with their weight, the time favourable for the vine had not yet come, nor did it come to pass that the Bride was invited to the task of its culture. But when they had passed away, and the dry earth appeared with its carpet of flowers, this was the sign that the season of culture had come. When was this, do you inquire? When, indeed, except in that season which saw the Flesh of Christ taking life again, and as it were reflowing, in the Resurrection. He is the first and chiefest Flower of the human race which has ever appeared on earth. For the Christ is called *the firstfruits of them that slept* (1 Cor. xv. 20). Jesus, I say, is *the Rose of Sharon, and the Lily of the valleys* (ii. 1), He who was supposed the Son of Joseph, He who was Jesus of Nazareth, which itself means a flower [or branch]. He then appeared as the first Flower of the Resurrection; but He did not appear alone. For many bodies of the saints who

slept arose with Him, and appeared upon our earth as bright and shining flowers. *They went*, in truth, *into the Holy City, and appeared unto many* (Matt. xxvii. 52, 53). Those, too, who first believed from among the people, the firstfruits of the saints, they were flowers. Their flowers were miracles which, like flowers, produced the fruits of faith. For after that rain of unbelief had a little passed, and had at least in part rolled away and ceased, then speedily followed that shower of grace (*voluntaria*) which the Lord reserved to His inheritance (Ps. lxviii. 9), and flowers began to appear. The Lord gave His blessing, and our earth yielded her flowers, so that in one day three thousand of the people believed, and in another they were five thousand (Acts ii. 41, and iv. 4); in so short a time did the number of flowers, that is, the multitude of believers, increase. Nor was the cold and frost able to prevail against the flowers which appeared, nor could it cause to perish, as is frequently the case, the fruit of life of which they gave promise.

9. For since all those who believed were filled with power from on high, there arose among them those who, strong in the faith, contemned the threats of men. They suffered, indeed, very many opposers; but they yielded not, nor ceased from proclaiming, to the utmost of their power, the great works of God It is that which is spoken of in a Psalm, if it may be spiritually interpreted: *They sow the fields, and plant vineyards, which may yield fruits of increase* (Ps. cvii. 37). In course of time the tempest was stilled, and, peace being restored to the earth, vines grew, and were propagated, and increased and multiplied beyond number. And then at length the Bride is invited, not, indeed, to plant the vines, but to prune and cultivate those already planted. And that was in due season, for the task required a time of peace. How could it be performed in time of persecution? How was it possible [for the saints] to *take in their hands two-edged swords, to execute vengeance upon the heathen, and punishments upon the people, to bind their kings with chains, and their nobles with fetters of iron, to execute upon them the judgment written* (Ps. cxlix. 6-9)—for all this is to be included in the task of pruning the vines; all these things are scarcely to be performed in peace even in a time of peace. So much for this subject.

10. This discourse might come to a close here if, according to my custom, I had given to each of you some words of counsel and warning with regard to the care of his own vineyard. For who has cut away, even to the quick (*ad unguem*), all things in himself which are superfluous, so as to have nothing which requires to be farther pruned? Believe me, those [evil tendencies] which are cut down shoot up again; those which have been driven away return; the fires which have been extinguished are, in a while, rekindled; and those desires which seemed fast asleep awake again. It is of little avail, therefore, to have pruned once; we must prune frequently, nay, if it were possible, always; because if you are honest with yourself, you will always find something within requiring to be sternly repressed. Whatever spiritual progress you

may make while you remain in this body, you err if you suppose that sins and vices are dead in you, because they are suppressed. Whether you are willing, or unwilling, the Jebusite dwells within your borders (Judg. i. 21); he may be subjugated, but cannot be exterminated. *I know*, says the Apostle, *that in me dwelleth no good thing*. But that is little in comparison with the confession which he goes on to make —that evil dwells in him. For he adds: *The good[1] that I would, I do not; but the evil which I would not, that I do. Now, if I do that I would not, it is no more I that do it, but sin that dwelleth in me* (Rom. vii. 15-17). Either, then, prefer yourself to the Apostle (for he it is who speaks thus), or confess with him that you, too, are not without indwelling sins. Now, virtue maintains the mid-place between impulses which, if yielded to in excess, become wrong; and thus it is that you have need, not only of sedulous self-denial, but also of circumcision. Otherwise, it is to be feared that our vine, being closely enfolded, or rather gnawed, by the vices which surround it on every side, should languish little by little without our perceiving it, or, if they get the upper hand, should be altogether suffocated. In face of so great a peril, I have but one counsel to give—that you watch with the greatest care, and cut away with prompt severity the first shoots of reviving vices as soon as they shall make their appearance. Virtue cannot increase at the same time with vice; and if the one flourish, it will not suffer the other to increase. Take away things superfluous, and those which conduce to salvation will have vigorous growth. Whatever you take away from things which minister only to pleasure, you add to those which minister to the soul's benefit. Let us give to self-denial its perfect work, and cut off the satisfaction of our desires and lusts that virtue may be strengthened thereby.

11. It is always, then, the time of pruning with us, my brethren, because there is always need of pruning; and I trust that with us, too, the time of winter has now passed away. Do you know of what winter I speak? Of that fear which is not joined with charity—which leads all to the beginning of wisdom, but perfects no one in it; inasmuch as advancing love casts out fear, as the spring banishes the winter. For the love of God is the spring of the soul, and if it has come to us, or, rather, because it has come to us (as it is just that I should consider is the case with you), all the winter rain must needs be dried: that is, all the anxious weeping which the bitter remembrance of past sin, and the fearful looking for of judgment, have drawn forth. Therefore (and I assert this without hesitation of most of you, if not of all) this winter rain has passed away, it is over and gone: and the flowers which are the signs of the milder and sweeter showers of spring begin to appear. For spring, too, has its showers,

---

[1] Mabillon omits *bonum*, with the earliest printed editions, and with five of the best MSS., as he says; the others admit the word, following, of course, the Vulgate, from which St. Bernard professedly quotes. It is obvious, also, that his argument requires the words 'good' and 'evil,' and is incomplete without them.—ED.

but these are sweet and fruitful. What is there more sweet and comforting than the tears of charity? The weeping of charity is inspired by love, and not by grief; it comes of the very depth of longing, or of the sympathy felt with those who weep. I do not doubt that with such a gracious rain as this your acts of obedience are bedewed : and I behold with joy that, far from being disfigured by murmuring, by sullenness and reluctance, they are accompanied by a spiritual gladness which renders them enlivening and happy. They are as flowers that you bear always in your hands.

12. If, then, the winter has passed; if the rain is over and gone; if flowers have at length appeared on our earth, and the sweetness and gentleness of grace, as a spiritual spring, indicates that the time of pruning for the vine has come, what remains but that we should set ourselves with all our strength to the doing of this work, so sacred and so necessary? *Let us,* as says the prophet, *search and try our ways* (Lam. iii. 40), and our disposition, so that each of us may consider himself to have made progress, not in supposing that there is nothing in him to blame, but in blaming and correcting that which he has found. If you have learned that there is an ever fresh need to examine yourself, your self-examination will not be perfunctory and useless; and as often as you shall have found that there is good reason for your scrutiny, so often will you feel that it ought to be repeated. If, then, you do this whenever there is need of it, you will do it always. Remember, in conclusion, that you have always need of help from on high, and of the mercy of Him who is the Bridegroom of the Church, JESUS CHRIST our Lord, who is, above all, God blessed for ever. AMEN.

SERMON LIX.

OF THE GROANS OF THE SOUL, WHICH SIGHS FOR ITS HEAVENLY FATHERLAND; AND OF THE COMMENDATION OF CHASTITY AND WIDOWHOOD.

'*The voice of the turtle is heard in our land.*'—Cant. ii. 12.

I AM obliged to allow that this is the second time that He who is of the heaven speaks of the earth; and that He mentions it with as much intimate knowledge of it, as affection, as if He were one of its citizens. It is the Bridegroom who speaks; and as, when He observed that the flowers had appeared, He did not say simply 'on the earth,' but 'on *our* earth,' so now He says: 'The voice of the turtle is heard in *our* land.' What can, then, be the reason for a mode of speech so unusual, not to say so unworthy of God? You will nowhere find, I think, that He has spoken thus of heaven, and that in no other place has He done so of earth. Observe, then, how kind and sweet it is of the God of heaven to say '*our earth.*' Listen, sons of men and earth-born ones: The Lord hath done great things for us (Ps. cxxvi. 3). He has a close relation with the earth, and with the Bride, whom it has pleased Him to draw from the earth to associate closely with Himself. Thus it is that He says *our land*. This phrase is not one of sovereignty, but of familiarity and of alliance. He speaks thus not as Lord, but as Bridegroom. What? He is Creator, and yet regards Himself as companion! It is Love that speaks, and love knows nothing of mastership. For this Song is a song of love, and it is appropriate to fill it with loving speeches only. Also this love is of God; nor has He it from any other than Himself, because He is the Source of love. And it is so much the more powerful and vigorous, inasmuch as He and love are but one. But those whom He loves, He treats as friends, not as servants. From being the Master, He becomes the Friend; for He would not call His disciples His friends, unless they were so in reality.

2. Do you perceive that even His Majesty yields to His Love? It is so, indeed, brethren; love looks up to no one, but neither does it look down upon any. It regards with an equal eye all who are united among themselves by a perfect bond of love; it combines together in its own self the loftiest with the lowest; nor does it merely make them to be equals, but makes them to be one. You think perhaps that God is excepted from this rule of love; but do you not know that *he that is joined unto the Lord is one spirit* (1 Cor. vi. 17)? Why do you wonder at this? He is made to be, as it were, one of us; and yet it is too little to say this, for He is made, not, as it were, one of us, but one of us in truth. It is too little for Him to be made equal to men; He is Himself made a man. Thus it is that He claims our earth as His, not as a mere possession, but as His birthplace and fatherland. Why should He not so claim it? It is from thence that He takes His Bride; thence is the substance of His Body; thence does He become a Bridegroom; and since He and His Bride are *one flesh* (Gen. ii. 4; Matt. xix. 5), why should they not have one fatherland also? *The heaven, even the heavens, are the Lord's,* saith the Psalmist; *but the earth hath He given to the children of men* (Ps. cxv. 16). It is, then, as Son of Man that He inherits the earth, as being Lord He has it in His power, as Creator He administers it, and as Bridegroom He shares it with His Bride. In saying, then, *our land*, He shows that He disclaims the possession of it in sole proprietorship, and does not disdain to share it with another. It is on this account that the Bridegroom so benignantly uses this phrase, and deigns to say *our land*. Now let us go on to consider other things.

3. *The voice of the turtle is heard in our land.* This is a sign that the winter has passed, a warning that the time of pruning and culture is at hand. That is according to the letter. Taking it in another sense, the voice of the turtle is not sweet in itself, but it announces things which are sweet. This is a little bird, and not of great cost to buy; yet, if you consider the matter, it is of no small value. Its

voice resembles more a moan of pain than a song of gladness, and this recalls to us our state of pilgrimage. Willingly do I listen to the voice of a preacher who arouses, not applauses for himself, but grief and sorrow for sin, in me. If you teach others to mourn, you will show yourself truly like the turtle; and if you desire to be persuasive [to penitence], you must effect this, not by declamation, but by being unfeignedly penitent yourself. Example is especially in this matter, as in many others, far more effectual than precept. Your voice will be persuasive and powerful if it be known that you are persuaded yourself of that which you are endeavouring to enforce on others. Actions speak louder and more effectively than words. Practise yourself what you urge upon others, and you will not only correct more easily what is wrong in me, but will free yourself from a great responsibility. It will not, then, apply to you if any should say: *They bind heavy burdens and grievous to be borne, and lay them on men's shoulders: but they themselves will not move them with one of their fingers* (Matt. xxiii. 4). Nor need you fear that reproach: *Thou, therefore, which teachest another, teachest thou not thyself?* (Rom. ii. 21).

4. *The voice of the turtle is heard in our land.* As long as men have received their reward for the worship which they render unto God only in the earth, and that land which flows with milk and honey, they do not at all realize that they are strangers and pilgrims upon the earth, nor mourn as the turtle in sad remembrance of their own country; but on the contrary, misusing the place of their exile as if it were their country and home, they have set themselves to eat the fat things of it, and drink the sweet. Thus it is that so long a time passes without the voice of the turtle being heard in our land. But when the promise of the kingdom of heaven has been made, when men have realized that they have not here a continuing city, and have begun to seek eagerly for that which is to come, then first the voice of the turtle is plainly heard sounding in the land. For when a holy soul sighs for the Presence of Christ, when it endures with pain to see the possession of His Kingdom deferred, when it hails from afar with sighs and groans the dear land it longs for, does it not seem to you that each soul which so bears itself on earth is as the chaste turtle which sits apart and utters its mournful note? Then it is, and thenceforward, that the voice of the turtle is heard in our land. How can it be otherwise than that the absence of Christ should move me to frequent tears and daily groanings? *Lord, all my desire is before Thee: and my groaning is not hid from Thee* (Ps. xxxviii. 9). Thou knowest, O Lord, *I am weary with my groaning;* but blessed is he who can say, like the Psalmist: *All the night make I my bed to swim; I water my couch with my tears* (Ps. vi. 6). Nor is it only I in whom these groanings are found, but all those who love His appearing. For what does He Himself say? *Can the children of the bridechamber mourn, as long as the Bridegroom is with them? but the days will come when the Bridegroom shall be taken from them, and then shall they* (mourn) (Matt. ix. 15); as if He had said: 'Then shall the voice of the turtle be heard.'

5. So it is, O dear Lord Jesus; those days have come. For the whole creation groaneth and travaileth in pain together until now, waiting for the manifestation of the sons of God (Rom. viii. 19-22). And not only they, but we ourselves also groan within ourselves, waiting for the adoption of the sons of God, the redemption of our body; knowing this, that whilst we are at home in the body, we are absent from the Lord (2 Cor. v. 6). Nor are those groans fruitless to which a response so kind and merciful is made from heaven, inasmuch as we hear: *For the oppression of the poor, for the sighing of the needy, now will I arise, saith the Lord* (Ps. xii. 5). That voice of groaning and complaint was heard in the time of the Fathers also, but seldom, since each of them retained his groans, as it were, within his own breast. Wherefore, also, one of them said: *My secret to myself, my secret to myself, woe is me* (Is. xxiv. 16, Douay). So, also, he who said: *My groaning is not hid from Thee* (Ps. xxxviii. 9), in declaring that from God alone was it not hidden, showed that it was hidden from others. And, therefore, it could not then be said, *The voice of the turtle is heard in our land*, since it was then a secret, known but to few, and not yet divulged to the multitude. But when the proclamation has been openly made: *Seek those things which are above, where Christ sitteth at the right hand of God* (Coloss. iii. 1); that plaintive cry of longing, the lament, as it were, of the turtledove, begins to belong to all, and the reason for it to be the same for all, since all know the Lord, as we read in the prophet Jeremiah: *They shall all know Me, from the least of them unto the greatest of them, saith the Lord* (Jer. xxxii. 34).

6. But if there are many who utter that plaintive cry, why does He speak of only one? The voice *of the turtle*, He says. Why does He not say, 'of the turtles?' Perhaps the Apostle resolves this difficulty, where he says that *the Spirit Himself maketh intercession for* the saints *with groanings that cannot be uttered* (Rom. viii. 26). Thus, in fact, it is. He who arouses in others those aspirations which groans manifest outwardly, is brought before us as Himself groaning. And however many there be whom you hear thus groan, it is one sound that the lips of all of them utter. Why should it not be, in fact, His voice, seeing that it is He who in the mouth of each forms the words of petition for the necessities that each feels? For the manifestation of the Spirit is given to every man to profit withal (1 Cor. xii. 7); to each one His Voice declares Him present, and makes Him manifest. Learn from the Gospel that the Holy Spirit has a voice. *The Spirit breatheth where He will, and thou hearest His voice, but thou knowest not whence He cometh or whither He goeth* (John iii. 8, Douay). But he, who was as a master who was himself dead,[1] teaching the dead letter of the Law to those who were similarly dead, did not know this. Nevertheless we, who have been brought from death unto life by the life-giving Spirit, we know, by His gracious illumination, and through our assured and daily

---
[1] *I.e.*, Nicodemus (John iii. 10).

experience, that our vows and aspirations come from Him, and ascend to Him, and there find mercy before the eyes of God. For when has God ever rendered the voice of His Spirit ineffectual? And He knows what His Spirit desires, inasmuch as He maketh intercession for the Saints according to the Will of God.

7. It is not only its plaintive cries which render the turtle acceptable, but also its chastity. For this merit it was judged a worthy offering for a Virgin Birth; and thus we read in the Scripture: *A pair of turtle-doves, or two young pigeons* (Luke ii. 24). And although the Holy Spirit is in other passages customarily spoken of under the figure of a pigeon or dove, yet that is a bird given to passion, and therefore not suitable to be offered in sacrifice to the Lord, except it were young and immature. But for the turtle-dove no age is prescribed, because its chastity at any age is recognised. It is content with one mate, and if he be lost does not take another, thus condemning a plurality of marriages among men. For although that is a remedy for incontinence, and therefore only a venial fault, yet that the incontinence itself should be so great is not creditable. It is a cause for shame that reason should be unable to do in man, and that in a matter of honour and uprightness, what nature is able to do in a bird. The widowed turtle may, in fact, be seen to practise all the tasks belonging to holy widowhood diligently and without weariness. You see it everywhere solitary; you hear it everywhere uttering its melancholy note; nor is it ever to be found perched upon any green bough; and from it you may learn to avoid as pestilential the ever green and vigorous shoots of pleasures. Add to this that it is most given to haunt mountain peaks and the loftiest summits of trees, and thus teaches us to despise earthly things and to love heavenly, a purpose especially appropriate to a state of chastity.

8. From all this it may be inferred that the note of the turtle is also a preaching of chastity. This utterance was not at first heard in the earth, but rather that other: *Increase, and multiply, and replenish the earth* (Gen. i. 28). To no purpose would that call to chastity have sounded, when the country of the resurrection (Luke xx. 35, 36) had not as yet been revealed, in which men, far more happily, *neither marry, nor are given in marriage, but are as the angels of God in Heaven.* Or was it the time for that utterance to be heard when every barren woman in Israel was held to be under a reproach, when the Patriarchs themselves had many wives at once, when the Law required a man whose brother died without children to raise up seed unto his brother? But when that commendation of eunuchs who had made themselves eunuchs for the Kingdom of Heaven's sake was heard from the mouth of the heavenly turtle (Matt. xix. 12), and when also the counsel of that other chaste turtle as regarding virgins was everywhere followed (1 Cor. vii. 25), then it might begin truly to be said that *the voice of the turtle has been heard in our land.*

9. Since both flowers, then, have appeared, and the voice of the turtle has been heard in our land, without doubt the Truth has been

made known both to hearing and to sight. For a voice is heard and a flower seen. By flowers are meant miracles, as I have explained above, which, joined to the impression made by the voice [of him who preaches the truth of the Gospel], brings forth the fruit of faith. For although faith cometh by hearing, the confirmation of the faith comes from sight. The voice has sounded, the flowers have shone, and truth has sprung up out of the earth by the confession of believing souls, word and sign thus concurring to the testimony of the faith. Those testimonies are rendered abundantly easy of belief when the flower attests the witness of the voice, the sight that of the hearing. The things that are heard confirm those that are seen, so that the testimony of two witnesses (I mean that of the ear and of the eye) establish the truth of that which they declare. Wherefore the Lord said : *Go your way, and tell John* (for He was addressing the disciples of that teacher) *what things ye have seen and heard* (Luke vii. 22). The certitude of faith could not have been expressed to them more briefly or more clearly. The same conviction was speedily brought about throughout the whole world, and by the same summary of argument. *What things*, He said, *ye have seen and heard*. O saying of little length, yet strong and effectual! I assert with assured belief that which I have perceived by the testimony of my own ears and my own eyes. The trumpet of salvation sounds, the miracles shine clear before the eyes of men, and the world believes. It is speedily persuaded of the truth of that which is asserted, when it is authenticated by actions so marvellous. Thus we read that the Apostles *went forth, and preached everywhere, the Lord working with them, and confirming the Word with signs following* (Mark xvi. 20). We read that He was transfigured on the mount in a cloud of wonderful brightness, and that nevertheless a Voice from Heaven bore witness to Him (Matt. xvii. 2-5). We read also of a Dove which similarly pointed Him out on the banks of Jordan, and of a Voice which bare witness to Him (Matt. iii. 16, 17). And thus it is that the mercy of God makes these two things, the voice and the outward sign, to concur everywhere to introduce the faith ; so making, by these two senses, as by two open windows, a wide opening for truth to reach the soul.

10. There follows, *The fig-tree putteth forth her green figs*. Of these we do not eat; their immaturity makes them unfit for use. They have the appearance, but not the taste, of good figs ; and in this they are perhaps made to describe hypocrites. Yet we do not altogether reject them, for we may perhaps have need of them another time. They will fall prematurely of their own accord, like grass growing upon the housetops, which withereth afore it groweth up (Ps. cxxix. 6), which, as I think, is spoken of hypocrites. Yet not without cause is mention made of them in this nuptial song. Doubtless they are of no use for food, but they may serve for another purpose ; for in a nuptial festival many other things beside viands are needed. I think that the subject ought not to be passed by altogether without mention ; but whatever be its significance I am unwilling to discuss it

within the narrow limits left me at the end of this Sermon; I defer it, therefore, to another time, which may be less occupied. I leave you to judge whether I am right in so doing; do you only obtain for me from God, by your prayers, that I may be enabled to explain, so as to conduce to your edification, what I think; and that all may be to the praise and glory of Him who is the Bridegroom of the Church, our Lord JESUS CHRIST, who is above all, God blessed for ever. AMEN.

SERMON LX.

OF THE INCREDULITY OF THE JEWS, AND OF THEIR SLAYING CHRIST, BY WHICH THEY FILLED UP THE MEASURE OF THEIR FATHERS.

'*The fig-tree putteth forth her green figs.*'—Cant. ii. 13.

THIS sentence depends on those which precede it. The speaker had said that the time for pruning and culture of the vine had come, and that this was shown as well by the appearance of flowers, as by the hearing of the note of the turtle-dove. He shows it by the production of green figs also, because the coming of spring is evidenced not only by the appearance of flowers and by the call of the turtle-dove, but by the fruits of the fig-tree. For the season is never more mild than when the fig-tree has produced its green fruit. The fig-tree has not flowers, but fruit, at the time when other trees flower. And as flowers appear and pass away, being useful only as a mark of, and a stage in the production of, the fruits which are to follow them, so is it with those fruits which appear for a time, but fall prematurely, and are themselves unfit to be eaten, but give place to others which attain ripeness. It is by this, as I have said, that the Bridegroom marks the advance of the season, and makes it the ground for earnestly urging the Bride not to be slothful in entering upon the work in the vineyard which has to be done, in its proper season, so that it be not lost. So much for the literal sense.

2. But what of the spiritual meaning? It is plain that here we must regard, not the fig-tree as being spoken of, but the people which it represents, since God's care is for men, not trees. Truly, the people is (as it were) a fig-tree; frail because of the flesh, of small sense and intelligence, of no high disposition, and whose earliest fruits (to carry on still the metaphor) are earthly and unripe. For it is not the object of popular desire to seek *first the kingdom of God and His righteousness* (Matt. vi. 33); but rather, as says the Apostle, to think of the things of this world, wherewith husbands may please their wives, and wives their husbands. Such shall have trouble in the flesh (1 Cor. vii. 28, 33), but we do not deny that at the last they

shall attain the fruits of faith, if they repent sincerely of, and confess, their faults, and especially if they make amends for the works of the flesh by almsgiving. The first fruits, then, which such persons produce are not properly speaking the whole products of their lives, but are like the green and immature fruits of the fig-tree. If they shall afterwards bring forth fruits worthy of repentance (Matt. iii. 8), for that is *not first which is spiritual, but that which is natural* (1 Cor. xv. 46), it shall be said to them: *What fruit had ye then in those things whereof ye are now ashamed* (Rom. vi. 21)?

3. But yet I think that we are not at liberty to interpret this passage of all peoples indiscriminately, but that one people in particular is intended. For the Scripture does not speak of trees, but of one tree: *The fig-tree putteth forth her green figs;* and, as I think, by that one is meant the nation of the Jews. In fact, how often does the Saviour seem to employ the same metaphor in the Gospel, in the parables which He delivered? For example: *A certain man had a fig tree planted in his vineyard* (Luke xiii. 6); and, again: *Behold the fig-tree, and all the trees* (xxi. 29); and to Nathanael it was said: *When thou wast under the fig-tree, I saw thee* (John i. 48). And again, it is a fig-tree upon which He pronounces a curse, because He has found upon it no fruit (Mark xi. 13, 14). Thus, that people is well compared to a fig-tree, which, although sprung from the root of the Patriarchs, which was good, was never willing to lift itself from the ground, or shoot upwards towards the sky; never responded to the goodness of its root, either by the greatness of its branches, the beauty of its flowers, or the abundance of its fruit. O tree stunted, knotty, and twisted, nothing answering to thy root is seen in thee: for thy root was holy. What appears in thy branches which is worthy of it? *The fig-tree putteth forth her green figs,* saith the Bridegroom. O evil seed, it is not from thy noble root that thou hast derived these! That which is in it is from the Holy Spirit, and all is refined and sweet which is produced by Him. Whence hast thou these figs crude and coarse? And, in truth, what is there in that people which is not crude and coarse, whether we consider their actions, their inclinations, their understanding, or even the rites with which they worship God? For their actions carried them [of old] into many wars, their inclinations are all devoted to the pursuit of gain, their intelligence stopped short in the thick husk of the letter of their Law, and their worship consists in shedding the blood of sheep and of cattle.

4. But someone says: Since that nation has never ceased to produce such crude fruit, then the time for pruning has been reached at an earlier period, since the two events are represented as contemporaneous. But that is not the case. We say that women are mothers, not when they are in travail, but when they have brought forth. And, similarly, we say that trees have flowered, not when the flowers have begun to appear, but rather when they have fallen. So also is it said here that *the fig-tree hath put forth*[1] *her green figs,* not when it has

---

[1] *Protulit* (Vulgate).

produced a few, but when it has produced them all—that is, when the production of them has come to an end. If you ask me at what period this took place with that [Jewish] people, I reply, when it slew Jesus Christ. For it was then that its malice was consummated, according as He Himself had foretold to them: *Fill ye up then the measure of your fathers* (Matt. xxiii. 32). Wherefore at the moment when He was about to yield up His spirit upon the Cross, He said: *It is finished* (John xix. 30). O what a consummation of its continual production of fruits crude and coarse did that fig-tree, so cursed and condemned to a perpetual sterility, at length reach! O how much worse were the last than the former ones! At first they were only useless, but the last came to be hurtful and poisonous. O nature not merely crude, but touched with viperous venom, to hate that Man, who not only cures the bodies of men, but saves their souls! O intelligence, coarse, dense, and, as it were, bovine, which did not recognise God even in His own works!

5. Perhaps the Jew will complain, as of a deep injury, that I call his intelligence bovine. But let him read what is said by the prophet Isaiah, and he will find that it is even less than bovine. For he says: *The ox knoweth his owner, and the ass his master's crib; but Israel doth not know, My people doth not consider* (Is. i. 3). You see, O Jew, that I am milder than your own prophet. I have compared you to the brute beasts; but he sets you below even these. Or, rather, it is not the Prophet who says this in his own name; but he speaks in the Name of God, who declares Himself by the very works He does to be God. *Though ye believe not Me*, He says, *believe the works;* and, *If I do not the works of My Father, believe Me not* (John x. 38, 37); and not even that aroused them to understand. Not the flight of demons, not the obedience of the elements, nor life restored to the dead, was able to expel from their minds that stupidity bestial, and more than bestial, which caused them, by a blindness as marvellous as it was miserable, to rush headlong into that crime, so enormous and so horrible, of laying impious hands upon the Lord of Glory. From that time, therefore, it could justly be said of them: *The fig-tree hath put forth her green figs*, inasmuch as the institutions of the Jewish Law began to draw towards their end, and, according to the ancient prophecy, on the coming of the new, the old should be abandoned (Lev. xxvi. 10). Even so do the green figs fall, and give place to the good figs which succeed them. 'As long,' says the Bridegroom, 'as the fig-tree continued to put forth its green fruit, I did not call upon thee, O My Bride, knowing that it could not, at the same time, produce good fruit. But now that those earlier ones have been put forth, I invite thee now in the due time, since, in the place of those that were useless, good and salutary fruits are about to appear.'

6. *The vines*, He continues, *in flower yield their sweet scent*, and this is the sign of fruit to come. This odour drives away serpents. It is said that when the vines are flowering every venomous reptile leaves the spot; they cannot endure the sweet scent of the flowers

in fresh bloom. Which I wish our novices to take particular notice of, and to act with corresponding trust and confidence, reflecting what manner of spirit they have received, that evil spirits cannot sustain even its first approaches. If their fervour is such at its beginning, what shall be its complete perfection? Let the fruit be judged from the flower, and the excellence of the savour of the one be estimated from the strength of the perfume exhaled by the other. *The vines in flower yield their sweet scent.* And, indeed, in the beginning it was so. Upon the preaching of the new grace of Jesus Christ followed newness of life in those who had believed, who had their conversation honest among the Gentiles (1 Pet. ii. 12), and were a sweet odour of Christ in every place (2 Cor. ii. 15). That sweet odour was the good testimony which was rendered to them, and which arises from good works, as perfume from a flower. And since, in the first period of the rising faith, the souls of the faithful were like spiritual vines covered with flowers and exhaling a pleasant odour, having a good testimony from those who were without, I think that what is here said applies not unfitly to them—that *the vines in flower yield their sweet scent.* To what end was this? It was that by this means even those who had not yet believed, reflecting on these good works, and being attracted by them to the faith, might themselves glorify God, and so to them also the odour of life might begin to be the means of life. It is then said of them, not undeservedly, that they sought not their own glory, but the salvation of others, by the good report which their actions obtained, and that they thus gave forth a sweet odour. For it would have been in their power to seek, after the example of certain others, to make a gain of godliness; for example, by ostentation or avarice. But that would have been not to give their good odour, but to sell it; and this they were careful not to do, because all their actions had charity for their sole motive.

7. But if the vines are believing souls; if their flowers are good works, and the odour they exhale the estimation they produce in the minds of others, what is the fruit they produce? It is *martyrdom;* yes, the blood of the martyr is truly the fruit of the vine. *When He shall give sleep to His beloved,* says the Psalmist, *behold the inheritance of the Lord are children, the reward, the fruit of the womb* (Ps. cxxxvi. 2, 3, Douay). I had almost said 'the fruit of the vine.' Why should I not call the Blood of the Innocent and the Just the most pure blood of the Vine—that red and most precious and approved lifeblood of the Vine of Sorek,[1] forced out by the winepress of suffering? For in the sight of the Lord the death of His saints is precious (Ps. cxvi. 15).

---

[1] *Sorech* or *Soreth.* The name is found three times only in Scripture—Gen. xlix. 11; Is. v. 2; Jer. ii. 21. The Hebrew root signifies tawny or reddish, according to Gesenius. The name is used in modern Arabic for a certain purple grape, grown in Syria, and highly esteemed; it is noted for its small berries and minute soft pips, and produces a red wine. The valley of Sorek, in the Philistine country (Judges xvi. 4), the home of Delilah, was perhaps so called from the growth of such vines ('Dictionary of the Bible,' s.v.).—ED.

So much as to that which is said: *The vines in flower yield their sweet scent.*

8. So, then, if we prefer to regard this passage as referring to the times of grace, this will be the meaning of it. But if we rather refer it to the Fathers (for the house of Israel is the vineyard of the Lord of Sabaoth), it will be explained thus: The Prophets and Patriarchs discerned as an odour of sweetness the future Coming and sacrifice of Christ in the Flesh, but did not give forth that odour in themselves, because they did not show forth in the flesh that which they felt in the spirit by anticipation. They did not give forth the odour of it in themselves, nor divulge their secret, awaiting its revelation in due time. Who, in fact, had then any comprehension of the wisdom which was hidden in a mystery, and not shown forth in the body? Thus the vines, indeed, did not then yield their sweet scent. But they did so afterwards, when, in the succession of generations, they brought into the world JESUS CHRIST, born of them, according to the flesh, of a Virgin Mother. It was then, I say, that those spiritual vines yielded in truth their sweet scent, since *the kindness and love of God our Saviour towards man appeared* (Tit. iii. 4), and the world began to have the presence of Him whom, while He was still absent, few had anticipated. That good man, for example, who, touching Jacob, had the feeling and anticipation of Christ, and said: *See, the smell of my son is as the smell of a field which the Lord hath blessed* (Gen. xxvii. 27). When he said this, he had the delight of this anticipation for himself, but he did not communicate it to any other person. But when the fulness of that time came in which *God sent forth His Son, made of a woman, made under the Law, that He might redeem those which were under the Law* (Gal. iv. 4), then, indeed, the sweet odour which was in Him diffused itself everywhere, so that the Church, perceiving it from the extremities of the earth, cried out: *Thy Name is as ointment poured forth* (Cant. i. 2), and souls, as young maidens, flocked towards its sweet perfume. Thus that vine yielded its sweet scent; and at that time other vines also, in which was the same odour of life, similarly gave it forth. Wherefore should they, from whom Christ came according to the Flesh, not have done so? It was said, therefore, that the vines yielded their sweet scent, either because faithful souls shed forth everywhere around them the good opinion which they aroused, or because the oracles and revelations of the Fathers were made openly known to the world, and their sweet odour went forth throughout all the earth, as the Apostle declares: *God was manifest in the Flesh, justified in the Spirit, seen of Angels, preached unto the Gentiles, believed on in the world, received up into glory* (1 Tim. iii. 16).

9 But it would be wonderful if neither the fig-tree nor those vines had in them anything which would serve to our edification. I believe, then, that this passage has a moral sense also; for, by the grace of God which is in us, we have also fig-trees and vines. The fig-trees are those whose characters are sweet and peaceable, and the

vines those of a more ardent and fervent spirit. Everyone among us who acts in union and peace with others, who lives among his brethren, not only without giving ground of complaint to any, but approving himself kind and helpful to all, and fulfilling towards them every office of charity, why may I not speak of him very fitly as a fig-tree? Yet if he have put forth crude and coarse fruits, it behoves him to cast them off; as, for example, the fear of judgment, which perfect love casteth out; and the bitterness of remorse for past sins, which is sure to yield to sincere confession, to abundant shedding of tears, and to the infusion of grace; and also other similar things, which are as the green figs which go before the good and sweet fruit. Such truths as these you are able by yourselves to reflect upon.

10. But that I may add here one more thought which occurs to me at the moment, may there not be counted among green figs such gifts as knowledge, prophecy, gifts of tongues, and the like? For these things must, like green figs, pass away, and give place to better, as the Apostle declares, asserting that prophecies shall fail, tongues cease, and knowledge vanish away (1 Cor. xiii. 8). The discernment of spiritual things shall exclude even faith in them, and the place of hope must of necessity be taken by sight. For that which a man sees why doth he yet hope for? Charity alone *never faileth*, but that charity only wherewith God is loved with all the heart, with all the soul, with all the strength, and with all the mind (Luke x. 27). Therefore I do not reckon this at all in the number of crude figs; I do not think that it is to be compared even to the fig tree, but to the vines. Now, those who are as vines show themselves severe rather than sweet; they act in a spirit full of ardour, are zealous for discipline, prompt and severe in rebuking vice, and applying to themselves very fitly that saying of the Psalmist: *Do not I hate them, O Lord, that hate Thee? and am not I grieved with those that rise up against Thee?* (Ps. cxxxix. 21). Also, *the zeal of Thine House hath eaten me up* (Ps. lxix. 9). The former seem to me to excel in love of their neighbour; the latter, in love of God. But let us make a pause under this vine and under this fig-tree, where the love of God and of our neighbour casts a delightful shade. Of each of these I am possessed when I love Thee, O dear Lord Jesus, who art my neighbour, because Thou art Man, and hast shown Thy love and mercy towards me, and who art, nevertheless, God over all, blessed for evermore. AMEN.

SERMON LXI.

HOW THE CHURCH FINDS THE RICHES OF DIVINE MERCY IN THE HOLLOWS OF CHRIST'S OPEN WOUNDS: AND OF THE FORTITUDE OF THE MARTYRS, WHICH THEY HAVE RECEIVED OF CHRIST.

' *Arise*,[1] *my love, my fair one, and come away.*'—Cant. ii. 13.

THE Bridegroom manifests His great affection by repeating the words of affection. For repetition is a sign expressive of affection; and that He again summons His Beloved to labour among the vines, shows how full of solicitude He is for the salvation of souls. That the vines denote souls, you have already heard; nor need I repeat what has been said upon that subject. Notice what follows. If I remember rightly, He has never yet clearly named the Bride in all this work except when He leads her to the vineyards, when He brings her near to the wine of charity. When she shall have come thither, when she shall have been perfected, He will make with her a spiritual marriage; and they two shall be, not one flesh, but one spirit, according to the saying of the Apostle: *He that is joined unto the Lord is one spirit* (1 Cor. vi. 17).

2. Then follow the words: *O My dove, that art in the clefts of the rock, in the secret places of the stairs, let Me see thy countenance, let Me hear thy voice.* He loves, and therefore goes on to speak words of love. He winningly calls her anew His dove; He says that He is hers, and claims her as belonging wholly to Him; it is no longer she who earnestly entreats that He will show Himself unto her, and speak to her; it is now He who in turn begs for these graces. He acts as a bridegroom, but as one who is modest and diffident, who shrinks from exposing himself to public gaze, who determines to enjoy his happiness in retirement, or, as it were, in the clefts of the rock, or in the hollows of the wall. Imagine, then, that the Bridegroom speaks thus to His Bride: 'Do not fear, My beloved, that the labour upon the vines to which I call you will interfere with or interrupt the enjoyment of our love. There will even be in it some advantage.' This is a kind of trifling founded upon the literal sense of the words. But why do I call it trifling, seeing that there is nothing serious in the literal explanation? The outward appearance of this passage is not worthy of our attention unless the Spirit shall help our infirmity to understand the inward meaning of it. Let us not, then, remain outside of this spiritual sense, lest it should seem (which God forbid!) that we desire to refer to what is impure and dis-

---

[1] Some editions repeat here 'make haste,' from verse 10; but not the earliest ones, nor the MSS.

honourable. Take heed that you bring chaste ears to this discourse of love; and when you think of these two who are its subject, remember always that not a man and a woman are to be thought of, but the Word of God and the devout soul. And if I shall speak of Christ and the Church, the sense is the same, except that under the name of the Church is specified not one soul only, but the unity, or rather the unanimity, of many souls. And do not think that by the clefts of the rock or the hollows of the wall are meant the hiding-places of those who work iniquity; reject from your minds every thought or suspicion of such works of darkness.

3. Another writer has thus expounded this passage, interpreting the clefts of the rock of the wounds of Christ. And rightly so, for *that rock was Christ* (1 Cor. x. 4). Precious are those clefts [to us], for they establish the faith of the Resurrection and the Divinity of Christ. *My Lord and My God*, said an Apostle (John xx. 28). Whence came that assured conviction (*oraculum*), if not from the clefts of the Rock? In these *the sparrow hath found an house, and the turtle a nest for herself, where she may lay her young* (Ps. lxxxiv. 3); in these the dove finds safety, and regards without fear the hawk that flies around. And therefore He says, *My dove that art in the clefts of the rock.* While the dove replies: *He hath exalted me upon a rock* (Ps. xxvii. 5), and again, *He hath set my feet upon a rock* (Ps. xl. 2). The man who is wise builds his house upon a rock, because there he need fear neither the force of the winds, nor the beating of the waves (Matt. vii. 24). What good does he not find upon that rock? Raised upon it, I stand firmly, and am safe. I am safe from the enemy; I am strong against accident; and all because I am lifted above the earth; for everything that is earthly is uncertain and perishable. Our conversation is in heaven, whence we need not fear ever to fall, nor ever to be cast down. Our rock, then, is in heaven; in it is strength, and on it security. Is it not said that the rock is a refuge for the conies (Ps. civ., 18)? And where, in truth, is there a firm and safe refuge for us who are weak, except in the Wounds of our Saviour? There I dwell with safety so much the greater, as He is so powerful to save. The world rages around me, the body weighs upon me, the devil lays snares for me; but I do not fall, for I am founded upon a firm Rock. Perhaps I have committed some great sin, my conscience is troubled, but I do not despair, because I remember the Wounds of my Lord; for He was wounded for our iniquities (Is. liii. 5). What sin is there so deadly that it may not be remitted through the Death of Christ? If, then, I keep in remembrance a remedy so powerful and efficacious, I cannot be terrified by any disease, however virulent it be.

4. Thus it plainly appears how greatly that man erred who said, *My iniquity is greater than I can bear* (Gen. iv. 13). Except that he was not among the members of Christ, nor did the merits of Christ pertain to him, so that he could have a dependence upon them, or say, as a member asserting an interest in that which belongs to His

Head, that they were His.[1] But as for me, that which is wanting in myself I claim with undoubting confidence in the Heart of the Lord, from which all mercy flows; nor is it without clefts through which that mercy flows forth. For [the soldiers] pierced His Hands, and His Feet, and His Side they pierced with a lance; and by these openings it is permitted to me to suck honey from the rock, and oil from the hardest crag; that is to say, to taste and see how sweet the Lord is. He was meditating thoughts of peace, and I knew it not; for who hath known the mind of the Lord; or who hath been His counsellor? But the nails wherewith He was pierced have become for me, as it were, master keys (*clavis, clavus*), to open for me the treasury of the Lord's Will. How can I do otherwise than see with clear vision through a cleft so broad? The nails cry aloud, and the wounds cry aloud, that God was in Christ, reconciling the world unto Himself. The sword passed through His soul, and came near to His Heart, that He might so learn to have a fellow feeling with our infirmities. Through the clefts of His Body the secret of His Heart is laid open, and that great mystery of goodness, the lovingkindness and mercy of our God, in which the Dayspring from on high hath visited us, is manifested to our thankful gaze. How can the Lord's wounds do other than exhibit His lovingkindness? and how has it ever shone forth more wondrously, O Lord, sweet and gentle, and of great mercy, than in the cruel wounds which Thou didst endure for our sake? There is no greater proof of compassion and mercy than this, that one should lay down his life for those who were destined and condemned to death.

5. The pitying mercy of the Lord is, then, all my merit. I am not altogether destitute of merits, as long as He deigns to have compassion upon me; and they will be increased just in proportion to the greatness of His mercy. What if I feel myself guilty of many offences? Where sin abounded, grace did much more abound (Rom. v. 20). And if the mercy of the Lord is from everlasting to everlasting (Ps. ciii. 17), I also will sing of the mercies of the Lord for ever (Ps. lxxxix. 1). Shall it be my own righteousness that I celebrate? Nay, O Lord; *I will make mention of Thy righteousness, even of Thine only* (Ps. lxxi. 16). For that is mine also, since Thou Thyself hast become my Righteousness. Have I any reason to fear lest the one righteousness should not suffice for both? It is not like that cloak of which the Prophet speaks, which was so narrow that it could not cover two (Is. xxviii. 20). *Thy righteousness is an everlasting righteousness* (Ps. cxix. 142). What is longer than eternity? And Thy Righteousness is eternal; and so ample as amply to cover me equally with Thyself. In me, indeed, it shall cover a multitude of

---

[1] This is the uniform reading of the old MSS. and the earlier editions. But Horst reads wrongly, *reum capitis membrum;* and Picard, *veri capitis membrum.* Our reading is genuine and easy, if in the former half of the sentence you understand *membrum* and supply *suam dicit*, so that the sense will be, *Sicut membrum rem capitis suam dicit.*

sins; but in Thee, O Lord, what does it cover but the treasures of Thy lovingkindness, the riches of Thy goodness to us? These are the treasures which are laid up for me in the clefts of the rock. Of what great variety of sweetness are these good things, hidden, indeed, now, but only from those who perish! For why is that which is holy given unto dogs, or pearls cast before swine? God has revealed them to us by His Spirit, and has made us enter into His holy things by these open clefts. How great an abundance of sweetness is found in them, what fulness of grace, and what perfection of virtues!

6. I will enter into those storehouses so richly filled, and, according to the counsel of the Prophet, will *leave the cities, and dwell in the rock* (Jer. xlviii. 28). I will be as it were a dove making her nest in the deepest recess of the cleft, so that, being set with Moses in the cleft of the rock, I may attain to see the Lord at least from behind as He passes by (Exod. xxxiii. 23). For who shall stand before Him and look upon His Face, that is, behold His unchangeable Glory, except he to whom it shall be vouchsafed, to be brought not only into His holy place, but into the Holy of Holies? Nor is that sight of the Lord a small favour, nor to be lightly thought of. Let Herod despise it if he will; as for me, I am far from thinking it a small thing, and the farther, the more despisable it seems to Herod. Even such a sight of the Lord has its own delights. Who knows whether God will not turn, and forgive, and leave behind Him a blessing? A time shall come when He shall show to us the light of His Countenance, and we shall be saved. But in the meantime, may He prevent us (*præveniat* = go before) with the sweetness of those blessings which He is wont to leave behind Him. Let Him now display to us His condescension, as it were, by a view of Him from behind, and reserve for another time the sight of His Countenance in its Glory. He is exalted high above all in His Kingdom, but upon His Cross He is all sweetness. Let Him begin with me by the latter vision, and in the other bestow upon me the fulness of joy. *Thou shalt make me full of joy*, it is said, *with Thy Countenance* (Acts ii. 28). Each vision is saving, and each is sweet; but the one is in supreme exaltation, the other in humility; the one in Glory, the other in mortal pallor.

7. For, as says the Psalmist of the dove: *The hinder parts of her back are covered with the paleness of gold* (Ps. lxviii. 14, Douay). He cannot be other than pale in death. But gold, though it be pale, is of more value than yellow and shining brass; so also the foolishness of God is wiser than men (1 Cor. i. 25). This gold is the WORD, the wisdom of God. This gold has rendered its colour pale, hiding the Form of God, and putting on the form of a servant. From the Church also He has taken her golden brightness, for she says: *Look not on me because I am black, because the sun hath looked upon me* (i. 6). Her back, then, also has the paleness of gold; she does not blush at the blackness of the Cross; she does not shudder at the scorching brands of the Saviour's Passion, nor fly from the livid

marks of His wounds. She even takes delight in them, and desires that her last end may be like these. It is on that account that the words are spoken which she hears from the Bridegroom: *My dove that art in the clefts of the rock;* because she dedicates herself with single-hearted devotion to the Wounds of Christ, and dwells in them with continual meditation. Thence comes the endurance which does not shrink from martyrdom; thence the complete confidence which she has in the Most High. The martyr can fear nothing who lifts his eyes to that bloodless and livid Face, by whose very paleness he is healed, and who nerves himself to show forth a glorious likeness of his Master's Death, even in the paleness of gold. Why should he fear to whom it is said by the Lord Himself: *Let Me see thy countenance?* (ii. 14). Why does He say this? I think it is not so much that He desires to see her, as that He desires to be seen by her. For what is there that He does not see? He has no need that anyone should show themselves to Him who sees all things, even though they be hidden. What He desires, then, is to be seen; the Leader full of kindness and bounty desires that the countenance and the eyes of His devoted soldier should be fixed upon His wounds, to draw from them strength and encouragement, and to render him stronger to endure his sufferings, through the power of His Example.

8. In truth, while the martyr is gazing at the Wounds of his Saviour, he will not feel his own. He stands intrepid and triumphant, though his whole body be a mass of wounds; and when the steel gashes his sides, he beholds the sacred blood of martyrdom spout forth from his body, not only bravely, but with gladness. Where, then, is the soul of the martyr? It is in a place of safety; in the Rock, in the Bosom of Jesus, which it enters through the open portal of His Wounds. If it were left to its own sensations only, assuredly the stabbing sword would be seen and felt; the pain would be found unendurable; it would succumb, and deny its Lord. But as it is abiding in the Rock, what wonder if it should endure as a rock endures? Nor if it is an exile from the body, is it wonderful that the pains of the body it does not feel. This is not the consequence of insensibility, but of the force of love. The senses are not lost, though they are controlled. The pain is felt, but the soul rises above it and scorns it. It is then from that Rock comes the fortitude of the martyr, and the power that is in him to drink of the cup of the Lord (Matt. xx. 22, 23). And that cup, so exciting in its passionate glow, how goodly is it! (Ps. xxiii. 5). Goodly, indeed; and that not less to the Leader who is keenly watching the struggle, than to the brave soldier who fights and conquers, for our strength is the joy of the Lord (Neh. viii. 10). How can it be otherwise than that the voice of a martyr's testimony, bravely sustained unto the end, should be to Him a cause of joy, since, in fact, He asks it so earnestly, in the words before us: *Let Me hear thy voice.* Nor will He delay, in His turn, to repay it according to His promise: *Whoso-*

ever, therefore, shall confess Me before men, him will I confess also before My Father which is in Heaven (Matt. x. 32). But let me cut short this sermon, for it cannot be finished at this time; and it would be excessively long were I to complete all that remains to be said upon this verse which I have begun to expound. Let me reserve it, therefore, to the beginning of the next sermon; and may all that I say, and the manner in which it is said, be a subject of satisfaction to Him, who is the Bridegroom of the Church, JESUS CHRIST our Lord, who is above all, God blessed for ever. AMEN.

SERMON LXII.

WHAT IS MEANT BY THE ABIDING OF THE FAITHFUL SOUL *IN THE CLEFTS OF THE ROCK*, AND WHAT *IN THE SECRET PLACES OF THE STAIRS*. THAT IT IS NEEDFUL RATHER TO SEARCH WHAT IS THE WILL OF GOD THAN TO SEARCH INTO HIS MAJESTY, AND THAT PURITY OF INTENTION IS NECESSARY TO THE PREACHING OF THE TRUTH.

'*My dove that art in the clefts of the rock, in the secret places of the stairs.*''—Cant. ii. 14.

IT is not only in the clefts of the rock that the dove finds a safe refuge; it is also in the secret places of the stairs. If, then, we take 'the stairs' as signifying, not a mere heaped-up pile of stones, but the assemblage of the Saints, may we not perhaps take the secret places or hollows in it to refer to the places left, as it were, empty in it by those Angels who, because of their pride, fell from Heaven, since those places are to be filled by men, even as ruins are built up with new and living stones? Wherefore the Apostle Peter says: *To whom coming, as unto a living stone, ye also as lively stones, are built up a spiritual house* (1 Pet. ii. 4, 5). Nor do I think that it will be far from the fact if we understand by it the guardianship of Angels, as in some sort acting as a wall (*maceria*) around the Lord's vineyard, which is the Church of the predestinate, since St. Paul says: *Are they not all ministering spirits, sent forth to minister for them who shall be heirs of salvation?* (Heb. i. 14). And the Psalmist: *The Angel of the Lord campeth about them that fear Him, and delivereth them* (Ps. xxxiv. 7). And if that be adopted, the sense will be that two things console the Church in the time and place of her pilgrimage— one referring to the past, the memory of the Passion of Christ; the other to the future, the thought and confident assurance of being received into the blessedness of the Saints. She looks forward and backward, and beholds each of these two with an earnest longing which never fails; each of them seems to her immeasurably sweet, and each provides her with refuge and consolation against her griefs and afflictions which she endures from evil men. The consolation is complete, since the Church knows not only what she has to look for, but also from whom she has to look for it. Her expectation is full of joy; nor is it doubtful, for it is founded on the Death of Christ. Why should she tremble at the greatness of the recompense, when she considers the value (*dignitatem*) of the price paid for it? What happiness she experiences in reflecting upon those clefts through which flowed that most sacred Blood, which was the price of her salvation! With what joy she traverses the hollows, the retreats, the mansions, which are so many, and so diverse, in the House of the Father, and in which He will place His children according to the diversity of their merits! And because she is not, for the present, able to enter into the heavenly home in reality, she enters it in the only manner which is possible to her, in spirit and by continual remembrance of it. But the time will come when she shall fill up those waste places; shall dwell in those hollows in body as well as in spirit; when she shall make light with the presence of the vast numbers of her children those heavenly habitations which their former denizens have left void; and then in the heavenly wall there shall appear no more empty hollows, but all shall rejoice in completeness and perfection.

2. Or, if you prefer the interpretation, let us say that by studious and pious souls these hollows are not found, but made. In what manner, do you ask? By the force of their thoughts and their desires. For that spiritual wall yields to the pious desire of the soul, just as soft stone yields to the edge of the mason's chisel; it yields to pure contemplation, to frequent prayer. For the prayer of the humble pierceth the clouds (Ecclus. xxxv. 17). Not, indeed, that it cleaves the spacious heights of this material atmosphere, as a bird cleaves them in its flight and by the beating of its wings; or that it pierces, as by the thrust of a sword, to the height of the dense firmament. But there are heavens which are holy, living, reasonable, which *declare the glory of God;* and these bend themselves, with a willing and gracious acquiescence, to our prayers: these allow themselves to be reached by our devout affections; these receive us into their bosom as often as we knock at the door of them with a pure and worthy intention. For to him that knocketh it shall be opened. It will, then, be allowed to each of us, even during this period of our mortality, to hollow out for himself caves of refuge, in whatsoever part he will, of this heavenly wall; even now to visit the Patriarchs and to salute the Prophets; even now to mingle with the glorious company of the Apostles and the noble army of Martyrs. It will be permitted to each, according as the fervour of his devotion shall bear up his soul as upon wings, to traverse in gladness and joy the dwelling place and the mansions of the blessed Virtues, from the least Angels to the loftiest Cherubin and Seraphin. And if he shall pause and knock

perseveringly at the door of those to whom he is most strongly drawn, according to the impulse of the Spirit, who quickeneth whom He will, it shall be speedily opened to him ; and making, as it were, a cave of refuge in the mountains, or rather in those holy souls, who willingly incline themselves to him in benignant kindness, he shall repose among them for a little while. Of every soul that acts thus, both the countenance and the voice are always acceptable to God : the countenance because of its purity ; the voice because of the praises it renders to Him (Ps. l. 23). And, in truth, the offering of thanks is fair in His sight ; wherefore, also, to such an one it is said : *Let Me see thy countenance ; let Me hear thy voice*. The voice is adoration in the mind that is occupied in contemplation ; the voice is giving of thanks. God takes great delight in such hollows as these, from which sounds forth the voice of thanksgiving to Him, the voice of adoration and praise.

3. Happy is the soul whose study it has been frequently to hollow out for itself caves of refuge on this wall, and still more happy if its refuge be in the rock. For it is open to us to hew and hollow out our refuge even in the Rock ; but for this is required a sharper edge, as it were, of purity, a stronger force of will and pious intention, and, furthermore, more prevailing merits of sanctity.[1] And who can be thought qualified in these respects? Surely he who said : *In the beginning was the Word, and the Word was with God, and the Word was God: the same was in the beginning with God* (John i. 1, 2). Does it not seem to you that this man is one who has plunged, and, as it were, whelmed himself in the abysses of the Word as in the depths of a sea, and who, from the recesses of the Heart of Jesus, has brought forth the very marrow of the deepest and most sacred Wisdom? What shall I say of him who was wont to speak wisdom among them who were perfect, even the hidden wisdom, which none of the princes of this world knew (1 Cor. ii. 6-8)? Did not that pious searcher, borne onward by a holy and religious, but penetrating, curiosity, pass through the first and the second heaven, and enter even into the third heaven in search of that wisdom ? And he has not been silent about it to us, but has set it forth faithfully in such faithful words as he could command. For he heard unspeakable words, which it is not lawful for a man to utter (2 Cor. xii. 4), that is to say, not to man ; and of these he would discourse to God only. Imagine, then, that God is consoling Paul, whose charity causes him to regret that he cannot make known this wisdom to his fellow-men, and saying to him : ' Why are you troubled because men are not capable of hearing and understanding the thoughts you have conceived? *Let Me hear thy voice*'—that is to say, 'If it is not permitted to you to reveal to mortal ears the thoughts you have in your mind, yet be consoled, inasmuch as your voice is acceptable and welcome to the Divine ears.' Do you see how that holy soul at one time is

---

[1] In most of the MSS. the word *sanctitatis* is wanting ; but all the printed editions have it, even the earliest.

sober because of its charity towards us, and at another beside itself
to God, and in the power of its purity (2 Cor. v. 13)? See also with
regard to holy David whether he was not himself that man of whom,
as if of another, he speaks with God: *The thought of man shall give
praise to Thee, and the rest of the thought make festival in Thine
honour* (Ps. lxxvi. 11). All, then, that the Prophet was able to make
publicly known, by his word or his example, of his prophetic consciousness, that he used to render public praise to God, and thanksgivings among the people of the Lord; while that which remained he
reserved for himself and for God, and together they made festival with
joy and gladness. This, then, is what he wished to make known to
us by the verse quoted: that is to say, whatever of the mystery of
wisdom he was able to arrive at by eager and attentive meditation,
he partly shared with the people, according to his ability, by the careful
preaching which he devoted to their salvation; and the remainder,
which the people were not capable of comprehending, he employed
in praises and thanksgivings to God. You see that nothing is lost
of holy contemplation, since that which cannot be expended to the
edification of the peoples is put to good use for the praise of God,
and is acceptable and agreeable to Him.

4. That being the case, it is clear that there are two kinds of contemplation: one, upon the state, the happiness, and the glory of the
heavenly City, with which either in action or in repose a multitude of
its citizens are occupied; the other, upon the majesty, the eternity,
and the Divinity, of the King Himself. The one may be said to
have relation to the wall, the other to the rock. But the more difficult
it is to hollow out this wall, the sweeter and more satisfying is the
result attained when it is done. Do not fear that with which the
Scripture threatens those who are searchers into Majesty (Prov xxv. 27).
Only bring to that search an eye which is pure and simple, then you
shall not be overwhelmed with glory, but shall be admitted [to behold
it]—that is, unless you seek not the glory of God, but your own.
Whosoever does this is indeed overwhelmed, but by [the looking for]
his own glory, not that of God; for in pursuit of that your heart is,
as it were, weighed down with desire of vainglory, and is unable to
lift itself up to the glory of God. But if that is driven out of our
soul we may then securely search[1] the Rock in which are hidden all
the treasures of wisdom and knowledge (Col. ii. 3). If you are still
doubtful, hear what the Rock Himself says: They that work in Me
shall not do amiss (Ecclus. xxiv. 22). Oh, that I *had wings like a
dove! for then would I fly away, and be at rest* (Ps. lv. 6). There
the gentle and simple soul finds rest, where the fraudful, the arrogant,
the covetous of vainglory, is overwhelmed. The Church is as a dove,
and therefore finds rest. The Church is as a dove, because it is
innocent and mournful. As a dove, I say, because it receives with
meekness the ingrafted word And it rests in the Word, that is, in
the rock; for the Rock is the Word. The Church, then, abides in

---

[1] *Scrutemur.* Another reading is *fodiamus.*

the clefts of the rock, through which she looks forth and beholds the glory of her Spouse; and yet she is not overwhelmed by that glory, because she does not arrogate it to herself. She is not overwhelmed by it, because it is not the Divine Majesty, but the Divine Will, into which it is her object to search. Sometimes, indeed, she ventures to contemplate that which belongs to His Majesty, yet not to scrutinize, but to adore. And if it is ever her lot to be transported into it by a sudden ecstasy, that is the Finger of God, who deigns thus to lift up man to Himself, not the temerity of man, presuming insolently to intrude into the deep things of God. For when the Apostle relates that he was caught up into Paradise, that he might excuse his venturing to glory (2 Cor. xii. 1, 2), what other mortal may presume by his own unaided efforts to introduce himself into the terrible sanctuary of this supreme Majesty, and to burst with eager gaze into the sight of its awful mysteries? I conclude that those who are here spoken of as searchers into the Divine Majesty are those who burst upon it of their own accord, not those to whom it is revealed in ecstasy. It is the former, therefore, that are overwhelmed by its glory.

5. A search into the Divine Majesty is, then, full of danger to be feared; but a search into the Divine Will [that we may obey it] is as safe as it is dutiful and pious. Why, indeed, should I not employ myself with all diligence in ascertaining what is the Will of Him to whom I owe obedience in all things? Glory and sweetness also come from the contemplation of His sweetness, from the beholding of the riches of His goodness and tender mercies. Then, indeed, we have beheld this glory, the glory as of the only begotten of the Father (John i. 14). That part of His glory which is here displayed is full of goodness, and truly paternal. That glory does not overwhelm me, though I bend all my powers to contemplate it; on the contrary, it impresses itself upon me. For when we with open face behold the glory of the Lord, we are changed into the same image from glory to glory, even as by the Spirit of the Lord (2 Cor. iii. 18). We are transformed in Him, when we are conformed to Him. God forbid that the conformity of man to the Divine likeness should be presumed to consist in the glory of His majesty, and not rather in a modest and complete obedience to His Will. This is my glory, if ever I shall be so happy as to hear it said of me: 'I have found a man after My own heart.' The Heart of the Bridegroom is the Heart of His Father, and of what character is that? *Be ye therefore merciful*, He says Himself, *as your Father also is merciful* (Luke vi. 36). It is this form and expression of countenance that He desires to see, when He says to the Church: *Let Me see thy countenance:* a form and expression of kindness and of piety. Such a countenance [the Church] lifts with all confidence towards the Rock, which it resembles. *They looked unto Him*, says the Psalmist, *and were lightened, and their faces were not ashamed* (Ps. xxxiv. 5). How, indeed, shall a humble soul be confounded by One who is humble, a holy soul by the God of holiness, a modest soul by Him who is modesty itself? The pure

countenance of the Bride will no more be abhorrent to the purity of the Rock, than virtue is abhorrent to virtue, or light to light.

6. But as the Church is not able as a whole to draw near at present to the piercing of the Rock, because it is not in the power of all who are in the Church to penetrate the sacred mysteries of the Will of God, or to apprehend by their own selves the deep things of His counsels, therefore the Bridegroom declares that she dwells not only *in the clefts of the rock, but in the secret places of the wall*. With respect, then, to those of her members who are perfect, who by the purity of their conscience and the quickness of their intelligence are emboldened and enabled to search and to penetrate the secrets of wisdom, the Church dwells in the clefts of the Rock. With respect to others, she dwells in the secret places of the wall; that is to say, those who either are not qualified to hollow out for themselves caves of refuge in the Rock, or do not presume to do so, should be content to contemplate in spirit the glory of the saints, and, as it were, to abide in the secret places of the wall. If there is anyone to whom not even this is possible, let the Church set before him Jesus Christ, and Him crucified, so that even he may abide, without any toil of his own, in the clefts of the Rock at the hollowing out of which he has not laboured. The Jews have laboured [to pierce them], and he, that he may be a believer, shall enter into the labours of the unbelievers. Nor let him fear to be repulsed, for he is called to enter in. *Enter into the rock*, says the Prophet, *and hide thee in the dust, for fear of the Lord, and for the glory of His majesty* (Is. ii. 10). To the soul that is feeble and undecided, such as is described in that verse in the Gospel in which one confesses of himself that he cannot dig, and to beg he is ashamed (Luke xvi. 3), a hollow is shown where he may hide in the earth until he gather strength and make spiritual progress, so that then even he may hollow out for himself clefts in the Rock, and with increased vigour and purity of mind may enter into the inner meanings of the Word.

7. And if we understand as referring to this hiding-place hollowed in the earth that passage in which it is said, *They have dug My Hands and Feet* (Ps. xxii. 17, Douay), it cannot be doubtful that the wounded soul which shall abide in it shall speedily recover health. For what is so efficacious to the healing of the wounds of conscience, as to the purifying of the intention of the soul, as assiduous meditation upon the Wounds of Christ? But until it is perfectly purified and healed I do not see how the words can be applied to it which are here spoken, *Let Me see thy countenance, let Me hear thy voice*. For how can the soul which is bidden to hide itself venture to show its countenance or lift up its voice? *Hide thyself*, it is said, *in the dust*. Wherefore? Because the countenance is not fair, nor worthy to be seen. Nor shall it be worthy to be seen as long as it is not capable of seeing. But when, by the sojourn made in the dust, it has made such progress in the healing of the inward eye that it is able to contemplate the glory of God with open face, then at length the soul shall

recount with confidence what it has seen, and shall be, both in voice and countenance, pleasing to the Lord. The countenance which is able to view fixedly the glory of God is necessarily able to please. For that it would not be able to do if it were not itself clear and pure, and transformed into the image of the glory which it contemplates. Otherwise it would recoil from that glory on account of mere unlikeness to it, as if stricken by a brilliance new and unbearable. Therefore, when a soul shall be pure and therefore able to behold unshrinkingly the pure truth, then it is that the Bridegroom will desire to behold its countenance and to hear its voice.

8. For how greatly He is pleased by the preaching of the truth when it is done with a pure intention is shown by the words which are added: *For sweet is thy voice.* And that the voice would not be pleasing to Him if the countenance were displeasing may be inferred from the remainder of the sentence: *And thy countenance is comely.* What is the beauty of the inward countenance except purity? The soul may please Him in very many respects without the voice of preaching; but without a pure intention it can please Him in none. To the impure Truth does not show itself, nor does Wisdom entrust itself to them. How, then, should they be able to speak of that which they have not seen? *We speak that we do know,* saith the Scripture, *and testify that we have seen* (John iii. 11). But you go and dare to give testimony about that which you have not seen, and to speak of that which you know not. Do you ask who it is that I say has not a pure intention? He who seeks for the praises of men; he who makes a traffic of the Gospel; he who preaches the Gospel as a means of livelihood; to whom gain is godliness; and who does not seek for spiritual fruit provided he obtains a gift. Such as these are wanting in pure intention; and though their mixture of motive hinders their beholding the truth, it does not hinder their discoursing of it as if they did behold it. Why do you act so hastily? Why do you not wait for light? Why do you presume to undertake the work of light before the light is with you? It is in vain that you rise before the light dawns upon you. The light, that is a pure intention, that is charity, which seeketh not her own (1 Cor. xiii. 5). Let this come first, that you speak not unadvisedly with your tongue, as one who setteth his foot at a venture. The truth is not discerned by the eye that is proud, but is clear to him that is upright and sincere. There is no truth which hides itself from the pure in heart, or that may not be uttered by him who is so. *But unto the wicked God saith, What hast thou to do to declare My statutes, or that thou shouldest take My covenant in thy mouth* (Ps. l. 16)? Many there are who, neglecting a pure intention, have tried to speak before they have seen the truth; and have either fallen into grave error, knowing neither what they say nor of what they affirm, or have incurred derision and contempt, inasmuch as they have taken upon them to teach others, while they have not themselves been taught. Let us pray Him who is the Bridegroom of the Church, JESUS CHRIST our LORD, to preserve us always from this twofold evil. He is above all, God blessed for ever. AMEN.

SERMON LXIII.

THAT A MAN WHO IS PIOUS AND WISE OUGHT TO CULTIVATE CAREFULLY HIS VINEYARD, THAT IS TO SAY, HIS LIFE, HIS SOUL, AND HIS CONSCIENCE; THAT THERE ARE TWO KINDS OF FOXES, NAMELY, FLATTERERS AND DETRACTORS; AND OF THE TEMPTATIONS OF MONKS IN THEIR NOVITIATE.

'*Take us the foxes, the little foxes, that spoil the vines: for our vines have tender grapes.*'—Cant. ii. 15.

IT is clear that it was not without real need that attention was called to the vineyards, since foxes are found among the vines, who are despoiling them. That is the literal sense of the words. But what of the spiritual? In the first place, we reject the common and familiar explanation altogether as absurd, insipid, and altogether unworthy to be received as the sense of a Scripture so sacred and authentic. Unless anyone is so dull of mind and devoid of reason as to imagine it a great thing to be taught here, after the fashion of the children of this world, to have a care for earthly possessions; to guard and defend the vines against the wild animals which attack them, for fear of possibly losing the fruit of the vine, in which is excess and riot, and of so losing at once their labour and their outlay. Assuredly great would be the loss if we should read and study the holy Book with so much care and deep veneration, only to be taught in it to protect our vines from foxes, lest if we should be negligent in our care of them, our cultivation should end in our purses being left empty. You are not so unskilled, nor so wanting in spiritual graces, as to understand the Scripture in so carnal a manner. Let us, then, seek the sense of them in the spirit. We shall, indeed, find, but in a sense more reasonable and more worthy of Scripture, the vines which have tender grapes, and the foxes which spoil them, and upon whom we may expend our labour in driving them away or capturing them, at once more honourably and to better purpose. Can you possibly doubt that it is needful to employ much more watchfulness to keep souls in safety than a crop of grapes, and that it needs much more vigilant care to avoid the snares of spiritual wickedness on account of the one than to capture marauding foxes on account of the other?

2. But now I must point out what these vines denote in a spiritual sense, and what these foxes. It will be your care, my dear sons, to apply, each to himself and to his own vineyard, whatever I may say in the course of this inquiry, that he may learn in what respect, and of what dangers, he has most necessity to take heed. To a wise man, then, this vineyard signifies his life, his soul, his conscience. For he who is wise ought to leave nothing in himself uncared for or desert. With the foolish man it is quite otherwise. You will find that with

him all things are lying neglected, dirty, and in disorder. Indeed, the foolish can hardly be said to have a vineyard at all, for how can there be a vineyard where nothing appears to be planted, nothing to be cultivated anywhere? The whole life of the foolish bristles, as it were, with thorns and briars growing wild; and is that a vineyard? Even though it was once one, it is so no longer, for it has gone back to the condition of desert. Where is the vine of virtue? Where are the grapes of good works? Where the wine of spiritual joy? *I went*, says the wise man, *by the field of the slothful, and by the vineyard of the man void of understanding; and lo, it was all grown over with thorns, and nettles had covered the face thereof, and the stone wall thereof was broken down* (Prov. xxiv. 30, 31). You see how the wise man ridicules the foolish, because he has left to perish by neglect the good endowments of nature and the gifts of grace, which he had perhaps received by the laver of Regeneration; which was, as it were, his original vineyard, planted by God and not by man; so that it is no longer a vineyard. And assuredly there can be no vine where there is no life. For I should regard the life of one who is void of understanding as rather death than life. How can there be life where there is barrenness? The tree that is dry and barren, is it not regarded as dead? Faggots and brushwood also are but dead wood. *He destroyed their vines with hail*, says the Psalmist (Ps. lxxviii. 47), showing that vines condemned to perpetual sterility are, in fact, deprived of life. So the man void of understanding, inasmuch as his life is useless, is dead while he liveth.

3. It is, then, the wise man alone of whom it can properly be said that he has a vineyard, or, rather, that he himself is one, that has life. He is a tree in the House of God which bears fruit, and is therefore living. For that very wisdom itself, by which a man becomes, and is called, wise, is a tree of life to them that lay hold upon her (Prov. iii. 18). How can he that takes hold upon her fail to have life? He truly lives, but by faith. For it is the just who is wise, and the just lives by faith (Heb. x. 38). And if the soul of the just be, as it is, the seat of wisdom, then he is truly wise who is just. He, then, whether you call him the wise or the just, because he never ceases to live, will never cease to have (or, rather, to be) a vineyard. For the vineyard and the life are in him the same thing. And the vineyard of the just is good, or, rather, the just is a good vineyard, since in him virtue is as the vine, his [good] actions the branches and shoots, the testimony of his conscience the wine produced, and his tongue, as it were, the wine press. *Our rejoicing is this*, says the Apostle, *the testimony of our conscience* (2 Cor. i. 12). Do you perceive how in the wise nothing is without its use? His discourse, his reflections, his manner of life, and all the rest of his conduct, what are they but entirely God's husbandry, God's building, and in one word, the vine of the Lord of Hosts? And since, as we are assured, even its leaves shall not fall withered to the ground (Ps. i. 3), what can perish which belongs to it?

4. But yet to such a vine as this there will never be wanting persecutions from without, nor snares from within. For *when goods increase, they are increased that eat them* (Eccles. v. 11). The wise man will be no less careful to keep his vine in safety than to cultivate it; nor will he suffer it to be devoured by foxes. Among the worst of these is the secret detractor, but the fawning flatterer is not less evil. Of both he who is wise will beware. He will direct his efforts, as far as in him lies, to 'take' those who practise such arts, but to take them by kindnesses and courtesies, by salutary admonitions, and prayers to God on their behalf. He will not cease to heap such coals of fire upon the head of the abusive person (Rom. xii. 20) and also of the flatterer; until he shall succeed, if possible, in drawing the envy from the heart of the one, and the dissimulation from that of the other, and thus fulfil the command of the Bridegroom: *Take us the foxes, the little foxes, that spoil the vines.* Does it not appear to you that a person is, as it were, 'taken,' whose countenance is covered with confusion, who blushes for his own judgment, and is himself the witness of the shame and regret that he feels, whether for having regarded with hatred a man most worthy of love, or for having loved with only a pretended and wordy affection him by whom, as he has at length (though late) experienced, he was loved in deed and in truth? He is evidently taken, and taken for the Lord, according to His own express command: *Take* [for] *us.* Would that I might be able thus to 'take' all those who oppose me without a cause, that I might gain them for Christ, or restore them to Him! That thus those who seek my life may be dismayed and confounded, that those who wish me evil may be turned backward and put to confusion, so that I for my part may be found obedient to the Bridegroom, and may take these foxes for Him,[1] and not for myself, is my earnest desire. But let us return to our text at the beginning, that our explanation may proceed in due order.

5. *Take us the foxes, the little foxes, that spoil the grapes.* This passage relates to morals; and, regarding it in a moral sense, we have already shown that these vines, spiritually understood, are nothing else than spiritual men, whose inward nature and faculties are all cultivated; which germinate, bear fruit, and bring forth a spirit of salvation, so that we are able to say of these vines of the Lord of Hosts what is said of the Kingdom of God, that it is within us (Luke xvii. 21). For we read in the Gospel that the Kingdom of God shall be given to a nation bringing forth the fruits thereof (Matt. xxi. 43). These are they which St. Paul enumerates, saying: *The fruit of the Spirit is love, joy, peace, longsuffering, gentleness, goodness, faith, meekness, temperance* (Gal. v. 22, 23). These fruits, then, are our progress in virtue. These are accepted by the Bridegroom, because He has a care of us. Do you think that it is of mere plants of earth that God has care? It is for men, not for trees, that the

---

[1] This is the reading of three MSS.; but two others, and the printed editions, read: *non modo in capiendo vulpes, sed et in capiendo ipsi.*

God Man has affection, and He regards our progress in holiness as His fruits. He observes diligently the season of these; He smiles to see them appear, and takes care and shows solicitude that, when they have appeared, they should not perish for us, or rather that they should not perish for Him; for He regards Himself as having the same interest in them as we. Therefore He commends, in His wise Providence, that the little foxes which lurk around them should be taken, lest they should ravage the fruits while still immature. And as if anyone should object, 'your fear is premature, for the time of fruit has not yet come.' He adds: 'That is not the case, for *our vines have tender grapes.*' After the flowers[1] the fruits do not delay; the former are no sooner fallen than the latter burst forth and begin to appear.

6. That is a parable which applies to the time which is approaching. Do you see [that these signify] those Novices? They have only lately come, they have only just been converted. We cannot say of them that our vine *has been* in flower, for it is flowering now. That which in the meantime you see appear in them is the flower, but the time of fruit has not yet come. The flower is their new and altered manner of life, their recently adopted rule, and stricter method of conduct. They have put on a mortified countenance, and a well regulated demeanour of their whole body. That which appears in them is, I confess, pleasing, for their outward man shows less care for dress and appearance, their speech is more sparing, their countenance more cheerful, their glances more modest, their movements more quiet and measured. But since they have practised these rules of life but a very little while, this very newness obliges us to regard them, so to speak, as flowers, and their actions as the hope of fruit, rather than as fruit themselves. I do not so much fear for you, my young sons, from the cunning of the foxes, since it is well known that their hostility is directed rather against fruits than flowers. Your danger comes from another direction. For you I fear the blasting of your flowers by the frost, rather than their being torn away by violence. It is the chilling north wind that I suspect, and the morning frosts, which are wont to cut off the early and untimely flowers and the fruits in their germ. Therefore it is from the direction of the north wind that you are threatened: for *who can stand before His cold?* (Ps. cxlvii. 17). If this freezing cold has once pervaded the soul (as happens but too often to it when the spirit is in a condition of relaxation and torpor), then, if there is no one (which may God avert) to hinder its further progress, it enters into the secret places of the heart, and into the inmost part of the soul; it stuns and paralyzes good dispositions, it closes up the avenues by which good advice and help might come, it troubles the light of the judgment, it fetters the impulses of the spirit; then, as it happens also to those who are suffering under a fever of the body, the soul undergoes sudden and vehement chills, its vigour is relaxed, a languor creeps

---

[1] The Vulgate reading is *vinea nostra floruit.*—ED.

over its powers, a horror of austerity is continually intensified, the fear of poverty troubles it more and more, the soul contracts, as it were, upon itself, grace ebbs away from it, life becomes wearisome, the reason is stupefied, the courage stifled, the recent fervour of the man rapidly grows cold, a fastidious and dainty lukewarmness gains ground in the soul, brotherly charity grows cold, pleasure begins to have attractions, the man falls into a false security, and the habitude of vice resumes its former prevalence. What shall I say more? The law is evaded, righteousness is rejected,[1] obligation proscribed, the fear of the Lord abandoned altogether. Finally, such a person yields himself to the last degree of shamelessness, he makes that leap which is rashness itself, that fall most disgraceful, shameful, and full of confusion and ignominy, from the sky into the abyss, from the pavement of a palace into a dunghill, from a throne into the gutter, from heaven into a swamp of mire, from the cloister into the outer world—yea, from paradise into hell.[2] It is not now the time to point out the origin and beginning of this downfall, or to show by what means it may be avoided, or by what strength it may be surmounted. That shall be the task of another day. At present let us proceed with what we have begun.

7. Our discourse must be brought back to those who are more advanced in virtue, and more stedfast in it; to the vine which has already flowered, whose flowers have nothing more to fear from the cold, though its fruits are not yet secure from despoiling foxes. It has yet to be explained at greater length what is to be understood spiritually by these foxes; why they are called 'little'; why the command is not that they are to be driven away, or to be slain, but that they are to be 'taken'; and how the different kinds of these are to be distinguished, so that my hearers may learn to know them, and to be more on their guard against them. But we must not enter upon this subject in the present sermon that we may not weary you, and that our devotion may not cease to be marked by willingness and zeal, through the grace and to the glory of Him who is the great Bridegroom of the Church, our Lord JESUS CHRIST, who is above all, God blessed for ever. AMEN.

[1] *Abdicatur*. Another reading is *abjudicatur*.
[2] A striking picture, indeed, of the fall of monks when in their novitiate. It may be compared with St. Bernard's 'Letters,' 107, 108, 395.

SERMON LXIV.

OF THE TEMPTATIONS OF MORE MATURE MONKS; BY WHAT FOXES THEY ARE INFESTED, THAT IS, BY WHAT TEMPTATIONS THEY ARE MOST TRIED. ALSO OF THE TAKING OF HERETICS, WHO ARE THE FOXES OF THE CHURCH.

' *Take us the foxes, the little foxes, that spoil the vines : for our vines have tender grapes.*'—Cant. ii. 15.

I AM now prepared to fulfil the promise I made. The foxes signify temptations. It is unavoidable that temptations should come. For who shall be crowned except he strive lawfully? (2 Tim. ii. 5). And what occasion is there for striving if there be no enemy to oppose? When, then, you enter into the service of God, endure constantly in fear, and prepare thy heart for temptation (Ecclus. ii. 1, 2), being assured that *all who will live godly in Christ Jesus shall suffer persecution* (2 Tim. iii. 12). Now, temptations are diverse according to the diversity of times. At the beginning of our spiritual course, when we are as tender and newly-planted flowers, it is evident that we are attacked, as it were, by the violence of cold. Of this I have spoken in a former sermon (No. LXIII., *n.* 6), and shown how we are to guard against this danger. As to those who are more advanced in holy things, the powerful enemies of good do not venture openly to oppose them, but are wont to lay wait for them in secret, like foxes full of cunning, and, though vices in reality, to put on the appearance of virtues. How many, for example, have I myself known who, when they had entered upon the ways of life, when they had even attained a high degree of perfectness, when they were going on well and safely, and making progress in the ways of righteousness, were, by the devices of these foxes, overthrown with shame and disgrace, and have lamented too late over the fruits of virtues which were blighted in them!

2. I have seen a man running well on his course, and lo, a sudden hesitation and scruple arises in him. Was not that due to one of these 'little foxes'? 'To how many,' he says, 'of my brethren and relations, of my friends and acquaintances, should I be able, if I were living in my own country and neighbourhood, to communicate of that good which I enjoy here alone? They love me, and would easily follow my advice. Why is this waste made? I will go thither, and in saving many of them I shall equally save myself. There is nothing to be feared in a mere change of place. What matters it where I am as long as I am doing a good work? And, in fact, I am without doubt the better placed where I am living a more useful and fruitful life.' Why repeat more of his reasoning? He goes whither he desires, and, unhappy man, he perishes : rather as a dog returned

to his vomit than as an exile who returns to his own land. He both comes to a miserable end himself and he fails to save any of his own people. Surely this was a 'little fox'; I mean the deceptive hope which he nourished of gaining over his friends. You are able to find out for yourself other and similar ideas to this in your own mind if you examine it closely.

3. Do you wish, nevertheless, that I should point out to you one more? I will do so; and even a third and a fourth, if I shall find that it renders you watchful to take those that you may perhaps discover in your own vineyard. It happens sometimes that a man who is making good progress in virtue, and who feels that God has poured upon him an abundance of heavenly grace, conceives a desire to preach, not indeed to his relatives and connections, according to that saying, *Immediately I conferred not with flesh and blood* (Gal. i. 16), but as if with a purer impulse, and with a design to be more powerful and more fruitful, to preach to strangers, and indeed to all. But still with great prudence. He fears to incur that malediction of the prophet upon him who shall withhold corn from the people (Prov. xi. 26), and to act against the precept of the Gospel if he should not preach to all, and, as it were, upon the housetops, what he has heard in the ear (Matt. x. 27). Now this is the temptation, so to speak, of a fox, and of one who is so much the more dangerous than the former, as he knows how to present himself secretly. But I will take him for you. First, Moses says: *Thou shalt do no work with the firstling of thy bullock* (Deut. xv. 19). And this is St. Paul's interpretation: *Not a novice, lest, being lifted up with pride, he fall into the condemnation of the devil* (1 Tim. iii. 6); and again: *No man taketh this honour unto himself but he that is called of God, as was Aaron* (Heb. v. 4); and still again: *How shall they preach except they be sent?* (Rom. x. 15). And we know that the function of a monk is not to teach, but to mourn for sin (St. Jerome, *Contr. Vigil.*). Out of these and similar reasons I weave my net; I take my fox, that he may not spoil the vine. From these considerations it is certain and clear that to preach in public is not expedient for a monk, is not becoming to a novice, nor, unless he be sent, even lawful. What destruction, then, to the conscience to violate at once all three of these rules! Therefore, whatever of this nature is suggested to the mind, whether it be by your own thoughts or by the prompting of an evil angel, recognise it always as the temptation of a wily fox presenting evil under the guise of good.

4. Look at another case. How many are there who, being fervent in spirit, have left their monasteries and taken upon them a solitary life, and who in the event have fallen back into lukewarmness, and by a careless, if not by an abandoned, way of living, have violated the law of the solitary? It is plain that this was the work of a fox where so extensive a devastation of the vineyard was made; that is, so deplorable an injury to the life and conscience of the man. He supposed that in a solitary life he should gather spiritual fruits with

much greater abundance than if he were in a community in which he obtained only the ordinary gifts of grace. And that imagination of his seemed good to him; but the issue of it showed that it was due to a fox, who was as usual spoiling the vine.

5. What shall I say of that excessive and superstitious abstinence as practised by some among ourselves, who disturb us so often, and render themselves so troublesome to themselves and to all? All the divisions which those singularities produce, do they not break up and lay waste the conscience of those who practise them, and destroy, as far as is in their power, that great vine which the Hand of God has planted, in destroying the unanimity which ought to exist among you all? *Woe to that man by whom the offence cometh!* (Matt. xviii. 7). *Whosoever*, says the Saviour, *shall offend one of these little ones* (Mark ix. 42)—severe are the words which follow, but how much more severe a sentence does the person deserve who gives scandal to a community so great and so holy! Assuredly, whosoever he is, a very severe judgment shall be passed upon him. But more of this another time.

6. Let us now consider what is said by the Bridegroom with regard to those small but cunning foxes which spoil the vines. 'Little,' not because they have little malice, but because of their subtlety. This kind of creature is by nature astute, and quick to inflict injury in secret. For this reason it seems to me well suited to be the type of certain very subtle vices, which are cloaked with an appearance of virtue, such as those of which I have already given some few examples. For they have, in fact, no other power to injure than that which they derive from passing themselves off as virtues, and thus deceiving by a kind of likeness which they have to the latter. They are either the vain imaginations of men, or the suggestions of evil angels, the angels of Satan, who transform themselves into the Angels of light (2 Cor. xi. 14), who prepare their arrows within the quiver (that is, in concealment) that they may privily shoot at the upright in heart (Ps. xi. 2). This is why, as I think, they are called 'little,' because, while other vices are, as it were, bulky, and show themselves openly, these are slender, subtle, and hard to be recognised, except by those who are perfect, experienced, and clear sighted, having their eyes enlightened to discern between good and evil, and especially by those advanced in the spiritual life, who are able to say with the Apostle, 'We are not ignorant of the devices [of Satan]' (2 Cor. ii. 11). Perhaps, too, this is the reason why the command of the Bridegroom is, not that they should be exterminated, or driven away, or slain, but that they should be taken; namely, because such little spiritual beasts (*bestiolas*) as these are full of craftiness, and require to be watched with the utmost vigilance and care, so that they may be taken (that is, caught in the trap of) their own craftiness. Therefore when their device is discovered, their fraud laid bare, their falseness demonstrated, then with the utmost fitness is it said that there is taken the little fox which spoiled the vine. It is thus, in fact, that we speak of a man being

taken in his discourse, as we read in the Gospel that the Pharisees took counsel that they might entangle Jesus in His talk (Matt. xxii. 15).

7. Thus, then, the Bridegroom orders the little foxes, which spoil the grapes, to be *taken*—that is, to be surprised, discovered, and convicted. This kind of pest alone has it for a distinct mark that if known and recognised it has no power to harm, so that for it to be discovered is to be vanquished. For who, except a person void of understanding, would step knowingly and wilfully into a trap that is discovered to him? It is sufficient, then, for temptations of that kind to be 'taken'—that is, to be uncovered and brought into the light; to those who have become aware of them they are harmless. It is not thus with other vices. For their attack is openly made, and their powers of injury are manifest; they take captive even those who are aware of them, they overcome the reluctant, but by open force, and not by guile. Therefore against those (as it were) ferocious brutes what is needed is not to seek them out, but to overcome and render them powerless. Against these 'little foxes' (who, because they are unable to hurt if discovered, have extraordinary powers of concealing themselves) it suffices that they be brought out into the light, for they have hiding-places, and taken in their own craftiness. For such reasons those foxes are described as 'little,' and ordered to be *taken*. Or again, they may be named thus to show that vices should be diligently observed in their earlier stages, that they may be taken while they are still young and small, and not allowed to grow greater, when they will both do more injury, and be with greater difficulty mastered.

8. If we understand these words in an allegorical sense, so as to take the vines as signifying Churches, and the foxes as heresies, or rather as the heretics themselves, the simple and natural sense is that heretics should be 'taken' rather than merely driven away. They should be taken, I say, not by force of arms, but by force of arguments, by which their errors are refuted, and they themselves, if possible, brought back to the true faith, and reconciled to the Catholic Church.[1] For this is the will of Him who desires all men to be saved, and to come to the knowledge of the truth (1 Tim. ii. 4). He shows here, in fact, that He desires this, since He says, not simply *Take the foxes*, but *Take us the foxes*. He desires, then, that they should be taken for Him. and for His Bride—that is, the Church Catholic, since He says: 'Take them for us.' Therefore the Churchman, who is skilled and learned, if he undertakes to argue with a heretic, ought to direct his endeavours to convince him that he has erred, and to convert him, bearing in mind that saying of the Apostle James: *He which converteth the sinner from the error of his way shall save a soul from death, and shall hide a multitude of sins* (James v. 20). If he is unwilling to be brought back, and is not convinced after a first and a second admonition, because he is entirely perverted, then, according to St. Paul, he is to be rejected (Titus iii. 10). In this

[1] Compare *Serm. in Cantic.* LXVI., *n.* 12; and Ep. CCCLXV.

case it would be preferable, as I consider, that he should be driven away, or even a restraint put upon his liberty, than that he should be allowed to spoil the vines.

9. Let it not, therefore, be supposed that a man has done a small or unimportant thing who has vanquished and refuted a heretic, who has disproved his heresy, who has distinguished clearly and plainly his fair-seeming theories from the truth, who has shown by obvious and irrefragable reasoning the faultiness and erroneous nature of his dogmas; and, in short, has subjugated that haughty and perverted intellect which set itself up against the knowledge revealed by God. He who has brought about such results as these has 'taken' the fox nevertheless, though not to his conversion and saving; he has taken him equally for the Bridegroom and the Bride, though after another manner. For the Church is strengthened in the faith, though that heretic be not raised up out of the mire of his errors; while the Bridegroom, without doubt, rejoices in the spiritual progress of His Bride, and the joy of the Lord is our strength (Neh. viii. 10). He who is so condescending as to associate Himself with us, regards our advantage as a matter in which He has an interest, and, therefore, bids the foxes be taken, not for Himself, but for us with Himself. Note the phrase, 'Take for us'—what can be more companionable and friendly? Does it not seem to you that He says this, as it were, like some father of a family, who possesses nothing separately for himself and his own advantage, but shares all things with wife and children and domestics? And He who thus speaks is God; yet He does not say this at all as God, but as the Bridegroom.

10. *Take us the foxes.* Do you see in how social and equable a manner He says this, He who has no companion or equal? He might have said, 'Take for me,' but He delights to associate others with Himself, and, therefore, preferred to say, 'Take *for us.*' O sweetness, O grace, O power of love! Is it possible that the Sovereign of all has become one of the mass of beings? Who has done this? It is Love; which is regardless of dignity, rich in condescension, powerful in affection, efficacious in persuasion. What more forceful than love? It prevails even with God. And yet, since it is Love, is there anything that is more gentle? What strength is that, I ask, which is so forceful for victory, so gentle in the face of violence? For the Lord emptied Himself (Phil. ii. 7), so that you might know it to be the effect of His great love, that His Fulness was poured forth and expended, that His loftiness was brought down to the level of others, and His unique position associated with them. With whom is it, O admirable Bridegroom, that you have so close and intimate an alliance? 'Take for us,' you say, 'the foxes.' For whom 'with you?' Is it for the Church gathered out of the Gentiles? That is composed of mortal and sinful beings. What she is, we know; but Thou, what art Thou, to be the devoted and eager spouse of this Ethiopian woman? (Num. xii. 1) Not another Moses, assuredly, but a greater than Moses. For Thou art

He who is fairer than the children of men (Ps. xlv. 2). But in saying this I have said too little : Thou art the brightness of the Eternal Life, the Splendour and express Image of the Person of God (Heb. i. 3) ; and finally, Thou art above all, God blessed for ever. AMEN.

NOTICE.

It seems to us opportune to introduce in this place the following letter, written to St. Bernard by Eberwin, Provost of Steinfeld, near Cologne, on the subject of the heretics of that time, which was the occasion of the two following sermons. I had thought with Horst and others that in these Bernard was treating of the Henricians, against whom he wrote his Letter 240. But the subjoined letter of Eberwin shows that those heretics, whose errors are refuted in the two following sermons, were others than the Henricians, since, while the latter infested Aquitaine chiefly, the former were found in Cologne and the neighbouring districts. However, it must be allowed that each class agreed in the same errors, and perhaps they were derived from the same source. I have spoken at greater length of these men in the General Preface, *n.* 6. I have no doubt that this Eberwin is the same as Eberwin, or Herwin, Abbot of Steinfeld, who is praised in Book vi. of the ' Miracles of St. Bernard,' *nn.* 22 and 26. He was unquestionably of the Order of Prémontré, which has still an abbey at Steinfeld.[1]

LETTER OF EBERWIN, PROVOST OF STEINFELD, TO ABBOT BERNARD,

RESPECTING THE HERETICS OF HIS TIME.

To the Reverend lord and father BERNARD, *Abbot of Clairvaux :* EBERWIN, *humble minister of the Abbey of Steinfeld, wishes that he may be made strong in the Lord, and may strengthen the Church of Christ.*

I REJOICE, as one that findeth great spoils, over your eloquent utterances, in which you are wont both by tongue and pen to bring to our mind the sweet and abundant graces of God ; and especially in the Canticle of the love of the Bridegroom and the Bride, that is, of Christ and the Church, so that we are able to say truly to the same Bridegroom : *Thou hast kept the good wine until now* (John ii. 10). He has set thee among us as a cupbearer of this precious wine ; do not cease to pour it forth, and do not hesitate, for it is not possible to exhaust the urns. Do not allow your bodily weakness, O holy father, to be an excuse, for in the discharge of that duty piety counts for more than bodily strength. Do not say that you are full of occupation ; I know not anything that ought to be preferred to a work so necessary as this to the common good. From

---

[1] *I.e.,* when Mabillon wrote, *circa* 1690.

that urn what an abundant stream you have, most holy father, already poured forth to us! From the first you have drawn to the satisfaction of all, and it has rendered those who have partaken of it wise and strong against the teaching and the force of the Scribes and Pharisees; the second has strengthened them against the arguments and the cruelties of the Gentiles; the third, against the subtle deceptions of heretics; the fourth, against false Christians; the fifth, against the heretics who shall appear towards the time of the end of the world, and of whom the Holy Spirit, by the mouth of an Apostle, speaks manifestly in these words: *In the latter times some shall depart from the faith, giving heed to seducing spirits and doctrines of devils; speaking lies in hypocrisy . . . forbidding to marry, and commanding to abstain from meats, which God hath created to be received with thanksgiving* (1 Tim. iv. 1-3). From the sixth the faithful shall receive exaltation and joy of spirit (*inebriabuntur*), and be strengthened against him who in this departure from the faith shall be revealed; I mean that son of sin, the man of perdition, who opposeth and exalteth himself above all that is called God, or that is worshipped; whose coming is after the working of Satan, with all power and signs and lying wonders, and with all deceivableness of unrighteousness (2 Thess. ii. 3-10). After this, since the sons of men will be exalted in spirit with the abundance of God's House, and the river of the pleasures which He bestows, a seventh will not be needful. You have in the meantime, O good father, poured forth sufficiently to all, from the fourth urn, for their correction, their edification, and their perfecting; to all, I say, whether they be beginners, those who are making progress, or who are going on unto perfection; and to the very end of the world it will be to their benefit against the coldness and the perversity which is in false brethren. Now is the time that you should draw from the fifth, and bring forth to us the wine from thence, against the new heretics who are now stirring almost everywhere, and casting forth the mud of the abyss throughout all the Churches, as if their chief was already beginning to be threatened with dissolution, and the day of the Lord was drawing nigh. And in the marriage song of Christ and of His Church that passage which you, my father, as you have yourself informed me, are now about to treat upon, namely, *Take us the foxes, the little foxes, that spoil the vines*, bears perfectly upon this subject, and conducts you naturally to this fifth urn. I entreat you, then, father, to distinguish between all the parts of the heresy of those persons, which have come to your knowledge, and by opposing to them the authorities and reasons of our holy faith, to destroy them.

2. There have been lately discovered among us in the neighbourhood of Cologne certain heretics, of whom some have made amends for their fault (*cum satisfactione*) and returned to the Church. Two among them, namely, he who was called their bishop, and his companion, have withstood us in an open assembly of clerics and laymen, in which the lord Archbishop himself was present, and some noble-

men of high rank, and defended their heresy by the words of Christ and His Apostle. But when they saw that they could make no progress, they requested that a day might be assigned to them on which they might bring forward men of their community who were well skilled in their faith. They professed that, if they saw that their teachers were unable to reply satisfactorily to the objections made to them, they were willing to submit to the Church; but that otherwise, they had rather die than give up their opinions. To these propositions reply was made by admonitions, continued during three days consecutively; but they were unwilling to yield or to come to a better mind. They were then seized and carried off by the people, who were transported by an excessive zeal; but quite against our will; and being cast into the fire by them, were consumed; and, which is a fact still more to be wondered at, they entered into and endured that torment of fire, not only with patience, but with joy. Here, holy father, I should wish, if I were present with you, to have your explanation, whence it is that those members of the devil have fortitude so great in their heresy as is scarcely equalled by those most sincerely attached to the faith of Christ.

3. This is their heresy: They say that the Church exists among them only, since they alone follow closely in the footsteps of Christ, and remain the true followers of the manner of life observed by the Apostles, inasmuch as they possess neither houses, nor fields, nor property of any kind. They declare that, as Christ did not possess any of these Himself, so He did not permit His disciples to possess them. 'But you,' they say to us, 'add house to house, and field to field, and seek the things of this world. So completely is this the case, that even those among you who are considered most perfect, such as the monks and regular canons, possess these things, if not as their private property, yet as belonging to their community.' Of themselves they say: 'We are the poor of Christ; we have no settled dwelling-place; we flee from city to city, as sheep in the midst of wolves; we endure persecution, as did the Apostles and the martyrs; yet we lead a holy and austere life in fasting and abstinence, continuing day and night in labours and prayers, and seeking from these only what is necessary to sustain life. We endure all this,' they say, 'because we are not of this world; but as for you, who are lovers of this world, you have peace with the world because you are, in fact, of it. False Apostles, adulterating the word of Christ, and seeking their own interests, have caused you and your fathers to wander far out of the right path; but we and our fathers are the descendants of the Apostles, we have remained in the grace of Christ, and shall remain until the end of the world. The distinction between us and you is to be found in those words which Christ spake: *By their fruits ye shall know them* (Matt. vii. 16). Our fruits are the following in the footsteps of Christ.' In respect of food, they forbid every kind of milk, that which is made of milk, and whatsoever is the product of that function. It is in this particular that their manner of living

is opposed to ours. In the reception of their Sacraments they cover the head with a veil, yet they have openly avowed to us that daily at their table when they eat they, according to the usage of the Apostles, consecrate, by saying the Lord's Prayer, their food and drink into the Body and Blood of Christ, so that by it they may be nourished as the members and body of Christ. They say that we do not hold the truth as to the Sacraments, but only a certain shadow of it, and tradition of men. They confess also plainly that besides the baptism with water, they give and receive a baptism with the Spirit and with fire, and are therewith baptized, adducing that testimony of John the Baptist, who, himself baptizing with water, said of Christ: *He shall baptize you with the Holy Ghost and with fire* (Matt. iii. 11), and in another place: *I baptize with water, but there standeth One among you whom ye know not* (John i. 26); as if he had thus wished to say, 'He shall baptize you with another Baptism beyond that of water.' And that such a Baptism ought to be bestowed by imposition of hands, they have endeavoured to show by the testimony of St. Luke, who, describing in the Acts of the Apostles the baptism of Saul (*Pauli*), which he received from Ananias at the direction of Christ, makes no mention of water, but only of the laying on of hands (Acts ix. 17, 18); and they pretend that whatever is found in the Acts, or in the Epistles of St. Paul, respecting the laying on of hands has reference to this baptism. Whosoever among them has received this baptism is called by them Elect; he has the power to baptize others, who shall be found worthy of receiving that baptism, and of consecrating at his table the Body and Blood of Christ. They previously receive him by the laying on of hands, from the number of those whom they call Hearers, into the ranks of the Believers; and thus he will gain the right to be present at their prayers, until, after sufficient proof of fitness, he shall be made one of the Elect. Of our Baptism they take no account. Marriage they condemn, but for what reason I have not been able to ascertain—either because they have no reason to give, or because they do not dare to avow it.

4. There are also in our country certain other heretics who differ in all respects from the former; indeed, it is by their mutual discord and contention that each kind of them is discovered to us. These latter deny that the Body of Christ is ever present (*fieri*) upon the Altar, because [they say that] the priests of the Church are none of them validly ordained (*consecrati*). According to them the Apostolic dignity has been corrupted by mixing itself with the affairs of this world, and as he who sits in the chair of Peter is not engaged in warfare for God, as was Peter, he has deprived himself of the power of consecrating and ordaining which was bestowed upon Peter. That power, therefore, which it does not itself possess, the Archbishops and Bishops, who live in the Church after the manner of the world, cannot receive from it, or derive the power of ordaining anyone. This they profess to derive from the words of Christ: *The*

Scribes and Pharisees sit in Moses' seat; all, therefore, whatsoever they bid you observe, that observe and do (Matt. xxiii. 2, 3); as if in these words He had said that to those who resemble the Scribes and Pharisees is accorded the power of preaching and government, but nothing more. Thus they make null the Priesthood of the Church, and condemn the Sacraments, except Baptism alone. Baptism they administer to adults only, and these they say are baptized by Christ, whosoever may be the minister of the Sacrament. They have no belief in the Baptism of little children, or [in any] except that of which it is said in the Gospel, *He that believeth and is baptized shall be saved* (Mark xvi. 16). They call every marriage fornication, except that contracted between two virgins, a man and a woman; and they support their belief by those words of the Lord, in which he replied to the Pharisees, *What God hath joined together let not man put asunder;* as if those [only] were joined together by God who were wedded according to the condition and mutual relation of our first parents; and they support this by that reply also which He made to the same opponents on the subject of a billet of divorcement: *From the beginning it was not so;* and also that which follows in the same place: *Whoso marrieth her which is put away doth commit adultery* (Matt. xix. 6-9). Further, they quote that saying of the Apostle: *Marriage is honourable in all, and the bed undefiled* (Heb. xiii. 4).

5. In the intercessions of the Saints they put no trust. They maintain that fasts and other mortifications of the flesh which are undergone for sins are not necessary for the just, nor even for sinners, because in the very day that a sinner has mourned over, and lamented, his sins, they are all remitted unto him; and other observances in the Church, which were established neither by Christ nor by His Apostles after Him, they call superstitions. They do not allow that there is any purgatorial fire after death, but hold that souls pass immediately on their going forth from the body either into eternal rest or eternal punishment, because of those words of Solomon: *If the tree fall toward the south, or toward the north, in the place where the tree falleth, there it shall be* (Eccles. xi. 3). And thus they regard as useless the prayers and oblations of the faithful for the dead.

6. Against all these forms of evil, so many and so varied, I entreat you, holy father, to let your solicitude be on the watch, and to direct the point of your sharp arrow upon these beasts of prey. Do not reply to us that that tower of David to which we fly for refuge is sufficiently strengthened with ramparts and bulwarks, that on it hang a thousand bucklers, and that it has a complete garrison of brave men. We wish, father, that this garrison should be, on account of our inexperience and backwardness, drawn together and combined by your care and zeal, that it may be more successful in finding out, and more effectual in resisting, this host of monsters. You should know also, my lord, that those who have returned to the Church have told us that they have a very great multitude of adherents scattered almost everywhere throughout the countries, and that among these they count

very many of our clerks and monks. Those who were burned said to us in their defence that this heresy has had a secret existence from the times of the martyrs even to our own day, and that it still remains in Greece and in some other countries. Such are those heretics who call themselves apostles, and have a pope of their own. Others there are who, though they do not acknowledge our Pope, yet allow that they have no other. Those emissaries (*apostolici*) of Satan have also among them (as they say) women vowed to continence, widows, and virgins; they have also their wives, some among the elect, others among the believers, as if to follow the example of the Apostles, to whom was conceded the power of taking about their wives with them. Farewell in the Lord.

SERMON LXV.

OF SECRET HERETICS, WHOSE PERVERSE DOCTRINES AND STUDIED CARE TO HIDE THEIR MYSTERIES ST. BERNARD SEVERELY CENSURES; ALSO OF THEIR SCANDALOUS BEHAVIOUR.

I HAVE already delivered to you two sermons upon one verse; I propose to deliver a third, if it will not weary you to listen. And I think it even necessary to do so; for though, as far as relates to our domestic vine, which is no other than yourselves, my brethren, I have, I think, sufficiently forearmed you, in the two preceding sermons, against the crafty advances of three kinds of foxes; namely, flatterers, calumniators, and certain seducing spirits who are skilled and experienced in presenting evil under the guise of good; yet that is not the case with the dominical, that is, the Lord's vine. I speak of that vine which has filled the earth, and of which we also are a part; a vine great and spreading, planted by the Hand of the Lord, redeemed by His Blood, watered by His Word, propagated by His grace, and rendered fruitful by His Spirit. The more carefully I have dealt with that which was of private and personal concern, the less valuable were my remarks with regard to that which was common and public. But it troubles me greatly, on behalf of that vine, to behold the multitude of its assailants, the fewness of its defenders, and the difficulty of the defence. The hidden and furtive character of the attack is the cause of this difficulty. For from the beginning the Church has had foxes; but they have been soon found out and taken. An heretic combated openly (indeed, that was the principal reason why the name was given, because the desire of the heretic was to gain an open victory), and was manifestly overcome. Those foxes, therefore, were easily taken. But what if a heretic, when the truth was set clear in the light before him, remained in the shadow of his obstinacy, and, bound (as it were) hand and foot in the outer darkness, withered away in solitude? Even then the fox was deemed to be 'taken' when his impiety was condemned, and the impious one cast out, thenceforth to live in a mere show of life without fruitfulness. From this to such an one, according to the Prophet, comes a sterile womb and dry breasts (Hos. ix. 14): because an error, publicly confuted, does not soon shoot up again, and an evident falsehood does not take root.

2. What shall we do to take those foxes, the most malignant and dangerous of all, who prefer the inflicting of severe injury to the enjoyment of open victory, and who crawl to, and steal upon, their purpose in order not to be seen? With all heretics the one intention has always been to obtain praise for themselves by the remarkable extent of their knowledge. But there is a heresy which alone is more malignant and more artful than others, since it feeds upon the losses of others, and neglects its own glory. It is instructed, I believe, by the examples of those ancient heresies which, when betrayed, were by no means suffered to escape, but were forthwith captured; and so is careful to actuate secretly, by a new method of mischief, this mystery of iniquity, and that with the greater freedom the less it is suspected. Furthermore, its promoters have met together, as it is said, at places appointed in secret, and concerted together their nefarious discourses. 'Take oaths, if needful; take them even falsely,' they say the one to the other, 'rather than betray the secret.' But at another time they do not consider it right by any means to swear, not even in the smallest degree, because of those words in the Gospel: *Swear not at all; neither by heaven . . . nor by the earth* (Matt. v. 34, 35), etc. O foolish and hard of heart, filled with the spirit of the Pharisees, ye, too, strain out a gnat and swallow a camel (Matt. xxiii. 24). To swear is not permitted, but to swear falsely, that is permissible, as if the allowance to do the latter did not carry with it the former also! In what passage of the Gospel, of which you do not, as you falsely boast, pass over one iota, do you find that exception? It is clear that you, both by superstition, forbid the taking of an oath, and, at the same time, wickedly presume to authorize a perjury. O strange perversity! That which is given only as a counsel of perfection—namely, *Swear not*—that they observe as rigidly and contentiously as if it were a positive command; while that which is laid down as an unchangeable law—namely, never to be guilty of perjury—they dispense with at their own will as a thing indifferent. No, say they; but let us not make known our secret. As if it were not to the glory of God to make known teaching [that is to edification] (Dan. ii. 28, 29)! Do they envy the glory of God? But I rather believe that they are ashamed to have their secret known, being conscious that it does not redound to their glory; for they are said to practise in secret things obscene and abominable, even as the hinder parts of foxes are offensive.

3. But I do not wish to speak of that which they deny; let them answer only to those which are known and manifest. Are they careful, according to the Gospel precept, not to give that which is

holy unto the dogs, or to cast pearls before swine? (Matt. vii. 6). But do not they who regard all who belong to the Church as dogs and swine, plainly confess that they are not of the Church themselves? For they consider that their secret, whatever it is, should be kept wholly from the knowledge of all, without exception, who are not of their sect. What their doctrine is they do not avow, and they adopt every means to avoid its becoming known; but yet they do not succeed. Reply to me, O man, who art wise above that which is meet, and yet more foolish than can be expressed in words. Is the secret which you are concealing of God, or is it not? If it is, why do you not make it known to His glory? For it is to the glory of God to reveal that which comes from Him. But if it is not, why do you put faith in that which is not of God, unless because you are a heretic? Either, then, let them proclaim the secret as coming from God to the glory of God, or let them confess that the secret is not of God, and thereby allow that they are heretics; or, at least, let them allow that they are manifestly enemies of the glory of God, since they are unwilling to make manifest a thing which would be conducive to that glory. For it is stated with preciseness in Scripture: It is the glory of kings to conceal a matter, but it is the glory of God to reveal discourse.[1] Are you not willing to reveal it? Then you do not desire to glorify God. But perhaps you do not receive this Scripture. Doubtless this is the case, for [sectaries] profess that they are followers of the Gospel, and the only ones. Let them, then, reply to the Gospel. *What I tell you in darkness*, saith the Lord, *that speak ye in light: and what ye hear in the ear, that preach ye upon the housetops* (Matt. x. 27). Now, it is not permitted to you to be silent. How long is that kept under the veil of secrecy which God declares is to be made known? How long is your Gospel to be hidden? I suspect that your Gospel is not that of St. Paul, for he declares that his Gospel is not hidden, or rather he says this: *If our Gospel be hid, it is hid to them that are lost* (2 Cor. iv. 3). Does not this apply to you who have among you a Gospel that is hidden? What is more plain than that you are in the way of being lost? Or perhaps you do not receive even the Epistles of St. Paul. I have heard that it is so with certain persons among you. For, although you all agree in differing from us, you do not all agree in all respects among yourselves.

4. But, at all events, you all receive, without exception, if I do not mistake, the words, the writings, and the traditions of those who were personally with the Saviour, as of equal authority with the Gospel. Now, did they keep their Gospel secret? Did they hide the weakness of the flesh in the Divine Son, the terrible circum-

---

[1] Thus St. Bernard quotes Prov. xxv. 2, and St. Gregory the Great ('Hom. in Ezech.,' Bk. i., *n.* 6) quotes it in the same sense. But the Hebrew, the Septuagint, the Vulgate, and after them the English A.V. and other versions, have the precisely opposite sense: 'It is the glory of God to conceal a thing,' etc. Perhaps our Saint may have taken the quotation from St. Gregory. It does not seem to occur elsewhere in this form, but see a similar passage in Tobit xii. 7.—ED.

stances of His Death, or the ignominy of His Cross? Did not their words, indeed, go forth into the whole world? (Ps. xix. 4). Where, then, is there in you that following of the Apostolic life and conduct of which you boast? They cry aloud, you whisper in secret; they teach in public, you in a corner; they *fly as a cloud* (Is. lx. 8), while as for you, you conceal yourselves in the darkness and in the cellars of your houses. What likeness to them do you display? Is it in that you do not indeed take women as travelling companions, but as inmates? Who could suspect those who raised the dead to life of anything unbecoming? Do you do likewise, and whatever be the circumstances in which you are found, I will be far from suspecting you. Otherwise you are rashly usurping to yourself the privilege of those whose sanctity you do not possess. To expose yourselves always to temptation and never to fall by it, is not that a greater miracle than to raise the dead? You are not able to do that which is less, and do you wish me to believe that you do that which is greater? You wish to be thought irreproachable. Let it be granted that you are so; yet suspicion is not wanting. You are to me a subject of scandal; take away the occasion of the scandal, that you may show yourself what it is your boast to be, a true follower of the Gospel. Does not the Gospel condemn that man who offends (*scandalizaverit*) even one member of the Church? And you are a scandal to the whole Church. You are a fox that spoils the vines. Help me, my friends, to take him, or rather do ye, O holy Angels, take him for us. He is crafty in the extreme; he is enveloped in his iniquity and impiety. Evidently he is so small and so subtle that he may easily elude the notice of men. But shall he elude yours also? It is to you, therefore, as the companions of the Bridegroom, that those words are addressed: *Take us the little foxes.* Do, then, that which you are commanded: take for us this little fox so skilled in dissimulation that we have so long been in pursuit of him in vain. Teach us and suggest to us in what manner his guile may be discovered. For this is to take the fox, because as a pretended Catholic he does much more injury than when made manifest as really a heretic.[1] For it is not in the power of man to discover what is in the heart of another man, unless indeed he is either enlightened to this end by the Spirit of God, or instructed by the care of the Angels. What sign will you give to make open and manifest to all this pernicious heresy which knows so well how to disguise itself, not only by words, but also by actions?

5. And, indeed, the recent spoiling of a vine shows clearly that the fox has been there. But I know not by what art that most crafty animal so conceals his footsteps, that it is by no means easy to be discovered where either his ingress or his egress was made. Though the mischief done is evident, the doer of it is not visible, and he hides his presence by the very destruction he has done. In fact, if you

---

[1] Some MSS. read *quam verus hereticus.* But others, and also the first editions, read as above.

interrogate him as to his faith, nothing is more Christianlike; or as to his conduct, nothing more unblamable; and he seems to justify his discourse by his actions. Such a man is seen, in order to give testimony of his faith, to frequent the Church, to honour the clergy (*presbyteros*), to offer his gifts, to make confession, to participate in the Sacraments. What can be more orthodox? Then as relates to character and conduct, he deceives no one, he exalts himself over no one, nor does violence to any. Furthermore, his cheeks are pale with fasts; nor does he eat the bread of idleness, but labours with his hands for his maintenance. Where, then, is the fox? We held him fast just now. How has he escaped from our hands? In what manner has he so suddenly disappeared? Let us pursue him, let us seek him; we shall recognise him by his fruits. Assuredly the spoiling of the vines is a proof that the fox has been there. Women have quitted their husbands, men have deserted their wives, to join themselves to these people. Clerks and priests, as well young as old (*intonsi et barbati*), often abandon their flocks and their churches, and are found in the throng, among weavers male and female. Is not that a terrible spoiling indeed? Are not these the doings of foxes?

6. But perhaps they do not all perform actions so unmistakable. and if they do there is no proof of the fact. How, then, shall we take these? Let us return to the former accusation, for there is no one among them but is involved in that. I ask, then, of some one of those people: 'My good man, who is that woman with you, and what is her relation to you? Is she your wife?' 'No,' he replies; 'I have taken a vow which does not allow me to marry.' 'Is she your daughter?' 'No.' 'What, then, is she your sister, or your niece, or, at least, a relation or family connection of yours?' 'No, she is not related to me in any way.' 'How, then, can you live safely thus? It is not permitted to you to act in this way. If you are not aware of it, let me remind you that the Church forbids it.[1] If you do not wish to give scandal to the Church, obey the command. If you do not do so, then, from that one fact, others will be, without doubt, inferred as probable, though they be not open and manifest.'

7. 'But' (he says to me) 'in what place of the Gospel do you find any proof that this is forbidden?' Very well, you have appealed to the Gospel; to the Gospel you shall go. If, then, you obey the Gospel, you will not give occasion for scandal, for this is a thing which the Gospel plainly forbids. And this scandal is just what you do give, in not conforming to the regulation of the Church. You had been previously under suspicion of despising the Gospel, and being an enemy of the Church, but now you are manifestly convicted of it. What think you of it, my brethren? If he remains obstinate, and will neither obey the Gospel, nor show any respect unto the Church, what room is there for hesitation? Does it not seem to you that the fraud is discovered, that the fox is taken? If he suffers a scandal to remain which he has it in his power to put an end to, he

[1] Can. iii., dist. 37, *de Cohabit. Clericor.*, Synod. Nicaen.

is convicted of disobedience to the Gospel. What ought the Church to do but to expel a person who is unwilling to take away scandal, so that she may not share his disobedience? For she has a commandment in the Gospel as to this, and it bids her not spare her own eye, or hand, or foot, if it be a cause of scandal, but to pluck out the one and cut off the other, and cast it away. *If he neglect to hear the Church*, it is said, *let him be unto thee as an heathen man and a publican* (Matt. xviii. 6-9, 17).

8. Have we reached any result? I think we have; we have taken the fox, since we have discovered his deception. Those pretended Catholics who were really destroyers of the Church have been made manifest. Even while you were taking with me sweet [and heavenly] food, I mean the Body and Blood of Christ, while we walked in the House of God as friends, a place for persuasion, or, rather, an opportunity for perversion, was found, according to the saying of Scripture: *An hypocrite with his mouth destroyeth his neighbour* (Prov. xi. 9). But now I easily, according to the wise admonition of S. Paul, avoid *a man that is a heretic after the first and second admonition, knowing that he that is such is subverted, and sinneth, being condemned of himself* (Titus iii. 10, 11), and that it behoves me to be on my guard, lest he cause my subversion also. It is, then, something gained, according to the word of the Wise, that transgressors should be taken in their own naughtiness (Prov. xi. 6), and especially those transgressors the weapons of whose warfare are deceit and snares. Open attack and defence they do not venture upon, for they are a despicable and rustic race, devoid of education, and wholly destitute of generous courage. In short, they are foxes, and little foxes. Even their errors are not defensible, not clever and able, nor even plausible, except only to country women and ignorant persons, such as are all those of their sect whom I have as yet seen. For I do not recall, among all their assertions which I have heard (and they are many), anything novel or extraordinary, but only commonplaces long since broached among the heretics of old, and by our divines confuted and crushed. Yet it ought to be shown, and I will endeavour to show, what absurdities[1] these are, being partly such as they have fallen into through incautiously taking one side or the other in questions disputed between Catholics, partly such as they have exposed themselves to by their dissensions with each other, and partly such as some of them who have returned to the Church have discovered to us, and this I will do, not that I may reply to them all (for that is unnecessary), but in order that they may be known. But that will be a task for another sermon, to the praise and glory of the Name of Him who is the Bridegroom of the Church, JESUS CHRIST our Lord, who is above all, God blessed for ever. AMEN.

---

[1] *Ineptiæ*. St. Bernard uses the same term, in the same sense, in the following sermon, *n.* 4; and see his Letter 190.

SERMON LXVI.

CONCERNING THE ERRORS OF HERETICS WITH RESPECT TO MARRIAGE, TO THE BAPTISM OF INFANTS, TO PURGATORY, TO PRAYERS FOR THE DEAD, AND TO THE INVOCATION OF THE SAINTS.

'*Take us the foxes, the little foxes, that spoil the vines.*'—Cant. ii. 15.

WITH these foxes I am still busied. They are those who wander out of the path and lay waste the vineyard. They are not content with quitting the road [of right], but turn the vineyard into a desert by their wicked falsehoods. It is not enough for them to be heretics; they must, as if to fill up the measure of their wrongdoing, be hypocrites also. These are they who come in sheep's clothing to strip the sheep and despoil the rams. Does it not seem to you that this is what they have done when, on the one hand, they rob the people of their faith, and, on the other, deprive the priests of their people? Who are these robbers? They are sheep in appearance, but foxes in cunning, and in their actions have the cruelty of wolves. They are men who desire to seem good, but are not; who desire not to seem evil, but are so. Evil they are, yet they wish to be thought good, lest they should be left alone in their evil; and they fear to appear evil, lest they should not thus have sufficient power for evil. For open malice has always been less dangerous; nor is a person who is good ever deceived, except by a pretence of goodness. They study, then, to appear good in order to do injury to the good, and shrink from appearing evil that they may thus give their evil designs fuller scope. For they do not care to cultivate virtues, but only to colour their vices with a delusive tinge of virtues. Under the veil of religion they conceal an impious superstition; they regard the mere refraining from doing wrong openly as innocence, and thus take for themselves an outward appearance of goodness only. For a cloak to their infamy they make a vow of continence. They think that infamy consists only in having wives, whereas it is marriage alone that is pure. Coarse they are, and stupid, and altogether contemptible; but, I assure you, not on that account to be disregarded; for they succeed in doing much evil, and their word eateth as doth a cancer (2 Tim. ii. 16, 17).

2. Nor has the Holy Spirit overlooked such as these, since He has plainly prophesied of them long since by the mouth of the Apostle: *Now the Spirit speaketh expressly, that in the latter times some shall depart from the faith, giving heed to seducing spirits, and doctrines of devils; speaking lies in hypocrisy; having their conscience seared with a hot iron; forbidding to marry, and commanding to abstain from meats, which God hath created to be received with thanksgiving* (1 Tim. iv. 1-3). It was evidently of those people that He spake. They forbid mar-

riage, they abstain from the food which God created; of which latter subject I will presently speak. But now see if all these things are not rather an illusion of demons than a mere mistake of men, according to that which had been foretold by the Holy Spirit. Ask of them who is the author of their sect; they will name no one. Yet what heresy has not had from among men its own leader (*hæresiarcham*)? The Manicheans had Manes for chief and for master; the Sabellians, Sabellius; the Arians, Arius; the Eunomians, Eunomius; the Nestorians, Nestorius. So is it with all the other plagues of this kind; each of them has some man for its master, from whom it has drawn at once its origin and its name. But what name or what title will you consider should be bestowed upon these people? Truly, none at all[1]; for their heresy is not of man, nor have they received it by man. God forbid that we should say that they had it by the revelation of Jesus Christ (Gal. i. 12), but, rather, and without doubt, as the Holy Spirit foretold, by the suggestions and artifices of seducing spirits, speaking lies in hypocrisy, and forbidding marriage.

3. They talk also with hypocrisy, and with a vulpine cunning pretend that they speak from mere love of chastity, whereas they have no other purpose than to foment and multiply impurity. It is so evident that this is their intention that I wonder how any Christian man could ever be persuaded that it was otherwise, unless, indeed, he were so wanting in insight as not to perceive that he who condemns marriage loosens the reins to every kind of uncleanness; or so full of wickedness, and absorbed in diabolical malignity, as to shut his eyes to what he cannot but perceive, and rejoice at the destruction of men. If you take away from the Church marriage, which is honourable and undefiled (Heb. xiii. 4), will you not fill the Church with persons guilty of every kind of uncleanness? Choose, then, which alternative you prefer; either that all these monsters of wickedness are saved, or that the number of the saved is reduced to the few who have kept continence unbroken; in the one case you include too few, in the other case too many. Neither of these alternatives is suited to the Saviour. What! shall infamy be crowned? Nothing is less suitable to the source of purity. Or, on the other hand, shall men be universally condemned, with the sole exception of the very few who have preserved their continence? That is not to be a Saviour. Continence is rare upon the earth; and if it were not for a very few persons that fulness of grace would have expired altogether. And how have we all received of that fulness (John i. 16) if a share of it is vouchsafed to those only who are continent? There is no reply that can be made to that argument, nor yet, I think, to the other

---

[1] I do not know how St. Bernard could have spoken thus, if these heretics of Cologne had been Henricians, and the name of their master Henry. It is true that the doctrines of these people and those of the Henricians were similar, as appears from his Letters 240, 241. Among these heretics of Cologne Eberwin distinguishes two classes, which distinction St. Bernard just touches upon at the end of Sermon LXV.

alternative. If there is for purity only a place in heaven, if there is no companionship between purity and impurity, just as there is no fellowship of light with darkness, then it is certain that no one who is unclean has any place in the land of salvation. If anyone thinks otherwise, an Apostolic voice shall convict him of error, asserting expressly: *They which do such things shall not inherit the kingdom of God* (Gal. v. 21). From what cavern shall this artful fox now creep forth? I think that he is taken in his burrow, in which he has made for himself two holes, one to enter by, the other to give him egress. This it is his custom to do. See now by what means each of these is closed to him. If he maintains that only the continent have a place in heaven, he denies salvation to the vast majority of people; if, on the contrary, he holds that those guilty of every kind of defilement have a place there equally with the continent, he causes purity to perish. But it is more accurate to say that he perishes himself, being unable to escape in either direction; and, thus shut up for ever, remains a prisoner in the pit which he has digged.

4. Certain persons among them, differing from the rest, declare that marriage is permitted, but only to those who are virgins. But I do not perceive on what ground of reason they make this distinction, except it be that they contend with each other to tear and rend asunder, each at his own pleasure, as it were with the teeth of serpents, the Sacraments of the Church, which are, so to speak, the bowels of their mother. For as to what they allege, that our first parents were virgins when their marriage took place: what is there in that fact, I ask, to prejudice the liberty of marriage, so that it may not be entered into between those who are not virgin? But I know not what declaration they whisper that they have found in the Gospel, which they wrongly imagine favours their absurd folly. I believe that it is the word which Our Lord spake after He had recalled that testimony in the book of Genesis: *God created man in His own image, in the image of God created He him: male and female created He them;* He then added: *What therefore God hath joined together, let not man put asunder* (Gen. i. 27; Matt. xix. 6). These, they say, were both virgins whom God joined together, and it was then not lawful to separate them; but no union of those who are otherwise [than virgin] shall be presumed to be from God. But who has told you that God joined those two together, *because* they were virgins? This the Scripture does not assert. But were they not virgins? replies the objector. They were; but it is not the same thing to unite those who were virgins, and to unite them because they were virgins. Again, although they were virgins, you will not find the fact even expressly stated [much less given as the reason for their union]. Their diversity of sex is expressly stated, not their virginity, since it is declared: *Male and female created He them*. And rightly so, for the marriage relation requires, not necessarily virginity of body, but difference of sex in the two persons who enter into it. With entire fitness, then, did the Holy Spirit, in the record of the institution of

marriage, make mention of sex, but preserve silence as to virginity, so as not to give occasion to those guileful foxes to misapply the text, which unquestionably they would have done with great willingness, but in vain. For what if the Holy Spirit had said that 'God created them virgins?' Would you not have forthwith inferred that it was permitted to virgins alone to be joined in marriage? How you would have assumed airs of triumph upon the strength of this single statement! How scornfully you would have rejected second and third marriages! How you would have insulted the Church Catholic, inasmuch as she willingly joins together even persons who have fallen and become infamous, because she regards this as assuredly the means for enabling them to pass from a state of shame to a state of honour! Perhaps you would even blame God for having commanded one of His prophets to take to wife a woman of that class (Hosea i. 2); but now the entire ground is wanting for your doing all this, and it pleases you to be a heretic of your own accord. For the statement that you have unjustly adduced to support your error is found, on the contrary, to destroy it; it does nothing in your favour, but much against you.

5. But now listen to another Scripture which ought to confound you entirely, or correct you, and which, at all events, crushes and pulverizes your heresy. *The wife is bound by the law as long as her husband liveth; but if her husband be dead, she is at liberty to be married to whom she will: only in the Lord* (1 Cor. vii. 39). It is St. Paul who allows to a widow to marry whom she will, and you, on the contrary, prescribe that none but a virgin shall marry; nor may she marry whom she will, but only a man who is likewise virgin. Why do you restrain the Hand of God? Why do you restrict the abundant benediction bestowed on marriage, and narrow to the virgin alone that which is vouchsafed to all her sex? St. Paul would not permit this unless it were lawful. But it is too little to say that he *permits* it; he also desires it to be done. *I will therefore,* he says, *that the younger women marry* (1 Tim. v. 14), and there is no doubt that he speaks of widows. What can be plainer than this? That therefore which he permits, because it is lawful, he also desires, because it is expedient. That, then, which is permitted, and is expedient, shall a heretic presume to forbid? He will convince men of nothing by this prohibition, except that he is a heretic.

6. It remains that we should correct those people a little on the other points included in the Apostolic prophecy. For they abstain, as is there predicted, from various kinds of food which God has created to be received with thanksgiving, and thus prove themselves to be heretics, not simply because they abstain, but because they abstain in an heretical spirit. For I, too, sometimes abstain from food; but my abstinence is a satisfaction for sins, and not due to superstition and impiety. Shall we blame St. Paul when he kept under his body, and brought it into subjection (1 Cor. ix. 27)? I will abstain from wine, because in it is excess (Eph. v. 18); or, if I

am weak, will use a little, according to the counsel of St. Paul (1 Tim. v. 23). I will abstain from eating flesh, lest it should too much pamper my flesh, and with it the lusts of the flesh. I will study to take even bread by measure that I may not, through fulness of stomach, stand wearily and reluctantly to pray to God, and that I may not be open to the reproach of the Prophet that I have eaten my bread in fulness (Ezek. xvi. 49). I will not accustom myself to drink immoderately even of pure water, lest it may excite in me feelings corrupt. It is quite otherwise with the heretic. He turns from milk, and all that is made of it; in fact, from everything which is the result of that function. That would be acting rightly and Christianly, if it were done, not because it was the result of that function, but from a motive of prudence.

7. But how does it come about that everything thus resulting is avoided in this manner? That minute scrutiny of kinds of food, so significantly expressed, is to me a cause for suspicion. If you bring forward this as a medical rule, I do not blame this care for the physical health, provided it be not excessive; for no one ever hated his own flesh. If as a part of the discipline of abstinence, that is, of the school of spiritual medicine, I even approve it as a virtue, by which you bring the flesh under due rule, and restrain its desires. But if, by the madness of the Manichean, you set bounds to the beneficence of God, so that the food which He has created and given to men to be partaken of with thanksgiving you, as a rash and ungrateful critic, pronounce unclean, and abstain from it as from an evil thing, then, far from praising your abstinence, I hold in execration your blasphemy, I hold you to be yourself impure, in considering that anything is impure in itself. *To the pure all things are pure*, says an excellent judge of things; and nothing is impure except to him who regards it as such; *but unto them that are defiled and unbelieving*, he adds, *is nothing pure; but even their mind and conscience is defiled* (Titus i. 15). Woe to you who reject food which God has created, judging it impure and unworthy to pass into your bodies; wherefore the Body of Christ, which is the Church, has rejected you yourselves as defiled and impure.

8. I am not unmindful that they boast that they, and they alone, are the Body of Christ; but that is not astonishing, since they persuade themselves also that they have the power to consecrate[1] daily at their tables the Body and Blood of Christ, to nourish them to become His members and His Body. For they boast that they are successors of the Apostles, and call themselves Apostolicals, though they are not able to show any sign of their apostolate. How long shall the lantern remain under a bushel? *Ye are the light of the world*, was said to the Apostles, and therefore are they set upon a candlestick, that they may enlighten the whole world. Let these successors of the Apostles be ashamed to be the light, not of the world, but of a bushel, and to the world to be but darkness. Let us

---

[1] See the Letter of Eberwin, p. 3.

say to them, Ye are the darkness of the world, and pass on to other things. They say that they are the Church, but they contradict Him who said, *A city that is set on a hill cannot be hid* (Matt. v. 14). Do you believe that the stone, which was cut out without hands, and then became a great mountain, and filled the whole earth (Dan. ii. 34, 35), is shut up in your caverns? Nor ought we to stop even here. Their opinion is content with whispering in private, and avoids being known openly. Christ has, and will always have, His entire inheritance, and the ends of the earth are His possession. Those who attempt to withdraw from Him this great inheritance rather cease to form a part of it themselves.

9. See now those detractors, those dogs. They make it a cause of ridicule against us that we baptize children, that we pray for the dead, that we entreat the suffrages of the Saints. They hasten to proscribe Christ in people at every age and of either sex; in children and in adults, in the living and in the dead; forbidding [the new Birth in Him through Baptism] to infants because of the weakness of their age, and to adults also because of the difficulty of continence. They deprive the dead of the succour of the living, and the living of the suffrages of the Saints who have died. But God forbid that it should be so. The Lord will not give up His people, who are as the sand of the sea; nor will He who redeemed all be contented with a small number, and those, heretics. For His Redemption is not small, but great and abounding. What is the pettiness of their number to the greatness of the price He paid? Those who attempt to empty it [of its efficacy], deprive themselves of it. Of what importance is it that an infant is not able to speak for himself, while the voice of the Blood of his Brother, and of a Brother so great and prevailing, cries to God from the ground for him? The Church, which is his Mother, arises and lifts up her voice on his behalf also. And what of the child himself? Does it not seem to you that in his inarticulate infantine cries he opens his mouth, gasping, if I may so speak, for the Saviour's fountains of grace, and crying out to God in his plaints, Lord, I am oppressed; undertake for me (Is. xxxviii. 14). It demands eagerly the help of grace, because it suffers violence from nature.[1] It cries because it is innocent and unhappy, because it is ignorant and small, because it is weak and doomed to suffer. All these things thus cry out together: the Blood of a Brother, the faithfulness of a Mother, the abandoned condition of the unhappy child, and the misery of it as abandoned; and these cries rise up to the Father; and He, because He is the Father, is not able to deny Himself.

10. Let no one object to me that a child has not faith, for its Mother [that is, the Church] communicates to it her own, wraps it in this faith, so to speak, as in a cloak, in the Sacrament of Baptism, which she bestows upon it; so that it becomes worthy to receive and to develop that faith in its purity, if not by its own active powers, yet with its passive assent. Is it not a short and narrow cloak which

---

[1] *A natura.* Other readings are: *ab origine* and *a peccato.*

cannot cover two? The faith of the Church is great. Surely it is not less than the faith of the Canaanitish woman, which we know was sufficient both for her daughter and herself. Therefore she had the happiness to hear: *O woman, great is thy faith; be it unto thee even as thou wilt* (Matt. xv. 28). Nor is it less than the faith of those who let down the paralytic through the roof before Jesus, and obtained for him the saving both of soul and of body. For we read: *Jesus, seeing their faith, said unto the sick of the palsy, Son, be of good cheer, thy sins be forgiven thee;* and a little after: *Arise, take up thy bed, and go unto thine house* (Matt. ix. 2-6). He who believes these things will be easily persuaded that the Church may presume with good reason, not only of the salvation of those little children who are baptized in her faith, but also of the crown of martyrdom for those infants who were slain for Christ. And as this is the case, those who are regenerate will not suffer prejudice from that which is said in another Scripture, *Without faith it is impossible to please God* (Heb. xi. 6); since they who have received the grace of Baptism for a testimony of faith are not without faith. Neither will they be hurt by that other declaration: *He that believeth not shall be damned* (Mark xvi. 16). For what is it to believe but to have faith? Therefore, also, a woman shall be saved in child-bearing, 'if they continue in faith and charity and holiness, with sobriety'[1] (1 Tim. ii. 15); and children shall be succoured by the Regeneration of Baptism. Adult persons also, who are not able to contain, redeem themselves by the thirtyfold (Matt. xiii. 8) fruit of marriage. The dead also, who shall have need of the prayers and sacrifices of the living, and shall be worthy of them, shall receive them by the good offices of the Angels; and from those who have already attained, comforts and consolations shall in no wise be wanting to the living, because of the affection which they have in God, who is everywhere, and the charitable care they feel for those who are absent; *for to this end Christ both died and rose and revived, that He might be Lord both of the dead and living* (Rom. xiv. 9). To this end, also, He was born as an Infant, and passed through all degrees of age, till He became a perfect Man, that He might be wanting to no age.

11. They do not believe that there remains a purgatorial fire after death; but that the soul, when released from the body, passes at once either to rest or to damnation. Let them, then, ask of Him, who declared of a certain sin that it should not be forgiven, 'neither in this world, nor in the world to come' (Matt. xii. 32), why He said this, if there were no forgiveness at all in the world to come. But it is not wonderful that those who do not acknowledge the Church should make light of the Orders of the Church; that they should not receive her Institutions; that they should despise her Sacraments,

---

[1] The readings vary here. In the Jumièges MS. it is, with the Vulgate, '*in fide et dilectione, cum sanctificatione et sobrietate*'; in the Colbertine, '*in fide cum sobrietate*'; in that of St. Germain, and in the earliest editions, '*in fide cum lenitate*.' (Mabillon prefers the last.)

and refuse to obey her commands. 'The successors of the Apostles,' they say, 'are all sinners, Archbishops, Bishops, and Presbyters, and therefore are not fit either to administer Sacraments or receive them.' Are, then, these two things, to be a Bishop and to be a sinner, so incompatible as that they can never be found in the same person? That is not the case. Caiaphas was a Bishop; and how great a sinner was he, who pronounced sentence of death upon the Lord? If you deny that he was a Bishop, the testimony of St. John, who declares that he was High Priest for that year, and prophesied (John xi. 51), shall convict you of error. Judas was an Apostle, and even chosen by the Lord; yet he was covetous, and a man accursed. Do you hesitate to allow that he had the apostolate whom the Lord Himself chose? He Himself said: *Have I not chosen you twelve, and one of you is a devil?* (John vi. 70). You hear that the same man was a chosen Apostle, and showed himself a devil; and do you deny that a man who is a sinner can possibly be a Bishop? The Scribes and Pharisees sat in Moses' seat; and those who did not obey them (as obedience is in like manner due to Bishops) were guilty, in fact, of disobedience to the Lord Himself, who gives these commands, and says: *Whatsoever they bid you observe, that observe and do* (Matt. xxiii. 2, 3). It is clear, then, that although they were Scribes, although they were Pharisees, although they were even the greatest of sinners, yet for the sake of the chair [of authority] of Moses which they occupy that saying, nevertheless, applies to them: *He that heareth you, heareth Me; and he that despiseth you, despiseth Me* (Luke x. 16).

12. There are many other erroneous and evil opinions which are urged upon this foolish and undiscerning people by those spirits of evil, who speak lies in hypocrisy; but it is not needful to make reply to all. For who is acquainted with all these errors? Besides, the labour of doing so would be unending; nor is it in the least necessary. For as for those people, neither are they convinced by reasons, because they do not understand them, nor corrected by the weight of authorities, for they do not receive them; nor are they influenced by persuasions, because they are entirely perverted. It has been shown by experience that they prefer to die rather than be converted. Of these men the end is destruction; at the last the fire awaits them. Long ago the type of them was shown forth in the foxes to whose tails Samson applied the fire (Judg. xv. 4, 5). Often the faithful have laid hands on some of them, and brought them into public notice. When they have been questioned upon those points of their belief on which they were suspected, they, according to their custom, refused entirely to give any answer; and when examined by the judgment of water,[1] they have been found liars. But when they have been discovered, and were not able to make denial, nor received the

---

[1] The ancients did not reject the proof by water, as is shown in a singular letter from Hincmar, Archbishop of Rheims, to Hildegar of Meaux. The method of performing this purgation is described in the *Analecta*, Bk. i., where it is said to have been instituted by Pope Eugenius II.

water at all; then taking, as the saying is, the bit in their teeth, they were so unhappy as to profess openly their impiety, to maintain it as the true faith, and to declare that they were prepared to suffer death on its behalf. Nor were those who were present less prepared to inflict it. Therefore the people, rushing in upon them, made of them new martyrs to their unbelief. Their zeal we approve, but we do not advise the imitation of their action, because faith is to be produced by persuasion, not imposed by force. Although it would, without doubt, be better that they should be coerced by the sword of him 'who beareth not the sword in vain,' than that they should be allowed to draw away many other persons into their error.[1]

13. Some persons are astonished that they go to their death, not only patiently, but, as it seems, even with joy; but such persons do not consider how great is the power of the devil, not only over the bodies, but also over the hearts of those whom, when once permitted, he has taken possession of. Is it not more astonishing still that a man should lay violent hands upon himself than that he should endure violence willingly from another person? But we know by experience that the devil has frequently exerted that power, namely, over many whom he has caused to drown or to hang themselves. Thus Judas hanged himself (Matt. xxvii. 5) doubtless by the instigation of the devil. Yet I find it still more strange, and a greater cause for wonder, that he should have been able to put it into the heart of Judas to betray his Lord (John xiii. 2) than that he should have caused him to hang himself. There is nothing resembling the constancy of the martyrs in the obstinacy of these men, because in the former it is piety, in the latter hardness of heart, that causes a contempt of death.[2] Also the Psalmist has said, perhaps with the voice of a martyr: *Their heart is curdled like milk; but I have meditated on Thy law* (Ps. cxix. 70, Douay), to show that although the suffering seemed the same, yet the intention was very different; for whilst the one was hardening his heart against the Lord, the other was meditating on His holy law.

14. This being the case, there is no need, as I have said, to say much against men who are foolish and obstinate in the extreme; it suffices to take note of them that they may be avoided. Wherefore, that they may be discovered, they must be obliged either to send away the women, by retaining whom in their houses they give scandal to the Church, or to leave the Church. It is much to be lamented that not only secular princes, but also, as it is said, certain of the clergy, and even of the order of Bishops, whose special duty it is to seek them out, support them for the sake of gain, and for the presents

---

[1] St. Bernard does not in any way contradict here what he had said in Sermon LXIV., *n.* 8, that heretics 'should be taken not by arms, but by arguments'; that is to say, if they remain quiet, and do not attempt to subvert others.

[2] St. Augustine expresses the same opinion in his *Opus Imperfectum contr. secund. Juliani responsion.* Bk. i.; and in *Lib. de Patientia*, cap. 17. It is following this Father that the Second Council of Orange, in its Can. 17, says: 'It is worldly cupidity that produces the constancy of the Gentiles; but the love of God produces the constancy of Christians.'

which they receive from them. 'How,' say they, 'shall we condemn men who do not confess error, nor are convicted of it?' That reason, or rather pretext, is frivolous. By this means alone, if there were no other, you will easily discover them; if, as I have said, you separate the one from the other, obliging the women to live with those of their own sex who have taken the same vow as themselves, and the men to do likewise. In this way you will have consulted both the interest of their vow, and their reputation, in giving them both witnesses and guardians of their good behaviour. If they do not submit to this, they will most justly be expelled from the Church to which they give scandal. Let this suffice, then, for the discovery of the wiles of those foxes that they may be known and guarded against by the Church, which is the beloved and glorious Bride of our Lord JESUS CHRIST, who is above all, God blessed for ever. AMEN.

SERMON LXVII.

OF THE WONDERFUL EXPRESSION OF THE LOVE OF THE BRIDE, WHICH IS CALLED FORTH BY THE AFFECTION OF HER BRIDEGROOM CHRIST.

'*My Beloved is mine, and I am His.*'—Cant. ii. 16.

HITHERTO we have had the words of the Bridegroom. May He now be present with us, and aid us worthily to expound the words of His bride, to His glory and to our salvation. For they are such as cannot be considered and discussed by us in a manner that is worthy of the subject unless He Himself shall be the guide of our words. For as they are sweet in the grace which they contain, so they are fruitful in senses and deep in mysteries. To what shall I liken them? They are as food which surpasses all other by a threefold excellence; delicious in taste, solid in nutriment, and efficacious as a remedy. It is thus with each word of the Bride. By the sweetness of its sound it charms the feelings; by its richness in teaching it nourishes and fertilizes the mind; and by the depth of the mysteries it contains it exercises and awes the spirit, and at the same time remedies in a wonderful manner the pride and inflation caused by knowledge. For if any one of those who perhaps seem to themselves learned, wishing to penetrate into these things with too curious a scrutiny, finds the powers of his intellect overpowered and baffled, and brought, as it were, into captivity, will he not be humbled and obliged to take these words for his own: *Such knowledge is too wonderful for me: it is high, I cannot attain unto it?* (Ps. cxxxix. 6). And without going any farther, with what a marvel of sweetness is the beginning of this sentence filled! For see what a declaration the **Bride** makes as a commencement: *My Beloved*, she says, *is mine, and*

I am His. Simple words they are, but how sweetly they sound! And this we shall treat of farther in the sequel.

2. She commences by love, and goes on to speak of Her Beloved, showing thus that she knows no other than He. It is clear of whom she speaks; not so clear to whom she is speaking. For it is not permitted to us to suppose that He is present, or that she is conversing with Him. This appears plainly from her calling to Him immediately afterwards, as if He were at a distance, to return to her: *Turn, my Beloved.* From this we are drawn to believe that, after having brought to a close what He had been saying to her, He had again, according to His custom, absented Himself from her, and that she continues, nevertheless, speaking of Him, who is never absent from her mind. Thus, in fact it is; and He continues to be upon her lips who did not depart, and never does depart, from her heart. That which is upon her lips comes forth from her heart, for of the abundance of the heart the mouth speaketh (Luke vi. 45). Therefore she speaks of her Beloved as one truly loved and truly deserving to be loved, inasmuch as she loves much. We know, then, of whom she speaks, but with whom we know not; nor can I conjecture, unless it be with her maidens, who cannot be absent from their mother when the Bridegroom has departed. But we shall better suppose, as I think, that she is speaking to herself, not to any other person; especially as her words seem abrupt and unconnected with what has been spoken before; plainly insufficient to be intelligible to an auditor, which in a conversation is the object intended. *My Beloved,* she says, *is mine, and I am His.* Nothing more? Then the discourse hangs suspended; or, rather, it is not suspended, but falls. Anyone who listens is held in suspense; he is not instructed, but is waiting to be so.

3. What, then, is the signification of her words: *My Beloved is mine, and I am His?* We do not comprehend what she says, because we do not feel what she feels. O holy soul, what is thy Beloved to thee, and what art thou to Him? What is, I pray thee, that mysterious gift which is reciprocally made each to the other, by Him and by thee, with so much kindness and familiarity? For thee is He, and for Him thou art. But is He to thee that which thou art to Him, or does He stand in some other relation to thee? If thou speakest for us, and for our understanding, speak forth clearly thy thought. How long dost thou hold our minds in suspense? Or is thy secret to be, according to the saying of the Prophet, for thyself? (Is. xxiv. 16). It is thus: the affection has spoken, not the understanding, and therefore what is said is scarcely understood. For what end, then, is this spoken? For no end at all, except it be that the Bride, having been vehemently affected, and filled with extreme joy and delight, by the long desired interview with her Beloved, when it has come to an end she is neither able to refrain altogether from speaking, nor yet, when she speaks, to express her feelings fully. Nor did she speak thus by way of expressing them, but in order not to be

altogether silent. Out of the abundance of the heart the mouth speaketh, but not in proportion to its abundance. The affections have their own language, in which they express themselves, even against their will. For instance, fear has its timid words, grief its mournful, and love its joyful ones. Are the lamentations of those who are in trouble, the sobs and sighs of mourners, the sudden and ungovernable screams and cries of those who are frightened or stricken, or even the yawns of the satisfied and sleepy, are these either caused by habit, aroused by reason, ordered by reflection, or shaped by premeditation? It is certain that all such expressions of feeling are not the products of a deliberate purpose, but are caused by sudden and unforeseen impulse. Thus burning and vehement love, especially that towards God, not being able to restrain itself, takes no heed of the order nor connection of the words it employs, nor even of their fewness, provided that it suffers no diminution of its vigour. Sometimes it does not seek for words, not even for articulate language at all, but is content with the wordless aspirations of the spirit alone. Thus it is that the Bride, burning inconceivably with holy love, seeks some relief and solace in the ardour which she endures, and in seeking it takes no heed of how she speaks, but, urged on by her love, bursts forth with the first words which come into her mouth. And what should she speak, except that with which her heart is so filled?

4. Recall to your mind the wording of this marriage song, from its beginning to this point, and see if, in the interviews and conversations of the Bridegroom with the Bride, He has ever addressed her with the same indulgent kindness as here, or ever held so many or so cheering discourses with her. What wonder, then, when her wishes have been satisfied to the full, that a burst of joy should come from her, rather than words? Or if she makes use of words, that they should burst forth without premeditation or studied completeness? For the Bride judges it not robbery to apply to herself the words of the Psalmist: *My heart hath uttered a good word* (Ps. xlv. 1), since it is with the same Spirit that she is filled. *My Beloved is mine, and I am His.* There is no prayer in the saying, and there is no conclusion drawn from it. What then? it is an outburst of feeling. In such an utterance what connection of sentiments, what solemnity of phrases do you seek? What laws or rules do you impose upon your own? It does not admit of your control, it does not wait for your careful and exact expression, it does not submit to your time, nor consult your convenience at all. It bursts forth of its own accord from within, without your will and even without your knowledge, forcibly rather than by choice. And it yields sometimes a good odour, sometimes a bad, according to the different qualities of the natures whence it arises. For a good man out of the good treasure of the heart bringeth forth good things; and an evil man evil things (Matt. xii. 35). The Bride of my Lord is a vase of good treasure, and sweet is the odour which comes from her.

5. I give thanks to Thee, O Lord Jesus, that Thou hast deigned to admit me at least to perceive that odour so sweet. Yea, Lord, so let me be admitted, even as the dogs, though of such small account, are allowed to eat of the crumbs which fall from their masters' table (Matt. xv. 27). This utterance of the feelings of Thy beloved is to me, I confess it, very agreeable; and of her fulness I receive, however little it be, with gratitude. The memorial of Thy abounding sweetness arises in me, and I am suffused with I know not what ineffable perfume of Thy love and condescension, so to speak, in those few words of hers: *My Beloved is mine, and I am His.* Let her, as it is fitting, eat and drink in Thy Presence, and rejoice exceedingly at the sight of Thee; yea, let her be transported out of herself for Thy sake, that for our sakes she may have full self-possession. Let her, then, be abundantly satisfied with the good things of Thy house, and let her drink of the river of Thy pleasures; but let there be for me, Thy poor servant, I entreat, at least a slight odour of those good things, breathed forth from the bosom of her fulness. The thought of Moses was uttered to my benefit, and from his words I gather the sweetness and greatness of the idea of creative power: *In the beginning God created the heaven and the earth* (Gen. i. 1). Isaiah also exhales the most sweet odour of mercy and redemption when he thus speaks: *He hath poured out His Soul unto death, and He was numbered with the transgressors; and He bare the sin of many, and made intercession for the transgressors* (Is. liii. 12), that they should not perish. And what odour equals in sweetness that of mercy? Good also is the utterance from the mouth of Jeremiah; and from that of David, when he said: *My heart is inditing a good matter* (Ps. xlv. 1). They were all filled with the Holy Ghost, and by their utterance replenished all things with His goodness. Do you ask for the utterance of Jeremiah? I have not forgotten it, I was preparing to give it to you. *It is good that a man should both hope and quietly wait for the salvation of the Lord* (Lam. iii. 26). That is his, I do not mistake; inhale its sweetness, the fragrance it brings of Him who recompenses righteousness, which excels the most exquisite perfume. He wills me, if I suffer for righteousness' sake, to await a recompense hereafter, and that I should not receive one at present, because the salutary wages of righteousness is from the Lord, not from the world. *If it tarry*, says the Prophet, *wait for it* (Hab. ii. 3). Therefore I will do what he exhorts me; I will wait for the Lord my Saviour.

6. But I am a sinner, and a long road still is before me to traverse, because salvation is far from sinners. Yet I will not murmur, and in the meantime I shall be consoled by the fragrance[1] of it. The righteous shall rejoice in the Lord, having tasted and known that of which I perceive the fragrance afar off. That which the righteous has in full view, he who is a sinner expects and waits for, and it is

---

[1] *Odore.* Horst adds *vel dolore;* but this is wanting in the MSS. and earliest editions.

that expectation which I call the fragrance of it. *For the earnest expectation of the creature waiteth for the manifestation of the sons of God* (Rom. viii. 19). To behold, is to taste and see how sweet the Lord is. Or is it rather the righteous who expects this, and the blessed who possesses it? *For the hope of the righteous shall be gladness* (Prov. x. 28). But the sinner has nothing to hope for. And, therefore, the sinner, not only because he is attached to the good things of the present time, but also because he is content with them, hopes for nothing from the future, and is deaf to that precept of the Lord: *Expect Me in the day of My Resurrection that is to come* (Zeph. iii. 8, Douay). Simeon was righteous because he waited for and already presaged Christ in the spirit, when as yet he did not as yet adore Him in the flesh. And in his expectation he was blessed, because through the odour of expectation he attained to taste, that is, to the beholding Him. For he says: *Mine eyes have beheld Thy salvation* (Luke ii. 25). Righteous also was Abraham, who desired and expected to see the day of the Lord; nor was he confounded in this hope, for *he saw it, and was glad* (John viii. 56). The Apostles, too, were righteous, for to them it was said: *Ye yourselves* [are] *like unto men that wait for their Lord* (Luke xii. 36).

7. Was not David righteous also when he said: *I waited patiently for the Lord?* (Ps. xl. 1). He is the fourth of those of whom I have said that they had longed for the Lord with all their heart (Ps. cxix. 131), whom I had almost passed over; but it is not advisable so to do. He opened his mouth and panted; then, when filled [with the consolations of the Lord], he not only poured out his heart in thankfulness, but sang for joy. O good Lord Jesus, how great is the fragrance and the sweetness which he has caused me to feel and experience in those utterances and songs, filled with that oil of gladness with which God, Thy God, hath anointed Thee above Thy fellows, from that myrrh and aloes and cassia out of the ivory palaces wherewith Thy garments are fragrant, because the daughters of kings have perfumed them in Thy honour and for Thy delight! (Ps. xlv. 8-10). O that Thou wouldest honour me so far as that I might meet that great prophet, Thy friend, in that day of solemn gladness, when he shall come forth from Thy chamber, singing his sacred marriage-hymn with the psaltery and joyful harp, overwhelmed with delights, steeped in perfumes of a sweetness beyond words, and diffusing them on every side! In that day, I have said, but rather in that hour; and perhaps it is not even an hour, but in that half-hour, according to that saying of the Scripture: *There was silence in Heaven about the space of half an hour* (Rev. viii. 1); therefore in that hour my mouth will be filled with gladness and my tongue with joy, when I shall feel the fragrance, I do not say of each Psalm, but of each verse of every Psalm, a fragrance far exceeding that of the most precious perfumes. What can be more fragrant than the utterances of St. John, who brings to me the solemn sweetness of the Eternal Generation and Divinity of the Word? What can I say of those of St. Paul, which

have filled the world with the odour of their great sweetness? In truth, the sweet savour of the knowledge of Christ was made manifest by them in every place (2 Cor. ii. 14, 15). And although the unspeakable words which he had heard he does not offer for me to listen to, he offers them for me to desire; and it is permitted to discern their fragrance, though to utter them is not lawful (2 Cor. xii. 4). I know not how it is, that those which are the most deeply hidden have the greatest charm, and that we sigh most eagerly for those which are denied to us. But now notice a similar fact with regard to the Bride, namely, how in the passage before us she, like St. Paul, does not wholly reveal her secret, and yet does not pass it over wholly unmentioned, as if she wishes to gratify us with somewhat of the fragrance of that treasure which she judges it not advisable as yet to lay open to our touch and taste, whether on account of our unworthiness or on account of our incapacity.

8. *My Beloved is mine, and I am His.* There can be no doubt that in this passage is apparent the flame of an ardent and reciprocal love of two persons, one for the other; while in this love appears also the supreme felicity of the one and the marvellous condescension of the other. For it is not an attachment and union between two persons who are of equal condition. Now, who could venture to lay claim to the full knowledge of what [the Church] glories in having received in this prerogative of love, and in having repaid it in turn by an affection so great, if not she, who by her eminent purity and holiness of body and of mind, has been found worthy to have experience in her own self of a fortune so exalted? It is in the sphere of the affections that this takes place, nor is it attained to by the reason, but by conformity of spirit. But how few there are who are enabled to say: *We all with open face, beholding as in a glass the glory of the Lord, are changed into the same image from glory to glory, even as by the Spirit of the Lord* (2 Cor. iii. 18).

9. But that what we read here may be brought in some degree under the grasp of the intellect I leave to the Bride her unique secret, to which it is not permitted to us to draw near, especially while we are so imperfect; and I propose to you something at once more easily understood, and of a more ordinary character, so that those who are as children in understanding may be able to grasp the sense and the relation of the words used by the Bride. To me, then, it seems that it will suffice for our dense and, as it were, popular apprehension if in saying *My Beloved is mine* we understand 'gives His thought and attention,' so that the sense will be: 'My Beloved gives His thought and attention to me, and I to Him.' Nor am I the first or the only one to suggest this sense, for the Psalmist has said before me: *I waited patiently for the Lord, and He inclined unto me and heard my cry* (Ps. xl. 1). You see here that the Lord gave attention to the Psalmist; you see also the patient waiting of the Psalmist for the Lord. For he who waits gives attention to him for whom he waits. The sense, then, of the Psalmist's words is the same

as of those of the Bride, nor are the words far different, only in the former they are used in another order; for he sets first that which she sets last, and conversely.

10. But in this the Bride has spoken more accurately, inasmuch as she does not put forward any merit of her own, but begins with the benefit she has received, and thus acknowledges that she has been prevented by the grace of her Beloved. She has well done in expressing herself thus. For who hath first given to Him and it shall be recompensed unto him again? (Rom. xi. 35). Hear also what St John thought on this subject. *Herein is love*, he says in his Epistle, *not that we loved God, but that He loved us* (1 John iv. 10). Though the Psalmist has not spoken of preventing grace, he has not denied, or been silent upon, following grace. But listen to his declaration upon that point in plainer terms in another place: *Thy mercy* (he was speaking to the Lord) *will follow me all the days of my life* (Ps. xxiii. 6, Douay). Hear also his declaration as to preventing grace; it is no less plain and unmistakable: *My God, His mercy shall prevent me* (Ps. lix. 10, Douay); and again to the Lord: *Let Thy tender mercies speedily prevent us, for we are brought very low* (Ps. lxxix. 8). It is with much beauty that the Bride a little farther on (if I do not mistake) uses again the same words, but not placing them in the same order; for she follows the order of the Psalmist, and speaks thus: *I am my Beloved's, and my Beloved is mine* (Cant. vi. 3). Why does she express herself thus? It is to show that she is more full of graces when she attributes all to grace, and ascribes to the Lord the beginning and the end of them all. Otherwise, how could she be full of grace if there were in her anything which was not of grace? There is no room for grace to enter where merit has already taken its place.[1] That full acknowledgment, then, of grace is itself a mark of the fulness of grace in her who makes it. For if there were in her anything which came from the soul as from itself, to whatever extent that existed, it must of necessity take the place of grace. Whatsoever you impute to merit you take away from grace. I will not have merit, because it excludes grace. I shrink from all that is of me that I may be my own: unless, perhaps, that is especially mine which makes me to be my own. Grace restores me to myself freely justified, and thus delivered from the slavery of sin. For where the Spirit of the Lord is, there is liberty (2 Cor. iii. 17).

11. O Synagogue, Bride insensate, which, despising the righteousness of God—that is, the grace of thy Bridegroom—and desiring to set up a righteousness of thy own, hast not submitted thyself to the righteousness of God! For this reason that unhappy one was repudiated, and is now no longer the Bride; which title belongs to the Church, to whom it is said: *I will betroth thee unto Me in*

---

[1] St. Bernard refers here to merit which does not come from grace, but which takes place above it and excludes it. Compare Sermon LXVIII., *n.* 6, and in S. Augustine, Ep. 105; 'Of Grace and Free Will,' cc. 6-8; 'Confessions,' Bk. ix., c. 13; *Enchiridion*, c. 107, etc.

righteousness, and in judgment, and in lovingkindness, and in mercies; I will even betroth thee unto Me in faithfulness (Hos. ii. 19, 20). Nor hast thou chosen Me, but I have chosen thee; nor have I found merits in thee for the reason of My choice, but have foreseen thy merits. It is, then, in faith that I have betrothed thee, not in the works of the Law; in faith, and in the righteousness which is by faith, not by the law. It remains that thou shouldest form a right judgment between Me and thee, the judgment in which I have betrothed thee; and recognise that I have done this, not because of thy merits, but purely of My goodness. This, then, is the judgment, that thou shouldest not extol thy own merits, nor prefer the works of the Law, nor boast that thou hast borne the burden and heat of the day; knowing that thou hast been betrothed in faith and the righteousness which is of faith; in mercies and in lovingkindness.

12. She, then, who is truly the Bride recognises these things, and confesses that she has received each kind of grace; that which is first, and is preventing grace; and that also which comes afterwards, to follow and to render perfect. Therefore she says now, *My Beloved is mine, and I am His*, attributing the beginning of the work of grace to her Beloved. But afterwards she says also: *I am my Beloved's, and my Beloved is mine;* and thus attributes to Him the ending and consummation of it also.

Let us now see, then, what is the meaning of those words she speaks, *My Beloved is mine*. If we are to understand with them 'gives attention to,' as I have already suggested, and as the Psalmist says, *I waited patiently for the Lord, and He inclined unto me*, I find that the words contain somewhat of no small interest and importance. But it is a subject worthy of our closest attention, and not to be entered upon to wearied ears and minds. If you please, it shall be deferred for a little while, and the sermon of to-morrow shall be commenced with it. Only let me ask you to pray, in the meantime, that I may be preserved from the encroachments of pressing cares, by the grace and mercy of Him who is the Bridegroom of the Church, JESUS CHRIST our LORD, who is above all, God blessed for ever. AMEN.

SERMON LXVIII.

HOW CHRIST THE BRIDEGROOM INCLINES UNTO AND GIVES ATTENTION TO HIS BRIDE, WHICH IS THE CHURCH; AND HOW SHE LIKEWISE INCLINES UNTO HIM. OF THE CARE WHICH GOD HAS FOR HIS ELECT. ALSO OF THE MERIT AND THE CONFIDENCE OF THE CHURCH.

HEAR now what I reserved from yesterday to say to you; hear the great joy which I have felt. And this joy is yours; hear it, therefore, and rejoice. I have felt it in one word of the Bride, and, after having been, as it were, perfumed with it, I have laid it by with care to share it with you to-day; and that so much the more gladly as the time seems appropriate for so doing. The Bride, then, has spoken, and has said that the Bridegroom inclines unto her. Who, then, is the Bride, and who is the Bridegroom? The Bridegroom is our God; and, if I venture to say so, it is we who are the Bride, with the rest of that multitude of captives whom He knows. Let us rejoice, for this is our glory[1]; we are among those to whom God gives attention. Yet how great is the disparity between Him and us! What are the children of men, the earth-born, before Him? According to the Prophet, *All nations before Him are as nothing; and they are counted to Him less than nothing, and vanity* (Is. xl. 17). What object, then, can there be in a comparison between persons so unequal? Either the one glorifies herself without measure, or the other loves without measure. Is it not a wonderful thing that she should thus claim as her own the attention and interest of her Bridegroom, and say, *My Beloved is mine?* Nor is she content even with this; she goes on to glorify herself still farther; she replies to Him as equal to equal, and gives assurance to Him in her turn. For she goes on to say, *And I am His.* An unexampled speech indeed: *I am His.* Nor is the other assertion less unexampled: *My Beloved is mine.* But the association of the two is still more wonderful than either of them separately.

2. What does not a pure heart, a good conscience, and a faith unfeigned, venture? 'To me,' she says, 'He gives attention.' Is it possible that a Majesty so great, upon which rests the government and administration of the universe, deigns to give attention to her, and that the Eternal God occupies Himself with the affairs, or, rather, the repose, of the affection and the aspirations of the Bride alone? It is evidently so. For she is the Church of the elect, of whom the Apostle says: *I endure all things for the elect's sakes* (2 Tim. ii. 10; see also 1 Cor. iii. 21). And who can doubt that 'the grace and mercy of God is with His Saints, and that He hath respect unto His chosen' (Wisd. iv. 15)? We do not, then, deny the providence of God over His other creatures; but the Bride claims for herself His especial care and regard. *Doth God take care for oxen?* (1 Cor. ix. 9). And there is no doubt that the same question may be asked with respect to horses, and to camels, to elephants, and to all the beasts of the earth; and similarly to the fishes of the sea, and the winged denizens of the air; in short, to everything that is upon the earth, with the sole exception of those beings about whom that declaration was made: *Casting all your care upon Him, for He careth for you* (1 Pet. v. 10). Does it not seem to you that this is as if the Apostle had said: 'Give attention unto Him, for He attends to you, and has an interest in you'? And notice that the Apostle Peter (for it is he who speaks) observes in his words the same order as does the Bride. For he does not say, *Casting all your care upon Him,* 'in order that

---

[1] Thus all the MSS. Horst adds: '*testimonium conscientiæ nostræ,*' words which do not harmonize with the rest of the passage.

He may care for you,' but ' because He careth for you '; and thereby he plainly shows that the Church of the Saints is not only beloved by God, but was beloved by Him before it had any love for Him at all.

3. It is quite evident that what the Apostle has said with regard to oxen has no reference whatever to the Church, since He who loved her, and gave Himself for her, cannot be said to be without care for her. Is not she that lost sheep in the parable, of which the care took precedence of even that for His flock in heaven? For the Pastor left those other sheep in the wilderness, and came down to earth to care for her; he sought for her diligently, nor when she was found did he even lead her back, but bore her back upon His shoulders; then there was instituted in Heaven a new festival of rejoicings with her and for her, and the peoples of the Angels were invited to the solemnity (Luke xv. 4-7, 10). What then? shall it be said that He has no care for her whom He deigned to carry back upon His own shoulders? She is not, then, deceived when she says: *The Lord thinketh upon me* (Ps. xl. 17); nor does she mistake when she says also: *The Lord will repay for me* (Ps. cxxxviii. 8, Douay), and makes any other assertion which marks the care which the Lord has for her. It is for that reason that she calls the Lord of Sabaoth her Beloved, and boasts that He who judges all things with tranquillity (Wisd. xii. 18, Vulg.) gives attention to her. Why should she not boast of this, since she has heard Him saying unto her · *Can a woman forget her sucking child, that she should not have compassion on the son of her womb? yea, they may forget, yet will I not forget thee* (Is. xlix. 15). Again, the eyes of the Lord are upon the righteous (Ps. xxxiv. 15); and what is the Bride, but the assembly of the righteous? What is she, but the generation of them that seek the Lord, who desire to behold the Face of the Bridegroom? For He does not give attention unto her without her rendering, in her turn, attention and devotion unto Him. Wherefore she expresses each of these truths, when she says: *My Beloved is mine, and I am His*. *He is mine*, because He is good and merciful; *I am His*, because I am not ungrateful. He bestows upon me grace from grace, and I render unto Him thanks (*gratiam*) for His grace; He has care for my deliverance, and I for His honour; He for my salvation, and I for obedience to His will. He has care for me and for no other, because I am His one dove, His undefiled, and I have care for Him and for no other; nor do I give ear to the voice of strangers, nor listen to those who say: *Lo, here is Christ;* or, *lo, He is there* (Mark xiii. 21). It is the Church that speaks thus.

4. But what shall we say of each of us individually? Are we to think that there is anyone among us to whom what is said by the Bride is capable of being applied? Anyone, do I say, among us? I should think that there is no one at all among the faithful members of the Church with respect to whom it may not justly be inquired whether the Bride's mystical saying is not realized in some degree in him. But between a single soul and the mass of souls there is a

difference of method. It was not on account of one soul alone that God [the Son] has done and suffered so many things when He performed and accomplished upon the earth the work of our salvation, but on account of a great number of souls which He would unite into one Church, and which would form one only Bride. Each to the other is the dearest of all; she clings to no other Spouse, nor does He give Himself to any other Bride. What may she not expect from a lover who took upon Him an enterprise so great? What may she not hope for from Him who descended from heaven to seek her? Nor has He only sought her, but has found and made her His own with a great price, that is to say, the Blood of the purchaser. Besides, she relies so much the more upon the favour shown to her, inasmuch as, looking onward to the future, she is not ignorant that the Lord hath need of her. To what end do you inquire? It is, says the Psalmist, ' to see the good of His chosen, to rejoice in the gladness of His nation, to glory with His inheritance' (Ps. cvi. 5). You will not think that this is a matter of small importance; nay, I say to you that all His works will remain imperfect, if this fail of being attained. Does not the end of all things depend on the state and consummation of the Church? If you take away this, it is in vain that the lower creation awaits the manifestation of the sons of God. If you take away this neither the Patriarchs nor the Prophets will reach their state of perfection, since St. Paul asserts that God has so provided for us that *they without us should not be made perfect* (Heb. xi. 40). If you take away this, the glory of even the holy Angels will be imperfect by the incompleteness of their number, nor will the City of God rejoice in the integrity of all its parts.

5. Whence, then, shall the design of God be fulfilled, and that great mystery of His mercy be accomplished? Whence shall be given to me those babes and sucklings, out of whose mouth God's praise is perfected? (Ps. viii. 2). Not Heaven, but the Church, has those babes in Christ, to whom the Apostle says, *I have fed you with milk, and not with meat* (1 Cor. iii. 2). And these are invited by the Psalmist to fill up, as it were, the praises of the Lord, saying, *Praise the Lord, ye children* (Ps. cxiii. 1, Douay). Do you think that our God will receive all the praise which is due to His glory, until the coming of those who shall sing on their own behalf in the presence of the Angels, *We have rejoiced for the days in which Thou hast humbled us, for the years in which we have seen evils* (Ps. xc. 15, Douay)? This kind of rejoicing the heavens have not known, except through the children of the Church. No one who has never known what it is not to rejoice ever rejoices after this fashion. Great is joy when it succeeds to sorrow, welcome is quiet after labour, the safe harbour after the shipwreck. Security is pleasing to everyone, but most of all to him who has been in fear of danger. Light is agreeable to all, but of especial sweetness to him who is escaping from the power of darkness. To have passed from death unto life doubles the charm of life. This it is that shall be the peculiar zest to me in

the banquet of heaven, and it will be distinct from that of the heavenly spirits themselves. I venture to assert that the blessed life of heaven itself is without this special blessedness which is mine, unless those whose is that blessed life deign to say that they enjoy it by their charity in me and through me. It seems, in truth, that something is added to the perfection of their joy from me, nor is this addition a small one; for the Angels rejoice at the repentance of a sinner. And if my tears of penitence are to the Angels a source of joy, what must my perfect happiness be to them? Every work of theirs has for its object the praise of God; but there is something wanting to His praise, if there is no one to say, *We went through fire and through water, but Thou broughtest us out into a wealthy place* (Ps. lxvi. 12).

6. The whole state of the Church, then, is happy and blessed, and the thanksgiving and glory which she renders to God is altogether below that which she owes to Him, not only for those benefits which she has already received from His goodness, but for those also which she has still to receive from it. For why should she be anxious with respect to her merits, to whom a stronger and more secure reason for glorying is supplied, in the purpose of God respecting her? God cannot deny Himself, nor does He undo that which He has done; as it is written, *Who declares . . . from ancient times the things that are not yet done* (Is. xlvi. 10). He will do them, without doubt; He will do them, nor will He be wanting to His purpose. Thus you ought not now to inquire on what merits we rest the hope of good things, especially when you bear in mind the words of the Prophet: *Thus saith the Lord God, I do not this for your sakes . . . but for Mine Holy Name's sake* (Ezek. xxxvi. 22). For merit, it suffices to know that our merits are not sufficient; but as it is enough for merit not to presume on merits of one's own, so it is enough for condemnation to be wholly without merits. Even infants, when regenerated in Baptism, are not wholly wanting in merits, but have the merits of Christ, of which, nevertheless, they render themselves unworthy, if, not through inability, but through neglect, they join to them no merits of their own; and this is, indeed, the peril of those who have reached the age of discretion. Make it, then, your care to have merits, but, having them, know that they have been given to you; hope for the fruit of them from the mercy of God, and you will escape every danger, whether of poverty, of ingratitude, or of presumption. A total want of merits is an injurious poverty, but a mistaken belief in one's wealth of merits is spiritual presumption. And therefore a wise man saith: *Give me neither poverty nor riches* (Prov. xxx. 8). Happy is the Church to whom neither merits are wanting without presuming, nor presumption without merits. She has ground for presumption, but not upon her merits; and she has merits, but for deserving, not for presuming; and, indeed, not to presume upon anything in herself, is not that very thing to deserve to presume upon her faith? Therefore she presumes the more securely [upon the

merits of Christ] that she does not presume [upon her own]; and she has no cause to fear being confounded in that on which she glories, since she has so much ground for glorying; for the mercies of the Lord are many, and His truth endureth for ever.

7. Why should not [the Church] securely glory, since mercy and truth are met together (Ps. lxxxv. 11) for a testimony of her glory? Whether, therefore, she says, *My Beloved is mine;* or, *I waited patiently for the Lord, and He inclined unto me;* or, *The Lord thinketh upon me* (Ps. xl. 1, 17); or uses other words of a similar kind which appear to express a degree of affection and singular favour with which she is regarded by God, she is enabled to claim all this without fear, since it is the Lord Himself who has given to her the ground for her confident assurance, especially as she sees no other Bride, no other Church, in whom those [prophecies], which must necessarily be fulfilled, can find their fulfilment. It is, then, clear that the Church need have no fear to appropriate to herself all these promises. But it is inquired whether it be permissible, also, for an individual soul, however holy and spiritual it be, to venture to attribute them in the same way to itself; for one single soul, however eminent in sanctity it may be, cannot be thought competent to attribute to itself all the prerogatives of that great multitude, faithful and Catholic, on whose account they were instituted. And therefore it would be the more difficult, as I consider, to find a soul (if, indeed, one such could be found) to whom this could be permitted. We will, however, essay this task, but in another discourse; because we do not wish to enter upon the paths of a discussion so intricate, and of which the issue is at present doubtful to us, before we have, in order to obtain the knowledge of that hidden word, lifted up our heart in prayer to Him who 'openeth and no man shutteth' (Rev. iii. 7), to Him who is the Bridegroom of the Church, JESUS CHRIST our Lord, who is above all, God blessed for ever. AMEN.

SERMON LXIX.

ALL THAT LIFTS ITSELF UP AGAINST THE KNOWLEDGE AND SERVICE OF GOD IS TO BE ABASED. IN WHAT WAY THE FATHER AND THE WORD COME INTO A SOUL THAT LOVES, AND TAKE UP THEIR ABODE IN IT; AND OF THE CLOSE RELATION THAT IS THUS ENTERED INTO BETWEEN GOD AND THE SOUL.

'*My Beloved is Mine, and I am His.*'—Cant. ii. 16.

IN the preceding sermon these words were said to be an utterance of the Church universal, occasioned by the promises made to her by God, as well for the life which now is as for that which is to come. The question proposed is whether a single soul can appropriate to itself, in a certain manner, those promises which are made to the whole community of souls. If it may not do so, then it behoves us to refer these words to the Church in such a way that they may not apply to the individual; and not these only, but all utterances of a similar kind in which great truths are expressed; as, for example, *I waited patiently for the Lord, and He inclined unto me* (Ps. xl. 1), and any others touched upon in the former sermon. If, on the contrary, anyone thinks that the individual soul is permitted to claim these promises, I do not contest that opinion; but it is needful to ascertain to whom that claim is permitted, for it is manifestly not open to all indiscriminately to do so. The Church of God has, without doubt, her spiritual men who serve God within her pale, not only faithfully, but also with confidence, who speak with God as with a friend, and whose conscience renders to them an approving testimony. But who are these? That is known only to God. Do you, nevertheless, hear what manner of men you ought to be if you wish to be of that number. Though I say this, I do so not as having had experience of this, but as one who desires to have it. Give me a soul which loves God, and Him only, and which deserves to be loved for His sake, to which to live is Christ, and not only so, but with which this has long been the case; which, whether in action or in repose, has God always before its eyes, and desires, with anxious care, to walk with Him at all times, to be of one mind with Him, and which is enabled so to be; give me, I say, a soul like this, and I do not deny that it is worthy of the care of the Bridegroom, of the regard of His Majesty, of the favour of the Sovereign, of the attention of the Ruler of all the earth, and if it desires to glorify itself it can do so without folly, provided it is mindful that 'whosoever glorieth, let him glory in the Lord.' In this manner one individual soul may venture to appropriate that which belongs only to many, but for a distinct reason.

2. For the causes which we have enumerated above give confidence to a holy and believing multitude, but there are two principal ones which give it to a holy soul separately. In the first place, the Divinity of the Bridegroom, being by nature wholly simple, is able to regard many persons as one, and one person as if many, without being divided by their diversity in the one case, or restricted by the singularity in the other; it is neither agitated by cares, nor troubled by disquietudes. Thus, though it be wholly occupied by one object, it is not absorbed by that object; nor, if occupied by many, is it spread over them. Secondly, which it is as sweet as it is remarkable to have experience of, so great is the condescension of the Word, so great is the benevolence of the Father and of the Word towards the soul well affected and well regulated (which is indeed the gift of the Father and the work of the Son) that they deign to honour it with their presence, and in such a measure that they not only come to it, but make their abode with it (John xiv. 23). For it is not enough that they come to it, unless they also bestow upon it their fulness. What is it for the WORD to come to the soul? It is to instruct it in

wisdom. And what for the Father to come? It is to touch it with the love of wisdom, so that it may be able to say: I *was a lover of her beauty* (Wisd. viii. 2). To love is of the Father, and therefore the coming of the Father is declared by the infusion of love. What would be the effect of knowledge without love? It would produce pride. And what of love without knowledge? It would be the cause of error. In fact, they were in error of whom St. Paul said: *I bear them record that they have a zeal of God, but not according to knowledge* (Rom. x. 2). It is not becoming for the Bride of the Word to be ignorant, and, on the other hand, the Father does not suffer her to be proud. For the Father loves the Son, and is always swift to cast down and destroy that which exalts itself against the knowledge of the Word, whether by moderating or by sharpening zeal, whereof the one is the effect of mercy, the other of justice. May He cast down, or, rather, destroy and reduce to nothingness, every rising of pride in me; and may He do this not by the fire of His anger, but by the gentle flowing of His love! May I be enabled to learn not to indulge in pride, yet to learn this not by the lessons of vengeance, but by the unction of grace! *O Lord, rebuke me not in Thine anger*, as [Thou didst rebuke] the Angel who exalted himself in Heaven, *neither chasten me in Thy hot displeasure* (Ps. vi. 1) as Thou didst man who offended in Paradise. Both of these meditated iniquity in seeking to exalt themselves, the one by power, the other by knowledge. For the woman foolishly believed the voice of the tempter when he promised: *Ye shall be as gods, knowing good and evil* (Gen. iii. 5). He had at an earlier period seduced himself, when he had persuaded himself that he should become like unto the Most High. For he who thinks himself to be something when he is nothing deceives himself (Gal. vi. 3).

3. But both one and the other of these eminences was cast down; but more gently in the case of man, according to the just judgment of Him who doeth all things in weight and in measure. For it was in fierce anger that the Angels were punished, or, rather, were condemned; but it was only a milder degree of displeasure that was felt by man. For in the midst of His wrath God remembered mercy. Wherefore the children of men are called to this day 'children of wrath,' but not 'of fierce anger.' If I were not born in the former state, I should not need a New Birth through Baptism; but if I were born in the latter state, either a New Birth would be unattainable to me or would profit me nothing if attained. Would you behold a child of fierce anger? If you have seen 'Satan as lightning fall from heaven,' that is to say, precipitated thence by the vehemence of the fierce anger of God, then you have learned what that anger is. Then He is not mindful of His mercy, for in His wrath He will indeed remember mercy; but it is not so when His fierce wrath burns as fire. Woe to the children of unbelief! to those, I mean, who, being descendants of Adam, have been born children of wrath, and have changed that wrath into fierce anger against themselves by

their diabolic obstinacy; the rod into a club, yea, rather into the hammer of destruction. For *they treasure up unto themselves wrath against the day of wrath* (Rom. ii. 5). Wrath treasured up, what is it but fierce anger? They have committed the sin of the devil, and are stricken with the same judgment as he. Woe also, though in a less terrible degree, to those who, having been born children of wrath, have not awaited the obtaining of the New Birth by grace. For having died in the same state in which they were born, children of wrath they shall remain. I say 'of wrath,' not 'of fierce anger,' because it is most piously believed, and the hopes and sympathies of humanity lead us to expect, that their penalties are of a far milder kind, since the infection of nature in them comes wholly from others.[1]

4. Therefore the devil has been judged in the fierce anger of God, because his iniquity was found hateful; while that of man has been judged but in anger, and in anger is corrected. Thus every kind of exaltation is repressed, as is also that which makes proud and leads to a headlong fall; for the Father is animated by zeal on behalf of the Son. For in both the one case and the other there is an injury to the Son, or rather there is [either] a usurpation of power against the Might of God, which is Himself, or a presumption of knowledge against the Wisdom of God, which also is no other than God Himself. O Lord, who is like unto Thee; who, except the Brightness of Thy Essential Being, the express Image of Thy Person? He alone is in Thy Likeness; He alone being Son of the Most High, and Himself Most High, thought it not robbery to be equal unto Thee (Phil. ii. 6). How can He be otherwise than equal to Thee, since Thou and He are one? His seat is on Thy Right Hand, not under Thy Feet. How can anyone be found so daring and so rash as to attempt to usurp the place of Thy Only Begotten Son? Let him be cast down. He sets a seat for himself on high; let the noxious chair of evil be overturned. Who is it that teacheth man knowledge? Is it not Thou, O Key of David, who openest and shuttest to whom Thou wilt? How, then, could the attempt be made without the Key to enter, or rather to gain access by violence to the treasures of wisdom and knowledge? For he who entereth not by the door, the same is a thief and a robber (John x. 1). Peter, then, will enter, who has received the keys; nor will he enter alone, for he shall admit me if he will; and if he will, shall shut out some other person, according to the knowledge and the power which has been conferred upon him.

5. And what are these keys? They signify the power of opening and shutting, and of distinguishing between those who should be admitted and those who should be excluded. These treasures are not in the serpent, but in Christ. And therefore the serpent was not able

---

[1] This is also the teaching of St. Augustine, who writes that 'children who die without baptism shall be in a state of condemnation which is the mildest of all.' —*De Peccatorum Meritis*, c. 16; also in *Contra Julianum*, Bk. v., c. 12; also Fulgentius *de Veritate Prædestinationis*, Bk. i., c. 14; and *De Incarnatione*, c. 30.

to bestow the knowledge which he did not possess, but He who did possess it bestowed it. Nor could he have a power which he had not received, but he had it who had received it. Jesus Christ bestowed it (Matt. xvi. 19); Peter received it. He was not rendered proud by his knowledge, nor is he therefore to be cast down from the power he has received. Wherefore? Because he in neither of these ways exalted himself against the knowledge of God, who laid claim to none of these powers beyond the knowledge of God, as did he who flattered himself in his own sight until his iniquity was found to be hateful (Ps. xxxvi. 2). How, indeed, should he have desired anything beyond the knowledge of God, who described himself as an Apostle of Jesus Christ, according to the foreknowledge of God the Father? (1 Peter i. 1, 2). And these things were said in respect of the zeal of God directed against the evil-doers, whether angel or man (for in both he finds perverseness), insomuch that He has destroyed in His wrath and fierce anger everything that exalts itself against the knowledge of God.

6. It is now needful to return to the zeal of mercy, that is, the zeal which is not inflamed against us, but is sent forth towards us; for the flame of zeal is, as we have already said, that of judgment, and has given us sufficient cause for fear in the examples which have been adduced of those so terribly punished. It is for that reason that I shall retire to a place of refuge from the face of the fierce anger of the Lord, namely, to that zeal of kindness which burns with sweet and efficacious expiation. Does not charity atone for sins? It does, and with power. I have read that it *covers the multitude of sins* (1 Peter iv. 8). But I ask: Is it not suitable also and sufficient to cast down and humble every exaltation of the eyes and of the heart? Assuredly, for it vaunteth not itself, and is not puffed up. If, then, the Lord Jesus deigns to come to me, or rather in me, not in the zeal of His fierce anger, nor even in wrath, but in love and in a spirit of gentle kindness, striving with me with a godly jealousy: since what is there that is so emphatically of God as charity? For that is indeed God. If, I say, He comes thus, then I know by that sign that He is not alone, but that with Him has come His Father also. For what is so Fatherly as this? And it is for this very reason that He is called, not only the Father of the Word, but also the Father of mercies (2 Cor. i. 3), because to Him it belongeth always to have pity and to spare. If I have ever felt that He has opened my understanding that I might understand the Scriptures (Luke xxiv. 45), either that I might be able to pour forth in preaching, as it were, from my inmost heart the wisdom which is from above, or that a deeper insight into Divine mysteries might be given me through an influx of light from heaven, or that the heavens themselves seemed to be spread over my soul and to let fall upon it the fruitful showers of meditation, then at such times it is not doubtful to me that the Bridegroom is present with me. For these rich gifts come to us from the Word, and of His fulness do we all receive these precious things. If, again, I am per-

vaded by a feeling of devotion humble and devout, but zealous and inspiring, if love of the truth, penetrating to my inmost being, produces in me a scorn and hatred of vanity, so that neither the increase of knowledge renders me proud nor the frequency of [the Divine] visitations exalts me, then I straightway feel that this is the effect of Paternal tenderness, and I do not doubt that the Father is with me. But if I shall have continued to persevere, as far as in me is, in sentiments and actions worthy of so great a Divine condescension, and the grace of God which was in me was not in vain, then I am assured that the FATHER and the WORD have taken up their abode in me; the One to nourish my soul, the Other to instruct it.

7. What a close and intimate relation this grace produces between the Divine Word and the soul, and what confidence follows from that intimacy, you may well imagine. I believe that a soul in such a condition may say without fear : *My Beloved is mine;* inasmuch as it is conscious that it loves God with a true and even a vehement affection, and therefore concludes that it is beloved in no less a degree by Him; and by the singular devotion, the care, the labour, the diligence, the earnestness wherewith it is animated in the incessant and ardent effort to find means to please God, which it readily, and without question, recognises in itself, it recalls the Lord's promise : *With what measure ye mete, it shall be measured to you again* (Matt. vii. 2). It is true that the Bride is prudent, and prefers to take for her part a deep thankfulness for grace bestowed, because she knows that her Beloved has prevented her in the bestowal of affection. It is for that she sets His Name first : *My Beloved is mine, and I am His.* From the attributes, then, which belong to God, she justly and confidently infers that by Him whom she loves, she is herself beloved. This is, in fact, the case. The love of God for the soul produces the love of the soul for God; the direction of the Divine thought upon a soul causes that soul to direct itself towards God, and His care and solicitude for it produces a similar care and solicitude in it towards Him. For, I know not by what affinity of nature it takes place, that when a soul has once attained to behold, with unveiled face, the glory of the Lord, it is speedily, as if by a necessary law, conformed to it, and transformed into the same image. God will then appear towards you, such as you shall have appeared towards Him. With an upright man (says the Psalmist) He will show Himself upright; with the pure He will show Himself pure (Ps. xviii. 25, 26). Why not, then, also loving with one who loves Him, attentive with the attentive, careful with the careful, and at leisure with the leisurely?

8. Lastly, He says : *I love them that love Me : and those that seek Me early shall find Me* (Prov. viii. 17). You see how He assures you, not only of His love, if you love Him, but also of the care and thought which He employs on your behalf, if He feels that you are careful in that which relates to Him. Are you keeping vigil? He will keep vigil too. Though you arise in the night itself, before the beginning of the morning watches, though you hasten as much as you are able

to 'prevent the night watches,' you will find Him there; you will not anticipate Him. You will act rashly if, in such a matter as this, you attribute any precedence in time, or any greater degree, to yourself rather than to Him; for His love is greater than yours, and it is before yours. If a soul is deeply assured of these glorious truths, can you wonder that it takes pride and pleasure, even for the very reason that it is assured of them. in the thought that this Majesty which is so great gives attention to it alone, as if He had no care for the rest of His creatures; nay, seems to set all other cares aside, and to guard it with an undivided devotion?

It is time that I should bring this sermon to an end. I will add only one thing, which seems marvellous, but is true, and is specially addressed to those spiritually minded who are among you: that a soul which beholds God beholds Him no otherwise than as if it alone were beheld by Him. It is, then, in this confidence that it declares that He gives attention to it, and that it gives attention to Him, and that it beholds nothing else but itself and Him. How good art Thou, O Lord, to the soul that seeks Thee! Thou comest to it; Thou dost embrace it; Thou showest Thyself to be its Bridegroom, its Spouse; Thou who art its Lord, yea, who art above all, God blessed for ever. AMEN.

SERMON LXX.

WHY THE BRIDEGROOM IS CALLED *BELOVED;* AND OF THE TRUTH, THE GENTLENESS, THE RIGHTEOUSNESS, AND THE OTHER VIRTUES, WHICH ARE CALLED *LILIES*, AND AMONG WHICH HE IS SAID TO FEED.

'*My Beloved is mine, and I am His: He feedeth among the lilies.*'—Cant. ii. 16.

WHO can now impute to the Bride presumption or insolence, because she declares that she has been admitted into fellowship with Him who feedeth among the lilies? Even if it were said, 'He feedeth among the stars,' I know not whether in consideration of that phrase, 'He feedeth,' it would seem to be a great thing thus to have with Him friendship or familiarity. For the phrase seems to have in it somewhat humble and unrefined. And when she says that He feedeth among the lilies, she seems by this note of humiliation to repel and remove from herself any charge of temerity. For what are lilies? According to the Word of the Lord they are *the grass of the field which to-day is, and to-morrow is cast into the oven* (Matt. vi. 28-30). What, then, is He who feedeth upon the grass, as a lamb or a calf? Evidently a lamb or a fatted calf. But you have, perhaps, carefully noticed that the lilies are referred to here, not as food, but as the place of His sojourn; nor is it said that He feedeth on the lilies, but *among the lilies*. So let it be. He does not feed on the grass as an ox; but what greatness can there be in one who is found among the grass, and lies down upon it to rest, like one of the crowd which surrounds Him; and what glory can there be to the Bride in having for her Beloved, one who acts thus? According to the literal sense, then, the modesty of the Bride, and the discretion with which she speaks, are sufficiently apparent, and it is clear that she rules her speech with judgment, and expresses her high fortunes in unassuming words.

2. But, nevertheless, she is not unmindful that He who feedeth is the same as He who giveth food to others; that He, though He abides among the lilies, yet reigns above the stars. But she makes mention the more willingly of the humble actions of her Beloved, because, as I have said, of His humility; but also because He began to be her Beloved from the time when He began to feed among the lilies. Nor was it only from that time that He did so, but from that fact. For He who in the heights is the Lord, in the depths is the Beloved; above the stars He reigns; among the lilies He loves. Yet even above the stars He loved, because at no time and in no place, being Himself the Essential Love, could He cease to love; but until He descended to be among the lilies, and was found to feed among them, He was not the object of love, nor did He become the Beloved. What! you reply; was He not loved by the Patriarchs and by the Prophets? Assuredly; but not before He was seen by them also, feeding among the lilies. They cannot be said not to have seen Him whom they foresaw, unless anyone is so entirely without discernment as to suppose that a person who sees in the spirit really sees nothing. Whence, then, were they Seers, for so the Prophets were called (1 Sam. ix. 9) aforetime, if they saw nothing? It was because they desired to see Him whom as yet they saw not. And they would not have been able to form the desire to see Him in the body if they had not seen Him in the spirit. But, I say, were they all prophets? Either they all wished to see, or faith was granted to all. As to all those who had the gift of spiritual vision, either they were Prophets, or they were acquiescent and in alliance with the Prophets. While as to those who had faith, to have believed, is to have seen. For it seems to me not a mistake to say that it is possible to behold a thing in spirit and by faith, and not only by the spirit of prophecy.

3. He, therefore, who giveth food to all flesh, in deigning thus to come down and to feed among the lilies, made Himself loved, because He could not be loved before He was known. Accordingly, when the Bride makes mention of her Beloved, she appropriately refers to this fact as the cause of His being known and loved. This feeding among the lilies is to be spiritually understood; to take it in a literal sense would be ridiculous. We will show, as far as we are able, what these spiritual lilies are. I think that it will behove us first to examine on what the Beloved 'feedeth among the lilies'; whether upon the

lilies themselves, or upon other plants and flowers hidden among them. That which appears to me the more difficult is that He is not said to give food to others, but Himself to feed. For that He gives food to others is not doubtful, nor is it unworthy of Him; but to say that He Himself feeds has a sound of indigence, and seems not capable of being attributed to Him, even spiritually, without doing some injury to His sovereign Majesty. I do not remember to have remarked in any part of this Canticle that He is said to feed; while you will remember with me that in one place He is said to make His flocks to feed. For the Bride there asks Him to show to her where He makes His flocks to feed and to rest at noon (i. 6). And now she says that He Himself 'feedeth,' which she has not asserted before; nor does she ask to have the place where He is pointed out to her, but herself names it expressly, '*among the lilies.*' The one fact she knew, the other she did not know; because it is not possible for her to be equally well acquainted with that which is lofty and in the heaven, and that which is lowly and on the earth. Lofty is the task, lofty also is the place; nor has access to it been granted as yet even to the Bride herself.

4. And therefore it was that He who giveth food to all men, and is their Pastor, emptied Himself of His glory even to the point of receiving food. He was found among the lilies; He was beheld in His state of poverty by the Church, which was poor, and was beloved for the very reason of their similarity in this respect. Nor was it for this cause alone, but also because of His truth, His gentleness, and His righteousness; because promises were fulfilled through Him; because iniquities were forgiven; because the demons and their chief were judged and condemned in their pride. Such, then, was He when He appeared, that He was deserving of being loved; for, while by His own Nature He was the purest Truth, to men He was gentle and kind, and on their behalf He was righteous. O Bridegroom truly to be loved, and to be embraced with every fibre of the heart's affection! Why should the Church hesitate or delay to commit herself with an entire devotion to one so faithful to His promises, so kind to forgive, and so strong and righteous to protect? The Psalmist had foretold of Him long before: *In Thy glory and Thy majesty ride prosperously.* What kind of flower has glory and beauty? The lily, I think; there is nothing more beautiful than that. So the Bridegroom is fairer than all. What, then, are these lilies from which He draws a beauty so rare? *Ride prosperously,* continues the Psalmist, *because of truth and meekness, and righteousness* (Ps. xlv. 3, 4). These are the lilies; the lilies, I say, growing out of the earth, and blooming brightly upon it; surpassing other flowers in beauty, and fragrant above all perfumes. Among these lilies is the Bridegroom, and from them is He surpassingly fair and beautiful. For otherwise, and regarding only the infirmity of the flesh, *in Him there is no form nor comeliness* (Is. liii. 2).

5. An exquisite lily, most fair in hue and marvellous in fragrance,

is Truth; for its brightness is that of the Eternal Light, the unspotted mirror of the Power of God, and the image of His goodness (Wisd. vii. 26). It is assuredly a lily which our earth has produced by a new benediction, and prepared before the face of all peoples, a light to lighten the Gentiles (Luke ii. 31, 32). As long as the earth was under a curse it brought forth thorns and thistles. But now, by the blessing of the Lord, Truth hath sprung out of the earth (Ps. lxxxv. 11), the beautiful Rose of Sharon, and the Lily of the valleys. Recognise it as a lily by the whiteness and brilliancy wherewith it shone by night upon the eyes of the shepherds, as soon as it had begun to flower; for the Gospel declares that *the Angel of the Lord came upon them, and the glory of the Lord shone round about them* (Luke ii. 9). It is well said, the glory *of the Lord*, for it was not the brightness of an Angel, but of this Lily, which surrounded those who were at Bethlehem. Recognise it as a Lily from the fragrance also, which reached even the Magi, who were at so great a distance. A Star indeed appeared to them, but those Wise Men would not have followed it had they not been inwardly drawn by the persuasive fragrance of this Lily. Assuredly Truth is a lily, of which the perfume animates faith and the brightness enlightens the understanding. Lift up now your eyes to the Person of the Lord Himself, who, speaking in the Gospel, says, *I am the Truth* (John xiv. 6). And see with how much reason Truth is compared to a lily. Notice, if you have never done so, how from the midst of this flower come forth five little rods of gold, beautifully arranged in the form of a crown, and surrounded by the white petals of the flower; and recognise in this a figure of the golden crown of Divinity in Christ, with the inviolable purity of His Human Nature; that is to say, Christ bearing the diadem wherewith His mother crowned Him (Cant. iii. 11). For that which His Father set upon His Head abides in the region of Light unapproachable, nor are you able, as yet, to behold Him wearing that. But of this we will speak at another time.

6. Truth, then, is a lily; so also is Gentleness; it has the whiteness of innocence, the fragrance of hope. 'Remnants there are,' it is said, 'for the peaceable man' (Ps. xxxvii. 37, Douay). The gentle and kindly is a man of good hope [for the future life], nor is he in the present life less an example of clemency and friendship. Does not the lily, which shines with the duties of charity, diffuse also the fragrance of hope? Add to this that just as truth has sprung out of the earth, so also has gentleness. Unless anyone doubts that the Lamb, the Ruler of the earth (Is. xvi. 1), that Lamb who was led to the slaughter, and opened not His Mouth (Is. liii. 7), was sprung from the earth. Not only Gentleness and Truth have sprung out of the earth, but also Righteousness; as says the Prophet: *Drop down, ye Heavens, from above, and let the skies pour down righteousness: let the earth open, and let them bring forth salvation, and let Righteousness spring up together* (Is. xlv. 8). That Righteousness is a lily, the Scripture teaches us, saying that the righteous *shall grow as the*

lily, and shall flourish for ever before the Lord (Hos. xiv. 5).[1] It is not, then, the case with this lily, that to-day it is, and to-morrow it is cast into the oven, since it shall flourish for ever; and that before the Lord, for the righteous shall be in everlasting remembrance, and shall not be afraid of evil tidings (Ps. cxii. 6, 7); that is to say, he shall not fear to have to listen to that terrible sentence by which sinners are bidden to go away into everlasting fire. To whom is the brightness of this lily not visible, except the person to whom it is unpleasing? It is a sun; but not that sun which rises upon the evil and upon the good. For those who shall say: 'The Sun of Righteousness hath not risen upon us' (Wisd. v. 6) have never even beheld His light. Far otherwise is it with them to whom it has been said: *Unto you that fear My Name shall the Sun of Righteousness arise with healing in His wings* (Mal. iv. 2). The whiteness of this lily, then, is among the just; its fragrance, indeed, extends even unto sinners, although in them it is not for good. For we have heard the voice of the righteous saying: *We are unto God a sweet savour of Christ, in them that are saved, and in them that perish: to the one we are the savour of death unto death, and to the other the savour of life unto life* (2 Cor. ii. 15, 16). Who, though he be the most abandoned of men, does not approve of the sentiments of a righteous man, although he does not love his actions? Happy is he who does not condemn himself in that which he approves. For it is a self-condemnation to approve that which is good, and yet not to love it; so that a person is not happy, but miserable, who is thus condemned by his own judgment. What can be more miserable than the condition of a person to whom the savour of life is a messenger, not of life, but of death? Or, rather, I should call it, not a messenger of death, but a deathstroke.

7. There are still many other lilies besides these which the Prophet has indicated to us in the character of the Bridegroom; I mean besides truth, and gentleness, and righteousness; nor will it be difficult for each of us to find for himself similar ones in the garden, so full of delights, of the Bridegroom. It abounds and superabounds in such; who can enumerate them? since there are as many lilies as virtues; and of virtues in the Lord of virtues there is no end. For in Christ there is the fulness of virtues, and, therefore, also the abundance of lilies. Therefore, perhaps, it is that He is Himself spoken of as the Lily, because He is wholly surrounded with lilies, and all events in His Life are, so to speak, lilies: His conception, His Birth, His manner of life, the words He spake, the miracles He did; His Sacraments, His Passion, His Death, His Resurrection, His Ascension. Which of all these events is there that has not a pure splendour and a sweet fragrance? Thus, for instance, in His Conception is apparent the brightness of heavenly

---

[1] This is not the reading of the Vulgate, which has, 'shall cast forth his root as Lebanon'; and the other versions agree in this. The quotation was probably made from memory.—ED.

light, from the abundance of the overshadowing Spirit; so that not even the holy Virgin would have been able to endure it, if it had not been tempered to her by the power of the Most High. His Birth was rendered full of light and beauty by the pure virginity of His Mother; His Life, by the sinlessness of His character; His words, by their truth unsullied; His miracles, by the purity of His Heart; His Sacraments, by the hidden power of His goodness and kindness; His Passion, by His willingness to suffer; His Death, by the freedom that He had not to die; His Resurrection, by the fortitude with which it has inspired His Martyrs; His Ascension, by the accomplishment in it of His promises. How exquisite also is the fragrance of faith in each of these mysteries, of the faith, I mean, which is ours, and fills our hearts and minds, though we have not beheld the brightness of that glory! For *blessed are they that have not seen, and yet have believed* (John xx. 29). May my part in these lilies be the odour of life which proceeds from them. It is faith which fills with that fragrance the nostrils (so to speak) of my soul, and fills it with so much greater abundance, because the multitude of the lilies is so great. It is that heavenly fragrance which softens the rigour of my exile, and renews in my heart without ceasing a desire and longing for my true country above.

8. Some of the companions of the Bridegroom also have their lilies, but not in great number. For though all have received the Holy Spirit, it is by measure, and by measure also have they received gifts and graces. It is He alone who possesses them without measure (John iii. 34), because He possesses all. It is one thing to have some lilies, and another thing to have lilies only. Whom can you show me, from among the sons of the captivity, who is so holy and entirely without guile, as to be able to cover all the land that is his with flowers like these? Not the infant of a day old is pure upon the earth (Job xiv. 4, 5, according to the LXX.). Great and successful is he who is able to train up in the plot of ground committed to him even three or four of these lilies, in the midst of such a thicket of thorns and thistles, which are the inveterate seeds of the ancient curse. As for me, who am poor, I shall think myself happy if I am enabled by diligent weeding to clear my little plot of land from that evil crop of iniquities and vices, and by careful cultivation to ensure the growth of even one lily, so that He who feedeth among the lilies may deign sometimes to find His place for so doing in my soul.

9. I have said 'even one lily,' but this is too little, and it was out of the poverty of my heart that my mouth spake. For one will not suffice; at least two are absolutely necessary. I refer to continence and to innocence, whereof the one without the other will not save. It will be in vain that I invite the Bridegroom to come to either one of these, for He is represented, not as feeding upon a lily, but *among the lilies.* My care, then, shall be to have lilies, so that He who feedeth among the lilies may not, because I have only a single one, turn away from His servant in displeasure. I set, therefore, inno-

cence first of all, and if I am able to join continence to it, I shall think myself rich in the possession of lilies. I am even, as it were, a king, if I am able to add to these, as a third lily, patience. And, indeed, the two former would suffice; but because they may be found wanting in the time of temptations, and the life of man upon the earth is marked by temptation (Job vii. 1), there is much need on that account of patience, which is, so to speak, the protector[1] and guardian of both. I think that if He who is the lover of lilies shall come, and shall find us in that condition, He will not, then, disdain with us to feed, with us to eat the Passover, since He will find great sweetness in the two former virtues, and great security shall be in the third. We shall see later on how He, who feeds and gives nourishment to all flesh, is here said Himself to feed. But now one thing is clear: that the Bridegroom not only appears among the lilies, but is to be found only among them, since every part of His character is a lily, that is, a virtue; and He Himself is the Lily, the Bridegroom of the Church, JESUS CHRIST our Lord, who is above all, God blessed for ever. AMEN.

SERMON LXXI.

OF SPIRITUAL LILIES, THAT IS, GOOD WORKS, OF WHICH THE FRAGRANCE IS A RIGHT INTENTION, AND THE COLOUR A GOOD REPUTATION; AND HOW THE BRIDEGROOM BOTH NOURISHES THESE, AND IS NOURISHED BY THEM. ALSO OF THE UNITY OF GOD THE FATHER WITH THE SON, AND OF THE HOLY SOUL WITH GOD.

THE conclusion of the last sermon shall form the commencement of this. The Bridegroom, then, is a Lily, but not a lily among thorns, because He did not commit sin, and thorns signify sin. It is the Bride of whom He has borne His testimony that she is *a lily among thorns* (Cant. ii. 2), and therefore if she should say that she had no thorns, she would deceive herself, and the truth would not be in her. As for Him, He has declared that He is the Rose, indeed, and the Lily, yet not among thorns. Instead of this, He says: *I am the Rose of Sharon, and the Lily of the valleys.* He makes no mention of thorns, because He alone among men has no need to say: *I am turned in my anguish, while the thorn is fastened* (Ps. xxxii. 4, Douay). Therefore He is never without lilies, because He is always without faults, because He is wholly and always white and glistering, fairer than the children of men (Ps. xlv. 3). Do you, then, who listen to, or who read these words, take heed that you have in your soul, and in your life, lilies that grow and flourish, if you wish to have Him who dwelleth among the lilies dwelling in you. Let

---

[1] *Tutrix*; another reading is, *nutrix*.

the blameless whiteness of your character and actions, let the fragrance they exhale, bear testimony that all your occupations, all your impulses, all your desires, are lilies. For characters have, as it were, their colour and their odour; nor are colour and odour the same thing in spirit any more than in bodies. Colour has regard to the right intention, fragrance to the good reputation of actions. *Ye have made our savour to be abhorred in the eyes of Pharaoh and in the eyes of his servants* (Exod. v. 21), said the Israelites, speaking of opinion. The intention of the heart, and the judgment of the conscience of the doer, give to an action its colour. Vices are black, and virtue white, and the conscience when consulted distinguishes between the one and the other. The Lord's declaration respecting the single eye and the eye that is evil (Matt vi. 22, 23) holds good, because there are certain lines of division between whiteness and blackness, as between light and darkness. That which comes forth from a pure heart and a good conscience is therefore white, and is virtue; and if, furthermore, good reputation follows it, it is a lily, since neither whiteness nor fragrance is wanting to it.

2. And although good reputation does not render virtue more great, it, nevertheless, renders it fairer and more illustrious. If there be any spot upon the intention, it will not fail to appear also upon that which that intention has produced; for the fault of the root reappears in the branches. And on this account, whatsoever it be that a corrupted root shall produce from itself, not without communication of its own corruption, for example, discourses, actions, or prayers, even though they seem to enjoy public esteem, it is not entitled to be called a lily, because, though it has an appearance of fragrant odour, it is wanting in colour. For how can that be a lily which has upon it a spot of discoloration? Nor will reputation avail to make that a virtue which the consciousness of bad intention convicts of being a vice. Virtue, indeed, will be content with a good conscience, where good report cannot possibly follow; but the fragrance of reputation will not suffice to excuse the fault of a conscience that is stained. Yet a man of virtue will, as far as he is able, provide things honourable, not only before God, but also in the sight of men (Rom. xii. 17), that he may truly be a lily.

3. But there is a whiteness of the soul which comes of the forgiving mercy of God, as He declares Himself by the mouth of the Prophet: *Though your sins be as scarlet, they shall be as white as snow; though they be red like crimson, they shall be as wool* (Is. i. 18). There is still another kind of whiteness with which a person clothes himself, who showeth mercy with cheerfulness. And if you consider the man charitable and gracious, who is described by the Psalmist, who *showeth favour and lendeth* (Ps. cxii. 5), will it not seem to you that this joy is, as it were, a whiteness and glory of kindness with which he is clad, and which appears as well upon his countenance as upon his work? On the contrary, when anyone gives with sadness and, as it were, by necessity, his brow and his

hands are so far from being white, that they gather blackness from the feelings of his heart. And therefore *God loveth a cheerful giver* (2 Cor. ix. 7). Does He love one who gives reluctantly and sadly? He who looked favourably upon Abel because of the willing heart which was expressed by the brightness of his countenance turned His Face from Cain, whose countenance fell, doubtless with sadness and jealousy (Gen. iv. 4, 5). Consider, then, of what a nature must be the colour of sadness and jealousy for God to turn away His Face from it. A poet has expressed aptly and elegantly that white brilliance of gladness which colours a deed of kindness, when he says in its praise :

     . . . '*Super omnia vultus*
  Accessere boni.' . . .[1]

Nor is it only the cheerful giver, but he also who giveth with simplicity (Rom. xii. 8), who is loved by God; for simplicity shows the whiteness of the soul. This I prove from the consideration of the contrary, for duplicity is a spot; nay, it is a stain. For what is duplicity but deceit and fraud? And he who acts deceitfully in the sight of God, his iniquity is found to be hateful (Ps. xxxvi. 2). Therefore it is that the man is called blessed unto whom the Lord imputeth not iniquity, and in whose spirit there is no guile (Ps. xxxii. 2). The Lord has well expressed in few words these two spots upon the soul, a feigned sadness, and deceit: *Be not as the hypocrites, of a sad countenance* (Matt. vi. 16). The Bridegroom, being virtue, takes pleasure in virtues; being a lily, He abides willingly among the lilies ; and being Himself of a pure whiteness, delights in those whose souls are white and pure.

4. Perhaps, also, this is the signification of 'feedeth among the lilies,' namely, that He delighteth in the whiteness and fragrance of virtues. Formerly, when He was in the Body, He was nourished with food in the house of Martha and Mary; he reclined, even in the body, among the lilies (I speak of them, for they were lilies), and at the same time was refreshed in spirit by the devotion and virtues of women. If, then, in that hour a Prophet, or an Angel, or some spiritual man, who was not unaware of the greatness of Him who there reclined, had entered, would he not have been lost in wonder at the condescension and familiar kindness shown by Him to those beings of pure mind and of modest, though earthly, body and of the weaker sex? and would he not have been able to bear true testimony, ' I have seen Him not only abiding, but also feeding, among the lilies ?' It is thus that the Bridegroom is found to feed among the lilies in a twofold manner, namely, in flesh and in spirit. I think, also, that He fed them in turn, but that was in spirit. But how did He nourish them spiritually by whom He was physically nourished? Did He not strengthen the timidity of those pious women, cheer their humility, enrich and render fruitful their devotion? But if you have seen that to Him to be nourished is to

[1] Ovid, '*Metamor.*,' Bk. viii., vv. 677, 678.

nourish, now notice also that, conversely, to nourish others is to be nourished Himself. What did the holy Patriarch, Jacob, say: *God, which fed me all my life long unto this day?* (Gen. xlviii. 15). He is a good master of a household who takes care for those of his house, and more especially in troublous days, who gives food to their hunger, yea, feeds them with the bread of knowledge and of life, and thus nourishes them for life eternal. But thus feeding others, He is, as I think, Himself nourished, and that with the food which is most agreeable to Him, I mean, with our progress in goodness; for it is a joy to the Lord to see us strong and courageous in good.

5. Thus, then, it is that, when He feeds others, He is Himself fed; and when He is fed He feeds others; at once refreshing us with His spiritual joy, and being Himself rejoiced with our spiritual advancement. To Him my penitence, my salvation, indeed, I myself, are, as it were, nourishment. Does He not, according to the phrase of the Psalmist, eat ashes as it were bread? (Ps. cii. 9). I am that ashes, for I am a sinner, and He, spiritually speaking, feeds upon me; He feeds upon me when He reproves and convicts me of my sin; I am swallowed when I am taught and trained; I am cooked when changed, and digested when transformed; finally, I am made one with Him when I am conformed unto His likeness. Do not wonder at this: it is that we may be more closely united to Him that He both feeds on us and is our food. Otherwise, our union with Him would not be perfect; for if I feed upon Him, but He not upon me, it will appear that, though He is in me, I am not yet in Him. If, on the contrary, He feeds upon me, but I do not upon Him, it will appear that, though I am in Him, yet He is not also in me; and in either of the two cases there is not a perfect union between us. But if He so feeds upon me that I may be in Him, and I in turn upon Him that He may be in me, how complete and strong is the bond[1] between us, since I am in Him, and He will, nevertheless, be in me.

6. Shall I make clearer what has been said by a comparison? Lift your eyes, then, to a truth of the highest order, which has much similarity, nevertheless, to that before us. If the Bridegroom Himself were in the Father in such wise that the Father were not in Him, or if the Father were so in Him that He was not in the Father, I venture to say that the union between them, if union it were, would stop short of being perfect. But now, as He is in the Father and the Father in Him, there is no defect in their union, but He and the Father are truly and Perfectly One. So, also, the soul, for which it is good to adhere to God (Ps. lxxiii. 28), does not regard itself as perfectly united to Him, until both He abides in it, and it in Him. Not that even then it may be said to be one with God, in the same manner as the Father and the Son are one, although *he that is joined unto the Lord is one spirit* (1 Cor. vi. 17). This I have read, but that I

---

[1] *Connexio;* so read the earliest editions and many MSS. Others have: *Erit perinde firma connexio et complexio integra.*

have not read. I do not speak of myself, I who am a person of very small importance (*nihil*), but assuredly there is no one in his senses, no one, I say, on earth or in heaven, who would arrogate to himself that saying of the Only Begotten Son of God: *I and the Father are One* (John x. 30). And yet I, though I am but dust and ashes, do not hesitate to say, in reliance upon the authority of Scripture, that I am one spirit with God, if, that is to say, I have ever been convinced by certain experience, that I am joined to the Lord, after the likeness of one of those who abide in charity, and by this abide in God, and God in them, feeding upon God,[1] and He upon them. For it is of such a union that, as I think, the words are said: *He that is joined unto the Lord is one spirit.* What then? The Son says: *I am in the Father, and the Father in Me: and We are One* (John x. 30, 38), while, as for the man, he says: 'I am in God, and God in me, and we are one spirit.'

7. But is it the case that as the Father and the Son, that They may be the One in the Other, and so be One, reciprocally feed upon each other, so God and man mutually penetrate each other by a kind of reciprocal manducation, and thus exist, if not as one being, yet as one spirit? By no means. For in the one case and in the other the indwelling is not after the same manner, and the unity of each is different. [[In fact,[2] the difference of unity, and the nature of that difference is indicated by the two words, *unus* and *unum* (that is, 'one' and 'the same substance'). For the former does not apply to the union between the Father and the Son, nor the latter to that between God and man. You, if you are already instructed in this mystery, will, if you make use of this opportunity, become so still more fully; and you should remark prudently, that by *unum* is denoted the unity of Substance or of Nature, while by '*unus*' is indeed denoted a unity, but one of a kind very different, because the Essence and Nature of God is far other than that of man, while it is evident that the Essence of the Father and of the Son is One. You see that this union between God and man is not in the fullest sense a unity, at least, not if it be compared with that other unique and sovereign Unity. For how can there be complete unity where there is plurality of nature and difference of substance? And yet a soul that is joined unto the Lord is said to be one spirit with Him, and is so in fact; nor is the plurality of substances any bar to this unity, since it is brought about, not by a confusion of natures, but by an agreement of wills. It is in this sense that many

---

[1] One MS. adds 'after a certain manner'; but the words are wanting in others, and, indeed, in the earliest editions.

[2] The parenthesis that we have here is wanting in the MSS. of Citeaux, of St. Germain, and of Jumieges; but it is found in others, and in the earliest editions. As for the second and much longer one, which follows a little later on, and extends from the middle of *n.* 8 to the middle of *n.* 10, it is, on the contrary, wanting in those earlier MSS. but is found in the later ones. Both the one and the other are superfluous. This diversity is caused by St. Bernard having retouched the passage, so that the first parenthesis of the former edition seems to be the second of the later one. We leave the reader to judge.

hearts are said to be one, and many souls one, as it is written: *The multitude of them that believed were of one heart and of one soul* (Acts iv. 32). This, then, as regards unity.

8. But what is that unity which does not come into being by the act of uniting, but which *is* from all eternity? Nor is it, like the other, produced by an act of mutual manducation, because it is not produced at all, but simply exists. It does not admit of conjunction, nor composition, nor any such thing, which is inconsistent with a perfect unity. To the Father and the Son, Nature, Essence, and Will, are not only one, but the same. For Nature, Essence, and Will, are Their Being and Substance. It must not, then, be said that the Unity, in which the Father and the Son are One, is a consequence following from their Natures, their Substances, or their Wills; it can in no sense be said to be caused or to come into existence, but it simply exists; in a word, it is not factitious, but original.]] The Father and the Son are the One in the Other. They are, in a manner which is not only ineffable, but also incomprehensible, capable of containing and being contained, but if They are capable of containing Each Other it is without Their being divisible; and if They are capable of being contained, it is without participation. For, as the Church sings in a hymn: 'In the FATHER the SON is wholly, and in the WORD is the FATHER wholly.'[1] The Father is in the Son, in whom He is always well pleased; and the Son is in the Father, of whom He is always the Begotten, and from whom He is never separated. Now it is by charity that man is in God and God in man, as says S. John: *He that dwelleth in love dwelleth in God, and God in him* (1 John iv. 16). It is by this consent and oneness of will that they are two in one spirit, or, rather, are one spirit. Do you perceive the distinction? It is not the same thing to be *consubstantial*, that is, of the same substance, and *consenting*, that is, concurring in the same will. Although, if you notice carefully, that difference in their unity is sufficiently indicated to you by the words *unus* and *unum*, since the former does not apply to the union of the Father and the Son, nor the latter to that between God and man. The Father and the Son cannot be said to be *one* [only], since the One is Father, and the Other is Son; yet They are declared to be, and are, one and the same Substance, because it is common to Both, nor has Each His singular Substance. On the contrary, God and man have not the same substance or nature, and, therefore, cannot be said to be *unum*. And yet, if they are attached to each other by the tie of love, they may, with perfect truth, be said to be *one spirit*. But that unity is brought about rather by the concurrence of wills than by the union of essences.

9. There is now made sufficiently clear (if I do not mistake) not only the diversity, but also the disparity, of these unities, the one existing in the same essence, and the other in diverse essences. What can differ more between themselves than the unity which exists between

---

[1] *Hymn. pro Feria Secund. ad Matutin.*

things of different kinds and between those of the same kind? The words *unus* and *unum*, as I have already said, mark the difference between the two kinds of unities, since by the word *unum* the essential unity between the Father and the Son is designated, and by *unus*, not this, but a mutual consent of affections and of will between God and man is so referred to. Nevertheless, it may very well be said that the Father and the Son are 'one' (*unus*), with the addition of some defining word; as, for example, one God, one Lord; and generally, with regard to all that relates equally to Each and not to One in particular. For Their Godhead or Their Majesty is no more diverse in Each than is Their Substance or Essential Nature; and all these, if you consider piously the matter, are not diverse in Them or divided, but are one. I have said too little: they are one and the same with Them. What shall we say of that unity in which, as we read, many hearts and many souls are one? I think that it does not merit the name of unity when compared with this, since it does not unite many things, but marks them singly as being one. Therefore that Unity, which is not brought about by any unifying act, but which exists from all eternity, is unique and supreme. Nor is it the effect of that spiritual manducation of which mention was made before, because it is not brought about, but it exists. Much less is it to be considered as due to any conjunction whatsoever of Essences or consent of Wills, for there is in it neither plurality of the one nor of the other. In Them, as has been said, there is one Essence and one Will; and where these are one there cannot be consent, nor composition, nor conjunction, nor any such thing. There must be at least two wills to unite in a common consent, and similarly there must be two essential existences for that consent to produce union. There is nothing like this in the Father and the Son, since there is in Them neither two Essences nor two [divergent] wills. These two things are in them but one, or, as I remember that I said before, these two things make but one in Them and with Them; and inasmuch as They abide Each in the Other, in a manner unchangeable[1] as it is incomprehensible, they are truly and uniquely One. Yet if anyone wishes to say that between the Father and the Son there is consent, I do not contest this, provided it be understood, not of a union of Wills, but of a unity of Will.

10. And yet we think that God and man abide each mutually in the other, but in a manner far different from that just referred to, because their substances and their Wills are distinct, and they abide each in the other in a manner far different; that is, they are not blended as to substances, but consentaneous as to wills. And this union is to them a communion of wills and a conformity in charity. Happy is this union if you have had experience of it, even though, compared with that more perfect union just referred to, it seem to be nothing at all. It was the saying of one who had experienced this: *It is good for me to draw near to God* (Ps. lxxiii. 28). It is indeed a

[1] *Incommutabiliter*. Another reading is *incomparabiliter*.

great good if you hold fast wholly to Him. Who, then, is it who perfectly does this except the person who, abiding in God as being loved by God, nevertheless draws God into himself by a reciprocal affection? Therefore, when God and man are mutually and perfectly attached (which is the case when they are mutually incorporate by close affection), I may without doubt say that by this God is in man and man in God. But man is indeed in God from all eternity, since he is beloved by God from all eternity, if, that is to say, he is of those who assert that He hath loved and accepted us in His dear Son before the foundation of the world (Eph. i. 4-6). But God is in man from the time that He is beloved by man. And, if this be the case, man indeed is in God even when God is not in man; but God is not in the man who is not in God. For although perhaps he loves for a time, he is not able to remain in the love of God if he is not loved of God; nor even, though loved, is he yet able to love Him. Otherwise, how shall that saying stand good: *He first loved us?* (1 John iv. 19). But when he who was loved before begins also to love, then man is in God and God in man. But he who never loves has plainly never been loved, and it is thus certain that he is not in God, nor is God in him. All this has been said to show the difference between that bond by which the Father and the Son are One, and that by which a soul which attaches itself to God is one spirit with Him, lest perhaps, when we read of the man who abides in love, that he abides in God and God in him, and also of the Son, that He is in the Father and the Father in Him, it should be thought that an adopted son of God enjoys the same prerogative as the Only Begotten.

11. These truths, then, having been made clear, let us return to Him who *feedeth among the lilies,* for it was from that point that we started to make this digression; whether it has been of interest and value it is for you to judge. I have already, as it seems to me, given two explanations of this passage. I have said that the Bridegroom, who is Himself the virtue and Brightness [of His Father], finds nourishment in the virtues of those upon whom He has shed the brightness of sanctity; and also that he receives sinners to penitence in His Body, which is the Church; and that it was to unite them with Himself that He was Himself made sin, who did no sin, that the body of sin might be destroyed in which sinners had once been incorporated, and that they might become righteousness in Him, being justified freely by His grace.

12. A third explanation which occurs to me I proceed to lay before you, and I think that it will suffice, not only for the explanation of the passage, but for the ending of this sermon. The Word of God is truth, and this is the Bridegroom. This you know; listen, then, to what remains. When a person hears this [Truth] and does not obey it, it remains empty and, so to speak, barren; it is sorrowful, and complains that it has been brought forward to no good purpose. But if the hearer has obeyed it, will it not seem to you that the Word has grown and taken to itself a body, because action is joined to word,

inasmuch as it is strengthened and reinforced by the fruits of obedience and the harvest of righteousness? Thence it is that He says in the Apocalypse: *Behold, I stand at the door and knock; if any man hear My Voice, and open the door, I will come in to him, and will sup with him, and he with Me* (Rev. iii. 20). It seems that the Lord gives approval to this explanation where He says in a prophet that His word shall not return unto Him void, but shall prosper, and accomplish that whereto He has sent it (Is. lv. 12). *It shall not return,* He says, *unto Me void or barren,* but as succeeding in all things; it shall be filled with the good actions of those who shall obey it in love. For, according to the usual manner of speaking, a word is said to be fulfilled when it has produced the effect intended by it; while, until it has done this, it is called empty and meagre and, so to speak, famishing.

13. But hear with what food the WORD Himself declares that He is nourished. *My meat,* He says, *is to do the will of Him that sent Me, and to finish His work* (John iv. 34). This is the utterance of the WORD Himself, and declares plainly that every good work is His nourishment; and, furthermore, that He finds it among the lilies, that is, among the virtues. That which is to be found, if it be so, beyond those limits, He *who feedeth among the lilies* will not touch, even though it seem to be, so far, good of its kind. For example, He will not accept alms from the hand of a robber or a usurer; nor, again, from the hand of a hypocrite who, when he bestows alms, causes a trumpet to be sounded before him that he may obtain the praise of men. He will by no means accept the prayer of him who loves to pray at the corners of the streets that he may be seen of men (Matt. vi. 2, 5). For the prayer of the ungodly will be abominable to Him (Prov. xxviii. 9). Without avail, also, will it be for one to offer his gift before the altar who is conscious that his brother has some cause of complaint against him (Matt. v. 23, 24). He had not respect unto the offerings of Cain, for the very reason that he was not well inclined towards his brother (Gen. iv. 5). As is testified by a holy prophet, He delighted not in the sabbaths and new moons and sacrifices of the Jews, so that He protested openly that they were abhorrent to Him, and asked: *When ye come to appear before Me, who hath required this at your hand?* (Is. i. 12). I believe that those hands had not the fragrance of lilies, and for that reason He who was wont to feed, not among thorns, but among lilies, disdained the gifts they proffered. Were not those hands filled with thorns of which He said: *Your hands are full of blood?* The hands of Esau were bristly, as if they had been covered with thorns, and therefore they were not admitted to minister to one who was holy.

14. I fear that there may be some among us also whose gifts the Bridegroom does not accept, because they have not the fragrance of the lilies. For if my own self-will is found, for instance, in the fasts which I make, the Bridegroom will not accept such fasting as that, because it savours not of the lily of obedience, but of the sin of my own self-will. The same thing is to be said, not only of fasting, but

of silence, of vigils, of prayer, of reading, of manual labour, and, in short, of every observance of the monastic life, where there is found in it, not obedience to a superior, but the prompting of our own self-will. I should consider that those observances, although good in themselves, are not to be numbered among lilies, that is, among virtues; but that the man whose services are of such a kind would hear from the Prophet the question: 'Is it such a service as this that I have chosen? saith the Lord' (Is. lviii. 3-5); and he adds: 'In the day of your fast ye find pleasure.' Self-will is a great evil, since it causes your good works not to be good for you. Such works need to [be altered, and] become lilies; for He who feedeth among the lilies will not taste of anything which is defiled with self-will. Wisdom is everywhere; she passeth and goeth through all things by reason of her pureness, nor can any defiled thing fall into her (Wisd. vii. 24, 25). So, then, the Bridegroom loves to feed among the lilies, that is, in pure and clear hearts. But how long shall this be? *Until the day break and the shadows flee away.* This passage is full of shadows and of difficulties; let us not enter into the thick wood of this profound mystery, except in the full light of day. But now, as my sermon has been unusually prolonged, the day has drawn to a close, and we are obliged unwillingly to withdraw from these lilies. I have not hesitated to expatiate at greater length than usual, because the fragrance of these flowers prevents anyone from being wearied or annoyed. There seems but little remaining of the verse before us; but of that little the meaning is deeply hidden, as is the case with all other parts of this poem. But He who reveals mysteries will come to our help, as I trust, when we shall have begun to knock [at the door]; nor will He shut the mouths of them that speak of Him. Rather is He wont to open those that are closed. He is the Bridegroom of the Church, JESUS CHRIST our Lord, who is above all, God blessed for ever. AMEN.

SERMON LXXII.

THE MEANING OF THE WORDS 'THE DAY BREAKS AND THE SHADOWS FLEE AWAY.' THE VARIOUS DAYS IN THE LIVES OF MEN EXPOUNDED. THAT THE RIGHTEOUS LIVE IN LIGHT, AND THAT A BRIGHTER DAY AWAITS THEM; BUT THAT THE WICKED, WHO ARE DEVOTED TO WORKS OF DARKNESS, CAN LOOK FORWARD ONLY TO ETERNAL NIGHT.

'*My Beloved is Mine, and I am His: He feedeth among the lilies: until the day break and the shadows flee away.*'—Cant. ii. 16, 17.

THE last part only of these clauses remains to be treated, and I am in doubt, in entering upon it, to which of the two preceding ones it ought to be joined, for I may connect it indifferently with either. For whether you say, *My Beloved is mine, and I am His, until the day break and the shadows flee away*, interposing only, *He feedeth among the lilies*, or following the literal order, *He feedeth among the lilies, until the day break and the shadows flee away*, you have in either case a sense perfectly good. There is only this difference, that if you join the '*until*' to the former sentence, *the day* is included in the sense; but if to the latter, *the day* is excluded from it. Are we to suppose that, in intimating that the Bridegroom will cease to feed among the lilies when the day shall have dawned, it is intended to declare that He will also cease to belong to the Bride and she to Him? By no means. Their relation shall endure for ever, with the sole difference that it shall then be as much happier as it shall be stronger, and as much stronger as it is freer and less impeded. It is necessary, then, to understand this word 'until' in the same way as that passage in the Gospel of St. Matthew where it is said that Joseph knew not Mary *until she had brought forth her firstborn Son* (Matt. i. 25). For he knew her not afterwards. Or, as in that verse of a Psalm: *Our eyes wait upon the Lord our God, until that He have mercy upon us* (Ps. cxxiii. 2); but not that they should be turned away from Him when He has begun to have mercy. Or, again, as that saying of our Lord to His Apostles: *Lo, I am with you alway, even unto*[1] *the end of the world*, for He will not cease to be with them after that event has taken place. But now see how this word *until* is to be understood if you connect it with the words, *My Beloved is mine, and I am His*. For if you refer it to *He feedeth among the lilies*, another sense must be put upon it. Now, there will be a good deal of difficulty in showing in what manner the Beloved ceases to feed among the lilies when the day begins to break. Is the day spoken of that of the Resurrection? But, then, why should it not please Him much more to pasture among the lilies, seeing that there is then a much greater abundance of them? So much as relates to the connection of the clauses.

2. Consider, now, with me, how, although (after the consummation of all things), the Bridegroom is in the midst of a Kingdom which is glorious with lilies, in which He takes the greatest joy and delight, yet it is not said that He feeds [among] them, as He had been accustomed to do up to that time. For where, then, are those sinners whom Christ makes one with Himself, having, so to speak, ground and masticated them with the teeth of an austere discipline, that is to say, with affliction of the flesh and heartfelt contrition? Nor, again, will the Bridegroom, who is the Word, any longer require for Himself the food of various works or actions of obedience, where the only action will be to enjoy repose, and the occupation [of the blessed] to contemplate God and be fully satisfied in Him. His food is, indeed, to do the will of His Father; but this refers to the present state, not to the future: for how can He be engaged in doing that which is fully done? And it is clear that then it will be complete and perfected. It is in that state that all the saints will know clearly what

---

[1] ἕως, until; Matt. xxviii. 20.

is that Will of God which is good, and acceptable, and perfect (Rom. xii. 2). And assuredly nothing remains to be done of that which is fully perfected. The occupation that is left is to find enjoyment in it, not to bring it about; to experience it, not to carry it into effect; to live in that Divine Will, not to exercise one's self in accomplishing it. Is it not of that very Will that we are taught of the Lord to pray earnestly that it may be done, as in heaven, so in earth (Matt. vi. 10), so that the carrying it out may not be a labour to us, but the fruits of it be then a delight? So, then, the Bridegroom, the Word, will no longer require the food of good works, because there every work will necessarily cease where all are filled with the abundance of wisdom. For they who are less in action shall receive wisdom (Ecclus. xxxviii. 25).

3. But let us now see if what we say is capable of standing with that sense of the words 'He feedeth among the lilies' in which some interpret them; namely, that He rejoices in the excellence, and, so to speak, in the whiteness of virtues. For we, too, have not passed over that sense among others. Shall we say, then, either that there are no virtues, or that the Bridegroom does not take pleasure in them? Either alternative is altogether extravagant. But see whether He does not take delight in them in any other manner; and if, instead of their being food to Him, they do not perhaps, and so to speak, serve Him as drink. During this life, and in this mortal body, there is no virtue of ours which is so purified from mortal frailty, and rendered so pure and sweet as to serve for the use of the Word in this way. But He who wills that all men shall be saved overlooks many things, and devotes His efforts, as it were, with pains and skill, to extract from that which cannot be used as a beverage somewhat agreeable and worthy to be food. A time shall come when virtue shall be capable of being pure and clear, so that instead of being masticated with labour and fatigue, or, rather, instead of wearying the eater, it shall give to him delight without weariness, but it is no longer as food that is eaten, but as a draught that is swallowed. It is that which the Lord promises in the Gospel: *I will not drink henceforth of this fruit of the vine until that day when I drink it new with you in My Father's Kingdom* (Matt. xxvi. 29). And He makes no mention of food. We read also in a Psalm: *Like a mighty man that shouteth by reason of wine* (Ps. lxxviii. 65); but here also food is not mentioned. The Bride is, then, conscious of this mystery when, having found and declared that her Beloved feedeth among the lilies, she names a time until which He deigns to do this, or, rather, has recognised and stated the time already fixed, saying, *until the day break, and the shadows flee away*. For she knew that after, He would rather drink (so to speak) of virtues than feed upon them. That, it may be said, agrees with the usual custom, that drink should follow food. He, then, who takes food here on earth shall taste of drink in heaven, and with as much greater sweetness as security; inasmuch as then He shall drink with ease, while now He partakes of them with labour, and, as it were, eats of them but in morsels.

4. Let us now set ourselves to consider what is that day and what are those shadows of which the Bride speaks: in what manner the one breaks, that is, appears, and by what power the others flee away. The expression here used is significant and singular, for it is only in this passage, I believe, that you will find the day spoken of as *breathing*.[1] For the winds are said to breathe, not the times. Man breathes, other animals breathe; and it is the air continually breathed which enables them to live. And what is this but wind? The Holy Spirit also breathes, and hence His Name. In what way, then, is the day, which is not a spirit, nor a wind, nor, indeed, a living creature at all, said to breathe? Although it is not, indeed, said to breathe, but, which is still more remarkable, to *aspire* [*spirans; aspirans*]. Nor is it less extraordinary that it is said, *and the shadows flee away*, since, at the rising of this visible and material light the shadows do not flee away, but are dissipated. The explanation of these things is to be sought outside the sphere of things corporeal. If we shall be able to find a spiritual day and spiritual shadows, then what is meant by the *aspiration* of one and the *fleeing away* of the other will become clearer. If it be considered that the day of which the Psalmist says: *A day in Thy courts is better than a thousand* (Ps. lxxxiv. 10), is a literal one, I know not what ought not to be understood in a literal sense. There is a day also which is taken in an evil sense, and which is named with malediction by the Prophets (Job iii. 3 and Jer. xx. 14). But let us by no means think that it is one of those visible days which the Lord has made. It is a day in a spiritual sense.

5. Who can doubt also that the shadow which rested upon Mary when she conceived (Luke i. 35) was a spiritual one? And so was it with that which is thus mentioned in the Prophet: *Under His shadow we shall live among the heathen* (Lam. iv. 20). But I think, nevertheless, that in this place by 'shadows' is meant those hostile powers which are called not 'shadows' only, but 'darkness' by an Apostle, where he speaks of *the rulers of the darkness of this world* (Eph. vi. 12); and that they designate also those of our race who are attached to these; who are children of the night, not of light, nor of the day. For when the day shall appear, these shadows shall not be entirely destroyed, while we see that material shadows not only disappear from the presence of the light of this world, but perish altogether. They shall not, then, be entirely destroyed, but shall be more miserable than if they were. They shall exist, but in a state degraded and subdued. Thus the Psalmist saith (and no doubt he refers to the prince of these shadows) 'he will crouch and fall when he shall have power over the poor' (Ps. ix. 10, Douay). His nature shall not, then, be annihilated, but his power taken away; his substance shall not perish, but the hour of darkness and its power shall pass. They are cast down that they may not see the glory of God; they are not blotted out of existence, that they may dwell for ever in the flame. Shall not the shadows be laid prostrate when the mighty

---

[1] *Aspiret*, Vulgate.

are cast down from their seat, and have been made a footstool? Speedily shall that come to pass. It is the last time : the night is far spent, the day is at hand. The day shall wax, the night wane[1] (Rom. xiii. 12). The night signifies the devil, the angel of Satan, though he transform himself into an angel of light. The night is Antichrist, whom the Lord shall consume with the spirit of His Mouth, and shall destroy with the brightness of His coming (2 Thess. ii. 8). And is not the Lord the day? Evidently He is the Day, which breathes and brightens, which puts to flight the shadows by the Breath of His Mouth, and destroys the phantoms [of the night] by the brightness of His coming. Or if you prefer to take the phrase 'flee away' in the sense of 'to be extinguished,' I do not oppose this. We see that the dark sayings and figures of Scripture are shadows ; so also are those ambiguous modes of speaking, those subtle phrases, and involved arguments, which obscure the light of truth rather than discover it. For in part we know, and in part we prophesy. But when the day breaks the shadows shall flee away ; for when the fulness of light is occupying every place, there is no spot left where shadows may linger. For when *that which is perfect is come, then that which is in part shall be done away* (1 Cor. xiii. 9, 10).

6. That would suffice, if the Scripture said simply that the day 'breathes,' and not that it 'aspires.'[2] But now I think it needful to add a few words to explain the reason of this small addition, and of the distinction which it indicates. For I, to speak truly, have long been persuaded that in the sacred and precious text of the Scripture not the smallest particle is without meaning and importance. Now, we are accustomed to make use of this word, to express the seeking something with eager desire, as, for example, when we say that such and such a person 'aspires' to this honour, or that dignity. There is denoted, then, by this word a marvellous abundance and power of the Holy Spirit to be manifested hereafter in that day when not only our souls, but even our bodies shall become spiritual, according to their manner, and when those who shall be found worthy shall be inebriated with the fulness of the House of the Lord, and shall drink to the full of the river of His pleasures.

7. There is still another way in which this passage may be taken. The sanctified day has already shone upon the holy Angels, breathing upon them, like a mighty wind, the sweetly flowing secrets of the eternal Divinity. For the Psalmist says : *The river of the flood thereof maketh glad the City of God* (Ps. xlvi. 4); but he refers to that City, to which it is said : Like as the habitation of all that rejoice is in thee (Ps. lxxxvii. 7). But when that day shall have breathed upon us also who dwell on the earth, it shall be not only a day of *breathing*, but also a day of *aspiring*, because it shall, as it were, open its bosom and admit us also. Or rather (that we may go farther back and treat of the course of events more at length) after the Creator had

---

[1] *Aspirabit, exspirabit.*
[2] *Spirans, aspirans.* The play upon words is untranslatable.—ED.

made man of the dust of the earth, He, as the truthful history narrates, *breathed into his nostrils the breath of life* (Gen. ii. 7). That then became for him a day *of inspiration.* But, lo, an envious night, pretending to be light, dashed against this day, for in promising to man a light of knowledge far more brilliant than he had, it enveloped our first parents, by the perfidious counsel given to them, with sudden darkness, with a deep and terrible obscurity. Woe! woe to them! they have not known nor understood; they walk on ignorantly in obscurity, taking darkness for light, and light for darkness. For the woman ate of the tree which the serpent had suggested (*dederat*) to her, which God had forbidden, and gave of it to her husband, and a new day, as it were, began to shine for them. For then the eyes of them both were opened, and that day became for them a day of conspiring, which destroyed the day of inspiration, and substituted for it an expiring day. Assuredly the subtlety of the serpent, the blandishments of the woman, and the weakness of the man, conspired and assembled together against the Lord, and against His Christ. Wherefore also the Lord and His Christ spake together: *Behold, the man is become as one of us* (Gen. iii. 22), because he had assented to the enticements of sinners, to the injury of each.

8. In this day we all are born. We all bear, in fact, impressed upon us as by cautery, the brand of that ancient conspiracy: Eve still lives in our flesh, and the serpent strives without ceasing, through the concupiscence which we derive from birth, to make us consenting parties to his rebellion. It is for that reason, as I have said, that the saints of the ancient law cursed that day, wishing that it might be short, and speedily turned to night, because it is a day of contention and contradiction, in which the flesh does not cease to revolt against the spirit, and during which the contrary law which abides in our members is in continual and unwearied contradiction to the law of our spirit. That is why it has become an *expiring day.* For then and thenceforth, what man is there who shall live and never see death? (Ps. lxxxix. 48). Let anyone say that pleases, that this is an effect of the wrath of God; I should nevertheless say that it is the effect of His mercy; so that the elect, on account of whom all things are done, should not so long be tormented by a contradiction full of trouble by which they also are led captive by the law of sin, which is in their members. For they abhor and endure with great reluctance that shameful captivity, that melancholy contradiction.

9. Let us hasten, then, to *respire* free from that old and injurious conspiration, because the days of man are few and brief (Job xiv. 1). Let the day of free respiration receive us and enlighten us, before a night of deep horror (*suspirans*) swallow us up, wrapping around us the thick glooms of the outer and everlasting darkness. Do you ask to what does this phrase (of *respiration*) refer, and in whom is it found? It consists in this, that the spirit begins in turn to mortify the deeds of the flesh. If you feel repugnance to these, you are breathing; if you are mortifying them by the spirit; if you crucify

the flesh with its affections and lusts, you have breathed. *I keep under my body*, says St. Paul, *and bring it into subjection, lest that by any means, when I have preached to others, I myself should be a castaway* (1 Cor. ix. 27). That is the utterance of a man who is breathing the free breath of the spirit; yea, rather who had already done so. *Go thou, and do likewise* (Luke x. 37), that you may show that you have breathed this inspiring air, and know that this day of inspiration has shone upon you. The night of death shall not prevail against this day of revival; it shines in the darkness, and the darkness comprehendeth it not. This light of life shall not fail even when life departs, and I think that to no one more fitly, than to him who dies thus, can these words be assigned: *Even the night shall be light about me* (Ps. cxxxix. 11). Why should he not see more clearly, being delivered from the shadow, or rather from the corruption of the body? When freed from corporeal bonds, he will doubtless be as free among the dead, and as one who sees among the blind. For like as once in former times, when throughout Egypt none could see clearly, the people of Israel alone had light amid the universal gloom, and beheld [the great work of] God; for the Scripture says: *All the children of Israel had light in their dwellings* (Exod. x. 23), so the righteous shall shine among the sons of darkness, and in the midst of the thick shadow of death, and shall have so much the clearer power of vision, as they are delivered from the shadows of the body. But as for those who have not previously breathed that inspiring air, nor sought for the light of that day, and on whom, therefore, the Sun of Righteousness has not risen; they shall pass from these shadows into deeper shadows still, so that those who are in darkness shall be in darkness still; while those who see, shall see more and more.

10. To this may be applied, not unfitly, the words spoken by Our Lord, that *whosoever hath, to him shall be given, and he shall have more abundance; but whosoever hath not, from him shall be taken away even that he hath* (Matt. xiii. 12). Thus it is also in death: for new light is added to those who already see, while from those who do not see is taken away the little which they seemed to have. For in proportion as the one class see less and less, so do the other see more and more clearly, until the night of sighs receives the one, and the day of light and aspiration the other; and these are the two extremes; that is, total blindness, and perfect sight. Then there will be nothing more to be taken away from those who have already been emptied of all, nor anything to be added to those who are filled; unless, indeed, the latter may expect to receive something more even beyond fulness, according to the promise made to them by the Saviour: *Good measure, pressed down, and shaken together, and running over, shall men give into your bosom* (Luke vi. 38). Does it not appear to you that the vessel which runs over must be something more than full? But you will hear calmly of this fulness superabounding, when you remember that you have read: [*The Lord shall reign*] *for ever and beyond* (Exod. xv. 18). He then shall be the

increase and crown of the day of aspiration. That day shall add, I say, to the measure of the fulness *inspired*, as to the abundance of the day *inspiring ;* working for us a far more exceeding and eternal weight of glory, so that the superabounding addition of honour should redound upon bodies also. For this cause it is, and to signify this, that the Holy Spirit has said, not '*spirans*,' but '*aspirans*,' adding the proposition '*ad*,' because those whom that day enlightens inwardly, it also adorns outwardly, and clothes them with a robe of glory.

11. I believe that will be sufficient by way of giving a reason for the word 'aspiring.' And if you wish to know, the day of *aspiration* is the Saviour Himself, for whom we wait; who shall change the body of our humility, that it may be fashioned like unto the Body of His glory (Phil. iii. 20, 21). He is also the day of *inspiration*, and by His operation makes us to respire previously in the light which He inspires, so that we also may be in Him a day of *respiration*, inasmuch as our inward man is renewed from day to day, and is renewed in the spirit of its mind according to the likeness of Him who created it, becoming day from the day and light from the light. There are, then, two days, one succeeding the other, in us: the day of *inspiration*, which is for the life of the body, and that of *respiration*, which is the sanctification by grace; and there remains a third, which shall be in the glory of the resurrection: it is manifest that the great mystery of the Divine goodness, which has been accomplished in the Head, shall be accomplished also sometime in the members of His Body, and the testimony of the prophet shall be fulfilled, who says: *After two days will He revive us ; in the third day He will raise us up, and we shall live in His sight ; then shall we know, if we follow on to know the Lord* (Hosea vi. 2, 3). It is He whom the Angels desire to contemplate, the Bridegroom of the Church, JESUS CHRIST our Lord, who is above all, God blessed for ever. AMEN.

SERMON LXXIII.

HOW CHRIST SHALL COME TO JUDGE IN HUMAN FORM, THAT HE MAY APPEAR DELIGHTFUL TO THE ELECT ; AND HOW HE IS LESS THAN THE ANGELS, YET LOFTIER THAN THEY.

'*Return, my Beloved, and be Thou like a roe or a young hart upon the mountains of Bether.*'—Cant. iii. 17.

WHAT? He is but just now gone, and you call Him back? What sudden need has arisen in so short a time? Have you forgotten anything? Yea, truly, the Bride has forgotten everything which is not He, even her own self. And though she is not devoid of reason, yet sometimes she seems for the moment to be deprived of it. Nor does it even appear that she retains in her feelings that modest self-restraint, which is always apparent in her actions. It is the violence of her love which occasions this. It is the same which in its triumph puts to silence every feeling of timidity, every consideration of fitness, or of deliberation; it causes her even to neglect times and seasons. For, as you see, the Bridegroom has scarcely left her side, than she calls upon Him eagerly to return. She entreats him even to hasten, to run with all the speed of the swiftest animals, such as the roe or the young hart. This is the literal meaning of the words, and this is the portion of the Jews.

2. But I will, as far as I have received from the Lord, seek out the spirit and the life in the deep and mysterious meaning of the sacred text; this is the portion which belongs to me, as a believer in Jesus Christ. Why should I not extract the sweet and salutary nourishment of the Spirit from the barren and tasteless mass of the letter, as I separate grain from chaff, the kernel from its shell, or marrow from the bone? With this mere letter, which, when tasted, savours only of the flesh, and when swallowed, brings death, I do not desire to have anything to do, but only with that teaching from the Holy Ghost which is hidden in it. For as the Apostle declares, The Spirit speaketh in a mystery (1 Cor. xiv. 2); but Israel, in place of the mystery, which is veiled, takes the veil which covers the mystery. Why is this, except that a veil is still upon their heart? Thus the literal meaning of the text is theirs, but its inner signification is mine; and thus there is to them a ministration of death in the letter, but to me life in the Spirit. For it is the Spirit which quickeneth (John vi. 64), inasmuch as it gives understanding; and is not understanding life? *Give me understanding and I shall live*, is the Psalmist's prayer to the Lord. Understanding does not remain on the surface of things, it is not superficial, it does not handle the outside with uncertain touch, like a blind man; but it penetrates to their depths, and often brings up from thence treasures of truth with eager grasp, as did the Psalmist when he said unto the Lord: *I rejoice at Thy word as one that findeth great spoil* (Ps. cxix. 144, 162). It is thus that the kingdom of truth suffereth violence, and the violent take it by force (Matt. xi. 12). But that elder brother in the Gospel (Luke xv. 25-30) who returned from the field is the type of that ancient and earthly-minded people which has learned to labour for an earthly heritage only, and groans with careworn and furrowed brow under the heavy yoke of the Law, which it bears throughout the burden and heat of the day. This people, I say, because it has no understanding, stands without even to the present time, and will not, even when invited by the Father, enter into the house of banqueting, thus depriving himself hitherto of any share in the music, and the dancing, and the fatted calf. Unhappy that he is, he refuses to make experience how good and joyful it is for brethren to dwell together in unity. All this has been said to show the distinction between the portion of the Church and that of the synagogue;

that the blindness of the one and the prudence of the other might be made more evident; and the happiness of the one be made more plain by contrast with the pitiable folly of the other.

3. Let us now examine the words of the Bride, and endeavour so to expound the chaste sentiments of her sacred love, that there may appear nothing that is contrary to reason in the sacred text, nor anything importunate or unbecoming. And if we bear in mind that hour when the Lord Jesus (for He is the Bridegroom) passed from this world unto the Father (John xiii. 1), and at the same time the state of mind in which the Church, His newly-wedded Bride, necessarily was when she saw herself deserted and left as a desolate widow, deprived of her only hope (I refer to the Apostles who had left all and followed Him, and had continued with Him in His temptations); if, I say, we consider these things, it will appear to us, I think, that it is not unreasonable nor unaccountable that the Bride should be so inconsolable for His departure, nor so urgent for His return, when she is left so solitary and in such distress. The affection that she feels for Him, and the need that she has for Him, forms, then, a twofold reason for thus appealing to Him; that since He cannot but ascend up where He was before, He will at least hasten His promised return. For that she desires and entreats that He would be like unto certain animals, and those the animals which are of greatest speed, is an indication of the eagerness of her desire, for which no return would be sufficiently prompt. Does she not ask for this daily when she prays, *Thy kingdom come* (Matt. vi. 10)?

4. Yet I think that she desires to point not less significantly to weakness as well as to speed, and that as well of sex in the *roe* as of age in the *young hart*. She desires, then, as it seems to me, that when returning to judgment He should appear, not in the Form of God, but in that Human Form in which He was not only born, but born as a little Child, and born only from that female sex which is the weaker of the two. Why is this? It is in order that from both the one and the other there may be a reminder to be gentle towards the weak even in the day of His wrath, and in the time of judgment to exalt mercy above judgment. For if He shall be strict to search out offences, who even of the elect shall stand in His presence (Ps. cxxx. 2)? The stars are not pure in His sight, and in His Angels He finds pravity (Job iv. 18; xxv. 5). Listen, then, to him who is elect and holy; hear what he says to God: *Thou forgavest the iniquity of my sin. For this shall everyone that is godly pray unto Thee, in a time when Thou mayest be found* (Ps. xxxii. 5, 6). Even the saints, therefore, need to entreat pardon for their sins, that they may be saved by the mercy of God, and must not trust in their own righteousness; for all have sinned, and all need mercy. In order, then, that when He is angry He may remember mercy, the Bride entreats of Him to appear in the garb of mercy, that is, in the Form of which the Apostle says: *Being found in fashion as a man* (Phil. ii. 7).

5. And, indeed, it is very necessary for us that it should be thus; for if, even with this moderating influence, so great is His equity in judgment, so awful the severity of the Judge, so lofty His majesty, and so changed the very appearance of all things, that, according to the Prophet, the day of His Coming does not bear to be thought upon (Mal. iii. 2, Douay), what would it be, do you imagine, if He who is a consuming fire (I mean the Almighty God) should come in all that immensity, and power, and purity of His Godhead, to put forth His power against a leaf (so to speak) which the wind driveth away, and to pursue the dry stubble (Job xiii. 25)? He is Man also, and who, says the Prophet, shall behold Him? *Who shall stand when He appeareth?* (Mal. iii. 2). How much less, then, could any among men endure the sight if He should manifest Himself to us without His Humanity: as God, unapproachable in His Glory, unattainable in His loftiness, incomprehensible in the greatness of His Majesty? But now, when His wrath is kindled but a little (Ps. ii. 12), how welcome and sweet towards the children of grace shall appear a glimpse of His Humanity! How it shall be to them a confirmation of faith, a strength to their hope, an increase in their confidence, because His grace and mercy is with His saints, and He hath respect unto His chosen (Wisd. iv. 15)! In fact, God the Father Himself hath given the power of judgment unto His Son; and not because He is His Son, but because He is the Son of Man (John v. 27). O truly He is the Father of mercies! He wills that men should be judged by a Man, in order that amid fear and apprehension of evils so great confidence might be given to the elect by the resemblance of nature. Holy David had predicted this formerly, in words which were equally a prayer and a prophecy: *Give the King Thy judgments, O Lord: and Thy righteousness unto the King's son* (Ps. lxxii. 1). To the same effect is the promise made by the Angels to the Apostles when, after Jesus had been taken up into heaven, they spake to the latter thus: *This same Jesus, which is taken up from you into heaven, shall so come, in like manner as ye have seen Him go into heaven* (Acts i. 11); that is to say, in that very form and substance of body.

6. It is very clear, from all these things, that the Bride had a certain access to the Divine plan, and that she was not ignorant of the mystery of God's supreme Will, which [hath chosen] the weak and harmless things of the world (1 Cor. i. 27); inasmuch as she indicates, in the spirit of prophecy, and in the words of one who utters prayer, that the nature which is weaker, or rather that which is lower (for then it shall no longer be weak), shall be set on high to judge; insomuch that He who shall shake heaven and earth by His power, while girded with power against the sinful and impenitent, shall yet show Himself gentle and kind, and, as it were, harmless, towards the elect. To this it may be added that, in order to discern the one from the other, He will need not only, as it were, the agility of the roe, but the piercing sight of the hart, so as to be able to discern, in so vast a multitude, and at the moment of so great a change

of condition, whom to fix upon, and whom to pass over, that He may not crush the righteous instead of the wicked, when He shall tread down the peoples in His wrath. For as to the wicked, it is necessary that the prophecy of David, or rather the word of the Lord speaking by his mouth, should be fulfilled; that *I will beat them small as the dust before the wind: I will cast them out as the clay in the streets* (Ps. xviii. 42, Vulg.); and also that another word, which He had spoken before by another prophet, should be accomplished, when, returning towards the Angels, He shall say [of the wicked]: *I have trampled on them in My indignation, and have trodden them down in My wrath* (Is. lxiii. 3, Vulg.).

7. But if anyone thinks that it would be preferable to understand the words of the Bride in this sense, that our fawn should pass over the wicked, and choose out the good in His bounds, I do not contest this, provided that discrimination is understood to be thus made between the evil and the good. For, if I remember rightly, such was also the sense which I put upon the words when I was expounding this verse in a former discourse (Sermon LIV.). But there that One is said to leap as a fawn upon some, and to pass over others, according to the dispensation of grace, and by the secret, though just, judgment of God; while here it is according to the final and varying recompense of merits. And perhaps the last words of the verse, which I had, indeed, almost forgotten, may seem to support that sense; for after having said, *Be Thou, my Beloved, like a roe or a young hart*, she adds, *upon the mountains of Bethel.* Now, in 'the House of the Lord' (which is the meaning of the word Bethel[1]) there are no mountains which are evil. Therefore the Bridegroom, leaping as a fawn upon them, does not crush and trample them, but causes them to rejoice, that the Scripture might be fulfilled which says: *The mountains and the hills shall break out before God into singing.*[2] There are, indeed, mountains which, according to the Gospel, faith, though it be as a grain of mustard seed, is able to remove (Matt. xvii. 20), but these are not the mountains of Bethel: and whichsoever these latter are, faith does not at all remove them, but renders them fruitful.

8. If by the mountains of Bethel be meant the Principalities and Powers, and all other bands of the blessed Spirits, as it is of them that we are to understand what is said, *Her foundations are upon the holy mountains* (Ps. lxxxvii. 1), this One, who appears as a fawn upon mountains so excelling in dignity, is assuredly not of small account or to be despised, being *made so much better than the Angels, as He hath by inheritance obtained a more excellent Name than they* (Heb. i. 4). For what if we do read in a Psalm that He is *made a little lower than the Angels* (Ps. viii. 5)? That He is in a lower place does not con-

---

[1] The word in the verse commented upon is not *Bethel*, 'House of God,' but *Bether*, 'House of division, or separation'; but most commentators treat them as identical. The latter word is not found elsewhere in Scripture. See the discussion in Corn. à Lapide, *in loc.*—ED.

[2] Is. lv. 12. The reading is, *before you.*

flict at all with His being better than they; nor have the Apostle and the Psalmist spoken in opposite senses, since they were animated by the same Spirit. For it was by His condescension, and not by any necessity, that He was made lower than the Angels; and far from that rendering His goodness less, it, on the contrary, renders it greater. Nor does the Psalmist say that He is less than the Angels, but that He is rendered lower than they; he extols the grace of His goodness without depreciating His greatness. For His Nature does not permit that He should be less than the Angels: and the cause of His being set below them explains and excuses that descent. He was, in fact, set below them by His own will, and on account of our necessity. Thus that abasement is but the effect of the compassion which He felt for us. What loss, then, is there by this humiliation? For His clemency and goodness has gained whatsoever His dignity may seem to have lost. Nor has the Apostle passed over in silence this great mystery of such extreme goodness, but says: *We see Jesus, who was made a little lower than the Angels for the suffering of death, crowned with glory and honour* (Heb. ii. 9).

9. Let this suffice in explanation of the comparison which the Bride makes of the Bridegroom to a fawn, and to show that she does thereby no injury to His dignity. Why do I say without injury to His dignity, when not even His weakness has remained without honour? He is [called] a fawn, He was a little Child. He is spoken of as like unto a roe, inasmuch as He was *made of a woman:* and yet He is *upon the mountains of Bethel*, yet He is *made higher than the heavens* (Heb. vii. 26). He does not say, 'who is' or 'who exists'[1] in the Heavens, but he says, *made higher than the heavens*, that it might not be thought that this was spoken of that Nature in which *He is that which He is*. But where he represents Him as preferred to the Angels, he does not say that He 'remains' or 'exists,' but that He is *made* better than they. From which it appears that not only according to that which He is from all eternity, but also according to that which He is in time, He is exalted far above all Principalities and Powers, and being the Firstborn of every creature, He is above every created being. Therefore *the foolishness of God is wiser than men: and the weakness of God is stronger than men* (1 Cor. i. 25). That the Apostle indeed asserts; but it seems to me that it would not be wrong to extend the assertion to the strength and the wisdom of the Angels. So, then, the present passage may conveniently be applied to the universal Church.

10. Now, as far as relates to the individual soul (for even one soul, if it love God dearly, wisely, and with passion, is the Bride), whosoever is spiritual may notice in himself what his own experience teaches upon this subject. As for me, I do not fear to make known to you

[1] In all the MSS. and in the earliest editions the reading here is *ens;* but Horst and others have *manens.* Thus you have *ens* in Sermon LXXV., *n.* 11, for which the editors have inserted *sedens.* Yet here (Sermon LXXIII. 9) is read a little farther on in the MSS., *manens vel existens.*

the experience of this kind which God has deigned to bestow upon me. For although it may perhaps appear trifling and worthless when heard, that does not affect me at all, because he who is spiritual will not despise me, while he who is not so will not understand me. But let me reserve this subject to another sermon, and perhaps there will not be wanting some who will be edified by that which the Lord, in answer to prayers, shall deign to inspire me with. For He is the Bridegroom of the Church, JESUS CHRIST our Lord, who is above all, God blessed for ever. AMEN.

SERMON LXXIV.

OF THE VISITATIONS OF THE BRIDEGROOM, THE WORD, TO THE HOLY SOUL, AND THE SECRECY WITH WHICH THEY ARE MADE. ST. BERNARD STATES HIS OWN EXPERIENCE OF THIS, WITH GREAT HUMILITY AND MODESTY, FOR THE EDIFICATION OF HIS HEARERS.

'*Return, my Beloved.*'—Cant. ii. 17.

SHE says, *Return*. It is manifest that He, whom she thus recalls, is not present; and yet that He had been present, not long before, since she seems to call Him back, in the moment of His departure. A recall which appears so untimely is a sign of the great love of the one, and of the great charm of the other. Who are they who are such followers after charity, whose affection is so devoted and so untiring, that it allows neither intermission nor rest in the pursuit of it? I remember that I promised to apply this verse to the Word and to the soul; but I confess that I have great need of the help of the WORD Himself in order that this may be done with ever so little an approach to a worthy treatment of the subject. Certainly this task would have befitted one who had more experience and a fuller knowledge of the secrets of Divine love than I; but I cannot allow myself to be wanting in what my office requires of me, nor do I wish to refuse your earnest requests. I see the danger before me; but you oblige me, so that I cannot avoid it. You oblige me (to use the words of the Psalmist) to exercise myself in great matters, and in things too high for me (Ps. cxxxi. 1). Alas! I fear that it may be said to me: 'Wherefore dost thou relate My delights, and take My mysteries into thy mouth?' Yet listen to me, for though I tremble to speak, I am unable to be silent. Perhaps my apprehension itself will be an excuse for my boldness, especially if it tend to your edification; and perhaps God will have regard to these tears also. *Return*, says the Bride. It is well. He departed; He is recalled. Who shall discover to me the mystery of this mutability? Who shall explain to me worthily the going and the returning of the

Word? Surely there cannot be inconstancy in the Bridegroom? Whither can He go, or whence return, He who fills all things? Or what movement locally in space can there be for Him who is Spirit? Or what movement of any kind whatsoever can be attributed to Him who is God? For He is absolutely immutable.

2. Let him comprehend these things who is capable of so doing. But let us in the exposition of this sacred and mystical discourse proceed carefully and with simplicity of purpose, and follow the example of the Scripture itself, which declares the hidden wisdom in our human words, indeed, but in a mystery; and which, in order to make God known to our powers of apprehension, makes use of figurative language, and imparts to human minds those precious truths, the unknown and invisible things of God, by means of similitudes drawn from things apparent to the senses, and, so to speak, proffers the draught of truth in cups formed of a material of little value. Let us, then, follow the example of this discourse; let us say that the WORD of God, who is God, and the Bridegroom of the soul, comes and goes to and from the soul as it pleases Him, provided only that we bear in mind that these events take place by the inward sense of the soul, not by the movements of the Word. For example, when the soul feels the influence of grace, it recognises that the Word is present; and when it does not feel this influence, it complains of His absence, and asks Him to return again, saying with the Psalmist: *My heart said unto Thee, Thy Face, Lord, will I seek* (Ps. xxvii. 8). And how should the soul do otherwise than seek Him, inasmuch as when that Spouse so dearly loved by her is withdrawn, it is not possible for her, I do not say to wish for, but even to think of, any other. Nothing then remains to her but to seek Him earnestly when He is absent, to recall Him when He departs. Thus, then, the Word is recalled; namely, by the earnest longing of the soul; that is to say, of the soul which has once had the happiness to taste how sweet is His goodness. Is not an earnest desire a voice? It is indeed, and a powerful one. For the Lord, says the Psalmist, has *heard the desire of the humble* (Ps. x. 17). When, then, the WORD departs, the one and constant cry of the soul, its single desire, its one and continual demand, is as it were a constantly repeated *Return*, until He come.

3. Show me now a soul that the Bridegroom-Word is wont frequently to visit, to whom intimate knowledge of Him has given boldness, in whom tasting has caused hunger, and contempt for all things repose, and I shall instantly assign to it the voice and the name of Bride, and apply to it the words that we are here considering. Such is, in fact, she who is here introduced as speaking. For she gives sufficient proof, in recalling the Bridegroom, that she has merited His presence, although not the full abundance of His graces. For otherwise it would be a call, not a recall, that she would give. That it is here a recall is marked by the word *Return*, and perhaps He withdrew Himself for that very reason, that He might be recalled with the

greater eagerness, and clasped the more firmly. For when He sometimes makes it appear that He would depart to a greater distance, it is not that He desires to do so, but to hear: *Lord, abide with us, for it is towards evening, and the day is far spent* (Luke xxiv. 28, 29). And, again, on another occasion, when He was walking on the sea, and the Apostles were in a boat and toiling hard in rowing, He made as though He would have passed by them, though He did not indeed desire to do so, but rather to prove their faith and draw forth their prayer. For as the Evangelist declares: *They were troubled, and cried out, supposing that it had been a spirit* (Mark vi. 49, 50). That pious simulation, or rather that salutary dispensation, which the Word, then in the body, sometimes made use of, the same Word, who is Spirit, does not cease to employ, but in a spiritual manner, with a soul that is devoted to Him. When He would pass away, He desires to be detained, and, when absent, to be recalled; for He, who is the Word of God, is not irrevocable. He goes and returns according to His good pleasure, He visits a soul at the breaking of the day, and suddenly puts it to proof by withdrawing Himself. If He come into a soul, it is the effect of His free and spontaneous grace; if He retire from it, it is similarly according to His will; but both the one and the other depend upon His judgment, and of this He alone knows the ground and reason.

4. It is, then, quite evident that changes take place in the soul by the going and returning of the Word. For He says: *I go away, and come again to you* (John xiv. 28); and again: *A little while and ye shall not see Me, and again a little while and ye shall see Me* (John xvi. 16). O truly *a little while!* but how long *a little while* may be! O kind and loving Lord, how canst Thou call the time in which I do not behold Thee 'a little while'? Saving the deference due to my Lord's word, it seems to me a *long* time, and even excessively long. Yet each of these estimates is true, for it is short if our merits be considered, but long if measured by our desires and prayers. You have each of these senses in that saying of the Prophet: *Though He tarry, wait for Him, because He shall surely come, He shall not tarry* (Hab. ii. 3). How can it be that He shall not tarry, and yet shall make delay, except that though He come with sufficient quickness, if our deservings be considered, He does not come quickly enough for our desires? Now, the soul that loves the Lord is carried away by the fervour of its prayers, is led on by its eager longing, forgets altogether the smallness of its merits, shuts its eyes to the majesty of the Bridegroom, and opens them only to the happiness which it hopes to enjoy; regards only His saving grace, and acts confidingly in that. Finally, without fear and without shame, it recalls the Word, and confidently asks for its former delights, calling Him with its habitual freedom, not Lord, but Beloved. *Return*, she says, *my Beloved;* and adds: *Be Thou like a roe or a young hart upon the mountains of Bether*. But of this more hereafter.

5. But now bear with my foolishness for a little. I wish to tell

you, as I have promised, how such events have taken place in me. It is indeed a matter of no importance. But I put myself forward only that I may be of service to you, and if you derive any benefit I am consoled for my egotism; if not, I shall have displayed my foolishness. I confess, then, though I say it in my foolishness, that the WORD has visited me, and even very often. But although He has frequently entered into my soul, I have never at any time been sensible of the precise moment of His coming. I have felt that He was present. I remember that He has been with me; I have sometimes been able even to have a presentiment that He would come; but never to feel His coming, nor His departure. For whence He came to enter my soul, or whither He went on quitting it, by what means He has made entrance or departure, I confess that I know not even to this day; according to that which is said: *Thou canst not tell whence it cometh and whither it goeth* (John iii. 8). Nor is this strange, because it is to Him that the Psalmist has said in another place: *Thy footsteps are not known* (Ps. lxxvii. 19). It is not by the eyes that He enters, for He is without form or colour that they can discern; nor by the ears, for His coming is without sound; nor by the nostrils, for it is not with the air but with the mind that He is blended; nor has He merely acted upon the air, but produced it (*infecit, fecit*); nor, again, does it enter by the mouth, not being of a nature to be eaten or drunk; nor, lastly, is it capable of being traced by the touch, for it is intangible. By what avenue, then, has He entered? Or perhaps the fact may be that He has not entered at all, nor indeed come at all from outside. For not one of these things belongs to outside. Yet it has not come from within me, for it is good, and I know that in me dwelleth no good thing (Rom. vii. 18). I have ascended higher than myself, and lo! I have found the Word above me still. My curiosity has led me to descend below myself also, and yet I have found Him still at a lower depth. If I have looked without myself, I have found that He is beyond that which is outside of me; and if within, He was at an inner depth still. And thus I have learned the truth of the words I had read: *In Him we live and move and have our being* (Acts xvii. 28); but blessed is the man in whom He is, who lives for Him, and is moved by Him.

6. You will ask, then, how, since the ways of His access are thus incapable of being traced, I could know that He was present? But He is living and full of energy, and as soon as He has entered into me He has quickened my sleeping soul, has aroused and softened and goaded my heart, which was in a state of torpor, and hard as a stone. He has begun to pluck up and destroy, to plant and to build, to water the dry places, to illuminate the gloomy spots, to throw open those which were shut close, to inflame with warmth those which were cold, as also to straighten its crooked paths and make its rough places smooth, so that my soul might bless the Lord, and all that is within me praise His Holy Name. Thus, then, the Bridegroom-Word, though He has several times entered into me, has never made His

coming apparent to my sight, hearing, or touch. It was not by His motions that He was recognised by me, nor could I tell by any of my senses that He had penetrated to the depths of my being. It was, as I have already said, only by the revived activity of my heart that I was enabled to recognise His Presence; and to know the power of His sacred Presence by the sudden departure of vices and the strong restraint put upon all carnal affections. From the discovery and conviction of my secret faults I have had good reason to admire the depth of His wisdom; His goodness and kindness have become known in the amendment, whatever it may amount to, of my life; while in the reformation and renewal of the spirit of my mind, that is, of my inward man, I have perceived, in a certain degree, the excellency of the Divine beauty, and have been rapt in wonder and amazement at His greatness and majesty, as I meditated upon all these things.

7. But when the WORD withdrew Himself, all these spiritual powers and faculties began to droop and languish, as if the fire had been withdrawn from a bubbling pot; and this is to me the sign of His departure. Then my soul is necessarily sad and depressed until He shall return and my heart grow warm within me, as it is wont, which indeed is the indication to me that He has come back again. After having, then, such an experience of the happiness derived from the indwelling WORD, what wonder that I should adopt for my own the language of the Bride, who recalls Him when He has departed, since I am influenced by a desire, not indeed as powerful, but at least similar to hers? As long as I live that utterance shall be in my mind, and I will employ, for the recalling of the WORD, that word of recall, which I find here in the word *Return*. And as often as He shall leave me, so often shall He be called back by my voice; nor will I cease to send my cries, as it were, after Him as He departs, expressing my ardent desire that He should return, that He should restore to me the joy of His salvation, the life-giving Presence of Himself. I confess to you, my children, that I take pleasure in nothing else in the meantime, until He is present who is alone pleasing to me. And this I pray, that He will not return empty, but full of grace and truth (John i. 14) as it is His wont to do, and as He did yesterday and the day before it. In which it seems to me that He will be *like unto a roe or a young hart*, for His truth has the piercing eyes of the one, and His grace the joy and lightsomeness of the other.

8. Each of these is necessary to me: truth, that I may not be able to hide myself before Him; and grace, that I may not desire to do so. If the one be not accompanied by the other, then either His severity is burdensome without His gladsomeness, or that may seem unmeasured without the gravity of the former, and thus the visitation of the WORD will be imperfect. For truth is bitter, if it be not seasoned with grace; and the fervour of devotion is sometimes unmeasured and tends to lightness, if it be not restrained by the bond

of truth. How many are there whom it has not profited to have received grace, because they have not accepted at the same time the regulating and restraining power of truth? They have taken too much pleasure in the enjoyment of grace; they have not sufficiently regarded the claims of truth; they have not imitated the gravity (as it were) of the roe, but have given themselves wholly to the lightsomeness of the young hart. Thence it has come about that they have been deprived of the grace which they had desired to enjoy by itself, and it has been possible to say to them, but too late: Go ye and learn what that meaneth, *Serve the Lord with fear, and rejoice with trembling* (Ps. ii. 11). For the holy soul which had said in its day of prosperity, *I shall never be moved* (Ps. xxx. 6), when it suddenly feels the Face of the WORD turned away from it, is not only moved, but grievously troubled, and thus learns by its affliction that with the gift of piety and devotion, it has need also of the steadying weight of truth. Therefore the fulness of grace consists not in grace alone, but also not in truth alone. What does it profit you to know what you ought to do, if there is not bestowed upon you also the will to do it? What does it profit you even to have the will, if you have not the ability? How many have I known to whom the knowledge of the truth was a cause of added sorrow, because, as they knew what the Truth required of them, they could not find an excuse in their ignorance when they did not do it?

9. This being the case, neither gift is sufficient without the other. Nor is this all, for it is not even an advantage to receive one without the other. How do we know this? We learn it from the Scripture: *To him that knoweth to do good, and doeth it not, to him it is sin* (James iv. 17); and, again: *That servant, which knew his Lord's Will . . . and did not according to His Will, shall be beaten with many stripes* (Luke xii. 47). That is, as regards truth. Now, as regards grace, it is written: *After the sop Satan entered into him* (John xiii. 27). This speaks of Judas, who, after he had received a gift of grace, because he did not walk in truth and sincerity with the Master of truth, gave place in himself to the devil. Listen, again: *He fed them with the finest of the wheat, and with honey out of the rock He satisfied them.*' Whom? '*The enemies of the Lord have lied unto Him*' (Ps. lxxxi. 16, 15). Those whom He had nourished with honey and with wheat lied unto Him and became His enemies, because they did not join truth to grace. Of whom it is said in another place: The children that are strangers have lied to me, strange children have faded away, and have halted in their path (Ps. xviii. 45, Douay). How could they do otherwise than halt, seeing that they were content to support themselves on one foot, that of grace, and not to use the other, that is, of truth? Therefore their time [of punishment] shall endure for ever (Ps. lxxxi. 15) with that of their prince, who also himself abode not in the truth, but *was a liar from the beginning* (John viii. 44), and therefore it was said to him: *Thou hast corrupted thy wisdom by reason of thy beauty* (Ezek.

xxviii. 17). I am unwilling to allow beauty in one who deprives me of wisdom.

10. Do you inquire what is that beauty so dangerous and so hurtful? It is the beauty which is thine. Perhaps you do not understand me when I say this, and I will put it in plainer language. It is the beauty which is of a personal and individual kind. We do not blame the gift of God, but the use which is made of it. For if you notice, it is not said that Lucifer lost wisdom by reason of beauty, but of *his* beauty. And if I do not mistake, the beauty of an angel is the same as that of a soul, that is, it is wisdom. For what is either the one or the other without wisdom, but a shapeless heap of unorganized matter? But with wisdom, either is not only formed and organized, but is full of beauty. But when it is appropriated in a selfish manner, it is forthwith lost, so that when it is said that he has lost wisdom by reason of his beauty, it is meant that he lost wisdom by his own wisdom. For when it is thus appropriated it is instantly lost. Because he was wise in his own eyes, because he did not give the glory to God, because he did not render back grace for grace, because he did not walk in grace and use it according to truth, but abused it according to his own will; that is the reason why he lost it, or rather that constitutes the loss of it. For to appropriate it thus is, in fact, to lose it. *If Abraham,* says the Apostle, *were justified by works, he hath whereof to glory, but not before God* (Rom. iv. 2). And thus it is with me. I am not in safety, because I have lost whatever I do not possess in God. What can there be, in fact, so completely lost as that which does not rest in God as its security? What is death, but the deprivation of life? And in the same way everlasting loss (*perditio*) is nothing else than alienation from God. Woe unto you who are wise in your own eyes, and prudent in your own sight! (Is. v. 21); of you it is said: *I will destroy the wisdom of the wise, and will bring to nothing the understanding of the prudent* (1 Cor. i. 19). They have lost wisdom, because their wisdom has caused them to be lost. How could they help losing all who were themselves lost? And how could those be otherwise than lost whom God knows not [as His own]?

11. Assuredly the foolish virgins, which are not, as I think, otherwise foolish, than as, believing themselves to be wise, they became foolish, these, I say, are doomed to hear from God, *I know you not* (Matt. xxv. 12). And also those who assumed glory to themselves because of the grace [to work] miracles which had been bestowed upon them, shall, notwithstanding these wonderful works, hear the same declaration, *I never knew you* (Matt. vii. 23). So that it is plainly evident, from all that has been said, that grace does not profit the individual when it is not accompanied by truth and sincerity of intention, but is rather a hindrance to him. Each of these is assuredly found in the Bridegroom. *Grace and truth,* says John the Baptist, *came by Jesus Christ* (John i. 17). If, then, the Lord Jesus Christ (who is the Word of God, the Bridegroom of the soul) knocks at the

door of my soul with only one of these two qualities, He will enter, not as Bridegroom, but as Judge. May God grant that this may never be the case with me! May He not enter into judgment with His servant! May He enter with peace, with joy and gladness; yet may He enter with aspect grave and serious, so as by the severe gravity of His look to repress any forwardness in me, and to purify the joy which I feel. May He enter with the agility of the roe and the piercing sight of the hart, so, as it were, to leap over my offences and to view them only with pity and forgiveness. May He enter as if descending from the mountains of Bethel, full of glory and of joy; as if coming forth from the Father, sweet, and full of goodness, so that He does not disdain to become and to be called the Bridegroom of the soul which seeks for Him: He who is above all, God blessed for ever. AMEN.

SERMON LXXV.

GOD IS TO BE SOUGHT IN DUE TIME, PLACE, AND MANNER. THAT NOW IS THE ACCEPTABLE TIME, IN WHICH ANYONE MAY FIND GOD FOR HIMSELF BY GOOD WORKS, AND MAY WORK OUT HIS SALVATION.

'*By night on my bed I sought Him whom my soul loveth.*'—Cant. iii. 1.

THE Bridegroom has not returned at the voice and according to the prayer of her who is recalling Him. Wherefore? It is that the yearning for Him may increase, that the affection may be proved, that the faculty of love may be exercised. It is not indignation, then, that actuates Him, but a concealment of love. But since, when called, He has not come, it remains that He should be sought, if, haply, He may be found. According to the words of the Lord, *He that seeketh findeth* (Matt. vii. 8). The words used to recall Him were, as you remember, such as these: *Return, my Beloved, and be Thou like a roe or a young hart.* When the WORD did not return at this call, for the reasons above given, the loving Bride became still more desirous of His presence, and set herself with increased earnestness to the task of seeking Him. First, she seeks Him *on her bed*, but finds Him not. Then she rises, makes a circuit of the city, goes and comes through the streets and squares, but she neither meets Him nor beholds Him at a distance. She questions those whom she meets, but learns no assured tidings of Him. It is not through one street only, or during one night, that she continues this search, and experiences this failure; for she says, 'I sought Him *by night* (*per noctes*).' What desire, and what ardour must she feel, that she does not blush to rise and appear in the night, to traverse the city, to interrogate openly and repeatedly all those she meets about her Beloved, not to be turned by any reason from following His footsteps, nor daunted by any difficulty; not to be held back by the love of ease and repose, by the sensitive modesty of a bride, nor by the terrors of the night! And, notwithstanding all this, the object of her wishes has not as yet been attained. Why is this? What can be the cause of a withdrawal so obstinate and so prolonged, which nourishes weariness, causes suspicions, is as a torch to enkindle impatience, as a stepmother to love, but a mother to desperation? If it is still a concealment of love on the part of the Bridegroom, that concealment is but too painful.

2. Granted that such concealment was useful and even kind in the meantime, until the Bride had set herself seriously to call upon Him, or to recall. But now, when she is thus seeking Him and calling for Him, what can be the object of any longer concealment? If the question here were of carnal spouses and of dishonourable loves, as the literal sense of the text seems at first to suggest, and such incidents should occur in them, I leave such matters to those whom they concern, for they do not concern me. But if it is my duty to respond to, and to satisfy, as far as my poor powers extend, the wishes and the needs of souls that seek the Lord, I ought to draw from the Holy Scripture, in which they trust that they have the word of life, something spiritual and life-giving, that they who are the poor of Christ may eat and may be satisfied, and that their hearts may find life. And what is the life of human hearts but my Lord Jesus Christ, of whom one who lived in Him said: *When Christ, who is our Life, shall appear, then shall ye also appear with Him in glory* (Col. iii. 4)? Let Him come, then, into the midst of us, so that it may be possible to say truly to us also: *There standeth One among you whom ye know not* (John i. 26). Though I do not know how the Bridegroom, who is Spirit, can fail to be recognised by spiritual men, who have made such progress in the life of the spirit, as to be able to say with the Prophet, *The Anointed of the Lord is a Spirit before our face* (Lam. iv. 20); and with the Apostle, *Though we have known Christ after the flesh, yet now henceforth know we Him no more* (2 Cor. v. 16). Is it not He whom the Bride was seeking? He is, in truth, the Bridegroom, both loving and lovable. He is, I say, the Bridegroom, as His Flesh is meat indeed, and His Blood drink indeed (John vi. 56); and all that He is He is in truth, for He is Himself no other than the Truth.

3. But why is it that this Bridegroom is not found when He is sought, especially when sought with so great and unwearied care, now on the couch, now in the city, or even in the streets and open places? Does not He Himself say, *Seek, and ye shall find;* and, *He who seeketh findeth* (Matt. vii. 7, 8)? To Him also speaks a Prophet: *The Lord is good . . . to the soul that seeketh Him* (Lam. iii. 25); and also holy Isaiah saith, *Seek ye the Lord, while He may be found* (Is. lv. 6). How, then, shall the Scriptures be accomplished? For she who here seeks the Lord is not of those to whom He says: *Ye shall seek Me, and*

shall not find Me (John vii. 34). But take note of three causes which occur to me, wherefore seekers are wont to be hindered in finding Him, namely, that they seek Him either not at the fitting time, or not in the fitting manner, or not in the fitting place. For if every time is proper to seek Him, why does the Prophet say: *Seek ye the Lord, while He may be found?* There will, then, without doubt, be a time when He may not be found, and therefore he adds, *Call upon Him while He is near*, because it will come to pass that He will not be near. By whom will He not be sought then? *Unto Me*, He saith, *every knee shall bow* (Is. xlv. 24). And yet He shall not be found by the wicked, whom the avenging Angels shall hinder from finding Him, and shall take them away, that they may not behold the glory of God. The foolish virgins shall complain, but to no purpose; for the door is shut, and He shall not go forth to them (Matt. xxv. 10). Let them take for themselves that which is said: *Ye shall seek Me, and shall not find Me.*

4. But now is the acceptable (*acceptabile*) time, now is the day of salvation (2 Cor. vi. 2); it is the time of seeking, and of calling upon, the Lord; for oftentimes, even before He is called, He is felt to be near. Hear, in fact, what He promises. *Before they call*, He says, *I will answer* (Is. lxv. 24). Nor does the Psalmist speak less decisively as to the acceptableness of the time present, for he says: *Lord, Thou hast heard the desire of the humble: Thou wilt prepare their heart, Thou wilt cause Thine ear to hear* (Ps. x. 17). If God is being sought by good works, then, while we have time, let us do good unto all men (Gal. vi. 10), especially since the Lord plainly warns us that the night cometh, when no man can work (John ix. 4). Do you expect to find in the ages to come some other time to seek God, some other opportunity to do that which is right, besides that which God has appointed for you, and in which He will be mindful of you? And, therefore, this is the day of salvation, because it is in it that God, who is our King before all the ages, has worked salvation in the midst of the earth (Ps. lxxxiv. 12).

5. Go, then, and await in the midst of hell the salvation which is already worked in the midst of the earth.[1] What profit will be to you those dreams of pardon, among the everlasting fires, when the season for pity shall have passed? There is no victim left to atone for your sins, when you shall be dead in sins. The Son of God is not crucified a second time: once He died, and now He dieth no more (Rom. vi. 9). His Blood, which was poured out upon the earth, does not descend into hell. All the sinners of the earth have drunk of it; there is none left for the demons to claim, that the flames which prey upon them may be quenched; nor for men who are the companions of demons. The Soul of the Saviour once descended into that place, but not His Blood; and this was the portion of

---

[1] Origen seems to be referred to, or at least the error ascribed to him, in this passage; just as St. Bernard notes other errors of the same writer in Sermon XXXIV., *De Diversis*, and Sermon LIV., *n*. 3, *in Cantica.*

those spirits who were in prison (1 Peter iii. 19). That was His one visitation to them, which was made then by the presence of His Soul, while His Body hung lifeless upon the Cross, on the earth. His Blood watered the earth, steeped it and made it glad; His Blood re-established peace on the earth, and also in the heavens; but hell had no part in that reconciliation. The Soul of the Saviour, as I have said, descended there once, and there worked redemption in part; so that it was not even that brief time without works of charity,[1] but to that He will add nothing. It is now, then, a fit and acceptable time to seek Him, in which he who seeks shall evidently find Him; if, that is to say, he seeks in the fitting manner, and place. For this is one cause which hinders those who seek the Bridegroom from finding Him; namely, that they do not seek at a fitting time. But this does not hinder the Bride, since she seeks Him and calls upon Him at the time which is fit. She seeks Him also neither with lukewarmness nor negligence, nor in a perfunctory manner, for she seeks Him with ardent and untiring earnestness, as she evidently ought to do.

6. There remains, then, the third obstacle, namely, that He is sought for in an unsuitable place. *On my little bed* (lectulo) *I sought Him whom my soul loveth*. But perhaps He for whom the whole world is too narrow should not be sought upon a 'little' bed, but upon a bed? Nevertheless, the little bed does not displease me, for I know that the Saviour was made a little Child. Cry out and shout, thou inhabitant of Zion, for great is the Holy One of Israel in the midst of thee (Is. xii. 6). But the same Lord, who is great in Zion, is found among us little, and weak; He has need to lie down, and even upon a bed that is little. Is not His tomb a little bed? or His cradle? or the womb of His Virgin-Mother? For the Bosom of His Father, who is so great, is not little, but great; and of it He speaks to the Son: From the womb, before the Daystar, I begot Thee (Ps. cx. 3, Douay). Though perhaps it may be thought more worthily that this womb is not a bed, and for rest, but a throne, and for rule. For abiding in the Father, He rules all things with the Father. Finally, faith undoubted teaches us that He does not recline, but sits, at the Right Hand of the Father; that Heaven is His throne, not His couch (Is. lxvi. 1), so that you may learn that among his own, that is, among the dwellers in heaven, He has the ensigns of power, not the solaces of weakness.

7. Rightly, then, does the Bride, when speaking of a little bed, call it *hers;* for it is manifest that whatever of weakness may appear in God [our Saviour] is not proper and natural to Him, but comes from us. He has taken from us all that He has suffered on our behalf: to be born, to be nourished with milk, to die, to be buried. The mortality of His Birth comes from me, the weakness of His Childhood comes from me, the pains of His Crucifixion, and His

---

[1] Thus the MSS. and earliest editions, except that some MSS. have *pietatis* for *charitatis*.

sleep in death come all from me. The former things have passed away, and behold! all things have become new. *By night on my bed I sought Him whom my soul loveth.* What! did you seek Him in that which is yours, who had already been received again into that which is His own? Had you not seen the Son of Man ascending up where He was before? In exchange for the stable, in exchange for the Tomb, He has taken possession of Heaven; and you seek Him still in your little bed? He is Risen; He is not here. Why do you seek in a bed Him who is strong, in a little bed Him who is great, in a stable Him who is pure and spotless? He has entered into [the exercise of] the powers of the Lord; He is clothed with beauty and with strength; and, behold, He who once lay under the stone of a sepulchre, now is enthroned above the Cherubim. He no longer reclines, He is sitting; and are you preparing for Him the comforts, as it were, of one who lies prone? To speak quite accurately, He is either seated to judge, or standing to help us.

8. For whom, then, I pray you, O holy women, do ye keep vigil? For whom do ye buy perfumes and make provision of fragrant oils? If ye knew how great He is, how free among the dead is that dead Man whom ye are going to anoint, you would perhaps petition that He should rather drop perfumes upon you. Is it not He whom His God hath anointed with the oil of gladness above His fellows? (Ps. xlv. 7). Blessed shall ye be if, when returning, you are able to make your boast, and say: *Of His fulness have all we received* (John i. 16). For it was in fact thus; and those holy women who had gone to anoint Him returned anointed themselves. How could they be otherwise than, as it were, anointed by the joyful and fragrant news of His Resurrection? *How beautiful are the feet of them that preach the gospel of peace and bring glad tidings of good things!* (Rom. x. 15). When sent by the Angel, they do the work of an Evangelist; they are made apostles to the Apostles themselves, and while hastening in the early morning to announce the mercy of the Lord, they say: 'We run in the fragrance of Thy perfumes.' From that time and thenceforth it was in vain that the Bridegroom was sought in that little bed, because, although the Church had known Him according to the flesh, that is, according to the weakness of the flesh, yet henceforth it knows Him [thus] no more. It is true that He was sought in this manner by Peter and John at the sepulchre, but they found Him not. Do you see with what singular fitness and suitableness each of them would be able to say: *In my bed I sought Him whom my soul loveth: I sought Him, but I found Him not.* For the Flesh of the Son of God, which was not of the Father, before going to the Father, put off, through the glory of the Resurrection, every trace of weakness; it was girded about with power, it was clad with light as it were with a garment, and adorned with all the glory and beauty which was befitting it, to present itself before the Father.

9. With great beauty also does the Bride say, not 'Him whom I love,' but 'Him whom my soul loveth,' because that affection belongs

truly and properly to the soul alone, with which anything spiritual is loved: as, for example, God, or an Angel, or a soul similar to itself. Of the same kind also is the love of righteousness, truth, piety, wisdom, and other virtues. For when a soul loves, or rather desires, somewhat according to the flesh, for example, food, clothing, property, or other things corporeal or earthly of that kind, that love should be considered as belonging rather to the flesh than to the soul. I say this to explain what the Bride says, in a manner somewhat unusual, though none the less appropriate, that her soul loves the Bridegroom, indicating clearly by this that He is a spirit, and is loved by her with an affection not carnal, but spiritual. So, also, it is well said that she has sought Him *each night.* For if, according to the Apostle, *they that sleep, sleep in the night, and they that be drunken are drunken in the night* (1 Thess. v. 7), so it may, as I think, be not unfitly said that those who are ignorant of the truth are so in the night, and, in consequence, those who seek it seek it in the night. For who seeks that of which he has possession openly? Now, the day makes manifest that which the night conceals, so that in the day you may find what in the night you had sought. It is, then, night for the soul as long as the Bridegroom is being sought, for if it were day He would be plainly seen in the midst, and would not be sought at all. And that is sufficient on this subject, except for the observation that though the Bride says she seeks Him not 'by night,' but 'by nights,' nothing is signified by the mere number.

10. It seems to me, however, if you have no better cause to suggest, that the reason may be something of this kind. That world has its nights, and they are many. What do I say? Not only has it nights, but it is itself almost an entire night, and is enveloped wholly in shadows. The unbelief of the Jews is a night; the ignorance of the Heathen, the obstinate error of heretics, even the carnal and animal mode of living of Catholics, each of these is a night. Is it not a darkness as of night when the things which are of the Spirit of God are not even perceived? So, also, as many sects as there are of heretics and schismatics, so many nights are there. To no purpose do you seek the Sun of Righteousness and the light of Truth, that is, the Bridegroom, through the gloom of these nights, for light hath no fellowship with darkness. But someone objects that the Bride is not so blind, nor so foolish, as to seek light in the darkness, or to expect to find her Beloved among those who know Him not nor love Him. What she says is, not that she is seeking Him now, but that she has sought Him; not 'I am seeking,' but *By night I sought Him whom my soul loveth.* And the meaning of these words is that when she was young she had but the thoughts and sentiments proportioned to the weakness of her age; that she sought the truth where it was not, wandering and not finding it, according as it is said in a Psalm: *I have gone astray like a lost sheep* (Ps. cxix. 176). In fact, she states that she was still, as it were, in a little bed, because she was of immature age and undeveloped intelligence.

11. But if that sense of the words be accepted, then the phrase 'on my bed' must be understood as if it were said 'being or reclining,' not, that is to say, 'I have sought on my bed,' but 'being on my bed I have sought'; that is, 'While I was still weak and incompetent, altogether unfitted to follow the Lamb whithersoever He should go, or to pursue the steep and arduous paths by which He ascended to the height of glory, I fell among many persons who, knowing my earnest desire, said to me: *Lo, here is Christ, or Lo, He is there* (Mark xiii. 21), and He was neither in the one place nor the other. Nevertheless, I do not regret to have fallen among them. For the more nearly I approached them and the more diligently I examined them, the more assured I became that the truth was not in them. For I sought it and did not find it, and what they falsely called day proved to be in truth but night.

12. Then I said in myself: *I will rise now and go about the city: in the streets and in the broad ways I will seek Him whom my soul loveth.* Now, you will observe that she must be reclining who says, *I will rise.* And this is said with much fitness, for how can she do otherwise than rise when she has heard of the Resurrection of her Beloved? But if thou, O blessed one, art risen with Christ, it behoves thee to seek those things which are above, and not to seek Christ here below, but to seek Him on high, where He sitteth at the Right Hand of the Father (Col. iii. 1). But she says: *I will go about the city.* To what purpose? For it is the wicked who do that. Leave that to the Jews, of whom their own Psalmist predicted: *They shall suffer hunger like dogs, and shall go round about the city* (Ps. lix. 7, Douay). If you shall enter into the city, then, according to another prophet, *behold them that are sick with famine* (Jer. xiv. 18), which doubtless would not have been the case if there had been in them the bread of life. He has arisen from the heart of the earth, but He has not remained upon the earth, for He has ascended up where He was before. For He who descended is the same who also ascended, the Living Bread who came down from heaven, the Bridegroom of the Church, JESUS CHRIST our Lord, who is above all, God blessed for ever. AMEN.

SERMON LXXVI.

OF THE GLORY OF THE BRIDEGROOM, IN WHICH HE SITS AT THE RIGHT HAND OF HIS FATHER, AND IS COEQUAL WITH HIM. HOW CAREFUL, WATCHFUL, AND DISCREET GOOD PASTORS OUGHT TO BE IN FEEDING THE SOULS GIVEN INTO THEIR CHARGE.

'*In the streets and in the broad ways I will seek Him whom my soul loveth.*'—Cant. iii. 2.

SHE thinks still as a child. I believe that she has supposed that immediately He came forth from the tomb, He presented Himself in public to teach the people as He was wont, and heal the sick, and thus to show forth His glory in Israel, to see if they would receive Him rising from the dead, who promised that they would receive Him if He would come down from the Cross. But He had finished the work which the Father had given Him to do: which she ought to have understood, indeed, from the words which He had spoken when hanging on the Cross, and about to give up His spirit (John xix. 30): *It is finished*. It was not for Him to show Himself anew to the masses of the people, who would not perhaps even thus have believed in Him. And He hastened to His Father, who would say to Him: *Sit Thou at My Right Hand, until I make Thine enemies Thy footstool* (Ps. cx. 1). For when He should have been lifted up from the earth, He would draw all things unto Him more powerfully as well as more Divinely. But she, in thinking that He was to be sought in the streets and open spaces, was influenced by an eager desire to enjoy His presence, and did not know that mystery; therefore, when having again failed, she repeats: *I sought Him, but I found Him not* (iii. 2), that the word might be fulfilled which He spake: *Ye shall not see Me . . . because I go to the Father* (John xvi. 16).

2. But perhaps the sense of her words is this: 'How shall they believe in Him whom they will not behold?' As if faith cometh from sight, and not rather by hearing! What marvel is it that you should believe that which you have seen? and what praise does it deserve not to disbelieve one's own eyes? But if we hope for that which we see not, we wait for it with patience; and patience is a merit. *Blessed are they who have not seen, and yet have believed* (John xx. 29). So, then, that He may not deprive her of the merit of faith, He withdraws Himself from sight, affording place for this virtue. Besides this, it is time now that He should betake Himself to His own place. You ask, What is His own place? It is the Right Hand of the Father. For as He is in the Form of God, He will think it not robbery to be equal with God (Phil. ii. 6). The place, then, of the Only Begotten is one in which He is out of the reach of every kind of outrage. There, indeed, let Him sit, not below the Father, but beside Him, that all may honour the Son even as they honour the Father. In this shall

appear His equality of dignity, if He is considered neither inferior nor posterior, to the Father. But the Bride has, in the meantime, regard to none of these things; she is, as it were, inebriated by her affection; she runs hither and thither, and seeks with her eyes for Him who is not now discernible by the eyes, but by faith. She does not think that Christ ought otherwise to enter into His glory than as having previously manifested the glory of His Resurrection openly to all the world, that impiety may be thereby confuted, the faithful made to rejoice, the disciples to glory, the peoples to be converted; so that after His Presence and His Resurrection shall have shown clearly the truth of His predictions, He shall at length be glorified by all. But you deceive yourself, O Bride. All these things must needs be fulfilled, indeed; but in their due time.

3. But now, in the meantime, see if it be not more in agreement with the supreme Righteousness, and more worthy of it, not to give that which is holy to dogs, nor to cast pearls before swine; if, according to the Scripture, the wicked should rather be taken away, and not behold the glory of God (Is. xxvi. 10); if faith should be not deprived of its merit, since that is assuredly more displayed and approved in believing that which is not seen; if thus that which is hidden from the unworthy is reserved for those who are worthy of it; if those who are filthy are filthy still, and those who are righteous become still more so (Rev. xxii. 11) if they do not sleep through weariness. Let the heavens and the heavens of heavens pass away and be confounded in their expectation rather than that the Almighty Father should be longer hindered from attaining the desire of His Heart, or the Only Begotten Son delayed longer (which would be a consummation in the highest degree unworthy) from entering into His glory. What is all the glory of mortals, thinkest thou, however great it may be, to be able to detain Him, for ever so small a time, from that glory which has been prepared by His Father from all eternity? Add to this that it is not fitting that the petition of the Son Himself should wait longer for its fulfilment. Do you ask, What was that petition? It was that in which He said: *Father, glorify Thy Son* (John xvii. 1). And yet I feel that He asked this, not as a suppliant, but as prescient of that which was to be. That is freely asked which it is in the power of Him who asks to receive. Therefore the request of the Son was the effect of providence, not of necessity, since He, with the Father, gives that which He from the Father receives.

4. It is proper here to remark that not only does the Father glorify the Son, but also the Son glorifies the Father; so that no one should say that the Son is less than the Father as receiving glory from the Father, inasmuch as He also glorifies the Father. For He Himself says: *Father, glorify Thy Son, that Thy Son also may glorify Thee.* But perhaps you still think that the Son should be considered inferior to the Father, because He seems, as if less glorious, to receive the glory of the Father, which He renders to the Father again. But hear that it is not so, for He says: *O Father, glorify Thou Me with Thine*

own Self with the glory which I had with Thee before the world was (John xvii. 5). If, then, the glory of the Son is not later than that of the Father, since it exists from eternity, it is plain that the Father and the Son are equally glorified. This being so, where is the Primacy of the Father? There is evidently Equality where there is Coeternity. And the Equality is to such a degree that the glory of Both is but one glory, as They Themselves are One. On that account, as it seems to me, it was that He says again : *Father, glorify Thy Name ;* and in so doing requests, in fact, nothing else than to be glorified Himself, since it is, beyond doubt, in Him, and through Him, that the Name of the Father would be glorified ; and He received a reply from the Father : *I have both glorified it, and I will glorify it again* (John xii. 28). And this reply of the Father is in itself no small glorifying of the Son. But He was glorified more highly and more amply still at the stream of Jordan, both by the testimony of John the Baptist, the pointing Him out by the Dove, and by the Voice of the Father, who said : *This is My Beloved Son* (Matt. iii. 14, 16, 17). And, most of all, He was glorified and exalted on Mount Tabor before the three disciples, both by that same Voice which was heard from Heaven, and also by the wonderful and unexampled transfiguration of His Body, and the witness that was borne to Him by the two Prophets who appeared in the same place talking with Him (Matt. xvii. 2-5).

5. It remains, then, that, according to the promise of the Father, He should be glorified yet once again, and that with the fulness of glory to which nothing more can be added. But where shall that glory be bestowed? It will not be, as the Bride supposed, in the streets and open places, unless, perhaps, in those of whom it is said : The streets [of Jerusalem] shall be paved with white and clean stones : and Alleluia shall be sung in its streets (Tobit xiii. 22, Douay). For it is in those that the Son has received from the Father a glory so great that its equal cannot be found, even among the dwellers in heaven. For *to which of the Angels said He at any time, Sit on My Right Hand?* (Heb. i. 13). Not only among the Angels, but also in the loftiest orders of the Blessed, none is found fit to receive this glory which superexcels all things. To not one of them has that announcement of singular and exceptional glory been made, to not one of them has it been given to see it realized in himself. The Thrones, the Dominations, the Principalities, the Powers, desire, without doubt, to contemplate it in Him ; but to compare themselves with Him they do not presume. It is, then, to my Lord only that it has been spoken, and upon Him only that it has been conferred by the Lord, that He should sit upon the Right Hand of His Glory as being coequal with Him in glory, Consubstantial in Essence, Like unto Him by Generation, not unequal in Majesty or in Eternity. It is there, it is there that he who seeks Him shall find, and shall behold His Glory : not glory as of one among others, but assuredly the glory as of the Only Begotten of the Father (John i. 14).

6. What doest thou, then, O Bride? Dost thou think that thou

art able to follow Him thither? Hast thou the ability or the boldness to introduce thyself into a secret so sacred, into a sanctuary so secret, as to contemplate the Son in the Father and the Father in the Son? Assuredly not. Where He is thou canst not follow Him now, but thou shalt follow Him hereafter. Yet do not cease to strive; seek Him, follow Him; let not that supreme glory, that unapproachable elevation, deter thee from seeking, nor make thee despair of finding Him. If thou canst believe, all things are possible to him that believeth (Mark ix. 22). *The word is nigh thee,* it is said, *in thy mouth, and in thy heart* (Rom. x. 8). Believe, and thou hast found [Him]. Those who are faithful know that Christ dwells in their hearts by faith (Eph. iii. 17), and what is nearer than this? Seek, then, with confidence, seek with zeal. The Lord is good to the soul that seeketh Him (Lam. iii. 25). Seek Him by your prayers, seek Him by your actions, find Him by your faith. What is there that faith does not find? It attains that which was not reached, it discovers what is hidden, it comprehends what is unlimited, it apprehends the farthest depths; it even contains, after a certain manner, in its comprehensive bosom, eternity itself. I say with confidence that the blessed and eternal Trinity, which I do not understand, I believe in, and thus hold by faith that which I do not grasp with the understanding.

7. But someone says: 'How shall she believe, without someone to instruct, since faith cometh by hearing, and hearing through the word of exhortation (Rom. x. 14, 17)?' For this God will provide. And see how they are already at hand who present themselves to instruct that new Bride, that soul who is to be united to a heavenly Bridegroom, in the truths that she needs to know; to deliver to her the faith, to teach her the form of piety and of true religion. For listen to what she goes on to say: *The watchmen that go about the city found me.* Who are these watchmen? They are those whom the Saviour pronounces blessed if He, when He shall come, shall find them watching (Luke xii. 37). How good are the sentinels who watch while we sleep, as if to give an account of our souls! How good the guardians who are wakeful in spirit, and pass the night in prayer; who seek out wisely the devices of the enemies, forestall the designs of the evil-disposed, lay bare their snares, escape their entanglements, shatter their nets, frustrate their plots! These are lovers of the brethren and of the people of Christ, who pray much for the people and for all the Holy City. These are they who, being careful and anxious for the sheep entrusted to them by the Lord, bear them on their heart at their waking, when the day breaks, to the Lord who made them, and offer intercession for them in the presence of the Most High. And though they thus watch and thus intercede, they do it, as knowing their own insufficiency to keep the city safe, and being conscious that *unless the Lord keep the city, the watchman waketh but in vain* (Ps. cxxvii. 1).

8. In fact, when the Lord thus instructs us, *Watch ye and pray,*

lest ye enter into temptation (Mark xiv. 38), it is plain that without this twofold exercise [of vigilance and prayer] by the faithful, and of sympathetic care on the part of the watchers, the city cannot be kept in safety, nor the Bride, nor the sheep. Do you inquire what is the difference between these? They are but one and the same; a city because it is an assembly of the faithful, a Bride because beloved, and a flock of sheep because of the kindness and care shown to it. Why is this Bride said to be a city? *I saw* (it is said) *the Holy City, new Jerusalem, coming down from God out of Heaven, prepared as a Bride adorned for her husband* (Rev. xxi. 2). It will plainly appear to you that the Bride is similarly called a *flock*, if you remember how earnestly the Saviour warned that first pastor (I mean St. Peter) to tend it with love when the sheep of it were for the first time committed to his charge. This that wise bestower of the trust (*creditor*) would not have done with such great care if He had not felt, from the witness of His own inmost heart, that this was the Bride of which He was the Bridegroom. Take good heed of this, O friends of the Bridegroom, if you are in truth His friends. But I have said too little in calling you simply *friends*. For it behoves those upon whom is bestowed the privilege of such familiar intimacy to be the very closest and dearest of friends to Him. It was not without a significant purpose that, when confiding the care of His sheep to St. Peter, He repeated so frequently, *Lovest thou Me?* (John xxi. 15-17). And I think that the significance of it was as if Jesus had said: 'If your conscience does not bear you witness that you love Me, that you love Me perfectly and entirely, that is to say, more than your own interests, more than your relatives, more even than your own self, so that the number of this threefold repetition of Mine may be fulfilled, then by no means do thou take upon thee this charge, nor in any wise presume to concern thyself with My sheep, for whom My Blood was poured forth.' An address which is indeed terrible, and capable of shaking the hearts of tyrants, however hardened.

9. Wherefore be ye watchful, whosoever of you have been chosen and called to the work of this ministry; take watchful heed, I say, to yourselves, and to the precious deposit which has been entrusted to you. It is a *city*; watch, then, to maintain it in safety and concord. It is a *Bride*; study to present her to the Lord decked with the precious jewels of abundant virtues. It is a *flock*; study diligently to give it needful pasture. And perhaps we may not unfitly explain by these three elements of pastoral duty the threefold question which the Lord addressed to St. Peter. Now, that the watch and ward over the city may be effective, it must be of three kinds: against the violence of tyrants, against the deception from heretics, and against the temptations of evil spirits. Again, the ornaments of the Bride ought to be of three kinds: of good works, of a saintly character, of high and noble principles. And the needful nourishment of the sheep is ordinarily indeed in the good pastures of the Holy Scriptures as being the heritage of the Lord; but there is a distinction in these.

For there are commandments which are imposed upon hard and carnal hearts, as a discipline and for the law of life; and there are miscellaneous masses[1] of dispensations, which are appointed on account of pity to those that are weak and of little courage; and there are counsels strong and solid, which are proposed from the inmost recesses of wisdom to those who have health and strength, and senses trained to discern good from evil. For to those who are as children, or, so to speak, as little lambs, is given the milk of exhortation and encouragement, not strong meat. To this end, good and careful pastors do not cease to feed their flock to fatness with salutary and encouraging examples, and preferably with their own rather than with those of others. For if they offer only those of other people, and not their own, this is to their shame, and, also, their flock do not profit. For if, to give an instance, I, who appear to bear the charge of pastor among you, should set before you the meekness of Moses, the patience of Job, the mercy of Samuel, the holiness of David, and other similar examples of various virtues, and be myself impatient and severe, unmerciful, and in no way holy, my discourse would, I fear, be void of all force and unction, nor would you care to listen to it. But this I leave to the Divine goodness, that it may supply what is wanting and correct what is amiss in my conduct towards you. The good pastor will also take care to have in himself that *salt* of which the Gospel speaks (Mark ix. 49), knowing that a discourse seasoned with salt is agreeable and also salutary. This is what I have for the present to say regarding the safe keeping of the city, the adorning of the Bride, and the nourishment of the flock.

10. Yet I wish to set forth the same truths somewhat more in detail, and with respect to those who, while they thirst for honours with excessive desire, and engage rashly to bear the burden of duties to which they are unequal, expose themselves thereby to very great peril, so that they may know what they are entering upon, according to the question that is asked in the Scripture: *Friend, wherefore art thou come?* (Matt. xxvi. 50). If I do not mistake, for the safe keeping of the city only, it is absolutely necessary that a man should be strong, faithful, and spiritually minded. He must be strong to repulse the assaults of its enemies, spiritually minded that he may discover their crafty devices, and faithful that he may not seek to advance his own interests. In the next place, for the elevation and training of souls (for this is what is signified and referred to in the adorning of the Bride), who does not at once perceive that a firm bond of discipline, as well as a sedulous diligence, is required? On that account everyone who is engaged in this ministry needs to burn with fervent zeal. It was with this that Apostle was fired who was so jealous for the glory of the Bride of the Lord, for he said: *I am jealous over you with godly jealousy, for I have espoused you to one husband that I may present you as a chaste virgin to Christ* (2 Cor. xi. 2). And, lastly, [a pastor must not be ignorant], for how can one who is so conduct

---

[1] *Olera.* The word implies a certain disdain and disapproval.—ED.

the Lord's flocks to the sweet pastures of the Divine oracles? But if he be a learned man, indeed, but not a good man, then it is to be feared that he will not so much nourish his flock by the abundance of his doctrine, as he will starve them by the barrenness of his life. Without having knowledge, then, and at the same time a good and praiseworthy life, it is mere rashness for anyone to take upon him the burden of this office. But see, I am obliged to come to an end, though I have not finished what I have to say upon this subject. We are called to another matter, to which it is an unworthy thing that this should give way.[1] I am pressed on all sides, and I know not which I ought to suffer the more impatiently, to be dragged in one direction, and repressed on another, though to endure the two together is worse than either separately. O servitude! O necessity! not what I desire, but what I hate, that I do. Notice, however, where we leave off, so that as soon as it shall be free to us to return to the subject, we may take it up from this point; in the Name of Him who is the Bridegroom of the Church, JESUS CHRIST our Lord, who is above all, God blessed for ever. AMEN.

SERMON LXXVII.

CONCERNING THE BAD PASTORS OF THE CHURCH. ALSO HOW THE BLESSED IN HEAVEN, AND THE ANGELS, COME TO THE AID OF THE ELECT, WHO ARE STILL PILGRIMS UPON THE EARTH.

WE are ready for a new departure. I described in the sermon of yesterday the leaders whom we should desire to have while we journey through this world, but I did not describe those whom we, in fact, have. And we find these latter to be wholly unlike the former. Not all of those whom you see at the present day surrounding the Bride on all sides, and who appear to take up the post at her right hand (to use a common phrase) as their own,[2] are the friends of the Bridegroom. Very few indeed are there among them who do not seek their own interests. They have a love for gifts, but they have not an equal love for Christ, because they have joined hands with mammon. See how they go about adorned and trim, clad in many and bright colours, like unto a bride coming out of her chamber. If you suddenly beheld such a person coming from afar, would you not take it to be the Bride herself rather than one of her guardians? From whence, do you suppose, comes this great

---

[1] These words indicate that the sermon was interrupted by necessity, and that some signal for the ending of it was made—either the signal for the common meal, or for some other occupation, which St. Bernard thought of inferior importance to his subject.

[2] *Addextrare*, a Low Latin word, and rare. It is not in Forcellini, and Du Cange gives but a few instances of its use. It is properly written *addexterare*.—ED.

abundance of all things to them, this magnificence in dress, this luxury at their tables, these masses of gold and silver vases, but from the property of the Bride? Thence it is that [the Church] is left poor and naked and in want, uncared for, wasted, pale and bloodless with famine. Assuredly this is not to adorn the Bride, but to despoil her; not to take care of her, but to destroy; not to defend her, but to expose her to danger; not to train her in good, but to abandon her to evil (*instituere, prostituere*); it is not to feed the flock, but to slaughter and devour it, and to such the Lord says: *Who eat up My people as they eat bread* (Ps. xiv. 4, and liii. 4); and in another Psalm: *They have devoured Jacob, and laid waste his dwelling-place* (lxxix. 7); and in a prophet: *They eat up the sin of My people* (Hosea iv. 8), as if He said: 'They exact the price of sins for their own profit, but for the sinners they do not take the care which is due.' Whom will you find among those who are set over the government of the Church who is not far more intent upon emptying the purses of those under his authority than of rooting up their sins? Or where will you find one who by his prayers turns away the Divine anger, and proclaims the acceptable year of the Lord? But let us speak of lighter evils: a heavier judgment awaits graver offences.

2. But yet it is in vain that we even remonstrate with them, for they do not listen to us. And if what I say is set down in writing, they disdain to read it; or, if they happen to read it, they inveigh against me, although they would with much more justice inveigh against themselves. Let us, then, leave those people, who are not finders of the Bride, but sellers, and let us rather inquire who are those by whom the Bride is found, as she herself states. Those of the present day, though they have indeed inherited the ministry in their place, have not inherited their zeal. All desire to be successors [of the Apostles], few to be imitators of them. Would that they were as watchful in the discharge of the functions of their offices as they are eager in soliciting some dignified appointment. Then they would carefully and watchfully keep her [the Church] who was found by them and entrusted to their charge; or rather they would be watchful for their own sakes, nor suffer it to be said of them: *My lovers and my friends stand aloof from my sore, and my kinsmen stand afar off* (Ps. xxxviii. 11). A complaint which is wholly just, and which applies to no period more justly than to our own. It is too little for our watchmen not to watch over us; they cause us positive and great harm. For they are plunged in a deep slumber, and do not awake even at the thunders of the Divine threatening, nor are stricken with fear even for their own peril. Thence it is that, having no concern for themselves, they have no concern for those under their charge; they allow them to perish, and perish with them.

3. But who are those watchmen by whom, as the Bride declares, she was found? They are the Apostles and Apostolic men. These are they who in truth guard the city, that is, the Church in which they are found, and that with so much the greater vigilance as they

see her struggling in these times against very grave perils of a domestic and internal kind, as it is written: *A man's enemies are the men of his own house* (Micah vii. 6). For they do not abandon her, on whose behalf they have resisted even unto blood, or leave her deprived of their help, but protect and guard her by day and night, that is, in their life and even in their death. And if *precious in the sight of the Lord is the death of His Saints* (Ps. cxvi. 15), I entertain no doubt that in death they do that with so much the greater ability, as in it their dignity and authority are so greatly strengthened.

4. 'You assert these things,' objects someone, 'as if you had seen them with your eyes, but they are altogether beyond the reach of human sight.' To which I reply: If you confide in the witness of your own eyes as faithful, the witness of God is greater. And He says: *I have set watchmen on thy walls, O Jerusalem, which shall never hold their peace day nor night* (Is. lxii. 6). But it is of the Angels, you rejoin, that this is spoken. I do not deny this; they are all ministering spirits (Heb. i. 14). But who forbids me to think the same of those who in power are not unequal to the Angels themselves, while they are perhaps as much more favourable to us by their sympathy and kindness as they are more nearly allied to us by nature? Add to this that they have endured the same sufferings and miseries in which we are now for a time involved. Will there not, then, be a profound compassion and interest for us aroused in those holy souls, since they doubtless remember that they themselves have passed through similar trials? Is not that saying theirs in the Psalms: *We went through fire and through water, but Thou broughtest us out into a wealthy place* (Ps. lxvi. 12). What? Will they, having passed through, leave us, their sons and their successors, in the midst of the fires and of the floods, nor even deign to stretch out a helping hand to us as we are struggling with dangers? Not so. It is well with thee, O holy Church, our Mother, it is well with thee even in this place of thy pilgrimage, for help comes to thee both from heaven and from earth. Those who keep thee neither slumber nor sleep. Thy guardians are the holy Angels; thy watchmen, the spirits and souls of the righteous. They do not mistake who think that thou art *found* by each of these orders of spirits, and that by each thou art equally guarded. And to each order there is a special reason for this their care of thee: to the one, that without thee they shall not be made perfect; to the other, that the fulness of their number will not be made up except from thee. For who does not know that when Satan and his accomplices fell from heaven, the number of the dwellers in heaven was diminished in no small degree? From thee, then, all these await their consummation: the one order that of their number; the other, that of their desires. Understand, then, that the words of the Psalmist apply to thee: *The just wait for me until Thou reward me* (Ps. cxlii. 8, Douay).

5. Notice, also, that it is not said that she has found them, but rather that they have found her; and that is, as I think, because that is the task to which they are called. For how shall they preach unless

they be sent? Now, in the Gospels we read that the Lord Himself said to the Apostles: *Behold, I send you forth* (Luke x. 3); and again: *Go ye into all the world and preach the Gospel to every creature* (Mark xvi. 15). Thus it was. She sought the Bridegroom, and to Him that was not unknown; for it was He who aroused in her mind the desire to seek Him, who bestowed upon her the desire to accomplish the precepts of the law, which is for a training unto life, provided that there was someone to instruct her and to teach her the way of wisdom. And He sent before her coming those who should plant and should water, that is to say, for her instruction and strengthening in every certitude of truth, and that they should bring her certain news of her Beloved, because He whom her soul truly loves, and whom she is seeking, is the Truth. And, in fact, who is the faithful and true love of the soul but He, in and through whom the soul is made to love the truth? I am gifted with reason, I am capable of truth; but it will avail me nothing if I am destitute of love for what is true. Of all these branches, of which the root is in me, He is the fruit. I am not in safety from the severing axe if I am found without Him. It is in Him, without doubt, that I am formed in the image and likeness of God, and am in this more excellent than all other living creatures. Thence it is that my soul ventures to aspire to the sweet and pure embrace of truth, and thus to rest in the love of Him with the most complete security and perfect sweetness, if only it may find grace in the eyes of a Bridegroom so august, and be found worthy to attain to this great glory, or rather if He will present her to Himself not having spot or wrinkle or any such thing. To how great a judgment, think you, will a man render himself liable, and of how great a punishment will he be worthy, who shall show himself regardless of so precious a gift of God? But of this let us speak at another time.

6. But now the Bride does not find Him whom she sought, and she herself has been found by those whom she sought not. Let those who do not fear to enter upon the ways of life without teacher or guide listen to this. They consider themselves to be equally disciples, and their own masters, in the spiritual art. Nor is even this enough for them; blind leaders of the blind, they heap together disciples to themselves. How many have been found to have been thus most perilously drawn aside from the right path! For as they were ignorant of the snares and devices of Satan, it has followed that those who had begun in the Spirit have finished their course in the flesh, and, being led away, have fallen into shameful and inexcusable excesses. Let such take care to walk heedfully; let them take an example from the Bride, who was unable to attain unto Him whom she longed for until she was met by those whose ministry she availed herself of to gain knowledge of her Beloved; that is to say, to learn the fear of the Lord. He who hesitates to give his hand to his legitimate teacher gives it to a seducer. And he who sends away his sheep to their pastures without a guardian is a shepherd, not of the sheep, but of wolves.

7. But now let us see in what sense the Bride declares herself to have been 'found.' For it seems to me that the word is employed in an unusual meaning, and that she speaks as if the Church had come only from one place; while, according to the word of the Lord, it came from the east and from the west (Matt. viii. 11), and from all the ends of the world. But neither has the Church been ever assembled unto one place where it might be found by the Apostles or by the Angels, to be directed or conducted unto Him, whom the soul of the Bride loveth. Could it have been found before it was collected? Evidently not, because it did not as yet exist. Wherefore if she had said that it was collected, or congregated, or (to use a term more applicable to the Church) gathered together by the preachers [of the Gospel], I should have simply passed that over without making any remark upon it. For they are the co-workers of God, whom also they heard speaking thus: *He that gathereth not with Me, scattereth abroad* (Matt. xii. 30). Nor would it have seemed strange to me if one should say that it was founded or built up by them. For they have done this in union with Him who says, as we read in the Gospels: *Upon this rock I will build My Church* (Matt. xvi. 18); and, *It was founded upon a rock* (Matt. vii. 25). But now she says none of these things, but, speaking in an unusual manner, says that she has been *found*, which makes us delay a little, and suspect that there is here some hidden meaning, which we ought to examine with greater care.

8. I wished, I own, to pass it over, and not to engage in an inquiry to which I feel myself not to be equal. But when I remember in how many obscure and difficult passages I have felt myself to be aided, even beyond my hope, when you lifted up your hearts in prayer on my behalf, I am ashamed of my want of faith; and blaming my fear, I undertake, though by no means with confidence, that which I timidly shrunk from. The accustomed help from the Lord will, I trust, not be wanting to me; and, in any case, the kindliness of my hearers will prevent what I have to say from being altogether without value. But with this the next sermon shall begin; for the present it is time to conclude. May He who is the Bridegroom of the Church, JESUS CHRIST our Lord, grant unto you not only to bear in mind the things which you have heard, but to love them ardently, and effectually to fulfil them in your actions. He is above all, God blessed for ever. AMEN.

SERMON LXXVIII.

THAT THE BRIDE, THAT IS TO SAY, THE CHURCH OF THE ELECT, WAS PREDESTINATED BY GOD BEFORE ALL AGES, AND PREVENTED BY HIS GRACE THAT SHE SHOULD SEEK HIM AND BE CONVERTED.

WE made a pause, if I remember rightly, at the word *found*, hearing with a kind of scruple the statement of the Bride that she was found by her preachers. We have stated the causes of our doubt and hesitation, and it seemed to us that here some hidden meaning was to be sought for; but this could not be done at the conclusion of a sermon, which point we had then reached. What remains, then, for us to do, but to fulfil now the promise which we made? In the exposition of this great mystery, which the Apostle of the Gentiles has interpreted as the holy and chaste union betwixt Christ and His Church (Eph. v. 32), and which is the very work of our salvation, three elements co-operate [and are to be taken into consideration]; God, the angelic race, and man. Why, indeed, should not God bring about, and take care for, these sacred nuptials of His Beloved Son? He does so in truth, and with entire willingness. He would assuredly be sufficient to accomplish it by Himself, and without the least help from these; nor could they, without Him, effect anything. That He, therefore, has associated them in the work of this ministry is not for the sake of assistance to Himself, but for good to them. For He has placed merit in works, as regards men, according to that saying: *The labourer is worthy of his hire* (Luke x. 7); and, *Every man shall receive his own reward according to his own labour* (1 Cor. iii. 8), whether he who plants in faith, or he who waters that which has been already planted. Now, if God employs the ministry of Angels to conduce to the salvation of men, does He not do it that Angels may be loved by men? For, that Angels love men is plain, especially from this, that Angels are not unaware of the fact that it is by men the ancient losses of their state are to be repaired and made good. And assuredly it was becoming that the realm of charity should not be ruled by other laws than those of mutual love between those who together are to reign, and by the pure affections of each, both to each other and to God.

2. But there is considerable difference in the manner in which these three causes act, according to the nobleness and dignity of each worker. For God doeth that which He wills, by His volition only; without stir, without motion, without alteration of place or time, of cause, or person. For He is the Lord of Sabaoth, who orders all things with peaceful and unquestioned power. He is also Wisdom, who sweetly doth order all things (Wisd. xii. 18, and viii. 3). An Angel acts without stir or agitation, but not without change of

time and place.¹ But a man cannot act without stir and eagerness of mind, nor is free, in acting, from movement of body and mind. For he is bidden to work out his salvation with fear and trembling (Phil. ii. 12), and to eat bread in the sweat of his face (Gen. iii. 19).

3. These things being explained, consider now with me that, in the glorious work of our salvation, there are three things which God, who is the Author of them, reserves unto Himself, and in which He anticipates all those who are helpers and co-workers with Him; these are predestination, creation, inspiration. Of which predestination had its beginning, I do not say from the founding of the Church, or even from this time or that time, for it is before all time. Creation, again, is coeval with time; while inspiration takes place in time, when and where God wills. According to predestination, then, there never has been any time when there was not a Church of the elect before the consciousness of God. If the unbeliever wonders at this, let him hear something at which he will wonder still more: that it has always been acceptable to God, and has always been loved by Him. Why should I not speak out boldly that hidden wisdom which has been made known to me from the Heart of God by that revealer of His high designs? I mean St. Paul, who has not hesitated to make known this secret which he had drawn, as he had so many others, from the riches of the Divine goodness. He says: *Who hath blessed us with all spiritual blessings in heavenly places in Christ, according as He hath chosen us in Him before the foundation of the world, that we should be holy and without blame before Him in love;* and he adds: *Having predestinated us unto the adoption of children, by Jesus Christ, to Himself, according to the good pleasure of His will, to the praise of the glory of His grace, wherein He hath made us accepted in the Beloved* (Eph. i. 3-6). And there is no doubt that these words are spoken with the voice and in the name of all the elect; and these *are* the Church. Who, then, even among the blessed spirits, could ever have been able to discover that Church in the deep bosom of the abyss of eternity, before the work of its creation was brought forth into the light of day, unless God, to whom is eternity itself, had chosen to reveal it?

4. But even when, at the command of its Creator, it had appeared, and was seen, under created forms and visible appearances, it was not at once recognised, either by men or Angels, because it was unfamiliar to them, being shadowed by the earthly likeness of man, and covered with the darkness of death. And not one of the sons of men hath entered into this life without this veil of universal confusion, One only excepted, He who enters it without stain of sin. He is Emmanuel, who, although He has taken from us, and put on for our sakes, the likeness of our sinful flesh, has not taken the reality of our sin. For the Apostle declares that He who appeared *in the likeness of sinful*

¹ In the MS. of St. Germain the reading is 'of body' (*quam corporali*). But I prefer *temporali*, as in the MS. of Citeaux, so as to answer more nearly to the preceding sentence, where it is said that God acts without alteration of place or time (Mabillon's Note).

flesh, and for sin, condemned sin in the flesh (Rom. viii. 3). All the remainder, whether elect or reprobate, have entered this life in the same manner, for there is no distinction; all have sinned, and all bear the livery[1] of the shame of sin. Because of this, therefore, although the Church was already called into being, and existed among created things, yet it could not be found or recognised by any creature, being marvellously hidden, for the time, both within the bosom of a blessed predestination, and within the mass of a miserable condemnation.

5. But [the Church] which Wisdom predestining had hidden from all eternity, and Creative Power had not produced when the world began,[2] the Divine Grace, which visits the earth, has in its due time revealed, according to the operation of that which I have named above, inspiration, because it consists of an inbreathing of the Spirit of the Bridegroom into human spirits for a preparation of the Gospel of peace, that is, to prepare a way for the Lord, and for the glory of His Gospel, into the hearts of all those who were predestined unto life, as many as they might be. It would have been in vain that the watchmen had toiled in preaching the Word, if this grace had not gone before. But now, seeing that the Word of God 'runneth very swiftly,' that the people of the nations are with ease turned unto the Lord, that their various tribes and languages concur in the unity of the faith, and that the ends of the earth are collected into the bosom of that one Church, Catholic and apostolic, which is the mother of us all, they have recognised the riches of that grace which was hidden from ages and from generations in the secret of an eternal predestination, and have rejoiced to have found her whom before all ages the Lord had chosen for Himself as His Bride.

6. Thus, then, as I think, it appears plainly not to have been without significance that the Bride declares that she was found by them; namely, as signifying that [the Church] was collected together, not [self] elected, and found before converted. For the conversion of each of the faithful ought to be attributed to Him, to whom it is necessary for all to say, as in the Psalm: *Convert us, O God of our salvation* (Ps. lxxxv. 4, Douay, partly). But I cannot, perhaps, apply the term of *finding* with such propriety to every soul, as the term of *conversion*. Or, rather, this is the state of the facts: The Lord cannot be said to *find* a soul, because He prevents (that is to say, is beforehand with) it; and prevention excludes *finding* (*inventionem*). What is there for Him to find to whom nothing is at any time unknown? *The Lord knoweth them that are His*, saith one (2 Tim. ii. 19); and what does He say Himself? *I know whom I have chosen*.[3] Plainly He refers to her whom from eternity He had foreknown: whom He chose, and loved, and formed; and therefore she could not be said to be *found* by Him. Yet I might safely say that she has been pre-

---

[1] *Caputium*; another reading is *pileum*.—ED.
[2] In the MS. of St. Germain, the reading is *nec creans Potentia satis in manifesto eduxerat*. The sense is the same.
[3] John xiii. 18. St. Bernard adds *a principio*, which is not in the Vulgate.—ED.

pared by Him that she might be found. For he that saw bare record, and we know that his record is true (John xix. 35). This is what he says: *I John saw the Holy City, new Jerusalem, coming down from God out of heaven, prepared as a bride adorned for her husband* (Rev. xxi. 2); and he was one of the watchmen who guard the city. And hear Him who is the Author and Preparer [of the Church] Himself, [and see Him] pointing her out, as it were, with His Finger to the watchmen, but under another metaphor. *Lift up your eyes*, He said, *and look on the fields, for they are white already to harvest* (John iv. 35). On this account the Lord of the Harvest invites His labourers to the work, when He has seen that all things were prepared, so that without much labour on their part they may be able to pride themselves on being *labourers together with God* (1 Cor. iii. 9). For what have they to do? They have to seek the Bride, and, when they have found her, to tell her of her Beloved. For they, because they are the friends of the Bridegroom, do not seek their own glory, but His. And they will not have to labour hard with regard to her, since she is already present, and is seeking Him with the devotion of her whole heart, inasmuch as her will has been prepared by the Lord.

7. Now, even while those watchmen have as yet said nothing to her, she anticipates her preachers, having been herself anticipated, and inquires of them: *Saw ye Him whom my soul loveth?* (iii. 3). Rightly, then, has she stated that she was found by those who guard the city, since she knows that she is already foreknown and anticipated by the Lord of the city, and that they find her such as she is, and do not make her so. Cornelius was thus found by Peter, and Paul by Ananias; but each of them had been previously found and prepared by the Lord. What preparation could be more complete than that of Saul, who had cried with submission, both of heart and voice: *Lord, what wilt Thou have me to do?* (Acts ix. 6). Nor was that of Cornelius less, since, by his alms and prayers which the Lord had inspired him to make, he had merited to attain unto the faith (Acts x. 4). Philip also found Nathanael; but the Lord, who saw him when he was under the fig-tree, had first found him. What was that seeing of him by the Lord but a preparation? And in the same way it is related that Andrew found his brother Simon; but that he was both foreseen and it was foreknown by the Lord that he should be called Cephas, which signifies 'Strong in faith' (John i. 41, 42, 45, 48).

8. We read of Mary, too, that she was found when she had conceived by the Holy Ghost (Matt. i. 18). I believe that the Bride of the Lord resembles in some degree His Mother in this respect. For unless she also had been found filled with the Holy Ghost, she would not have questioned with such confidence those who found her, respecting Him, whose is the Spirit. She would not have endured that they should have declared to her to what end they had come, but she spake to them herself, and, indeed, out of the fulness of her heart: *Saw ye Him whom my soul loveth?* She knew that the eyes which had seen Him were blessed, and in her admiration for those

who had had that blessing, she said: 'Are you not they to whom it has been given to see Him, whom so many prophets and kings desired to see, and have not seen? Are you not they who have merited to behold Wisdom in the flesh, the Truth in bodily form, God in Man? Many there are who say, Lo, He is here, and Lo, He is there; but I think it safer for me to give credence to you, who have eaten and drank with Him, after He rose from the dead.' I believe what has been said will suffice respecting the inquiry made by the Bride, of the watchmen, but if not, it shall be supplied in another sermon. But even now, and from this, it has been made abundantly clear, that [the Church] has been prevented by the Holy Spirit, and found by them who guard the city, because it is she whom God has foreseen and predestined before all ages, and prepared to be an everlasting joy, throughout eternal ages, to His dear Son, that she may be holy and immaculate in His sight, growing as a lily, and flourishing for ever before the Lord and Father of my Lord JESUS CHRIST, the Bridegroom of the Church, who is above all, God blessed for evermore. AMEN.

SERMON LXXIX.

OF THE STRONG AND INDISSOLUBLE LOVE WHEREWITH THE SOUL HOLDS TO ITS LORD; ALSO OF THE RETURN OF THE BRIDEGROOM AT THE ENDING OF THE AGE, TO SAVE THE SYNAGOGUE OF THE JEWS.

'*Saw ye Him whom my soul loveth?*'—Cant. iii. 3.

O LOVE, violent, vehement, burning, impetuous, which dost not suffer anything else to be thought of, but, despising all things in comparison, art content with thyself! Thou confoundest ranks, takest no count of custom, ignorest all measure; thou dost triumph in thy own self over all the rules of opportuneness, of reason, of reticence, of prudence, or of judgment, and bringest them under control. Every thought and word of hers is full of thee, has regard to thee and to nothing else, so entirely hast thou taken possession of her, both in heart and tongue. She says: *Saw ye Him whom my soul loveth?* As if they knew what was the subject of her thoughts. 'Dost thou ask for news of Him whom thy soul loveth, and has He not a name? Who art thou; and He, who is He?' I speak thus, because of the strangeness of this address, and the singular disregard of names, in which this passage appears very different to other Scriptures. Whence, in this epithalamium, the words are not so much to be considered as the feelings which underlie and prompt them, because the sacred affection which is plainly the entire subject of this whole canticle is thus to be estimated, that is, not by word only, or by language, but in deed and in truth. Love speaks in it everywhere, and if anyone desires to obtain a knowledge of those things which are read in it, a spirit of love is necessary to him that he may do so. In vain will one who is without love attempt to listen to or read this Song of Love; the cold heart cannot comprehend or appreciate its language, full of feeling and fire. Just as one who is unacquainted with Greek or with Latin cannot understand a person who speaks in either of those languages, and so with other things, so is it with the language of love; it is strange and barbarous to one who does not love, and to him will be but as sounding brass and a tinkling cymbal (1 Cor. xiii 1). But as they (I mean the watchmen) have received from the Spirit the ability to love, they understand what the Spirit speaks, and are able to respond on the spot to the words of love addressed to them; and even to respond in the same language, that is, in feelings of affection and acts of kindness.

2. They do, indeed, instruct her so well concerning Him about whom she inquires, and that in a brief time, that she says: *It was but a little that I passed from them, but I found Him whom my soul loveth.* She says well *a little*, because their reply to her was brief and comprehensive; that is, they delivered to her the Creed, which is a concise statement of the Faith. And what follows is in similar terms. It was expedient indeed that the Bride should pass by them, through whom she should learn the truth, but also that she should pass beyond them. And if she had not passed beyond them she would not have found Him whom she sought. And you may be assured that they themselves urged this very thing upon her. For they did not preach themselves, but Christ Jesus their Lord, and He is assuredly both beyond them and above. Wherefore also He says: Come unto Me, all ye that be desirous of Me (Ecclus. xxiv. 19). Nor was it enough to pass *to* Him, but she is taught to pass *through* to Him. Because He whom she was seeking had also *passed through*. For not only did He pass from death unto life, but He passed through death unto glory. It was indispensable, then, that the Bride should likewise pass through unto Him, otherwise she could not succeed in reaching Him, not having followed His footsteps whithersoever He went.

3. And to explain more clearly what I say: if my Lord Jesus had risen indeed from the dead, but had not ascended into heaven, it could not be said of Him that He had passed through, but only that He had passed away; and consequently the Bride in seeking Him must pass away from others, but need not pass beyond them. But as, in ascending into heaven, He has passed beyond Resurrection, the Bride says with accuracy, not simply that she has passed, but that she has passed beyond, inasmuch as by faith and devotion she has followed Him even unto the heavens. Therefore to believe the Resurrection is a passing, but to believe the Ascension is a passing beyond. And perhaps she knew the one and did not know the other (which I remember that I said one day when I was treating the subject[1]). Therefore, having been instructed by them in that which

---
[1] Sermon I., *in Festo Paschæ*.

was wanting to her, namely, that He who had risen from the dead had also ascended into heaven, she also has thither ascended, that is, has passed beyond [this sphere of outward things], and has found Him (Heb. iv. 14, and compare Collect for Ascension Day in the Common Prayer Book of Church of England). How could she fail to do so, when arising in heart and mind[1] unto the place where He is in body? *It was but a little that I passed from them.* Rightly does she say from *them;* for our Head has preceded and transcended in two respects both His apostles, and all other His members who are upon the earth; that is to say, by His Resurrection (as I have already mentioned) and by His Ascension. And yet in each case Christ is the first-fruits. He has gone before, and our faith has gone before also. Where has it not followed Him? If He has ascended into heaven, it is there; if He has gone down into hell, it is there also; and if He has taken wings with the morning, and dwelt in the utmost parts of the sea, *even there*, it declares to Him, *shall Thy Hand lead me, and Thy Right Hand shall hold me* (Ps. cxxxix. 8-10). And, finally, is it not according to this faith that He, the Father of the Bridegroom, He, who is supremely Powerful and supremely good, has raised us up, and made us to sit at His Right Hand?[2] So far to explain what the Church has said: *I passed beyond them:* because she has passed beyond her own self in abiding, by her faith, in regions whither she has not as yet attained in fact. I think that it is now clear why she has said, 'I have passed beyond,' rather than said simply 'I have passed.' Let us now go on to the words which follow.

4. *I held Him, and would not let Him go, until I had brought Him into my mother's house, and into the chamber of her that conceived me.* Thus it is that from that time and thenceforward, the people of Christ have never been without either faith upon the earth or charity within the Church. Floods have come, and winds have raged, and beat upon it, and it has not fallen, for it was founded upon a rock (Matt. vii. 25). That Rock is CHRIST. Therefore neither the wordy diatribes of philosophers, nor the cavils of heretics, nor the swords of persecutors, have ever been able, nor shall they ever be able, to separate it from the love of God, which is in Christ Jesus (Rom. viii. 39), so strongly does the Church hold to Him whom her soul loveth, so firmly convinced is she that it is good to hold fast to God. 'Good it is,' says the prophet Isaiah, 'for the soldering'[3] What is more tenacious than this solder, which is not dissolved by water, nor parted by winds, nor even severed by sword strokes? For many waters, we are told, cannot quench love (Cant. viii. 7). *I held Him, and would not let Him go.* And the holy Patriarch also said: *I will not let Thee go, unless Thou bless me* (Gen. xxxii. 26). She also will not let Him go, and perhaps her attachment is stronger than that of the Patriarch, for not even for the sake of a benediction can she consent

---
[1] Another reading is *fide.*
[2] In some copies it is added *in cœlestibus.* See Eph. ii. 6.
[3] Is. xli. 7, not used in a literal sense.

to part with Him. 'I desire,' she says, 'not even Thy benediction, but Thee.' *Whom have I in heaven but Thee? and there is none upon earth that I desire beside Thee* (Ps. lxxiii. 25). I will not let Thee go, even if Thou hast given me Thy blessing.

5. *I held Him, and would not let Him go.* Nor does He, perhaps, desire less to be held, for He says: *My delights were with the sons of men* (Prov. viii. 31), and in the Gospel He gives the promise: *Lo, I am with you alway, even unto the end of the world* (Matt. xxviii. 20). What bond of union is stronger than that which is compacted by the perfect and earnest willingness of the two who are parties to it? *I held Him*, she declares. But, nevertheless, she is held fast in return by Him whom she holds, as in another place she says to Him: *Thou hast holden me by my right hand* (Ps. lxxiii. 24). And she who holds and is holden, how can she possibly fall? She holds to the Lord by the firmness of her faith, by the fervency of her devotion. But yet she could not long hold fast to Him, were she not also held by Him. It is the power and the mercy of the Lord by which she is held. *I held Him, and would not let Him go, until I had brought Him into my mother's house, and into the chamber of her that conceived me.* Great is the charity of the Church, inasmuch as she does not grudge her choicest delights even to her rival, which is the Synagogue. What goodness can be greater than to be prepared to communicate even to her enemy, Him whom her soul loves? And yet it is not wonderful, inasmuch as *salvation is of the Jews* (John iv. 22). To the place whence He came forth, let the Saviour return, that the remnant of Israel may be saved (Rom. ix. 27). Let not the branches be ungrateful to the root, nor the children to their mother. Let not the branches grudge to the root the sap which they themselves have derived from it, nor the children grudge to their mother the milk which they have drawn from her bosom. Let the Church hold firmly the salvation which Judæa has lost; let her hold it fast, until the fulness of the Gentiles be come in, and so all Israel shall be saved (Rom. xi. 25, 26). She would wish to come in common to the common salvation, which is partaken by all, in such a manner, that no part is taken away from any. This she does, and more What more? She chooses the name and the grace of His Bride. This is over and above the gift of salvation.

6 This degree of charity would be incredible, were it not that the words of the Bride, here recorded, compel us to believe it. For she has said, if you have noticed, that she wishes to bring Him to whom she holds so closely, not only into the house, but into the chamber, of her mother, which is the sign of a singular prerogative. It would be sufficient for salvation that He should enter the house; but that He enters into the secret of the chamber is a sign of special grace. *This day*, saith the Lord, *is salvation come unto this house* (Luke xix. 9). When the Saviour had entered the house, how could it be otherwise than that those of the house should be saved? But she that merits to receive Him in the chamber has for her part His secret gift.

Salvation is for the whole house, but the higher and sweeter gifts are reserved for those, for whom they are prepared by the Father. *Until I had brought Him into my mother's house,* she says. Of what house does she speak, but of that of which the Lord had foretold to the Jews: *Behold, your house is left unto you desolate?* (Luke xiii. 35). He has done what He had said, according to His declaration made by a prophet: *I have forsaken Mine house, I have left Mine heritage* (Jer. xii. 7); and now the Bride promises to bring Him back to it, and to restore to her mother's house its lost salvation. And as if even this were a little thing, hear what a promise of good she adds thereto: *And into the chamber of her that conceived me.* He who enters into the marriage chamber is the Bridegroom. Great is the power of love! The Saviour had gone forth from His home and from His heritage with indignation and wrath; and now He is so far turned from the fierceness of His anger, so won to forgiveness and grace, as to return not only as a Saviour, but as a Bridegroom. O daughter [of this house], blessed art thou from the Lord, who dost quench the indignation, and restore the heritage. Blessed art thou of thy mother, for it is by thy good deed that the wrath of the Lord is turned away, that salvation is brought back to her; that He is brought back who says to her: *I am thy Salvation* (Ps. xxxv. 3). Nor is even this enough, for He adds: *I will betroth thee unto Me for ever: yea, I will betroth thee unto Me in righteousness, and in judgment, and in loving kindness, and in mercies* (Hos. ii. 19). But remember that she who wins these kindnesses for her mother is the Bride. How can she be willing to yield her Bridegroom, and such a Bridegroom, to another; nay, desire to do so? But it is not to be understood thus. It is as a good daughter that she desires this great good for her mother, yet not to give it up, but to communicate it. It is sufficient for both; and, indeed, they are not two, but one in Christ. For He is our Peace, who has made both one; that there may be one Bride, and one Bridegroom, JESUS CHRIST our Lord, who is above all, God blessed for ever. AMEN.

SERMON LXXX.

AN ACUTE AND PROFOUND ARGUMENT RESPECTING THE IMAGE OR WORD OF GOD, AND THE SOUL, WHICH IS CREATED IN THAT IMAGE: AND CONCERNING THE ERROR OF GILBERT, BISHOP OF POICTIERS.[1]

SOME of you, as I have learned, find a reason for discontent, because, while I have for some days past taken pleasure in occupying you with the profound and wonderful mysteries contained in the words of the Bride, the discourses which I have delivered to you have been too little seasoned with moral reflections,

---

[1] This sermon was preached after the Council, held at Rheims in the year 1148, in which Gilbert was condemned.

or even altogether without them. That is indeed different from my usual custom. But permit me to return again to those subjects which I have already expounded. For I cannot proceed without taking a brief retrospect of these. Tell me, then, if you remember, from what part of the Scripture it was that I began to deprive you of this satisfaction that you desire, that so I may commence afresh from that point. It is my task to repair your loss, or, rather, I trust to the Lord, in dependence upon whom I do all things, that He will do so. From what point, then, shall I begin again? From this verse, if I do not mistake: *On my bed I sought Him whom my soul loveth.* From that verse and henceforward my one endeavour was to disperse the dense cloud of mystery in which these allegories were enveloped, and to bring forth into the light of knowledge the sacred and mysterious joys of Christ and His Church. But now let us go back and seek out the moral senses of these words. That which may be for your benefit cannot be disagreeable to me. And this will be done with considerable fitness, if we apply what has been said of Christ and the Church in a similar way to the WORD of God and the soul.

2. But someone will say to me: 'Why do you join these two together? What relation is there between the WORD and the soul?' Much in every way. In the first place, there is so close an affinity between the nature of the One and that of the other, that the One is the Image and Likeness of God, the other made after that image. In the second place, the resemblance that is between them is a witness of that affinity. For the soul has been created, not only after the image, but in the likeness of it. Do you ask, In what respects is it like? Listen first, and hear in what respects it is in the Image of the Word. The WORD is truth, and wisdom, and righteousness, and these constitute the image. Of what is it the image? Of [Him who is] Truth, and Wisdom, and Righteousness. He who is the Image is, then, Righteousness of Righteousness, Wisdom of Wisdom, Truth of Truth, yea, Light of Light, and in a word, God of God. None of these can be predicated of the soul, because it is not [at the present] the Image of God. But it is capable of these excellences, and desirous of them, and, therefore, perhaps is shown to be in the image of the WORD. It is of creatures the loftiest, since it is capable of that greatness, and the desire it feels for that is a mark of its uprightness. For we read that God made man upright (Eccles. vii. 29); and as for his greatness, his capacity, as has been said, is a conclusive proof of it. For it is of necessity that he who is in a certain image should be in conformity with that image, and not merely share in the empty name of the image; inasmuch as the archetypal Being Himself bears not His Name simply for the name's sake, but because it is expressive of His attributes. But you are told of Him who is the Image of that archetypal Being, that He was in the Form of God, and thought it not robbery to be equal with God (Phil. ii. 6). You see that His uprightness is shown by His being in the Form of God, and His greatness by His equality with Him; so

that uprightness being compared with uprightness, and greatness with greatness, it becomes manifest that the Image, and that which is made in that image [*i.e.*, the soul], correspond in one of these respects ; while the Image, and that Being of whom He is the Image, correspond in both. For it is He of whom you have heard holy David sing in a Psalm : *Great is our Lord, and of great power* (Ps. cxlvii. 5) ; and again, *The Lord is upright . . . and there is no unrighteousness in Him* (Ps. xcii. 15). Of that great and righteous God He is the Image, so that He is great, and He is righteous ; and it is from Him that the soul, that is made in His image, has its likeness.

3. But I inquire : Has He who is the Image of God nothing more than the soul which is made in His likeness, for we ascribe to it also to be great and to be righteous ? Assuredly, there is a very great difference. The one has received those qualities in a measure : the other has them according to His equality [with the Father]. Is there not still another difference ? There is this : Upon the one either creation or condescending goodness has conferred them : but they belong to the other by His generation. And there is no doubt that this is a sign of far higher dignity. No one can fail to see that the one receives these qualities only by the bounty of God ; but the Other has from God His very Nature and Substance, which is a condition far more exalted. For the Image of God is consubstantial with Him ; and all that He appears to communicate to the same Image of Him is Essential to Both, not accidental. Notice also still another particular in which He who is the Image of God is immeasurably superior. To be great and to be righteous ; who does not know that those two qualities are distinct in their nature ? Yet in Him they are but one. And even more : they are one *with* Him. Not only is it with Him the same thing to be righteous and to be great, but His greatness and His righteousness are no other than His Being. It is not thus with the soul. Its greatness and its righteousness are both distinct from itself and distinct from each other. For if, as I have said above, the soul is great because it is capable of things eternal, and righteous because it yearns for the goodness everlasting, then the soul which does not desire nor seek for the things which are above, but those which are upon the earth, is not upright, but is bent downwards, and so ceases to be always great, though it remains always capable of eternal existence. For even if the soul should never receive it, it will always retain this capability ; and thus the saying of the Scripture is realized, *Surely man passeth as an image* (Ps. xxxviii. 7, Douay), yet only in part, so that the immeasurable superiority of the WORD, as possessing these qualities in their completeness, may clearly appear. For how is it possible that the WORD should fall from being righteous and great, since He is Himself greatness and righteousness? Man, on the contrary, possesses these qualities in part, lest if he were wholly deprived of them, no hope of salvation should remain to him. For if [the soul] should cease to be great, it would cease also to be

capable of salvation, inasmuch as it is from this capacity, as I have said, that its greatness is derived. How, then, could it possibly hope for that which it was not capable of receiving?

4. It is, then, by the greatness which it still retains, even after having lost its righteousness, that man passes through this world in the image [of the WORD]; only he limps (so to speak) on one foot as he walks, and he has become an alienated son. For of such it was, I think, that these words were spoken: The children that are strangers have lied unto me, strange children have faded away, and have halted from their paths (Ps. xviii. 46, Douay). With great fitness are they styled *strange children;* for they are *children*, because they have re tained that which made them great; and yet they are *strange*, because of the loss of their original righteousness. Nor would he have said *have halted*, but 'have fallen,' or something like that, if they had divested themselves entirely of the image in which men were made. So then, now, man passes through the world in the image of the WORD so far as relates to greatness; but as relates to righteousness, he, so to speak, halts; he is troubled and despoiled of that image; and the Scripture speaks thus of him: *Every man walketh in a vain shew; surely they are disquieted in vain.* Altogether in vain, for it goes on to say: *He heapeth up riches, and knoweth not who shall gather them* (Ps. xxxix. 6). And why is he ignorant, except that he bends down towards things low and earthly, and treasures up for himself nothing but earth? He does not know in the least for whom he is gathering those things which he confides to the earth, whether for the moths to devour, or for thieves to break through and steal, for robbers to pillage, or for fire to destroy. And therefore it is in the person of that unhappy man who contorts himself towards the ground, and broods over none but earthly things, that the melancholy declaration is made in the Psalms: *I am troubled; I am bowed down greatly; I go mourning all the day long* (Ps. xxxviii. 6). He has experience in himself of the truth in that saying of the Wise Man: *God hath made man upright; but they have sought out many inventions* (Eccles. vii. 29). And at once the voice of ridicule is addressed to him: *Bow down, that we may go over* (Is. li. 23).

5. But how have we arrived at this point? Was it not thus, that we wished to show that greatness and righteousness (which are the two excellences that we had determined to be in the Image of God) are not one in the soul and with the soul, as we have shown it to be of faith that they are one in the WORD and with the WORD. And as to righteousness, it is quite plain from what has been said, that it is distinct both from the soul itself and from the greatness of the soul, since even when it no longer exists, the soul endures, and is still great. But in what way shall it be shown that the greatness of the soul is distinct from the soul itself? For this cannot be done in the same manner in which the distinction between the soul and its righteousness was demonstrated; the soul cannot be deprived of its greatness as it may be of its righteousness. Yet the greatness of the

soul is not the soul itself; for although the soul is not found without its greatness, yet the greatness itself is found also without (*extra*, beyond) the soul. Do you ask where? In the Angels. For the Angels are great in the same manner as the soul, namely, by the capacity they have for things eternal. It has been shown clearly that the soul is distinct from its righteousness, because it may be deprived of that righteousness; why, then, should it not be distinct from its greatness, which it cannot claim to be exclusively its own? If, then, the one of these qualities is not in every soul, and the other is not found in the soul alone, it is plain that both the one and the other is distinct from the soul. Also, no form is that of which it is the form. Now, the greatness of the soul is its form. For it cannot be said not to be the form of the soul because it is inseparable from it. All differences of substance are of this nature, not only those which are so proper to one thing that they cannot belong to any other, but also certain others which are common to many natures. The soul, then, is not [the same as] its greatness, even as the blackness of a crow is not the crow, nor the whiteness of snow the snow, nor the faculty of reason or of risibility is the man who possesses them; and yet you will never find a crow without blackness, snow without whiteness, nor a man without the faculty of reason or of risibility. Thus also the soul and the greatness of the soul, although inseparable, are distinct from each other. How can they be otherwise than distinct, when the one is in the subject [in which it inheres], and the other is the subject and the substance? The only Nature which is supreme and uncreate, that is, God the Holy Trinity, possesses for Itself alone this pure and unique simplicity of Essence, that there is not found in it one thing and another thing, here and there, one time and another time. For it abides in its own Self, It is all that It has, and what It is; It exists always, and in a manner unchanging and unchanged. All that in other natures is separated or different, is in it united and rendered alike, so that in It, number does not cause plurality, nor diversity change. It contains all places, and not being contained in any, sets in due order all things, each in its place. Beneath it pass all times; it is not subject to them. The future it does not await; it does not hold anything in remembrance as past, nor experience any as being present.

6. Let us withdraw ourselves, beloved, let us withdraw ourselves from those teachers of novelties, not dialecticians, but heretics, who, in their extreme impiety, argue that the greatness in which God is great, the goodness in which He is good, the wisdom in which He is wise, and the righteousness in which He is righteous, and lastly, the Divinity in which He is God, is not God. 'He is God,' they say, ' by His Divinity, but the Divinity is not God. Perhaps it does not condescend to be God, because it is so great that it makes God to be what He is.' But if It is not God, what is It? For either It is God, or something which is not God, or It is nothing at all. Now, you do not allow that It is God; you do not pretend, I suppose, that It is

nothing; then you confess that It is so necessary to God, that without It He could not be God, but that by It He is [that which He is]. If, then, there be something which is not God, either it will be less than He, or greater than He, or equal. But how can it be less than He, seeing that it is by it He is God? It remains, then, that you should allow it to be either greater than He, or equal. But if it be greater, then It and not God is the Supreme Good; while if it be equal, there are two, each of which is the Supreme Good; and either conclusion is contrary to the Catholic Faith. We are of the same opinion respecting the greatness, the goodness, the righteousness, the wisdom of God, as respecting His Divinity, and I hold that they are all one in God and with God. For He is good from no other source or reason than that which makes Him great; nor is He otherwise righteous and wise than He is great and good; nor, in fact, is there any other source or reason for any of His attributes than there is for His Divinity. He is in His own Self the Source of all.

7. But the heretic says: 'What? Do you deny that He is God by His Divinity?' No; but I maintain that the same Divinity by which He is God is God Himself, that I may not be obliged to allow that there is anything more excellent than God. For I say also that He is great by greatness, but is Himself that greatness, that I may not rank anything as greater than God. And I confess that He is good by goodness, but that this goodness is no other than Himself, that I may not seem to recognise anything as better than He; and so with all other attributes. It is with gladness and confidence that I am going onward in the path of truth, that I adopt the conclusion of him who said: 'God is great with no other greatness than that which He Himself is; for otherwise that greatness would be greater than God.' This was Augustine, the strongest hammer who has ever crushed heretics.[1] If, then, any such thing may be properly said of God, it may more fitly and correctly be asserted that God is greatness, goodness, righteousness, wisdom, than to say God is great, good, righteous, or wise.

8. For this reason it was that in the Council lately held at Rheims by Pope Eugenius, that exposition made by Gilbert, Bishop of Poictiers, in his comment upon the words of Boethius' *De Trinitate*, which are themselves perfectly sound and orthodox, was deservedly adjudged by the Pope and the other Bishops to be perverse and altogether suspicious. For the Bishop commented upon them thus: 'The Father is Truth, that is, He is true; the Son is Truth, that is, He is true; the Holy Ghost is Truth, that is, He is true. And these Three together are not three truths, but one Truth; that is to say, One Being who is true.' O explanation obscure and perverse! How much more appropriate and true it would be to say, on the contrary: 'The Father is true, that is, He is Truth; the Son is true, that is, He is Truth; the Holy Ghost is true, that is, He is Truth. And these Three are One Being who is true, that is, They are One Truth.'

[1] *De Trinitate*, Bk. V., c. 10, *n.* 11.

Which, indeed, he would have done had he deigned to imitate holy Fulgentius, who says: 'One only Truth of One God, or rather one Truth which is One God, does not allow the service and the worship which is due to the Creator to be rendered to a creature' (*Lib. de Fide Orthod. ad Donat.*, cap. 5). He was a good defender of the faith who spoke so truly of the Truth, who had opinions so pious and Catholic respecting the true and pure simplicity of the Divine Substance, in which there can be nothing which is not Itself, and Itself is God. That book of the Bishop beforenamed contained other passages which differed from the rectitude of the faith, one of which I will quote as an example. For where his author (Boethius) says: 'When it is said, God, God, God, this refers to the Substance,' our commentator adds: 'Not what the Substance is, but by what It is.' But God forbid that the Church Catholic should assent to that proposition that there is any substance or anything at all by which God is, and which is not God.

9. But it is not against him personally that I say these things, since he, in the same Council, acquiescing humbly in the opinion of the other Bishops, has condemned with his own mouth both these and other statements which were found worthy of blame; but on account of those persons who are said to be still perusing and transcribing that book, against the apostolical prohibition promulgated at the same place, and who persist obstinately in following that Bishop in opinions which he has himself abandoned, preferring to have him for a master in his error, rather than in the correction of it. And we have spoken not only for them, but on your account I have thought it desirable to make this digression, taking occasion from our having to consider the difference between the Image [of the Word] and the soul which has been made in that Image, so that those who perhaps may at some time have drunk of those stolen waters, and have thought them pleasant (Prov. ix. 17), may reject them by the taking of this antidote, and, being purged in the stomach of their soul, may listen to that which remains to be said, according to my promise, of the resemblance of the soul to the WORD. Thus they shall draw with joy from purer fountains; not mine, but those of the Saviour, the Bridegroom of the Church, JESUS CHRIST our Lord, who is above all, God blessed for ever. AMEN.

SERMON LXXXI.

OF THE SIMILARITY AND LIKENESS OF THE SOUL TO THE WORD, IN RESPECT OF ITS IDENTITY OF ESSENCE, ITS IMMORTALITY OF EXISTENCE, AND ITS FREEDOM OF WILL.

IT was not without good reason that the inquiry was made in the last discourse, what affinity there was between the human soul and the WORD. For what can there be in common between a Majesty so great and a poverty so extreme, that a greatness which is so exalted and a lowliness so humble should be said to be associated, as if upon an equality, in the manner and with the love of a pair who are espoused to each other? For if we assert this with truth, then great is the reason for rejoicing and confidence; but if falsely, then ours is an audacity to be greatly punished. And therefore it was necessary to inquire what was the affinity between these two, which, indeed, we have already ascertained in many respects, but not altogether. For who is so undiscerning as not to see the correspondence between the image and that which is formed after the pattern of that image? We have shown in the sermon of yesterday, if you remember, both that the WORD is the Image of God and that the soul is made in that image. And we have proved in that also the close relation between the soul and that Image of God, since not only is it made in that image, but also after the likeness of it. But we have not yet declared in every particular that in which this likeness principally consists. Let us now address ourselves to this task, so that the soul, recognising more fully what its origin is, may be filled with a noble shame to degenerate from it by an unworthy manner of living, or, rather, that it may study with earnest care what it shall recognise as being corrupted in itself by sin, and thus ruling itself by the help of God in a manner worthy of its origin, may be enabled to draw near with modest confidence to communion with the WORD.

2. Let it recognise, then, that from this original Divine likeness it draws a natural simplicity of substance, by which to be is to it the same as to live, although not always to live well or happily; and in this it has a likeness to the Image of the WORD, though not an equality with It. This is a degree of relationship, but only a degree. That to live should be synonymous with living in perfect goodness and happiness is the supreme height of moral greatness, and to this height it does not attain. If, then, the WORD, because of His greatness, has this unique prerogative, and the soul, because of its likeness to the WORD, has the attribute that for it to exist is to have life, though it does not attain to the lofty perfectness of the WORD, yet the affinity of natures, and the privilege of the soul, are manifest herein. To express this more clearly: It is in God alone that 'to live' is the same as 'to live in perfect goodness and happiness,' and He is the Essence

absolutely pure and absolutely Eternal. The second degree is that in which 'to exist is to have life'; this is the condition of the soul, and this is to be like unto God. From that degree, though a lower one, it is possible to ascend, not only to the life of goodness, but also to that of happiness; not that, even for the soul that has attained to it, existence and goodness are one and the same, because, although the WORD glorifies it by His likeness, the disparity that ever exists between Him and it obliges it to say: *Lord, who is like unto Thee?* (Ps. xxxv. 10). Yet it is for the soul a promotion of extreme value, because from it, and from it alone, is it possible to ascend unto the life of blessedness.

3. There are two classes of beings which have life: those who are conscious of it, and those who are not conscious. The former rank above the latter, and above both the one and the other are those in whom life and thought are the same. Life, and that which lives, are not in the same degree; much less are life, and those which live not. Life is, indeed, the soul which is living; but it lives not other whence than from itself, and on this account we speak of it with propriety, not so much as living as being itself life. Thus it follows that the soul, when infused into a body, gives life to it; but that body does not, by the presence of life in it, become itself life, but living. From whence it clearly appears that it is not the same thing even to a living body to exist and to live, since it may exist and yet not live. Much less shall those things which are without life rise into this rank. It does not even follow that everything which is said to have life, or which has it in fact, will be able forthwith to attain to this point. There is a life of the lower animals, and a life of trees; the former has consciousness, the latter is without it. Yet in neither is it the same thing to exist and to live, since, according to the opinion of many persons,[1] their life has been in the elements before it was in the limbs of the one class, or the branches of the other. And, according to this view, when their life ceases to animate them, they cease to live, but they do not cease to exist. They are equally unloosed and dissolved, as if they were not merely bound together, but intertwined.[2] For the life of these things is not simple in its nature, but compounded out of many elements. And therefore it is not reduced to nothingness, but separated into parts, of which each returns to that whence it had its origin; for example, that which is of an airy nature to the air, that of a fiery nature to the fire, and the rest in like manner. To this kind of life, then, it is by no means the same thing to exist and to live, since when it does not live, it still exists.

4. Now, none of these things in which that is the case, can ever progress or rise into that higher life of goodness and blessedness, since they have not been able to attain even that grade which is below it. The soul of man alone can reach that higher life, inasmuch as it

---

[1] Query, the followers of Empedocles.
[2] *Solvuntur et dissolvuntur: alligatæ, colligatæ.* The meaning of the sentence is not quite clear.—ED.

is seen to have been constituted as life by Him who is the Life, simple [in its nature], by Him who is simple in His Essence, as He is Infinite, and immortal by Him who is Immortal; so that it is not far from the supreme degree in which existence is identical with perfect happiness, in which He dwells for ever who alone is infinitely Blessed and infinitely Powerful, who is King of kings and Lord of lords. The soul, then, has received, by the condition in which it is, the power of attaining blessedness, though it is not now blessed; and to that supreme grade it is advancing as much as it is able to do, yet without reaching it. For, as we have already said, even when it shall attain blessedness, yet that blessedness will not be to it the same thing as its life. We allow to it a resemblance; we deny to it equality. For example, God is Life; the soul also is life; it is, then, like unto God, but it is not equal to Him. It is like unto Him, because it is life; and its life is in itself, because it is not only living, but also lifegiving (*vivens, vivificans*), as also He is Himself all these things. But yet to Him it is unequal, inasmuch as a creature is unequal to its Creator. It is wholly unequal, inasmuch as neither would it have existed if it had not been created by Him, nor would it live unless He bestowed life upon it. It would not live, I say; that is, in the spiritual life, not the natural. For it lives immortally in the natural life, and that necessarily, even though spiritually it does not live. But of what kind is that life, in which it would be better not to have been born, than not to have the power to die? It is rather death than life, and that a death the more cruel, as it is the effect of sin, not of nature. For the death of the wicked is very evil (Ps. xxxiv. 22, Douay). The soul, then, which lives according to the flesh is dead while it lives, since it were good for it not to live at all rather than to live in such a manner. And, indeed, from that living death it can have no resurrection ever, except through the word of life; or, rather, through Him who is the WORD, who is the Life, and bestows life.

5. But, farther, the soul is immortal; and in this respect also it is like unto the WORD, but not equal to Him. For the immortality of the Divine Nature is so far above, and surpassing every other, that the Apostle says of God: *Who only hath immortality* (1 Tim. vi. 16). Which is spoken of Him, as I think, because He alone is unchangeable in and by His Nature who says: *I am the Lord; I change not* (Mal. iii. 6). For the immortality which is true and perfect is no more susceptible of change than it is of ending, since every change is a likeness of death, and an anticipation of it. Everything which changes, in passing from one state to another, necessarily dies, so to speak, to that which it is, in order to begin to be that which it is not. If, then, there are as many deaths as there are changes, where is the immortality? And to this vanity everything created is made subject, not willingly, but by reason of Him who hath subjected the same in hope (Rom. viii. 20). And yet the soul is immortal, because its life is in itself, and as it cannot fall away from itself, so it cannot fall away from its life. But since it is plain that in thoughts and

feelings it is subject to change, while it recognises in its immortality its likeness to God, it ought also to recognise how far, indeed, it falls short in comparison with Him to whom alone complete and perfect immortality belongs, with whom is no variableness, neither shadow of turning (James i. 17). Yet the present discussion has shown that the dignity of the soul is by no means small, since it appears to draw near to the nature of the WORD in two respects : in the simplicity of its essence, and the endlessness of its life.

6. But there is still another resemblance which occurs to me, and which I will by no means pass over, for it contributes no less than the other particulars to the greatness of the soul, and perhaps renders it even more like unto the WORD. This is Freedom of the Will, a quality plainly Divine, and which shines forth in the soul like a jewel set in gold. It is by this that there is in the soul the power of distinguishing and the freedom of choosing between good and evil, that is, between life and death, between light and darkness, and other things similarly opposed, which present themselves before the consciousness of the soul. That eye of the soul is a close discerner and authoritative judge between opposed alternatives ; as a clear-sighted observer it discerns, as a free and independent judge it decides. On this account its decision is said to be free, because it is open to be influenced by the determination of the will, and can carry out the decision when made, into action. Thence also is man capable of merit. For every action done by you, and which you were free to do or to leave undone, is rightly imputed to you for merit or demerit, according as it is good or evil. And as a person is rightly praised, both he who, having it in his power to do evil, has not done it, and he who, being free not to do good, has, nevertheless, done it ; so also a person is justly blamed who, being able not to do evil actions, has done them, or to do good ones, has not done them. For where there is no liberty of action there is no merit. On this account it is that animals, which are without reason, have likewise no merit, because they are wanting both in freedom [of will] and in the power of deliberation and judgment. They are directed by the leadings of their senses, carried away by their impulses, and are under the dominion of their appetites. For they have not the power of judgment, by which to reflect upon their actions or control them ; nor, indeed, have they the faculty of forming a judgment, that is, reason ; and they are not judged, because they are not capable of forming a judgment. How can creatures who have not received the gift of reason be reasonably called to account for their actions?

7. Man alone is not put under a constraint by his nature, and therefore man alone among living beings is free. And yet he also, by the intervention of sin, suffers a kind of violent constraint ; but this arises not from his nature, but from his own will, and he is not thereby deprived of the liberty which is natural to him. For that which is done voluntarily is done freely. And, indeed, it is by sin it is brought about that the corruptible body weighs upon the soul ; but

this is not by its own weight, but by its love for that which is amiss. For that the soul which was capable of falling by its own action is not capable of rising again by its own action is the fault of the will, which, being weakened and prostrated by the corrupted and vicious affections of the corrupt body, is no longer capable of an equal love for righteousness. And thus, I know not how, it happens that the will, having fallen by sin into a state so changed and miserable, imposes upon itself a strange and sad necessity, and that of such a kind, that being voluntary, it forms no excuse for the will, while the will, being led away by the false good which attracts it, has no power of resisting the necessity, a voluntary necessity, if it may be so called. For there is a pleasing violence, which overcomes by flattering, and flatters while overcoming; and then the will, become a traitor to itself, and having once consented to that which is evil, is no longer able to free itself by its own strength, yet can found no reasonable excuse upon its own weakness. From thence comes that complaint of one who groaned under the yoke of that necessity: *O Lord, I am oppressed: undertake for me* (Is. xxxviii. 14). But knowing, on the other hand, that he could not justly make complaint against the Lord, when it was his own will that was in fault, take notice of what he adds: What shall I say, or what shall He answer for me, when I myself have done it?[1] He was weighed down by a heavy yoke, but it was the yoke of a voluntary servitude; and that servitude excited pity, but the assent of his will to it rendered it inexcusable. For it was the will which, when it was free, made itself the slave of sin by consenting to sin, and it was also the will which, by submitting itself to sin, made the servitude a willing one.

8. Some one, perhaps, will thus reply to me: 'Take heed of what you say. Do you call that voluntary, which it is plain to all the world is done under constraint? It is true that the will has rendered itself subject, but it does not remain in that state of subjection willingly; it is held captive in spite of itself.' Very good; you allow at least that it is held captive. But consider that it is the *will* of which you say this. Do you assert, then, that the will is not willing? But the will is not constrained against itself. It is not will at all unless it wills. The word expresses the action of one who exercises a power of determining, not of one who has no such power to exercise. If the will is constrained willingly it constrains itself. What, then, shall it answer, or what excuse shall it make to God, since its action is its own? What has it done? It has made itself a servant. Wherefore it is said: *Whosoever committeth sin is the servant of sin* (John viii. 34). On this account, when it has sinned (and it has sinned when it has determined to obey a sinful impulse) it has made itself a servant of sin. But it becomes free if it no longer does the bidding of sin. But while it chooses to abide in the same servitude it goes on following the temptation to sin. Yet it is not retained in

---

[1] Is. xxxviii. 15. The Vulgate has *fecerit*, not *fecerim*. St. Bernard takes notice of each of these varieties of reading in Sermon *de Diversis*, iii., *nn.* 5, 6.

bondage unwillingly, from the very fact that it is the will. If, then, it has made itself a slave voluntarily, it is also voluntarily that it remains in its bondage. What, then, shall it reply in excuse for itself, since its servitude (and this is always to be borne in mind) has been, and is, its own doing.

9. 'But you will not make me disbelieve' (says an objector) 'in the necessity under which I labour, which I experience in my own self, and against which I continually struggle.' Where, then, I ask, do you feel this constraint? Is it not in your will? You do not, then, will with too little strength what you will of necessity. You will strongly what you are unable not to will, whatever strength of resistance you exert. Now, where there is the power to will, there is liberty. And in saying this I refer to the liberty which is by nature, not that which is spiritual and by grace; namely, that *liberty wherewith*, as says the Apostle, *Christ hath made us free* (Gal. v. 1). And the same Apostle, speaking of that liberty, says: *Where the Spirit of the Lord is, there is liberty* (2 Cor. iii. 17). It is thus that the soul is at the same time free, and enslaved by this necessity which, as unhappily as strangely, is voluntarily incurred; free, by the possession of the power of will, and enslaved, by the pressure of necessity. And farther, which is at once stranger and more deplorable, it is guilty because it is free, and a slave because it is guilty; and thus by a strange paradox is a slave because it is free. Unhappy man that I am, who shall deliver me from this servitude so shameful? Unhappy I am indeed; but I am free. Free, because I am a man; unhappy, because a slave. Free, because I am in the likeness of God; unhappy, because I am contrary to Him. *O Thou Preserver of men! why hast Thou set me as a mark against Thee?* (Job vii. 20). For indeed Thou hast in a sense done that, the doing of which Thou hast not hindered. But, in other respects, it is I who have set myself *where I am, so that I am a burden to myself* (*Ibid.*). It is indeed most just and right that he who is Thy enemy should be mine also, and that he who opposes Thee should oppose me too. In truth, I have become contrary to Thee and to my own self also, and I find in my members a revolt against my own soul and against Thy law. Who shall set me free from my own hands? That which I would, that do I not; and it is not another person, but my own self, who hinders me. So also that which I hate, that do I; and it is no other person, but my own self, who obliges me to do it. I would that this prevention on the one hand, and this compulsion on the other, were so violent that my actions ceased to be voluntary, for then perhaps I might be excused; or that it were so far voluntary that it was not violent, for so perhaps I might be corrected. But now no opening for escape appears on either side for me unhappy, whom, on the one hand, the assent of my will renders, as I have said, inexcusable; and on the other, necessity renders incapable of being corrected. Who shall deliver me from the hands of a sinner, from the hand of the unrighteous and cruel man? (Ps. lxxi. 4).

10. Someone asks me, perhaps, 'Of whom am I complaining?' Of myself. It is I who am that sinner, that man unrighteous and cruel. A sinner I am, for I have, in fact, sinned; and unrighteous, because I persist voluntarily in violating the law of righteousness. For my will itself is as a law in my members warring against the Divine Law. And because the Law of the Lord is of right a law unto my soul, as it is written: *The Law of his God is in his heart* (Ps. xxxvii. 31), for that very reason it is that my will is found in opposition to my own self, which is the height of iniquity. For to whom am I not unjust, when I am unjust to myself? 'He that is evil to himself,' it is said, 'to whom will he be good?' (Ecclus. xiv. 5). I am not good, I confess, [even to myself], for in me is no good thing. Yet I am consoled for this, because even a saint said: *I know that in me (that is, in my flesh) dwelleth no good thing* (Rom. vii. 18). Nevertheless he makes a distinction when he says, *in himself*, and explains that he means, 'in his flesh,' because of the law of contradiction [to the Law of God], which is in it. For that better law is also in the soul. Is not the Law of God good? If, then, he is evil, because of the law of evil which is in him, why is he not good by reason of the law of good which is in him likewise? Will you say that the law of evil is his own because it is in his flesh, and that therefore he is evil because his law is evil, and not also that he is good because of a law which is good? That cannot be the case. The Law of God is in his soul, and so in his soul as to be the law of his soul. He is a witness of this, who says: *I see another law in my members, warring against the law of my mind* (Rom. vii. 23). Is that *his* which is in his flesh, and not that which is in his soul? I say that it is his even more. Why should I not say what the same master of the spiritual life says: *With the mind* (that is, following the impulse of the spirit which is myself) *I myself serve the law of God, but with the flesh the law of sin* (vii. 25). He shows very clearly by those words, which law he regards as being his own, since he considers the evil which is in his flesh as being alien to him, for he says: *It is no more I that do it* [the evil], *but sin that dwelleth in me* (vii. 20). And it is perhaps for that very reason that he has declared expressly that he found another law in his members, because he regarded it as foreign to him, and coming from without. Therefore I venture (yet not, I think, rashly) to add something more, that St. Paul was not a sinner on account of the evil which he had in his flesh; but rather good on account of the good which he had in his soul. Is he not good who consents unto the law of God, that it is good? For although he confesses that he is in captivity to the law of sin, this he does in the flesh, not in the soul. For *with the mind he serves* the law of God, though *with the flesh the law of sin*, and which of these two ought the rather to be attributed to St. Paul, you can easily judge. For my part, I confess that I have no difficulty in coming to the conclusion that that which was of the spirit was more truly his than that which was of the flesh; and this is not my belief alone, but it was that of St. Paul himself, as

is shown by what he has said, which I have quoted above: *If I do that I would not, it is no more I that do it, but sin that dwelleth in me.*
11. This will suffice respecting liberty. In the treatise which I have written on Grace and Free Will you will perhaps find other points discussed, in which the soul is made after the image and likeness of God; but nothing, I think, contrary to what is said here. That treatise you have read, and what has just now been said you have heard; which of the two you rather approve I leave to your judgment, and if there is anything in either which approves itself to you, in this I rejoice and will rejoice. However that may be, you will bear in mind that we have remarked upon three great qualities as distinguishing the nature of the soul: its simplicity of substance, its immortality, and its liberty of will. And I think that it will appear very clear to you that the soul, by these three points of resemblance in the qualities which are its birthright and are natural to it, has no small affinity to the WORD, the Bridegroom of the Church, JESUS CHRIST our LORD, who is above all, God blessed for ever. AMEN.

SERMON LXXXII.

HOW THE SOUL, WHILE STILL REMAINING LIKE UNTO GOD, LOSES BY SIN A PORTION OF ITS LIKENESS TO HIM IN ITS SIMPLICITY, IMMORTALITY, AND LIBERTY.

WHAT think you, my brethren? Does it appear to you that we can go back and take up again the order of exposition from which we have digressed, since the affinity of the soul with the WORD, to establish which was the object of the digression, must be now quite clear to you? We might do so, as it seems to me, only for one thing; that there still remains, as I feel, some little obscurity in the various parts of the expositions which have been given. I do not wish to steal anything from you. I do not willingly pass over anything that I think would be useful to you. How could I dare to do so, especially of those truths which I receive only in order that I may communicate them to you? I know a man who once, in the course of an address that he was making, held back some part of what the Holy Spirit suggested to him, not unfaithfully, but perhaps with a want of reliance on His aid for the future, with the purpose of reserving it for another occasion, that he might have something to say when treating on the same subject again; and that man seemed to hear a voice, which said to him: 'As long as you shall withhold this you shall receive nothing else.'[1] What if he had kept back this thought, not for the supply of

[1] St. Bernard is here borrowing one of St. Paul's turns of phrase (2 Cor. xii. 2), and speaking of himself. This is declared by Cæsar of Heisterbach, who, in his sermon for the Octave of Christmas, speaks thus: 'One day he was treating upon

his own need, but from a feeling of jealousy that his brethren should be advanced by it? Would it not have been just that the very knowledge which he seemed to have should be taken away from him? May God keep such a feeling far from him who is your servant, as He has always done as yet! May that inexhaustible fountain of saving wisdom deign to impart itself unto me as constantly and abundantly, as it is true that I have always, without grudging, shared with you what I have received, and have poured forth again upon you whatever He in His goodness has so far showered upon me. If I should fail to bestow liberally upon you, how could I hope that God would bestow liberally upon me?

2. There is, then, among the various observations that have been made, something which may, I fear, be a stumbling-block to you, unless it be made very clear. And, if I do not mistake, there are some standing here to whom what I wish to say may be the occasion of some scruple. That threefold likeness to the WORD, which we have assigned to the soul, or, rather, have observed that it was impressed upon the soul, do you remember that it appeared to us to inhere in it inseparably? Now, does not that seem to conflict with some statements of Scripture, as, for example, with this out of the Psalms: *Man that is in honour and understandeth not is like the beasts that perish* (Ps. xlix. 12, 20); and this: *They changed their glory into the similitude of an ox that eateth grass* (Ps. cvi. 20); and this, which is plainly stated in the Person of God: *Thou thoughtest that I was altogether such an one as thyself* (Ps. l. 21); and many others, which seem to assert with one voice that, after the commission of sin, the likeness to God in man was altogether effaced? What, then, shall we say to these statements? That these three qualities are not in God, and that therefore we must seek for others, in which consist the resemblance that the soul has to Him? or that they are indeed in God, but are not in the soul, so that in these respects it has no resemblance to God? or that, though they are in the soul, they are not in it *necessarily*, and therefore are not inseparable from it? God forbid that either of these alternatives should be the fact. These qualities are in God; they are also in the soul, and are in it always. Nor have we any reason to repent of what has been stated upon these points, since it is founded on certain and indubitable truth. But when the Scripture speaks of the unlikeness of man to God which has been brought about, it does so, not because that likeness which previously existed was effaced, but because another has been laid over it. The soul has plainly not put off its original form, but has put on over it one which is foreign to it. The latter is added, but the former is

---

some subject, and a thought came to him which, though it would have been in place at the time, he proposed to himself to reserve till the end, where he thought he should be in want of matter, and he heard a voice saying to him, "If you keep back this, nothing else shall be given to you."' 'So truly was it,' says Manrique, 'not he that spake, but God in him.' See on the same subject, Sermon *in Cantic.*, xviii., *n.* 2.

not lost; and that which is subsequent may hide the earlier and natural lineaments of the soul, but cannot obliterate them. Thus it is said by the Apostle: *Their foolish heart was darkened* (Rom. i. 21), and by a prophet: *How is the gold become dim, how is the most fine gold changed!* (Lam. iv. 1). The gold laments that it has become dim, but it still remains gold; its beautiful colour has changed, but the ground of the colour is not fundamentally changed. The pure and simple nature of the soul remains unshaken in its essential character, but it is concealed from view by a thick film of human fraudfulness, and pretence, and hypocrisy.

3. How incongruous is the mixture of duplicity with the natural simplicity of the soul! What an unworthy action to raise a structure so poor on a foundation so precious! It was with this duplicity that the serpent concealed his cunning purpose when, in order to deceive the first woman, Eve, he took upon himself the character of an adviser, and pretended to be her friend. It was with this that the first dwellers in the earthly Paradise, after they had been led into disobedience by him, endeavoured to conceal their nakedness and shame by the shelter of a leafy tree, by girdles of leaves, and by words of excuse (Gen. iii. 7, 8, 12, 13). From that time and thenceforward the poison of hypocrisy has spread deeply and widely, and has infested the whole of their posterity. Whom is there of all the children of Adam who, I will not say wishes the entire truth in every instance to appear, but even suffers it to do so? Nevertheless, the fundamental truthfulness of the soul persists [in conflict] with original duplicity in every soul, and confusion is increased by the simultaneous presence of the two; and its immortality also continues, but an immortality shadowed and rendered sombre by the encroaching clouds of the death which belongs to the body. For although it is not deprived of life, it is unable to claim the full benefit of that life for its body. But of the soul which does not hold fast its own spiritual life, what shall I say? For *the soul that sinneth it shall die* (Ezek. xviii. 4). Does not that twofold death into which it falls, render the immortality (of what kind soever it may be) which it still retains, gloomy and unhappy to the last degree? Add to this that the desires which it has for earthly things (which, indeed, all tend towards its destruction) render still more dense the clouds and darkness in which it is enveloped, so that a soul existing in such a state has, as it were, a countenance pallid and deathlike, nay, the very image of death. Why does not the soul, being immortal, desire things which are eternal and immortal like itself, so as to appear that which it really is, and to live that life for which it was intended? But it delights in and seeks for things which are quite contrary to these; it conforms itself to things which are mortal and perishable, by leading a life far degenerated from the nobleness of its nature, and blackens, as it were, the glory of its immortality by daily converse with, and preference for, things which are dingy and defiled. How can a longing desire for mortal things fail to assimilate the immortal to mortality and make

it unlike to itself? For 'He,' saith the Wise Man, 'that toucheth pitch shall be defiled therewith' (Ecclus. xiii. 4). In the enjoyment of things that are mortal it is itself clothed with mortality, and though it does not put off its robe of immortality, it dims the brightness of it by the stains and similitudes of death.

4. Consider, for instance, how Eve, by attaching herself to things that were mortal, though herself an immortal soul, soiled the glory of her immortality by the mould of mortal things. Since she was immortal, why did she not contemn things that were perishing and transitory, and content herself with those that were unchangeable and eternal, similar to her own nature? *She saw*, saith the Scripture, *that the tree was good for food, and that it was pleasant to the eyes, and a tree to be desired to make one wise* (Gen. iii. 6). That beauty, O woman, that sweetness, that desirableness, is not thine; and if it belongs to thee because thou art in part made of the dust of the earth, is not thine alone, but thou hast it in common with all the living creatures of the earth. That which is truly thine is of another nature, and comes from another source; it is eternal, and comes from eternity. Why dost thou set upon thy soul another likeness, or, rather, a deformity which is strange to it? For what it desires to possess, that it fears to lose; and that fear is a kind of colour, which stains its free will, which hides it, and renders it like unto itself. How much more worthy of its origin would it be that it should desire nothing, so that it should fear nothing; and that, thus guarding its inborn freedom from servile fear, it should remain in its pristine beauty and strength! Alas! it is not so; its perfect hue has faded. Thou dost fly, and hidest thyself; when thou hearest the voice of the Lord God thou lurkest in a hiding-place. Why is this, but that Him whom thou didst once love, now thou dost fear; and that a slavish fear has taken the place of the beauty of thy freedom?

5. That necessity voluntarily incurred, and that law of contradiction imposed upon the members (of which I have spoken in another discourse), weighs upon the same liberty, and at the same time allures and enslaves by means of its own will, a creature free by nature; covers it with confusion and ignominy, so that it obeys, though unwillingly, the law of sin which is in its flesh. Because, then, it has neglected to guard the original nobleness of its nature by innocency of life, it has followed, by the just judgment of its Creator, that it is not stripped of the freedom which belongs to it, but clad with its *own confusion as with a mantle* (Ps. cix. 29). Well is it said, *as with a mantle*, that is, a garment which is folded or doubled (*diploide*), because while its liberty remains, that being necessarily inherent in the will, yet its manner of conduct, which is servile, imposes upon it constraint and necessity. The same thing may be remarked of the simplicity of the soul, as of its immortality; and if you observe closely you will find nothing in that also which is not covered, as it were, with a double mantle of likeness and unlikeness. Is not that like a doubled mantle, where deceit is not inborn, but is laid upon truthful-

ness, is attached and, as it were, sewn to it by the sharp needle of sin; as also death to immortality, and necessity to freedom? For this duplicity of disposition does not destroy the essential truthfulness of the soul, nor does death, whether it be the voluntary death of sin, or the necessary death of the body, disprove the immortality of the soul by its nature; nor, again, does the necessity which follows a voluntary servitude destroy the freedom of the will. Thus these evils are adventitious; they do not follow from the good gifts which are natural, but are superinduced upon them; they disfigure, without destroying them; and trouble their action, though they do not nullify it. Thence it is that the soul is unlike to God, and unlike even to itself; thence it is that it is compared unto beasts that perish, and made like unto them (Ps. xlix. 12, 20); thence it is that, as we read, they have changed their glory into the similitude of an ox that eateth grass (Ps. cvi. 20); thence it is that men, like foxes, have winding earths, as it were, of duplicity and fraud; and, as they have made themselves like unto foxes, shall have the destiny of foxes; for, according to the saying of Solomon, *that which befalleth the sons of men befalleth beasts: even one thing befalleth them* (Eccles. iii. 19). Why should not one who has lived like the beasts have a death like theirs? He has attached himself to earthly things, and delighted in them, like the beasts; like the beasts also he must leave them. And there is still another point. What wonder is it that we should go forth from this life similarly to the beasts, since we come into it in a similar manner? Whence is it, except from their resemblance to the lower animals, that there is in human creatures so much ardour in the indulgence of the passions, so much pain in parturition? Thus it is that the human creature, in his conception and his birth, in his life and his death, is compared unto the beasts that perish, and made like unto them.

6. What shall I say of the fact that a creature who is free does not subdue appetite and rule it as a queen, but, on the contrary, follows and obeys it as a servant? Does not such a creature rank itself among animals without reason, and make itself like unto them whom their nature has not called to liberty, but has placed in a state of servitude, to follow and obey their lusts and appetites? Is it not with justice that God is revolted at being considered and represented as like unto a man such as this? And therefore it is that He says: *Thou thoughtest* [wickedly] *that I was altogether such an one as thyself;* and declares, *I will reprove thee, and set thee in order before thine eyes* (Ps. l. 21). It is not for a soul that sees and knows itself, to think that God is like unto it, especially such a soul as mine, which is unrighteous and a sinner. For it is to such that the stern accusation is addressed: 'Thou thoughtest, *O wicked one*,' not 'O soul,' or 'O man,' *that I was altogether such an one as thyself*. But if the wicked one be set, as it were, before his own eyes, and made to stand face to face, if I may so speak, with the ghastly and discoloured countenance of his inner man, so that he cannot avoid beholding the manifold

uncleanness of his conscience, nor ignore it when beheld; but, on the contrary, recognizes, even against his will, the defilement of his sins, and the deformity of his vices; then he will by no means be able to think that God is like unto him, nay, the difference which he will see will be so great that I think he will be driven to cry, Lord, *who is like unto Thee?* (Ps. xxxv. 10), which, indeed, was spoken with reference to that voluntary and novel unlikeness. For the first resemblance still remains; and it is that which renders the later unlikeness still more displeasing. Oh, how great a good is the one, and how great an evil the other! And by the close contact and contrast of the two the effect of each in its kind is heightened.

7. When the soul discerns in itself two things so different and so opposed, how can it do otherwise than cry out, between hope and despair: *Lord, who is like unto Thee?* By so great an evil it is drawn towards despair, but by so great a good it is recalled towards hope. Thence it is that the more it is offended by the evil which it beholds in itself, the more ardently it aspires to the good which it also descries, and the more it desires to become wholly like unto Him in whose image it has been formed; that is to say, to be simple, upright, fearing God, and departing from evil. Why should it not be able to depart from that which it has been able to approach, or to draw near to that from which it has been able to withdraw? Yet for either of these movements, I must not omit to say, grace must be relied upon, not nature, nor even laborious effort. For it is wisdom that prevails over vice (Wisd. vii. 30), not nature nor labour. Nor is ground for hope wanting, for it is the WORD to whom it turns for help. The noble relationship of the soul to the WORD, and the enduring likeness which it has to Him, of which, during the last three days, I have been discoursing, is not barren or ineffective with the WORD. He deigns to admit into the fellowship of His Spirit that which is like unto Him by nature. Like seeks like assuredly, according to the natural order. Listen to His voice as He calls to the soul: *Return, return, O Shulamite: return, return, that we may look upon thee* (Cant. vi. 13). He would not look upon her while she was unlike unto Him, but when she shall be in His likeness will behold her, and admit her also to the vision of Himself. For *we know that when He shall appear, we shall be like Him; for we shall see Him as He is* (1 John iii. 2). Believe, then, that when it is inquired: *Lord, who is like unto Thee?* the words refer rather to a thing that is difficult than to one which is absolutely impossible.

8. Or, if you prefer to take it thus, it is a cry of admiration. Assuredly it is a likeness wonderful and admirable, which accompanies the vision of God, or, rather, it is that vision itself. For I understand this of the vision which is brought about by love, for in love is that vision and that likeness. Who does not stand amazed at the great love of God in recalling to Himself a soul by which He has been scorned? It is with justice, then, that that wicked one, who was represented in a former sermon as usurping to himself the like-

ness of God, is severely censured, since in loving iniquity he is not able to love either himself or God, as it is written: *He that loveth iniquity hateth his own soul* (Ps. x. 6, Douay). The iniquity, then, which is in part the cause of the unlikeness between God and the soul, being taken out of the way, there shall be between them a spiritual union perfect and entire, a mutual discernment and vision, a reciprocal love. *When that which is perfect is come, then that which is in part shall be done away,* and there shall be between God and the soul a perfect and consummated affection, a full knowledge, a vision manifest, a firm union, an indivisible society, a perfect similitude. Then the soul shall *know, even as also it is known* (1 Cor. xiii. 10, 12); then shall it love even as it is loved, and the Bridegroom shall rejoice over the Bride, because knowledge and love are reciprocal between them. He is JESUS CHRIST our Lord, who is above all, God blessed for ever. AMEN.

SERMON LXXXIII.

OF THE MANNER IN WHICH THE SOUL, HOWEVER CORRUPTED IT MAY BE WITH EVIL HABITS, IS STILL ABLE, BY A CHASTE AND HOLY LOVE, TO RECOVER ITS RESEMBLANCE TO THE BRIDEGROOM, THAT IS, CHRIST.

I HAVE, during three days, devoted myself, as far as the time prescribed by our rule for me to address you would permit, to show you the close relation and resemblance of the soul to the WORD. What usefulness is there in all that endeavour? There is this. We have shown that every soul, though it may be burdened with sins, caught in the net of evil habits, taken captive by the allurements of sinful pleasures; though it be as a captive in exile, confined in the body as in a prison, submerged and fixed fast in mud and clay, closely bound to its members, weighed down by cares, absorbed in business, saddened by fears, afflicted by sorrows, led astray by errors, anxious because of forebodings, uneasy through suspicions, and, lastly, an alien on the earth, in which it finds so many enemies, and, according to the saying of a prophet, defiled with the dead and counted with them that go down into hell (Baruch iii. 11); although a soul, I say, be thus under condemnation and thus despairing, yet, as I have shown, it is able to find in itself, not only reason for breathing freely in the hope of mercy and forgiveness, but also for daring to aspire to the heavenly nuptials of the Word; nor does it fear to enter into alliance with God, and to bear the sweet yoke of love with Him who is the King of Angels. For why should it not venture to come confidently into the presence of Him by whose image and likeness it sees and knows that it is still honoured and ennobled ? Why should even a Majesty so great be a cause of distrust to a being to whom its own origin gives a ground for confidence? All that it has to do is to preserve with care the original purity of its nature by a pure and honourable life; or, rather, to study to adorn and embellish by good and virtuous thoughts and actions, as by rich colours, that illustrious image which has been impressed upon the depths of its nature at its creation.

2. Why, then, does it remain inactive? Labour and industry are assuredly a great gift of nature; and if we do not employ it to its fullest extent, will not all those good inclinations which are left in us by nature be hindered in their working, or remain, as it were, inactive and powerless? This would indeed be an injury to the Creator. That is the reason why God our Creator has willed to preserve always in the soul a clear sign of its Divine origin, so that it should be continually admonished by the resemblance which it has to the WORD, either to remain with Him, or to return to Him, if it has been induced by any motive to quit His Presence. It does not leave Him, as by change of place, or by steps taken with the feet; but it leaves Him in the manner of a spiritual substance, that is to say, by its purposes and affections, when it renders itself unlike Him, and degenerates from the nobleness of its origin, by the evil of its conduct and life, and thus becomes distinctly worse. That unlikeness, nevertheless, does not amount to an abolition of its nature; but it is a grave fault, for good raises up nature as much by comparison with itself, as by conjunction [with evil] it is defiled. But this return of the soul is its conversion, that is, its turning to the WORD; to be reformed by Him, and to be rendered conformable to Him. In what respect? In charity. For it is written: *Be ye followers of God, as dear children: and walk in love, as Christ also hath loved us* (Eph. v. 1, 2).

3. It is that conformity which makes, as it were, a marriage between the soul and the WORD, when, being already like unto Him by its nature, it endeavours to show itself like unto Him by its will, and loves Him as it is loved by Him. And if this love is perfected, the soul is wedded to the WORD. What can be more full of happiness and joy than this conformity? what more to be desired than this love? which makes thee, O soul, no longer content with human guidance, to draw near with confidence thyself to the WORD, to attach thyself with constancy to Him, to address Him with confidence, and consult Him upon all subjects, to become as receptive in thy intelligence, as fearless in thy desires. This is the contract of a marriage truly spiritual and sacred. And to say this is to say too little; it is more than a contract, it is a communion, an identification with the Beloved, in which the perfect correspondence of will makes of two, one spirit. Nor is it to be feared that the inequality of the two who are parties to it should render imperfect or halting in any respect this concurrence of wills; for love has no respect of persons. It is from affection, not from reverence, that it is named love. Let one who is struck with horror, with astonishment, with fear, with admira-

tion, rest satisfied with honouring; but in one who loves all these feelings are merged in affection. Love is filled with itself; and in the soul to which it has once come, it overcomes and transforms all other feelings. Therefore the soul which loves, in loving, is regardless of all else. He who justly deserves to be honoured and admired, and regarded as a miracle of perfectness, yet loves rather to be loved. They are Bridegroom and Bride. What other bond or constraining force do you seek for between spouses, than to love and to be loved? This bond overcomes even that which nature has drawn most closely, namely, the bond between parents and children. *For this cause*, says the Saviour in the Gospel, *shall a man leave father and mother, and shall cleave to his wife* (Matt. xix. 5). You see how powerful is this feeling in those who are wedded; not only does it prevail over all other feelings, but even over itself.

4. It is to be added that this Bridegroom is not only loving, He is Himself Love. Is He not also Honour? Anyone who pleases may maintain that He is; but I have not, in fact, read any such thing. I have read that *God is Love* (1 John iv. 16); not that He is honour, or dignity; though it is not to be understood that God does not desire to be honoured, for He says: *If I be a Father, where is Mine honour?* He says that as a Father. But if He declares Himself to be a Bridegroom, will He not change the word, and say: 'If I be a Bridegroom, where is the love that is due to Me?' For he had previously said: *If I be a Master, where is My fear?* (Mal. i. 6). God, then, requires that He should be feared as Lord, honoured as Father, but as Bridegroom, loved. Which of these three is highest and most to be preferred? Surely it is love. Without it fear is painful, and honour without attraction. Fear is servile as long as it is not rendered free by love; and honour which is not inspired by love is not truly honour, but flattery. Certainly honour and glory are due to God, and to Him alone; but neither of these will He receive, if they be not, as it were, seasoned with the honey of love. Love is alone sufficient by itself; it pleases by itself, and for its own sake. It is itself a merit, and itself its own recompense. It seeks neither cause, nor consequence, beyond itself. It is its own fruit, and its own object and usefulness. I love, because I love; I love, that I may love. Love, then, is a great reality, and very precious, provided that it recurs to the principle on which it rests, that it is kept in continual relation with Him who is its origin, and draws from that pure source waters that flow continually in greater abundance. Of all the feelings, affections, and movements of the soul, love is the only one by which the reasonable creature is able to respond to its Creator, and even in some sort to repay, though not upon equal terms, the goodness which it has received from Him. For example, if God is displeased with me, should I be at liberty to feel displeasure towards Him? Certainly not: I tremble, and humble myself before Him, and entreat His pardon. So also, if He accuses me, He is not to be accused by me in return, but the justice of His accusation is to be instantly

recognised. Nor, if He shall judge me, will I judge, but will adore. When He saves me, He does not ask of me salvation in return; nor does He who restores freedom to all need that He should Himself be freed. If He exercises the authority which He has over me, my part is to do Him service; if He commands, my duty is to obey; and it is not for me to require of the Lord either the service, or the obedience, that I properly render to Him. Now, you see what a great difference there is in all these respects with regard to love! For when God loves us, He desires nothing else than to be loved, because He loves us that He may be loved by us, knowing that those who love Him become blessed by their love itself.

5. Love, then, is a great reality, but there are degrees in it. The Bridegroom stands highest of all. For though children have affection for their parents, yet they think of their heritage, and in the fear of losing that, they have more respect than love for him from whom they expect it. That love I hold in suspicion which seems to be produced only by the hope of acquiring something. It is weak; for if that hope be withdrawn, it is either extinguished altogether, or greatly diminished. It is impure, since it is founded on the hope of something else. Love that is pure is not mercenary; it does not draw strength from hope, nor is it weakened by distrust. This is the love which is felt by the Bride, because all that she is is only love. The very being of the Bride, and her only hope, consists in love. In this the Bride abounds; with this the Bridegroom is content. He seeks nothing else from her; she has nothing but this to give. Thence it is that He is Bridegroom, and she is Bride. This belongs exclusively to a wedded pair, and to it none other attains, not even a son. For He cries out to His sons: *Where is My honour?* and does not say: 'Where is My love?' reserving the prerogative of the Bride. Thus we see that a man is bidden to honour his father and his mother (Deut. v. 16), and no mention is made of love; not because parents are not to be loved by their children, but because many children are disposed more to honour parents than to love them. It is true that the honour of a king loves judgment (Ps. xcix. 4); but the love of the Bridegroom, or rather of the Bridegroom who is Himself Love, requires only love and faithfulness in return. Let it, then, be permitted to the Bride to love in return. How could she do otherwise who is the Bride, and the Bride of Love? How can Love fail to be loved?

6. Rightly, then, does she renounce all other affections, and devote herself wholly and entirely to Him who is Love, since she can make return to Him by a love which is reciprocal. For when she has poured herself forth entirely in love, what would that be in comparison with the ever-flowing and inexhaustible source of love? Not with equal fulness of resource flows that stream from Love and from the creature that loves Him, from the soul and from the WORD, the Bridegroom and the Bride, the Creator and the creature; and the thirsty wayfarer might as well be compared with the fountain that satisfies his thirst. What then? Shall the vow of the Bride, the deep

aspirations of her heart, her loving ardour and undoubting confidence, perish and become of none effect because she is unable to contend with a Giant who runs His course, to dispute the palm of sweetness with honey, of gentleness with the lamb, of whiteness with the lily, of brilliance with the sun, or of charity with Him who is Himself Charity and Love? No. For although, being a creature, she loves less than He by whom she is loved, because she is less; yet if she loves with her whole self, nothing can be wanting where the whole being is offered. Wherefore, as I have said, to feel such love as this constitutes a spiritual marriage between the soul and the WORD, since it is not possible for a soul to love thus, and yet not to be greatly loved; and in the consent of the two parties consists a perfect marriage. Unless anyone should feel a doubt whether the soul is not first loved, and with a greater affection, by the WORD. Assuredly, it is both anticipated in loving, and surpassed in love. Happy is the soul whose favoured lot it is to be prevented with the benediction of a delight so great! Happy the soul to which is granted to experience the delight of that communion so sweet, which is nothing else than a love holy and pure, sweet and delightful, as calm as it is sincere: a love mutual, endearing, powerful, which makes of two, by their close union, not, indeed, one flesh, but one spirit, as St. Paul declares: *He that is joined unto the Lord is one Spirit* (1 Cor. vi. 17). And now upon these subjects let us listen to her whom *that unction which teaches of all things*, and a frequent experience, has rendered more learned than all others in this mystery. Though perhaps it will be better to defer that subject to the beginning of another sermon, so that we may not confine an important matter within the limits of a sermon just upon the point of closing. So, then if you approve, I will break off this discourse before reaching the end of the subject, in order that to-morrow we, as souls that are a-hungered, may assemble in good time to taste with eagerness those delights which it is the exceeding great reward of the holy soul to enjoy from the WORD, and with the WORD, who is her Bridegroom, JESUS CHRIST our Lord, who is above all, God blessed for ever. AMEN.

SERMON LXXXIV.

THAT THE SOUL, SEEKING GOD, IS ANTICIPATED BY HIM; AND IN WHAT CONSISTS THAT SEARCH FOR GOD IN WHICH IT IS THUS ANTICIPATED.

'*By night on my bed I sought Him whom my soul loveth.*'—Cant. iii. 1.

IT is a great good to seek God. I think that, among all the blessings of the soul, there is none greater than this. It is the first of the gifts of God; the last degree of the soul's progress. By no virtue is it preceded; to none does it give place. To what virtue is that added which is not preceded by any? And to which should that give way which is the consummation of all virtues? For what virtue can be ascribed to him who is not seeking God, or what limit prescribed to one who is seeking Him? *Seek His Face evermore* (Ps. cv. 4), says the Psalmist; nor do I think that when a soul has found Him, it will cease from seeking. God is sought, not by the movement of the feet, but by the desires of the heart; and when a soul has been so happy as to find Him, that sacred desire is not extinguished, but, on the contrary, is increased. Is the consummation of the joy the extinction of the desire? It is rather to it as oil poured upon a flame; for desire is, as it were, a flame. This is, indeed, the case. The joy will be fulfilled; but the fulfilment will not be the ending of the desire, nor therefore of the seeking. But think, if you can, of this earnest love of seeking God as being without any deprivation of Him, and of the desire for Him as without anxiety or trouble of mind. His Presence excludes the one, and the abundance of His graces prevents the other.

2. But now observe why I have made these introductory remarks. It is that every soul among you which is seeking God should know that it has been anticipated by Him, and has been sought by Him before it began to seek Him. For without this knowledge it might be that out of a great blessing might arise great harm, if, when it has been filled with the good gifts of the Lord, it treats those gifts as if they had not been received from Him, and so does not render to God the glory of them. It is, doubtless, in this way that some who appeared very great before men, because of the graces which had been conferred upon them, were counted as the least before God, inasmuch as they did not render back to Him the glory which was due on their account. But in saying this, I have used inadequate terms. To spare you, I have spoken of 'greatest' and of 'least,' but I have not thus expressed my thought in all its force. I will make clearer the distinction which I have tried to mark. I ought to have said that he who is the best of men becomes in this way the worst. For it is a thing certain and without doubt that such a person becomes as blameable as he before was praiseworthy, if he ascribe to himself the praise of that which was excellent in him. For this is one of the worst of crimes. Someone will perhaps say, 'God forbid that I should be of that mind; I fully recognize that by the grace of God I am what I am; but suppose that a person should try to take for himself a little spark of glory for the grace that he has received, is he, therefore, a thief and a robber?' Let one who speaks thus listen to the words: *Out of thine own mouth will I judge thee, thou wicked servant* (Matt. xix. 22). For what can be more wicked than the servant usurping to himself the glory which belongs to his Lord?

3. *By night on my bed I sought Him whom my soul loveth.* The soul seeks the WORD, but it had been previously sought by the WORD. For otherwise, when it had been once driven out or cast forth from the presence of the WORD, it would have returned no more to obtain the sight of the good things it had lost if it had not been sought by

the WORD. Our soul, if abandoned to itself, is a spirit which goes to and fro, but does not return. Listen to a fugitive and wandering soul, and learn what it complains of, and what it seeks: *I have gone astray like a lost sheep: seek Thy servant* (Ps. cxix. 176). O man, dost thou desire to return? But if that depends upon thy own will, why dost thou entreat help? Why dost thou ask for from another what thou hast in abundance in thy own self? It is plain that he does desire this, and is not able to perform it; he is a spirit which goes to and fro, and returns not; though he who has not even the wish to return is farther removed still. Yet I would not say that the soul which longs to return, and desires to be sought, is wholly exposed and abandoned. For from whence comes this willingness which is in it? It comes, if I do not mistake, from its having been already sought and visited by the WORD; nor is that visitation fruitless, since it has so worked in the soul as to produce that good will, without which a return would not be possible. But it does not suffice to be sought once only, so great is the languor of the soul, and so great the difficulty of the return. What if the will of a soul is to return? The will lies inoperative, if it be not supported by the power to do so. For, *to will is present with me*, says the Apostle, *but how to perform that which is good I find not* (Rom. vii. 18). What is it, then, that the Psalmist seeks in the passage which I have quoted? He plainly seeks nothing else than to be sought: which he would not seek if he had not been sought; and yet again, which he would not seek if he had been sought sufficiently. This latter grace, indeed, is what he entreats: *Seek Thy servant;* that is, that what it has been granted to him to desire, it may be granted to him also perfectly to attain, according to the good pleasure of God.

4. Yet it does not seem to me that the present passage is capable of being applied to a soul such as this, which has not attained the second grace, and, though desiring to approach Him whom she loves, has not the ability to do so. For how can the words which follow be made to apply to such a soul; namely, that she rises and goes about the city in the streets, and in the broad ways seeks her Beloved (iii. 2), seeing that she herself needs to be sought? Let her do this as she is able; only let her remember that, as she was first beloved, so she was first sought; and to that she owes it that she herself loves and is engaged in seeking. Let us, too, pray, beloved, that those mercies may speedily anticipate us, for we are brought into extreme need of them. But I do not say this of you all; for I know that very many of you are walking in the love wherewith Christ hath loved us, and are seeking Him in simplicity of heart. But there are some (I say it with sorrow) who have not yet given us any mark of this saving and preventing grace being in them, and therefore no sign of their salvation; they are men who love their own selves, not the Lord, and seek their own interests, not those of Jesus Christ.

5. *I have sought*, says the Bride, *Him whom my soul loveth*. It is to this that the goodness of Him who has anticipated you in seeking

you and loving you first, it is to this that His goodness is calling and arousing you. You would not seek Him at all, O soul, nor love Him at all, if you had not been first sought and first loved. You have been anticipated by a twofold benediction, that of love and of seeking. The love is the cause of the seeking; the seeking is the fruit and the clear proof of the love. You have been loved, so that you might not fear that you were sought for to be punished; you were sought for, that you might not complain that you were loved to no purpose. Each of these two great and unmistakable favours has given you courage, has removed shyness and timidity, has touched your feelings, and disposed you to return. Hence arises that zeal and ardour in seeking Him whom thy soul loveth; because, just as you were not able to seek Him, until you had first been sought, so now that you have been sought, you are not able to do otherwise than seek Him.

6. Again, never forget whence it is that you have come hither. And that I may apply the better to myself what has been said (which is the safer course), is it not thou, O my soul, who, having left thy first Bridegroom, by whose side all had been well with thee, hast broken the faith first pledged to Him, and gone after others? And now that thou hast sinned with them to the full, and art perhaps fallen into contempt with them, dost thou impudently and with effrontery desire to return to Him, to whom thou hast behaved with so much pride and insolence? What? when thou art fit only to hide thyself, dost thou seek the light, and though more deserving of correction than favour, dare to run unto the Bridegroom? Wonderful it will be if you do not find a Judge to condemn you instead of a husband to receive you. Happy is he who shall hear his soul replying to these reproaches: 'I do not fear because I love, and also I am loved; nor could I have loved unless He had first loved me. Let those fear who have no love; but for the soul that loves there is nothing to be feared. How can those who have no love do otherwise than be under constant apprehension of injury? But because I love, I no more doubt that I am loved than I doubt of my own love; nor can I possibly fear His countenance, whose affection for me I have assuredly felt. In what have I felt it, do you inquire? In this: that not only has He sought me, unhappy as I am, but has caused me to seek Him, and to feel sure of succeeding in my search. Why should I not respond to Him in His search, to whom in His affection I respond? Why should He be angry at my seeking Him, who, when I showed contempt for Him, forgave it? He sought me when I contemned Him, why should He contemn me when I seek Him? Benign and gentle is the Spirit of the WORD, and gentle is His greeting to me; He makes me aware of His kindness towards me, He whispers to me and convinces me of the earnest love of the WORD for me, which cannot be hidden from Him. For He searcheth the deep things of God, and knows that the Divine thoughts are thoughts of peace, and not purposes of vengeance. How can I be otherwise

than encouraged to seek Him, who have had experience of His clemency, and am persuaded of His reconciliation with me?'

7. My brethren, to think seriously of these truths is to be sought by the WORD; to be persuaded of them is to be found by Him. But not all are capable of receiving that Word. What shall we do for the little children among us, I mean those who are still in the stage of beginners (*incipientes*), and yet are far from being without understanding (*insipientes*), since they possess already the beginning of wisdom, being subject one to the other in the fear of Christ? How, I say, shall we cause them to believe that the spiritual life of the Bride is marked by such experiences as these, since they know nothing as yet of such feelings themselves? But I send them to one, to whom they cannot refuse credence. Let them read in a book [of Scripture] that which they fail to discern in the heart of a fellow man, and therefore will not believe. For it is written in one of the Prophets: *If a man put away his wife, and she go from him, and become another man's, shall he return unto her again? shall not that land be greatly polluted? but thou hast played the harlot with many lovers, yet return again to Me, saith the Lord* (Jer. iii. 1). They are the words of the Lord, and it is not permitted to doubt or hesitate. Let them believe what they have not experienced, that by the merit of their faith they may one day attain the fruit of experience. I think that now it has been sufficiently explained what it is to be sought by the WORD, and how this is necessary, not for the WORD, but for the soul, so that the soul which has experienced this knows Him both more fully and more happily. It remains to be treated of in the next discourse how souls that thirst for Christ seek Him by whom they have been sought; or rather that we should learn that from her, who is brought before us in these verses, as seeking Him whom her soul loveth, Him who is the Bridegroom of the soul, JESUS CHRIST our Lord, who is above all, God blessed for ever. AMEN.

SERMON LXXXV.

OF THE SEVEN NEEDS OF THE SOUL, ON ACCOUNT OF WHICH IT SEEKS THE WORD. WHEN THE SOUL IS ONCE REFORMED, IT DRAWS NEAR TO CONTEMPLATE CHRIST, AND TO ENJOY THE SWEETNESS OF HIS PRESENCE.

'*By night upon my bed I sought Him whom my soul loveth.*'—Cant. iii. 1.

FOR what cause does she thus seek? That has been already stated, and it would be superfluous to repeat it; yet, for the sake of some who were not present when that question was treated, I will give a short summary of the causes, to which even those who were with us on the former occasion will not find it troublesome to listen. For not all that was to be said could be finished then. The soul seeks the WORD, and accepts His correction with willingness and joy, so that she may obtain enlightenment and the knowledge of Him, that by His support she may attain to virtue, and be reformed according to wisdom, that she may be conformed unto His likeness and rendered by Him fruitful in good works, and, finally, may be happy in the enjoyment of His Presence. For all these causes the soul seeks the WORD. I do not doubt that there are many others, but in the meantime these are what occur to me. Anyone who is disposed to do so may easily discover others in himself. For our unhappinesses are many, the needs of our soul numerous and unlimited, and our anxieties uncounted. But more richly and fully still does the WORD superabound in good things, insomuch that He surpasses our badness by His wisdom, overcoming evil with good. And now hear the reason for these statements which I have made. In the first place, see how the soul consents, as I said first, to the Divine correction. We read that the WORD speaks thus in the Gospel : *Agree with thine adversary quickly, whiles thou art in the way with him, lest at any time the adversary deliver thee to the judge, and the judge deliver thee to the officer* (Matt. v. 25). What can be more prudent? It is the advice of the WORD, who declares solemnly, if I do not mistake, that He is an adversary to us, because He opposes Himself to our carnal desires, as when He says : *It is a people that do err in their heart* (Ps. xcv. 10). Thou, then, who hearest this, if thou shalt begin in a just fear to flee from the wrath to come, wilt be, I think, solicitous to know in what manner thou mayest agree with that adversary who seems to menace thee with a wrath so terrible. Now, that is impossible, unless thou shalt disagree with thyself, unless thou shalt become an adversary to thine own self, unless thou shalt combat with thyself in continual and untiring struggle ; in short, unless thou shalt renounce thy rooted habitudes and inborn affections. That is indeed a struggle hard and stern ; and if thou shalt attempt it in thy own powers alone, it is as if thou shouldst try to arrest a rushing torrent with a finger, or to make the river of Jordan flow backwards. What canst thou do, then? Thou must seek the WORD, by whose grace it is that thou art enabled to give a glad acquiescence to His will. Fly for help to Him who opposes thee [in evil], by whose help thou mayst become such that He will oppose thee no longer, that He who now threatens thee will approve and applaud thee, and that the grace which He imparts may be more effectual to transform thee than the most violent anger.

2. This is the first necessity, as I think, which brings the soul to seek the WORD. But if you know not what He, to whose will you have already given consent, really desires, will He not say of you that you have a zeal for God, but not according to knowledge? (Rom. x. 2). And that you may not think such ignorance a light thing, remember that which is written, that if any man know not he shall not be known (1 Cor. xiv. 38, Douay). Would you know what I should counsel you to do in this strait? In the first place, my advice is that you should have recourse to the WORD, and He will teach you His ways, for fear lest you, wishing to do good, but not knowing how, should only wander from the right road in your course, and go to and fro in a pathless wilderness. For the WORD is Light, as it is said in the Psalms: *The entrance of Thy words giveth light: it giveth understanding to the simple.* Blessed art thou if thou also art able to say: *Thy Word is a lamp unto my feet and a light unto my path* (Ps. cxix. 130, 105). In no small degree has your soul profited, if your will is changed and your reason enlightened, so that you are enabled both to desire that which is good and to recognise it when it appears to you. In the one gift your soul has received life; in the other, vision. For the soul was dead when it willed that which was evil, and blind when it was ignorant of good.

3. Now your soul lives, now it sees, now it is established in good; but all this is by the help and by the working of the WORD. If it stands upright, it is because it has been lifted up by the hand of the WORD, and set, as it were, upon two feet, devotion and understanding. It stands upright, I repeat; but yet let it take as spoken of itself that which is said: *Let him that thinketh he standeth take heed lest he fall* (1 Cor. x. 12). Do you think that the soul, which was not able to arise by its own strength, will by its own strength be enabled to stand? I should suppose not. What? It was by the WORD of the Lord that the heavens were made (Ps. xxxiii. 6), and shall a being which is but earth stand without Him? If it were able to stand by itself, why was it that a man, formed also of the earth, prayed thus: *Strengthen Thou me according unto Thy Word* (Ps. cxix. 28)? He had even experienced that he could not stand by himself, since he says: *Being pushed, I was overturned that I might fall, but the Lord supported me* (Ps. cxviii. 13, Douay). Does anyone inquire what it was that thus pushed? It was not one only; it was the devil, it was the world, it was perhaps some man. What man, do you rejoin? In truth, every man is a tempter such as this to and for himself. Marvel not at this.

To such a degree is every man a tempter to himself, and an occasion of falling, that you need not fear the temptation put before you by another person, if you can keep your own hands from working destruction to you. *For who*, says the Apostle, *is he that will harm you, if ye be followers of that which is good?* (1 Peter iii. 13). By your own hands I mean the consent of your will. If, when the devil suggests to you, or the world persuades you to do, anything which is not right, you refrain from giving an inward consent to it, nor allow your members to be the instruments of iniquity, then you have not permitted sin to reign in your mortal body ; in resisting the promptings of evil you have approved yourself the follower of good, and the temptation has done you good rather than harm. For it is written : *Do that which is good, and thou shalt have praise* (Rom. xiii. 3). They are confounded who sought to harm your soul, and you shall sing : *If they shall have no dominion over me, then shall I be without spot* (Ps. xix. 14, Douay). You have shown yourself to be animated by a holy emulation if, under the guidance of wisdom, you have had affection for your own soul (Ecclus. xxx. 23), if you have kept your heart with all diligence (Prov. iv. 23), if, according to the precept of the Apostle, you have kept yourself pure (1 Tim. v. 22). Otherwise, even though you should gain the whole world, but suffer loss to your soul, we shall certainly, as the Saviour Himself teaches, regard you as not being a follower of that which is good.

4. There are, then, three adversaries by whom you are threatened. Of these the devil impels to evil by malice and jealousy, the world by the tempest of vanity, while man himself is burdened by the weight of his own corruption. The devil impels you indeed to evil, but he does not overthrow you, if you do not give him your help by yielding assent to his wicked suggestions. Thus we read : *Resist the devil, and he will flee from you* (James iv. 7). It is he who in his envy tempted and overthrew those who were upright in Paradise, for they did not resist him, but consented to his evil suggestions. It is he who, by his pride, cast himself down from the height of heaven, and that without impulse from any other; thus you may learn what very grave cause man also, because of the weight by which he is oppressed in his own nature, has to fear that he may fall. The world also impels to evil, because it lieth in wickedness (1 John v. 19). Its impulse is felt by all, but it overthrows only those who are of it, that is, who are consentient with it in mind and will. I desire not to be the friend of the world, lest I fall. For he who desires to be a friend of this world becomes thereby an enemy of God, and this is the most calamitous fall it is possible to make. From this it appears that man is to himself the principal occasion of falling, since he can fall by his own impulse, and without any impulse from another person, but cannot fall without his own impulse, whatever instigation he may receive from others. Now, which of these three adversaries ought chiefly to be resisted ? Plainly, that one which is more importunate, as it is in more intimate relation with us, which is sufficient by itself

to make us fall, and without which no other adversaries are able to effect anything against us. Not without cause does the wise man declare: *He that ruleth his spirit is better than he that taketh a city* (Prov. xvi. 32). This is of great importance to you; you have need of great strength, and of that strength with which you can be endued only from on high. That strength, if it be perfect, will easily render the soul victorious over itself, and, consequently, invincible by all other adversaries. For it is a spiritual strength, which knows not how to yield when in defence of the right. Or, if you prefer to express it thus, it is a spiritual strength which stands firm and unshaken, with good reason, and on behalf of the right. Or, again, thus: a spiritual strength, which, as far as in it lies, directs and rules all things according to reason.

5. Who shall ascend into the hill of the Lord? Whosoever shall take upon him to ascend to the top of that mountain, that is to say, to attain the perfection of virtue, must consider how arduous is that ascent, and how easy to fall without the assistance of the WORD. Happy is the soul which excites the joy and the astonishment of the Angels who behold it, so that it hears them speaking of it thus: *Who is this that cometh up from the wilderness, leaning upon her Beloved?* (viii. 5). For otherwise she labours to no purpose, if she does not lean upon God (*nititur, innititur*). She will acquire new forces in her struggle with herself, and thus becoming the stronger, will bring all things into subjection to reason. She will regulate anger, fear, cupidity, and joy, as a skilful charioteer (if I may so speak), driving the chariot of the soul; she will bring into captivity every carnal affection, and subject all the senses to the control of reason and the practice of virtue. How can all things fail to be possible to a man who depends in his endeavours upon Him who can do all things? How firm a ground of confidence is that saying: *I can do all things through Christ which strengtheneth me* (Phil. iv. 13). Nothing shows more clearly the Almighty power of the WORD, than that He makes all those whose hope is in Him to be, as it were, all powerful. For *all things are possible to him that believeth* (Mark ix. 23). Is not he all-powerful to whom all things are possible? Thus it is that the soul, if it does not presume upon its own powers, but is strengthened by the WORD, will be able so to rule over itself that no unrighteousness shall have dominion over it. It is thus, I say, that the soul, resting upon the WORD, and endued with power from on high, cannot possibly be either overthrown or brought into subjection by any open violence, secret guile, or enticing allurement.

6. Would you have no fear of violence from without? Then let not the foot of pride find place within you; so the hand of the violent shall not cast you down. *There are the workers of iniquity fallen* (Ps. xxxvi. 12). It was thus that the devil and his angels fell. They were impelled to evil by no force from without; nevertheless, they were not able to stand, but were driven forth from Heaven. He did not stand fast in the truth, who did not rely upon the WORD, but

trusted in his own strength. It was for that reason, perhaps, that he desired to *sit*, because he was not able to stand upright. For, he said: *I will sit upon the mount of the congregation* (Is. xiv. 13). But the judgment of God was otherwise; he neither stood nor sat, but fell headlong, as we are told by the Lord Himself: *I beheld Satan as lightning fall from heaven* (Luke x. 18). Therefore let the soul that stands, if it does not desire to fall, not trust in its own strength, but lean upon the WORD. The WORD Himself warns us: *Without Me ye can do nothing* (John xv. 5). That is most truly the case; without the WORD we can neither stand firm in the good to which we have attained, nor rise up towards any fresh good. Do you, therefore, who as yet art standing firm, give glory to the WORD, and say: *He set my feet upon a rock and ordered my goings* (Ps. xl. 2). It is needful that the same Hand which has raised you up should hold you firm and prevent you from falling. Thus much is by way of explanation of what I said, that we have need of the WORD, that we may be supported by Him and enabled to attain unto virtue.

7. In the next place, let us consider what I have also asserted, namely, that it is by the WORD we are reformed according to wisdom. The WORD is wisdom, and He is strength. Let the soul, then, draw wisdom from Him who is wisdom, and strength from Him who is strength; and let each of these gifts be ascribed to the WORD alone. Otherwise, if either be ascribed to some other source, or arrogated to the soul itself, let it be said also that the river does not flow from the spring, the juice of the grape from the vine, or light from the orb of day. It is a faithful saying: *If any of you lack wisdom, let him ask of God, who giveth to all men liberally, and upbraideth not: and it shall be given him* (James i. 5). This the Apostle expressly states; and I think it is not otherwise with regard to strength. For strength is nearly allied to wisdom; it is a gift of God, coming down from Him who is the Father of the WORD, and to be ranked among the best gifts. If anyone should think that it is in all respects identical with wisdom, I do not contest it; but that perfect resemblance is in the WORD, not in the soul. For those excellences, which in the WORD are one because of the unique simplicity of the Divine nature, have not in the soul the same action; but accommodate and distribute themselves, as if diverse, according to its different and various necessities. According to this principle, then, it is one thing for the soul to be acted upon by strength, and another for it to be directed by wisdom: one thing for it to be strengthened by power, and another for it to be delighted by sweetness. For although wisdom be powerful, and power sweet; yet that we may attach to words each their proper signification, we attach to power the sense of a certain vigour in the soul, and to wisdom that of calmness and composure, accompanied by a kind of spiritual sweetness. This I take to have been specified by the Apostle when, after having given many exhortations relating to spiritual strength, he added with regard to sweetness: *In sweetness, in the Holy Ghost* (2 Cor. vi. 6, Douay). It is, then, an honour,

indeed, to stand firm, to resist, to repel force by force, which are regarded as the works of strength and courage; but it is also a labour. For it is not the same thing to defend your honour with toil and danger, and to possess it in peace. Whatsoever strength laboriously prepares, wisdom makes use of and enjoys; and that which wisdom ordains, contemplates, regulates, strength carries into effect.

8. 'The wisdom of a scribe cometh by his time of leisure,' saith the Wise man (Ecclus. xxxviii. 25, Douay). The very leisure, therefore, of wisdom is a labour; and the more leisurely wisdom is, the more laborious it is in its own way. But virtue, the more it is exercised in its own sphere of action, the more illustrious it is; and the more it prevails over difficulties, the more it is approved. And if anyone should define wisdom as the love of virtue, I do not know that he would be far wrong. But where love is, there a task, whatever it be, is not a mere labour, but a pleasure and a joy. And perhaps the name '*sapientia*' is derived from 'sapor,' since it is, as it were, the seasoning of virtue, to which it gives taste and savour, and which, in default of it, remains tasteless and insipid. Nor should I object if anyone should define wisdom to be the love of, and taste for, good. But we have lost this taste almost from the very appearance of our race upon the earth. From the moment in which sense has prevailed, and the venom of the old serpent has occupied and corrupted the palate of the heart, it has begun to have no longer a taste for that which is good, and a depraved and injurious taste has begun to enter in. Thence it is that *the imagination of man's heart is evil from his youth* (Gen. viii. 21); that is, from the folly of the first woman. It is, then, the folly of the woman that was the cause of our losing the taste for good, and that because the malicious cunning of the serpent deceived her inexperience. But the very reason which made that malice appear to have gained the victory for a time, occasions it the mortification of defeat for all eternity. For, lo! Wisdom once more has wholly filled the heart and the body of a woman; so that as by a woman we had become deformed by falling into folly, so by a woman we should be reformed unto wisdom. And now wisdom constantly prevails over malice in those souls into which it has entered, destroying and replacing by a better that taste for evil which malice brought with it. Wisdom, when it enters into the soul, renders insipid all the pleasures of the flesh, purifies the understanding, heals and restores the palate of the heart. Thus, with the restoration of its powers, it begins to desire that which is good, and to desire wisdom itself, than which there is nothing better.

9. How many good actions are done in which, notwithstanding, those who do them have no real delight, because they are not impelled to do them by a taste and love for them, but are, in a measure, forced to do them by the compulsion of reason, or of circumstances, or even by necessity! And, on the contrary, how many there are who, though they do wrong, do not take pleasure in evil, but are led into it rather by fear, or by some desire which they wish to satisfy, than by any

satisfaction in wrongdoing! But those who act from deliberate purpose either are wise, and delight in goodness for its own sake, or they are of evil disposition, and find pleasure in evil as such, without being drawn to it by the hope of some advantage. What, indeed, is iniquity but the taking pleasure in what is evil? Happy is the soul which has delight only in whatever is good, and distaste and hatred for whatever is evil! This it is to be reformed unto wisdom; this is to have had happy experience of the victory of wisdom in one's own self. For that in which the predominance of wisdom over malice is most plainly shown is when, by the exclusion of all delight in evil, which is nothing else than evil itself, the soul feels itself to be wholly occupied by a deeply seated approval of, and delight in, that which is good. It is, then, to power we have to look for the ability bravely to endure tribulations, and to wisdom for the ability to rejoice in them. To strengthen thy heart, and wait patiently upon the Lord, that is the work of power; to taste and see how sweet is the Lord, is the gift of wisdom. And as each gift shows to the greatest advantage in its appropriate virtue, so modesty of mind approves the man who is wise, constancy the man who is full of power. And it is with fitness that we put wisdom after power, because power of soul is, as it were, the firm foundation upon which wisdom raises for itself the complete edifice of the Christian character. But it is needful that the knowledge of the good should precede each of these, for there is no point of agreement between the light of wisdom and the darkness of ignorance. And a good will also is needful, for 'into a malicious soul wisdom shall not enter (Wisd. i. 4).

10. Now, having taken note that by the change of its will from evil to good the soul has recovered life, spiritual health by the instruction which God bestows, stability by the gift of strength, and, lastly, maturity by that of wisdom, it remains that it should obtain the gift of beauty, without which it is not able to please Him who is fairest among the sons of men. For she knows that it is said: *The King shall greatly desire thy beauty* (Ps. xlv. 11). How many good gifts to the soul, the gifts of the WORD, have we enumerated: knowledge, goodwill, power, wisdom; and yet we do not read that either of these is *desired* by the WORD; only of '*thy beauty*' is this said. So the Psalmist also says: *The Lord hath reigned, He is clothed with beauty* (Ps. xciii. 1, Douay). How can He fail to desire that she who is at once His likeness and His Bride should be clad with a similar garment of beauty to Himself? The closer is her resemblance to Him, the dearer will she be. In what, then, consists this beauty of the soul? Is it not in this, that she is called *honourable*? Let us take that meaning provisionally, if no better occurs to us. But honour appears in the outward behaviour; not that it consists in this, but it is by this that it is recognised. Its origin and its dwelling-place are in the conscience, and the testimony of a good conscience is its glory. When the truth shines forth in the soul, and the soul beholds itself in the truth, there is nothing brighter than that

light, nothing more glorious than that testimony. But of what nature is the image thus displayed? It is that of a soul chaste, modest, self-restrained, circumspect, admitting nothing which tends to obscure the glory of the testimony thus rendered; conscious of no wrongdoing which should make it ashamed in the presence of the truth, and oblige it to hide its countenance, as if confused and repelled by the Divine light. This is without doubt that beauty which God takes most pleasure in beholding, among all the excellences of the holy soul; and this we name and define as *honour*.

11. But when the splendour of this beauty is diffused abundantly throughout the heart, so as to fill it wholly, it is of necessity that it should become visible also without, and be not as a light hidden under a bushel, but rather as a lamp shining in a dark place, and which cannot be concealed. Thus casting the bright illumination of its rays upon the body, it makes the latter an image of the soul, and diffuses itself through all its faculties and senses, insomuch that every action, every word, look, motion, every laugh (if it should ever give way to laughter) should be mixed with gravity and full of self-restraint. When, then, all the movements of the body, all its gestures and habits, are grave, pure, and modest, far removed from all boldness and licence, from all lightness and luxury, but adapted to righteousness, and to every duty of piety, then the fairness of the soul shall be visible, provided there be no secret guile to obscure it. For it may be that all these things are put on and simulated, and do not come naturally out of the abundance of the heart. And to display this spiritual beauty in all its lustre, we will define, if you please, this *honour*, and show in what it consists. It is the *candour* of the soul, which is solicitous to unite the testimony of a good conscience within with spotlessness of reputation without, or in the words of the Apostle: *Providing for things honest, not only in the sight of the Lord, but also in the sight of men* (2 Cor. viii. 21). Blessed is the soul which has clothed itself in that beauty of holiness, that pure whiteness of innocence, by which it may claim a glorious likeness, not to the world, but to the WORD; of whom we read, that He is the Brightness of the everlasting Light (Wisd. vii. 26); *the Brightness of the glory of God, and the express Image of His Person* (Heb. i. 3).

12. From this degree the soul which is in such a condition ventures to think of union with the WORD. Why should she not do so, when she sees that the more she resembles Him, the more fitted she is for that spiritual marriage? The loftiness of His Majesty does not terrify her, because her resemblance associates her with Him, her affection unites her to Him, her profession of obedience and loyalty constitutes a betrothal. And this is the form of that profession: *I have sworn, and will perform it, that I will keep Thy righteous judgments* (Ps. cxix. 106). This the Apostles had followed when they said: *Behold, we have forsaken all, and followed Thee* (Matt. xix. 27). Similar is that saying which, referring to a carnal marriage, signified, nevertheless, the spiritual union which is betwixt

Christ and His Church: *For this cause shall a man leave his father and mother, and shall be joined unto his wife, and they two shall be one flesh* (Eph. v. 31); and by the Psalmist the Bride glorifies herself in these terms: *It is good for me to draw near to God: I have put my trust in the Lord God* (Ps. lxxiii. 28). When, then, you shall see a soul which, having left all, cleaves unto the WORD with every thought and desire, lives only for the WORD, rules itself according to His will, nay, becomes, as it were, fruitful by the Word, which is able to say with sincerity, *To me to live is Christ, and to die is gain* (Phil. i. 21), then you may have much assurance that this soul is wedded to the Word, and is His Bride. The heart of her Spouse trusteth in her, knowing her to be faithful, inasmuch as she has despised all things in comparison of Him, and counts them as dung (Phil. iii. 8), that she may win Christ, and be found in Him. Such the Lord knew him to be of whom He said: *He is a chosen vessel unto Me* (Acts ix. 15). Assuredly the soul of the Apostle St. Paul was, as it were, a faithful spouse and a tender mother, as was shown by his touching words: *My little children, of whom I travail in birth again until Christ be formed in you* (Gal. iv. 19).

13. But notice that in this spiritual marriage there are two ways of travailing in birth, different, though not contrary; since saintly souls, as holy mothers, either bring forth souls by preaching, or by meditation develop spiritual intelligences. In the latter kind of travail it sometimes happens that the soul is so transported out of itself, and entirely detached from the bodily senses, that, though conscious of the WORD, it has no consciousness of itself. This is the case when it is drawn on by the ineffable sweetness of the WORD, and, as it were, stolen from itself, or, rather, it is rapt out of itself to enjoy the Presence of the WORD. The mind is affected in one way when it is rendered fruitful by the WORD, and in another when it enjoys the Presence of the WORD. In the one it is full of care for the necessity of its neighbour; in the other it is filled with enjoyment of the sweetness of the WORD. And, indeed, a mother has joy in her offspring, as a Bride in the kindness of her spouse. Dear and precious are children, who are the pledges of affection; most sweet also the devotion of the beloved. So also it is a good work to save many souls; but to depart and to be with the WORD, that is far better. But when does that happen to us, or how long does it endure? Sweet is that communion; but how seldom does it occur, and for how brief a time does it last! And this is the final reason of those for which, as I remember I stated above, the soul seeks the WORD; namely, that it may attain to spiritual joy through Him.

14. Perhaps it will be asked of me by someone who hears this, What is it to enjoy the WORD? I reply, Let that be asked rather from him who has had the happiness to experience it. Even though it were given to me to have that great blessing, how can you think it possible that I should explain a mystery which is incapable of being put into words? Hear one who had known it: *Whether we be beside*

ourselves, it is to God: or whether we be sober, it is for your cause (2 Cor. v. 13). That is to say, It is one thing for me to have communion with God, and of that God alone is the judge; it is quite another for me to be in familiar speech, my brethren, with yourselves. It has been permitted to me to have experience of that great blessing; it is not at all permitted to me to express it in speech. And in the reference which I have just now made to it, I adapt my words, so as to speak, as you are able to receive what I may say. O thou who art full of curiosity to know what it is to enjoy the WORD, prepare thy heart for that, not thy ear. The tongue cannot reveal it, it is taught only by grace. It is hidden from the wise and prudent, and it is revealed to babes. Humility, my brethren, is a great and lofty virtue, by which that which is not taught is promised; which is worthy to attain what is beyond the province of teaching; worthy of the WORD, and to receive by the WORD that which it is not itself capable of expressing in words. Why is this? Not because of any merit of its own, but because such is the good pleasure of Him who is the Father of the WORD, the Bridegroom of the soul, JESUS CHRIST our Lord, who is above all, God blessed for ever. AMEN.

SERMON LXXXVI.

OF THE CAUTION AND MODESTY BECOMING TO THE SOUL IN SEEKING THE WORD, AND OF THE PRAISE OF MODESTY.

I BELIEVE that nothing more will be expected of me upon the subject of the soul's reasons for seeking the WORD, for I have already sufficiently stated them. Come, then, let us continue to expound what remains of the verse before us, as far only as relates to morals. Notice, then, in the first place, the *modesty* of the Bride. I know not whether there is any virtue which man can attain more beautiful than this. This before all I would desire to take, so to speak, in my hands, and to gather it as a fair flower to present to those who are young among us. Not that those who are more advanced in it ought not to preserve it with every care, but because the grace of a tender modesty shines out more fairly and becomingly in those who are of a more tender age. What is there more amiable than a young man who is modest? How fair, and even splendid, does this jewel of virtues show on the countenance and in the life of the young! What a certain and unmistakable mark it is of goodness of character, and of that which may be one day hoped for from them! It is, as it were, a rod of correction to such an one, which is constantly present before his mind, which chastens the affections and the thoughtless actions of an age which is wont to be artful and deceptive, and which restrains its light or insolent actions. What is there more contrary than it to coarse speech, or to any kind of impurity? It is the sister of continence. There is no mark so plain and unmistakable as this, of dove-like simplicity: and therefore it is the proof of innocence. It is a lamp which burns without ceasing in a modest soul, so that nothing impure or unbecoming can attempt to enter there without being instantly discovered. Thus it acts as the destroyer of vices and promoter of inward purity, the special glory of conscience, the guardian of good fame, the ornament of life, the seat and the first-fruits of virtue, the glory of nature, and the token or ensign of everything honourable. What grace and beauty the very colour in the cheeks called up by modesty imparts to the countenance!

2. Modesty is an excellence so natural to the soul, that even those who do not fear to act wrongly are ashamed to let it be perceived, as the Lord Himself declares: *Every one that doeth evil hateth the light* (John iii. 20). And again, St. Paul says: *They that sleep, sleep in the night; and they that be drunken are drunken in the night* (1 Thess. v. 7); that is to say, the works of darkness, which are deserving of darkness everlasting, shroud themselves in darkness of their own accord. It is, however, important to distinguish here between the modesty of men who are not ashamed to do such actions, but blush to have them discovered, and therefore conceal them, and that of the Bride, who does not merely conceal them, but rejects them absolutely, and drives them away. Thus the Wise Man declares: There is a shame which bringeth sin: and there is a shame which is glory and grace (Ecclus. iv. 21). The Bride seeks the WORD; seeks Him at night, and on her couch, but modestly and timidly; and this modesty is glorious, not sinful. She seeks to find Him for the purifying of her conscience, for the obtaining of the testimony, that she may say: *Our glory is this, the testimony of our conscience* (2 Cor. i. 12, Douay). *By night on my bed I sought Him whom my soul loveth* (Cant. iii. 1). Her modesty, if you notice, is indicated to you both by the place and the time. What is there so congenial to a modest mind as secrecy? Now, the night and the couch ensure that her prayer is secret. And, in fact, we are bidden, when we desire to pray, to enter into our bedchamber (Matt. vi. 6), no doubt for the sake of secrecy. That is, indeed, to be done as a measure of precaution, lest if we pray in the sight of men human praise may hinder the effect of our prayer and deprive us of its fruit. But we learn from it also a lesson of modesty; for what course is so appropriate to modesty as to avoid even the praises that are due to it, and to fly from vainglory? It is, then, clear that the Son, who is the teacher[1] and pattern of modesty, has expressly bidden us to seek for secrecy in our prayers, so as to promote modesty. What can be so unbecoming, especially in a young man, as an ostentation of sanctity? It is to be borne in mind also that at that age it is particularly needful to make a beginning of religious obedience, according to the saying of Jeremiah: *It*

---

[1] *Magister;* another reading is *minister.*

is good for a man that he bear the yoke in his youth (Lam. iii. 27). The prayer which you are about to offer will be well recommended if you cause it to be preceded by modesty, saying : *I am very young and despised : but I forgot not Thy justifications* (Ps. cxix. 141, Douay).

3. It is needful that he who desires to offer acceptable prayer should observe not only the right place, but also the right time to do so. A time of leisure is the fittest and most convenient, and especially during the deep silence which night brings; for then prayer arises most freely, and is most pure. *Arise*, says a prophet, *cry out in the night; in the beginning of the watches pour out thine heart like water before the face of the Lord* (Lam. ii. 19). How securely during the night does prayer arise to heaven, unwitnessed, save by God alone, and by the holy Angel, who receives that prayer to present it before the Altar of Heaven! How acceptable and clear it is, being rendered translucent by humility and modesty! How serene and peaceful, since it is troubled by no sound nor interruption! And lastly, how pure and sincere, as being free from the soiling dust of earthly care, nor deflected by the praise and flattery of human witnesses! For these reasons it was that the Bride, who is as modest as she is prudent, sought the silence of the night, and the retirement of her chamber, to pray, that is, to occupy herself in seeking the WORD. For these two objects are one. Otherwise you do not pray aright, if in prayer you seek some other object than the WORD, or seek it otherwise than on account of the WORD, since in Him are all things [that you ought to seek]. In Him are the remedies for the wounds of your soul, in Him the help for necessities, supplies for all defects, abundance for the soul's progress in holiness, and, in a word, all things that man ought to have or to desire, all things that he needs, all things that are good for him. It is, then, wholly without cause that anything but the WORD is asked of Him in prayer, for He Himself is all things. For although we sometimes seem to ask those temporal good things of which we have need, if it is for the sake of the WORD that we ask them (as indeed it is fit and right we should do), it is not properly those good things themselves for which we are making petition, but for Him on whose account and for whose service we are asking them. Those whose rule of conduct it is to make use of all things so as to endeavour to deserve well of the WORD, know the truth of what I say.

4. We shall not regret examining still farther the mysteries indicated by this mention of the *bed* and of the *night*, to see if there be some spiritual truth concealed in it, which it will be for our benefit to discover. If, for example, by the *bed* we understand the weakness of our human nature, and by the *night* its ignorance, then we shall be thus taught that it is not without good cause that the Bride seeks with such touching and painful earnestness the WORD, who is the Power of God and the Wisdom of God, that she may be fortified by His presence against each of these evils, which are to be attributed to the fault of origin. What can be more fitting than that Power

should be opposed to weakness, and wisdom to ignorance? And that no doubt may linger in the hearts of the simple regarding this interpretation, let them hear what is said in a Psalm: *The Lord will strengthen him upon the bed of languishing; Thou wilt make all his bed in his sickness* (Ps. xli. 3). That is as relates to the *bed*. And as to the *night* of ignorance, what can be plainer than the statement in another Psalm: *They know not, neither will they understand; they walk on in darkness* (Ps. lxxxii. 5)? which expresses with preciseness that state of ignorance into which the whole human race are born. It was into this, as I think, that the blessed Apostle St. Paul both confesses that he was born, and glories that he has been delivered from it, saying: *Who hath delivered us from the power of darkness* (Col. i. 13). And on this account he says also: *We are not* [children] *of the night, nor of darkness* (1 Thess. v. 5); and also he says (Eph. v. 8) to all those who are elect: *Walk as children of light.*

Thus far had the holy Bernard written, when death arrested his proceeding farther with the work. This very Sermon was evidently left unfinished, and on that account is so much shorter than the rest, and wanting in the usual Ascription and Doxology.

[The Sermons on the Canticles were continued by a disciple of St. Bernard, Gilbert, first Abbot of St. Mary of Hoiland (Swineshead Abbey, in the County of Lincoln), and apparently a countryman of our own. He carried the Exposition on as far as v. 10, in forty-eight Sermons, and then '*similiter præventus morte*' died, about A.D. 1200, at least his name cannot be traced in the records any farther than that date.]

S. J. E.

INDEX.

A.

ACTIVE life, the, more necessary than the contemplative, 48.
Air, said to be the abode of demons, 327.
Ambition, a temptation, 222.
Ambrose, St., xiii.
Angels, why they need bodies, 25 ; nature of their bodies, 27 ; cannot by themselves reach unto human minds, *ib.* ; assist men in prayer and praise, 35 ; nature and manner of their love to God, 104 ; Archangels, the, 105 ; Powers, *ib.* ; Dominations, 106 ; Thrones, *ib.*, Seraphin, 107 ; Cherubin, *ib.* ; in what sense they are redeemed, 125 ; mystically called stars, 169 ; guardian Angel, his offices to a holy soul, 204 ; they watch over the faithful, 249 ; impart Divine truths, 257 ; are acquainted with the invisible verities of God, 321 ; called mountains and hills, 322 ; how the fallen Angels were punished, 422 ; their places are to be filled by human souls, 476.
Animals, in what sense they have spirit, 25 ; it does not survive their body, *ib.*
Anselm, St., his idea of *creatura mundi*, 25.
Apostles, the supposed inebriation of, 298.
Apples, mystically interpreted, 308.
Aquinas, St. Thomas, xiii. ; as to Angelic bodies, 27
Athanasius, St., xii.
Augustine, St., xii. ; as to Angelic bodies, 27 ; his love for the name of Jesus, 83 ; on Baptism, 423.
Avarice, mystically interpreted, 249.
Avaricious, the servant rather than the master of his wealth, 120.

B.

BAPTISM, the deliverance at the Red Sea a type of, 247 ; heretical errors respecting, 404.
Beams, mystical meaning of, 286.
Berengar, disciple of Abaelard, his *Apologeticum*, 170.

Bernard, St., his preaching, 1, 2, 3, 4 ; preparation, 3 ; his experience of spiritual coldness, 77 ; his lament for his brother Gerard, 164 ; protests his unworthiness, 196 ; laments his many occupations, 197 ; his favourite text, 269 ; his relics, 270 ; his desire to preach Jesus only, 269 ; his assiduity in celebrating, 305 ; his satisfaction at good results from his sermons, 309 ; humility of, 334 ; his modesty, 457 ; his personal experience of Divine visitations, *ib.*, of Divine suggestions, 501 ; Bible of, xix.
Bernard des Portes, suggests sermons, 2.
Bethel, or Bether, house of, 452.
Bishops, how highly to be revered, 65 ; not rashly to be criticised, *ib.* ; their office not to be sought by ambition, *ib.*
Blackness, mystical sense of, 150 ; outward, frequently a sign of inward comeliness, 151 ; as applied to St. Paul, 152 ; to the Saviour, 154 ; to the Bride, 153.
Blessed dead, whether they can feel sympathy for the living, 159 ; the felicity of, 216 ; their care for the faithful on earth, 476.
Blessedness, the future, to be derived from God Himself, 57.
Body, the, its complaint against the soul, 147 ; why created upright, *ib.* ; compared to a tent, 155.
Bonaventura, St., xii.
Bossuet, Bishop, xiv.
Brentius, J., xii.
Bridegroom, the, is the Divine Son, 43 ; breasts of the, are Patience and Clemency, 46 ; the four perfumes of the, 123, 129, has many chambers, 137 ; mercy and judgment the attributes of, 333 ; how He is said to have *stood*, 336 ; is present everywhere in His Divinity, 337 ; His coming mystically stated, 341 ; calls to duty, 347 ; His great love to mankind, 387 ; gives attention to the Church, 415 ; the signs of His Presence in the soul, 424, 454 ; why called Beloved, 426 ; feeds among

the lilies, 427, 432 ; of His Glory with the Father, 468-470 ; of His returning at the end of the age, 483.
Bride, the Church called the, 78 ; why desiring to be drawn after Christ, 116 , is black, yet comely, 149 ; adornment of the, 167 ; beauty of consists in virtues, 168 ; the qualities of, 214 ; called the fairest, 243 ; loved by the Saviour, 251 ; what constitutes its beauty, 252 ; compared to a turtle-dove, 254 ; the ornaments and necklaces of, 256 ; is called to duty by the Bridegroom, 347 ; the expression of her love to Him, 408, 415 ; limits of her knowledge, 471.

C.

CAMPHIRE, mystically interpreted, 271.
Canticles, Book of, to be entrusted to wise and devout minds only, 8 ; is without preface, 9 ; in Scripture, how they differ, 10.
Carnal delights compared to wine, 48.
Cassiodorus, xii.
Castellio, S., xiv.
Cedar, mystical meaning of the, 282.
Centurion, the, depended upon hearing, that is, faith, rather than sight, 179.
Chamber of the Bridegroom, mystical sense of, 132, 136 ; chambers of God, of Providence, of judgment, and of mercy, 138.
Chancellors, said to be so-called from sitting behind *cancelli*, 339.
Chariots of Pharaoh, the, 247, 250 ; their horses and drivers, *ib.*
Charity, need of, 104 ; necessary with faith to uprightness, 149 ; is the measure of souls, 174 ; is the best gift, 188 ; want of, a great fault, 189 ; what it is to set in order in the soul, 300 ; of feeling and of action compared, 302.
Chastity, commendation of, 354.
Cherubin, the, 107.
CHRIST, His self-emptying a ground of hope, 57, 58 ; why He suffered so greatly to redeem mankind, 59 ; the Church His Body, 66 , His Name compared to sweet ointment, 79 ; how we should love Him, 111 ; love to Him according to the flesh, 113 , comparison between two ways of loving Him, 115 , most men desire His Glory rather than His Cross, 117 ; in what sense He is a Redeemer to the Angels, 126 ; how unworthy it is not to follow Him, 127 ; various motives for doing so, 128 ; all perfections united in the Life of, 130 ; in what sense said to be black, 153 ; likeness to Him the glory of the Christian, 154 ; called the true Solomon, 168 ; said to have incurred blackness for the sake of man, 177 ; His glory and beauty, 183 ; not discerned in His humiliation by the Jews, 184 ; the faithful soul lives in the shadow of, 207 ; communicated to some souls as Bridegroom, to others as Physician, 207, 208 ; His Life on earth compared to an aurora, 217 ; His perfect humility, 266 ; meditation upon His sufferings and Passion, how helpful, 267 ; compared to a bundle of myrrh, *ib.* ; the Vision of Him, 278 ; His manifold Perfections, 280 ; called Rose of Sharon and Lily of the Valley, 287, 289 ; is our pattern and also our recompense, 289 ; what is meant by the Shadow of, 295 ; compared to an apple-tree, 293 ; is by Nature superior to the children of grace, 295 ; death terrible without Him, 338 ; the Passion of, the strength of martyrdom, 370 ; virtues of, called lilies, 426 ; manifested that He might be loved, 427 ; comes in human form to judge, that He may be delightful to the elect, 448 ; less than the Angels, yet loftier, 448, 453 ; why He ascended into Heaven, 468.
Church, the prayer of the, for the diffusion of the grace of the Gospel, 75 ; is black, yet comely, 149 ; is composed both of Angels and men, 171 ; said to have heavens, 175 ; is both humble and sublime, 176 ; complaint of against persecuters, 186 ; called a vineyard, 193 ; was increased through persecution, 194 ; its privilege is to be universal, 195 ; the four temptations of, 223 ; injured by the evil lives of Christians. 224 ; of the state and composition of, 281 ; the end of all things depends on its consummation, 418 ; how gathered, 478 ; of the elect, predestinated before all ages, 479 ; not at first recognised, 480 ; how formed, 481 ; how continually protected, 485 ; charity towards the Synagogue, 486.
Cistercian Churches, plainness of, xvii.
Clairvaux, the community at, some insubordinate members of, 284 ; request to the brethren of, not to disturb their Abbot for trifling causes, 318.
Confession, a sincere, of sin, a proof of spiritual life, 85 ; the three kinds of, 86 ; what is a wrong kind of, 91 ; must be made with simplicity, 92 ; with faith, 93.
Consolation and exhortation yielded by the Spouse, 49.
Contemplative life, the, not so necessary as the active, 48 ; the use of contemplation, 103 , three ways of, called storerooms, 130 ; how to be attained, 283 ; leads to ecstasy, 314.
Contrition, in what it consists, 86.
Conversion, a sign of, 343.
Countenance of the soul, the intention so-called, 253.
Cure of souls, the, how great a hindrance is avarice to, 50.

INDEX 531

Curtains of Solomon, mystical sense of, 155, 156, 167.
Cypress, mystical meaning of the, 282.
Cyril, St., of Jerusalem, xii.

D.

DAVID, example of, 70, 213 ; his patience, 225, 411 ; his marriage hymn, 412.
Day of inspiration, 446 ; of respiration, 448.
Daybreak, mystically explained, 444.
Death of the soul, 315 ; of the body, 316 ; is terrible without Christ, 338.
Despair, comes from ignorance of God, 243.
Detraction, the vice of, 142 ; destroys charity, 145 ; different kinds of, 146 ; detractors called foxes, 380.
Deutz, Rupert of, xiii.
Devotion, a spiritual perfume, 49 ; of what composed, 52 ; glorifies God, 53.
Dionysius Carthusianus, xiii.
Discretion, the importance of, 299 ; the regulator of all the virtues, 300.
Divine Service, how it should be shared in, 291.
Dominations, an order of Angels, 106.
Dublin, St Mary's Abbey at, 5
Durand, John, 5.

E.

EBERSBERG, William, Abbot of, xii.
Eberwin, Provost of Steinfeld, 4 ; his letter to St. Bernard, 388.
Ecstasy, two kinds of, 299 ; is reached by the way of contemplation, 314 ; is an approach to the Angelic life, 316.
Elijah and Elisha, the Divine instruments in working miracles, 71.
Elisha, the staff of, 85.
Enemy, an, with what feeling to be regarded, 306.
Engedi, explanation of, 271, 272.
Envy, in anywise to be avoided, 301 ; the inward consent to, constitutes sin, 302.
Epiphanius, Bishop, xii.
Ernald, Life of St. Bernard, 2.
Estius, as to Angelic bodies, 27.
Eucharist, the Holy, sometimes intermitted among the Cistercians, 305.
Eusebius of Cæsarea, xii.
Ewald, G. H. A. von, xiv.
Example, a good, to be given by pastors, 473.
Exhortation and consolation yielded by the Spouse, 49.

F.

FAITH, separation from charity fatal to, 148 ; has a surer cognition than experience, 182 ; compared to a shadow, 206 ; without works is dead, 296 ; denoted by flowers, 309 ; prepares the soul for the Vision of God, 320.
Faithful, the, signified by vineyards, 192.

Fasting, heretical errors respecting, 403.
FATHER, the, His Unity with the SON, 432, 435, 436.
Fear, the threefold, of the loss of grace received, 324, 330 ; typified by water, 331.
Figs, green, mystically interpreted of imperfect actions, 359 ; of knowledge and prophecy, 365.
Fire of God, consumes and yet blesses, 344.
Flatterers, called foxes, 380.
Flesh, the prudence of the, is death, 192 ; concupiscence of the, extinguishes compassion for others, 274.
Fleury, Church History, xvii.
Flower of holiness, threefold : virginity, martyrdom, and good works, 287 ; flowers of the field, the garden, and in the chamber, contrasted, 288 ; called types of Christ, 289 ; mystically interpreted, 308.
Force, a Hand of God, 33.
Foxes, flatterers and detractors called by that name, 378, 380, 386.
Free will of the soul discussed, 504.

G.

GARDEN OF THE BRIDEGROOM, mystical sense of, 132.
Genebrand, Bishop, xii.
Gentleness, the virtue of, called a lily, 426.
Geoffrey, ' Life of S. B.,' 2.
Gerard, brother of St. Bernard, the saint's lament for his death, 157 ; his thoughtfulness for his brother, 159 ; prudence and ability in management of affairs, 160 ; his joy in the hour of death, 164 ; scene at the death of, *ib.*
Gerhard, John, xiii.
Gerlach, O. von, xiii.
Gerson, J., xii.
Ghislerius, Michael, xiii.
Gifts, there are diversities of, 299 ; a cheerful giver, 434
Gilbert de la Porrée, Bishop, 4, 487.
Gilbert of Hoiland, continues the sermons, 5, 528.
Gilboa, Mountains of, mystically interpreted, 327.
Ginsburg, Dr. C. D., xiv.
GOD is a pure Spirit, 22 ; spoken of in Scripture as having Hands, and Feet, and Mouth, 23 ; is the Principle of Being to all things, 23 ; has no need of bodily organs as instruments, 23 ; makes use of the agency of His creatures, 28 ; acts by the *fiat* of His Will, 29 ; Mercy and Judgment called His Feet, 31 ; Force and Liberality called His Hands, 33 ; is perfectly known only when perfectly loved, 42 ; anticipates the prayers of pious souls, 46 ; His benefits to be remembered as a

532 SERMONS ON THE SONG OF SONGS

means of consolation, 57; praise and glory are to be rendered to Him, 67; not every kind of thanksgiving acceptable to Him, 68; Name of, revealed to Moses, 81; appeal of the nations to, 82; as Father, forgives, as Creator, judges, 90; love of, for human souls, 99; three ways in which He is loved, 109; aspiration of a penitent soul to, *ib.*; the consciousness of the blessed dead absorbed in, 159; the Vision of by the soul, 201; how to draw near to Him, 202; how manifested to the Patriarchs, 203; His manifestation cannot be described, 205; His Presence in the soul not continuous, 208; His great lovingkindness, 244; His severest anger is to inflict no chastisement, 261; duty of thankfulness to, 311; goodness of, in entering into relation with the soul, 314; the visitations of to be reverently observed, 340; by what signs they may be known, 341; fire of, consumes and yet blesses, 344; Voice of, calls for obedient service, *ib.*; not to be rashly sought into, 375; His love for the soul, 425; His will to be perfectly accomplished, 442; is to be sought in due time, place, and manner, 461; what is the right time, 463; the right place, 464; contrast between His action and that of creatures, 479, 480; the Image or WORD of, 487; seeks first the soul, 512.

Gold, denotes the Divine splendour, 257.
Good works, denoted by fruits, 309; called lilies, 432; vitiated by a bad intention, 433.
Grace, necessity of, 118, 211; not to be counted on unthinkingly, 119; we must co-operate with, 212; preventing and following grace, 414; grace and truth both needful, 459.
Great souls obtain great blessings, 212.
Green, Dr. W. H., xiv.
Gregory of Nyssa, xii.
Gregory, St., the Great, xiii.
Grotius, Hugh, xiv.
Guerric, Abbot of Igny, 6.
Guignard, M., his account of the relics of St. Bernard, 269.
Gulielmus Parvus, xiii.
Guyon, Madame, xii.

H.

HAURÉAU, M., *Des Poèmes Latins attribués à St. Bernard*, 290
Havernick, xiii.
Hearing, rather than sight, the way to religious truth, 179.
Heaven, in what sense a holy soul is called this, 167.
Hengstenberg, xiii.
Herder, xiv.
Heresies, temptation from, 223; [Heretics] should be met by reasoning, not by force, 386; the arguments of St. Bernard against, 393, 401, 407, 477.
Herod, not worthy to behold the Messiah, 16.
Hills, interpreted of heavenly spirits, 319; otherwise of demons, 324.
Hinds, mystically interpreted, 317.
Hitzig, xiv.
Holy Ghost, gifts of the, are the Kiss bestowed upon the Church, 38; the Holy Ghost is the Kiss from the Father to the Son, 39; is the Goodness of Each, 39; is not accorded to the angels, 38; His approach to the soul to be sedulously observed, 95; His operations upon souls called infusion and effusion, 100.
Holy women, the, 465.
Honorius of Autun, xii.
Hope of life, itself a harvest, 240; the soul reposes in, 313.
Humility, combined with spiritual greatness, a rare and high virtue, 69, 224; a preparation for great graces, 225; is both laudable and safe, 242; two kinds of, 259; signified by spikenard, 262; contrast between enforced and voluntary, 265; a qualification for the crown of martyrdom, 290; the consummation of righteousness, 291.
Hug, L., commentator, xii.

I.

IBN EZRA, xi.
Ignorance, the parent of falsehood and doubt, 96; two kinds of, to be avoided, 227; a cause of degradation, 231, 232; what kind is not hurtful, 234; ignorance of God the cause of despair, 243.
Incarnation, the, expected by the Prophets, 10, 11; mystically called the 'Kiss of God,' 11; to win the love of men a principal object of the, 113; called a descending upon the hills, 323; the means by which Christ gained an experimental knowledge of human necessities, 335.
Inebriation of the Apostles, the supposed, 298.
Infants are regenerated in baptism, 404, 419; the merits of Christ are attributed to, *ib.*
Inspiration, 481.
Isaac, how deceived, 181.
Isaiah, the prophet, 411.
Isidorus Hispalensis, xii.
Israel holds to the literal meaning of the text of Scripture, 449.

J.

JEREMIAH, his book of Lamentations, 88, 411.
Jerome, St., xii.
Jesus, the Name of, St. Bernard's hymn on, 84, 290; manifold excellences of the Saviour's character, 84; a saving

INDEX

antidote against sin, 85 ; called the Flower of the human race, 351 ; the Blood of, called the fruit of the vine, 363 ; His Wounds places of refuge, 367 ; why He is Judge of mankind, 451 ; His Ascension, 484.
Jews, the incredulity of, 360 ; their intelligence called bovine, 362.
Job, his saying on the nature of wisdom, 181.
John, St., of the Cross, xii.
Joseph, example of, 69.
Judgment, and mercy, called the Feet of God, 31, 32 ; Day of, a cause of fear to the sinner, 90, 450 ; how to escape it by penitence, 332.
Justus Argelitanus, xii.

K.

KAISER, xii.
Kedar, tents of, mystical sense, 155, 156.
Keil, xiii.
Keys of the kingdom of heaven, what is meant by, 423.
Kimchi, David, xi.
Kiss, meaning of, in the Canticles, 9 ; explained as the Incarnation, 13 ; of the Lord's Feet, explained as penitence, 18 ; of His Hand, as strength to make progress in holiness, 19 ; of His Lips, as spiritual communion with Him, 22 ; only to be comprehended by those who have experienced it, 18 ; for the perfect only, 20.
Kistemacher, xiv.
Knowledge, what kind of is for our good, 233 ; the right motive for, 235 ; unused and unfruitful is hurtful, 236 ; of self, is necessary, *ib*. ; a motive to humility, 237 ; of God, needful to salvation, *ib*. ; two kinds of, 238 ; the right kind of, will not minister to pride, 241.

L.

LAPIDE, CORN. A, xiii.
Laquearia, what is meant by, 282.
Lazarus, a type, 345, 346.
Lessing, xiv.
Liberality, a Hand of God, 33.
Life, the present, full of dangers, 292.
Lily of the valleys, 290 ; the Hûleh lily, 292 ; the virtues called lilies, 426.
Love, a uniting force, 355 ; shown by the Bridegroom to mankind, 387 ; of God for the soul, 425 ; is not mercenary, 510 ; is small compared with the love of God, 511.
Lowth, Bishop, xiv.
Lucifer, envied the human race, 97 ; desired to rule over it, 98.

M.

MABILLON, Dom John, his Introduction, ix, 1-6.

Macarius, xii.
Maimonides, Moses, xi.
Malice, mystically interpreted, 249.
Man, his degeneration from his first state, 230.
Marriages, plurality of, condemned, 358 ; heretical errors respecting, 399, 401.
Martha, a type, 345 ; the Lord in her house, 435.
Martyrdom, called the flower in the field, 289 ; the fruit of the vine, 363 ; the strength of, derived from the Passion of Christ, 370.
Mary, a type, 346.
Mary Magdalene, 51 (*note*).
Mary, the Blessed Virgin, her great love for Jesus, 191 ; her overshadowing a support to her, 207, 444 ; her purity, 230 ; how found, 482.
Maximus, Confessor, xii.
Mercy and Judgment, called the Feet of God, 31, 32.
Messiah, His Coming longed for. 14 ; His Human Nature a ground of confidence, 15.
Michael, Psellus, xiii.
Michaelis, J. D., xiv.
Modesty, frequently found with knowledge, 342 ; praise, especially in the young, 524.
Monks, singularity in, blamed, 108 ; their too great regard for their bodily condition blamed, 199 ; temptations of, 220 ; the younger, called nascent fruits, 381 ; of their fate, 382 ; the elder, of their temptations, 383.
Montalembert, Comte de, his purpose of writing the life of St. Bernard, 269.
Moses, Divine manifestation to, 213.
Mountains, interpreted of heavenly spirits, 319 ; of angels and men, 324.
Myrrh, the sufferings of Christ compared to a bundle of, 267.

N.

NAME of Christ, the, compared to sweet ointment, 79 ; is a salutary medicine, 80; expresses His Power and His Beneficence, *ib*. ; the means of salvation, 81 ; why compared to oil, 82 ; is light and nourishment, *ib*. ; St. Bernard's hymn on, 84.
Nations, the, their appeal to God, 82.
Necessity, the ' maxim of law ' respecting, 305.
Night, a type of the weakness of human nature, 527.

O.

ORIGEN, the error of, as to a crucifixion of the Lord in the air, 326 ; Homilies, xii.
Osorius, Hierono., xii.

P.

PASTOR, a good, qualities of, 103; must use patience and gentleness towards souls, 150; how he should feed his flock, 229; is not consoled by being merely clear of personal blame, 262; qualities needful for, 472; must give a good example, 473; of those who are bad, 474.
Patience, of, 224.
Patriarchs, how God was manifested to the, 203.
Paul, St., his distinction between his life and himself, 198; his allowance of the use of wine, 200; his struggle against the law of the flesh, 338, 353.
Penitence, a spiritual perfume, 49; acceptable to God, 51; enables the soul to escape judgment, 332.
Perfumes, the three spiritual, are Penitence, Devotion, and Piety, 49; of the holy women, 64; the four, of the Bridegroom, 125, 129.
Persecutions, the many, endured by the Church, 187; yet they increase it, 193, 223.
Peter Lombard, Bishop of Paris (Master of the Sentences), as to Angelic bodies, 27.
Peter, St., why blamed by the Lord, 112; zeal in defending Jesus, 349; the keys given to, 424.
Pharaoh, mystically interpreted of the devil, 247; the chariots of, 249.
Philip, St., the Lord's reply to, 213.
Piety, a spiritual perfume, 49; the most excellent of all, 60; of St. Paul, 61; of Job, ib.; of Joseph, ib.; of David, 62; of the holy women, 63, 64.
Piscator, John, xiii.
Poverty, Evangelical, possesses all things, 120.
Powers, an order of Angels, 105.
Prayer, earnest, does not remain unanswered, 298; what kind of, is acceptable, 526.
Preachers, the threefold cord entrusted to, 87; should resemble a reservoir rather than a canal, 101; signs of those who are faulty, 102; duty of preaching imposed, 258; require a pure intention, 371, 377; the desire to preach sometimes a temptation, 384.
Predestined to salvation, happy state of those in that condition, 141; how they are without sin, ib.
Pride, not permissible in an Angel, much less in a man, 328; secret, the evil consequences of, 329.
Principalities, an order of Angels, 106.
Psalms, how to find pleasure and sweetness in the, 36.
Puffendorf, Von, xiii.
Pure intention, necessary for those who pray, 37.

R.

RAINS, mystical sense of, 351, 353.
Rashi, R. Solomon ben Isaac, xi.
Rectitude, in what it consists, 146.
Redemption, the manner in which accomplished, the benefits of, 57.
Renan, E., xiv.
Repentance, the need of, 103.
Richard of St. Victor, xii.
Riches, the master rather than the servant of the avaricious, 120.
Righteousness called a lily, 426.
Roes, mystically interpreted, 317.
Roos, M. F., xiii.
Rosenmuller, xii.

S.

SAADIAS, R., xi.
Sacrament of the Altar, St. Bernard upon the, 215; is food and consolation to the soul, 219.
Saints, the glory of the, due to God, 71.
Salisbury, John of, his Polycraticus, 235.
Salmeron, xiii.
Samaritan, the good, 272.
Scripture, Holy, threefold sense of, 132; declares Divine truths in a figurative manner, 455.
Self-denial needs to be continually renewed, 353.
Self, the love of, 8.
Sensuality mystically interpreted, 249.
Separation worse than death, 158.
Seraphin, the, 107.
Seven, the number, mystical signification of, 86, 88.
Shadows, mystically explained, 441, 444.
Shepherds, the, their vision, 16; evil pastors are hurtful to their flocks, 219.
Simeon, his gladness at Christ's coming, 16.
Sins, called walls between God and man, 335; enfeeble the qualities of the soul, 506.
Sixtus of Sienna, 5, 35.
Sleep of the body, 315.
Sleep, those blamed who indulge in during service, 35.
Solitude, the real nature of, 255; the solitary life unwisely chosen, 384.
Solomon, curtains of, mystical sense, 156.
SON, the, His unity with the FATHER, 432-436.
Song of Songs, the title, 7, 10.
Sorrow, gives a zest to joy which follows, 418.
Soul, the ardent love of for God, 33; called the Bride of the Lord, 34; its three great faculties (reason, will, and memory), 57, 58; a depraved soul not able to love God, 147; a holy soul called heaven, 167; whether it has its origin in heaven, 170; how said to be heaven, 172; is measured by the charity

INDEX 535

it possesses, 174; its union with the WORD not imaginary, but not corporeal, 204; what the devout soul ought to seek, 214; aspirations of, 218; how lamentable for it to leave God for created things, 228; souls that are carnal and worldly called women, 245; what constitutes its beauty, 252; its solitude, 255; its twofold beauty, 275; how it speaks to God the WORD, 279; sleep of the, 315; its aspirations towards heaven, 354; said to abide in the clefts of the Rock, 371, 373; how it belongs to the Lord, 417; how the Father and the WORD enter into, 420; the love of God for it causes it to love Him, 425; unity with God of the holy soul, 432; its love to the Lord, 483; is in the image of the WORD, 488; its greatness and righteousness, 490; its immortality and freewill, 494, 497; this partly lost, 501; is enfeebled by sin, 506; how able to recover its likeness to Christ, 507; conformed to Him by love, 508; is sought first by God, 511; the seven needs of, wherefore it seeks the WORD, 515; devotion and understanding, the two feet of, 517; cannot be overthrown against its will, 518.

Speech, said to be sometimes unmeasured and involuntary, 410.

Spirits, the four orders of, 24; compared to mountains and hills, 319.

Starke, 'Synopsis,' xiii.

Stars, virtues called by this name, 172.

Storehouse of the Bridegroom, mystical sense of, 132.

Storrs, Dr. R. S., xxii.

Synagogue, the, desirous to monopolize the knowledge of God, 75; said to be as a repudiated bride, 414.

T.

TALMUD of Jerusalem and of Babylon, xi.

Temptations, four kinds of, 221.

Teresa, St., of Jesus, xii.

Thankfulness, duty of, 311.

Theodoret, Bishop, xii.

Thomas, St., his request to the Lord, 213.

Thoughts, good, are from God, but evil from ourselves, 210.

Thrones, the, an order of Angels, 106.

Thrupp, J. F., xiv.

Truth, called a lily, 426.

U.

UNBELIEF, called a night, 466.

Unity, the, of the Divine Persons, 432, 435, 436.

Upright, why man was created in that state, 146.

V.

VAINGLORY a temptation, 222.

Vineyards, the souls of the faithful spoken of as, 192; souls and Churches spoken of as (and as vines), 348, 363; to be carefully cultivated, 378.

Virgins, the foolish, 460.

Virtues, the, an order of Angels, 105; compared to stars, 172; called lilies, 426; called the drink of the WORD, 443.

Vision of God, the, 201; the Beatific, *ib.*; not to be attained in this life, 202; cannot be described, 205; faith a preparation for, 320.

Visitations of the Lord to be reverently observed, 340; by what signs known, 341, 457, 458.

W.

WALLS between God and man, sins compared to, 335.

Watchmen, the Apostles called thus, 471, 475; the qualities needful for, 472.

Water, the ordeal by, 406.

Widowhood, commendation of, 354.

Windows, Christ's experiences of the weaknesses of men called thus, 336.

Wine, comparison of, with carnal delights, 48; St. Paul's allowance of the use of, 200.

Winter, mystical sense of, 349, 354.

Wisdom, true, 8; of the world, *ib.*; contrasted with that of Christ, 199; gives all things their right value, 306; description of a man who is truly wise, 307; called the beauty of a soul, 460.

WORD, the, His Flesh not subject to perishableness, 230; how He speaks to the soul, 279; in what sense said to have hands, 311; typified by gold, 369; signs of His coming to the soul, 457; of His departure, 458; is the Image of God, 487; what it is to enjoy communion with, 524.

Wordsworth, Bishop Christopher, xiv.

Works, relation of faith to, 149.

World, love of the, 8.

Wounds of Jesus a place of refuge, 367.

Z.

ZEAL, the, needed by spiritual guides, 136; danger of, without discretion, 299.

Zöckler, Dr. Otto, xiv.

THE END.

www.ingramcontent.com/pod-product-compliance
Lightning Source LLC
Chambersburg PA
CBHW052044290426
44111CB00011B/1608